Thomas D. Lea The New Testament

Its Background And Message

BROADMAN & HOLMAN PUBLISHERS

Nashville, Tennessee

4210–78
0-8054-1078-3

Dewey Decimal Classification: 225
Subject Heading: Bible. N.T.—History\ Bible. N.T. Study
Library of Congress Card Catalog Number: 93-46945

Library of Congress Cataloging-in-Publication Data
Lea, Thomas D.
The New Testament: its background and message / Thomas
D. Lea.
p. cm.
Includes bibliographical references
ISBN 0-8054-1078-3
1.Bible. N.T. —Introductions.   2. Bible. N. T.—Text-
books.
I. Title.
BS2330.2.L3871996
225.6'1—dc20   93–46945
                                                         CIP

01 02 03 04 05 06 01 00 99 98 97 96

To my wife Beverly,
whose love for the study of
the New Testament constantly
challenges and informs me

Contents

Abbreviations   ix

Introduction   1

Part 1: The Background to the New Testament

1. The Political History
   of Palestine During the Intertestamental Period   5
2. Life in the World of the New Testament   27
3. The Religious Background to the New Testament   43
4. The Canon, Text, and Genre of the New Testament   65

Part 2: The Life of Jesus and the Gospels

5. Learning About Jesus   79
6. The Synoptic Problem   107
7. The Four Gospels   127
8. The Birth, Childhood, and Early Ministry of Jesus   167
9. Jesus' Ministry in and Around Galilee   189
10. The Later Judean and the Perean Ministry   223
11. The Final Week of Jesus' Life—
    Crucifixion and Resurrection   245

Contents

Part 3: The Growth of the Early Church in Acts

12. Introduction to the Acts and the Role of Peter
    in Early Christianity (Acts 1–12)   281
13. The Role of Paul in the Spread of Christianity
    (Acts 13–28)   303

Part 4: The Epistles of Paul

14. An Overview of Paul's Life   331
15. Paul's First Writings
    (A Survey of Galatians and 1 and 2 Thessalonians)   365
16. Paul's Chief Writings
    (A Survey of Romans and 1 and 2 Corinthians)   393
17. Paul's Captivity Epistles
    (Ephesians, Philippians, Colossians, and Philemon)   437
18. The Pastoral Epistles   469

Part 5: Hebrews, the General Epistles, and Revelation

19. The Epistle to the Hebrews   501
20. The Epistle of James   519
21. The Epistles of 1 and 2 Peter   533
22. The Johannine Epistles   559
23. The Epistle of Jude   575
24. The Revelation   585

Glossary of Terms   614
Names Index   623
Subject Index   627

Abbreviations

Books of the Bible

Gen.	Jer.	Acts
Exod.	Lam.	Rom.
Lev.	Ezek.	1, 2 Cor.
Num.	Dan.	Gal.
Deut.	Hos.	Eph.
Josh.	Joel	Phil.
Judg.	Amos	Col.
Ruth	Obad.	1, 2 Thess.
1, 2 Sam.	Jon.	1, 2 Tim.
1, 2 Kings	Mic.	Titus
1, 2 Chron.	Nah.	Philem.
Ezra	Hab.	Heb.
Neh.	Zeph.	James
Esther	Hag.	1, 2 Pet.
Job	Zech.	1, 2, 3, John
Ps. (*pl* Pss.)	Mal.	Jude
Prov.	Matt.	Rev.
Eccles.	Mark	
Song of Sol.	Luke	
Isa.	John	

Commonly Used Reference Works

AB	Anchor Bible
ANF	The Ante-Nicene Fathers (All references to Apostolic Fathers are from this source.)
BSac	*Bibliotheca Sacra*
BNTC	Black's New Testament Commentary
BST	The Bible Speaks Today
CBQ	*Catholic Biblical Quarterly*
EBC	Everyman's Bible Commentary
EGGNT	Exegetical Guide to the Greek New Testament
EvQ	*Evangelical Quarterly*
ExpTim	*Expository Times*
GNBC	Good News Bible Commentary
Hermeneia	*Hermeneia: A Critical and Historical Commentary on the Bible*
HNTC	Harper's New Testament Commentary
HTR	*Harvard Theological Review*
ICC	International Critical Commentary
Int	*Interpretation*
IVPNTC	InterVarsity Press New Testament Commentary
JETS	*Journal of the Evangelical Theological Society*
JSNT	*Journal for the Study of the New Testament*
JSOT	*Journal for the Study of the Old Testament*
Loeb	Loeb Classical Library (All references to Josephus and Greek and Latin classics are from this source.)

NAC	New American Commentary
NCB	New Century Bible
NCLB	New Clarendon Bible
NIBC	New International Bible Commentary
NICNT	New International Commentary on the New Testament
NIGTC	New International Greek Testament Commentary
NPNF	Nicene and Post-Nicene Fathers (All references to Eusebius are from this source.)
NovT	*Novum Testamentum*
NovTSup	Novum Testamentum, Supplements
NTS	*New Testament Studies*
SNTSMS	Society for New Testament Studies Monograph Series
SJT	*Scottish Journal of Theology*
SWJT	*Southwestern Journal of Theology*
TynBul	*Tyndale Bulletin*
TCB	The Century Bible
TNTC	Tyndale New Testament Commentary
TJ	*Trinity Journal*
WBC	Word Biblical Commentary
WC	Westminster Commentary
WEC	Wycliffe Exegetical Commentary
WUNT	Wissenschaftliche Untersuchungen zum Neuen Testament (Scientific Investigations on the New Testament)

Introduction

Many New Testament surveys provide an excellent background for a discussion of questions of authorship, date, and circumstances for the writing of the New Testament books. Information about these issues can consume so much of the interest of the author and the readers that little time or space remain for a discussion of the content of the books of the New Testament.

This survey seeks to strike a balance between a discussion of the critical issues of authorship, date, purpose, and background and the investigation of the content of the book. Both types of information are included in this survey with a determined attempt to make certain that the student learns the content of each New Testament book. This book will be useful in teaching New Testament survey in beginning college and seminary classes. It will provide a fresh assessment and evaluation of questions of an introductory nature and seek to deal with the most recent discussions about the content of each New Testament book.

Each chapter begins with questions intended to alert the reader to issues discussed in the chapter. Summary questions intended to help the reader review the material are included at the end of each chapter. Most chapters include an annotated bibliography that identifies additional sources for further study of the issues discussed in the chapter.

Part 1 contains background material for the New Testament. The four chapters in this section discuss the historical development, social setting, and religious background of the New Testament period and development of the New Testament canon.

Part 2 studies the life of Jesus as narrated in the four Gospels. Two introductory chapters assess various critical approaches to the life of Jesus and the synoptic problem. A harmonistic perspective following the organization of A. T. Robertson's *Harmony of the Gospels* is used to discuss the life of Jesus.

Part 3 focuses on the growth of the early church in Acts. This section includes critical information on the writing of Acts and a discussion of the roles of Peter and Paul in the spread of Christianity.

Part 4 investigates the epistles of Paul. An introductory chapter surveys the life, literary contributions, and theology of Paul. The other chapters discuss his early writings, major Epistles, captivity Epistles, and pastoral Epistles.

Part 5 is a multi-chapter study of Hebrews and the general Epistles. Part 6, in a single chapter, is a study of the Book of Revelation. A glossary at the conclusion of the survey includes definitions of various New Testament terms and concepts encountered in the discussions within this book.

The theological perspective of the author is evangelical and Baptist. These two features are an important influence in the presentation of the material in this book.

In some chapters I found it more convenient to comment on issues that related to all the books studied within the chapter without commenting again on the issues separately for each individual book. For example, I thought it best in chapter 18 to make general comments for all the Pastorals before elaborating on the specific purpose and occasion for each letter. Students should examine headings in the chapters that deal with multiple books to be certain they do not omit important information relevant to their study.

This survey was written during a year's sabbatical from my teaching responsibilities at Southwestern Baptist Theological Seminary spent at Cambridge University in England. I express heartfelt thanks to former President Russell Dilday and Theology Dean Bruce Corley for granting the leave and supporting the project.

Introduction

My wife Beverly enjoyed the sabbatical with me and encouraged me with interested inquiries and faithful prayers. During the writing process I served as interim preacher of a church in the European Baptist Convention in the village of Little Stukeley near RAF Alconbury, the home of a large American military installation. I received unceasing encouragement and persistent support from these faithful Christian friends.

The Political History of Palestine During the Intertestamental Period

1

Guiding Questions

1. List the various powers controlling Palestine during the intertestamental period and the dates of their control.

2. Give the names of any Jewish leaders who were important for Jewish history during the time of control by foreign powers. What was their distinctive contribution to Jewish history?

3. List some of the religious developments among the Jews during the intertestamental period.

4. Identify the leaders of the Herodian dynasty whose activities appear at some point in the New Testament record.

5. Explain the cultural developments that took place among the Jews during the intertestamental period.

Introduction

The final historical sections of the Old Testament describe Judea as part of the Persian Empire. The last ruler mentioned by name in the Old Testament is Darius the Persian (Neh. 12:22). He may be identical with Darius II, who served from 423–405 B.C. Because several kings named Darius ruled in Persia, the identification is not certain.

When we turn to the New Testament about four hundred years later, the ruling monarch is Augustus; he represents the power of Rome (Luke 2:1). Between these two pillars of history the ebb and flow of wars, struggles, hopes, and defeats passed over Palestine. How will a knowledge of the political history of the times help us interpret the New Testament?

First, knowing the political history of this period helps us make a more accurate interpretation of the text of the New Testament. Names of government leaders such as Tiberius Caesar, Claudius Caesar, Pilate, Herod the Great, and Gallio appear in the New Testament. These men made decisions that had consequences for individual Christians and the early church. We can more wisely grasp the significance of their actions when we know something about them and their individual history.

Second, knowing some of the details of political history helps us to present a more lifelike description of the events narrated in Scripture. Understanding the cruelty of Herod the Great, the hesitancy of Pilate, and the boldness of Paul's appeal for a trial before Caesar makes the New Testament more vivid and alive. Knowing the details of New Testament events gives the personalities a dimension of reality that forbids us from relegating their actions and personalities to the realm of the mystical and mythical.

Third, it is important for us to recognize that the New Testament presents a theological interpretation of history. When readers realize that the historical and political details are verifiable, they feel a greater pressure to come to grips with the theological content of Scripture.

Fourth, the New Testament itself is often remarkably silent about the historical and political dimensions of this period because the writers could assume that their first readers knew the personalities and political entities they mentioned. They could also assume that their readers understood the contributions of Alexander the Great and his successors to the life of the New Testament era. Two thousand years later we cannot assume that modern readers know and understand the significance of these details. Therefore, it is important to introduce readers to this information in a survey of the New Testament.

We will explore this history from the standpoint of the powers presiding over Palestine during the intertestamental period. In consecutive order, these powers or ruling groups were Babylon, Persia, Greece, Egypt, Syria, Maccabees, and Rome.

1) The Babylonian Period

In 597 B.C. Nebuchadnezzar, king of Babylon, ended Jewish independence by conquering Judea and capturing Jerusalem. The Babylonian king deported the Jewish king, Jehoiachin, along with his family and court, to Babylon. Nebuchadnezzar installed Jehoiachin's uncle on the throne of Judah and changed his name from Mattaniah to Zedekiah (2 Kings 24:10–17). Nebuchadnezzar actually held authority over Judah from perhaps 604 B.C., but after 597 B.C. his control was more thorough and absolute.

Zedekiah had pledged to serve the king of Babylon (2 Chron. 36:13), but he later asserted his independence and dabbled in political intrigue with Egypt (Jer. 37:5–10). Nebuchadnezzar moved an army to oppose Zedekiah's rebellion, laid siege to Jerusalem, and captured the city in 586 B.C. (Jer. 39:1–10). The walls of Jerusalem were demolished. Babylonian forces captured the fleeing Zedekiah and brought him to the king. In a brutal display of cruelty, Nebuchadnezzar killed the sons of Zedekiah, blinded him, and carried him bound to Babylon.

To maintain some law and order, Nebuchadnezzar appointed Gedaliah as governor of Judah. However, factions in Judah still produced strife and discontent. Gedaliah was eventually assassinated. Some of the insurgents escaped to Egypt and took Jeremiah (against his will) with them (Jer. 40–43).

Nebuchadnezzar had taken some of the most devout and competent Jews into captivity in Babylon. There the prophet Ezekiel helped to mold segments of this group into a body that would provide the leadership needed to replace those fallen in Jerusalem. He promised that God would revive his people spiritually and restore them to their homeland in Palestine (Ezek. 36:22–28).

During the Babylonian captivity the practice of synagogue worship developed among the Jews. In the absence of a temple, godly Jews banded together to learn and apply the law. Teachers of the law took the place of the temple priesthood in providing spiritual leadership for the people. The study of the law replaced animal sac-rifices, and ethical obedience replaced temple ritual. Jeremiah had predicted a seventy-year captivity for the Jews (Jer. 25:11–14). In 539 B.C. Cyrus, king of Persia, captured Babylon by diverting the water of the Euphrates from its normal channel. Cyrus and the Persians inherited the mantle of authority in the Middle East. Under Cyrus the Jewish captivity in Babylon ended for some of the Jews.

The Persian Period (539–331 B.C.)

In the first year of his reign, Cyrus issued a decree allowing the Jews to return home. He released some of the captured temple treasures to them and promised to rebuild the temple at his own expense (Ezra 6:3–5).

Most of the Jews remained in the more settled and prosperous surroundings of Cyrus's kingdom, but a group of forty-two thou-sand, led by Sheshbazzar, returned to Jerusalem around 537 B.C. (Ezra 1:5–11; 2:64). They began to rebuild the temple, but the work languished because of opposition from the residents of Pales-tine (Ezra 4:1–5). Because of the urgent preaching of Haggai and Zechariah, the work resumed around 520 B.C., and construction was completed within four years (Ezra 4:24; 6:1–15).

Detailed records of events in Palestine are not available for the next sixty years, but in 458 B.C. Ezra the scribe led a second group from Babylon to return to Palestine (Ezra 7:1–7). Around 446 B.C. a third group returned to Palestine under the leadership of Nehemiah, cupbearer of the Persian king Artaxerxes (Neh. 2:1–8). Nehemiah led the people in repairing the city walls quickly, and the security of the city was established once again (Neh. 6:1–16). Nehemiah instituted various economic and social reforms, and Ezra led in calling the people back to the observance of the law (Neh. 8:1–12).

The reforms under Ezra and Nehemiah produced a group of strong devotees to God's law. They remained faithful to God's demands despite the deceptive pressures of Hellenism and the later faithlessness of the priesthood. During this period the demand for intensive study of the law produced the scribes, who copied the law and became experts in its interpretation. We will meet scribes on several occasions in Jesus' ministry. This same period also saw the development of the "Great Synagogue," a body which sought to administer the law, and later developed into the Sanhedrin in New Testament times.

Persian control of Palestine lasted until Alexander the Great defeated the Persians at the battle of Arbela in 331 B.C.

3) The Grecian Period (331–320 B.C.)

Even during the period of Persian rule over Palestine, Greek influence in the area had developed rapidly. Greek traders carried their commerce and civilization to the entire Mediterranean world. Greek musical instruments and weapons appeared in Babylon as early as 600 B.C. Then the conquests of Alexander the Great of Macedonia followed and accelerated the spread of Greek culture, known as Hellenism.

Philip, the father of Alexander, had forged Macedonia into a mighty military machine. During his lifetime he made the Greek city-states the tributaries of Macedonia, and he was poised on the verge of additional conquests when he died in 337 B.C.

Alexander had his father's aggressive character and military skills. The Greek philosopher Aristotle had tutored Alexander in the ideals of Hellenism, and Alexander developed a deep devotion to Hellenistic culture and tradition. In 334 B.C. he led his forces across the Hellespont into Asia Minor where he defeated Persian forces at the battle of Granicus. Successive victories at Issus (333 B.C.) and Arbela (331 B.C.) established Alexander as master of the ancient Middle East. His far-flung kingdom included Egypt, Palestine, and Syria and extended to the Indus River in modern India. As he conquered, he established colonies that became centers for spreading Hellenism.

Alexander encouraged his soldiers to marry Oriental women, thus enhancing the blending of Greek and Oriental cultures. He educated Persians in the Greek language. His military successes turned him more and more into an arbitrary, oriental despot. A lifestyle of revelry impaired his health. He finally contracted fever and died in 323 B.C. at the age of thirty-three.

At his death four of his generals divided his kingdom among themselves. Two of these generals developed empires which are important for New Testament history. In Egypt the rulers bore the name Ptolemy and established their capital in Alexandria. The seductive Cleopatra, who died in 30 B.C., was the last of the Ptolemaic rulers. In Syria the rulers carried the name of either Seleucus or Antiochus. They made Antioch their capital. The Roman general Pompey ended the history of this empire by conquering it in 64 B.C.

Although the ruling power in Palestine after Alexander was not geographically centered in Greece, all subsequent Palestinian rulers increased the influence of Hellenism. Alexander had passed the legacy of Hellenism to both the Ptolemaic and the Seleucid empires. Even Rome was so highly influenced by Hellenistic culture that Greek became a common street language. The Roman satirist Juvenal, whose life spanned much of the first and early second century A.D., said, "I cannot abide . . . a Rome of Greeks."[1]

The Ptolemaic Period (320–198 B.C.)

Alexander's premature death in 323 B.C. precipitated a power struggle among his leading generals. The four generals who emerged victorious from the struggle became known as the *diadochi*, a derivative from a Greek word meaning "successors."

Ptolemy I was one of Alexander's most competent generals. He shrewdly accepted headship of Egypt in 323 B.C., avoiding any immediate conflict with other powerful generals. In 320 B.C. he deposed the governor of Palestine and added its territory to his kingdom.

In Alexandria, Egypt's capital city, Jewish influence was strong. Alexander had admitted Jewish colonists to full citizenship. Ptolemy I transferred many Jews and Samaritans to Egypt. These new immigrants fell fully under the influence of Hellenistic culture. Hellenism also flowed into Palestine itself through the influence of Greek cities in the area and trade between Palestine and Egypt.

Generally, the Egyptian rulers treated the Jews well. Under Ptolemy Philadelphus (285–246 B.C.) the Old Testament was translated into Greek. The appearance of this translation indicated that

---

1. Juvenal, *Satire* 3.60–61 (Loeb). Unless otherwise noted, all references to Greek and Roman classical writers are taken from the Loeb Classical Library, published by Harvard University Press.

Jewish residents in Egypt were becoming more proficient in the use of Greek than in the use of their native Hebrew. Jewish tradition taught that this translation was the work of seventy-two Jewish scholars. The translation, known as the Septuagint, is commonly designated by the Roman numerals LXX, since seventy is the nearest round number to seventy-two.

Writers of the New Testament frequently used the Septuagint whenever they quoted the Old Testament. Although the quality of the Greek translation is uneven, it is useful to show how Jewish scholars interpreted the Hebrew Scriptures at that time.

During the period of Egyptian hegemony over Palestine, the Egyptians and the Syrians constantly fought. The battles between these regional powers were frequently fought on Palestinian soil. In 198 B.C., at Paneas, near the foot of Mt. Hermon in Northern Palestine, Antiochus III of Syria decisively defeated Ptolemy V of Egypt. After this battle, control of Palestine passed from Egyptian to Syrian hands.

5) The Syrian Period (198–167 B.C.)

In attempting to assert its authority over Palestine, Syria faced a divided nation. Many Jews, led by the high priest Onias III, supported the Ptolemies of Egypt. Their opponents from the wealthy house of Tobias supported Syria. For some years a struggle ensued between the pro-Egyptian Oniads and the pro-Syrian Tobiads.

The Oniads initially prevailed over the Tobiads, and their dominance continued until the Syrian ruler Antiochus IV (175–163 B.C.) came to the throne. Antiochus was a committed Hellenist and an egotist. He assumed the name "Epiphanes," suggesting that he was the incarnation of the Olympian Zeus on earth. In a mocking twist of irony the Jews dubbed him "Epimanes," the madman.

Antiochus had aggressive plans for using funds from Palestine and especially from the Jerusalem temple. He found a Jewish turncoat willing to work with him as a pawn. Jason, brother of the high priest Onias III, promised huge sums of money to Antiochus's treasury, and in return for an appointment to the high priesthood he promised to cooperate with Antiochus in introducing Hellenistic customs into Jerusalem.

11

After his appointment to office, Jason established a gymnasium with a race track in Jerusalem. Here Jewish boys exercised in the nude after the Greek custom. This practice understandably produced outrage among devoted Jews. Races opened with invocations to pagan deities. Jewish priests even began to leave their duties to attend these events. Although these developments enticed many Jews to adopt pagan customs, they also produced an opposing group called "Hasidim," meaning "the pious ones."

Prior to a planned invasion of Egypt, Antiochus replaced Jason with another Jew, Menelaus, who had offered a higher tribute to Antiochus. Pious Jews deeply resented the sale of the sacred office of high priest to the highest bidder. As an added offense to the Jews, Menelaus may not have belonged to a priestly family. The description of this display of treachery by Menelaus appears in 2 Maccabees 4.

In 169 and 168 B.C. Antiochus made forays into Egypt to add it to his kingdom. After initial successes, his attempts to annex Egypt proved futile. The Roman legate, Popilius Laenas, protecting the ambitions of his government, confronted Antiochus outside Alexandria, drew a circle on the ground around him, and demanded his promise to withdraw from Egypt before he stepped out of the circle. Antiochus, unable to resist the armed might of Rome, grudgingly withdrew from Egypt.

Fuming inwardly from a wounded ego, Antiochus headed back to Syria. He then went to Jerusalem to defeat an effort by Jason to regain the priesthood. Antiochus took Jerusalem; killed large numbers of men, women, and children; entered the temple; and confiscated the holy vessels and offerings he found there. He built a strongly fortified citadel on the western hill of Jerusalem, garrisoned it with troops loyal to him, and left it behind to enforce his victory.

Back in Antioch, he decreed steps for ending Jewish worship in Jerusalem (see 1 Macc. 1:41–60; 2 Macc. 6:1–2 for descriptions of his actions). His purpose had little to do with his devotion to Hellenistic religion, but he wanted to unify his kingdom on a religious basis and to control the offerings pouring into the Jerusalem temple. After his decree it became a capital offense to practice circumcision, observe the Sabbath and other religious festivals, and even to own copies of portions of the Old Testament. Pagan sacrifices became compulsory in the temple and at altars throughout the country. Antiochus ordered the erection of a statue of Olympian Zeus in the temple and even had a sow sacrificed on the sacred altar.

He failed to reckon with the stubborn commitment of the Jews to follow their religion. Many Jews courageously chose martyrdom rather than compromise their faith. Stories of such religious heroism appear in 2 Maccabees 6:18–7:42. Courageous survivors of Antiochus's withering persecution began to prepare themselves for armed resistance to the despotic decrees.

In 167 B.C. a band of Jews gathering around an aged priest named Mattathias from the village of Modin (or Modein), about ten miles northwest of Jerusalem, sparked a revolt against Syrian power. Although the struggle against Antiochus and Syria dragged on for years, the effective control of Syria over Palestine was finished.

6) The Maccabean Period (167–142 B.C.)

To enforce his religious policies, Antiochus dispatched a royal emissary to the village of Modin to force the offering of pagan sacrifices. The legate attempted to bribe Mattathias, the village priest, with promises of wealth and honor if he would lead the people in offering sacrifices. Mattathias adamantly refused. When a compromising Jew stepped forward to comply with the agent's order, Mattathias killed the offerer and the agent and fled with his five sons to nearby hills (1 Macc. 2:1–28).

Although Mattathias died within a year of this episode, he vested military leadership in his third son, Judas. Judas proved to be a nearly invincible military leader. With stealth and sudden attacks he routed armies of superior numbers sent against him by Antiochus. His exploits earned him the nickname of Maccabeus, "the Hammer." The Maccabean family also was called Hasmonean after the name of an earlier ancestor, Hasmon.

In 164 B.C. Judas wrested religious freedom from the Syrians. Antiochus rescinded his ban on the Jewish religion, and Judas was able to lead the Jews in the worship of Jehovah in a purified temple. Modern Jews still commemorate this event in their annual celebration of the

Feast of Lights or Hanukkah. Although Judas obtained religious freedom, he still sought to win full national autonomy, and he carried on his struggle for complete victory. Antiochus died in 163 B.C.; rivalry and strife among his would-be successors aided the Jews in their quest for freedom.

Judas was killed in battle in 160 B.C., and his brother Jonathan received the mantle of leadership. Jonathan wrested further land and freedom from the Syrians. In a surprising move for a Maccabee, he accepted the appointment of the office of high priest from an aspirant to the Syrian throne in 152 B.C. Captured in battle by a Syrian general, Jonathan was put to death in 143 B.C. and was succeeded by his brother Simon.

Simon continued military and political pressure until 142 B.C., when a claimant to the Syrian throne offered Simon national release from tribute and taxation in return for his military and political support. The leader, Demetrius II, did not withdraw all Syrian forces from Palestinian soil, but Simon continued a military struggle and subdued the citadel in Jerusalem which had been established there by Antiochus IV. From then until the rise of the Roman Empire, the Jews enjoyed national autonomy.

In the period of peace that followed, a grateful Jewish nation recognized the leadership of Simon and his family. Simon was awarded the office of hereditary high priest, and the Jewish people vested in him religious, military, and political authority. This threefold responsibility of the single office of high priest was a distinct departure from biblical teaching and previous Jewish practice.

The Hasmonean family brought to Jewish life a zeal for the law along with significant military and administrative skills. Descendants of the Hasmonean family continued to rule after 142 B.C., but their political aims and intrigues alienated most of the religiously minded Hasidim in the nation. In an ironical twist, later descendants of the Hasmonean branch became supporters of Hellenism and were corrupted by their own use of power and wealth. In many ways the original hopes of the Maccabean revolt had been realized by 142 B.C. After that time many of the descendants of the Maccabees who served as rulers abandoned the first aims and goals of their forefathers and pursued personal agendas that were often secular and influenced by Hellenism. Although those Jewish rulers who served after 142 B.C. were Maccabees, we will use the term Hasmonean to distinguish them as descendants who had different agendas from their forefathers.

7) The Hasmonean Period (142–63 B.C.)

After he attained freedom for the Jews, Simon's reign was brief but prosperous. Jewish religious life revived, and economic conditions improved. Though Simon was able to push back military threats from Syria, he succumbed to internal strife. In a display of unbelievable treachery, Simon's son-in-law, Ptolemy, murdered Simon and two of his sons. A surviving son, John Hyrcanus, escaped and repulsed the military efforts of Ptolemy.

Hyrcanus continued the military conquests which his father had made and virtually became a Jewish king. His cruelty alienated many godly Jews and pushed Hyrcanus into a reconciliation with wealthy Jews who had sympathies for Hellenism. During his lifetime we see the initial development of groups that later became the Pharisees and the Sadducees of the New Testament period. The Pharisees were the descendants of the Hasidim who had initially joined with the Maccabean brothers in their efforts to win Jewish freedom. The Sadducees became a wealthy party with priestly influence and a love for Hellenism.[2]

Hasmonean successors to the high priestly office were uniformly corrupted by a lust for power. Murder, deceit, and treachery came to characterize the dynasty. Aristobulus I, the sucessor to Hyrcanus I, was the first Hasmonean to call himself king in his official activities. Two developments concluded this period and prepared the way for the political situation we meet in the New Testament.

1. Antipater, an Idumean who was a skilled political climber, manipulated his way into favor with Hyrcanus II, the Hasmonean high priest who reigned after 67 B.C. Hyrcanus became the tool of a group of wealthy Jews led by Antipater, the father of Herod the Great of New Testament times.

---

2. Josephus, the Jewish historian, indicated that Hyrcanus initially followed the Pharisees but later became a Sadducee (*Antiquities of the Jews* 13.10.6). References to Josephus are taken from Whiston's numbering unless otherwise indicated.

2. The general chaos in Palestine attracted the attention of Rome. Antipater urged Hyrcanus to cooperate with Rome, but Hyrcanus's ambitious brother Aristobulus II began a civil war in order to seize leadership from his brother. Ultimately, the Roman general Pompey invaded Palestine, subdued Aristobulus, and reduced the Jewish territory of Judea to a Roman province. Although Rome established its power over Judea in 63 B.C., the Jews retained a semblance of Hasmonean leadership under Hyrcanus II and his successor Antigonus, whose death in 37 B.C. marked the end of the Hasmonean dynasty.

8) The Roman Period (63 B.C. on)

The city of Rome was founded in 753 B.C. as a union of small villages on the Tiber River in central Italy. In the fifth century B.C. Rome developed a republican form of government which vested power in the people and their chosen representatives.

Rome grew by making alliances with nearby cities and by waging wars of expansion against its neighbors. In 275 B.C. Rome defeated aggressive attacks by the Hellenist King Pyrrhus of Epirus and became the master of central and southern Italy. In 146 B.C., after two centuries of battles, Rome defeated its chief rival, the North African city of Carthage. In the same year Macedonia and Achaia in Greece became Roman provinces. Nearly a century later Pompey completed the conquest of much of the eastern Mediterranean by subduing Syria and Judea.

The military conquests of Julius Caesar helped him to seize power in Rome. His enemies feared his ambition and successfully plotted his murder in 44 B.C. Out of the chaotic struggle for power between rival Roman bodies, Octavian, Caesar's nephew, seized control. He secured his position with a stunning victory over the forces of Antony and Cleopatra in a naval battle near Actium, Greece, in 31 B.C. His victory led Rome from a period of aggressive expansion into a period of relative peace known as the *Pax Romana* or Roman peace.

1) Augustus (27 B.C.– A.D. 14)

Octavian's victories allowed him to become Rome's first emperor. In 27 B.C. an appreciative Roman Senate named him commander-in-chief of the Roman armed forces. He received the name Augustus, literally "the majestic one," a title indicating the esteem the Romans held for him.

Augustus initiated many religious, political, and economic reforms. To administer the far-flung empire, he divided the provinces of Rome into two major types. The more peaceful provinces such as Greece were governed by the Senate and had a leader known as the proconsul, usually appointed for a term of a single year. Gallio (Acts 18:12) was a New Testament proconsul. Alongside the proconsul in these senatorial provinces the emperor usually appointed another officer, the procurator, who watched over financial affairs of the province. The more restive provinces such as Palestine were governed directly by the emperor and had a leader known as a propraetor or prefect. The prefect retained his office at the discretion of the emperor. Pontius Pilate served as prefect of Judea from A.D. 26–36.[3]

From the standpoint of the New Testament, Augustus is important because he was the emperor under whom Jesus was born (Luke 2:1). He ordered the census connected with Jesus' birth.

Augustus could boast that he found Rome brick and left it marble. His efficient administration replenished the treasury, restored confidence in the government, and strengthened Rome's influence throughout its empire. At his death, his adopted son, Tiberius, was chosen to succeed him.

Tiberius (A.D. 14–37)

Tiberius came to power at the age of fifty-six after a lifetime of service in the Roman government. His haughty, suspicious bearing contributed to his general lack of popularity. In the latter part of his term of service, a series of domestic difficulties and political conspiracies brought out such cruelty in Tiberius that those suspected of the slightest opposition to him often faced death. At his death in A.D. 37 the country collectively breathed a sigh of relief.

---

3. Some disagreement exists over the proper name to use for the office of Pilate. A. N. Sherwin-White suggested that the correct title to use for the office in the period before Claudius (A.D. 41–54) was "not *procurator* but *praefectus.*" See A. N. Sherwin-White, *Roman Society and Roman Law in the New Testament* (Oxford: Clarendon Press, 1963; reprint, Grand Rapids: Baker, Twin Brooks Series, 1978), 6–9.

Tiberius was the emperor during whose lifetime Jesus ministered, died, and rose from the dead. After the emperor's name is mentioned in Luke 3:1, he plays no active part in the biblical story.

3.) Caligula (A.D. 37–41)

The Roman Senate named Caligula the successor to Tiberius. He experienced early popularity with a series of highly-approved political measures. He released political prisoners, reduced taxes, and provided public entertainment. Eventually, signs of mental weakness and an oppressive arrogance emerged. He demanded worship as a deity and instructed his representative in Syria to erect his statue in the Jerusalem temple. The legate wisely delayed action until Caligula's death in A.D. 41. His reckless tyranny led to his assassination by a group of imperial guards. No action of Caligula is mentioned in Scripture.

4.) Claudius (A.D. 41–54)

At the death of Caligula, the praetorian guard, that is, the emperor's special bodyguards, appointed Claudius as emperor. He had lived in relative obscurity during the reigns of Tiberius and Caligula. An early illness, perhaps a form of infantile paralysis, left him with a repulsive physical appearance. A drooling mouth caused some to think him mentally deficient. His appearance was deceptive, for he proved to be a far more able ruler than his contemporaries would have anticipated.

Claudius made a determined attempt to restore the earlier Roman religion to a place of significance with the people. The Roman writer Suetonius states that Claudius expelled the Jews from Rome because of some disturbances surrounding one "Chrestus."[4] This expulsion of Jews affected Priscilla and Aquila, Paul's well-traveled missionary companions (Acts 18:2).

---

4. Suetonius, *The Lives of the Caesars* 5.25.4. It is uncertain whether Suetonius was referring to a Jew named "Chrestus" or misunderstood the name "Chrestus" for "Christus." If the latter is true, it may indicate that unbelieving Jews were causing disturbances over the preaching of Jesus as the Christ. See also the statement by Gill and Gempf that the disturbance "was the result of a Messianic superstar creating trouble in Rome but not the Christian's Messiah." See Bruce W. Winter, ed. *The Book of Acts in Its First Century Setting*, vol. 2, *The Book of Acts in Its Graeco-Roman Setting*, ed. David W. J. Gill and Conrad Gempf (Grand Rapids: William B, Eerdmans Publishing Co., 1994), 99.

5) Nero (A.D. 54–68)

Agrippina, the scheming mother of Nero, manipulated her husband Claudius into designating Nero, her son by a former husband, as his legal heir. Nero came to the throne at the young age of seventeen. His youth made it wise for him to follow older, experienced advisors for his first five years. During this time he managed to rule with effectiveness.

In A.D. 59 he murdered his dominating mother and assumed full control of the government. The results constituted a political disaster. His careless administrative policies emptied the treasury, and he used violence and cruelty to fill it again.

Nero had the temperament of an artist rather than that of a politician. He read his poetry in public, played the lyre before audiences, and sang at public performances.

During his reign a disastrous fire swept away ten of Rome's fourteen wards. Nero was accused of having the fire set deliberately to provide space for a new palace. He accused Christians of causing the disaster in order to divert any blame from himself. He unleashed severe local persecutions on Christians after the blaze.[5] Church tradition suggests that both Peter and Paul were martyred during the reign of Nero.[6]

Nero's draconian measures in government incited a revolt against his rule. He fled Rome and was killed by a former slave acting on Nero's orders. The revolt against Nero's authority led to three rapid changes of emperors during the years A.D. 68–69. Order was not restored until Vespasian's soldiers captured Rome and installed him as emperor.

5.) Vespasian (69–79)

Vespasian was involved in a siege of Jerusalem when his soldiers declared him the Roman emperor. Leaving the military affairs of Jerusalem in the hands of his son Titus, he proceeded to conquer

---

5. For different opinions on Nero's role in the fire, contrast Suetonius, *The Lives of the Caesars* 6.38.1 with Tacitus, *Annals* 15.38. Suetonius confidently asserts that Nero set the fire openly, but Tacitus only acknowledges the existence of a rumor concerning Nero's involvement in the fire.

6. Eusebius, *Church History* 2.25 (NPNF). All references to Eusebius are taken from NPNF.

the country of Egypt and cut off the supply of grain to Rome. A lieutenant of his set out for Italy, where he captured and sacked Rome. His victory led to Vespasian's assumption of the imperial office.

As an emperor Vespasian's strict and frugal habits plucked order from the chaos which Nero had caused. He built the famous Colisseum. He died in office in A.D. 79, leaving his position to Titus. His name is not linked with any New Testament events, but during his lifetime, Christianity grew rapidly throughout the Mediterranean world.

7. Titus (79–81)

Titus's most important link with the biblical world occurred in A.D. 70, when he captured and destroyed Jerusalem. His name is not mentioned in Scripture. His brief reign did not allow opportunity for significant accomplishments. During his reign the fiery destruction of Pompeii and Herculaneum occurred when Mt. Vesuvius erupted.

8. Domitian (81–96) Brother of Titus.

After Titus's death the Senate bestowed power on his younger brother Domitian. He was an autocratic ruler who tried forcibly to suppress foreign religions. Church tradition attributed the persecution of Christians to him, but extensive information about his actions is lacking.[7] His persecution probably provided the background against which the apostle John wrote the Revelation.

Local Rulers in Palestine

In Palestine the Romans used local rulers to carry out Roman policy. Herod the Great, an Idumean by birth, was the first non-Jewish ruler appointed to office by the Romans.

Herod the Great (37 B.C.–A.D. 4). The political craftiness of Herod's father Antipater offered his son a powerful beginning to a political career. The Roman Senate approved Herod's kingship, but he had to win the office by military means. His non-Jewish background caused most Jews to resent his presence. His capacity for scheming, cruel behavior appears in the biblical story of his slaugh-

---

7. Ibid., 3.17–18.

ter of the children in Bethlehem (Matt. 2:16–17). Herod's unscrupulous character explains his duplicity in dealing with the Magi from the East (Matt. 2:1–12).

Despite his cruelty and suspicious attitude, Herod had excellent administrative abilities. He provided free grain during famine and free clothing in other calamities. He constructed many impressive buildings and was also reponsible for the refurbishing of the Jerusalem temple. The temple was redecorated with white marble, gold, and jewels and became renowned for its splendor and lavish appearance. Additionally, Herod strengthened the defenses of Jerusalem by building or repairing a sturdy wall around the city.

His many marriages (nine or ten wives!) led to unbelievable domestic discord and competition for his throne. To prevent his scheming sons from deposing him, Herod killed at least three of them and at least two of his wives. As a practicing Jew, Herod would not normally kill a hog in order to eat pork. The fact that he had no scruples against killing his own sons reportedly prompted Augustus Caesar to remark about Herod, "It is better to be Herod's pig than his son."

Herod's final days were filled with displays of violence and hatred. His death in A.D. 4, likely of intestinal cancer, found him haunted by the memory of the atrocious murders he had committed.

Herod's Successors. At Herod's death three of his sons inherited separate parts of his kingdom. Archelaus became ethnarch of Judea, Samaria, and Idumea. The term *ethnarch* was used to describe the ruler over an ethnic group such as the Jews. He served from 4 B.C. to A.D. 6, when his distasteful rule provoked the Jews to ask Augustus to replace him. His reign over Judea led Joseph to take Mary and Jesus to live in Galilee rather than return to Judea (Matt. 2:22). After Archelaus's banishment from the Judean throne, the Romans generally ruled Judea through a prefect or propraetor who answered to the Roman emperor. Pontius Pilate was in the line of these prefects.

Herod Antipas was appointed *tetrarch* (a general designation of subordinate rulers) of Galilee and Perea and reigned from 4 B.C. to A.D. 39. John the Baptist rebuked him for divorcing his wife to marry Herodias, the wife of his half brother (Mark 6:17–20). Jesus labeled him "that fox" (Luke 13:32) and later stood trial before him (Luke 23:7–12).

Herod Philip was appointed tetrarch of Iturea, Trachonitis, Gaulanitis, Auranitis, and Batanea. He was fair and just in his dealings and served in this position from 4 B.C.–A.D. 34. Apparently Herod the Great also had another son named Philip. This Philip never ruled over any territory and is known in Scripture only because he was the first husband of the Herodias whom Herod Antipas married (Mark 6:17).

Two later descendants of Herod are also important because they are mentioned in the Bible. Herod Agrippa I, grandson of Herod the Great, executed James the Apostle and imprisoned Peter (Acts 12). He served as king over all Palestine (A.D. 37–44) before succumbing to a tragic death described in Acts 12:20–23. A great grandson, Herod Agrippa II, became tetrarch of Chalcis and other small territories in A.D. 50. He is important as the Agrippa before whom Paul gave his dramatic testimony in Acts 26.

Later Events in Palestine

When Titus destroyed Jerusalem in A.D. 70, temple worship ceased. Jewish rabbis who had fled the city established a school in the coastal town of Jamnia to carry on the traditions of the Pharisees. The Roman emperor Hadrian (A.D. 117–138) erected a pagan temple over the location of the Jewish temple and banned the practice of circumcision. The Jews revolted again under the leadership of Bar Cochba (also spelled Kokhba). Many regarded him as the Messiah. In A.D. 135 the Romans crushed the revolt, rebuilt Jerusalem as a Roman city, and banned Jews from entering the city. The Jewish nation lost any significant political existence until it appeared again in A.D. 1948.

Conclusion

Political changes in Russia, Germany, China, India, the Middle East, and Africa in the last century altered the course of world history. Political developments we cannot change touch our lives, mold our futures, and restrict our choices. Christians in all lands can respond more wisely to their own political dilemmas when they know and understand political transformations in other lands and times. When we understand the political developments of the New Testament period, we can interpret its message with greater insights.

Many statements with political implications are included in the New Testament. Jesus asked, "Whose portrait is this? And whose inscription?" (Matt. 22:20). At Jesus' trial Pilate demanded, "Are you the king of the Jews?" (Mark 15:2). The Jews who accused Jesus shouted to Pilate, "If you let this man go, you are no friend of Caesar" (John 19:12). In Luke 3:1–2 Luke mentioned the political leaders Tiberius Caesar, Pontius Pilate, Herod Antipas, Herod Philip, Lysanias, Annas, and Caiaphas. All of these questions, statements, and observations in the Gospels are political in nature.

Paul's Jewish opponents accused him of "persuading the people to worship God in ways contrary to the law" (Acts 18:13). The charges against the persecuted Christians in Hebrews 10:32–34 are political in nature. James warned readers that rich men were "the ones who are dragging you into court" (James 2:6). Peter urged his readers to "Submit . . . to every authority instituted among men" (1 Pet. 2:13). In a similar emphasis Paul directed his Roman friends to "submit . . . to the governing authorities" (Rom. 13:1). Political realities are also present in these passages.

Because of the political undercurrents in so much of the New Testament, we must be alert to the developments which lie beneath the politically-tinged statements and commands so that we can understand and apply the New Testament more wisely.

For Further Discussion

1. How did God use the events of the intertestamental period to prepare for the coming of Christ and the birth of the church?

2. Do you see examples in Christian history of Christian leaders who have used some of the same methods to defend their positions that Herod the Great used in his own defense?

3. What are some similarities of culture, political experience, and linguistic usage that residents throughout the New Testament world share in common?

Bibliography

Primary Materials

Austin, M. M. *The Hellenistic World from Alexander to the Roman Conquest.* Cambridge: Cambridge University Press, 1981. Selection of ancient sources on Greek history.

Barrett, C. K. *The New Testament Background: Selected Documents.* Rev. ed. London: SPCK, 1987.

Josephus, Flavius. *Antiquities of the Jews.* 7 vols. Loeb Classical Library. Cambridge: Harvard University Press, 1976–88.

———. *The Jewish War.* 2 vols. Loeb Classical Library. Cambridge: Harvard University Press, 1989.

Lewis, Naphtali, and Reinhold Meyer. *Roman Civilization, Sourcebook II: The Empire.* Rev. ed. New York: Harper & Row Publishers, Inc., 1966.

Plutarch. *Lives.* Vol. 7, *Alexander and Caesar.* Loeb Classical Library. Cambridge: Harvard University Press, 1971.

Suetonius. *The Lives of the Caesars.* 2 vols. Loeb Classical Library. Cambridge: Harvard University Press, 1964.

Suggs, Jack, Katharine Doob Sakenfield, and James R. Mueller, eds. "1 & 2 Maccabees." In the *Oxford Study Bible.* New York: Oxford Univeristy Press

Tacitus. *Histories and Annals.* 4 vols. Loeb Classical Library. Cambridge: Harvard University Press, 1962–63.

Secondary Materials

Bruce, F. F. *Israel and the Nations.* Grand Rapids: William B. Eerdmans Publishing Co., 1963. Historical sketch of the period leading up to and including the intertestamental period.

———. *New Testament History.* Garden City, N.Y.: Doubleday, 1971. Historical sketch primarily of the period beginning with the Herods and extending to the end of the New Testament era.

Enslin, Morton Scott. *Christian Beginnings: Parts I and II.* New York: Harper & Brothers, 1938; Harper Torchbooks, 1956. Good overview of political developments during the intertestamental period.

Filson, Floyd V. *A New Testament History.* Philadelphia: Westminster Press, 1964. A study primarily of the history of the New Testament era, beginning with Jesus and extending through the apostolic church.

Grant, Michael. *The Jews in the Roman World.* Dorset: n.p., 1984. Information concerning the impact of the Roman world on Judaism.

Gundry, Robert H. *Survey of the New Testament.* Rev. ed. Grand Rapids: Zondervan Books, 1981. Brief treatment of intertestamental history.

Jones, A. H. M. *The Greek City from Alexander to Justinian*. Oxford: Oxford University Press, 1939. Excellent political and social history of Greece.

———. *Studies in Roman Government and Law*. Oxford: Basil Blackwell Inc., 1960. Study of select issues, many relating to Roman practices evident in the New Testament.

Koester, Helmut. *History, Culture, and Religion of the Hellenistic Age*. Vol. 1, *Introduction to the New Testament*. Philadelphia: Fortress Press, 1982. Excellent overview of the political developments preceding the New Testament era.

Lea, Thomas D., and Tom Hudson. *Step by Step Through the New Testament*. Nashville: Baptist Sunday School Board, 1992. New Testament survey primarily for lay people.

Puskas, Charles B. *An Introduction to the New Testament*. Peabody, Mass.: Hendrickson Publishers Inc., 1989. Excellent bibliographical information on intertestamental period.

Reicke, Bo. *The New Testament Era*. Philadelphia: Fortress Press, 1968. Detailed historical background for the intertestamental period.

Sherwin-White, A. N. *Roman Society and Roman Law in the New Testament*. Oxford: Clarendon Press, 1963. Reprint, Grand Rapids: Baker, Twin Brook Series, 1978.

Tarn, W. W., and G. T. Griffith. *Hellenistic Civilisation*. 3d ed. London: Edward Arnold & Co., 1952. Excellent sourcebook concerning Hellenism's impact on Judaism.

Tenney, Merrill C. *New Testament Survey*. Grand Rapids: William B. Eerdmans Publishing Co., 1961. Brief, but excellent survey of intertestamental period.

2 Life in the World of the New Testament

Guiding Questions

1. What were the basic differences between daily life in Palestine and in the Roman Empire?

2. How did the people of the first century live, eat, dress, work, travel, learn, and enjoy entertainment?

3. How did the people of the first century observe the institutions of marriage and death?

Life in the New Testament era pulsated with many of the same dynamics of contemporary daily life. Families needed to earn a livelihood in order to have shelter, food, clothing, and some form of entertainment.

- Education was provided for the younger generation.

- Marriages took place.

- Death was inevitable.

- Human corruption and disagreements led to crime and struggles.

- Business and commerce developed, thus necessitating the need for transportation and some form of communication.

- Class distinctions existed.

Information about life in the New Testament world comes from two chief sources: ancient writers, who described habits of daily life; and archaeology, which has unearthed many previously unknown facts about living conditions and practices of this period.

Home Construction

A home in New Testament times varied from the tent of the desert bedouin, to the stucco or sun-dried brick of Palestine, to the brick or concrete of Rome.

Desert Tents

The portable tents of the bedouins were made of animal skins and could be enlarged as families grew. A number of families placed their tents close together to form a camp. As a tentmaker Paul probably did not make tents for bedouins but for military personnel who found the portability of tents useful in transitory military life (Acts 18:1–3).

Palestine

Many houses in Palestine were constructed from stone because it was cheap and readily available. Smaller stones were packed into the gaps between larger stones, and a layer of mud was plastered over the interior. Larger houses may have had a double thickness of stones. In the Jordan Valley it was easier to build houses with mud bricks because of the availability of rich, thick mud.

The roof of a house in Palestine was usually made by placing wooden beams across the top of the walls, covering them with brush, and placing a layer of mud or clay on top. This roof had to be rolled after each heavy rain in order to flatten it out.

The rooftop of a Palestinian home was reached by an outside staircase or in some cases even a wooden ladder propped against the wall. These roofs were surrounded with a parapet to prevent accidental tumbling from the roof. Washing clothes took place on the roof, and vegetables and fruits were dried there. Peter prayed atop a roof in Joppa (Acts 10:9–20). One of Jesus' most spectacular miracles occurred when he was teaching in a crowded home in Capernaum (Mark 2:1–12). Four men, unable to bring their paralyzed friend to Jesus because of the crowd, climbed to the roof, made a hole in it, and lowered their friend to Jesus.

Homes for poor people were constructed of very perishable material, and all traces of them have long been destroyed. Homes for the rich and privileged were made of more durable materials, and most of the remains discovered by archaeologists come from these homes. Some wealthy inhabitants of Palestine such as Herod the Great built elaborate palaces.

Poorer Palestinians could normally afford only a single-room dwelling. In such a home part of the room was on a higher level than the rest. Sitting, sleeping, and cooking took place on the higher level, and livestock and other animals inhabited the lower level. The floor was made of packed earth or stone.

Homes in Palestine generally had no windows. The absence of windows blocked the heat of direct sunlight from the interior and offered protection against the entry of a thief.

Homes in Rome

The rooms of Roman homes were often built around an unroofed courtyard with the more expensive homes having rows of pillars surrounding the courtyard. Roman homes were generally built of more durable material than those in Palestine, and conveniences such as central heating, baths, and plumbing were not uncommon. Oil lamps provided lighting, and floors were decorated with elaborate mosaics. Homes for lower- and middle-class people in the Roman Empire often consisted of flats in apartment houses.

Food

The daily diet for the average Palestinian of New Testament times probably consisted of vegetables, fruit, and bread. Sometimes the vegetables were flavored by boiling them with herbs. Meat was an expensive luxury, reserved for festive occasions (Luke 15:23). In northern Palestine fish provided a source of protein.

Palestinians normally ate two meals each day, at midday and in the evening. In the evening people relaxed over their food after a long day of work. They ate, talked, told stories, sang, and eventually went to bed. The Gospels indicate that Jesus sometimes ate meals as a guest (Mark 2:15–17). Apparently hosting guests was fairly common.

In New Testament times guests on formal occasions often reclined or lay down on couches as they ate their meals. It is easier to understand the events of the Last Supper if those present were reclining with their heads facing the table (John 13:23–30). In more informal meals individuals sat around the tables.

Bread was made from either wheat or barley, with barley more commonly used by poor people (note the relative prices of wheat and barley in Rev. 6:6). Olive oil was a vital ingredient for cooking. Individuals drank water, but its frequent impurity led many to use wine more commonly (cf. 1 Tim. 5:23).

Wealthy Romans, with a diet that included far more delicacies and richly prepared food than the rather spartan Palestinian fare, may have had four meals each day. In addition to meals corresponding to our breakfast, lunch, and dinner, they had an afternoon break around 4:00 P.M. for eating and drinking. Dinner was not eaten until 8:00 or 9:00 P.M.

Clothing

In biblical times both men and women wore a tunic, that is, a garment fitting loosely from shoulder to knee or ankle. The tunic was simple to cut and sew and could be worn year-round. Color and embroidery distinguished special clothes from those worn on ordinary occasions. In Palestine women commonly wore veils to cover their heads. Everyone except the poorest who went barefoot wore open leather sandals. These sandals consisted of a flat sole secured by thongs across the instep and between the toes.

In cooler weather a cloak was usually worn over the tunic. Women sometimes wore brightly colored outer garments. Because a cloak provided protection from the cold, it was regarded as securely belonging to its owner. Normally, not even a litigant could take a cloak from its owner. In Matthew 5:40 Jesus appealed for his followers to give their cloak freely to someone who tried to sue only for the shirt or tunic.

The cloth used to make these garments was frequently wool and sometimes linen. Sometimes the cloth would be left in its natural color, but the use of dyes was not uncommon. Bleaching was used to produce white cloth.

Social Classes

In Roman society class distinctions were based primarily on wealth. Senators, military leaders, wealthy landowners, and important businessmen enjoyed great luxury. Beneath them were the humble people without any capital and tradesmen, who because of the possession of some capital, were slightly higher on the social scale. Slaves did most of the work, and no strong middle class existed.

Among the Jews some class distinctions existed, but even the poorest Jew felt that in the eyes of Yahweh he was accepted in a way that paralleled the wealthiest son of Abraham. In practice, however, the chief priests and other leading officials of the temple constituted an upper class.

In Israel, special contempt was reserved for the tax collectors or publicans who assisted the hated Romans and often took money from the poor illegally. Jews in Judea also looked with disdain on the residents of Galilee because of the mixing of races which took place there.

Slavery was so widespread in the Roman Empire that slaves may have outnumbered the free. Debtors, criminals, and war prisoners were often condemned to slavery. Many slaves, particularly those taken from battles, were more skilled and educated than their masters. A large number of early Christians were slaves (Eph. 6:5–9). Slavery also existed among the Jews, but the number of slaves was smaller, and their treatment was significantly more humane (Lev. 25:39–46).

Languages

It is quite possible that Jesus was trilingual. When Jesus read the Isaiah scroll in the synagogue (Luke 4:18–19), it would have been normal to read in Hebrew. Jesus apparently had no difficulty doing this.

He may also have spoken Greek. Even though we find no Greek quotations among his words, Greek was the language of business and diplomacy, especially in Palestine. When Pilate interrogated

Jesus in John 18:33–37, he would normally have used Greek. Since he did not call for an interpreter, it is possible that Jesus conversed with him in Greek.

We know that Jesus also used Aramaic. His utterance of such phrases as "Talitha, cumi" (Mark 5:41) and "Eloi, Eloi, lama sabachthani" (Matt. 27:46) is evidence of this usage.

Proof of the trilingual nature of much of Palestinian culture appears in the inscription at the cross of Christ written in Hebrew (probably Aramaic), Greek, and Latin (John 19:20). Jesus' disciples would have likely been able to use several of these languages.

Jewish Population

The Jewish population in Palestine during Jesus' lifetime has been estimated at five or six hundred thousand.[1] The total population of Jerusalem has been estimated as ranging from twenty-five to thirty thousand, but during Jewish festivals this number increased by many times.[2] Estimates of the total number of Jews in the Roman Empire are from four million[3] to seven or eight million. Daniel-Rops, who makes the higher suggestion, estimates that one Roman in ten was a Jew.[4]

Jews outside Palestine, known as the "Diaspora," were thus considerably more numerous than those living inside its boundaries. Rome and Alexandria, although not predominantly Jewish, were the two largest centers of Jewish population in the world. These Jews were not totally absorbed into pagan society, but they were much more open to non-Jewish practices. Few of them abandoned the Jewish faith, but most observed the law in a more relaxed manner than those who lived in Palestine.

Some areas of Palestine, such as Galilee, had a majority of Gentiles. The province of Judea was the chief population center for Judaism.

---

1. Joachim Jeremias, *Jerusalem in the Time of Jesus* (Philadelphia: Fortress Press, 1969), 205.

2. Ibid., 77–84. This figure for Jerusalem population represents a reduction from his earlier estimate of a range from 55,000 to 95,000 (see p. 83, n. 24).

3. Robert H. Gundry, *A Survey of the New Testament*, rev. ed. (Grand Rapids: Zondervan, 1981), 21.

4. Henri Daniel-Rops, *Daily Life in the Time of Jesus* (New York: Hawthorn, 1962), 58.

Industry, Labor, and Commerce

Among the basic industries operating in New Testament times were the manufacture of clothing and pottery, metal working, and construction. As a carpenter, Jesus had a trade which was vital to the welfare of the New Testament world (Mark 6:3). All industry operated in small, local shops because transporting raw materials and finished products could not be done economically.

Silversmiths (Acts 19:24) and ivory carvers made products intended to appeal to more wealthy clients. A list of raw materials, expensive foods, perfumes, and other products for the wealthy appear in Revelation 18:11–17, showing the existence of luxury industries.

Although some small industry and craft work appeared in Palestine, most of the area was pastoral and agricultural in the first century. In the area around the Sea of Galilee fishing was an important source of income.

The practice of trading was common among both the Jews and Gentiles (see James 4:13–16). Among Jews, grain import and export and banking were large business enterprises. Some Jews handled the business of exporting grain from Egypt to Rome and other cities. Detailed banking practices were also common in the Roman world. Trade guilds united professionals with similar skills, insisted on just compensation and working hours, and provided assistance to distressed members (observe the functions of the guild in Acts 19:25–27).

Transportation and Communication

Even though the Romans constructed a vast road network in the first century, the majority of people did not venture far from home. No public transportation services had scheduled travel. Hotels on travel routes were often dangerous and were hotbeds of immorality. Roadside brigands made even short trips dangerous (the parable of the good Samaritan in Luke 10:25–35 accurately reflects this travel danger).

In Israel three international roads ran north to south. The Way of the Sea (mentioned in Matt. 4:15 as a quote from Isa. 9:1–2) followed the coast along the narrow strip of land between the sea and the desert. The Sinai Road passed through Shechem, Jerusalem,

Hebron, and Beersheba in its route through the southern part of Palestine known as the Negev to Egypt. A third road, known as the King's Highway, began in Damascus and passed east of the Jordan to Elath on the Gulf of Aqabah. A branch of this road extended into Arabia.

Rome constructed its road system to facilitate the movement of soldiers and commerce throughout the empire. In contrast with Palestinian roads, the Roman roads were durably constructed. The Appii Forum (Acts 28:15) was a rest stop along the Appian Way leading to Rome. The Egnatian (or Ignatian) Way carried land traffic across Macedonia between the Aegean and Adriatic Seas en route to Rome. Paul would have followed a portion of this route on his travels through Macedonia from Philippi to Thessalonica (Acts 17:1).

Even though much traffic moved via land in the first century, water was the primary commercial means of transportation, and Alexandria was the chief port for shipping grain from Egypt throughout the empire. Paul was aboard an Alexandrian grain ship when he was shipwrecked (Acts 27:6).

Government communications moved over the highways and across the bodies of water. Sometimes private businesses hired couriers to carry messages. Writing materials for communication included papyrus, broken bits of pottery (known as ostraca), and wax tablets. Leather and parchment (made from animal skins) provided more durable writing material. Local messages were announced by town criers or by posting on public bulletin boards.

Education

Prior to a few centuries before Christ no schools existed for most children, and sons were probably taught the fundamentals of reading and writing by their fathers. In about the second century B.C. synagogue rabbis assumed the role of teachers for boys beginning at age six. Pupils who learned from the rabbis sat on the ground surrounding the teacher and repeated what the rabbis taught them. The teaching chiefly consisted of religious instruction based on the Torah. Seats and other classroom conveniences did not appear until a later date. The only education provided for girls was the informal domestic education given to them by their mothers in the home.

The development of education among the Jews may indicate a response to the influence of Hellenism. Education played an important role among the Greeks, and a person was expected to demonstrate vigorous intellectual effort until at least age eighteen. Hellenistic education was available for boys and girls.

In the Roman Empire slaves often served as teachers. Pupils studied philosophy, mathematics, music, literature, and rhetoric. For senior scholars additional instruction was available in such subjects as astronomy and architecture. Centers such as Alexandria, Carthage, Tarsus, and Marseilles were special locations which offered advanced training and often drew distinguished lecturers to speak to large and interested audiences.

Science and Medicine

Medical practice in Palestine was crude and frequently contained elements of superstition and magic. Until Greek times medical diagnosis was the responsibility of the priest. The Pentateuch itself contained some of the medical principles of the Israelites (see the instructions concerning hygiene, for example, in Lev. 15).

Common diseases in biblical times included malaria, typhoid, dysentery, leprosy, tuberculosis, pneumonia, and smallpox. Eye diseases and deafness were also common in Palestine, as seen in Jesus' work of healing people with these afflictions (Mark 7:31–37; 10:46–52).

In New Testament times, doctors existed both among the Jews (see Mark 5:25–26) and the Romans (Col. 4:14). For the Romans, training involved apprenticeship to experienced doctors and education in medical schools of the time. Amputations, tracheotomies, and cranial surgery were performed on patients. Such operations used neither anesthetics nor antiseptics and must have been painful and often fatal.

Among medical instruments used by physicians were lancets for opening abscesses, and various types of razors, forceps, and catheters. Ointments, herbs, and varieties of minerals were among medications used by physicians.

Although medical knowledge in the first century was rudimentary, those who had the training used it intelligently for the relief of human suffering. Medical skills were more common outside of

Palestine. Here Roman and Greek influence led in the adoption of a more scientific approach to the discipline.

Entertainment

Feasting, singing, and dancing were among the most popular forms of entertainment in the world of the Bible. Any cessation of these common experiences was evidence of national disaster (note the disaster described in Rev. 18:21–24).

People celebrated military victories with singing and dancing. Feasts and festivals often included musical activity in order to increase the merriment of the occasion (Luke 15:25–32). Musicians used stringed instruments resembling the harp, wind instruments such as the flute (Matt. 9:23), and percussion instruments such as cymbals and tambourines. Although music was often used in moments of joy and celebration, sad and mournful dirges were common during periods of bereavement.

People of biblical times also played various types of games. Archaeological excavations have uncovered board games involving the use of dice. The rules of these games are now lost. Outdoor games included running, throwing, wrestling, and shooting. Paul taught lessons on the Christian life, using images drawn from the world of athletics (1 Cor. 9:24–27).

The Romans provided public games for entertainment which included killing men or animals. War captives, slaves, and condemned criminals often became gladiators who fought with one another to maim or kill an opponent. The Roman emperor Constantine officially abolished these shows in A.D. 313 because they were incompatible with Christianity.

In Palestine children played in the streets and often copied the actions of their parents. Rattles, balls, and dolls were among the toys made for children.

Marriage

Our society assumes that marriage should be based on the mutual love of the participating couples, but this idea would have been strange to those living in New Testament Palestine. Marriages were arranged by the fathers of the couple. In New Testament times rabbis fixed the minimum age for marriage at twelve for girls and thirteen for boys, but some waited additional years in order to learn a trade and accumulate money for the price of the marriage.[5]

After the proposal for marriage was made, the fathers began financial negotiations. The marriage price was seen as compensation given to the father of the prospective bride for the loss of a worker. The bride was not mere property, and during times of personal need she may have received the marriage price back for her own use. The amount paid was not dependent so much on the desirability of the bride as on the wealth and standing of the bride's father.

After the agreement on the marriage price, the couple was viewed as engaged. This relationship was more binding than contemporary engagements. If plans for the wedding failed, the responsible party often bore a financial penalty. During this period of engagement no sexual relations were permitted. It was this fact which led Joseph to consider "putting away" Mary during their period of engagement (Matt. 1:18–25).

In the wedding ceremony the bridegroom went with a company of friends to take the bride-to-be from her father's house. The bride was transported in a litter to the bridegroom's house with well-wishers singing wedding songs along the way. Upon arrival, the parents of the groom would repeat a traditional blessing for happiness and a fruitful marriage. Games, dancing, and merriment continued throughout the evening, and celebration of the marriage lasted for at least a week. On the first evening the pair vanished in order to consummate the marriage. After this the young couple returned to share in the celebration with songs and dancing.

Among the Jews divorce was often obtained on rather flimsy grounds. In biblical times only men could initiate a divorce. Women had no legal protection from the court.

Funerals

Death was an occasion for a public display of grief and emotion. Crying, weeping, and beating the breasts were common expressions of grief. Some tore their outer clothes and wore sackcloth.

---

5. J. A. Thompson, *Handbook of Life in Bible Times* (Downers Grove, Ill.: InterVarsity Press, 1986), 85.

Some mourners threw earth over their heads, rolled in the dust, or sat dejectedly among ashes. Professional mourners, usually women, were often hired to compose and sing lamentations for funeral processions. The period of mourning usually lasted for seven days.

Burial came quickly after death. The Palestinian heat caused bodies to decompose quickly, possibly creating a health risk. Coffins were generally not used, but wealthy people cut chambers in rocks for burial. In New Testament times bodies were wrapped with linen cloths, and the folds of the cloth were filled with aromatic spices (John 19:38–42).

The Greek custom for funerals was to prepare the body for burial by washing the body and clothing it in a white garment. Near relatives and professional wailers gathered to weep loudly and to tear their hair or cut their cheeks. The funeral procession followed immediately in hot climates, but it could be delayed a few days in regions of more moderate climate. Cremation was the usual Greek method for disposal of the body. If burial did occur, a wooden or stone coffin was used. On certain annual days after the funeral it was customary to bring offerings of wine, oil, milk, or a mixture of honey and some liquid to pour on the grave.

Crime

Life was cheap, and murder was common in the New Testament era. The murderous rage of Herod the Great is recorded in Matthew 2:16–18. Parents sometimes "exposed" girls and deformed and unwanted infants by abandonment in an alley, on a hillside, or in the city center. In addition, robbery, extortion, and blackmail were practices as common then as now.

Punishment for criminals was outrageously brutal. The Romans used crucifixion as a sadistic method of punishment. To punish other criminals, Romans used a scourge fitted with strips of leather or cords with a pellet of bone or metal at the end. Each blow of the scourge cut and mangled the flesh. Other types of punishment for criminals involved imprisonment (Rev. 1:9), banishment, or forced labor.

Among the Jews, crimes against religion were regarded with the greatest detestation. The practice of idolatry, magic, or blasphemy received the penalty of death. In New Testament times decisions on capital crimes could not be made by the Jews. Such decisions belonged to their Roman overlords (John 18:31). Stoning was a Jewish form of capital punishment, but its practice in Acts 7:58–60 probably represents a mob reaction rather than a punishment sanctioned by the Romans.

[handwritten: – Soldiers]

The Roman Army *[handwritten: – Legionaries – Praetorian guards]*

The Roman Army was a volunteer organization, and its enticing terms of service attracted numerous volunteers. The length of service was twenty years, but regular soldiers often served for longer periods. The daily pay rate for the soldier was a denarius, and with this money he purchased equipment and other necessities. If he did not enter the army as a Roman citizen, he received citizenship upon his entry. At the conclusion of his service he received a lump sum of money and a piece of land.

Under the reorganization by Augustus, recruitment became a matter for the various provinces to handle individually. The result was that those serving in Palestine during the New Testament era were likely recruited from that region rather than from the western regions of the Empire.

The army was divided into legions of infantry consisting of six thousand men. Each legion was divided into ten cohorts of six hundred soldiers, and these in turn were divided into three maniples, containing two hundred each. In New Testament times Pilate probably had four regular legions quartered in Palestine. In addition to these regular legionnaires there were auxiliary troops comprised of men who were not normally Roman citizens but who obtained citizenship at the completion of their term of service.

The most frequently mentioned army officer in the New Testament is the centurion, the leader of one hundred men. Most centurions were Romans with steady leadership skills and proven courage. Centurions appearing in the New Testament are uniformly men of character (Acts 10:1–8). Another army officer mentioned in the New Testament is the tribune. Each legion had six tribunes. Claudias Lysias (Acts 23:16–30) held the rank of tribune. Some tribunes commanded cohorts, but these cohorts probably contained more than the six hundred soldiers mentioned earlier.

The Praetorian guards became the special bodyguards of the emperor. As an elite group they received double the rate of pay of ordinary legionnaires. Paul's reference to the "palace guard" (Phil. 1:13) may refer to this special group.[6]

The people of the first century did not have the advantages of modern science, education, and technology, but they devised their own responses to meeting the basic needs of life. Jews, Greeks, and Romans showed flexibility and creativity in responding to their culture and climate to provide life's necessities. We can easily identify today with the construction of buildings and types of food the Graeco-Roman world provided. The current influence of Judaeo-Christian religions allows us also to appreciate many of the institutions of Judaism, such as marriage.

For Further Discussion

1. How did cultural practices of the first century prepare for the coming of Christ and the development of the church?

2. List some factors which might cause differences in practice and outlook among Palestinian Jews and Diaspora Jews.

3. Did the social practices of early Christianity more resemble those of Palestinian Jews or Diaspora Jews? Explain your answer.

4. List some areas in which the advent of Christianity affected the social customs of the Graeco-Roman world.

Bibliography

Primary Materials

Barrett, C. K. *The New Testament Background: Selected Documents.* Rev. ed. London: SPCK, 1987.

Danby, Herbert. *The Mishnah.* London: Oxford University Press, 1933.

Finegan, Jack. *The Archaeology of the New Testament.* Princeton: Princeton University Press, 1969.

Jeremias, Joachim. *Jerusalem in the Time of Jesus.* Philadelphia: Fortress Press, 1969.

---

6. Some translators adopt the translation of "palace" and view the term as a reference to the residence of the emperor or governor.

Suetonius. *The Lives of the Caesars*. 2 vols. Loeb Classical Library. Cambridge: Harvard University Press, 1964.

Tacitus. *Histories and Annals*. 4 vols. Loeb Classical Library. Cambridge: Harvard University Press, 1962–63.

Secondary Materials

Bloch, Abraham P. *The Biblical and Historical Background of Jewish Customs and Ceremonies*. New York: KTAV Publishing House Inc., 1980.

Bouquet, A.C. *Everyday Life in New Testament Times*. New York: Charles Scribner's Sons, 1953.

Corswant, W. *A Dictionary of Life in Bible Times*. New York: Oxford University Press Inc., 1960.

Daniel-Rops, Henri. *Daily Life in the Time of Jesus*. New York: Hawthorn, 1962.

Gundry, Robert H. *A Survey of the New Testament*. Rev. ed. Grand Rapids: Zondervan Books, 1981.

Johnson, Luke T. *The Writings of the New Testament*. Philadelphia: Fortress Press, 1986.

Lohse, Eduard. *The New Testament Environment*. Rev. ed. Nashville: Abingdon Press, 1976.

Thompson, J. A. *Handbook of Life in Bible Times*. Downers Grove, Ill.: InterVarsity Press, 1986.

The Religious
3 Background to the
New Testament

Guiding Questions

1. What were the various options of religious belief and practice open to non-Christians in the Graeco-Roman era?

2. Describe the religious institutions to which Jews in the New Testament era devoted themselves.

3. Describe the features of the non-Christian and Jewish religious scene that assisted or influenced the spread of Christianity.

Paganism

The Graeco-Roman Pantheon

The religion of early Rome was animism. In the largely rural society farmers worshipped those gods which personified the forces they faced daily, gods of the field, forest, and stream. They appealed to their gods to aid them in sowing and harvesting. These gods had no distinct personalities, and we may best view them as influences or sources of power.

As Rome made contact with Greece, the Romans adopted the personalities and fables of the Greek gods into their own pantheon but changed their names. Zeus, the father of the gods to the Greeks, became Jupiter (Acts 14:12). Hera, the wife of Zeus, became Juno. Poseidon, the god of the sea, was renamed Neptune. Hermes, the messenger of the gods for the Greeks, became Mercury (Acts 14:12). All the deities named by the Greek poet Homer in his classic writings were adapted to their Roman equivalents.

When Augustus became sole ruler of the Empire in 27 B.C., he tried to build solidarity in the state by promoting the old Roman religion. He built temples, recruited candidates for the priesthood, and restored some of the ancient rites and festivals. However, even Augustus's organizing genius could not turn the devotion of Roman citizens back to their ancestral gods. Roman nobility had a nostalgic place for the ancient religion, but most Roman citizens became involved in the personal cults developing at that time.

The repulsive immoralities and petty bickerings of the Graeco-Roman deities contributed to a general decline in their public worship. Philosophers scorned them, and moralists warned that their bad examples would corrupt the young.[1] One factor that accelerated the decline in worship of the Greek pantheon was the defeat of Greece by Rome. Romans were reluctant to worship gods who seemed too weak or fickle to help them.

Several features characterized Graeco-Roman religion.

- Graeco-Roman religion was nonexclusive. A Roman who worshipped one deity could also give devotion to another deity. In Christianity such a compromise of worship would be unthinkable.

- In Graeco-Roman religion the power of fate was thought to be quite strong. This belief led to a faith in astrology and a gullible respect for all forms of magic.

- Graeco-Roman religion was corporate. Religion was to be practiced by society at large; it was not viewed as an essentially private matter.

- Religion and morality were separated. The rules governing religions were those of ritual purity rather than ethical or moral guidelines.

---

1. Plato, *Republic* 2.378; 3.390.

The practices of ancient paganism demonstrate the accuracy of Paul's charges in Romans 1:18–32. There Paul pictured a religion which began by rejecting the knowledge of God and concluded by perverting all moral values. Pagan worshippers were guilty of creating gods whose existence was solely in the empty caverns of their own minds.

Domestic and Rural Religion

The worship of the Greek and Roman gods appeared most often in the cities of the Graeco-Roman world under state sponsorship. In private homes and in the rural countryside individual citizens willingly preserved traditions from earlier periods. Events such as eating, birth, and death involved many religious customs. Greeks believed their countrysides were inhabited by demons or spirits. To placate these nature spirits, they stacked piles of stones by the roadways. Travelers would add other stones to the heap or place food on the stack as an offering to the deity.

Many Roman homes had a niche which served as a shrine to spirits whom they called lares, shadowy beings which were thought to watch over and protect the family and the household. The lares received offerings before every meal and at other regular intervals. They were also worshipped at crossroads as protectors of travelers. The average Roman respected these animistic deities more than they did the great Roman pantheon headed by Jupiter and Juno.

Emperor Worship

In the first century the Roman senate moved gradually to ascribe divinity to the Roman emperor. This practice was influenced by long-standing traditions from the Greek East. Some Roman emperors such as Augustus saw emperor worship as a useful tool to encourage patriotism and inspire political unity in the Empire. Others such as the insane Caligula openly sought worship for themselves.

After Augustus brought peace to the Empire, he was regarded as a savior, and some thought his accomplishments were indicative of his divinity. Romans accepted the idea that the destiny for the ruler's soul was different from that of the general population. Prior to Augustus, Julius Caesar had accepted honors which ascribed deity to himself. Augustus encouraged this feeling toward himself, but he moved cautiously lest he offend more conservative elements in Rome. He encouraged the emperor cult more vigorously in the provinces than in Rome itself. In his lifetime he accepted the status of more than human but not fully divine. After his death in A.D. 14 the Senate ascribed deity to him. All subsequent first-century emperors supported the worship of deceased emperors. Tiberius, Claudius, and Vespasian did not encourge expressions of adoration, though Caligula, Nero, and Domitian manipulated circumstances to produce such expressions.

Many Romans viewed emperor worship as merely a harmless patriotic duty. The Christian claim was that there was only "one God, the Father" and "one Lord Jesus Christ" (1 Cor. 8:6). The Christian refusal to practice emperor worship brought fierce persecution on believers.

The Mystery Religions

Graeco-Roman citizens did not find true satisfaction from either devotion to the Roman pantheon or the practice of emperor worship. Most citizens wanted a more personal faith that would ensure contact with the deity and offer hope in times of stress and trouble. Mystery religions attempted to fill this void. Some of the devotees to the mysteries and other pagan religions later found the reality they were seeking through making a commitment to Jesus Christ. Seeking religious truth made them prime candidates for Christian evangelism.

Many mystery religions originated in the East in pre-Christian times, but the Eleusinian mystery existed in Greece for many centuries prior to the New Testament era. The cult of Cybele developed in Asia. Devotion to Isis and Osiris or Serapis infiltrated the Roman world from Egypt, and Mithraism began in Persia. Each mystery differed in small details, but certain common traits appeared in all. The myth revolved around a god who had died and had experienced a resuscitation. Pageantry involved introductory ceremonies with secret rites, mystical formulae, symbolic washings, and fellowship meals. Each initiate was given a promise of immortality, and was thought to participate in the experience of the god who died and revived.

The mysteries eliminated class distinctions by placing rich and poor, master and slave, prominent and insignificant on the same level. They provided an outlet for emotions in religious experience, an opportunity that was entirely lacking in state-sponsored rituals.

They emphasized the personal aspect of religion more than the corporate aspect. The New Testament does not mention the mystery religions directly, but debates about their influence on the New Testament have persisted among scholars. Peter's use of the term "behold" (1 Pet. 2:12) involves a word frequently employed to describe the act of viewing the sacred objects of a mystery religion. The usage does not suggest that Peter was ever a devotee of a mystery religion, but it shows that Christians did sometimes use the same vocabulary as the mysteries.

Because the beliefs of the mysteries were a carefully guarded secret, it is difficult to know precisely what they taught their followers. However, some information about the beliefs of the mysteries became available in the second, third, and fourth centuries A.D. We know that many mysteries were pre-Christian in origin. The beliefs and practices of some mysteries appear to be similar to certain teachings of Christianity. These similarities may indicate that Christians (after the first century) and adherents to the mysteries may have borrowed or been influenced by one another, although there is little evidence that Christians in the first century were indebted to the mysteries. The following examples reveal both similarities and striking contrasts between Christianity and the mysteries.

- The death of Jesus is uniformly presented in the New Testament as a redemptive event (2 Cor. 5:21; 1 Pet. 3:18), but the deaths of the gods of the mysteries lack redemptive value.

- The event of Jesus' death and resurrection relates to a historical figure, but the myths of the deaths and rebirths of the mystery deities are related to the cycle of vegetation.

- Jesus experienced a bodily resurrection, but the gods of the mysteries came back to life only in part or in another realm of history.[2]

---

2. See J. G. Machen, *The Origin of Paul's Religion* (New York: Macmillan Co., 1928), 211–90, for an apologetic on the originality of Christian ideas. For a discussion of the beliefs of selected mystery religions, see Everett Ferguson, *Backgrounds of Early Christianity* (Grand Rapids: Wm. B. Eerdmans Publishing Co., 1987), 197–240.

- In the myths of the Phrygian deity Attis, there is a restoration to life for Attis. The restoration, however, involves only the preservation of his body from decay, the growth of his hair, and the ability to move his little finger. This is hardly a parallel with Jesus' death and resurrection.

Gnosticism

The term Gnosticism is derived from a Greek word referring to knowledge. Its very name implies that this religion offered salvation by presenting added knowledge for those who sought it. Those who followed the path of Gnosticism felt that the primary spiritual problem of humanity was not sin, which demanded forgiveness, but ignorance, which demanded new insight.

The major beliefs common to the Gnostic system included the following :

- Knowledge was superior to faith, and certain enlightened Christians had a special knowledge of the truth.

- Matter was evil; matter served as the source of all other evil; matter and spirit were distinct.

- Evil originated with a creature known as the demiurge, who was distinct from the God of the Old Testament and could have no contact with material creation.

- Christ was not human and his sufferings on the cross were regarded as unreal.

- Asceticism was the means of achieving communion with God.

- Adoption of an attitude of indifference toward the human body which led to antinominanism.

Not all Gnostic systems promoted all of these emphases, but they were generally present in most Gnostic belief statements. Among the features of "added knowledge" was the idea that this world was too evil to have been created by a good god. Gnostics believed that the chief god produced a series of emanations, also known as aeons, with each emanation inferior to the one from which it sprang. The last of these emanations created the world.

Thus, the world created was evil, but it was not created by the actions of the good god. Anyone wishing to receive salvation was forced to renounce the material world and seek the invisible world. This teaching led to two different moral emphases.

1. Some responded to Gnosticism by practicing asceticism. They tried to prevent the body from becoming involved in evil and curbed the appetites of the body.

2. Others responded to Gnostic teaching by denying the reality of the body and suggesting that bodily acts had no significance. They abandoned themselves to bodily appetites and indulged the body.

Gnosticism was an eclectic movement. It contained remnants of pagan thought, Judaism, and distortions of Christianity. The movement did not develop fully until the mid-to-late second century, but the ideas which led to Gnosticism were present in the first century and are reflected in the New Testament.

In Colossians 2:21 Paul revealed evidence of ascetic practices indicated by the warning: "Touch not; taste not; handle not." The reference to the "worship of angels" (Col. 2:18) showed a possible Gnostic doctrine of emanations which related the true God to the physical universe. Paul attempted to correct these errors by presenting the person and work of Christ. He described Christ as one who had the fulness of the Godhead dwelling in him (Col. 1:19) and as the one who held all creation together (Col. 1:17).

Paul warned Timothy not to give attention to the "ideas of what is falsely called knowledge" (1 Tim. 6:20). Some have suggested that the presence of the term *knowledge* is proof that Paul was opposing a form of Gnosticism. In contrast to this interpretation is the idea that the essential elements of Gnosticism are not present in 1 Timothy or the other Pastorals. The Pastorals do not contain evidence of a belief that a hierarchy of lesser spiritual beings related human beings to God. Nor do they include a discussion of the use of this knowledge to assist the soul in escaping from the world of matter. Paul's words indicate that Gnostic-like ideas circulated in the New Testament world, but these ideas do not represent fully developed Gnosticism.

In 1 John the apostle discussed the knowledge of God (1 John 5:20) and a heresy that appeared to deny the reality of Christ's body (1 John 4:1–3). John insisted that the knowledge of God which he discussed was not reached by heeding Gnostic speculations but by the obedience of faith (1 John 2:7–11). He also affirmed the historical reality of Jesus (1 John 2:22) and condemned licentious behavior (1 John 3:9).

In 1945 at Nag Hammadi, or Chenoboskion, Egypt, an entire early Gnostic library was discovered. The library dated from the mid-second century and contained many of Jesus' Gospel sayings in a distorted form. The writings emphasize that salvation consists of receiving knowledge imparted by Jesus, and they present evidence that Gnosticism borrowed from Christianity rather than the reverse. The documents of these sources provide valuable evidence for studying the origins and teachings of early Gnosticism. However, the study of these documents has revealed nothing that would contradict the earlier summary of the main teachings and emphases of Gnosticism. [3]

The Philosophies

Greek philosophy represented an effort by intelligent thinkers to address concerns relating to world problems and questions. The answers given to life questions by the various philosophies were too abstract for most people to grasp, but they always held an appeal for the educated elite.

- Epicureanism defined pleasure as the absence of pain and advocated that pleasure was life's highest good. It did not always lead to wanton sensuality, but it did promote a self-centered lifestyle.

- Stoicism emphasized that perfect self-control was the aim of life. Stoics viewed events as decreed by providence and felt that the universe was to be accepted, not changed. Paul encountered both of these philosophies in Athens (Acts 17:18).

---

3. For an excellent discusion of the chief beliefs, development, and possible influences of Gnosticism see *The International Standard Bible Encyclopedia*, rev. ed., s.v. "Gnosticism" by A. M. Renwick.

- The Cynics of the first century used shocking behavior to show their disdain for comfort, affluence, and social position. They abandoned all standards and were utterly indecent in talk and action.

- The Skeptics rejected all standards of right and wrong and insisted that all moral judgments were relative. Following their position would logically lead to complete moral and intellectual paralysis.

These philosophies have modern counterparts which appear under different names. Despite their pretentious beliefs, they actually had influence on a small number of first-century people.

Judaism

The Literature of Judaism

The variety of literature produced by Judaism shows the farflung geographic reach and theological diversity among Jews of the Graeco-Roman period and clearly demonstrates that Judaism had considerable variety and was not merely a legalistic monolith.

The Old Testament in the first century appeared in three different translations.

1. The original Hebrew was used in priestly observances in Palestine.

2. Diaspora Jews used the Greek translation Old Testament, known as the Septuagint. Jewish legend indicates that seventy-two scholars labored to produce the Septuagint, and the Roman numerals LXX, the nearest round number to seventy-two, symbolize the Septuagint. Translated in Egypt at the request of Ptolemy II Philadelphus (285–246 B.C.), this version became the Bible of the early church.

3. Targums were original oral translations which were gradually being written in Aramaic. They often contained imaginative material not found in the Hebrew text.

The term *Apocrypha* (literally "hidden books") refers to the books, generally from the intertestamental period, containing history, fiction, and wisdom literature. Protestants do not recognize these books as canonical, but the writings do contain useful historical information and some acceptable moral teaching. Catholics often accept them under the label of "deutero canonical." The Apocrypha includes such historical books as 1 and 2 Maccabees, wisdom literature such as the Wisdom of Solomon and Ecclesiasticus, and edifying but largely fictitious stories such as Tobit, Judith, and the additions to Daniel.

A second group of Jewish writings excluded from the canon is known as the *Pseudepigrapha.* The term designates the books as falsely inscribed with the name of an authoritative Old Testament personality in order to gain a degree of acceptance. Apocrypha and Pseudepigrapha are misleading terms, for there is much that is hidden about the Pseudepigrapha, and some false inscriptions appear in the Apocrypha. None of the Pseudepigrapha were ever serious contenders for canonical status, and this is the chief reason for giving them a special category. Among the books in this category are 1 and 2 Enoch (not written by the biblical Enoch), the Assumption of Moses, the Letter of Aristeas, and 3 and 4 Maccabees. The fact that Jude quotes from 1 Enoch (vv. 14–15) and apparently from the Assumption of Moses (v. 9) shows that some of the Pseudepigrapha had wide usage, even though they never received canonical authority.

The Dead Sea Scrolls were discovered in caves near Qumran on the Dead Sea during the late 1940s and early 1950s. Many Bible scholars view them as coming from the Essenes, a small Jewish sect who lived a rigidly legalistic existence in this vicinity. The documents contain biblical manuscripts, sectarian writings, and some previously known apocryphal and pseudepigraphal works. Studying them can enlarge our knowledge of the messianic beliefs and liturgical practices of Palestinian Judaism.[4]

Apocalyptic writings appear in the Old Testament, the Apocrypha, Pseudepigrapha, and the Qumran writings. This literature employed vivid symbols to reveal God's control over the events of history. Many apocalyptic writings are pseudonymous. The book of 1 Enoch is an example of a pseudonymous apocalypse.

---

4. F. F. Bruce describes the insights which a knowledge of the Dead Sea Scrolls can give to New Testament study in "The Dead Sea Scrolls and Early Christianity," in *A Mind for What Matters* (Grand Rapids: William B. Eerdmans Publishing Co., 1990), 49–64.

The Jewish writer Philo lived in Alexandria, Egypt, between 30 B.C. and A.D. 50. His writings represent an attempt to make Judaism acceptable to the educated Greeks of his day. The Jewish writer Josephus was born in A.D. 37/38 and died between 110 and 120. His most important works present a survey of Jewish history, particularly the Jewish war with Rome from A.D. 66–70.

Rabbinic literature represents a collection of decisions by rabbis about interpretations of Old Testament law. The tradition was originally oral, but was later written down. Much of this material developed after the destruction of the Jewish temple in A.D. 70. The material differed in content in Palestine and in Babylon, and it grew in size as it was compiled over centuries. The Palestinian Talmud from the fourth century A.D. contains the *Mishnah*, law developed through the second century A.D., and the *Gemarah*, comments on the Mishnah dating from the third to the fifth centuries. Two famous schools of rabbinical interpretation were the more moderate school of Hillel and the strict school of Shammai.

Jewish Theology

The chief emphasis of Judaism was the unity and transcendence of God. The Jewish creed in Deuteronomy 6:4 affirmed monotheism in contrast to the multitude of deities in the pagan world. Jews also taught the possibility of a relationship with God by emphasizing the fatherhood of God.

God created human beings to keep all of his commandments and thereby establish a relationship with him. Jews emphasized the need for obedience both to the moral law and the ceremonial law.

The Old Testament period had placed a strong emphasis on the fate of the Jewish nation. During the intertestamental period, the focus changed. The testing of the individual became a growing emphasis and the doctrine of individual resurrection emerged. The suggestion of a resurrection is found in the Psalms (note Peter's interpretation of Psalm 16 in Acts 2:22–36) and also in the Prophets (Isa. 26:19), but the idea of a resurrection is not a clear emphasis of the Old Testament.

During the intertestamental period the doctrine of the advent of a political deliverer, the Messiah, also gained strength. Jewish literature on this subject does not suggest that the Messiah is divine and it does not focus on his redemptive suffering for human beings.

Most Jews anticipated that God would use a human being to bring deliverance from Rome by military force. Some felt, however, that God himself would bring the deliverance and then present the Messiah as ruler.

Judaism was a fiercely nationalistic religion, but it attracted Gentile adherents. Male proselytes to Judaism underwent circumcision. God-fearers (Cornelius in Acts 10:1–2 is an example) practiced the moral aspects of Judaism but did not submit to circumcision and rigid Jewish regulations. The lofty monotheism and more enlightened morality of Judaism attracted Gentiles who were repulsed by pagan superstition and immorality.

The Sects of Judaism

Palestinian Judaism reflected the normal trend toward sectarianism, but it had a greater unity than other religions of the Graeco-Roman world. All Jewish sects professed devotion to the law, but their practice of obedience to the law varied from mere opportunism to punctilious performance. Even the groups mentioned below had various subdivisions that emphasized particular aspects of the law.

Pharisees. The Pharisees were the largest and most influential Jewish group in New Testament times. They accepted the directives of the oral and the written law. Originating with the Hasidim during the time of the Maccabean revolt, they were strongly established during the New Testament period. They received the entire Old Testament canon but gave strong attention to a rigid observance of the oral law or tradition. They were supernaturalists, believing in the existence of angels and spirits, the immortality of the soul, and the resurrection of the body. Although many Pharisees deserved Jesus' strong denunciations (see Matthew 23), many others were virtuous, as seen in the example of Nicodemus (John 3:1–17). Pharisaism survived to become the pattern of modern orthodox Judaism.

Sadducees. Many relate the name of the Sadducees to Zadok, the high priest during the days of David and Solomon. The children of Zadok comprised the priestly hierarchy during the time of captivity (2 Chron. 31:10), and the name persisted as the title of the priestly party during the days of Christ. Historically the Sadducees developed from the priestly supporters of the Hasmonean dynasty during the intertestamental period. Sadducees accepted the Torah or

Law as having a higher authority than the Prophets and the Writings. Smaller in number than the Pharisees, they were anti-supernaturalists who did not believe in a bodily resurrection and denied the existence of spirits and angels (Mark 12:18–27). In the New Testament the Sadducees were wealthy political opportunists who joined readily with any group who could assist them in retaining power and influence. They were the priestly party, and their influence disappeared with the destruction of the temple in A.D. 70.

Essenes. The Essenes are not mentioned in the New Testament, and much of our information about them comes from the Jewish historian Josephus.[5] They seem to have been a small ascetic group with very stringent requirements for admission. They probably separated from the Pharisees in disgust over the political aims of the Hasmonean rulers. They refused to practice the sacrificial ritual of the Jerusalem temple because they viewed it as captive to a corrupt priesthood. They did not practice marriage and grew only by receiving converts. Essenes held all property in common. They were sober and restrained in their habits and resembled the Pharisees in their theology. Many scholars identify the Essenes with the residents of the Qumran community near the Dead Sea.

Zealots. Zealots were revolutionaries fanatically dedicated to the overthrow of Roman power. They refused to pay taxes to Rome and initiated several revolts against their Roman overlords. One revolt resulted in the destruction of Jerusalem in A.D. 70. Though the term Zealot came to be attached to those who led in the uprising of A.D. 70, its use in the New Testament (Luke 6:15) may have been a non-political designation.

Herodians. The Herodians comprised a small minority of influential Jews who supported the Herodian dynasty and, by extension, the Romans who installed the Herods in office. They are not mentioned outside the Gospels (Mark 3:6), where they joined with the Pharisees to plot the death of Jesus.

Scribes. The scribes were technically a professional group rather than a religious or a political group. Scribes interpreted and taught the Old Testament law and gave judicial opinions on cases brought before them. In Jesus' time most of the scribes were Pharisees, but not all Pharisees had the theological skill demanded of a scribe.

---

5. Josephus, *Wars of the Jews* 2.8.2–13.

Scribes in the New Testament come under the same condemnations given to the Pharisees (Matt. 23:2, 13, 15, 23, 25, 27, 29).

The Temple

The original temple of Solomon was destroyed when the troops of Nebuchadnezzar sacked and burned Jerusalem in 586 B.C. The second temple was rebuilt during the restoration—urged by the prodding from the prophets Haggai and Zechariah (Ezra 6:13–15). This temple had been defiled, desecrated, cleansed, and repaired; it was still standing when Herod the Great gained control of Jerusalem in 37 B.C. In the eighteenth year of Herod's reign (20–19 B.C.) the king began a rebuilding of the temple in a project not completed until A.D. 62 or 64. The statement in John 2:20 implies that the work was still underway in Jesus' lifetime.

The rebuilt temple contained white marble with a large portion covered in gold. The reflection of sunlight from the temple gave it a dazzling visual appearance. The temple was divided into various sections called courts. The outer court was known as the Court of the Gentiles and was accessible to all people. Probably the temple cleansing mentioned in John 2:13–22 and in Matthew 21:12–13 occurred in this section. A barrier separating the Court of the Gentiles from the interior of the temple contained a sign warning Gentiles to stay out of the area under penalty of death. The incident in Acts 21:27–29 is evidence for the prohibition of the presence of Gentiles. Within the deeper interior of the temple were special courts reserved for Jewish women (Court of the Women), Jewish men (Court of Israel), and the priests.

The sanctuary of the temple contained a Holy Place and a Most Holy Place. It retained the same dimensions and furniture prescribed in the Old Testament (see Heb. 9:1–4; Exod. 25–26) except for the absence of the ark lost in the destruction of Solomon's temple. Annually on the Day of Atonement the high priest entered the Most Holy Place to atone for the sins of the people (Heb. 9:7; Lev. 16).

The Jews maintained a police corps to preserve order within the temple. Its chief officer was known as the "captain of the temple" (Acts 4:1; 5:24–26).

Within the daily life of the temple, priests presided over offerings in the morning and the afternoon, and sacrifices for Caesar and the

Roman nation were also offered. Sabbaths and various festivals and holy days necessitated additional ceremonies in the busy life of the temple. The cessation of these sacrifices by order of the captain of the temple signaled a Jewish revolt against Rome in A.D. 66.

The priesthood contained twenty-four courses or orders, each of which served a week at a time twice a year. During the great festivals all the courses were available. Most of these priests lived outside of Jerusalem and came to the city when they were on duty in the temple (Luke 1:5–25). A great social and spiritual gulf existed between the priestly aristocracy living in Jerusalem and the village priests who regularly officiated in the temple.

The temple was the worship center of Judaism. Jesus preached in the temple courts, and the early church met in a section of the temple known as Solomon's Porch (Acts 3:11; 5:12). As the Gentile church developed later in the first century, contact between the church and the temple ceased.

Festivals and Holy Days

The Jewish religious calendar called for the observance of a weekly Sabbath, some less significant monthly festivals, and seven annual festivals. Three important festivals—Passover, Pentecost (Feast of Weeks), and Tabernacles brought large numbers of pilgrims to Jerusalem (Luke 2:41). Most Jews refrained from interpreting the biblical commands concerning these festivals (Exod. 23:17; Deut. 16:16) as mandating attendance three times a year. Jews who resided far from Jerusalem contented themselves with attendance once in a lifetime.

The Jewish observance of the Sabbath as a holy day of rest maintained Jewish separatism from surrounding peoples. Prior to New Testament times the day had become both a day of rest and a day of assembly for the principal synagogue service. Family and friends also shared a common meal on this day. The Mishnah tractate Shabbath prohibited thirty-nine classes of work on the Sabbath. Religious Jews were quite careful in their observance of these laws (see Mark 3:1–6), but the majority of Jews were unconcerned about such details.

The Jewish year contained twelve lunar months with an intercalary month added whenever it was needed to bring the lunar year into line with the solar year. The following chart names, explains the purpose, and gives the approximate date of the Jewish feasts. Because of differences between solar and lunar calendar systems, the equivalents in our months can only be approximate.

All of the feasts with the exception of the last two, which developed during the exile, are mandated in the Mosaic law.

Name	Purpose	Date
Passover and Un-leavened Bread (John 13:1)	Marking the Exodus from Egypt and the beginning of grain harvest (Lev. 23:10–14)	Nisan 14, 15–21 (April)
Pentecost, or Weeks (Acts 2:1–4)	Completion of grain harvest and commemoration of the giving of the Law	May–June
Trumpets, or Rosh Hashanah	Beginning of Jewish civil year	Sept.–Oct.
Day of Atonement, or Yom Kippur (Acts 27:9)	Time of national repentance, fasting, and atonement	October
Tabernacles, or Booths (John 7:2–3)	Commemorating the wilderness wanderings and the completion of the grape harvest. A joyous, popular feast	October
Lights, Dedication, or Hanukkah (John 10:22)	Marking the rededication of the temple by Judas Maccabeus; brilliant lights in home and temple	December
Purim	Noting the deliverance of Israel in the time of Esther	March

Sanhedrin

Because the Romans permitted Jews to deal with many of their own religious and domestic laws, many local legal bodies functioned. The most important of these courts was the Sanhedrin, a body that met daily in the area of the temple—except on the Sabbath and important holy days. The high priest presided over the meetings of this court, and both Pharisees and Sadducees were members. In New Testament times the Sadducees had the chief influence in the Sanhedrin. The New Testament refers to the Sanhedrin with the term "council" or "chief priests, elders, and scribes" (Mark 15:1). Nicodemus (John 3:1–12) was a member of the Sanhedrin.

In the New Testament period the Sanhedrin could not carry out capital executions; it was forced to appeal its decisions to the appropriate Roman official (John 18:31). If the regulations of the Mishnah tractate Sanhedrin were in force in New Testament times, the practices at Jesus' trial were in serious violation of Jewish law.

Synagogue

The destruction of the temple during the Jewish exile led the Jews to emphasize the study and application of Old Testament law. This attitude contributed to the establishment of the synagogue as a pillar of Jewish practice. The exact time of the origin of the synagogue is uncertain, but many scholars have suggested that synagogues first appeared during exilic or postexilic gatherings of Jews to read and study the law. By the first century, synagogues were widely located throughout Palestine and the Diaspora. It was customary to form a synagogue whenever as many as ten Jewish men resided in a community.

The synagogue served as the center of religious, social, and educational life for the Jewish communty. Jews gathered weekly for the study of the law and the worship of Jehovah. During the week children were instructed in the Jewish faith and learned to read and write. The synagogue also served as a center for receiving offerings for the poor and administering charity to the needy.

The synagogue was organized around a head or president (Mark 5:22), who likely was elected by vote from the body of elders. He presided over synagogue services and intervened in any disputes

(Luke 13:14). The elders had general responsibilities for spiritual care of the congregation. An officer known as a *hazzan* cared for the building and its contents, blew the trumpet announcing the Sabbath day, and sometimes taught in the school at the synagogue. Perhaps the official of Luke 4:20 who received the scroll of Scripture from Jesus held this office. The use of the term *rabbi* as a reference to an ordained scholar belongs to the period after the destruction of the temple in A.D. 70. In the New Testament the term was largely used to address Jesus or others as an authoritative teacher or master (Matt. 23:7; Mark 9:5; John 1:38; 3:2).

The synagogue building was normally a substantial stone structure, often elaborately furnished. Each synagogue had a chest containing the law scroll. The speaker's platform was raised, and the congregation sat on stone benches around the walls or on mats or wooden chairs in the center of the room. To read from the scroll, the speaker stood. To preach, he sat down (Luke 4:16–20).

The synagogue service consisted of a recitation of the Jewish creed known as the Shema (see Deut. 6:4–5). This recitation was accompanied with praises to God known as the Shemone Esreh and was followed by a ritual prayer. The term *Shemone Esreh* suggests that there were eighteen benedictions of praise, but the actual number of benedictions varied by time and place. The reading of the Scriptures was followed by a sermon, explaining the portion which had been read. A blessing by a priest closed the service. In the absence of a priest a prayer was substituted.

Jesus regularly attended and participated in synagogue services. Paul made synagogues his initial point of contact in the cities he visited (Acts 13:5). Some early Christian worship may have taken place in the synagogue, for the term translated "meeting" or "assembly" in James 2:2 is the Greek term for synagogue. The church and the synagogue separated as it became apparent that most synagogue members rejected the gospel and resented a Christian presence. The church and the synagogue still have similar features in the prominence given to Scripture, prayer, and the sermon.

Diaspora Jews

Palestine was the homeland of the Jewish race, but in the first century the majority of Jews in the Roman Empire lived outside the borders of the Holy Land. They were known as the Diaspora, a term designating them as being scattered abroad. Large cities of the Roman Empire, such as Alexandria and Rome, had large Jewish populations, and even the smaller communities often had a Jewish colony.

Two groups stood out among the Diaspora. The Hebraists, or the Hebrews, were those Jews who retained not only the Jewish faith but also the use of the Hebrew or Aramaic language and Hebrew customs. Most of the Hebraists lived in Palestine, but Paul, raised outside of Palestine, said that he was raised "according to the strict manner of the law of our fathers" (Acts 22:3). The Hellenists absorbed the Graeco-Roman culture and ceased to be Jews except in matters of faith. They spoke Greek, adopted the customs of their neighbors, and often closely resembled their Gentile neighbors. Both classes of these Jews appear in Acts 6, and a looming division between them threatened the unity of the church. Generally the Hellenists who became Christians were more open to the wider application of the Old Testament Scriptures (note evidences of this openness in Stephen's speech in Acts 7:44–58).

Conclusion

Pagan religions struggled to provide answers to life's basic questions for those who struggled with suffering, hopelessness, and feelings of isolation. Such religions emphasized rules of ritual purity, not moral righteousness. Although some found hope in the answers of pagan religious ideas, these religions still presented a quagmire of religious confusion.

Judaism based its teachings on the revelation of a God who called for moral righteousness. The institutions of Judaism demonstrated these ideas of God. Nevertheless, Jews universally fell short of the moral commitment which their religious views commended.

For Further Discussion

1. What parallels do you see between the varieties of pagan religious practices in the New Testament era and the present variety of religious practices in secular western society?

2. List some contemporary philosophical movements which have beliefs or practices similar to the philosophies of the New Testament era.

3. List the beliefs or practices of the Pharisees, Sadducees, and Essenes which you either accept or reject. What change in their beliefs or practices would make the group acceptable to you?

4. What similarities and differences do you see between the activities in Jewish synagogues and those in modern churches?

Bibliography

Primary Material

Barrett, C. K. *The New Testament Background: Selected Documents*. Rev. ed. London: SPCK, 1987.

Charles, R. H., ed. *Apocrypha and Pseudepigrapha of the Old Testament*. 2 vols. Oxford: Clarendon Press, 1913.

Charlesworth, J. H., ed. *The Old Testament Pseudepigrapha*. 2 vols. Garden City, N.Y.: Doubleday, 1983–85.

Foerster, W. *Gnosis*. 2 vols. Oxford: Clarendon Press, 1972–74.

Kee, Howard Clark. *The Origins of Christianity: Sources and Documents*. Englewood Cliffs, N.J.: Prentice-Hall Press, 1973.

Robinson, J. M., et al. *The Nag Hammadi Library in English*. 3d ed. San Francisco: Harper & Row Publishers Inc., 1988.

Suggs, Jack M., et al., eds. *The Oxford Study Bible* (Revised English Bible with Apocrypha). New York: Oxford University Press, 1992.

Theron, Daniel J. *Evidence of Tradition*. Grand Rapids: Baker Book House, 1958.

Vermes, Geza. *The Dead Sea Scrolls in English*. 3d ed. London: Penguin Books, 1987.

Secondary Material

Bruce, F. F. *Biblical Exegesis in the Qumran Texts*. Grand Rapids: William B. Eerdmans Publishing Co., 1959.

———. *New Testament History*. Garden City, N.Y.: Doubleday, 1971.

Daube, David. *The New Testament and Rabbinic Judaism*. London: Athlone Press, 1956.

Davies, W. D., and Louis Finkelstein, eds. *Cambridge History of Judaism*. 2 vols. Cambridge: Cambridge University Press, 1984–89.

Dupont-Sommer, A. *The Essene Writings from Qumran*. Cleveland: World, 1961.

Ferguson, Everett. *Backgrounds of Early Christianity*. 2nd ed. Grand Rapids: William B. Eerdmans Publishing Co., 1993.

Filson, Floyd V. *A New Testament History*. Philadelphia: Westminster Press, 1964.

Glover, T. R. *The Conflict of Religions in the Early Roman Empire*. London: Methuen & Co., 1909. Reprint, Washington, D.C.: Canon, 1974.

———. *The World of the New Testament*. Cambridge: Cambridge University Press, 1931.

Grant, R. M. *Gnosticism: An Anthology*. London: Collins Publishers, 1961.

———. *Gnosticism and Early Christianity*. New York: Columbia University Press, 1959.

Guignebert, C. *The Jewish World in the Time of Jesus*. London: Kegan Paul, Trench, Trubner & Co., 1939.

Gundry, Robert H. *A Survey of the New Testament*. Rev. ed. Grand Rapids: Zondervan Books, 1981.

Kee, Howard Clark, and Franklin W. Young. *Understanding the New Testament*. Englewood Cliffs, N.J.: Prentice-Hall Press, 1957.

Koester, Helmut. *History, Culture, and Religion of the Hellenistic Age* Vol. 1 of *Introduction to the New Testament*. Philadelphia: Fortress Press, 1982.

Logan, A. H. B., and A. J. M. Wedderburn, eds. *The New Testament and Gnosis*. Edinburgh: T & T Clark, 1983.

Lohse, Eduard. *The New Testament Environment*. Rev. ed. Nashville: Abingdon Press, 1976.

Machen, J. C. *The Origin of Paul's Religion*. New York: Macmillian Co., 1928.

Moore, G. F. *Judaism*. 3 vols. Cambridge: Harvard University Press, 1927–30.

Safrai, S., and M. Stern. *The Jewish People in the First Century*. 2 vols. Philadelphia: Fortress Press, 1974–76. Excellent summary of traditions and institutions of Judaism at beginning of Christian era.

Safrai, S., M. Stone, M. J. Mulder, et al. *The Literature of the Jewish People in the Period of the Second Temple and Talmud*. 3 vols. Philadelphia: Fortress Press, 1984–88. Content and analysis of Jewish writings during beginning of Christian era.

Schurer, E. *The History of the Jewish People in the Age of Jesus Christ (175 B.C.–A.D. 135)*. 3 vols. Revised and edited by G. Vermes, et al. Edinburgh: T & T Clark, 1973–87.

Tenney, Merrill C. *New Testament Survey*. Grand Rapids: William B. Eerdmans Publishing Co., 1961.

————. *New Testament Times*. Grand Rapids: William B. Eerdmans Publishing Co., 1965.

Wilson, R. M. *The Gnostic Problem*. London: Mowbray, Imprint of Cassell PLC, 1958.

Yamauchi, E. M. *Pre-Christian Gnosticism*. Grand Rapids: William B. Eerdmans Publishing Co., 1973.

4 The Canon, Text, and Genre of the New Testament

Guiding Questions

1. Explain the criteria used by Christians to determine the New Testament canon.

2. What are the sources of evidence for the development of the New Testament canon?

3. What are the sources of information used in the task of textual criticism?

4. List and define the four most prominent genres in New Testament writings.

The Canon

Twenty-seven books, known as the New Testament canon, comprise the Christian New Testament. Although these books were written early in Christian history, the slow process of communication in the New Testament world delayed the circulation of these writings among believers. When the New Testament books did begin to circulate, many other writings, such as additional gospels, acts of Christian leaders, additional epistles, and apocalypses appeared. Some groups accepted these additional writings; others rejected them. Some of the writings now in the New Testament required a long time to gain acceptance throughout the church. How did Christians determine which books to include? What were their criteria for selection? Can we reconstruct the selection process?

Two Definitions

Christians use the name New Testament for the second part of the English Bible. The term is derived from the Latin *Novum Testamentum*. The Latin term is a translation of the Greek *He Kaine Diatheke*, meaning literally "The New Testament." The term *testament* can refer to the final will of someone who is deceased, but it can also refer to an arrangement made by one person which may be accepted or rejected by another party. The party examining this testament has the freedom to decide the appropriate response to it, but after the testament is accepted its terms cannot be altered. Both parties are then bound by the agreement.

In English we use the term "covenant" to describe this relationship. It is accurate for us to use the term "New Covenant" to refer to the arrangement God made through Christ for a new manner of dealing with human beings. God established the terms, and human beings are given the choice to either accept or reject them. Once they accept the terms, both humans and God are bound to complete the requirements of the covenant. Our New Covenant contains a revelation of God's holiness through a sinless Son. Those who respond to the revelation in God's Son become members of God's family (John 1:12), experience the forgiveness of sins, and are sealed to God by the Holy Spirit (Eph. 1:13–14).

Our English term *canon* is derived from the Greek word *kanon*. Originally it referred to a straight rod or a ruler which was used as a test for straightness or a measurement of length. It also came to symbolize anything which constituted a rule, norm, or standard. We use the term in the latter way in contemporary English when we refer to the trends or rules of fashion as the canons of fashion.

The Greek word for canon appears in the New Testament four times. In 2 Corinthians 10:13, 15, 16 it refers to an area or sphere of ministry that God determined for Paul. The word also appears in Galatians 6:16, where it describes the standard that Paul wants believers to follow.

In Christian history the term *canon* was first used to describe doctrines which constituted the basic beliefs and practices of the church. It was a synonym for orthodoxy in belief and practice. As time passed, it also came to refer to those Scriptures which Christians regarded as normative for the church and which contained approved doctrine. These books became the canon of the New Testament.

Determining Canonicity

The criteria for determining canonicity are difficult to determine precisely. Some books were quickly and widely received. Others appear to have been severely questioned and little used. Some books were accepted into the authoritative collection of Scripture in one locale but omitted in other places.

The most important criterion for determining canonicity is inspiration. Paul stated this principle in 2 Timothy 3:16 by suggesting that "all Scripture is given by inspiration of God." Originally Paul's statement referred to the inspiration of the Old Testament, but the term *Scripture* came to be used also in reference to New Testament writings (2 Pet. 3:16).[1] An inference from Paul's statement is that whatever God inspired is Scripture, and whatever God did not inspire is not Scripture. Notice that this use of the term *inspiration* is a precise and limited usage. The writings of a Christian teacher today might be inspiring, but we would not insist that they appear in the New Testament. When we speak of Matthew or Romans as inspired, we use the term *inspired* in a special sense.

How did early Christians determine the presence of inspiration? Not all New Testament books claimed inspiration. What method did the church use to demonstrate that the books in the canon deserved to be there? Three elements guided church leaders.

1. Church leaders often appealed to the agreement of the book with what they called "the rule of faith." This meant that the

---

1. In fairness, it should be observed that not all New Testament interpreters view 2 Peter 3:16 as designating the New Testament writings as "Scripture." For a discussion of the issue, see Michael Green, *2 Peter and Jude*, TNTC, rev. ed. (Grand Rapids: William B. Eerdmans Publishing Co., 1987), 160–62. Green supports the view that Peter designated the New Testament as "Scripture."

teaching of the book followed the beliefs the church regarded as acceptable and correct.

2. The book had to demonstrate apostolicity. This criterion required authorship by an apostle or by the associate of an apostle (as in the instance of Mark and Luke).

3. The church applied the test of universality. This required that the book be accepted by a broad geographical segment of the church.

These three criteria can be described as orthodoxy, apostolicity, and universality.

The fact that the church accepted the present twenty-seven books as canonical does not suggest that the church created the canon or that the church caused the books to be thought of as inspired. The acceptance of these books indicates only that the church recognized their divine origin. God's people had already sensed that these books had inherent authority. The church was ratifying what committed Christians had already accepted.

It is important to understand that early Christians produced and used many more writings than we have in our New Testament canon. The subapostolic writings were written in the period soon after the death of the apostles, and included among others, the Epistle of Barnabas, 1 and 2 Clement, the Epistles of Ignatius, and the Epistle of Polycarp to the Philippians. Among the subapostolic writings the Didache, the Shepherd of Hermas, and 1 Clement briefly enjoyed canonical status in sections of the church. Dated somewhat later than these subapostolic writings, we also have a group of writings known collectively as the New Testament Apocrypha.[2] These later writings

---

2. We must distinguish these from the Old Testament Apocrypha, many of which were written during the intertestamental period. The New Testament Apocrypha, dating from the New Testament period, contain different "Gospels," "Acts," and apocalyptic writings. They are fantastic, fanciful writings often conveying heresy and lacking the truthfulness of the canonical New Testament. A collection of these writings appears in E. Hennecke, *New Testament Apocrypha*, 2 vols. (Philadelphia: Westminster Press, 1963–66). Hennecke's collection brings together documents from different places and various periods of time. Some of them are Coptic documents found at Nag Hammadi in Egypt in 1945. The term "New Testament Apocrypha" was not a term used in the early church, but it has become a convenient name used to designate the many non-canonical writings from the early centuries which have been discovered in recent years.

included alternate gospels with such titles as The Gospel of the Hebrews, The Gospel of Peter, and The Gospel of Philip. This collection also includes legendary accounts of Jesus' life, later acts of the apostles, and later apocalypses that are written as imitations of the Book of Revelation. The church sifted through these documents and determined that they lacked the marks of authenticity needed for inclusion in the canonical list. The fact that a document was written in ancient times did not prove that it was worthy of inclusion among the canonical writings of the period.

Christians did not use the criteria for canonicity in a mechanical fashion. Sometimes one criterion was more important than another. The opinion of a powerful church leader might also be important. These criteria, however, came to be generally adopted in the church during the period of the second century, and the church did not vary widely from them in succeeding centuries.

Evidence of the Developing Process

The first Christians had none of the books of the New Testament, since the books were in the process of being written. However, they did possess the Old Testament, oral teaching about Jesus' ministry and redemptive work (1 Cor. 15:1–4), and direct revelation from God coming through Christian prophets (Acts 21:10–14).

Evidence of the growth of the canon appears in the use of canonical writings by early Christian writers. The subapostolic writings make reference to the writings we now hold to be canonical. The use of the canonical writings in these and later documents is evidence of the acceptance of the canonical writings in various divisions of the church. This type of evidence represents the best proof available up to the end of the second century.

A second source of evidence appears in the opinions of certain writers or ecclesiastical councils.

- The Canon of Marcion, appearing in A.D. 140, provoked strong oppposition among early Christians, for Marcion's canon contained only a mutilated Gospel of Luke and ten of Paul's epistles (excluding the Pastorals). Doubtless, the appearance of a heretical canon such as that of Marcion helped to prod Christians into naming the books they believed to be genuine.

- The Muratorian Canon, dating from A.D. 170, did not mention James, Hebrews, and the Petrine epistles, and expressed doubt about the Revelation of John, but it accepted the other New Testament writings as canonical.

- The Festal Letter of Athanasius in A.D. 367 accepted all twenty-seven New Testament writings.

- The Third Council of Carthage in A.D. 397 received the full complement of New Testament writings. After this time there was general agreement on the content of the New Testament canon.

A third source of evidence of canonicity comes from the contents of ancient manuscripts. For example, the fourth-century Codex Sinaiticus contains the entire New Testament and part of the Old in the sections that have been preserved. The New Testament portion contains the *Epistle of Barnabas* and the *Shepherd of Hermas* in addition to the twenty-seven canonical works. The contents of other ancient manuscripts provide similar evidence.

Some Difficulties

Some books were accepted into the canon in spite of difficult questions raised in various segments of the church. Uncertainty about the authorship of Hebrews led some sections of the church to question its inclusion. The difference in style between 1 Peter and 2 Peter led many to hesitate to add 2 Peter to the canon. Shorter books such as 2 and 3 John required additional time to be accepted. The unusual style and apocalyptic content of Revelation caused many to question its inclusion.

Completing the Process

When a gospel or an epistle had been written, it remained in the possession of the individual or the church that received it. These originals were copied and circulated. Copies circulated between churches, and some churches may have sent individuals to make copies at the locations where the originals were found. By this process churches throughout the Christian world would gradually obtain a somewhat complete set of the New Testament documents.

In the process of this circulation and copying the originals were lost or destroyed.

The process of completing the canon required time so that the church could read and evaluate the books. Differences of opinion about certain books continued to appear during the centuries when the canon was being formed. Those who compare the writings of the subapostolic period and the New Testament Apocrypha will see clearly that the canonical writings reflect a different quality in their content from the excluded writings. Those who accept the idea of a canon feel that God's guidance led the church to select those books which were inspired and to reject those which were not inspired.

Closing the Canon

Jesus taught the full authority of the Old Testament as Scripture (Matt. 5:17–19; John 10:35). He affirmed that his own words were equally authoritative (note the authoritative claim inherent in his statements in Matt. 5:22, 28, 32, 34, 39, 44). He led his disciples to expect the Holy Spirit to instruct them in the significance of his ministry (John 14:26; 16:12–15). The New Testament canon contains the authoritative record of Jesus' life and the interpretation of its significance. Christians have closed the canon and limited its content to the apostolic books. This action expresses the belief that what God has revealed in Christ is both sufficient and complete (Heb. 1:1–4).

The New Testament Text

None of the original manuscripts of the New Testament (also known as autographs) exist, and the ancient manuscripts we possess are only copies of copies of the originals. Although the existing manuscripts have enormous areas of agreement, they also have disagreements. Most of the differences in manuscripts deal with spelling, word order, the presence or absence of conjunctions and articles, and other less important features. The science of textual criticism has allowed us to make considerable progress toward restoring the original text of the New Testament. What materials are available for the use of the textual critics? How do they use these materials?

The Writing Materials

Papyrus is a writing material made from a reed that grows along the Nile River. In damp climates papyrus often rotted quickly, but in dry climates such as Palestine and Egypt the written material can endure for centuries. The New Testament books were likely originally written on papyrus. Other writing materials such as parchment and vellum were available, but their use generally began in the fourth century. By then the church was wealthier and sought to use a more durable material than papyrus. Originally parchment referred to a writing material made from sheep and goat skins, and vellum referred to material made from calves. Today the terms are practically interchangeable.

Many of the ancient writers used a scroll form (note the term "roll" in Luke 4:20, a reference to the Old Testament), but some of the books may have been written in codex form with the separate pages bound together. Normally a writer dictated his words to a secretary known as an *amanuensis*. Tertius, whose name appears in Romans 16:22, was the amanuensis of Romans.

Early manuscripts used the uncial script, consisting of all capital letters. Later manuscripts used the more easily reproduced cursive script in small (minuscule) letters. The earliest manuscripts lacked word divisions, punctuation marks, and chapter and verse divisions. The printer R. Stephanus first used verses in his edition of 1551.

The Materials of Textual Criticism

Three primary types of material are available for use by textual critics. As critics use these materials, they can decide between variant readings to determine the more likely original reading.

1. Scholars use manuscripts of the Greek New Testament. A papyrus manuscript (known as P52) containing a section of John 18 is usually dated around A.D. 135. It is the oldest extant section of the New Testament. Two fourth-century uncial vellum manuscripts, known as Codices Sinaiticus and Vaticanus, are the most useful uncial writings. Later manuscripts, written in the small minuscule script, appeared frequently from the eighth century on. Some of these minuscules contain an earlier text version, but many of them are not useful in textual criticism because their text is a later one.

2. Scholars use ancient versions of the New Testament. Translations in Syriac and Latin are especially useful because some of these translations appeared two hundred years before the major uncial manuscripts. Other useful versions appear in various dialects of Coptic, the language of ancient Egypt. Less useful versions include those in Armenian, Gothic, Ethiopic, Georgian, Arabic, and Slavonic. In each instance the textual student translates the version back into Greek to determine the text lying beneath the version.

3. Textual students use quotations in the writings of the early church fathers and lectionaries (New Testament readings used in early liturgy). These writings are useful because we know when and where the author lived and can determine the type of text being used at that time in that area.

The Practice of Textual Criticism

Textual scholars have developed careful rules for carrying out their studies to arrive at the best reading. Generally textual scholars prefer the text containing the oldest reading and the reading which is supported in the widest number of geographical areas. Sometimes, however, the oldest reading is not the best reading, for some variant readings appeared quite early and were often copied.

Early copies of the New Testament were made one by one as individuals and churches asked for copies of the New Testament. Later copies of the New Testament were made by trained scribes who simultaneously transcribed a number of copies from dictation. Errors of the ear and eye could creep into copies through this system, and textual critics allow for this in determining the best readings.

Usually textual critics prefer the shorter reading because copyists more commonly added to the text rather than deleting from it. They also prefer the more difficult reading because scribes tended to make expressions easier rather than harder to understand. Students also prefer the reading which best explains the origin of other readings.

The application of these principles is not a merely mechanical process. Skill and judgment are demanded in assessing the evidence and in determining the most probable reading.

The materials for the practice of New Testament textual criticism are quite numerous. By contrast, the materials for determining the text of the writings of Plato or the Roman poet Virgil are few in number and are separated from the originals by as much as fourteen hundred years. New Testament textual criticism has assisted us by providing access to substantially the same text which the first-century writers produced.

Modern Translations

Even before the Reformation, various English versions of the Bible began to appear. John Wycliffe published an English Bible, based on the Latin text, in 1382. William Tyndale published his first edition of the English New Testament at Worms in 1525. Bishops confiscated the available copies when they were brought to England, and Tyndale was burned at the stake for heresy in 1536. In 1560 English Protestants produced the Geneva Bible. This Bible became the means of helping the English people to understand biblical doctrine.

Roman Catholics published the Douay Version in 1582. The King James Version was completed in the reign of James I of England in 1611. It is the first of the English versions still in active use.

The discovery of new manuscripts and changes in English speech led to an English Revised Version (1881) and the American Revised Version (1901). The twentieth century has spawned a proliferation of versions, many undertaken to update the language of the King James. Among these are the Revised Standard Version (1952), the New American Standard Bible (1963), the Jerusalem Bible (1966), Today's English Version (1966), the New English Bible (1970), and the New International Version (1978). A revision of the New English Bible (the Revised English Bible) was published in 1989, and a revision of the Revised Standard Version appeared in the same year.

Genre in the New Testament

The term *genre* is a literary category that denotes the style, form, or general content of a literary production. The question of the genre into which the New Testament writings fit is an important one, and in recent years discussions about genre have become increasingly prominent.

The issue is significant because understanding the genre of literature provides guidance in reading it correctly. Some Christians read the prophecies of Revelation like the weather forecast in a newspaper. An engagement ring means one thing to an ecstatic young lady who writes her feelings about it in a diary and another to a chemist who records its specific gravity and metallic content in a scientific report. The resurrection of Jesus means something quite different to the reader who regards the Gospels to be truthful history in contrast with what it means to one who is convinced that the Gospels are mythical presentations of truth. In each of these examples the question of genre is an important issue.

Four broad categories of genre appear in the New Testament: biography (in the Gospels); letters (written by Paul, James, Peter, Jude, and John); history (in Acts); and a combination of prophetic, apocalyptic, and letter forms (in Revelation).

The Gospels are biographies of Jesus, but biographies with unique content and purpose. The Gospels do not profess to be comprehensive historical accounts of Jesus' life, for they lack details about his childhood and growth into maturity as well as a complete account of his ministry. The Synoptics focus more on Jesus' Galilean ministry, while John's Gospel also emphasizes his Judean ministry. All four Gospels lack chronological precision in reporting Jesus' life.[3] Each Gospel is written with a specific purpose or aim, and each Gospel writer selected the content of the Gospel with that purpose in mind (note John's guiding purpose in John 20:30–31).

We may classify Paul's writings as letters, but the defining features of each Pauline letter vary slightly. Romans is a letter that presents a theological argument, and 1 Corinthians is a letter that responds to needs and questions among the Corinthians. A distinctive feature of all of Paul's letters is their occasional nature. Each letter is generally written in response to a specific occasion or need

---

3. Where the Gospels speak about chronology, they are accurate (see John 1:29, 35 where "next day" is a chronological note). However, sometimes chronological development in Jesus' ministry is described with a rather vague "after this," and lengths of time are given as "a few days" (John 2:12). The given chronology of the Gospels is trustworthy, but it is not intended to be overly precise.

of the church which received it. We will be wiser and more accurate interpreters if we understand the situation which produced the letter as we attempt to apply its teaching.

The Book of Acts contains history, but Luke presents this history with the aid of theological interpretation. The Christian history presented in Acts is not exhaustive, for little report is given of the spread of Christianity in Asia and Africa. Acts intends to show the work of the Holy Spirit in spearheading the spread of the gospel from Jerusalem to Rome. In Acts, Luke presents the normal church as a body of believers following the direction of God in spreading the gospel wherever God prepares an opening (see Acts 2:41–47).

The Revelation of John has been called an apocalypse, a prophecy, and an epistle or letter. Traces of all three of these genres appear in Revelation. The epistolary genre appears in chapters two and three in the letters to the seven churches. Reference is made to "prophecy" in Revelation 1:3. Apocalyptic characteristics are seen in the extensive use of symbolism, the communication of messages by angels using visions, and an expectation of divine deliverance in the near future (see "near" in Rev. 1:3). Recognizing the genre of Revelation will warn us against interpreting it entirely as prewritten history and will guide us to apply more wisely its emphasis on divine sovereignty (Rev. 4:8, 11) and redemption in Christ (Rev. 5:1–14).

For Further Discussion

1. How would you answer members of a group who argue that the canon of the New Testament is still open?

2. Are translations of the Scripture as inspired as the original writings? Why or why not?

3. Explain the meaning of John's warning in Revelation 22:18–19. Do these words prohibit the use of Scripture translations?

4. How does the historical information in the Gospels and in Acts differ from the historical information appearing in a daily newspaper?

Bibliography

Primary Material for the Subapostolic Writings and New Testament Apocrypha

Grant, R. M., et al. *The Apostolic Fathers.* 6 vols. New York: Thomas Nelson Publishers, 1964–1968. With helpful interpretive notes.

Hennecke, E. *New Testament Apocrypha.* Edited by W. Schneemelcher. Translated by R. McL. Wilson. 2 vols. Philadelphia: Westminster Press, 1963–66. With extensive introductions and notes.

James, M. R. *The Apocryphal New Testament.* Oxford: Clarendon Press, 1953.

Lake, Kirsopp. *The Apostolic Fathers.* 2 vols. Loeb Classical Library. Cambridge: Harvard University Press, 1912–13. Greek and English text with notes.

Discussions of the Canon

Bruce, F. F. *The Canon of Scripture.* Downers Grove, Ill.: InterVarsity Press, 1988.

Farmer, William R., and Denis M. FarKasfalvy, O. Cist. *The Formation of the New Testament Canon.* New York: Paulist Press, 1983.

Gamble, Harry Y. *The New Testament Canon.* Philadelphia: Fortress Press, 1985. Excellent, brief overview of questions about the canon.

Green, Michael. *2 Peter and Jude.* TNTC. Rev. ed. Grand Rapids: William B. Eerdmans Publishing Co., 1987.

Metzger, Bruce M. *The Canon of the New Testament.* Oxford: Clarendon Press, 1987. Excellent tracing of the historical development of the canon. Practical content.

Ridderbos, H. N. *The Authority of the New Testament Scriptures.* Philadelphia: Presbyterian and Reformed Publishing Co., 1963. Explains the theological necessity for the canon.

Tenney, Merrill C. *New Testament Survey.* Grand Rapids: William B. Eerdmans Publishing Co., 1961. Especially pp. 401–13.

Thiessen, H. C. *Introduction to the New Testament.* Grand Rapids: William B. Eerdmans Publishing Co., 1954. Especially pp. 3–30.

Westcott, Brooke Foss. *A General Survey of the History of the Canon of the New Testament.* 7th ed. New York: Macmillan Co., 1896. Excellent historical survey of development of canon.

Discussions of Textual Criticism

Aland, Kurt, and Barbara Aland. *The Text of the New Testament*. Translated by Erroll F. Rhodes. Grand Rapids: William B. Eerdmans Publishing Co., 1987. Technical but full discussion of textual criticism.

Greenlee, J. Harold. *Introduction to New Testament Textual Criticism*. Grand Rapids: William B. Eerdmans Publishing Co., 1964. Good introduction for those beginning the study of the discipline.

Metzger, Bruce M. *The Text of the New Testament: Its Transmission, Corruption, and Restoration*. 3d ed., enlarged. New York: Oxford University Press, 1992. A thorough, but readable discussion of textual criticism.

Discussions of Versions of the New Testament

Bruce, F. F. *The Books and the Parchments*. Rev. ed. Westwood, N.J.: Fleming H. Revell Co., 1953. See especially pp. 209–226.

————. *History of the Bible in English*. 3d ed. New York: Oxford University Press, 1978.

Lewis, Jack P. *The English Bible: From KJV to NIV*. Grand Rapids: Baker Book House, 1981.

Metzger, Bruce M. *The Early Versions of the New Testament*. Oxford: Clarendon Press, 1977.

Genre in the New Testament

Aune, David E. *The New Testament in Its Literary Environment*. Philadelphia: Westminster Press, 1987. Thorough scholarly discussion of genre in the New Testament.

Puskas, Charles B. *An Introduction to the New Testament*. Peabody, Mass.: Hendrickson Publishers Inc., 1989. Especially pp. 109–157.

5   Learning About Jesus

Guiding Questions

1. Explain how we arrive at definite dates for the birth, ministry length, and death of Jesus.

2. Discuss the geographical areas in which Jesus carried out his ministry.

3. Develop a general chronological outline for the ministry of Jesus.

4. Describe the characteristics of Jesus' teaching that made him so effective in communicating with an audience.

5. List primary and secondary sources for information on the life of Jesus and evaluate their effectiveness.

Undertaking the study of Jesus' life forces us to ask a variety of questions about him. Where will we look for information on Jesus? In what geographical areas did Jesus minister and serve? Is the information in our Gospels historically reliable and trustworthy? How did Jesus' teaching contribute to the fulfillment of his purpose in the divine plan? It will also be important to correlate some events in Jesus' life with dates on secular calendars and to obtain an overview of the chronology of Jesus' life.

Sources

The four Gospels, Matthew, Mark, Luke, and John, are our primary sources for learning about Jesus. Even though some of the Epistles were probably written before the Gospels, we are correct in using the Gospels to provide both factual and theological information about Jesus.

References to Jesus outside the Gospels are so few in number that they provide little help in reconstructing his life. The Jewish historian Josephus designated Jesus as a wise man who "wrought surprising feats" and stated that after his crucifixion "on the third day he appeared to them restored to life."[1] Many experts consider these comments to be a Christian interpolation into the text. The second-century Roman historian Tacitus referred to Jesus' death and the presence of a Christian community in Rome as he discussed Nero's persecution of Christians.[2] Suetonius referred to the same persecution by Nero by stating that "punishment was inflicted on the Christians, a class of men given to a new and mischievous superstition."[3] The younger Pliny wrote to the emperor Trajan in the opening years of the second century A.D. that Christians in his section of Asia Minor "sang in alternate verses a hymn to Christ, as to a god."[4] Lucian, the satirist of the second century, scorned Christians and described Jesus as the first "lawgiver" of Christians and a "crucified sophist."[5]

These references are of no value in providing trustworthy information about Jesus. However, they do provide evidence of his life and death and of the rapid spread of Christianity as far as Rome.

Some sayings of Jesus appear in literature outside of the Gospels. These sayings are known as *agrapha*, a term derived from the Greek word meaning "unwritten." The materials are obviously written down, but they are designated as "unwritten" because they do not appear in the text of the Gospels. Sayings spoken by Jesus are also

---

1. Josephus, *Antiquities* 18.63–64, Loeb Classical Library, English translation by Louis H. Feldman (Cambridge: Harvard University Press, 1981). Observe the notes by the translator, who discusses the view that these words come from a Christian interpolator.
2. Tactitus, *Annals* 15.44.
3. Suetonius, *The Lives of the Caesars* 6.16.
4. Pliny, *Letters 10.96*
5. Lucian, *The Passing of Peregrinus* 13.

called "dominical" sayings, a term taken from the Latin word for "lord." Acts 20:35 contains a dominical saying that is part of the agrapha. Other agrapha appear in documents found in Egypt such as the Oxyrhynchus papyri and the *Gospel of Thomas*. The Oxyrhynchus finds, first discovered in 1897, contain some information clearly influenced by the canonical Gospels. Some of the information, however, consists of words and incidents expanded and embroidered by the vivid imagination of the writer. *The Gospel of Thomas*, discovered in Nag Hammadi, Egypt, around 1945, lacks the narrative story of a gospel. It clearly was not written by Thomas. Some of the sayings in the writing are altered versions of the canonical Gospels. Still others are totally different from anything found in the New Testament.[6] Scholars do not believe these finds contribute reliable information about the life and teachings of Jesus.

Luke's opening verse referred to written records that he used to produce his Gospel. None of these records has survived, with the possible exception of Mark. However, after the apostolic period many apocryphal writings appeared with the purpose of providing information for the curious about the life of Mary, the childhood of Jesus, and the correspondence of Pilate. These documents, frequently called the "Infancy Gospels," are an unequal collection of pious imagination and outright falsehood and provide no assistance in assessing the life and impact of Jesus.[7]

The Geography of Jesus' Homeland

Jesus spent most of his active life in Palestine, a territory of no more than ten thousand square miles, about the size of the state of

6. A collection of the Nag Hammadi finds appears in James M. Robinson, *The Nag Hammadi Library in English*, 3d ed., rev. (San Francisco: Harper & Row, 1988). Logion 20 (p. 128) resembles Matt. 13:31–32 in defining the kingdom of heaven as "like a mustard seed, the smallest of all seeds. But when it falls on tilled soil, it produces a great plant and becomes a shelter for birds of the sky." Logion 7 (p. 127) says, "Blessed is the lion which becomes man when consumed by man; and cursed is the man whom the lion consumes, and the lion becomes man." No Gospel parallel exists for this saying.

7. For a collection of these writings see M. R. James, *The Apocryphal New Testament* (Oxford: University Press, 1953). Some of these writings also appear in Hennecke, *The New Testament Apocrypha*, vol. 1, ed. W. Schneemelcher, trans. R. Mcl. Wilson (Philadelphia: Westminister, 1963).

Vermont. When Jesus was an infant, Joseph took him and Mary to Egypt to escape the wrath of Herod (Matt. 2:13–15). During his ministry Jesus visited Tyre and Sidon (Matt. 15:21). On the few occasions when he crossed the Jordan River, he did not travel far into the trans-Jordan territory (Matt. 19:1).

In the New Testament era Palestine had three geographical divisions of political importance: Galilee in the far north, Samaria in the central section, and Judea in the south. Judea had the heaviest concentration of Jewish population. Galilee had a large Gentile population living among the Jews. Samaria had a mixed-race population whose people viewed the Jews with contempt. Most of Jesus' ministry took place in rugged Galilee and between Galilee and Jerusalem.

The eastern edge of Palestine borders the western edge of the Arabian desert. The western edge of Palestine, from Mt. Carmel to Gaza, had a shoreline of about one hundred miles on the Mediterranean Sea. From Mt. Hermon, near Caesarea Philippi (Matt. 16:13) in the north, to the southern tip of the Dead Sea covers about 160 miles. In the north the distance from the Mediterranean Sea to the Sea of Galilee is twenty-eight miles at the narrowest point. In the south the distance from the Mediterranean to the Dead Sea is fifty-four miles. The Jordan River, rising near the foot of Mt. Hermon and flowing into the Dead Sea, divided the land from north to south. East of the Jordan are the areas of Perea, not mentioned by name in the New Testament, and the Decapolis (Mark 7:31).

The terrain of Palestine changes quickly and provides a variety of landscapes and climates. The climate of the coastal plain is mild. Its fertile soil makes it an agricultural wonderland. The coastal plain begins in the southern desert and ends at Mt. Carmel in the north. Joppa (Acts 9:43) was a popular coastal harbor.

Moving inland from the coastal plain, a traveler encounters the hill country (Luke 1:39). This rocky, barren land has a moderate climate. Many of its inhabitants raised grain and grapes and kept cattle. Lakes, valleys, and plains provided outlets for fishing and farming. Trade routes honeycombed the area. In the north some of the hills reach an elevation of almost four thousand feet. Jerusalem in the south has an elevation of almost twenty-six hundred feet. Most of the population of Palestine lived in this hilly area, with significant numbers in all the major areas of Galilee, Samaria, and Judea.

Located next to the hill country, the Jordan Valley is part of a gigantic rift in the earth beginning in the Taurus Mountains, continuing through Palestine and Arabia, passing into the Red Sea, and finally ending in Africa. The Jordan flows directly from the Sea of Galilee into the Dead Sea, which has no outlet. The river bed varies in width from a mere trickle to a body some two hundred feet across. During rainy seasons sections of the gorge fill with muddy water. Floods sometimes wash away existing roads.

The Sea of Galilee is a small lake thirteen miles long and eight miles wide at its greatest expanse. It is 682 feet below sea level. Sudden rushes of wind produce violent storms on the lake (Mark 4:35–41). On the western shore of the Sea of Galilee in Jesus' day was the city of Capernaum, used by Jesus as his base for travels throughout the area (see Mark 2:1). On the eastern bank the hillsides are steep, and the territory is somewhat barren (note the presence of a steep bank in Mark 5:13).

The Dead Sea functions as an evaporating basin which has collected minerals and salts for centuries. The surface of the Dead Sea is 1,290 feet below sea level, and its bottom is 1,300 feet lower than its surface. Nothing can grow in the sea itself, but in New Testament times the tropical climate of the area permitted the raising of fruits and other crops which could not tolerate the more extreme temperatures of the higher elevations.

The eastern plateau across from the Jordan River stretches into the Arabian desert. In New Testament times the area east of the Jordan near the Sea of Galilee was known as the Decapolis, a name literally meaning "ten cities" (Mark 7:31). The region extended both north and east of the Jordan River. Originally built by Alexander the Great, the cities were an outpost of Hellenistic culture adjacent to the heartland of Judaism. Although some Hebrews lived in the area, the majority of the population was Gentile.

The Historical Study of Jesus' Life

Christians who lived prior to the eighteenth century viewed the Gospels as historically reliable pictures of the life of Jesus. Their main problem in describing his life was to harmonize the facts of the four Gospels to produce a smooth flow of events. The period of the eighteenth century, known as the Enlightenment, ended this trust in the historical accuracy of the Gospels. Those who followed the philosophical views of the period questioned the Gospel miracles and viewed the historical accounts of the Gospels as suspect.

Originally, those who responded to this philosophical movement found naturalistic explanations for the miracles. Later, D. F. Strauss published a life of Jesus (1835) and insisted that the Gospels presented truth, but truth of a religious nature. Strauss viewed the Gospels as myths, stories which indicated the religious beliefs of the readers. Many who followed in Strauss's footsteps attempted to peel away centuries of what they viewed as theological dogmatism in order to reach the real Jesus, who was seen as a humble teacher from Nazareth. At the beginning of the twentieth century the German scholar Adolph Harnack presented a picture of Jesus as a teacher of high ethical ideals who gave sacrificial service to mankind.

In 1906 Albert Schweitzer dropped a theological "bombshell" on the scholarly world when he published his famous *Quest for the Historical Jesus*. Schweitzer showed that each of the earlier "lives" of Jesus had been little more than a projection of the writer's own philosophical outlook in the first century. Schweitzer himself did not promote an orthodox view of Jesus, but he put to death the movement that viewed Jesus as little more than a Galilean religious teacher. Schweitzer felt that Jesus expected the imminent arrival of God's kingdom on earth and anticipated that he would become the Messiah. Jesus promised the disciples that God would send the Messiah to establish the kingdom before they completed their preaching mission in Galilee (Matt. 10:23). When their preaching did not bring in God's kingdom, Jesus determined that he would surrender his own life to force the kingdom to appear. Schweitzer felt that Jesus mistakenly undertook these actions and that his determination to die was a useless and unnecessary act. In Schweitzer's view Jesus' example of unselfishness means something to our time, but we ourselves can only approach him as "One unknown, without a name."[8] Jesus' actions remained something of an enigma to Schweitzer.

---

8. Albert Schweitzer, *The Quest for the Historical Jesus* (New York: Macmillan Co., 1950), 403.

Schweitzer's chief accomplishment was to call attention to the obvious eschatological emphasis in Jesus' teaching, but his complete portrait of Jesus has not compelled widespread acceptance. Schweitzer overlooked statements by Jesus that the kingdom had already arrived (Matt. 12:28). He failed to present an adequate explanation of why Jesus would present significant amounts of ethical teaching to his disciples if he felt the world would end soon. Schweitzer's view that the kingdom in Jesus' teaching is still future is called "consistent eschatology." Schweitzer did not believe in this eschatology, but he emphasized that Jesus both accepted and taught it.

Rudolph Bultmann pioneered an even more skeptical approach to the New Testament. His studies in form criticism convinced him that we could trust very little of the Gospel accounts for factual information about Jesus. The early church, in Bultmann's opinion, had thoroughly doctored the accounts. This inability to know truly the historical Jesus did not trouble Bultmann. He felt that the necessity was to experience Jesus today by personal encounter. He assumed that the *kerygma* of the early church provided the foundation for the theology of the New Testament, but he was indifferent to the question of whether or not this *kerygma* rested on the message and ministry of Jesus.[9] He insisted that faith was a decision which by its very nature could not depend on the work of a historian. Bultmann felt that we must strip away the legendary myths which early Christians added to the Jesus story in order to encounter the true Jesus. In light of the New Testament emphasis on the historicity of recorded incidents (see Luke 1:1–4; 1 Cor. 15:1–8), Bultmann's approach met with increasing opposition, even from those with a more liberal mindset.

Bultmann and many others who investigated the same problems were involved in trying to separate the *Jesus of history* from the *Christ of faith*. The term *Jesus of history* refers to Jesus as he actually was. The term *Christ of faith* refers to Jesus as Christians believed him to be. Most Christians have assumed that the Jesus described in the Gospels is the same as the Christ in whom they place their trust for salvation. Bultmann and some other scholars insisted that

---

9. Rudolph Bultmann, *Theology of the New Testament*, 2 vols. (New York: Charles Scribner's Sons, 1951–55), 1:3.

the Christ in whom Christians had come to believe differed substantially from Jesus as he actually was.

Most Christians who have studied the Gospel accounts recognize that they do not contain enough material for a full biography of Jesus. The Synoptics show a degree of uniformity in describing Jesus' ministry, but the Gospel writers did not intend to provide a complete historical harmony of Jesus' life. Sometimes the writers arrange their material topically, and this makes it difficult to relate the chronology of events in one Gospel to that in another.

Christian conscience also recognizes that a knowledge of historical facts alone cannot compel faith. When Peter preached at Pentecost he assumed that his hearers knew the relevant facts about Jesus' life (Acts 2:22), but Peter appealed to the resurrection of Christ as the foundation for faith in his hearers (Acts 2:33–38). The Gospels are not indifferent to Jesus' life history, but they are primarily theological interpretations of the historical life of Jesus. Many current New Testament scholars accept the fact that the Gospel accounts of Jesus' life are an authentic abridgment written by passionate proponents of Christianity who selected their material to compel faith in Christ.[10] The differences among the Gospels do not imply error or creation of material but all reflect different arrangement and presentation in order to convey meaning. The Gospel accounts are not always written in a strict chronological order, but they should receive complete trust as documents which correctly proclaim the redemption in Christ and urge us to place our faith in him. The Gospel accounts of the life, death, burial, and resurrection of Jesus provide a trustworthy foundation for our faith in him.

The Teaching of Jesus

The Greek verb for teach (*didasko*) appears in the Gospel of Matthew ten times in reference to Jesus' teaching activities. This

---

10. Craig L. Blomberg authored a recent, thorough work intended to present evidence for accepting the historical trustworthiness of the Gospels. See his book *The Historical Reliability of the Gospels* (Downers Grove, Ill.: InterVarsity Press, 1987). For a more popular presentation of the historical trustworthiness of Scripture, see Joel B. Green, *How to Read the Gospels & Acts* (Downers Grove, Ill.: InterVarsity Press, 1987), especially pp. 69–98.

emphasis on teaching is also prominent in Mark and Luke. In John's Gospel the same emphasis on teaching appears with Jesus using lengthy discourses to communicate his message to the multitudes.

Jesus' Method

Those who heard Jesus' teaching were gripped by the authority with which he spoke (Mark 1:22). He did not depend on references to his predecessors, but he freshly interpreted God's message in an engaging manner and this resulted in listening and acceptance. Notice the presence of the phrase, "I tell you," in Matthew 5:22, 28, 32, 39, 44 as evidence of his personal authority.

Jesus' best known teaching method was the parable. Using either an extended story or a short, pithy statement, he conveyed spiritual truth by comparing it to familiar facts from daily life. The meaning was often so clear that the listener(s) needed no additional interpretation to understand the message. When Jesus told the parable of the two debtors in Luke 7:40–50, Jesus' host Simon understood that Jesus had given his proud attitude a stinging rebuke. To have asked what the parable meant would resemble asking a master humorist to explain his jokes.

Jesus also used pungent figures of speech to communicate truth. He frequently used the epigram, a terse statement which would grab the attention of his audience like a barb on wire grabs the skin (see Matt. 9:12–13). He also used hyperbole, intentional exaggeration, to communicate his point (see Matt. 5:29–30, where Jesus did not require either eye surgery or amputation). Some of Jesus' teachings have a rhythmic quality, evident even in English translations. This poetic quality would assist in easy memorization by his followers (see Luke 6:27–28).

Jesus occasionally used arguments in his teaching, but the basis of his arguments centered around the interpretation of Scripture. He did not argue from abstract premises or philosophical assumptions. His arguments in Matthew 22:23–45 reflect this trait.

Jesus' occasional use of questions and answers stimulated listeners. Usually his questions dealt with some form of deep human need or spiritual problem. The pressing question of Matthew 16:26 compelled his hearers to come to grips with the issue. Jesus not only used questions in his teaching; he also responded positively to questions from his followers (Mark 4:10–20).

Jesus sometimes used object lessons to communicate concrete truth to his listeners. He washed the feet of the disciples to impress them with their need for humility (John 13:3–11). He called a little child to him to discuss childlike faith (Matt. 18:1–5), and he described unselfish giving as he watched a destitute widow drop two small coins into the temple offering box (Mark 12:41–44). Jesus probably spoke the parable of the sower within viewing distance of a farmer tossing out seed (Luke 8:4–15).

Jesus helped his listeners understand and remember his teachings by the use of frequent repetition. Notice his threefold prediction of his death in Mark 8:31; 9:31; 10:33–34. Some of his sayings in the Sermon on the Mount may have been repeated on more than one occasion.

Jesus promoted learning by focusing on the performance of a project. In dealing with his disciples, he told them how to minister and what they could expect to encounter. Then he sent them out, allowed them to learn, and concluded this practicum with a reporting session (Luke 9:1–10).

One factor further promoting Jesus' skill as a teacher was his personal example. He lived what he taught to others. He taught by deed and by word. His own life remains an example for us to imitate in our devotion to him.

The Content

Jesus' teaching is scattered throughout the Gospels. It frequently appears in blocks, some of which represented a monologue (Matthew 5–7), while other teaching was apparently given in the context of dialogue (John 8:12–59). Jesus spoke on moral and theological subjects. In the Sermon on the Mount he spoke about sexual morality (Matt. 5:27–32), revenge (Matt. 5:38–42), and forgiveness (Matt. 6:14–15). He discussed the nature of God (John 4:41–44) and his own role in the divine plan (John 12:27–36). He also presented practical instructions when he prepared his disciples for their coming persecution (John 16:1–4).

Jesus did not organize his teaching into a system. He centered it around his own person. The frequent appearance of the "I am" sections in John's Gospel shows this trait (John 6:35; 8:12; 14:6). As a boy he told Joseph and Mary of his awareness of a special obligation to his heavenly Father (Luke 2:49). With his enemies he used language which reflected his awareness of his preexistence and deity (John 8:42, 58–59). He accepted the worship his followers offered him (John 20:28–29).

Concerning specific doctrinal topics, Jesus taught about the Holy Spirit (John 16:8–11), and emphasized that only one born of the Spirit could enter God's kingdom (John 3:5). He did not make a systematic presentation of a doctrine about Scripture, but he stressed its reliability (John 10:35). He did not teach extensively about the church, but he declared that he had founded it (Matt. 16:18). He promised eternal life and security for those who knew him (John 10:28), and he promised a return to bring his followers to a heavenly home with him (John 14:3).

A major emphasis of Jesus' teaching was the kingdom of God. The term referred to God's rule over the hearts of men (Luke 17:21), culminating in an establishment of some type (Matt. 6:10). Jesus regarded the kingdom as having already begun in his own person (Matt. 12:28), but as yet to come in its fullness after his death and resurrection (Luke 22:16).

Jesus did not hesitate to proclaim the importance of his own mission. He knew that he had come to preach the gospel (Luke 4:43) and to call sinners to repentance (Matt. 9:13). He recognized that God had sent him to offer his life as a ransom for many (Mark 10:45). Just before his crucifixion he reported to the Father the successful accomplishment of his mission (John 17:4).

Jesus explained to Nicodemus how he could participate in God's kingdom. The first requirement involved regeneration (John 3:3), which demanded both repentance (Mark 1:14–15) and faith (John 6:47). Repentance involved both moral and theological change. Morally it demanded that a person turn to Christ in obedience (Mark 8:34–35). Theologically it demanded a correct belief in who Jesus was and is (Matt. 11:27). Faith demanded a complete trust in Christ alone for deliverance from sin. Jesus used the example of the little child to demonstrate the humility needed to come to him (Mark 10:13–16).

Dates in Jesus' Life

Several factors make it difficult to give precise dates to the events of the New Testament era. First, since secular historians often looked contemptuously on Christianity, they seldom referred to incidents involving the church. Second, various peoples in history have used quite different methods to reckon chronology, thus resulting in differences. The Romans followed a solar calendar introduced under Julius Caesar, but they reckoned dates more often by their distance from the beginning of an emperor's term. Jews used a lunar calendar of twelve months which annually fell short of a solar calendar by ten or eleven days. The production of a calendar that dated events from the birth of Christ was a later development first undertaken in A.D. 525 by Dionysius, a Scythian monk. In reasoning back to the year of Christ's birth Dionysius erred by several years.[11]

Birth of Christ

Biblical evidence indicates that Jesus was born before the death of Herod the Great (Matt. 2:1–12), during a period that corresponded with a census ordered by Augustus in the time when Quirinius was governor of Syria (Luke 2:1–2). At the same time a star led wise men from the East to find Jesus in Jerusalem (Matt. 2:9–11). All three of these features provide assistance in identifying the date of Jesus' birth, but we must investigate each feature separately.

The Jewish historian Josephus mentions the occurrence of a lunar eclipse just before the death of Herod.[12] Astronomy suggests that the most probable date for this eclipse was March 12, 4 B.C. Herod's death probably occurred within a month of the eclipse.

The date of the census during the governorship of Quirinius is a much-debated issue of New Testament chronology. Evidence that Quirinius served as governor over Syria during the period before Christ is uncertain. Also uncertain is the nature of the census. Was it a registration of taxable persons and objects, or was it an occasion for the official assessment of the taxes? Evidence exists to suggest

---

11. For an explanation of the development of this calendar, see Harold Hoehner, *Chronological Aspects of the Life of Christ* (Grand Rapids: Zondervan Books, 1977), 11–12. Hoehner also discusses many of the issues relating to the date for Christ's birth, length of ministry, and death.
12. Josephus, *Antiquities* 17.6.4.

that Quirinius was in an authoritative position in Syria at the time of Christ's birth, and that the registration of people for taxation could have been ordered in 8 B.C. It might have required several years for the decree of the census to be executed. If so, Jesus' birth could have occurred somewhere in the period from 7 to 5 B.C.

Matthew's account of the movements of the star which guided the wise men seems to refer to a single miraculous event. It would be impossible to date the occurrence of such a miracle.

Church tradition has established the date of the celebration of Jesus' birth on December 25 for the western church and January 6 for the eastern church. The presence of the shepherds outside watching their flocks (Luke 2:8) would not normally occur during the cool season of winter. Jesus was born sometime during 6 or 5 B.C., but it is difficult to determine exactly the precise season or date of his birth.

The Length of Jesus' Ministry

John's Gospel provides the most useful information for computing the length of Jesus' ministry. John mentions the occurrence of at least three Passovers during Jesus' ministry (2:23; 6:4; 12:1). This in itself implies a length of at least two years. However, it is not certain that John mentioned all of the Passovers observed during Jesus' ministry, since providing a chronicle of these feasts was beyond his purpose.

John 5:1 mentioned an unnamed feast in Jerusalem, but identifying this feast is difficult. Even if we cannot precisely identify the feast, we may still be able to estimate the passage of time in John's Gospel. The Passover of 2:23 occurred in the spring. The mention of time in 4:35 (the approaching harvest) suggests that nine months have passed since the events of 2:23. John also mentioned a Galilean ministry of Jesus in 6:1–3 preceding the Passover in 6:4. It is likely that Jesus' ministry in 6:1–3 exceeded three months. If this is so, an unnamed Passover may have occurred between those mentioned in 2:23 and 6:4.

If Jesus' ministry involved a fourth Passover, the total length of his ministry would be at least three years. Even if his ministry encompassed only three Passovers, it still may have lasted nearly three years. Thus, three years is a reasonable length to suggest for his ministry.

The Death of Jesus

An effort to determine an exact date for Jesus' death will often produce different analyses of the available information. My analysis is no exception to that principle.

Luke located the beginning of the ministry of John the Baptist by relating it to the periods of service of a number of Roman and Jewish officials (Luke 3:1–2). We know that Jesus' ministry began shortly after that of John. The only chronological information given by Luke was "the fifteenth year of the emperor Tiberius." Tiberius succeeded to the throne after Augustus died in A.D. 14. However, many scholars have felt that Luke may have reckoned the beginning of Tiberius's reign not from the time of Augustus's death, but from the time when Augustus elevated Tiberius to be coemperor with him, that is, A.D. 11. If we follow this system, the fifteenth year of Tiberius's reign began in A.D. 26, and Jesus' baptism took place in late 26 or early 27. Adding three years for the duration of Jesus' ministry, we find that Jesus' death would have occurred in A.D. 29 or 30.

During Jesus' first Passover (John 2:23) his Jewish opponents stated that the temple had been in the process of construction for forty-six years (John 2:20). This process of remodeling began in 20–19 B.C. The Passover about which John wrote in 2:23 would then have occurred somewhere around A.D. 26 or 27. If we add three additional years to these calculations to allow for at least three additional Passovers, we would arrive at A.D. 29 or 30 as the year of Jesus' crucifixion. This approximates the time which we identified in the previous paragraph. It seems safe to suggest that the death of Jesus likely occurred in A.D. 29 or 30.[13]

The Chronology of Jesus' Life

Because no Gospel provides exhaustive data on the life of Jesus, it is impossible to construct a full biography of his life. Sometimes the order of events is not chronological, for each writer felt free to

---

13. Contrast this date with Puskas, who advocates a date of A.D. 33. Note that the chief difference in the calculations involves the time of beginning the reign of Tiberius. See Charles B. Puskas, *An Introduction to the New Testament* (Peabody, Mass.: Hendrickson Publisher Inc., 1989), 162–68.

present material according to his own objective. These facts create differences of opinion on the correct order of events in Jesus' life. The following outline parallels the opinions of many scholars and includes only the larger blocks of material and periods of time in Jesus' life.

Birth and Early Years

Both Matthew and Luke provide information about the birth and early life of Jesus. They indicate that Mary gave birth to Jesus by the biological miracle of the virgin birth.

Luke provides information about the visit of the shepherds to Bethlehem in connection with the birth. He also includes the story of Jesus' presentation in the temple on the eighth day after his birth (Luke 2:8–38). Matthew tells the story of the visit of the wise men (the Magi) and Herod's slaughter of the innocent children in Bethlehem (Matt. 2:1–18).

Matthew includes the sojourn in Egypt (Matt. 2:19–23), and Luke narrates the visit of the twelve-year-old Jesus to Jerusalem for the Passover. Here Jesus amazed the Jewish scribes by his insights into God's plans (Luke 2:41–50). The New Testament is virtually silent about his life between the age of twelve and the events just prior to the beginning of his public ministry (Luke 2:51–52).

The Period of Preparation

Before Jesus began his public ministry, three important incidents related to his work took place:

1. the ministry of John the Baptist;

2. the baptism of Jesus;

3. the temptation of Jesus.

Matthew and Luke present the most complete information about these incidents, but Mark makes a brief allusion to all three.

John the Baptist fulfilled the role of announcing the beginning of a new era. He maintained a link with the past by following the methods and moral appeals of the ancient prophets. But he broke with the past by heralding the advent of God's messenger and by calling even Jewish leaders to a baptism of repentance (Matt. 3:1–12; Luke 3:1–17).

Jesus' baptism concluded John's work. For Jesus, baptism signified a commitment to God's plan and an identification with the needs of a sinful people. The descent of the Spirit in the form of a dove marked the inauguration of Jesus' public ministry (Matt. 3:13–17; Luke 3:21–22).

In the temptations Satan tested Jesus' commitment to follow the divine plan for his life (Matt. 4:1–11; Luke 4:1–13). Jesus overcame all the temptations by quoting Scripture, and his victory better equipped him to strengthen his followers in their temptations (Heb. 5:8–10).

Jesus' Early Judean Ministry

Only John's Gospel provides information about Jesus' early ministry in Judea. During this period Jesus made contacts with those who would later become his committed disciples (John 1:19–42). During this same period he made a detour into Galilee, where he performed the first of his miraculous signs, the wedding at Cana (John 2:1–11). In Jerusalem he cleansed the temple and spoke with Nicodemus (John 2:13–3:21).

Jesus' Galilean Ministry

Although the major block of Jesus' work in this period took place in Galilee, John's Gospel shows that Jesus made periodic forays into Judea (John 7:1–14). This section can be divided into three chief periods.

1. The first period includes Jesus' work up to the time of choosing the twelve disciples. During this period Jesus delivered the Sermon on the Mount (Matthew 5–7) as well as other teachings (Mark 1:35–39). He also performed miracles of healing that included those listed in Mark 1:40–3:12. This period is characterized both by popularity (Matt. 4:23–25) and opposition (Mark 2:1–12). As Jesus appointed the twelve disciples, he sent them out with instructions for their initial preaching tour and the subsequent missions they would undertake in the Christian church (Matt. 10:1–42).

2. The second period ends with the withdrawal of Jesus from northern Galilee. It was a time when Jesus continued to teach and perform miracles, and included the development of more intense opposition by the official religious leaders in Jerusalem. Controversy erupted when Jesus' healing of a blind and speechless man led to a charge that he was empowered by

Satan (Matt. 12:22–32). During this period Jesus often taught in parables (Matt. 13:1–53; Mark 4:1–34). He met rejection in his hometown of Nazareth (Matt. 13:53–58), and the death of John the Baptist demonstrated that following the will of God could be costly (Mark 6:14–29). After Jesus fed the five thousand (see Matt. 14:13–21, but the event is also mentioned in all four Gospels), he encountered further rejection in a dispute with Pharisees sent from Jerusalem (Matt. 15:1–20; Mark 7:1–23). Following this disagreement he focused his efforts in the Gentile areas around Tyre and Sidon (Mark 7:24–31).

3. In the third period Jesus ministered largely outside of Galilee and returned there only as he traveled toward Jerusalem for the final time. In the Gentile districts of the North he fed the four thousand (Matt. 15:32–39) and received Peter's great confession at Caesarea Philippi (Mark 8:27–37). He also manifested his glory in the transfiguration (Luke 9:28–36) and began to prepare his disciples for his death by predictions of his passion (Mark 9:30–32). He returned through Galilee as he traveled toward Jerusalem (Mark 9:33–50).

The Final Journey to Jerusalem

This period of Jesus' ministry is a difficult period to organize chronologically. Matthew and Luke present only brief summaries of Jesus' activities, and Luke combines much material into a travel document with the individual parts tied together very loosely.

Luke 9:51 describes the beginning of Jesus' journey toward Jerusalem, a journey which finally concluded in 19:28. In Luke 10:38 he is in Bethany, the home of Mary and Martha. In 17:11 he is passing through the area between Samaria and Galilee heading toward Jerusalem. These passages indicate a very loose chronological link. The entire section is sometimes called the Perean ministry, a name taken from the territory of Perea on the east side of the Jordan. The section contains teaching on prayer (11:2–4), some memorable parables (12:13–21), and a barbed attack on the Pharisees (13:10–17). The incidents mentioned in John 7–10 likely fit in this chronological period. In Luke 15 Jesus offered a rebuke to the Pharisees by showing God's concern for sinners, a concern which these Jewish leaders did not share. He also included an appeal for disciples (Luke 16:1–13) and an additional warning to the Pharisees (16:19–31). He gave additional teaching about prayer (Luke 18:1–14) and aroused the Jewish leaders to plot his death by raising Lazarus from the dead (John 11:1–53).

After the Jewish leaders decided to seek his death, Jesus withdrew from public appearances in Judea to the town of Ephraim. There he remained until the Passover season approached (John 11:54).

As Jesus approached Jerusalem for the final time, he met the rich young ruler (Mark 10:17–31) and made a final prediction of his coming death (Mark 10:32–34). His arrival at Bethany placed him on the threshhold of his final week of ministry and sacrifice (John 11:55–12:11).

The Week of the Passion

It is possible to present a rough daily outline of the activities of Jesus during this significant week. Each Gospel presents supplementary detail, and by harmonizing the incidents a more complete picture emerges. However, the materials of the Gospels do not present a full chronological development of the week.

Jesus began this climactic week with the triumphal entry on Sunday (Mark 11:1–10). On Monday he cleansed the temple (Mark 11:15–19). On Tuesday he became involved in discussions with the Jewish religious leaders (Mark 11:27–12:37), and he presented the apocalyptic discourse on the Mount of Olives (Mark 13:1–37). His Wednesday activities are not mentioned, but on Thursday he ate the Passover meal with his disciples (Mark 14:12–25) before his betrayal and arrest (Mark 14:43–52).

After the arrest, his trial had two divisions. In the Jewish phase of the trial he appeared before Annas (John 18:12–14, 24), Caiaphas (Mark 14:53–64), and the entire Sanhedrin (Mark 15:1). In the Roman phase of the trial he appeared before Pilate (Mark 15:1–5), Herod Antipas (Luke 23:6–12), and again before Pilate (Luke 23:13–25). Jesus suffered on the cross from approximately 9 A.M. until 3 P.M. (Mark 15:25–41). His burial took place quickly to avoid leaving his dead body on the cross during the Sabbath (Mark 15:42–46). When the women arrived at the tomb the next morning, it was empty (Mark 16:1–8). Subsequently Jesus appeared to Mary Magdalene (John 20:11–18), two disciples on the road to Emmaus (Luke 24:13–32), the ten disciples meeting in an upper room (John 20:19–25), and the eleven disciples, including Thomas (John

20:26–31). He presented the Great Commission to the assembled disciples in Galilee (Matt. 28:16–20).

Outline for a Harmonistic Study of the Gospels

I. Introduction: The Background to Jesus' Life
   A. Luke's prologue (Luke 1:1–4)
   B. John's prologue (John 1:1–18)
   C. The genealogies of Jesus (Matt. 1:1–17; Luke 3:23–38)

II. The Birth and Childhood of Jesus
   A. Pronouncement to Zecharias of John's birth (Luke 1:5–25)
   B. Pronouncement to Mary of Jesus' birth and Magnificat (Luke 1:26–56)
   C. Birth, naming, and childhood of John (Luke 1:57–80)
   D. Pronouncement to Joseph of Jesus' birth (Matt. 1:18–25)
   E. Jesus' birth attended by the shepherds (Luke 2:1–20)
   F. Circumcision, naming, and presentation of Jesus in the temple with Simeon and Anna (Luke 2:21–40)
   G. Worship of wise men and experiences of Jesus' infancy (Matt. 2:1–23)
   H. Visit to the temple (Luke 2:41–52)

III. Preparation for Jesus' Ministry Throughout Palestine
   A. Ministry of John the Baptist (Matt. 3:1–12; Mark 1:1–8; Luke 3:1–18)
   B. Baptism of Jesus (Matt. 3:13–17; Mark 1:9–11; Luke 3:21–22)
   C. Temptation of Jesus (Matt. 4:1–11; Mark 1:12–13; Luke 4:1–13)
   D. John's witness to Jesus (John 1:19–34)
   E. The first disciples (John 1:35–51)
   F. Changing water into wine at Cana of Galilee (John 2:1–12)
   G. Cleansing the temple (John 2:13–22)
   H. Challenge to Nicodemus to be born again (John 2:23–3:21)
   I. The overlapping ministries of John and Jesus (John 3:22–36)
   J. John's imprisonment and Jesus' departure to Galilee (Matt. 4:12; Mark 1:14; Luke 3:19–20; 4:14; John 4:1–4)
   K. The Samaritan woman at the well (John 4:5–42)

IV. The Ministry in Galilee

 A. Beginning the ministry in Galilee with the healing of a nobleman's son and making a home in Capernaum (Matt. 4:13–17; Mark 1:14–15; Luke 4:15; John 4:43–54)

 B. Additional contact with the first disciples (Matt. 4:18–22; Mark 1:16–20; Luke 5:1–11)

 C. Beginning ministries in Capernaum including teaching, healing, and exorcising (Matt. 4:23–25; 8:14–17; Mark 1:21–39; Luke 4:31–44)

 D. Cleansing a leper (Matt. 8:2–4; Mark 1:40–45; Luke 5:12–16)

 E. Forgiving and healing a paralytic (Matt. 9:1–8; Mark 2:1–12; Luke 5:17–26)

 F. The call of Matthew–Levi (Matt. 9:9–13; Mark 2:13–17; Luke 5:27–32)

 G. Debate over fasting (Matt. 9:14–17; Mark 2:18–22; Luke 5:33–39)

 H. Healing the lame man at the pool of Bethesda (John 5:1–47)

 I. Reaping and eating grain on the Sabbath (Matt. 12:1–8; Mark 2:23–28; Luke 6:1–5)

 J. Healing the man with the withered hand on the Sabbath (Matt. 12:9–14; Mark 3:1–6; Luke 6:6–11)

 K. Withdrawing from the multitude (Matt. 12:15–21; Mark 3:7–12)

 L. Selecting the Twelve Apostles (Mark 3:13–19; Luke 6:12–16)

 M. The Sermon on the Mount (Matt. 5:1–8:1; Luke 6:17–49)

 N. Healing of a centurion's servant (Matt. 8:5–13; Luke 7:1–10)

 O. Bringing back to life the widow's son in Nain (Luke 7:11–17)

 P. The doubts of John the Baptist (Matt. 11:2–19; Luke 7:18–35)

 Q. Rebuke to the Galilean cities (Matt. 11:20–30)

 R. Jesus anointed by an immoral woman (Luke 7:36–50)

 S. The women who followed Jesus (Luke 8:1–3)

T. Jesus accused of the unpardonable sin (Matt. 12:22–37; Mark 3:19–30)

U. The sign of Jonah (Matt. 12:38–45)

V. The spiritual family of Jesus (Matt. 12:46–50; Mark 3:31–35; Luke 8:19–21)

W. Parables of the kingdom (Matt. 13:1–53; Mark 4:1–34; Luke 8:4–18)

X. Quieting the storm (Matt. 8:18, 23–27; Mark 4:35–41; Luke 8:22–25)

Y. The Gadarene demoniac(s) (Matt. 8:28–34; Mark 5:1–20; Luke 8:26–39)

Z. Twin miracles: healing the woman with the flow of blood and raising the daughter of Jairus (Matt. 9:18–26; Mark 5:21–43; Luke 8:40–56)

AA. Healing the blind men and the man who could not speak (Matt. 9:27–34)

BB. The rejection at Nazareth (Matt. 13:54–58; Mark 6:1–6; Luke 4:16–30)

CC. Sending out the disciples (Matt. 9:35–11:1; Mark 6:6–13; Luke 9:1–6)

DD. The fear of Herod after beheading John the Baptist (Matt. 14:1–12; Mark 6:14–29; Luke 9:7–9)

EE. Feeding the five thousand (Matt. 14:13–23; Mark 6:30–46; Luke 9:10–17; John 6:1–15)

FF. A nature miracle: walking on the water (Matt. 14:24–36; Mark 6:47–56; John 6:16–21)

GG. The message on the bread of life (John 6:22–71)

HH. The source of true defilement (Matt. 15:1–20; Mark 7:1–23; John 7:1)

II. Healing the daughter of a Syro–Phoenician woman who had faith (Matt. 15:21–28; Mark 7:24–30)

JJ. Feeding the four thousand (Matt. 15:29–38; Mark 7:31–8:9)

KK. The sign of the Messiah (Matt. 15:39–16:4; Mark 8:10–12)

LL. The leaven of the Sadducees and Pharisees (Matt. 16:5–12; Mark 8:13–26)

MM. The confession of Peter, the keys of the kingdom, binding and loosing (Matt. 16:13–20; Mark 8:27–30; Luke 9:18–22)

NN. First prediction of the passion (Matt. 16:21–26; Mark 8:31–37; Luke 9:23–25)

OO. The transfiguration (Matt. 16:27–17:8; Mark 8:38–9:8; Luke 9:26–36)

PP. The relationship between John the Baptist and Elijah (Matt. 17:9–13; Mark 9:9–13)

QQ. The exorcism of the boy possessed with a demon (Matt. 17:14–20; Mark 9:14–29; Luke 9:37–42)

RR. Second prediction of the passion (Matt. 17:22–23; Mark 9:30–32; Luke 9:43–45)

SS. Payment of the temple tax (Matt. 17:24–27)

TT. A childlike attitude and discipleship (Matt. 18:1–14; Mark 9:33–50; Luke 9:46–50)

UU. The practice of forgiveness, the parable of the unmerciful servant (Matt. 18:15–35)

VV. A challenge to discipleship (Matt. 8:19–22; Luke 9:57–62)

WW. Jesus at the Feast of Tabernacles (Luke 9:51–56; John 7:2–10)

V. The Later Ministry in Judea and the Ministry in Perea

    A. Jesus' discussion at the Feast of Tabernacles (John 7:11–52; 8:12–59)

    B. Healing the man born blind (John 9:1–41)

    C. Jesus as the Good Shepherd (John 10:1–21)

    D. Sending out the seventy (Luke 10:1–24)

    E. The parable of the good Samaritan (Luke 10:25–37)

    F. Mary and Martha (Luke 10:38–42)

    G. Parables on prayer (Luke 11:1–13)

    H. Jesus' defense against an accusation of being linked with Satan, the parable of the empty house, the sign of Jonah, and developing a healthy spiritual vision (Luke 11:14–36)

    I. Woes on the Pharisees (Luke 11:37–54)

    J. Instruction on hypocrisy, greed (parable of the rich fool), watchfulness, and the appearance of the messianic kingdom (Luke 12:1–59)

    K. The parable of the fruitless fig tree (Luke 13:1–9)

    L. Healing on the Sabbath of a woman bent over and the parables of the mustard seed and leaven (Luke 13:10–21)

    M. Jesus' claim to be one with God (John 10:22–42)

N. The narrow door and Jesus' sorrow for Jerusalem (Luke 13:22–35)

O. Sabbath healing of a man with dropsy, teaching on humility, and the parable of the messianic banquet (Luke 14:1–24)

P. The cost of discipleship (Luke 14:25–35)

Q. The parables of the lost sheep, the lost coin, the prodigal son, and the elder brother (Luke 15:1–32)

R. The parables of the unjust steward and the rich man and Lazarus (Luke 16:1–31)

S. Caring for young believers, faith, and service (Luke 17:1–10)

T. The raising of Lazarus (John 11:1–44)

U. The Sanhedrin's plot against Jesus (John 11:45–54)

V. Healing the ten lepers (Luke 17:11–19)

W. The advent of the kingdom (Luke 17:20–37)

X. Parables on persistence and humility in prayer (Luke 18:1–14)

Y. Divorce and remarriage (Matt. 19:1–12; Mark 10:1–12)

Z. Jesus and the little children (Matt. 19:13–15; Mark 10:13–16; Luke 18:15–17)

AA. The rich young ruler (Matt. 19:16–30; Mark 10:17–31; Luke 18:18–30)

BB. The parable of the laborers in the vineyard (Matt. 20:1–16)

CC. Third passion prediction with the selfish request of James and John (Matt. 20:17–28; Mark 10:32–45; Luke 18:31–34)

DD. Healing of the blind man Bartimaeus (Matt. 20:29–34; Mark 10:46–52; Luke 18:35–43)

EE. Jesus and Zacchaeus (Luke 19:1–10)

FF. The parable of the pounds (Luke 19:11–28)

VI. The Passion Week in Jerusalem

A. The arrival of Passover pilgrims in Jerusalem and the Sanhedrin's plot against Jesus and Lazarus (John 11:55–12:1, 9–11)

B. Anointing of Jesus by Mary of Bethany (Matt. 26:6–13; Mark 14:3–9; John 12:2–8)

C. The triumphal entry (Matt. 21:1–11; Mark 11:1–11; Luke 19:29–44; John 12:12–19)

D. Cursing the fig tree and cleansing the temple (Matt. 21:12, 13, 18, 19; Mark 11:12–18; Luke 19:45–48)
E. The Greeks seeking to see Jesus and a warning against unbelief (John 12:20–50)
F. The withering of the fig tree (Matt. 21:19–22; Mark 11:19–25)
G. Question about Jesus' authority (Matt. 21:23–27; Mark 11:27–33)
H. Parable of the two sons (Matt. 21:28–32)
I. Parable of the vineyard (Matt. 21:33–46; Mark 12:1–12; Luke 20:9–19)
J. The parable of the marriage feast (Matt. 22:1–14)
K. Paying taxes to Caesar (Matt. 22:15–22; Mark 12:13–17; Luke 20:20–26)
L. Sadducees' question about the resurrection (Matt. 22:23–33; Mark 12:18–27; Luke 20:27–40)
M. The greatest commandments (Matt. 22:34–40; Mark 12:28–34)
N. The deity of the Davidic Messiah (Matt. 22:41–46; Mark 12:35–37; Luke 20:41–44)
O. Denunciation of the scribes and Pharisees (Matt. 23:1–39; Mark 12:38–40; Luke 20:45–47)
P. The widow's offering (Mark 12:41–44; Luke 21:1–4)
Q. The Olivet discourse (Matt. 24–25; Mark 13:1–37; Luke 21:5–38)
R. The plan for the betrayal (Matt. 26:1–5; Mark 14:1, 2, 10, 11; Luke 22:1–6)
S. Preparing for the last supper (Matt. 26:17–19; Mark 14:12–16; Luke 22:7–13)
T. Observing the last supper
   1. Washing the disciples' feet (Matt. 26:20; Mark 14:17; Luke 22:14–16; John 13:1–20)
   2. Departure of Judas Iscariot (Matt. 26:21–25; Mark 14:18–21; Luke 22:21–23; John 13:21–30)
   3. Prediction of Peter's denials (Matt. 26:31–35; Mark 14:27–31; Luke 22:31–38; John 13:31–38)
   4. Instituting the Lord's Supper (Matt. 26:26–29; Mark 14:22–25; Luke 22:17–20; 1 Cor. 11:23–26)

5. The farewell discourses in the Upper Room (John 14–16)
6. Jesus' prayer for his disciples (John 17)
U. Jesus in Gethsemane (Matt. 26:30, 36–46; Mark 14:26, 32–42; Luke 22:39–46; John 18:1)
V. The arrest of Jesus (Matt. 26:47–56; Mark 14:43–52; Luke 22:47–53; John 18:2–12)

VII. Jesus' Trial and Crucifixion
   A. The trial before the Jews
   1. Hearing before Annas (John 18:12–14, 19–23)
   2. Hearing before Caiaphas and the Sanhedrin (Matt. 26:57, 59–68; Mark 14:53, 55–65; Luke 22:54, 63–65; John 18:24)
   3. Peter's denials (Matt. 26:58, 69–75; Mark 14:54, 66–72; Luke 22:54–62; John 18:15–18, 25–27)
   4. Official condemnation of Jesus by Sanhedrin (Matt. 27:1; Mark 15:1; Luke 22:66–71)
   B. The suicide of Judas Iscariot (Matt. 27:3–10; Acts 1:18–19)
   C. The trial before the Romans
   1. First hearing before Pilate (Matt. 27:2, 11–14; Mark 15:1–5; Luke 23:1–5; John 18:28–38)
   2. Hearing before Herod Antipas (Luke 23:6–12)
   3. Second hearing before Pilate (Matt. 27:15–30; Mark 15:6–19; Luke 23:13–25; John 18:39–19:16)
   D. Jesus' crucifixion (Matt. 27:31–36; Mark 15:20–25; Luke 23:26–33; John 19:16–18)
   E. The events at the crucifixion site (Matt. 27:37–50; Mark 15:26–37; Luke 23:34–43, 46; John 19:19–30)
   F. Tearing of the veil of the temple (Matt. 27:51–56; Mark 15:38–41; Luke 23:44, 45, 47–49)
   G. Burial of Jesus (Matt. 27:57–66; Mark 15:42–47; Luke 23:50–56; John 19:31–43)

VIII. Jesus' Resurrection, Post–Resurrection Appearances, and Ascension
   A. The empty tomb (Matt. 28:1–4; Mark 16:1)
   B. The women at the tomb (Matt. 28:5–8; Mark 16:2–8; Luke 24:1–8; John 20:1)
   C. The coming of Peter and John to the tomb (Luke 24:9–12; John 20:2–10)

D. Appearance of Jesus to Mary Magdalene (John 20:11–18)
E. Appearance of Jesus to the other women (Matt. 28:9–10)
F. Sanhedrin's bribe of Roman guards for the tomb (Matt. 28:11–15)
G. Appearance of Jesus to the disciples on the Emmaus Road (Luke 24:13–35; 1 Cor. 15:5a)
H. Appearance of Jesus to the disciples without Thomas (Luke 24:36–43; John 20:19–25; 1 Cor. 15:5b)
I. Appearance of Jesus to Thomas (John 20:26–31)
J. Appearance to the disciples at the Sea of Galilee and the restoration of Peter (John 21)
K. Appearances of Jesus to the Eleven, the five hundred, James, and the Great Commission (Matt. 28:16–20; 1 Cor. 15:6–7)
L. The ascension of Jesus (Luke 24:44–53; Acts 1:3–12)

For Further Discussion

1. To what lengths should we go today to make the message of the gospel understandable to modern people? To make it acceptable to modern people?

2. In what respects would the biographical information about Jesus in the Gospels differ from the biographical information which a modern biographer would present?

3. Compare and contrast the teaching methods and techniques of Jesus to those advocated by modern educators.

4. How important is accurate historical information in providing a foundation for believing and accepting the gospel message?

Bibliography

Secondary Sources

Sources of Information about Jesus

France, R. T. *The Evidence for Jesus.* Downers Grove, Ill.: InterVarsity Press, 1986. Excellent review of evidence about Jesus both inside and outside the New Testament.

The Geography of Jesus' Homeland

May, Herbert G., ed. *Oxford Bible Atlas.* 3rd ed. New York: Oxford University Press, 1984. Useful discussion and maps for understanding the geographical development of Jesus' life.

Turner, George A. *Historical Geography of the Holy Land.* Grand Rapids: Baker Book House, 1973.

The Study of Jesus' Life

Althaus, Paul. *The So-Called Kerygma and the Historical Jesus.* Trans. by David Cairns. Edinburgh: Oliver and Boyd, 1959. Insightful study of Bultmann's demythologizing program by a German who insists on the value of the historical picture of Jesus in the Gospels.

Blomberg, Craig L. *The Historical Reliability of the Gospels.* Downers Grove, Ill.: InterVarsity Press, 1987. A sympathetic examination of evidence for trusting the facts and message of the Gospels.

Bultmann, Rudolph. *Theology of the New Testament.* 2 vols. New York: Charles Scribner's Sons, 1951–55.

Dunn, James D. G. *The Evidence for Jesus.* London: SCM Press Ltd., 1985. Defense of the reliability of the historical presentation about Jesus.

Green, Joel B. *How to Read the Gospels and Acts.* Downers Grove, Ill.: InterVarsity Press, 1987. A popular defense of the historical reliability of the New Testament historical books.

Hennecke, E. *New Testament Apocrypha.* Edited by W. Schneedmelcher. Translated by R. McL. Wilson. 2 vols. Philadelphia: Westminster Press, 1963–66.

Henry, Carl F. H., ed. *Jesus of Nazareth: Saviour and Lord.* Grand Rapids: William B. Eerdmans Publishing Co., 1966. Symposium by largely American evangelicals on problems of historicity and interpretation in the New Testament.

Hoskyns, Sir Edwyn, and Noel Davey. *The Riddle of the New Testament.* London: Faber and Faber Ltd., 1936. An apologetic work pointing out that historical facts alone cannot bring one to faith in Jesus Christ.

Longman, Tremper, III. *Literary Approaches to Biblical Interpretation.* Grand Rapids: Zondervan Books, 1987. Introduction to literary criticism in New Testament study.

Marshall, I. Howard. *I Believe in the Historical Jesus.* Grand Rapids: William B. Eerdmans Publishing Co., 1977. Thoughtful defense of the historical trustworthiness of the Gospels.

Robinson, James M. *A New Quest of the Historical Jesus.* Missoula, Mont.: Scholars' Press, 1979. Appeal for a new investigation of the "historical Jesus" problem by a student of Bultmann.

Schweitzer, Albert. *The Quest for the Historical Jesus*. New York: Macmillan Co., 1950.

The Teaching of Jesus

Branscomb, Harvie. *The Teachings of Jesus*. New York: Abingdon Press, 1931. A study primarily of the content of Jesus' teaching.

Bruce, F. F. *The Hard Sayings of Jesus*. Downers Grove, Ill.: InterVarsity Press, 1983. Interpretation and application of some of Jesus' more enigmatic teachings.

Burney, C. F. *The Poetry of Our Lord*. Oxford: Oxford University Press, 1925. A study of the use of Hebrew poetry in Jesus' teaching.

Manson, T. W. *The Teaching of Jesus*. Cambridge: Cambridge University Press, 1951. See pp. 89–312 for emphasis on Jesus' content.

Puskas, Charles. *An Introduction to the New Testament*. Peabody, Mass.: Hendrickson Publishers Inc., 1989. See especially pp. 181–90 for emphasis on content of Jesus' message.

Chronological Information on Jesus' Life

Hoehner, Harold W. *Chronological Aspects of the Life of Christ*. Grand Rapids: Zondervan Books, 1977. Thorough study of significant dates in Jesus' life.

Reicke, Bo. *The New Testament Era*. Philadelphia: Fortress Press, 1968. See especially pp. 106–7.

Historical Development of Jesus' Life

Gundry, Robert H. *A Survey of the New Testament*. Rev. ed. Grand Rapids: Zondervan Books, 1981. See especially pp. 112–15.

Tenney, Merrill C. *New Testament Survey*. Grand Rapids: William B. Eerdmans Publishing Co., 1961. See especially pp. 201–8.

6   The Synoptic Problem

Guiding Questions

1. Describe the three types of critical approaches to the Gospels known as form criticism, source criticism, and redaction criticism, giving their purposes, methods, and an evaluation of their usefulness.

2. Explain the use and purpose of each of the suggested documents in the four-document hypothesis.

3. Evaluate the reasons given for accepting Markan priority.

4. Evaluate the usefulness of literary critical approaches to the New Testament.

At the end of the eighteenth century the German biblical scholar J. J. Griesbach named Matthew, Mark, and Luke the "synoptic Gospels." The term *synoptic* comes from a Greek word meaning "a seeing together." Griesbach selected the word because the first three Gospels have a high degree of similarity in their discussion of Jesus' life and ministry. Several features characterize this similar presentation of Jesus' life.

1. The Synoptics have the same general historical arrangement. Starting with the baptism and temptation of Jesus, they cover with varying detail his public ministry in Galilee. All three

Gospels suggest that Peter's confession at Caesarea Philippi was the turning point of Jesus' ministry. After this crucial event they narrate the final journey to Jerusalem and Jesus' arrest, trial, crucifixion, and resurrection.

2. In many sections the verbal content of the Synoptics is similar. A comparison of the verbal agreements in the healing of the leper in Matthew 8:1–4; Mark 1:40–45; and Luke 5:12–16 will show the extent of this similarity. In some instances two of the Gospels have a similar style and wording in comparison to the third. Frequently Matthew and Luke have similar wording for material common to them but missing in Mark (see Matt. 3:7–10; Luke 3:7–9).

3. Despite the similarities between the Gospels, many differences in arrangement and vocabulary appear. For example, all three Gospels have interesting differences in the details of the story of the healing of the man with the withered hand (Matt. 12:9–14; Mark 3:1–6; Luke 6:6–11). Matthew placed the incident in a different order than Mark and Luke. Luke later (14:1–6) repeated another incident with verbal similarities to the Matthean account. The Synoptics also narrate Jesus' passion in a generally similar sequence, but they contain many variations of detail and wording.

Such similarities and differences have caused thoughtful Christians to ask, "How can these things be?" What could cause the appearance of so many similarities and, at the same time, so many differences? Why do we have more than one Gospel?

These observations and questions represent the essence of the Synoptic problem. In the following sections we will review some of the suggested solutions.

The Development of the Synoptic Gospels

The opening sentences of Luke, known as the prologue, describe the process by which the author gathered the material for the Gospel (see Luke 1:1–4). These verses show that Luke recognized three stages in the development of his work.

1. He referred to those "original eyewitnesses," who had handed down the traditions to him and others.

2. He described the writers who had drawn up "an account of the events" which had occurred.

3. He spoke of his own role in making a careful investigation and in writing "an orderly narrative."

These three stages consecutively refer to: the period of oral tradition, the period of written sources, and the period of final composition. We will investigate each of these stages of writing and other features which extend beyond these three.[1]

The Period of Oral Tradition: Form Criticism

The first Christians did not have any written copies of the Gospels. They did have accounts of the life and teaching of Jesus which were circulated in units. Some of these may have been linked together in a chronological sequence. Paul's reference in 1 Corinthians 15:3 to the "tradition" he received refers to oral tradition. During this period the information about Jesus was largely passed on by word of mouth and some portions of written material. The study of this period of gospel transmission involves the discipline of form criticism. Historically, interest in form criticism developed after an investigation of the written sources for the Gospels. However, the discipline of form criticism focuses on the first stage in the process of Gospel writing, that is, the stage of the oral tranmission of the Gospel accounts.

Development of Form Criticism. Form criticism was initially used by Scandanavian scholars in the study of the development of traditions in the Old Testament. They formed their techniques by noting how Scandanavian folk tales developed. In the twentieth century German scholarship led in the application of this discipline to the study of the New Testament. Rudolph Bultmann was the best known form critic. He believed that most of the Gospel material was distorted or even fabricated in order to support the theological beliefs of the early

---

1. For a more complete discussion of these stages in the development of the Gospels, see D. A. Carson, Douglas J. Moo, and Leon Morris, *An Introduction to the New Testament* (Grand Rapids: Zondervan Books, 1992), 19–60.

church.[2] Bultmann suggested that the New Testament contained myths that were theologically but not necessarily historically true. He advocated "demythologization," a process of stripping away miraculous features and doctrinal additions that he believed modern people could not accept. Most advocates of form criticism shared at least five common assumptions.

1. The stories and sayings of Jesus first appeared in small self-contained units. The only exception to this principle was in the passion section, which many form critics viewed as an independent unit from the outset. Scholars give the name *pericope* to an individual unit or section of the Gospel story.

2. The stories and sayings of Jesus assumed the standard forms or structures that appear in the Gospels. Form critics disagree on the number and nature of these forms. Bultmann advocated at least four.

- The apophthegm, a short story ending with a saying of Jesus (Mark 2:15–17).

- The miracle story, a story presenting information about Jesus' miraculous deeds (Matt. 9:18–26).

- The "legend," a story that magnifies the greatness of Jesus (Luke 2:41–52).

- The dominical saying, a teaching of Jesus that does not end in a single pithy statement (Mark 4:3–20).

3. The form of a story or saying allowed a critic to discover its place in the life of the early church, due to the assumption that the existence of the story sprang out of a definite need or condition in the early church.

4. As members of the Christian community passed along the sayings, they put the material into forms and also modified the content to meet community needs. This view suggests that the church added to, changed, or altered these stories so that they

---

2. Rudolph Bultmann and Karl Kundsin, *Form Criticism*, trans. by F. C. Grant (New York: Harper Torchbook, 1962). See p. 71, where Bultmann says, "Indeed, it must remain questionable whether Jesus regarded himself as Messiah at all, and did not rather first become Messiah in the faith of the community."

are not necessarily accurate historically. Form critics disagree among themselves about the extent to which the early church changed and developed Gospel materials.

5. Some form critics developed criteria for determining the age and historical trustworthiness of particular stories. They named these criteria *laws of transmission*. These so-called laws of transmission are founded upon the assumptions that in passing on information groups usually:

- lengthen their stories,

- add details,

- fit stories to their own language,

- preserve and develop only what meets their needs and promotes their beliefs.

Using these laws, form critics concluded that shorter Gospel materials lacking in detail, containing Semitic features, and not fitting into the interests of the early church are likely to be more historically reliable and written at an earlier date.

Evaluation of Form Criticism. Many form critics are skeptical of the historical trustworthiness of the Gospels. However, the discipline of form criticism need not conclude with a negative judgment about the historicity of material in the Gospels. Form criticism is correct in suggesting that there was a period during which the Gospel materials were passed along primarily in an oral fashion. Also, the early church surely must have influenced the manner in which the material was handed down. Doubtless, early Christians inserted much of the material into the Gospels because it met needs in the life of the church.

However, it is necessary that those who use form criticism for a more beneficial purpose and those who use it to support historical skepticism cautiously evaluate its strengths and weaknesses before adopting its platform. Below we will explore some of the strengths and weaknesses of form criticism.

- Form critics assume that in the earliest period of transmission the Gospel material circulated orally in disconnected units. However, it is likely that some material was written during this time. Additional materials may have been linked together to form fuller literary units. For instance, some of the original eyewitness material in Luke 1:1–4 could have been circulated in writing.

- Form critics tend to use the literary forms in a rigid, inflexible manner. Some forms in the Gospels are mixed, that is, they retain features of more than one form (note Mark 2:1–12, which is both a miracle story and an apophthegm). Thus, the classification of forms should be general and not too specific.

- The claim that a form can be clearly indentified from its setting in the early church is suspicious. We do not have sufficient information to make such a dogmatic identification.

- The use of the laws of transmission to attribute the early stories and sayings to the church rather than to Jesus is a tenuous procedure at best. Sometimes oral transmission does not lengthen the material.[3]

- The suggestion that the church fitted material to its own needs causes some form critics to accept as authentic only the material that clearly lacks reference to the interests and beliefs of the early church.[4] It hardly seems possible that Gospel material could emerge from the incubator of the early church without containing some evidence of attention by the early church. To dismiss the material that identifies with the interests of the early church as inauthentic defies sound judgment and common sense. It is important to consider that some Gospel material was preserved because it was true, not merely because it supported the biases or the teaching of the early church.

---

3. E. P. Sanders, *The Tendencies of the Synoptic Tradition*, SNTSMS 9 (Cambridge: Cambridge University Press, 1969), 46–87.

4. Carson, Moo, and Morris, *An Introduction to the New Testament*, 23, suggest that a more radical form critic would tend to accept Mark 13:32 as authentic because here Jesus addressed the crowd with a suggestion of his ignorance of the time of his return. Such a premise runs counter to the expected views of the early church, and some form critics would thus regard the statement as authentic on that account.

- We must consider the impact of the eyewitnesses of the original events recorded in the Gospels. Eyewitnesses (note the appeal to eyewitnesses in John 1:14; 1 Cor. 15:5–8; and 1 John 1:1–4) would oppose the wholesale creation or mutilation of Gospel events. Their role in securing the accuracy of the Gospel material must not be ignored.

The British New Testament scholar C. H. Dodd popularized a contrasting approach to the acceptance of an unbalanced form criticism. He detected a common pattern in early Christian preaching that included the following elements:

- The prophecies are fulfilled, and Jesus' coming has inaugurated the new age.

- Jesus was born of the seed of David.

- He died according to the Scriptures to deliver us out of this evil age.

- He was buried.

- He rose on the third day according to the Scriptures.

- He has been exalted at God's right hand.

- He will come again as judge and savior of mankind.[5]

Dodd called this pattern the *kerygma*, a term taken from the Greek word for "proclamation." This kerygma was evangelistic preaching used in making converts. As time passed, the outline of the kerygma was expanded to include stories about Jesus, memorable sayings of Jesus, and parables. Dodd felt that the expansion of Christianity into geographical areas without eyewitnesses of the events in Christ's life led to the writing of the Gospels as permanent records. Also, the death of the original eyewitnesses created the need for accurate records. Dodd contended that Mark's Gospel was an expansion of this kerygma in written form. He also referred to the *didache* as the teaching needed by believers for growth and spiritual life. Dodd's distinction between the kerygma and the

---

5. C. H. Dodd, *The Apostolic Preaching and Its Development* (New York: Harper-Collins Publishers, 1944), 17.

didache is often difficult to maintain, and the outline of preaching may not have been as rigid as Dodd proposed.

Dodd viewed the Gospels as the final stage in a process of oral tradition. His approach preserves the integrity of the Christian message accepted by the early church, and is an alternative approach to a radical form criticism that might view the events of the Gospels as largely the creation of the early church.

The Period of Written Sources: Source Criticism

Some written material containing Gospel incidents must have appeared even in a period of predominantly oral transmission. As apostles and early eyewitnesses aged or passed away, the demand to put their materials into writing would increase. Source critics ask the question, What written sources did the Gospel writers use to produce their writings?

Development of Source Criticism. In 1771 the German literary critic G. E. Lessing suggested that the relationships among the Gospels stemmed from a single original Gospel written in Hebrew or Aramaic. This suggestion was adopted by some and modified by others, but it has not received widespread attention in this century.

In 1797 the German critic J. G. Herder suggested that the unique contents of the Gospels developed from the rapid transformation of the Jesus tradition into a rather fixed oral summary. The suggestion has been expanded and altered, but only a few scholars support it today.

The best solution to explain the Synoptic problem stems from a theory of interdependence. This view suggests that two of the Gospel writers used one or more of the Gospels and perhaps additional documents in preparing their material. This view accounts for the minute agreements in detail and also for the differences between the Gospels.

Augustine, the great North African theologian, suggested that Matthew was the first written Gospel, followed consecutively by Mark and Luke. Those who follow this suggestion generally feel that the later Gospels used their predecessors to produce a final copy. J. J. Griesbach published a treatise in 1789 defending the order of composition as Matthew, Luke, and Mark. He also argued that each later Gospel used the contents of its predecessor(s). Although Griesbach's view has experienced a great resurgence in popularity recently, his view of interdependence has not been widely accepted.[6]

The most common source critical view of Gospel origins is called the "Two-Source" hypothesis. Proponents of this position assert Markan priority, that is, Mark is the earliest Gospel. They also call for the use of a now lost document to which they give the name of Q, an abbreviation taken from the German word *Quelle*, meaning "source."

Evidence for Markan priority includes:

- Matthew contains nearly all of Mark's material, and Luke contains about half of the material.

- Matthew and Luke often repeat the exact words of Mark (Matt. 8:1–3; Mark 1:40–42; Luke 5:12–13).

- Matthew and Luke do not depart together from the Markan sequence of events.

- Matthew and Luke sometimes appear to alter the wording of Mark in order to clarify or smooth out difficult or grammatically awkward statements in Mark. (Both Matthew and Luke omit Mark's statement that Jesus' family viewed him as "mad" [Mark 3:21; Matt. 12:22–32; Luke 8:19–21].)[7]

The existence of Q was suggested because of the presence in Matthew and Luke of very similar material not contained in Mark. (An example is Matt. 3:7–10 and Luke 3:7–9) If the document Q existed, it likely would have been a collection of Jesus' sayings with little narrative content. The acceptance of the Q-hypothesis has varied widely. Some argue that the agreement between Matthew and Luke varies too much to come from a common document.

The most elaborate proposal of a theory of interdependence came from the writings of the British New Testament scholar B. H. Streeter in 1924. Streeter accepted the priority of Mark and the existence of Q. He also proposed a document designated as M to

---

6. A contemporary exponent of Griesbach's views is W. R. Farmer, who offers a thorough critique of Markan priority in *The Synoptic Problem* (Dillsboro, N.C.: Western North Carolina Press, 1976).

7. Ralph Martin discusses Markan priority in greater detail in *New Testament Foundations*, vol. 1: *The Four Gospels* (Grand Rapids: Eerdmans, 1975), 140–43.

refer to those sayings of Jesus distinctive to Matthew (see Matt. 13:24–30) and another document designated as L to refer to the sayings of Jesus distinctive to Luke (see Luke 15:11–32). Although his proposals have not received general agreement, they continue to be a classic statement of a suggested solution.

Evaluation of Source Criticism. Although Markan priority is not held today with the same confidence of a generation ago, it still remains a widely supported assumption. However, the very existence of Q is still uncertain. The discovery of the Gnostic *Gospel of Thomas* shows that collections of Jesus' sayings did circulate, but whether or not a document exactly like Q ever existed is debatable. Even more doubtful is the existence of the suggested documents M and L. Both Matthew and Luke may have used Mark, but the extent of their use likely varied with each Gospel. Their use of Mark or any other historical source does not render their testimony any less credible. They may have used Mark with the conviction that the Markan testimony was trustworthy and with a desire to report a common tradition about Jesus. If they ever reworked Mark's details in their own writing, it may have been done with the purpose of preventing an erroneous interpretation or the addition of details.

The process by which the Gospels developed is so complex that no source-critical hypothesis will likely provide a full explanation of their development. If source hypotheses are used, it is important not to view them as a "scissors-and-paste" method. Any documentary hypothesis should be seen as a working theory that will continue to undergo modification as new data are discovered and observed.

The Period of Final Composition: Redaction Criticism

Form criticism focuses on the materials used in the oral stage of Gospel transmission. Source criticism investigates the documents prominent during the written stage of Gospel development. Redaction criticism focuses on the activity of the author in the production of the Gospels. W. Wrede, a German scholar of the late nineteenth and early twentieth centuries, pictured Mark as a theologian who added to his Gospel the references Jesus made urging silence concerning his messiahship (see Mark 1:34). Wrede argued that Mark added these references to explain why only a small number of people were accepting Jesus as Messiah during his lifetime. Few scholars today accept this "messianic secret" motif, but many now accept the idea that Mark was a theologian who imposed his viewpoint on the historical events he encountered.

Three other German scholars led in emphasizing the theological activity of the evangelists in their writings. Writing successively about Matthew, Mark, and Luke, the German biblical scholars, Gunther Bornkamm, Willi Marxsen, and Hans Conzelmann, insisted that the Gospel writers structured the account of events based on their theological viewpoints.

Description of Redaction Criticism. Redaction critics insist that the Gospel writers not only delivered traditions to their audiences, but they also changed and modified these traditions to introduce their own viewpoint and special emphases.

The term *tradition* refers to whatever source the Gospel writer had in hand as he wrote. It could have been written or oral, but by the time the Gospels were written in their entirety much of the material available to the writers was in written form. The evangelist modified the tradition as he carried out the redaction. Redaction critics are interested in the Gospel as a literary whole, and they pay close attention to the work of the author in selecting and editing the material. Evidence of this redactional activity is thought to appear in the following features.

- The choice to include or exclude material. Matthew's inclusion of the Sermon on the Mount (chaps. 5–7) in contrast to Luke's abridged treatment of this address (see Luke 6:20–49) suggests that Matthew had an abiding interest in instructing the church about Jesus and the law.

- The arrangement of material. The change in the order of the temptations in Matthew and in Luke indicates a different emphasis of the respective writer.

- Additions to the document. Luke's inclusion of the reference to Jesus' praying all night prior to his selection of the disciples is evidence of a special emphasis on prayer in Luke (see Luke 6:12).

- Alteration of words. Matthew pronounces a blessing on the "poor in spirit" (Matt. 5:3), and Luke pronounces a blessing on the "poor" (Luke 6:20). Redaction critics view this as an indication of Lucan interest in economic concerns.

As redaction critics find evidence of these kinds of changes, they note recurring patterns and attribute them to special interests and theological concerns of the respective evangelist. Based on this emphasis, the critic then tries to determine a setting in which the writing of the Gospel may have taken place. For example, Matthew's interest in the law may indicate that he wrote within a Jewish setting or for a Jewish-Christian community.

There is nothing inherently improbable about the possibility that the writers of the Synoptics included, excluded, arranged, added, or altered the material they received. Difficulty arises only if the assertion is made that the Gospel writers changed the facts they received about the life of Jesus.

Evaluation of Redaction Criticism. Some redaction critics make far more specific conclusions about the theological concerns of the evangelists than the evidence allows. Since we do not possess exact copies of the documents which Matthew and Luke used, we cannot determine with certainty who changed what. Also, it is not always true that differences between the Gospels suggest theological concerns. Sometimes differences may be due to a concern for historical accuracy. Redaction critics also commonly assume that what is distinctive or unique about a Gospel writer is an indication of his theological concern. This assumption fails to observe that we might find theological concerns more obviously present in areas of commonality than in areas of difference.

Sometimes decisions about the setting of a particular Gospel are deduced in a far more specific manner than the evidence warrants. Matthew's emphasis on the importance of the law in the Sermon on the Mount certainly indicates a subject of interest to the Jews. To make the details more specific than this, however, is unwarranted.

It is unnecessary to use redactional criticism to attach historical skepticism to the Gospels. Many redactional critics assume that the Gospel writers had little concern for historical accuracy. One can scarcely read the words of Luke 1:1–4 without feeling that Luke had a concern for historical accuracy. It cannot be denied that Matthew, Mark, and Luke redacted some of the material they received. However, their rerrangement, omission, or rewording need not detract from the historicity of the events recorded.

New Testament students often distinguish between the *ipsissima verba* and the *ipsissima vox* of Jesus. The former refers to the actual words of Jesus. The latter calls for the authentic voice of Jesus. It is much more likely that the Gospels contain the authentic voice of Jesus, rather than his actual words. We need not claim that the Gospel writers have always quoted Jesus verbatim, but we do need to believe that in all instances they have provided us with an accurate summary in their own words. We can believe that the Gospel writers were free to select, summarize, or reword a statement with a synonym without affecting its historical accuracy.

Redaction criticism has made many helpful contributions to the study of the New Testament. Among these is the emphasis that the evangelists wrote with theological interest, and were seeking to apply their understanding of Jesus' teaching to the life of the early church. We would add that they were also reporters who sought accurately to report what Jesus said.

Redaction criticism also helps us focus on the distinctive contribution of each Gospel. The report of Jesus' life did not appear in a single monolithic Gospel but in four Gospels, with each making a creative contribution to our grasp of Jesus' life. This four-dimensional presentation adds a richness we would not have if we possessed only a single narration of Jesus' life.

The Development of Literary Criticism

Form criticism, source criticism, and redaction criticism all approach the study of the writing of the Gospels from a diachronic perspective. That is, they all follow the development of the Gospels over a period of time. A new type of criticism, one that features a synchronic approach, is also developing. This approach places the Gospels side by side to be read as they are. It assumes that the Gospels are in their fixed canonical form and is not interested in the process by which they came to be that way. A common name for this criticism is *literary criticism*.[8]

---

8. For a sympathetic introduction to literary criticism, see Edgar V. McKnight, *The Bible and the Reader* (Philadelphia: Fortress Press, 1985). For a helpful survey and critique of the movement, see Tremper Longman III, *Literary Approaches to Biblical Criticism* (Grand Rapids: Zondervan Books, 1987).

Many literary critics look at the text as it stands and as it functions in the Christian community. They do not often seek to locate meaning in the author's intention but in their own understanding. Meaning comes to the surface in the encounter between the text and the reader. The meaning is often seen as dependent on so-called *deep structures* in the text. This term refers to common and universal ways of expressing truths. A critical discipline known as *structuralism* seeks to locate these structures, classify them, and use them in interpretation.

Literary criticism has a proper concern when it expresses interest in a study of the Gospels in themselves. A return to a study of the text is always welcome. However, this type of criticism often becomes quite subjective upon arriving at the meaning of the text. When literary critics jettison the concept of the author's meaning, they launch the meaning of the text onto the sea of their own subjectivity. Also, some of their categories of interpretation are derived from modern literature such as the novel. This practice fails to take the unique nature of the Gospel materials into account.

Moving Toward a Synoptic Consensus

No overarching hypothesis is possible in solving the Synoptic problem. However, several directions of movement toward a solution are obvious.[9] It is important to observe that the Gospels received recognition as authoritative at a very early period of Christian history. If this is so, it raises an interesting question about any sources which the Gospel writers used. Obviously the readers could distinguish between the authority of the Gospels and the lack of this specific authority in the sources which the writers used.

It is also important to see the Gospels as unique. Since Jesus is himself unique, it is not difficult to see that they too must be in that category. We must be prepared for some differences between Synoptic studies and general literary studies. If we recognize this uniqueness, we will not too quickly appeal to non-Christian parallels (as is true in form criticism and in some varieties of new literary criticism) for guidance in solving the Synoptic problem.

---

9. For an enlarged discussion of this issue, see Donald Guthrie, *New Testament Introduction*, 3d ed. (Downers Grove, Ill.: InterVarsity, 1970), 220–36. His discussion in his 4th edition, pp. 1029–45, also carries helpful insights.

Marshall, I. Howard, ed. *New Testament Interpretation*. Grand Rapids: William B. Eerdmans Publishing Co., 1977. For discussions of various critical methodologies, see pp. 126–95, 285–333. Contains many examples of balanced use of all the critical methodologies.

Martin, Ralph P. *New Testament Foundations*. Vol. 1, *The Four Gospels*. Grand Rapids: William B. Eerdmans Publishing Co., 1975. See particularly pp. 119–60.

Moule, C. F. D. "Jesus in New Testament Kerygma." In *Essays in New Testament Interpretation*. Cambridge: Cambridge University Press, 1982.

Stein, Robert H. *The Synoptic Problem*. Grand Rapids: Baker Book House, 1987. Excellent discussions of source, form, redaction, and literary criticism by a leading evangelical New Testament scholar.

Stonehouse, Ned B. *Origins of the Synoptic Gospels*. Grand Rapids: William B. Eerdmans Publishing Co., 1963. Groundbreaking usage of critical methodology in Gospel studies by the late American evangelical New Testament scholar.

Tenney, Merrill C. *New Testament Survey*. Grand Rapids: William B. Eerdmans Publishing Co., 1961. See particularly pp. 131–39.

Thiessen, H. C. *Introduction to the New Testament*. Grand Rapids: William B. Eerdmans Publishing Co., 1954. See especially 101–29.

Critical Approaches to the New Testament

Form Criticism

Bultmann, Rudolph, and Karl Kundsin. *Form Criticism*. Translated by F. C. Grant. New York: Harper Torchbook, 1962.

Dodd, C. H. *The Apostolic Preaching and Its Development*. New York: Harper Collins Publishers, 1944.

Dunn, James D. G. "The Gospels as Oral Tradition." In *The Living Word*. Philadelphia: Fortress Press, 1988. An appeal for the general authenticity of the oral traditions contained in the Gospel accounts.

Henderson, Ian. *Myth in the New Testament*. London: SCM Press Ltd., 1952. A fair but perceptive analysis of Bultmann's call for "demythologizing" the New Testament.

Hughes, P. E. *Scripture and Myth*. Tyndale Monographs, no. 2. London: Tyndale Press, 1956. A severe critique of Bultmann's plea for demythologization.

McKnight, Edgar. *What Is Form Criticism?* Philadelphia: Fortress Press, 1969. An appreciative survey of the discipline of form criticism.

Sanders, E. P. *The Tendencies of the Synoptic Tradition*. SNTSMS 11. Cambridge: Cambridge University Press, 1969.

Stein, Robert H. "An Early Recension of the Gospel Traditions?" *JETS* 30 (June 1987): 167–83. An affirmation of the reliability of the sayings and stories about Jesus contained in the New Testament.

Taylor, Vincent. *The Formation of the Gospel Tradition.* 2d ed. London: Macmillan Co., 1935. Introduction to form criticism by an English New Testament scholar who uses the discipline moderately.

Source Criticism

Farmer, W. R. *New Synoptic Studies.* Macon, Ga.: Mercer University Press, 1983. Gospel studies largely dealing with source criticism, but exploring other options.

————.*The Synoptic Problem.* Dillsboro, N.C.: Western North Carolina Press, 1976.

Streeter, B. H. *The Four Gospels: A Study of Origins.* London: Macmillan Co., 1936. Classical statement of the four-document hypothesis of source criticism.

Redaction Criticism

Perrin, Norman. *What Is Redaction Criticism?* Philadelphia: Fortress Press, 1970. A discussion of the origins, development, and significance of the discipline by an enthusiastic supporter.

Literary Criticism

Longman, Tremper, III. *Literary Approaches to Biblical Interpretation.* Grand Rapids: Zondervan Books, 1987. A survey of the field which shows awareness of both the pitfalls and promises of the discipline.

McKnight, Edgar V. *The Bible and the Reader.* Philadelphia: Fortress Press, 1985.

————.*Post-Modern Use of the Bible.* Nashville: Abingdon Press, 1988. Contemporary study of the usage of various literary approaches to Bible study.

McKnight, S. "Literary Criticism of the Synoptic Gospels." *TJ* 8 (spring 1987): 57–68.

Patte, Daniel. *What Is Structural Exegesis?* Philadelphia: Fortress Press, 1976. Sympathetic introduction to structuralism and its usage in Bible study.

History of Critical Methodologies

Noll, Mark A. *Between Faith and Criticism.* San Francisco: Harper & Row, 1986. Study of the development of critical methodologies among American and British evangelicals.

General Information on Critical Studies

Marshall, I. H. "An Evangelical Approach to 'Theological Criticism.'" *Themelios* 13 (April/May 1988): 79–85.

7   The Four Gospels

Guiding Questions

1. Distinguish between the external and internal evidence for such issues as the authorship and dating of the Gospels.

2. Present the external and internal evidence for the authorship of each Gospel.

3. Explain a method for arriving at the date for the writing of each of the four Gospels.

4. Give the unique features in each of the four Gospels.

5. Discuss the purpose for the writing of each Gospel.

6. Present a brief discussion of the plan and content of each Gospel.

The Gospels represent a unique style of literature, different from the styles of ancient writings and from many modern writings. Unlike other ancient miracle narratives the Gospels contain much more than an outline of miracles or a succession of "hero stories." They are not memoirs or notes by either Jesus or the human author. The Gospels, unlike modern biographies, omit historical background information, character analysis, and an investigation of the inner life of the main character. The Gospels are good news in that they represent a proclamation of Jesus' actions for our salvation written from a specific theological perspective. The writers intend to convince readers that their proclamation is true and requires a decision.

The Gospel of Matthew

Authorship

Evidence concerning the authorship of Matthew's Gospel comes from two sources: external and internal evidence. External evidence represents the opinion of leaders in the early church. Internal evidence is found within the Gospel. We will depend on both sources of evidence to establish authorship, for insights from external evidence often require supplementary help from the internal content of the writing.

The church historian Eusebius presented the opinions of Papias about Matthew's Gospel with this statement: "Matthew wrote the oracles in the Hebrew language, and every one interpreted them as he was able."[1] These words raise three issues for interpretation. First, what does Papias mean by the term "oracle"? Second, what does it mean to say that Matthew wrote in the Hebrew language? Third, in what sense did "interpretation" occur?

In context the term *oracle* most likely refers to a Gospel, but we have copies of Matthew's Gospel only in the Greek tongue. Nothing in Matthew's Gospel suggests that it is a translation from a Semitic original, for its content simply does not read like Greek translated from an Aramaic source. If Matthew had translated from a Semitic original into Greek, why would he have included the Semitic originals and Greek translations of a few terms such as "Golgotha" (Matt. 27:33)? Because of this and other difficulties some scholars feel that the term *oracle* refers not to the Gospel but to a collection of messianic proof texts drawn up in Hebrew or Aramaic by Matthew and later used in his Greek translation of the Gospel. Others suggest that Papias used the term to refer to the Q source, a collection of special sayings and events appearing in Matthew and Luke but not in Mark. Because we lack clear evidence to support either of these options, it is difficult to evaluate them.

---

1. Eusebius, *Church History* 3.39.16 (quoted from NPNF).

Since we have no support for these alternate suggestions, it is quite likely that Papias was commenting about Matthew's Gospel and not about some source used to write it.

In answer to the second question, Gundry suggested that Matthew wrote our present Greek Gospel in a Hebrew style, but not necessarily using the Hebrew language.[2] If this were Papias's meaning, there would be no question about a Semitic original or of Matthew's translation from it. This emphasis would also match well with the clear Hebraic flavor of the Gospel. Against this view is the fact that this clearly is not the most obvious meaning of Papias's statement. Most early interpreters of the phrase understood Papias to be saying that Matthew first wrote his Gospel in a Semitic language, probably Aramaic. However, in the absence of evidence for a Semitic original of Matthew's Gospel, Gundry's suggestion offers the most promising understanding of Papias's words.

The meaning of the term *interpreted* depends on the meaning assigned to the previous two phrases. If the oracle written in Hebrew were an Aramaic original of the Gospel, then an interpretation could be a translation into Greek. Since we lack any evidence that Matthew is a translation of an Aramaic original, this does not seem to be a likely meaning. It is also possible that the term *interpreted* refers not to translation but to application and explanation of content. With this meaning Papias would be suggesting that the readers of the Gospel applied and explained it to their audiences so that they could understand it and live according to its precepts.

Two facts stand out from the previous discussion. First, it is likely that the term *oracle* refers to Matthew's Gospel. Second, it is unlikely that the Gospel ever appeared in a Semitic original. Exactly what Papias meant in his statement is uncertain, but if he intended to suggest the existence of a Semitic original, the accuracy of his opinion is questionable. Even if he were in error about the original language of the Gospel, it seems likely that he is correct in attributing the writing to the apostle Matthew. This is the unanimous opinion of the early church, and this alone provides strong evidence for its veracity.

---

2. Robert H. Gundry, *A Survey of the New Testament*, rev. ed. (Grand Rapids: Zondervan Books, 1981), 82.

Some modern scholars deny that the apostle Matthew wrote the first Gospel. One important reason for this denial is the difficulty of Matthew's apparent use of Mark's Gospel.[3] Matthew was an apostle. How could he, the argument goes, use the writings of someone who lacked the dignity of an apostle? One answer to this question is that Matthew was not deferring to Mark but rather to Peter, whom early tradition views as the source of much of Mark's material.

Other opponents to Matthaean authorship suggest that Matthew wrote Q and that early Christians attached Matthew's name to the Gospel because the unknown writer used so much of Q in his Gospel. However, if there were such a document as Q, there would be no reason to preclude Matthew's authorship of both Q and the Gospel. Others who question the apostolic authorship of the Gospel claim that a school of interpretation with special interest in the Old Testament wrote Matthew and that the document was attributed to the apostle although it came through the joint labors of many in this school.

The discipline of redaction criticism insists that many of the sayings in the Gospel come not from the lips of Jesus but from the Matthean church. Those who follow this discipline focus more on the differences between Matthew and Mark than upon the similarities of the Gospels. This in itself is a precarious assumption. Redaction criticism performed a service in alerting us to the unique intents and purposes of Matthew, but it extends beyond the evidence when it suggests that the church, not Matthew accurately reporting Jesus' words, provided the content of the Gospel.

The early church attributed the Gospel to the apostle Matthew without exception. It seems unlikely that early Christians would select a relatively obscure apostle as the author unless it were true. If we view the first Gospel as the work of the apostle Matthew, we can find internal evidence that corroborates the assumption.

- The organizational method of the Gospel, built around five discourse or teaching sections, reflects the tidy mindset of one who could have been a tax collector.

---

3. For additional information on this issue see the discussion of the Synoptic problem in chapter 6.

- This is the only Gospel that contains the story of Jesus' payment of the temple tax (17:24–27), a fact of great interest to a publican.

- The account of the call of Matthew to discipleship (9:9–13) uses the name "Matthew" rather than the name "Levi," which appears in both Mark (2:13–17) and Luke (5:27–32). The fact that the list of apostles in Matthew 10:3 refers to Matthew as "Matthew the publican" whereas the lists in Mark, Luke, and Acts designate him only as "Matthew" is helpful. It may reflect that Matthew viewed himself as unworthy of the place of apostle given him by Christ.

Date

Dating the Gospel of Matthew is difficult because the writing does not contain clear links with secular history. Several features of the Gospel cause some scholars to date it later, perhaps in the eighties or nineties. Those who are suspicious of predictive prophecy feel that the statement of 22:7 that "the king . . . sent his troops . . . and burned their city" points to the destruction of Jerusalem in A.D. 70 and reflects a later insertion after the event itself. Others who do not harbor a suspicion of the presence of predictive prophecy feel that the Matthaean interest in the church (Matthew alone of Gospel writers uses the term—in 16:18 and 18:17) shows a later period when a delay in Christ's return produced a deeper interest in the doctrine of the church. In opposition to this view we should note that Paul showed an unusual interest in the church in his writings, and all of these are prior to A.D. 70. Also, there is evidence that Matthew wrote to evangelize Jews, and he could have done this more easily before A.D. 70, because after A.D. 70 the relationship between church and synagogue worsened. A date prior to A.D. 70 seems more likely.

The Plan

The Gospel of Matthew presents Jesus as Messiah (12:28; 21:1–11) and the church as God's new people who have temporarily replaced the covenant nation of Israel (21:41–44).

The Gospel begins with the birth and early life of Jesus (1:1–2:23) followed by a section showing the preparation of the Messiah for ministry (3:1–4:25). The section of preparation includes the ministry of the forerunner John the Baptist, the expression of the Father's approval in Jesus' baptism, and the commitment of Christ to obedience, displayed in the temptations.

After these chapters the first of five discourse sections appears. These sections include the Sermon on the Mount (chaps. 5–7), the commission to the disciples (chap. 10), the parables (chap. 13), encourgement to humility and forgiveness (chap. 18), and the Olivet Discourse (chaps. 24–25). Each discourse is a sermon-length message with appropriate dialogue sometimes interspersed, which concludes with the formula, "It came to pass when Jesus had finished these sayings that. . . . "

In the Sermon on the Mount Jesus taught the meaning of true righteousness. The authority of his teaching provided evidence of his messianic origin (7:29). Proof of Jesus' messiahship is also presented in a section of healing miracles, nature miracles, and memorable teachings (8:1–9:38).

In the commission to the disciples Jesus appointed and sent them out with instructions that prepared them for persecution (10:16–22). He promised a reward for those who devoted their lives to his service (10:39–42). From 11:1–12:50 Matthew narrated the development of opposition to Jesus' messiahship.

Jesus used the parables of the kingdom to explain the meaning of the kingdom. He used the parable of the sower to teach his disciples that the soil in the listener's heart determined the response of the listener to the message of Jesus (13:3–9, 18–23). He used the parable of the mustard seed to teach that the kingdom would begin small, almost imperceptibly, but would grow to an imposing conclusion (13:31–32). From 13:54–17:27 Matthew presented critical events in Jesus' ministry, including the increasing opposition at Nazareth (13:54–58), Peter's great confession (16:13–20), Jesus' transfiguration (17:1–5), and the predictions of Jesus' suffering and death (16:21; 17:22–23).

In 18:1–35 Jesus challenged his disciples to display humility and mutual forgiveness, qualities of life believers must practice in the kingdom. Matthew followed this chapter with a collection of Jesus' teachings and miracles on his journey to Jerusalem (19:3–20:34), including the rich young ruler (19:16–22) and the healing of two blind men outside of Jericho (20:30–34).

The final week of Jesus' life on earth began with the triumphal entry (21:1–11). Following this entry, Jesus' teaching continued to inflame opposition against him (21:33–46; 23:1–39). In the Olivet Discourse (chaps. 24–25) Jesus prepared his disciples for coming persecution, promised his return in great glory, and urged his followers to be morally alert in their obedience.

In 26:1–27:66 Matthew narrated the betrayal, trial, crucifixion, and burial of Jesus. The final chapter presents the Resurrection and concludes with the challenge to carry the gospel to all nations.

Geographically, Matthew's Gospel covers a fairly narrow section of territory, as can be seen below.

Chapter	Location
Chapters 1 and 2	Bethlehem, Egypt, Nazareth
3:1–4:11	Jordan River Valley
4:12–13:58	Galilee
14:1–18:35	Galilee, north of Galilee
19:1–20:34	Journey to Jerusalem
21:1–28:20	Jerusalem

Primarily, Matthew shows Jesus' ministry in Galilee with a brief trip north into the areas of Tyre and Sidon followed by a return to Galilee and a trip onward to Jerusalem.

Features

The early church viewed Matthew as written largely for a Hebrew audience,[4] and evidence supporting this view is easily seen. It is easy to recognize that in the Sermon on the Mount Matthew deliberately highlighted those incidents from Jesus' life that contrast his teaching with Moses. In 5:21, 27, 31, 33, 38, 43 Jesus quotes a saying from the Pentateuch and contrasts it with his interpretation. By this action Jesus implied that he is greater than Moses. A Jewish audience would observe this type of comparison carefully.

---

4. Origen, *Commentary on John* 1.6. Also, note Eusebius, who quotes Origen's opinion with the identical emphasis in *Church History* 6.25.

Matthew contains a repetitive emphasis on Jesus' fullfilment of the law and Old Testament prophecy (1:22–23; 2:15, 17–18, 23); and traces Jesus' genealogy (1:1–17) back through David to Abraham, a fact that would attract the interest of Jewish people. Also, Matthew frequently designates God as "Father in heaven" (6:1, 9), a phrase mentioned rarely in Mark and Luke. Jews would be accustomed to the reverent substitution of "heaven" for the name of God. Matthew alone of the Gospels refers to the "kingdom of heaven," a phrase that appears as "kingdom of God" in Luke and Mark (cf. Matt. 13:11 and Mark 4:11). Matthew also contains a full additional chapter in the Olivet Discourse beyond Mark and Luke, a fact likely reflecting Jewish interest in eschatology. Matthew mentions Jewish customs without including an explanation, while in Mark the same passages may include an explanation for the benefit of Gentile readers (cf. Matt. 15:1–3 and Mark 7:1–4). Sayings included in Matthew's Gospel sometimes reflect a special Jewish flavor (for example, "go rather to the lost sheep of the house of Israel" [Matt. 10:6]). In the Resurrection narrative Matthew counters the Jewish charge that Jesus' disciples had themselves stolen his body (28:11–15).

These features may well indicate that Matthew wrote his Gospel in order to evangelize Jews and to confirm them in their faith. However, Matthew exhorts his readers to extend the gospel beyond the Jews alone.

The Great Commission appeals for Jesus' followers to carry the gospel to all nations (28:19–20). In 2:1–12 the magi (wise men), who are Gentiles, come to worship Jesus just after his birth. Matthew inserts Jesus' quote that "many will come from the east and west, and . . . sit down with Abraham, and Isaac, and Jacob in the kingdom of heaven. But the children of the kingdom shall be cast out into outer darkness" (Matt. 8:11–12). In the parable of the wheat and tares Jesus indicates that "the field is the world" (13:38), and he warns the Jews that God will transfer the kingdom from them to others (21:33–43). As previously mentioned, Matthew's use of the word *church* is unique among the Gospels (16:18; 18:17). These verses indicate that Matthew's Gospel has a universal outlook.

Matthew also contains evidence of a quest for organization, a feature which a tax collector such as Matthew would need in his work. He frequently chooses those sources from the teachings of

Jesus that reflect organization. In addition to the fivefold structure of the discourses, there are many groupings of three and seven in the Gospel. The genealogy of Jesus contains three sections (1:17). The thirteenth chapter of Matthew contains seven parables, and chapter 23 contains seven woes specifically directed against the scribes and Pharisees. No doubt, the numerical groupings are dependent on Jesus' own usage, but Matthew's selection of these elements shows his preference for them beyond what appears in the other Gospels.

Provenance

Matthew's Gospel has no specific information concerning its place of origin, but its Jewish nature suggests that it was written from Palestine or Syria, perhaps from Antioch. Many Jewish converts from Palestine migrated there after persecution broke out (Acts 11:19). The fact that this church sent Paul on the first mission among the Gentiles (Acts 13:1–3) makes the suggestion more plausible. An additional fact supportive of an Antiochean background is the use of the Gospel by the second-century Christian leader Ignatius, who was bishop of Antioch.[5] No issue of significance depends on determining the place of writing.

Purpose

Unlike John's Gospel, Matthew lacks a precise statement of purpose. However, indications of its purpose have already appeared in our study of the characteristics of the Gospel.

- Matthew wrote with a special purpose of reaching Jewish people.

- Matthew was concerned that the readers understand the person and work of Jesus in order to make an intelligent decision about him (Matt. 12:28).

- Matthew shows a profound interest in preserving the teachings of Jesus. This is particularly evident in his discourse sections.

The content of the Gospel of Matthew suggests that he wrote primarily to ethnic Jews to present the gospel and lead them to

---

5. Ignatius, *Epistle to the Smyrneans* 7.

make an intelligent commitment to Christ. After that commitment, Matthew wanted them to understand Jesus' teaching so that they might grow, obey him, and fulfill the Great Commission (Matt. 28:19–20).

Outline of Matthew

I. The Birth of the Messiah (1:1–2:23)
   A. Genealogy and birth (1:1–25)
   B. The worship, flight, and return of the Messiah (2:1–23)

II. The Words and Works of the Messiah (3:1–18:35)
   A. Preparation for the Messiah's ministry (3:1–4:25)
      1. The ministry of John the Baptist (3:1–12)
      2. The baptism of Jesus (3:13–17)
      3. The temptation of Jesus (4:1–11)
      4. Initial ministry of the Messiah in Galilee (4:12–25)
   B. First discourse: the Sermon on the Mount (5:1–7:29)
   C. Proofs of Jesus' messiahship by word and deed (8:1–9:38)
   D. Second discourse: the commission to the Twelve (10:1–11:1)
   E. Opposition to Jesus' messiahship (11:2–12:50)
   F. Third discourse: the parables of the kingdom (13:1–52)
   G. Critical events in Jesus' messiahship (13:53–17:27)
   H. Fourth discourse: instructions about humility and forgiveness (18:1–35)

III. The Commitment of the Messiah to the Divine Task (19:1–20:34)

IV. The Passion of the Messiah (21:1–28:20)
   A. Opponents of the Messiah (21:1–23:39)
   B. Fifth discourse: preparation for persecution and Christ's return (24:1–25:46)
   C. Death and resurrection of the Messiah (26:1–28:20)

The Gospel of Mark

Authorship

The church historian Eusebius quoted the early Christian leader Papias as saying, "This also the presbyter said: 'Mark, having become the interpreter of Peter, wrote down accurately, though not indeed in order, whatsoever he remembered of the things said or done by Christ.'"[6] Papias's words, which are attributed to John the elder, state two facts about Mark's Gospel. First, Mark served as the interpreter of Peter. This likely means that Mark used Peter as a source of information in writing the second Gospel and helped to make Peter's views known. Second, possibly in defense of Mark against those who questioned the accuracy of the Gospel, Papias described Mark as writing accurately but not in order. At points Mark may not have followed a correct chronological order in recording events in Jesus' life, but instead, he may have grouped his materials together by similarity of subject matter. For example, Mark 2:1–3:6 is a collection of stories reflecting the theme of conflict development with the scribes and Pharisees. Papias may have understood that sometimes Mark followed a thematic principle of organization rather than a chronological plan.

Other early Christian leaders joined with Papias in attributing the authorship of the second Gospel to Mark. Markan authorship of the second Gospel is an uncontested fact emerging from early Christian writings. The result is that Mark's Gospel has the testimony of Peter as an eyewitness to events. Peter's contribution to Mark's writing helps to explain the vividness and freshness which sets Mark apart from the other Gospels (note the description of the grass in 6:39 as "green," a fact not mentioned in the other Gospels).

Also undisputed is the identity of this Mark. Early Christians identify him with John Mark of Acts 12:12. This is the young man who left his Jerusalem home to accompany Paul and Barnabas as an assistant on the first missionary journey (Acts 13:5). For reasons that later proved unacceptable to Paul (Acts 15:37–41), Mark left Paul and Barnabas on the journey and returned to Jerusalem (Acts 13:13). Barnabas took Mark on a separate journey with him (Acts 15:39). During Paul's final days of Roman imprisonment, Mark was of much help to him (2 Tim. 4:11).

Mark's presence does not appear in the Gospel unless it is at the point where a young man following Jesus after his arrest was captured by Roman soldiers (Mark 14:51–52). As the soldiers grasped his garment, he slipped from it and fled into the night. Logically, the presentation of this incident points more to Mark than to anyone else.

---

6. Eusebius, *Church History* 3.39.15.

Early Christian sources described Mark as "stump-fingered," a reference likely describing a congenital deformity of some kind. This liability may well have prevented his involvement in strenuous manual labor and might have prepared him to serve more as a scribe or record keeper, a task which he might have performed for Barnabas and Paul on the first missionary journey (Acts 13:5).

Date

Giving a specific date to Mark's Gospel is difficult. Irenaeus suggested that Mark wrote his Gospel following Peter's death, but other early Christian leaders omit this information and cause us to question the accuracy of Irenaeus.[7] Some who question the validity of predictive prophecy feel that the reference to the "abomination of desolation" in 13:14 was written after the fall of Jerusalem in A.D. 70.

Mark's Gospel contains strong appeals for believers to follow Jesus in a commitment of discipleship (Mark 8:34–36). This emphasis would fit well with the period of persecution instituted by Nero in the mid-sixties. However, it is not necessary to limit the time of writing to that decade, for Christians were always liable to persecution for their faith, even apart from the time of Nero.

The most likely time for the writing of Mark's Gospel appears to be in the late fifties. Mark could have contacted Peter in Rome by this time. Mark's emphasis on persecution suggests that his readers were facing opposition and difficulty. If we date Mark in the fifties, we could affirm that Mark was the first Gospel to be written. If Acts were dated in the early sixties, Luke could have used Mark in writing both his Gospel and Acts.

Plan

The Gospel is organized according to a simple plan. It begins with the ministry of John the Baptist and briefly summarizes the baptism and temptation of Jesus (1:1–13).

---

7. Irenaeus, *Against Heresies* 3.1.1. Clement of Alexandria, as quoted by Eusebius in *Church History* 6.14.6–7, suggests that Peter was still alive when Mark wrote. In the same location Eusebius quotes Clement as stating that the Gospels with genealogies were written first. If this were true, it would make Mark and John subsequent to Matthew and Luke.

From 1:14–9:50 the Gospel describes the ministry of Jesus in and around Galilee. This section contains a description of Jesus' miracles but few lengthy teaching materials. A growing opposition to Jesus is also chronicled. During this period Jesus travelled into the area of Tyre and Sidon and the Decapolis (Mark 7:24–37). Near the area of Caesarea Philippi he received Peter's great confession (8:27–33).

Following the ministry in Galilee he traveled to Jerusalem through Perea and Judea (10:1–52). In this section Mark listed such memorable teaching from Jesus as his contact with the rich young ruler (10:17–22) and with the sons of Zebedee, James and John (10:35–45).

From 11:1–16:20 Mark outlined Jesus' final week of passion and victory. Mark positioned this section to demonstrate its importance in Jesus' ministry.

Geographically Mark follows an order similar to that of Matthew. Jesus' early ministry began in Galilee, and near the conclusion of this Galilean ministry Jesus moved into the area of Tyre, Sidon, and the Decapolis. Passing through Capernaum briefly (9:33–37), he headed with determination toward Jerusalem where he spent the final week of his life on earth.

Features

Several stylistic features are unique to Mark's Gospel.

- Mark focuses on the actions of Jesus. The Gospel omits the birth narrative of Jesus and places far more emphasis on his deeds than on his words. The Gospel also contains some forty repetitions of the Greek adverb translated "immediately" (see, for example, 1:10, 18, 20–21), an expression that gives the impression of the rapid development of activity. Even though Mark's Gospel focuses more on Jesus' actions, it indicates that Jesus taught extensively but omits the words he used (2:13; 6:2, 6, 34; 10:1).

- Mark focuses on Jesus' emotional life. The Gospel mentions the compassion of Jesus (1:41; 6:34; 8:2), his indignation (3:5; 10:14), his sorrow (14:33–34), and the sighing of Jesus (7:34; 8:12).

- Mark gives special attention to Jesus' preparation of the disciples for future ministry. More clearly than in the other Gospels, Mark states Jesus' purpose for selecting the Twelve Apostles (3:14–15). The Gospel also identifies their shortcomings so that Jesus' patient dealing with them might be apparent (5:31; 9:10–13; 10:13–14).

- Mark's Gospel contains a high Christology. The first verse designates Jesus as Son of God. This position is later corroborated by the Father (1:11; 9:7), by demons (3:11; 5:7), by Jesus himself (13:32; 14:61–62), and by the centurion at the cross (15:39).

Provenance

Several statements from early Christian writers suggest that Mark wrote his Gospel while he was in Rome. Early tradition suggests that Peter was martyred in Rome, and Papias's earlier-quoted statement that Mark was Peter's interpreter points to his presence in Rome. Both Clement of Alexandria and Irenaeus also add testimony for a Roman origin of writing. The anti-Marcionite prologue to Mark indicates that Mark wrote his Gospel in Italy.[8] The reference to Mark in 1 Peter 5:13 places him at Rome with Peter, and this provides additional information about the likelihood of a Roman origin for Mark's Gospel.

Destination

Internal evidence suggests that Mark wrote for a Roman audience. His explanation of Jewish customs implies that he wrote to a Gentile audience unacquainted with Jewish practices (7:3–4). He frequently translated Aramaic expressions so that his Roman audience could understand them (3:17; 5:41; 7:34; 14:36; 15:34). Furthermore, Mark sometimes used Latin equivalents to explain Greek expressions (12:42; 15:16). If we assume that the Rufus of Romans 16:13 is the same as the Rufus of Mark 15:21, then this person was living in Rome when Mark wrote his Gospel.

---

8. These prologues were early introductions to the New Testament books specifically written against the early Christian heretic Marcion.

Purpose

Like Matthew, Mark did not include a statement of purpose. Some modern scholars suggest that Mark wrote to provide a document for liturgical use in religious services. However, his arrangement lacks the expected smoothness if intended for use in worship.

W. Wrede felt that Mark wrote to cover up Jesus' failure to proclaim that he was Messiah.[9] In Wrede's view Mark invented the idea that Jesus was the Messiah and put into his mouth words which prohibited the public disclosure of this secret (1:34; 8:30). Wrede felt that Mark did this in order to give the appearance that Jesus privately taught his messiahship, even though in reality Jesus did not do this.

Several reasons help to explain why Jesus would be interested in preventing the publicity of his messiahship.

- The Jews held a conception of the Messiah that stressed his power as a politician and military ruler. Jesus would not want them to perceive him in this way.

- The Jews lacked a concept of deity in their view of the Messiah. Jesus' reference to himself as a divine Son of Man was an effort to correct this erroneous view (see Mark 14:62, a reference to Dan. 7:13–14).

- If Jesus had allowed a premature revelation of his messiahship, it would have subjected him to a quick arrest and trial.

These reasons suggest that it is not necessary to think that Mark invented the idea that Jesus concealed his messiahship.

Internal evidence from the Gospel assists us in understanding why he wrote. The opening verse shows that Mark was concerned about presenting the gospel of Jesus Christ. Furthermore, the content of the Gospel reveals that Mark sought to emphasize the person and work of Jesus (8:31; 9:31; 10:33–34); the need for humans to repent (1:15); and the servant aspect of Jesus' work with a special focus on its culmination in Jesus' death (10:45). Mark's emphasis on

---

9. W. Wrede, *The Messianic Secret* (Cambridge: James Clarke, 1971). See also the discussion about Wrede in chapter 6 in the section entitled "The Period of Final Composition: Redaction Criticism."

the gospel presents a pattern for the church to imitate—that is Christians must continue to preach the gospel.

Mark may have had a subsidiary purpose for emphasizing that persecution was the expected lot of believers. In writing to Roman Christians he could have stressed the certainty of reward if they persisted in obedience to Christ despite serious persecution (10:29–30).

The Ending of Mark

The conclusion of Mark's Gospel is a problem for textual critics. Some of the most reliable manuscripts of Mark end at 16:8. Others add a longer ending, which appears in the KJV as verses 9–20. A lesser known short ending also exists. The short ending does not seem to come from Mark, and the ending of verses 9–20 appears to be an attempt by a scribe to present a summary of post-Resurrection appearances in order to provide a suitable conclusion. This long ending also suggests that the ability to perform miracles is proof of genuine Christianity (16:17–18), but Jesus himself suggested that love for Christian brothers and sisters is the foremost proof (John 13:35).

The textual section in dispute does not affect a significant Christian doctrine. Also, the issue does not concern biblical inspiration, but only whether or not a scribe or some other person has copied an addition to Mark's writing.

It is unlikely that either verses 9–20 or the short ending is a legitimate writing from Mark. The other options are that the Gospel ends at 16:8 or that the original ending was lost. Of these two options the best choice seems to be to conclude the Gospel at 16:8. If the book ends at 16:8, then the final word of the Gospel is the Greek conjunction *gar*, meaning "for." Additional support for ending at 16:8 developed as students of Greek syntax found several examples of Greek sentences ending with the term. A decision cannot be reached with certainty, but accepting an ending at 16:8 seems to be the most viable option.

Outline of Mark

I. Introduction: The Beginning of the Gospel (1:1–13)

II. The Works and Words of Jesus in and Around Galilee (1:14–9:50)

    A. Initial ministry in Galilee (1:14–45)

        1. Call of the first disciples (1:14–20)

        2. Miracles of deliverance and healing (1:21–45)

    B. Initial opposition to Jesus (2:1–3:35)

    C. Parables of Jesus (4:1–34)

    D. Miracles asserting Jesus' power (4:35–5:43)

    E. Growing opposition to Jesus (6:1–8:26)

    F. Instructions to the disciples (8:27–9:50)

III. The Journey to Jerusalem (10:1–52)

    A. Instruction to inquirers (10:1–31)

    B. Prediction of the passion (10:32–34)

    C. Warning to the faithless (10:35–52)

IV. The Works and Words of Jesus in Jerusalem (11:1–16:20)

    A. The presentation of the Messiah (11:1–26)

    B. The final development of opposition (11:27–12:44)

    C. Instructions for the present and the future (13:1–37)

    D. The suffering of the Savior (14:1–15:47)

    E. The Resurrection of the Savior (16:1–20)

The Gospel of Luke

Authorship

Luke's Gospel is the longest single book of the New Testament. If we assume that Luke also authored Acts, then Luke made the largest quantitative contribution to the New Testament.

Several features point to the identity of the author of Luke and Acts. Both books begin with dedications to Theophilus. Acts 1:1 speaks of a "first work," and this allows us to link Luke and Acts togther as a single work. The style of writing for Luke and Acts is similar. Both reflect an interest in historical facts, and both use an excellent quality of Greek.

We can use data from Acts to show the likelihood of Lucan authorship for both writings. Acts contains several sections in which the writer used the first person plural pronoun "we" to suggest that he accompanied Paul on those occasions he wrote about.

These "we" sections appear in Acts 16:10–17; 20:5–21:18, and 27:1–28:16. The first section describes Paul's journey from Troas to Philippi; the second pictures Paul's final journey to Jerusalem; and the third traces his journey from Caesarea to Rome.

Whoever wrote Acts must have travelled with Paul to Rome. If we assume that the prison Epistles were written from Rome, we should find information in them about Paul's companions at this time. Among those who were with Paul in Rome were the following: Epaphras (Col. 4:12), Epaphroditus (Phil. 2:25), Timothy (Phil. 2:19), Tychicus (Col. 4:7), Mark (Col. 4:10), Jesus called Justus (Col. 4:11), Aristarchus (Col. 4:10), Onesimus (Col. 4:9), Luke (Col. 4:14), and Demas (Col. 4:14). Of the companions, Aristarchus, Tychicus, Timothy, and Mark are mentioned in the third person at some point in Acts and thus could not be the author of the book. Demas later deserted Paul (2 Tim. 4:10) and is not likely the author of the book. Epaphroditus joined Paul after his arrival in Rome and could not have described the voyage to Rome. Epaphras also apparently arrived in Rome at a later date (Col. 1:8). No tradition supports the authorship of the third Gospel by either Jesus (Justus) or Onesimus. Logically Luke becomes the best choice for the author of the book. Since the author of Acts is also the author of the third Gospel, we suggest that Luke authored both writings.

In addition to the use of internal evidence to arrive at Lucan authorship, we also have ample early testimony for this position. Such early Christian leaders as Irenaeus[10] and Tertullian accepted Lucan authorship. The Muratorian Canon, an early listing of canonical writings, also supports Luke as author.

Luke wrote as a Christian historian. He intended that his Gospel and Acts serve as a single volume dealing with the beginning and growth of the early church. Probably the early church separated Luke and Acts because of its desire to include his Gospel with the other three Gospels. It is more accurate to speak of Luke's writings as Luke-Acts.

---

10. Irenaeus, *Against Heresies* 3.1.1. Irenaeus wrote as if there were no question of Lucan authorship when he said, "Luke also, the companion of Paul, recorded in a book the Gospel preached by him."

Luke is usually viewed as a Gentile Christian. In Colossians 4:10–11 Paul refers to Aristarchus, Mark, and Jesus Justus as Jewish believers. Later he sends greetings from Luke, apparently designating him as a Gentile. Others view the descriptions of Aristarchus, Mark, and Jesus Justus as a designation that they are Jewish Christians of the stricter type. They feel that Luke is a not-so-strict Hellenistic Jew.[11] Early church tradition suggests that he may have been a native of Antioch, but this is not certain. His excellent use of Greek commends him as a person of education and competence.

Colossians 4:14 refers to Luke as a physician. Scholars have closely examined the vocabulary of Luke-Acts to look for evidence that the author was a student of medicine. In 1882 W. K. Hobart published *The Medical Language of St. Luke*. He concluded that the writer of Luke used words and phrases which reveal his medical background. More recent researchers suggested that Hobart may have overstated his case. Most who investigate the issue today contend that the language of Luke-Acts is compatible with what a medical man could write, but the usage is not sufficient to prove that he must have been a physician. For additional information about Luke, see the section titled "Luke the Man" in chapter 12.

Date

The date of Luke's Gospel is linked to the writing of Acts. Acts ends abruptly with Paul imprisoned in Rome, where he waited two years for his trial before Caesar. When the book closes, we ask, "What has happened to Paul?" Luke does not tell us if he was condemned, martyred, released, or retained in prison for a longer time.

The most obvious solution to explain an ending at this point is that Luke described all the events that had occurred up to the time of the writing of Luke-Acts. When Luke wrote, Paul was still awaiting trial. Paul was imprisoned in Rome in the early sixties, and it is best to date the writing of Acts during this period.

---

11. E. E. Ellis asserts that "the balance of probabilities favors the view that Luke was a hellenistic Jew" in *The Gospel of Luke*, NCB, rev. ed. (Grand Rapids: William B. Eerdmans Publishing Co., 1981), 53. See also the discussion by John Wenham, "The Identification of Luke," *EQ* 63 (January 1991): 3–44. Wenham feels that "the balance of probability is in favor of Luke being one of the seventy, the Emmaus disciple, Lucius of Cyrene, and Paul's kinsman" (p. 43).

An additional fact that supports this date comes from one of Luke's purposes for writing Acts. He sought to show that Christians were innocent of the charges brought against them by the Roman government. It is more logical to see Luke writing with this purpose before Nero viciously persecuted Christians in A.D. 64. Luke would have written his Gospel at a slightly earlier time.

Other factors supporting a date in the early sixties include the lack of any reference to Neronian persecution of Christians and the failure to refer to the martyrdom of James, the brother of Jesus, at the same time.

Luke used the phrase "Jerusalem surrounded by armies" (Luke 21:20) to describe events prior to Jesus' return. Some have seen in this description a reference to the destruction of Jerusalem in A.D. 70 and have called for a date of writing after A.D. 70. This type of reasoning overlooks the possibility of a genuine prediction of the siege of Jerusalem by Jesus and also conflicts with other data previously discussed.

Plan

Luke's Gospel follows a plan similar in content to that of Matthew and Mark. It begins with a lengthy presentation of the birth and early life of Jesus. The story of the visit of the angel Gabriel to Mary to announce the birth of Jesus is included (1:26–38). The birth of John the Baptist is recorded in 1:57–66. In connection with Jesus' birth the story of the angels and the shepherds (2:1–20) and the presentation of Jesus in the temple (2:21–40) are narrated. The Gospel of Luke provides our only information on the boyhood of Jesus (2:41–52).

From 3:1–4:13 the Gospel of Luke presents the early ministry of Jesus, the ministry of John the Baptist, the baptism of Jesus, and the temptation of Jesus.

Jesus' public ministry in Galilee extends from 4:14–9:50. This section abounds with preaching tours (4:42–44), miracles and healings (5:1–11; 7:11–17; 8:40–56), and occasions for teaching (6:17–49). The section concludes with the recognition of Jesus' messiahship (9:18–27) and Jesus' instruction about messiahship (9:46–50).

Jesus makes a long journey to Jerusalem in 9:51–19:44. This section of Luke, often called Luke's central section, is a travel document written more to emphasize the fact of the journey to

Jerusalem than to give precise locations of events during the journey. The section begins with Jesus determined to go to Jerusalem (9:51–62). Many of Jesus' most notable parables appear in this section (10:25–37; 15:1–32). Some locations do not appear to fit the sequence of a consecutive itinerary (10:38–42). Other incidents take place without any indication of location (11:1–10). The fact that much of the travel occurs on the eastern side of the Jordan has led some scholars to designate this section as the Perean ministry of Jesus. Perea was the name given to this eastern section of Palestine, but the name does not appear anywhere in Luke or, for that matter, in the New Testament. The section concludes with Jesus' entrance through Jericho (19:1–10) into Jerusalem (19:28).

In Luke's Gospel after Jesus enters Jerusalem, he spends his final week teaching in the city, faces the Crucifixion, and experiences the subsequent glory of the Resurrection (19:28–24:53). The Gospel of Luke reports Jesus' teaching about authority (20:1–8) and eschatology (21:5–36). The road to the Crucifixion begins with Judas's betrayal of Jesus (22:1–6), and continues with Jesus' appearance before Pilate (23:1–5, 13–25) and Herod Antipas (23:6–12). The Resurrection story begins with an angelic announcement to the women (24:1–11) and includes the story of Jesus' appearance to the men on the road to Emmaus (24:13–35). A brief account of the Ascension appears in 24:50 to 53, but this event is narrated more fully in the opening chapter of Acts.

Luke's Gospel has numerous historical references (3:1–2) and contains many of our most beloved parables from Jesus. It begins with the piety expressed in Judaism and moves into the Gentile world to present a savior who came to seek and to save all the lost, Jew and Gentile (19:10).

Features

Luke's Gospel is unique in its demonstration of Jesus' interest in those who were normally outcasts from Jewish society. This includes Gentiles (2:32), moral outcasts (7:36–50), social outcasts (19:1–10), and the economically deprived (14:12–14). The good Samaritan, an object of hatred to many Jews, draws warm commendation from Jesus (10:29–37). In the story of the rich man and Lazarus Jesus destroyed the Jewish conception that the possession of wealth was an indication of divine favor (16:19–31). The story also demonstrates an interest in the pauper Lazarus. While Jesus did not condemn wealth as such, he warned that only an attentive listening to the prophetic message of the Bible could lead one beyond wealth to genuine repentance.

Luke was also interested in women and their role in Jesus' ministry.

- Mary, Elizabeth, and Anna are all mentioned, in the story of Jesus' nativity (chaps. 1–2).

- Mary, the sister of Martha (10:38–42) and the poor widow (21:1–4) are commended.

- The women who surrounded the site of Jesus' crucifixion (23:27–31) and their activity in reporting his resurrection (23:55–24:11) are given attention.

The Gospel of Luke also focuses on those stories illustrating Jesus' social skills.

- Jesus is pictured socializing with Pharisees and publicans (7:36–50).

- Jesus' interest in the needs of ordinary people is revealed (7:11–17).

- Jesus' ability to relate easily to the wealthy (19:1–10) and the lowly (9:37–43) is demonstrated.

Jesus appears as a savior with broad sympathies and ideal skills of relationship. He is no pale-faced ascetic. On several occasions the Gospel of Luke highlights Jesus' practice and teaching on prayer.

- Jesus is shown to be praying at his baptism (3:21), after busy days of ministry (5:16), and before selecting the disciples (6:12).

- Two parables of Jesus are recorded on prayer (11:5–13; 18:1–8).

- Jesus' expression of prayer concern for Peter is included (22:31–32).

The work of the Holy Spirit receives special attention in Luke.

- The Gospel of Luke reveals that John the Baptist was filled with the Holy Spirit from his mother's womb (1:15).

- The Holy Spirit is involved in Mary's conception of Jesus (1:35).

- At the naming of John the Baptist, his father Zechariah is filled with the Holy Spirit (1:67).

- The Holy Spirit leads Simeon to anticipate seeing the Messiah before his own death (2:25–27).

- After being tempted, Jesus returns to Galilee with the power of the Spirit (4:14).

- Before the Ascension, Jesus promises the disciples that they will receive power from above (24:49).

The presence and work of the Holy Spirit also produce joy in the advent and spread of Christianity. Mary expresses joy (at the birth of Christ) in the praise of the Magnificat (1:46–55). The term *Magnificat* appears in the Latin translation of 1:46 and refers to Mary's joy when she recognizes God's goodness to her. Further examples of joy and praise in Luke include Jesus' exultation in 10:21, the joy of the owner in finding the lost sheep in 15:5–7, and a description of the joy inspired by the Ascension in 24:52–53.

Luke's prologue expresses concern for presenting a reliable account of events. Luke's interest in history is revealed in several references such as 2:1–2 and 3:1–2. Luke's conviction that God's salvation appeared in the life, death, resurrection, and ascension of Jesus (note the emphasis on the approach of "the time" in 9:51) is clearly demonstrated. An understanding of these events in Jesus' life was being sorted out in the early church. Luke can correctly be called a theologian of redemptive history.

Hans Conzelmann made an important contribution to Lucan studies in noting that to Luke all history pivots on Jesus.[12] Conzelmann is correct in viewing Jesus as the end of the old order and the start of the new order. However, his work also contains questionable features. For example, he claims that Luke viewed the return of Christ as futuristic instead of imminent, and consequently the Gospel of Luke emphasizes the ethics of the Christian life rather than

---

12. Hans Conzelmann, *The Theology of St. Luke* (London: Faber & Faber Ltd., 1960).

the expectation of an imminent return. However, the Gospel of Luke does stress the nearness of God's judgment (10:9, 11; 18:7–8), and there is little basis for suggesting that Luke's eschatological hope differed from that expressed in the other Gospels.

Provenance

Early tradition is uncertain about the provenance of Luke's Gospel with both a Roman and a Grecian origin receiving some support. If Luke wrote his Gospel near the time of the writing of Acts, it seems appropriate to place the origin in Rome, where Paul remained in prison. The lack of sufficient evidence, either external or internal, makes it impossible to be dogmatic about the place of writing. An origin in Rome is a logical conjecture.

Destination

Nothing in Luke's Gospel helps us identify a clearly targeted audience. However, many features of the Gospel suggest that he wrote primarily for Gentiles while not intending to neglect the Jews. The dedication to Theophilus (1:1–4) and the linking of the start of John the Baptist's ministry with secular rulers (3:1–2) suggest Gentile recipients. The designation of Theophilus as "most excellent" indicates that he was a person of rank. The name "Theophilus" means "lover of God," and some feel that Luke used it as a symbol of godly people everywhere. Although an unlikely conclusion, it cannot be disproven.

Luke does not express the interest in the fulfillment of Messianic prophecy as we find in Matthew. This omission points toward his aim at a Gentile audience. Further indications of an interest in the Gentiles appear in the description of Jesus as a light to the Gentiles in 2:32 and the fact that the genealogy of Luke (3:23–38) begins with Adam as the progenitor of the human race rather than Abraham as in Matthew's Gospel. The descent from Adam would be a fact of universal interest to all human beings, both Jews and Gentiles.

Purpose

The prologue of Luke's Gospel (1:1–4) provides the clearest statement of his purpose in writing. Luke's Gospel maintains that he used eyewitness reports and written accounts and that he also made his own careful investigation. His statements suggest that he wrote with three aims in mind.

1. He intended to be accurate. His own investigation (1:3) and his reference to historical events (3:1–2) demonstrate that he intended to provide a trustworthy account of Christian beginnings.

2. He wrote in order. Since Luke himself does not always follow chronological order (note that this is true in 9:51–19:27), we should define order as including more than a detailed chronology. Perhaps he meant that he was presenting a thorough account of Christian beginnings in contrast with some earlier written records which were brief and incomplete.

3. He wrote to give his readers a certain basis for their knowledge. He wanted them to know that the events which he narrated occurred as he described, and he provided a foundation for their belief in these events. The fulfillment of this final purpose is a logical outgrowth of his aim for accuracy.

Outline of Luke

I. Prologue: Dedication to Theophilus and Statement of Purpose (1:1–4)

II. Birth and Early Life of Jesus (1:5–2:52)
  A. Announcement of birth of John the Baptist (1:5–25)
  B. Announcement of birth of Jesus (1:26–38)
  C. Mary's response to the announcement (1:39–56)
  D. Birth and early life of John the Baptist (1:57–80)
  E. Birth of Jesus (2:1–7)
  F. Visit of the shepherds (2:8–20)
  G. The naming and presentation of Jesus (2:21–40)
  H. Jesus' temple visit (2:41–52)

III. Jesus' Early Ministry (3:1–4:13)
  A. The ministry of John the Baptist (3:1–20)
  B. The baptism of Jesus (3:21–22)
  C. The genealogy of Jesus (3:23–38)
  D. The temptation of Jesus (4:1–13)

IV. Jesus' Galilean Ministry (4:14–9:50)

    A. Rejection of Jesus in Nazareth (4:14–30)
    B. Early ministry in Galilee (4:31–6:11)
    C. The selection of the disciples (6:12–16)
    D. The sermon on the plain (6:17–49)
    E. Jesus' responses to needy people (7:1–8:3)
    F. The parable of the sower (8:4–18)
    G. Miraculous activities of Jesus (8:19–56)
    H. Sending out the Twelve (9:1–9)
    I. Feeding the five thousand (9:10–17)
    J. Peter's great confession (9:18–27)
    K. The Transfiguration (9:28–36)
    L. Object lessons of Jesus (9:37–50)

V. The Journey to Jerusalem (9:51–19:27)

    A. The characteristics of a true disciple (9:51–10:24)
    B. The parable of the good Samaritan (10:25–37)
    C. Teaching about obedience and prayer (10:38–11:13)
    D. Development of opposition (11:14–12:12)
    E. Warning about greed and anxiety (12:13–59)
    F. A ministry of teaching and healing (13:1–14:35)
    G. Parables on God's forgiveness of sinners (15:1–32)
    H. Parables on the use of money (16:1–31)
    I. Teaching on forgiveness, faith, and gratitude (17:1–19)
    J. Parables on the coming of the kingdom (17:20–37)
    K. Parables on prayer (18:1–14)
    L. A commendation of humility (18:15–17)
    M. The rich young ruler (18:18–30)
    N. Prediction of Jesus' death and resurrection (18:31–34)
    O. The approach to Jerusalem (18:35–19:27)

VI. Jesus' Final Week, Crucifixion, and Resurrection (19:28–24:53)

    A. Events of the Passion Week in Jerusalem (19:28–22:53)
    B. The trial of Jesus (22:54–23:25)
    C. The crucifixion of Jesus (23:26–49)
    D. The resurrection of Jesus (24:1–12)
    E. The postresurrection ministry of Jesus (24:13–49)
    F. The ascension of Jesus (24:50–53)

The Gospel of John

Authorship

The simple style and vocabulary of John's Gospel conceal a depth that encourages study and reflection. The tradition that the apostle John authored the Gospel has generated considerable discussion and intense investigation. Those who examine the same external and internal evidence sometimes reach different conclusions.

The most important external information about authorship of the Gospel comes from Polycarp, who was martyred at Smyrna in Asia Minor in A.D. 156 at the age of eighty-six. Polycarp claimed to be associated with the apostle John, and information about this relationship appears in Eusebius's rendition of statements by Irenaeus.[13] Concerning the authorship of the Fourth Gospel, Irenaeus said, "John, the disciple of the Lord, who also had leaned upon His breast, did himself publish a Gospel during his residence at Ephesus in Asia."[14] Irenaeus identified the fourth evangelist as John and linked him with the beloved disciple mentioned in John 13:23. We may feel that ultimately Irenaeus's information originated with the witness of Polycarp. Information concerning Johannine authorship of the Fourth Gospel comes not only from Irenaeus but also from Clement of Alexandria and Tertullian. Even though much of this evidence appears in a period later than we might wish, we discover that the evidence is virtually unanimous in affirming Johannine authorship of the Fourth Gospel.

Some find a flaw in this impressive testimony by noting the words of Papias, another contemporary of Polycarp, who may also have been a student of John. Eusebius quoted the words of Papias and found evidence of the existence of another John, whom he des-

---

13. Eusebius, *Church History* 5.20.5–6. In his statement Eusebius quotes Irenaeus as saying, "I am able to describe the very place in which the blessed Polycarp sat as he discoursed, and his goings out and his comings in, and the manner of his life, and his physical appearance, and his discourses to the people, and the accounts which he gave of his intercourse with John and with the others who had seen the Lord."

14. Irenaeus, *Against Heresies* 3.1.1.

ignated as John the Elder.[15] However, an examination of the statement of Papias suggests that he was probably using the term *elder* as a reference to an apostle, and the statement thus becomes another witness for authorship of the Fourth Gospel by the apostle John.

The internal evidence for Johannine authorship has also been much disputed. Leon Morris developed more extensively the earlier classic approach of B. F. Westcott in which he argues progressively that the author of the Fourth Gospel was: a Jew, a Palestinian, an eyewitness, an apostle, and John the Apostle.[16] The claim of the author to be an eyewitness appears in 1:14 and 19:35. The knowledge of personal names (Nathanael in 1:45 and Malchus in 18:10) together with vivid details (six water jars in 2:6) also supply evidence of an eyewitness. The writer knows Palestinian topography from the period before A.D. 70 (5:2 and 19:13).

The key issue concerning authorship hinges on the identification of the "beloved disciple" in the Gospel. The beloved disciple first appears at the last supper, where he reclines next to Jesus and fields a question from Peter to Jesus (13:23–25). At the cross he receives a special commission from Jesus to care for Mary (19:26–27). At the empty tomb he races ahead of Peter to arrive first at the tomb (20:2–9). In 21:24–25 he is identified as the one who "wrote these things." If we assume that writing involves the production of the material, and that "these things" is a reference to

---

15. Eusebius, *Church History* 3.39.4–5. The statement is: "If, then, any one came, who had been a follower of the elders, I questioned him in regard to the words of the elders—what Andrew or what Peter said, or what was said by Philip, or by Thomas, or by James, or by John, or by Matthew, or by any other of the disciples of the Lord, and what things Aristion and the presbyter John, the disciples of the Lord, say." It is important to note that in the first listing of the name of John, he is placed with the other apostles, who are called "elders." In 1 Pet. 5:1 Peter linked an "elder" with those who had "witnessed the sufferings of Christ," a clear reference to the apostles. Hence, the apostles could also be called elders. Since in both instances John is called an"elder," the evidence suggests that it is the same apostle John who is discussed.

The probability is that Papias is not making two lists which distinguish between apostles and elders of the first generation and those of the second generation. He is likely distinguishing between those first-generation witnesses who have died and those who are still alive. If this is the distinction, then both Aristion and John the elder (also the Apostle) are still alive at the time of Papias's statement. Those in the first list are now dead. This double reference points toward a single individual named John who in both instances is the apostle John.

16. Leon Morris, *Studies in the Fourth Gospel* (Grand Rapids: William B. Eerdmans Publishing Co., 1969), 218–53.

the entire book and not merely to chapter 21, then the beloved disciple is the author of the Fourth Gospel.

The beloved disciple is one of the seven mentioned in chapter 21. Since Peter, Thomas, and Nathanael are mentioned in 21:2, it seems obvious that none of them is the beloved disciple. Of the sons of Zebedee, mentioned also in 21:2, James cannot be the beloved disciple, for he was martyred during the reign of Herod Agrippa I (Acts 12:1–2) and could not have lived long enough to lend credence to the belief that he would not die (see 21:23). It hardly seems likely that either of the two unnamed disciples in 21:2 could be the beloved disciple, for they are obscure personalities. The traditional interpretation that John the Apostle is the beloved disciple is a reasonable choice. Some might object that it would be prideful for John to style himself as "beloved," but the usage of this term could also be an expression of wonder at God's love for one who was formerly known as a "son of thunder" (Mark 3:17).

Another difficulty appears in the identity of "we" of 21:24. Is this a group of church leaders witnessing to the trustworthy testimony of the beloved disciple, or is it a modest claim by the beloved disciple that his own testimony is true? Although difficulties emerge with either choice, it seems better to understand this statement as a self-effacing claim by the beloved disciple for a reliable testimony.

One popular theory behind the production of the Fourth Gospel, widely accepted today, is that the Gospel is the product of a group or community around John preoccupied with studying, teaching, and writing. Many today feel that this "school" was involved with the production of the Gospel through several editions and stages. Among chief proponents of this view are Raymond Brown[17] and R. Alan Culpepper.[18] Although it is impossible to disprove the suggestions of Brown and Culpepper, following

---

17. Brown proposed this theory first in his *The Gospel According to John* (Garden City, N.Y.: Doubleday, 1966), and he followed up with additional proposals in his *The Community of the Beloved Disciple* (New York: Paulist Press, 1979). In the earlier book he argued that John the son of Zebedee was the beloved disciple, but he did not identify him with the writer of the Fourth Gospel. In the latter book he viewed the beloved disciple as outside the circle of the apostles.

18. R. Alan Culpepper, *The Johannine School* (Missoula, Mont.: Scholars Press, 1975). Culpepper concludes that a Johannine School, similar to other ancient schools, grew up around John, but he leaves open the applications to be drawn from his conclusion. See pp. 287–90.

their suggestions involves accepting more difficult assumptions than accepting the testimony of the Gospel to be the product of the beloved disciple whom we have identified with John, the son of Zebedee. The best solution to all the issues, in my judgment, is that John the Apostle is the author of the Fourth Gospel.

Date

Dates for the writing of the Fourth Gospel vary from before A.D. 70 to a period well into the second century, with most of the suggestions falling between A.D. 80 and 100. The discovery in 1935 of a fragment of John 18 forced the abandonment of the second-century dates. The fragment, known as the Rylands Fragment and numbered as p52, dates from A.D. 135 and suggests that the original writing of the Gospel occurred several decades earlier. An earlier date allows time for copying and carrying the Gospel even to the deserts of Egypt, where it was found.

J. A. T. Robinson advocated an earlier date for the Gospel by suggesting that the temple was still standing when the Gospel was written. He added, "I do not therefore believe that there is anything in the language even of the Johannine prologue which demands a date later than the 60s of the first century."[19] Despite Robinson's careful discussion, his approach has not received widespread acceptance.

Although dogmatic statements about date are not permissible, more external and internal details point to a later (late first century) rather than an earlier date. Irenaeus suggested that John was the final evangelist to produce his Gospel.[20] The statement about the death of the beloved disciple (21:23), if taken as a reference to John the Apostle, tends to support a later date. The language of John's Gospel concerning Jesus' deity (for example, 10:30) and preexistence (1:1; 8:58) tend also to fit best in a later date. The failure to mention the destruction of the temple in A.D. 70 is hard to explain if the book were written shortly after A.D. 70 but easier to under-

---

19. J. A. T. Robinson, *Redating the New Testament* (Philadelphia: Westminster Press, 1976), 284. Robinson suggests that the language of 2:20 presupposes that the temple was still standing when the statement was written. He also indicates that the expression in 5:2 shows an acquaintance with a pre–A.D. 70 topography of Jerusalem.
20. Irenaeus, *Against Heresies* 3.1.1.

stand if it were written in the late 80s or early 90s. Given the evidence, the closest estimate that can be made is that the Fourth Gospel was written during the last fifteen years of the first century.

Plan

John's Gospel begins with a prologue that declares the preexistence and incarnation of Jesus as the word of God (1:1–18). From 1:19–10:42 Jesus discloses signs of his messiahship.

Within this section the Gospel focuses on the early ministry of Jesus (1:19–4:54). Here we witness two of the signs of Jesus (2:1–11; 4:43–54) and overhear a dialogue between Jesus and Nicodemus (3:1–15) and between Jesus and the Samaritan woman (4:7–42). Jesus' movements within this section alternate between Galilee and Jerusalem.

From 5:1–7:53 we see additional signs from Jesus, but by this time Jesus encounters increasing resistance. The sabbath healing of the paralytic at the pool of Bethesda in Jerusalem precipitates a reaction from the Jews and a monologue by Jesus (5:1–47). After feeding the five thousand, Jesus claims that he is the true bread of life (6:1–58). After his appearance in Jerusalem for the Feast of Tabernacles, the Jewish leaders engage in a bitter quarrel over Jesus amongst themselves (7:10–52).

The record of the woman caught in adultery (7:53–8:11) is not a part of the original text of John. The material from 8:12–10:42 narrates the works and words of Jesus with highly escalated confrontation. After Jesus' claim to be the "I am" (8:58), the crowd attempts to stone him. Jesus issues an incisive denunciation of the Pharisees in 9:39–41. From 10:1–39 Jesus presents himself as the Good Shepherd and claims to be one with the Father.

From 11:1–12:50 the Gospel of John includes material that shows the preparation for the crucifixion of Jesus. The raising of Lazarus by Jesus (11:1–44) pushes the Jewish leaders to determine to kill him (11:45–53). In 12:3–7 Mary anoints Jesus in anticipation of his death, and in the triumphal entry in 12:12–19 Jesus openly announces his messiahship.

In the farewell discourses (13:1–17:26) Jesus provides instructions to prepare the disciples for his departure. In 13:1–17 he urges them to practice mutual service to one another. In 13:21–16:33

Jesus prepares them for the advent of the Holy Spirit. Jesus prays for the unity of the disciples in 17:1–26.

The arrest and trial are in 18:1–19:16. The crucifixion and burial are narrated in 19:17–42. The resurrection and some post-resurrection appearances are found in 20:1–31.

The final epilogue (21:1–25) contains Peter's restoration to service along with an appeal for all believers to focus on their God-given field of service.

Features

The style of John's Gospel involves a simple profundity. The simplicity comes from two sources. The terms used by John (*light, darkness, life*) are familiar terms and do not involve abstract concepts at first reading. The writing style includes much *parataxis*, a type of connection between sentences which uses more coordinate clauses (connected by "and" or "but") than subordinate clauses (connected by "because" or "in order that"). This produces a flowing text which is easier to read.

This simplicity nevertheless contains great depth in content. The simple presentation of words involves theological depth concerning such subjects as the deity of Christ (10:30), the incarnation (1:14), and preexistence (1:1).

John's Gospel includes an emphasis on "signs." In John's terminology a sign is a miracle, a supernatural event that points to Jesus' divine origin. In addition to the Resurrection John described seven signs (2:1–11; 4:46–54; 5:2–9; 6:1–14; 6:16–21; 9:1–7; 11:1–44), and indicated that Jesus performed many other signs not written in the Gospel (20:30).

John's Gospel emphasizes Jesus' attendance at the religious feasts of the Jews. Three Passovers are mentioned (2:23; 6:4; 13:1) with an unnamed feast in 5:1, which, if another Passover, would clearly add an additional year to Jesus' ministry. The Feast of Tabernacles (7:2) and the Feast of Dedication are also mentioned (10:22).

John's Gospel supplements the information in the Synoptics with an emphasis on the Judean ministry of Jesus. The Synoptics also suggest Jesus' ministry in Judea (note the visit with Mary and Martha in Luke 10:38–42), but John's Gospel gives the fullest account of his ministry there (note that the events from 2:13–3:36 occur in Judea).

John's Gospel presents the deity of Jesus in bold, straightforward language and deeds. The words of Jesus claim his deity (10:30). The deeds of Jesus prove his deity (5:36). Two Christological items absent from the Synoptics but included in the Fourth Gospel are the preexistence of Christ (1:1, 8:58; 17:5) and the designation of Jesus as "Logos" (1:1, 14). The humanity of Jesus, although less emphasized in the Fourth Gospel, is not absent. Mention of the Incarnation (1:14) implies his humanity, and such features as human compassion (11:35, 38) and exhaustion (4:6) clearly present the human Jesus. Another feature of John which supports Jesus' claims to deity is the presence of "I am" passages. In seven passages (6:35; 8:12; 10:7, 9; 10:11, 14; 11:25; 14:6; 15:1) Jesus claimed for himself an attribute which could only properly be given to God.

John's Gospel recounts many lengthy discourses of Jesus with questions, answers, and dialogue (4:7–42; 5:1–47). John probably paraphrased the words of Jesus and summarized Jesus' discourses in his own words. However, such Synoptic passages as Matthew 11:25–27 and Luke 10:21–22 also present a Jesus who spoke in a manner similar to the style of the Fourth Gospel.

John's unique method of presentation allowed him to make many significant theological contributions. John used the actions of Jesus to emphasize the inner significance of his work (13:12–17). His words sometimes carry the possibility of double meaning. His reference in 3:3 to being "born again" suggests either being born anew or being born from above. John often wrote using theological themes in pairs, as in his use of "light" and "darkness" and "life" and "death." He emphasized the coming of the Holy Spirit (16:8–11) and the concept of predestination or election (6:37).

C. H. Dodd popularized the phrase "realized eschatology" to describe the Johannine emphasis that God immediately gives eternal life to believers (5:24). This emphasis affirms that believers already have a foretaste of heaven in the here and now. It should not be taken as a denial of a future completion of eternal life (perhaps this was the error denounced in 2 Tim. 2:17–18), but it should alert believers to the realization that eternal life is both an already and a not yet.

John's use of such terms as *life, eternal, and light* was earlier taken as an indication that John reflected a hellenistic portrait of Jesus. Further evidence supporting this view came from the material in John's Gospel that presented Jesus as a sort of "divine man" who went about performing miracles and mighty works. In the last fifty years the discovery and reading of the Dead Sea Scrolls have shown that John's religious vocabulary also appeared in first-century Judaism. It is now less fashionable to speak of John's Gospel as presenting a Hellenistic portrait.[21] Many modern students now agree that John was deeply dependent on the Old Testament for some of his primary insights.

Provenance

Much disagreement exists about the place of origin of John's Gospel. Some have suggested Alexandria in Egypt on the basis of John's similarity to Philo, who also discussed the concept of "logos." Irenaeus declared that John wrote while he was in Ephesus.[22] Other patristic evidence uniformly supports Irenaeus.

Determining the origin is not significant in the interpretation of this Gospel, and it is difficult to speak with certainty of a specific location. The solid patristic backing gives Ephesus a weak nod of approval, but an Ephesian origin should not be held with too much tenacity.

Destination

The Fourth Gospel does not suggest a probable audience. If one decides that John wrote while he lived in Ephesus, it seems likely that he would compose it for residents near Ephesus. The question of destination is uncertain, but it is linked with the understanding of the purpose of the Gospel.

Purpose

John included a more precise statement of purpose in his Gospel than the other Gospel writers. John's purpose statement in 20:30–31 suggests several features.

- John was selective. His Gospel suggests that he knew many others signs performed by Jesus, but that he selected to record in writing only some of them.

---

21. C. H. Dodd followed this line of thought in his *The Interpretation of the Fourth Gospel* (Cambridge: Cambridge University Press, 1953), when he spoke of John bringing the concept of eternal life into "the context of Greek philosophical thought" (p. 150).
22. Irenaeus, *Against Heresies* 3.1.1.

- The Gospel is evangelistic. This is the obvious meaning of 20:31. John wrote to help others believe in Jesus as the Christ.

- The Gospel focuses on the Jews. Jews would be most concerned about the question of the identity of the Messiah, the Christ. Some have suggested that those most concerned about this question would be those Jews and Jewish proselytes who understood the meaning of "the Christ" and were seeking to learn more from the Christians with whom they were in dialogue. Diaspora Judaism may best fit this context.[23]

It is also possible that John wrote with a subsidiary purpose of correcting the misplaced emphasis of a group which had grown up around the figure of John the Baptist. Acts 19:1–7 shows that John the Baptist had some followers in Ephesus during the time of Paul. The Gospel of John emphasizes that Jesus was superior to John the Baptist and that Jesus had an affirmation of his superiority even from the heavenly Father (3:25–30; 5:33–40). These facts may indicate an interest in countering the influence of a group of devotees to John the Baptist.

Some have suggested that John engaged in a polemic against Judaism. It is true that unbelieving Jews are frequently singled out for their opposition to the gospel (5:10–18; 6:41–42; 11:47–54), but Jewish resistance to the gospel is also apparent in the Synoptics. John's Gospel appears to give an accurate picture of the historical opposition of unbelieving Jews. During the last part of the first century Jews added a benediction against heretics to their synagogue liturgy to drive out all Jewish Christians who might be present at the services.[24] Some maintain that the benediction gave the occasion for John to encourage Jewish believers to suffer banishment from the synagogue without retracting their Christian

---

23. D. A. Carson, Douglas J. Moo, and Leon Morris, *An Introduction to the New Testament* (Grand Rapids: Zondervan Books, 1992), 171.

24. This benediction has had several variant renderings. Gundry gives the reading as: "For the excommunicate let there be no hope, and the kingdom of pride do Thou quickly root out in our days. And let the Christians and the heretics perish as in a moment. Let them be blotted out of the book of life, and with the righteous let them not be written. Blessed art Thou, O Lord, who subdueth the proud." See Robert H. Gundry, *Survey of the New Testament*, rev. ed. (Grand Rapids: Zondervan Books, 1981), 104; n. 33. The existence of the "Benediction against Heretics" in the first century is still debated, but many scholars accept its existence and use during the latter part of the first century.

commitment. Although the apostle might have known of the benediction in 9:22 and 16:1, it is difficult to use these texts to prove that John's purpose was to provide encouragement to wavering Jewish Christians.

The Text of John 7:53–8:11

Most modern textual critics contend that John 7:53–8:11 was not part of what the apostle John originally wrote. These verses are absent from most of the early Greek manuscripts, and the early church fathers do not refer to this narrative in their commentaries. Some later manuscripts which include the narrative mark it to indicate hesitation about its authenticity. Some manuscripts place it after John 7:36; 7:44, or 21:25. Others even place it after Luke 21:38. No theory to explain the origin of this passage has been widely accepted.

It is certainly possible that the substance of the story represents an authentic incident from Jesus' life. However, the likelihood that John originally included it in his Gospel is remote.

Outline of John

I. Prologue: Jesus as the Eternal, Incarnate Word of God (1:1–18)

II. Jesus' Initial Ministry to the World (1:19–10:42)

    A. The early ministry of Jesus (1:19–4:54)

        1. Initial contact with the disciples (1:19–51)

        2. The first sign, changing water into wine (2:1–11)

        3. Cleansing the temple (2:12–17)

        4. Explanation of the temple cleansing (2:18–25)

        5. Dialogue with Nicodemus (3:1–21)

        6. The contrast of Jesus with John the Baptist (3:22–36)

        7. Dialogue with the Samaritan woman (4:1–42)

        8. The second sign, healing the son of the nobleman (4:43–54)

    B. Developing opposition to Jesus (5:1–7:52)

        1. Healing the invalid man at Bethesda pool (5:1–9a)

        2. Dialogue on the authority of Jesus' words (5:9b–47)

        3. Feeding the five thousand (6:1–15)

        4. Walking on water (6:16–21)

        5. The bread of life discourse (6:22–71)

        6. Ministry at the Feast of Tabernacles (7:1–13)

      7. Opposition to Jesus' messianic claims (7:14–52)

   C. Radical confrontation with Jesus (8:12–10:42)

      1. The light of the world discourse (8:12–59)

      2. Healing the man born blind (9:1–41)

      3. Jesus as the Good Shepherd (10:1–21)

      4. The claim to deity (10:22–42)

III. The Preparation for the Crucifixion (11:1–12:50)

   A. The death and resurrection of Lazarus (11:1–44)

   B. The decision to kill Jesus (11:45–54)

   C. The movement toward the Cross (11:55–12:36)

   D. The rejection of Jesus' signs (12:37–50)

IV. Preparation of the Disciples for Jesus' Departure (13:1–17:26)

   A. The appeal to live as servants (13:1–20)

   B. The treachery of Judas (13:21–30)

   C. The approaching departure of Jesus (13:31–14:31)

   D. The coming of the Holy Spirit (15:1–16:33)

   E. Jesus' prayer for his disciples (17:1–26)

V. Arrest, Trial, Crucifixion, and Resurrection of Jesus (18:1–20:31)

   A. The arrest of Jesus (18:1–12)

   B. The trial of Jesus (18:13–19:16)

   C. The crucifixion of Jesus (19:17–37)

   D. The burial of Jesus (19:38–42)

   E. The resurrection of Jesus (20:1–31)

VI. Epilogue: The Restoration of Peter and Authentication of the Gospel (21:1–25)

For Further Discussion

1. List the advantages and disadvantages of having four Gospels instead of a single Gospel.

2. How does the content of the Gospels present you with a firmer historical basis for your acceptance of the facts of Jesus' life?

3. How would you answer a sincere question from a friend who ponders how to distinguish in the Gospels between the words of Jesus and the opinions of the church?

4. Which Gospel most clearly presents the following information:

- a historical basis for Christianity;

- material aimed at unbelieving Jews;

- material aimed at unbelieving Gentiles;

- Jesus of action?

- Present either internal or external evidence from the Gospel for your answer.

5. Which Gospel would you use today to reach:

- white middle-class Americans;

- minority groups;

- those skeptical of the historicity of the Gospel materials;

- those with an interest in the teachings of Jesus?

- Give evidence for your answer.

Bibliography

General Information on the Gospels

Carson, D. A., Douglas J. Moo, and Leon Morris. *An Introduction to the New Testament*. Grand Rapids: Zondervan Books, 1992.

Gundry, Robert H. *A Survey of the New Testament*. Rev. ed. Grand Rapids: Zondervan Books, 1981.

Guthrie, Donald. *New Testament Introduction*. 4th ed. Downers Grove, Ill.: InterVarsity Press, 1990.

Harrison, Everett F. *Introduction to the New Testament*. Grand Rapids: William B. Eerdmans Publishing Co., 1964.

Johnson, Luke T. *The Writings of the New Testament*. Philadelphia: Fortress Press, 1986.

Kummel, W. G. *Introduction to the New Testament*. London: SCM Press Ltd., 1966.

Martin, Ralph P. *New Testament Foundations*. Vol. 1: *The Four Gospels*. Grand Rapids: William B. Eerdmans Publishing Co., 1975.

Robinson, J. A. T. *Redating the New Testament*. Philadelphia: Westminster Press, 1976.

Tenney, Merrill C. *New Testament Survey.* Grand Rapids: William B. Eerdmans Publishing Co., 1961.

Thiessen, H. C. *Introduction to the New Testament.* Grand Rapids: William B. Eerdmans Publishing Co., 1954.

Special Information on Matthew

Bornkamm, Gunther, Gerhard Barth, and Joachim Heinz Held. *Tradition and Interpretation in Matthew.* 2nd ed. London: SCM Press Ltd., 1982. Redaction critical studies of Matthew's Gospel.

France, R. T. *Matthew.* TNTC. Grand Rapids: William B. Eerdmans Publishing Co., 1985. Introduction and commentary for Matthew's Gospel by a British evangelical.

————. "Matthew's Gospel in Recent Study." *Themelios* 14 (January/February 1989): 41–46.

Gundry, Robert H. *Matthew.* Grand Rapids: William B. Eerdmans Publishing Co., 1982. Commentary on Matthew's Gospel based on redaction critical studies.

Stendahl, Krister. *The School of St. Matthew.* Philadelphia: Fortress Press, 1968. A discussion of the writing of Matthew's Gospel by an individual or a group using the Old Testament to instruct believers.

Special Information on Mark

Cole, Alan. *Mark.* TNTC. Rev. ed. Grand Rapids: William B. Eerdmans Publishing Co., 1989. Commentary and introduction on Mark by a British evangelical.

Hooker, Morna D. *The Gospel According to Mark.* BNTC. London: A & C Black Publishers Ltd., 1991. Commentary and introduction to Mark's Gospel by a well-read British scholar who advocates a later date for Mark.

Hurtado, L. W. *Mark.* GNBC. San Francisco: Harper & Row, 1983. Commentary and brief introduction to Mark by a Canadian evangelical, who writes for a non-specialist audience.

————. "The Gospel of Mark in Recent Study." *Themelios* 14 (January/February 1989): 47–52

Wrede, W. *The Messianic Secret.* Cambridge: James Clarke and Co. Ltd., 1971.

Special Information on Luke

Conzelmann, Hans. *The Theology of St. Luke.* London: Faber & Faber Ltd., 1960. Redaction-critical study of Luke's Gospel.

Ellis, E. Earle. *The Gospel of Luke.* NCB. Rev. ed. Grand Rapids: William B. Eerdmans Publishing Co., 1981. Commentary and introduction to Luke by a Baptist evangelical.

Geldenhuys, Norval. *Commentary on the Gospel of Luke.* NICNT. Grand Rapids: William B. Eerdmans Publishing Co., 1951. Commentary and introduction to Luke by a late South African evangelical.

Marshall, I. H. "The Present State of Lucan Studies." *Themelios* 14 (January/February 1989): 52–57.

Wenham, John. "The Identification of Luke." *EQ* 63 (January 1991): 3–44.

Special Information on John

Beasley-Murray, George R. *John.* WBC. Waco, Tex.: Word Inc., 1987. Commentary and introduction to John by a British evangelical.

Brown, Raymond. *The Community of the Beloved Disciple.* New York: Paulist Press, 1979.

———. *The Gospel According to John.* AB. Garden City, N.Y.: Doubleday, 1966. Commentary and introduction to John by a Roman Catholic scholar.

Carson, D. A. "Selected Recent Studies of the Fourth Gospel." *Themelios* 14 (January/February 1989): 57–64.

———. *The Gospel According to John.* Grand Rapids: William B. Eerdmans Publishing Co., 1991. Commentary and introduction on John's Gospel by a strong defender of Johannine historicity.

Culpepper, Alan R. *The Johannine School.* Missoula, Mont.: Scholars Press, 1975.

Dodd, C. H. *The Interpretation of the Fourth Gospel.* Cambridge: Cambridge University Press, 1953.

Ellis, E. E. "Background and Christology of John's Gospel: Selected Motifs." *SwJT* 31, no. 1 (1988): 24–31.

Morris, Leon. *The Gospel According to St. John.* NICNT. Grand Rapids: William B. Eerdmans Publishing Co., 1971. Commentary and introduction to John by an Australian evangelical.

———. *Studies in the Fourth Gospel.* Grand Rapids: William B. Eerdmans Publishing Co., 1969.

Sanders, J. N. *The Gospel According to St. John.* HNTC. New York: Harper & Row Publishers Inc., 1968.

8 The Birth, Childhood, and Early Ministry of Jesus

Guiding Questions

1. Contrast the manner in which each Gospel begins its account of Jesus' life and ministry.

2. List the details of Matthew and Luke concerning the birth and childhood of Jesus.

3. Explain the significance of Jesus' baptism and temptation in his preparation for ministry.

4. Explain the basis for confidence in the accuracy of the Gospel accounts concerning miracles.

Only Matthew and Luke present information about Jesus' birth and childhood. Mark begins his account with the ministry of John the Baptist, and John also refers to the ministry of the Baptist after making a brief statement about Jesus' preexistence.

The reports of Jesus' early ministry focus on his work in Judea with periodic trips back into Galilee. John's Gospel is our primary source of information for Jesus' journeys during this period. All three of the Synoptics report the ministry of John the Baptist and the baptism and temptation of Jesus.

The Lucan Prologue (1:1–4) #1[1]

Luke's prologue states the source and purpose of the Gospel. Luke probably used both oral and written sources in his writing. These sources were based on the accounts of eyewitnesses and thus have a significant claim for accuracy. Luke's purpose was to verify the certainty of the Gospel for Theophilus. His "orderly" account need not have been chronological, but may have been more logical and complete than the sources he used.

The Johannine Prologue (1:1–18) #2

John's prologue provides a preview of the contents of the Gospel. Many of the central themes of the Gospel first appear in the prologue: life, light (1:4); darkness (1:5); witness (1:7); world (1:10); glory, truth (1:14). John began his story of Jesus prior to creation (vv. 1–5). Jesus' earthly ministry began with the witness of John the Baptist (vv. 6–8). The next empasis in the prologue is the coming of Jesus as the Word along with reactions to him (vv. 9–13). This coming of Jesus was nothing less than an incarnation (v. 14) of the eternal Word into human flesh. John the Baptist witnessed to the priority of Jesus both in time and position (v. 15). We also find an explanation of the complementary relationship between Moses and Jesus (vv. 16–18).

The "beginning" to which John refers in verse 1 was the beginning of all things, the start of the universe. John used the term *Word* (Greek: *logos*) because it had rich associations in both Greek and Jewish thought. Among the Greeks it described the rational principle holding all things together (Stoicism) or the ideal man from whom all human beings develop (Philo). In the Old Testament the term *word* was linked to God's activity in creation (Ps. 33:6) and to his communication to the Old Testament prophets (Isa. 38:4). This

---

1. The paragraph numbers in the text follow the numberings used in A. T. Robertson, *A Harmony of the Gospels* (New York: Harper & Row Publishers Inc., 1950). Gospel harmonies accomplish two purposes. First, the editors place in parallel columns the text of the Gospels where they view the contents as identical. Second, the editors arrange the incidents in the most likely chronological order according to their opinion. Robertson's *Harmony* has remained widely accepted over several generations. A harmony enables a reader to obtain a developing chronological view of the incidents of Jesus' life. A disadvantage to its use is that it makes it more difficult to note the distinctive emphases of each Gospel.

same word of God brought about deliverance and rescue (Ps. 107:20). The Old Testament used the term to describe the self–expression of God in creation and salvation. John used the term to describe God's ultimate self-disclosure in his Son. Pagan readers would be familiar with the term, but they would be drawn to reflect on it because of the new meaning of personification in Christ that John gave to it.[2]

In verse 1 John affirmed three truths about God's Word, Jesus.

1. He was "in the beginning," an affirmation of the divine preexistence.

2. He was distinct from God the Father ("with God"), but enjoyed fellowship with him.

3. He possessed deity ("was God").

In verses 6–8 John affirmed the witness of the Baptist toward Christ. John was sent from God to bear witness to Jesus as the light. The purpose of John's witness was to lead people to believe in the light (1:35–37). Those who responded to John's witness became children of God by divine creation (1:12–13). John also affirmed in his witness the temporal and spiritual priority of this Word. The term *temporal priority* refers to Jesus' preexistence (v. 1), and *spiritual priority* describes his lordship.

With a masterful condensation John described Jesus' entrance into the human race in clear, straightforward language. The Word so entered the human race that the one who had always been God (v. 1) now became a man whose name was Jesus (v. 14). The glory revealed in this "enfleshed" Word was not raw power or external pomp but grace and truth. These terms reveal the moral excellence of God's character.

Although no human being has ever observed the glory of God's face, the person of Jesus revealed him. In stating that Jesus "declared" God, John used the term from which we derive our English word *exegesis*. We might say that in word and deed Jesus is the exegesis of God the Father.

---

2. For a brief summary of the background of the term *logos*, see D. A. Carson, *The Gospel According to John* (Grand Rapids: William B. Eerdmans Publishing Co., 1991), 114–17.

The Genealogies of Jesus
(Matt. 1:1–17; Luke 3:23–38) #3

Jews kept ancient genealogical records with great care because they were important in such legal issues as inheritance of property and marriage. The birth stories and genealogical lists in Matthew and Luke present Jesus as a descendant of David and make it clear that Joseph was the legal, but not the actual, father of Jesus. Matthew traced Jesus' genealogy from Abraham with forty-one links to Joseph arranged in three sets of fourteen generations. Matthew omitted three generations of kings in v. 8 (note Ahaziah, Joash, and Amaziah in 1 Chron. 3:11–12 after the mention of Joram and compare with Matt. 1:8), and his use of the term "begat" does not indicate a father-son relationship but shows a direct line of descent.

Luke worked back from Joseph through David and Abraham to Adam, using seventy-seven names. From Abraham to David the two genealogies agree closely, but from David to Joseph the lists differ radically. Matthew's genealogy follows the list of successors to Judah's throne through Solomon. Luke's list passes through Nathan, another son of David. How can we explain the difference?

We should take both genealogies seriously, for both writers had access to reliable genealogical information. Three primary suggestions have been offered to explain the differences.

1. Some suggest that Matthew's Gospel provides the genealogy of Joseph, the legal father of Jesus, and Luke's Gospel provides the genealogy through Mary, the actual lineage of Jesus. This interpretation views the statement "Joseph, the son of Heli," as "Joseph, the son-in-law of Heli." The Gospel of Luke, however, does not mention Mary, and it was not normal to provide a genealogy through the mother. Luke's genealogy focuses on the unique situation of a virgin birth, and we do not know just how the genealogy would appear in the absence of a human father.

2. Some explain the differences by referring to the practice of levirate marriage. The early Christian leader Africanus (c. A.D. 220) suggested that Heli (Luke 3:24) died childless and that Jacob (Matt. 1:15–16), who had the same mother but a different father, married the widow of Heli and fathered Joseph. If

we follow this view, Matthew's Gospel provides Joseph's genealogy through his actual father Jacob, and Luke's Gospel provides Joseph's genealogy through his legal father Heli.

3. J. G. Machen suggested that Matthew named the legal
   descendants of David, those men who were the official line of
   succession to the throne. Luke, in turn, listed the descendants
   of David in that branch of the Davidic family to which Joseph,
   Mary's husband, belonged. This view assumes that Jacob, the
   father of Joseph in Matthew, died without offspring, and the
   line of succession then passed to the descendants of Heli.[3]

Matthew's genealogy includes four women: Tamar, an adulteress;
Rahab, a harlot; Ruth, the Moabitess, whose late night approach to
Boaz could be questioned (Ruth 3:1–14); and the wife of Uriah,
Bathsheba, seduced by David. Their inclusion suggests a theme of
grace operating even in the genealogy of Jesus. The development
of Luke's genealogy through David to Adam indicates Jesus' messianic qualifications and his connection with the entire human race.

The Announcement to Zechariah (Luke 1:5–25) #4

For two weeks each year priests from the villages of Palestine
journeyed to Jerusalem to officiate in the temple. The priests were
divided into twenty-four orders, and Zechariah belonged to the
division of Abijah. The godly character of this village priest stands
in stark contrast to the self-seeking worldliness of the high priests
who lived in Jerusalem and controlled the wealth of the temple.

Since there were more priests present for service than needed, it
was necessary to cast lots to assign tasks. Whenever a priest was
chosen by lot to burn incense in the temple, he was disqualified
from performing that task in the future. Offering the incense was a
thrilling, once-in-a-lifetime opportunity.

Zechariah was chosen to officiate, and it was during this time that
the angel Gabriel (1:19) announced to Zechariah that he and his
wife Elizabeth would have a son. This son would live like a Nazarite,

---

3. See the discussion in J. G. Machen, *The Virgin Birth of Christ* (London: Marshall, Morgan, & Scott, 1930; reprint, Grand Rapids: Baker, Twin Brooks Series,
1965), 188–209. For a thorough, more recent discussion of the two narratives, see
R. E. Brown, *The Birth of the Messiah* (Garden City, N.Y.: Doubleday, 1977).

never touching wine or strong drink. He would prepare for the advent of the Messiah and be Spirit-filled from his birth. When Zechariah responded with disbelief, the angel left him mute.

Zechariah completed his service in the temple unable to speak and then returned home with Elizabeth. The reason for her five-month hiding is unclear. Perhaps her childlessness had been the occasion for earlier reproaches, and she now wanted to remain alone until it was obvious that God had removed the blight of childlessness from her.

The Annunciation to Mary and the Birth of John (Luke 1:26–80) #5–8

Luke narrated the birth of Jesus from the viewpoint of Mary (1:25–56). When the angel Gabriel appeared to Mary to announce that she would conceive and give birth to Jesus, Mary was perplexed (v. 34). Gabriel reverently described God's sovereign activity in causing the conception and birth. Gabriel was apparently the first to inform Mary of her kinswoman Elizabeth's pregnancy (vv. 36–37). Mary's final response expressed submission and heroism. Mary was not yet married, and the penalty for adultery was death (Deut. 22:23–24). Even though there is no evidence that the penalty was carried out often, the threat still existed. When Mary saw the will of God, she accepted it regardless of the possible consequences.

Mary visited Elizabeth and returned home after a three-month stay (v. 56). Elizabeth's response to Mary indicated that she recognized Mary's child as the Messiah. She showed no trace of jealousy, and with surprising humility she deferred to the greater blessing which God had given to Mary.

Mary's song of praise in 1:46–56 is called the Magnificat from its opening words in the Latin translation. It has close parallels to Hannah's song after the birth of Samuel (1 Sam. 2:1–10).

Elizabeth gave birth to John (1:57). The Jews had a custom of naming a male child when he was circumcised on the eighth day after his birth (Lev. 12:1–3). Friends and relatives assumed that the child would receive his father's name, but the parents insisted on the name John, which means "the Lord is gracious." When Zechariah was again able to speak, he uttered a hymn of joy named the Benedictus from its opening word in Latin (v. 68).

The Annunciation to Joseph (Matt. 1:18–25) #9

Matthew wrote his narrative from the viewpoint of Joseph. Matthew may have wanted to defend the virgin birth against its detractors,[4] and he may have also tried to establish the legitimacy of Jesus' Davidic link through his adoption by Joseph.

A Jewish betrothal or engagement period represented a binding contract which lasted at least a year. The man was already viewed as the husband (v. 19), but the woman continued to live with her family, and no physical relationship was consummated. Matthew made it clear that Mary's pregnancy was due to the Holy Spirit.

Although stoning was required by the Old Testament law for premarital unchastity (Deut. 22:23–24), the Jews permitted divorce for this offence. Joseph was unwilling to humiliate Mary publicly, and he considered the alternative of a private divorce before two witnesses. Joseph might have suspected unfaithfulness by Mary, or he may have been unwilling to present himself as the father of Jesus. God used the appearance of an angel in a dream (cf. 2:13, 19, 22) to instruct Joseph to proceed with the marriage. Joseph's response to the dream compares favorably to Mary's response to Gabriel (Luke 1:38).

In subsequent verses (21, 23) the meanings of the names "Jesus" and "Emmanuel" are related to the child. Matthew also suggested that the birth of Jesus fulfilled Isaiah's prophecy of the virgin birth (Isa. 7:14). Isaiah used the Hebrew term *almah*, meaning "young

---

4. Origen mentions scurrilous rumors about the illegitimacy of Jesus' birth which he denounces in *Against Celsus* 1.28, 32. The rumors suggest that an unnamed carpenter to whom Mary was married drove her from the home because of her adultery. She later bore a child to a soldier named Panthera. Origen denounced these as efforts by his opponent Celsus to hide from the miracle of the virgin birth. The existence of these rumors in Origen's lifetime suggests that they may have surfaced even earlier and opens us to the possibility that Matthew was opposing rumors like them.

C. E. B. Cranfield presents an argument favoring the historicity of the virgin birth when he says that if the virgin birth were not historical, "It is . . . difficult . . . to explain at all convincingly how the early Church came during the first century to affirm it." See his article "Some Reflections on the Subject of the Virgin Birth," *SJT* 41 (1988): 188.

woman," and Matthew used the Greek term *parthenos*, meaning "virgin," to show that the woman chosen to fulfill Isaiah's prophecy would be a young, unmarried woman. Isaiah's original statement likely prophesied a double reference of events. It referred to an unusual birth (perhaps the unusual birth of the righteous Hezekiah as a descendant of the evil Ahaz; see 2 Kings 18:1–7) during the lifetime of the recipient Ahaz and also to a more distant messianic fulfillment.

References to other children of Mary (Matt. 13:55–56; Mark 6:3) indicate that she did not remain perpetually a virgin. Matthew implies that Joseph refrained from sexual relations with Mary until after the birth of Jesus (v. 25).

The Birth, Infancy, and Childhood of Jesus (Luke 2:1–52; Matt. 2:1–23) #10–19

Luke linked Jesus' birth to a census taken during the service of Quirinius in Syria. The decree was likely an administrative directive which set the process of the census in motion. Quirinius served as governor of Syria in A.D. 6, during which time he carried out a census. Scholars have also found inscriptions suggesting that Quirinius executed military functions in Syria during the period between 10 and 7 B.C. No record for the biblical census exists outside of Luke, but there is nothing impossible about the Lucan information (see additional discussion in chap. 5 under the subject "Birth of Christ").

The government edict required Mary and Joseph to return to their ancestral city, Bethlehem. The traditional location of Jesus' birth is in a stable, but it is also possible that he was born in a poor home which housed both people and animals, or in a cave. Swaddling clothes are long strips of cloth which could be wrapped repeatedly around the child.

Angels announced the birth to shepherds near Bethlehem (Luke 2:8–20). These shepherds hurried off to view the unlikely spectacle of the birth of a savior in the humble surroundings of a stable. They provided a proper setting for the presentation of another shepherd-king who resembled David.

Jesus was circumcised on the eighth day in accord with Jewish law, but Luke placed more emphasis on the naming of Jesus on that

occasion than on the circumcision. On the fortieth day after Jesus'
birth his parents took him to the temple for the ceremony of
redeeming the firstborn (Exod. 13:2, 12, 15). At the same time
Joseph and Mary gave the specified offering for purifying the
mother after childbirth (Lev. 12:1–5). The offering of the turtle-
doves or pigeons implies the poverty of Joseph and Mary (Lev.
12:6–8). Simeon and Anna, two godly Jews, recognized Jesus as the
Messiah. Simeon warned that Jesus would cause "standing" or "falling" in Israel, a reference to Jesus' ability to produce both faith and
disbelief in his listeners (Luke 2:34).

Matthew's story of Jesus' birth was intended to convince Jews
that he was the Messiah. Matthew presented Jesus as the true king
of the Jews in contrast to the self-seeking Herod (Matt. 2:2). The
wise men, the Magi, were a Persian priestly caste, who probably
served as magicians or astrologers. Somehow they had escaped the
blinding influences of pagan thought, and they came seeking the
Messiah. Matthew probably included this story as an appeal for the
Jews to follow their example. The star they saw likely represented a
miraculous occurrence with no parallel in astronomical history.
Matthew reminded his readers that Jesus was born in Bethlehem in
fulfillment of a prophecy (Micah 5:1–2). Herod's subjects would
have recognized the hypocrisy in his instructions to the Magi, but
as foreigners the Magi might have been deceived. Miraculous guidance by God prevented them from carrying the information back to
Herod (Matt. 2:12). The fact that Herod later slaughtered the
infant boys in Bethlehem under the age of two does not imply that
this was Jesus' age at the time but suggests that Herod was leaving a
margin for error.

The subsequent childhood of the Messiah typified aspects of
Israel's national history. Just as God protected the nation of Israel
in Egypt, so he protected his son, the Messiah, in Egypt (Matt.
2:15). Just as Jews grieved over those exiled at the time of the Babylonian captivity, mothers in Bethlehem grieved over the loss of
their infants due to Herod's murderous decree (Matt. 2:17). The
passage in Matthew 2:23 does not refer to a specific Old Testament
verse, but it may point to Jesus' residence in Nazareth as a
fulfillment of Isaiah 11:1. Isaiah named the Messiah a "shoot" or a

"branch," and the Hebrew word used is linked etymologically with Nazareth.

Only Luke presents information about Jesus' boyhood (Luke 2:39–52). At the age of thirteen Jewish boys became full participants in Judaism. Jesus' parents may have taken him there when he was twelve years of age to acquaint him with the temple and its festivals. Jesus' reply to his parents in Luke 2:49 indicates a developing messianic consciousness at an early age. As an obedient son Jesus dutifully returned to Nazareth with his parents. Luke chronicled the development of Jesus intellectually ("in wisdom"), physically ("in stature"), spiritually ("favor with God"), and socially ("favor with man") (Luke 2:52).

The Ministry of John the Baptist
(Mark 1:1–8; Matt. 3:1–12; Luke 3:1–18) #20–23

Luke located the beginning of John's ministry in the fifteenth year of Tiberius Caesar. This date is equivalent to our A.D. 26 or 27.[5] Although John ministered in an area near the Essene community at Qumran, we have no evidence that he ever belonged to the group. He appears to be a single, ascetic prophet with remarkable sensitivity to God's calling.

John urged the Jews to repent in expectation of the imminent arrival of God's kingdom. This preparatory work by John fulfilled prophecies by Isaiah and Malachi, but Mark mentioned only Isaiah, the more prominent of the two prophets. The Jews were to show their repentance by undergoing baptism.

Only proselytes to Judaism were baptized at this time. The method of this baptism was self-administered immersion. John startled the Jews by calling on them to be baptized for repentance. John's preaching placed proud Jews in the same category as spiritually needy Gentiles and ruled out any benefit that they may have received for descending from Abraham. John's ascetic dress resembled that of Elijah (2 Kings 1:8). His spartan diet was nutritious (although repulsive to modern westerners!) and easily obtainable in his locale.

---

5. For further information on this issue, see the discussion of "The Death of Jesus" in chapter 5.

Using almost identical words, Matthew and Luke present samples of John's preaching. The Pharisees and Sadducees came for baptism either out of curiosity or for public show. John compared them to snakes fleeing a grass fire (Matt. 3:7; Luke 3:7). This reaction of John indicates that he doubted their genuineness and did not heartily welcome them as prospective converts! Luke demonstrated his customary interest in social problems (3:10–14) and quoted John's description of genuine repentance. As evidences of repentance, John demanded that the general public, publicans, and soldiers display generosity, honesty, and kind treatment.

The most important component of John's message concerned his relationship to the Messiah. John preached a coming judgment that was to be executed by the Messiah. The unrepentant, comparable to chaff, could expect divine judgment. The repentant, comparable to wheat, could expect a baptism of the Holy Spirit and fire.

Laborers threshed wheat grain by treading the wheat on a threshing floor to remove the kernels from the chaff. The resultant mixture was thrown into the air with the aid of a winnowing fork ("fan"), and the wind blew the chaff aside to be gathered and burned. The wheat kernels were stored in a granary.

John's ministry accomplished three purposes.

1. He prepared for the Messiah's advent by raising expectations and calling for repentance (Matt. 3:2; Luke 3:3).

2. He explained the nature of the Messiah's mission (Matt. 3:11; Luke 3:16).

3. He inaugurated the Messiah's ministry by baptizing him (Matt. 3:13–17; Mark 1:9–11; Luke 3:21–22).

The Baptism of Jesus
(Matt. 3:13–17; Mark 1:9–11; Luke 3:21–23) #24

The baptism of Jesus marked his entrance into public ministry. Since John's baptism normally signified repentance, he protested the request to baptize one who had no sin (Matt. 3:14).[6] Although

---

6. We are not told how John identified Jesus. Even though John grasped the sinlessness of Jesus, his total understanding of Jesus' mission seems at this point to have been incomplete. John 1:31–34 suggested an insight that came to John after the baptismal experience.

none of the Gospels specifically state a reason for the baptism, Jesus likely insisted on undergoing the rite in order to identify with the people of God who repent.

After Jesus' baptism God demonstrated his approval with both a visible and an audible commendation. Visibly, the Spirit descended in the form of a dove. Luke's reference to a "bodily form" like a dove (3:22) suggests that the "bodily form" refers to the shape of the vision and not to the way that the form descended. The bestowal of the Spirit represented Jesus' commission for ministry, not the initial experience with the Spirit. Audibly, the voice of the Father from heaven identified Jesus with the Davidic Messiah ("You are my beloved Son," taken from Ps. 2:7) and with the Servant of the Lord ("In you I am well pleased," taken from Isa. 42:1). The three persons of the Trinity each have a role in the baptism event.

The text contains no hint that Jesus became Son of God at his baptism. Mark has already clearly identified the Messiah as God's Son (Mark 1:1). This event did not cause Jesus to become something that he had not previously been, but it launched him on the mission for which God had prepared him and defined it according to Old Testament expectations.

The Temptations of Jesus
(Matt. 4:1–11; Mark 1:12–13; Luke 4:1–13) #25

These temptations did not comprise the complete collection of Jesus' conflicts with the devil (see Matt. 16:23 for additional devilish harassment), but they did test Jesus' relationship with the Father, newly revealed at the baptism. Only Jesus himself could have been the source of this information. Explanations of the different order of the temptations in Matthew and Luke are conjectural, but most scholars agree that Matthew's order is chronological, while Luke may have changed the order of the final pair of temptations to climax the testing in the Jerusalem temple. The temptations may have been either inward and mental, outward and more physical, or a combination of all.

The fact that Jesus was led by the Spirit into the wilderness (Matt. 4:1) suggests that God, not the devil, initiated and controlled the progress of the tests. Jesus' forty-day fast reminds us of

Moses' experience at Sinai (Exod. 34:28). The text does not indicate whether Jesus' fast was total or if he was limited to subsist on the meager fare that the wilderness could provide. Either way Jesus experienced real hunger.

The chief emphasis in each temptation appears to be Jesus' personal relationship with God. The "if" in the devil's approach for the first temptation is not an indication that the devil doubted Jesus' sonship but assumes that he is God's son and suggests that such a son as Jesus need not tolerate physical deprivation. Jesus realized that his hunger was a divine experience designed to teach him the lesson of Deuteronomy 8:3. He refused to seek material comfort and pledged uncompromising obedience to the Father's plan.

If we follow Matthew's order, the second temptation questions Jesus' absolute confidence in the protection promised by the Father in Psalm 91:11–12. Jesus refused to follow the devil's suggestion to force God's hand and, learning from Israel's experience at Massah (Deut. 6:16), he pledged himself to a relationship of trust which did not require any form of inspection.

Still following the Matthaean order, the devil next makes a direct assault on Jesus' loyalty to the Father. Jesus refused to consider any easy route to world domination by compromise with the devil and, taking a quote from Deuteronomy 6:13, he abruptly dismissed him, using the name "Satan"[7] for the first time (Matt. 4:10).

God now provided the help which Jesus earlier refused to request (Matt. 4:11). The ministry of the angels included the provision of food. Satan departed from the arena for the moment, but he would return later.

Jesus quoted sections of Scripture in which the nation Israel faced temptation and failed. At the outset of his mission God's Son faced the same tests and succeeded. Trials such as these equipped Jesus to be a merciful and faithful high priest who can offer help to the tempted (Heb. 2:18; 4:14–16).

---

7. The term *Satan* is a Hebrew term equivalent in meaning to the Greek term *devil* (Grk. *diabolos*). Both terms picture him as an accuser.

The Witness of John the Baptist to Jesus
(John 1:19–34) #26–27

The Jews expected a variety of messianic figures, and the Jewish leaders in Jerusalem wanted John to categorize himself in relation to these eschatological hopes. To a delegation seeking to learn who he was, John denied relationships to the Messiah, Elijah, or any other great prophet. He identified himself as a forerunner for the Messiah and boldly suggested that his ministry was a fulfillment of Old Testament prophecy (Isa. 40:3). When the interrogators asked John the source of his authority to baptize, John implied that he had divine authority for his actions, but he explained that he was insignificant compared to the one to whom he witnessed.

John used two descriptive phrases to identify Jesus. First, he was the "lamb of God." Jesus was a sacrificial lamb who could resolve the problem of sin, not only for Jews but for the entire world. Second, he was a "Holy-Spirit baptizer." God told John that the man on whom the Spirit descended was the one who would baptize with the Holy Spirit. The descent of the Spirit after Jesus' baptism identified this role of Jesus to John.[8]

Initial Contact with the Disciples
(John 1:35–51) #28

The initial contact of Jesus with the disciples was not technically a "call" to discipleship, but it was the first exposure of these disciples to Jesus. The subsequent prompt response of some of these disciples to his call in Mark 1:16–20 is more understandable with the initial contact in the background.

First to experience contact with Jesus are Andrew and an unnamed disciple, probably the apostle John. Andrew attracts his brother Simon to Jesus by presenting Jesus as the Messiah. The term *Messiah* is the transliteration of a Hebrew or Aramaic term meaning "anointed one." The term *Christ* has the same meaning in Greek and was originally applied to Jesus as a title, not as a name. Jesus greeted Peter by calling him a name which described what

---

8. See footnote 6 (in ref. to Matt. 3:14) for an effort to harmonize this passage with John's ability to grasp the sinlessness of Jesus prior to the act of baptism.

Jesus could help him become. The English translation for Cephas (Aramaic) or Peter (Greek) is "rock" or "stone."

After Philip had contact with Jesus, he left to return to his friend Nathanael. Nathanael, a native of Cana in Galilee (John 21:2), responded with ambiguous interest when Philip identified Jesus as the one to whom the Scripture pointed. His skeptical response showed that even Galileans loathed Nazareth, but Jesus' commendation of his honesty and display of special knowledge resolved his doubts. Nathanael spoke more truthfully than he realized when he identified Jesus as the Son of God. Jesus promised Nathanael that he would receive divinely sent proof that Jesus was the Messiah designated by God.

The First Sign (John 2:1–12) #29–30

Jesus' address to Mary (v. 4) as "dear woman" followed by the statement that "My time has not yet come" was a gentle rebuke to her. Jesus was reminding her that any work of his ministry must be done in response to the Father's will, not at her suggestion.

The stone pots held about twenty gallons each. Their contents were used for Jewish ritual washings, and as such they represent the old practices of Judaism which Jesus would replace with the new wine of Christianity (cf. Mark 2:22) and the greater freedom of the gospel. Apparently, the miracle was semi-public because only the servants and the disciples recognized its occurrence. The master of ceremonies for the feast remarked with amazement and jest that the host saved the good wine until last.

Normally marriage feasts were week-long activities, and it was an inexcusable social embarrassment to run out of wine before the completion of the feast. This miracle shows Jesus' involvement in the ordinary activities of life and makes it impossible to view him as an other-worldly ascetic. The miracle is also a "sign," John's term for a miracle. This sign prompted responsive disciples to put their faith in Jesus. Not all who saw the miracle responded with faith. The servants saw the sign, but did not perceive the glory with the eyes of faith.

Excursus on Gospel Miracles

Now that we have seen Jesus' first miracle, we need to explore the validity and significance of miracles. The synoptic Gospels picture

Jesus as involved in acts of healing, exorcisms, and nature miracles. John's Gospel mentions healing and nature miracles, but contains no references to exorcisms. It is important not to detach the miracles of Jesus from his teaching and the general course of his life. The discipline of apologetics studies the Gospel miracles as supernatural evidences of Jesus' divinity. Some critical study focuses on the teaching of Jesus to the exclusion of his miracles. Form criticism sometimes views the miracles as products of pious imagination, produced by churches which were eager to present Jesus as a divine man.

The advent of modern science led some thinkers to view miracles as violations of the laws of nature. Skeptical philosophers like David Hume denied that the laws of nature can be violated. With a mindset such as this no amount of historical evidence is sufficient to verify a miraculous event. Hume suggested that the actual evidence for miracles was weak and inconclusive, accepted only by ignorant, obscure people.

A wiser approach is to begin with the evidence for a theistic world view and then interpret miracles as the action of a personal God in nature and history. If we accept a personal creator who can use powers beyond human understanding whenever his purpose requires it, miracles become feasible. C. S. Lewis used this approach to defend miracles.

At least two features contribute to making the miracle stories of the Gospels credible reports of actual events. First, the miracles reported in the Gospels came from eyewitnesses who endured imprisonment, exclusion, torture, and death for their belief in Jesus. At unbelievable costs they felt compelled to proclaim the life, death, and resurrection of Jesus. They could have lived much more comfortably if they had either admitted that their testimonies were false or simply refused to witness. Eyewitness reports of the resurrection of Christ are especially compelling.

1. Paul based the evidence for the Resurrection on the reports of many different witnesses, who saw Jesus at many different times and places (see 1 Cor. 15:3–8). The variety of evidence and the integrity of the reporters make their testimony an indisputable witness to truth.

2. The Gospel accounts of Jesus' ministry began to be written within half a century after Jesus' death. This brief interim is

too short to allow the development of mythology, since eye-witnesses, both friendly and unfriendly, would still be alive to restrain any inaccurate reporting.

The miracles in the Gospels are credible reports worthy of our confidence, but it should not follow that the chief evidence for Christianity's presence among contemporary believers lies in their ability to duplicate these miracles. The New Testament itself locates the evidence for vital Christianity in the moral transformation of believers by the gospel rather than upon their ability to produce miracles (see John 13:34–35; 1 Pet. 2:12).[9]

The Cleansing of the Temple (John 2:13–22) #31

The synoptic Gospels place a temple cleansing near the conclusion of Jesus' ministry (Matt. 21:12–13; Mark 11:15–17; Luke 19:45–46). Some scholars insist that either John or the synoptic writers have changed the chronological order for theological reasons. It is not impossible, however, that Jesus would begin and conclude his ministry with a protest against the materialistic greed of the temple leaders. In favor of the Johannine order supporting two cleansings is the appearance of a definite time connection between the events in John 2:11 and 2:13. Also, the details of the cleansing in John contain some different information—for example, Jesus' reference to the Resurrection as a sign of his right to prescribe temple worship—from that in the Synoptics.

The cattle, sheep, and doves were used by Jews in temple worship. Their sale in the temple precincts was a convenience and service for worshippers coming from a distant location. The money changers provided the special Tyrian coin necessary for payment of the temple tax. This coin was used as a standard because of its purity, and travelers would not normally have brought it with them. The merchants made a profit on their sales, but Jesus' objection

---

9. Among useful works defending the presence of the miraculous in the Gospels are Craig Blomberg and David Wenham, eds., *The Miracles of Jesus*, vol. 6 of *Gospel Perspectives* (Sheffield: *JSOT*, 1986); Colin Brown, *Miracles and the Critical Mind* (Grand Rapids: Wiliam B. Eerdmans Publishing Co., 1984); and C. S. Lewis, *Miracles: A Preliminary Study* (New York: Association, 1958). Hume's attack on miracles appears in "Of Miracles," #10 of *Enquiries Concerning the Human Understanding and Concerning the Principles of Morals*, reprinted in *Hume's Enquiries*, ed. L. A. Selby-Bigge, 2d ed. (Oxford: Clarendon Press, 1902), 109–31.

was not as much to their dishonest business practices as to their crass commercialism in the house of God. Noisy commerce usurped worship and prayer in the temple. The common people probably sympathized with Jesus' actions and made it difficult for the authorities to take punitive measures against him.

When the Jewish leaders questioned Jesus' right to interfere with temple activities, he challenged them to destroy "this temple, and I will raise it in three days." His hearers understood it on a purely physical level and viewed his words as a threat against the temple itself (cf. Mark 14:57–58). Only later did his disciples realize that he was referring to his resurrection and suggesting that he replaced the temple as the true center of worship (cf. Acts 7:44–50, in which Stephen teaches that God cannot be limited merely to a temple).

Nicodemus Learns of the New Birth (John 2:23–3:21) #32

Jesus' performance of miracles gained followers, but he recognized the inadequacy of their response merely to the miraculous. His response to them could have led to the creation of a popular messianic movement, but their superficial faith led him to hold himself aloof from their enthusiasm. Miracles alone cannot cause faith (see John 10:32), but God is sometimes pleased to use them to help produce or strengthen faith (John 3:2; 20:19–29).

The designation of Nicodemus as a "ruler of the Jews" identifies him as a member of the Sanhedrin. Nicodemus's observation of Jesus' miraculous powers stimulated him to come to Jesus with his confession. Jesus' challenge that he needed to be born again may also suggest that he needed to be born "from above," by the power of God from heaven. Jesus called Nicodemus to move toward him with a spiritual commitment which went beyond a mere faith in Jesus' miraculous powers. The change with such a regeneration would be comparable to beginning life over again, but this time the believer would have a nature from heaven.

Jesus' appeal to be born "of water and spirit" (v. 5) uses the two nouns to symbolize the thoroughness of conversion. "Water" symbolizes the cleansing from impurity, and "spirit" represents the complete transformation of the heart which empowers a person to wholly follow God.

This renewing work of the Spirit finds its foundation in Jesus' descent from heaven in the Incarnation and his ascent back to heaven following the events of the Cross (vv. 13–14). Jesus compared the redemptive effects of being lifted up on the cross to the delivering effect of Moses elevating the serpent in the wilderness (see Num. 21:8–9).

Jesus and John the Baptist (Matt. 4:12; Mark 1:14; Luke 3:19–20; 4:14; John 3:22–4:4) #33–34

Jesus and John the Baptist had preaching and baptizing ministries that overlapped chronologically. Jesus himself did not baptize, but he carried on this ministry through his disciples (4:2). Although large numbers of hearers were coming to John, even larger crowds flocked to hear Jesus (3:25–26).

When John observed the resentment toward Jesus' success, he unhesitatingly pointed out that Jesus' ministry had the greater significance. John was a forerunner or herald of Jesus and resembled the best man at a wedding ("friend of the bridegroom"). Jesus was the bridegroom. The increasing prominence of Jesus flooded John with joy, not jealousy. He conceded that Jesus would grow more in importance in God's plan of redemption while he slipped aside into insignificance. His attitude reflects a humble acceptance of God's will, and this attitude must forever guide modern believers.

Jesus' subsequent departure for Galilee (see 4:3) prevented conflict between his ministry and that of John the Baptist and protected Jesus from the immediate malicious designs of the Pharisees. The shortest travel route from Judea to Galilee lay through Samaria, and this geographical fact dictated Jesus' trip through the area (4:4).

Jesus and the Samaritan Woman (John 4:5–42) #35

Jesus arrived at the Samaritan town of Sychar at midday and remained at the well, exhausted from his journey, while his disciples went into town to obtain food. When Jesus asked the Samaritan woman for a drink of water, she was astonished because Jews normally would not share the same drinking vessels with Samaritans.

Jesus' promise of living water aroused the woman's curiosity. Jesus may have used the term "living water" because it could refer either to fresh, running water from springs or could serve as a metaphor for the cleansing power of God in her life (Isa. 1:16–18). The woman viewed Jesus' promise as a reference to the provision of flowing spring water, a provision which could spare her from the drudgery of returning to draw water from the well. She later came to see that the term "living water" referred to the spiritual power available through Jesus himself.

When Jesus revealed his knowledge of her immoral background, she saw his spiritual insight and asked him about the proper place for worship (v. 20). Jesus answered that the location of worship was immaterial and called the woman to a style of worship directed by the Holy Spirit and centered on the truth which he revealed (v. 24). When Jesus identifed himself as the Messiah, the woman believed in him and later convinced some of her townspeople to believe (vv. 28–29, 39–42).

For Further Discussion

1. Suggest a modern term instead of "Word" which John might have used in order to identify Jesus as God's method of communicating with human beings.

2. Evaluate the various options available for harmonizing the differences between the genealogies of Jesus in Matthew and Luke.

3. Compare and contrast the response of Mary and Joseph to the angelic revelations they received.

4. List Matthew's references to the Old Testament in the birth and infancy stories of Jesus and explain how the Old Testament reference is used.

5. Explain how the temptations of Jesus prepared him to be a more understanding savior.

6. List and evaluate the steps through which Jesus took the Samaritan woman in bringing her to faith in him.

Bibliography

Brown, R. E. *The Birth of the Messiah*. Garden City, N.Y.: Doubleday, 1977.

Carson, D. A. *The Gospel According to John*. Grand Rapids: William B. Eerdmans Publishing Co., 1991.

Cole, R. Alan. *Mark*. TNTC. Rev. ed. Grand Rapids: William B. Eerdmans Publishing Co., 1989.

Cranfield, C. E. B. "Some Reflections on the Virgin Birth." *SJT* 41 (1988): 188.

Ellis, E. Earle. *Luke*. NCB. Rev. ed. Grand Rapids: William B. Eerdmans Publishing Co., 1981.

France, R. T. *Matthew*. TNTC. Grand Rapids: William B. Eerdmans Publishing Co., 1985.

Machen, J. G. *The Virgin Birth of Christ*. London: Marshall, Morgan & Scott, 1930. Reprint, Grand Rapids: Baker, Twin Brooks Series, 1965.

Morris, Leon. *Luke*. TNTC. Rev. ed. Grand Rapids: William B. Eerdmans Publishing Co., 1988.

Robertson, A. T. *A Harmony of the Gospels*. New York: Harper & Row Publisher Inc., 1950.

Tasker, R. V. G. *John*. TNTC. Grand Rapids: William B. Eerdmans Publishing Co., 1960.

9 Jesus' Ministry in and Around Galilee

Guiding Questions

1. Consider Jesus' Galilean ministry. Where was his base of operation? What method of ministry did he use? What was the general reponse to his ministry there?

2. What reasons did the scribes and Pharisees present for opposing Jesus in Mark 2:1–3:6?

3. Explain how Jesus selected, trained, and used the twelve disciples.

4. Summarize the contents of the major teaching sections of Jesus' Galilean ministry in the Gospel of Matthew.

5. What truths about Jesus' ministry did the kingdom parables (Matthew 13; Mark 4) reveal?

After Jesus arrived in Galilee from his trip through Samaria (John 4), he engaged in ministry primarily in Galilee of perhaps a year and a half. During this time Jesus made Capernaum his headquarters, and from this strategically located city on the Sea of Galilee he traveled throughout the area. It is impossible to reconstruct his journeys with chronological precision, but traces of these trips appear in the Gospels (Mark 1:39; Luke 4:14–15; 8:1–3). Although most of Jesus' actions during this time take place in Galilee, he made periodic trips back to Judea (John 5:1–47).

During much of this period Jesus became more popular with the masses, although Jewish religious leaders steadily opposed his actions and teaching (Mark 2:1–3:6). After the feeding of the five thousand, Jesus' popularity seems to have plummeted with the masses, as his would-be followers, shocked by the exclusiveness of his demands, left him (John 6:60–71). After this decline in public acceptance, Jesus spent more of his time in training and preparing his chosen disciples.

Jesus' Return to Galilee (Matt. 4:13–17; Mark 1:14–15; Luke 4:14–15; John 4:43–54) #36–38, 40

Jesus left Samaria, where he had received an open-hearted welcome, and returned to Galilee, his homeland, where those who responded to him were likely more attracted by his miracles than by belief in his messiahship. They did not give him the honor he deserved as Messiah.[1]

During the period of his ministry in Galilee, Jesus made Capernaum the center of his activities (Matt. 4:13–16). The story in John 4:46–54 resembles the healing of the centurion's servant in Matthew 8:5–13, but the details are sufficiently different to suggest that we are dealing with two distinct incidents. The nobleman showed his faith in Jesus by approaching Jesus for a favor and by accepting Jesus' word about the healing of his son. This was not the second miracle which Jesus performed, for he had done many miracles in Judea not recorded in John's Gospel (see John 2:23). This is, however, the second miracle performed by Jesus in Galilee (see John 2:11).

Section 39 in Robertson's *Harmony* should be equated with #69. At this point Luke was probably arranging his material topically rather than chronologically.

---

1. This interpretation assumes that the response of the Galileans resembled that of the Judeans mentioned in John 2:23–25. The welcome given by the Galileans was superficial and inadequate. Jesus' rebuke in John 4:48 is not limited to the nobleman alone, but its plural form suggests that Jesus was rebuking all the Galileans for their flawed faith. The nobleman's acceptance of Jesus' work indicated that he, unlike other Galileans, trusted the person of Jesus and was interested in more than signs and wonders.

The First Disciples
(Matt. 4:18–22; Mark 1:16–20; Luke 5:1–11) #41

Matthew and Mark report the same incident, but Luke reports another instance of Jesus' call of Peter. It is difficult to know whether it is earlier or later than the account in the other two Synoptics. All three incidents probably followed the initial meeting of Jesus with Andrew, Peter, Philip, and Nathanael in John 1:35–51.

Jesus called these disciples not only to listen and learn but also to join him in "fishing" for human beings. This was the first time Jesus asked the disciples to disrupt their normal life activities to follow him. The fact that Zebedee had hired servants (Mark 1:20) suggests that James and John came from a background of greater wealth than Andrew and Peter. Both pairs of men left all that they had—the minimum requirement for a follower of Jesus.

A Busy Ministry in Galilee (Matt. 4:23–25; 8:2–4, 14–17; Mark 1:21–45; Luke 4:31–44; 5:12–16) #42–45

Much of the ministry of Jesus in this section takes place in Capernaum on the Sabbath. In the synagogue in Capernaum Jesus taught without relying on rabbinic authorities as precedents for his teaching. This assumption of personal authority amazed his hearers.

The demon-possessed man witnessed to the person and work of Jesus, but he recoiled from his purity. Jesus confronted the demoniac, muzzled his testimony, and freed him from the demon's power. Jesus' muzzling of the demoniac showed his refusal to accept involuntary testimony of his deity from evil powers. The deliverance amazed the crowd, but it did not lead to a response of faith and commitment.

After leaving the synagogue, Jesus entered Peter's home and found Peter's mother-in-law sick with a fever. Jesus touched the woman and she was instantly healed. She showed her grateful devotion by serving him food.

These two miracles occurred on a Sabbath, but they did not attract attention as violations of the Sabbath. The healing of the demoniac was somewhat involuntary; and the healing of Peter's mother-in-law was a private event. Orthodox Judaism allowed healing on the Sabbath only when life was in danger. The setting of the sun (Mark 1:32) signaled the end of the Sabbath, and crowds of sick and oppressed people surrounded Jesus. Mark distinguished those who were sick from those who were demon possessed (Mark 1:32).

Jesus refused to accept demonic testimony of his deity because such statements by the powers of evil only represent an empirical fact, not a morally transforming insight. Such confessions by demonic powers are far removed from saving faith (see James 2:19).

Jesus extended his ministry outside of Capernaum throughout all Galilee (Mark 1:39). While his disciples were resting after an exhausting Sabbath, Jesus arose to begin the day in communion with his heavenly Father. Peter was doubtless puzzled that Jesus viewed the throngs of people seeking him as a sign to move on to other areas. Matthew summarized Jesus' work as "teaching in their synagogues, preaching the gospel, and healing diseases" (4:23).

Mosaic law quarantined all lepers, and this prohibition of contact with society must have added to the misery of the leper (see Leviticus 13–14). Rabbinic practice warned Jews against getting near a leper, and Jesus' touching the leper must have shocked those who saw it. Jesus' act of touch brought healing to the leper rather than defilement to Jesus, and he directed the healed leper to present himself to the priest and make the required offerings (see Lev. 14:2–20). This would prove his healing and demonstrate Jesus' power to the priest. Jesus prohibited publicity of the healing in order to avoid attracting followers who were merely curious. The well-intended disobedience to this command by the healed leper only hindered the work of Jesus.

The Beginning of Opposition to Jesus
(Matt. 9:1–17; Mark 2:1–22; Luke 5:17–39) #46–48

Jesus healed the paralyzed man in response to the faith of those who carried him (Mark 2:1–12). Scripture does not indicate the attitude of the sick man, but Jesus' offer of forgiveness to him suggests that he was more conscious of his spiritual burden than his physical need. The scribes saw the logic behind Jesus' claims to forgive sin and recognized that he was claiming a divine prerogative. Since they assumed that he was a mere mortal, they felt that they detected blasphemy in his words. Jesus volunteered to produce a sign of his power by healing the paralytic before them. If we answer

Jesus' question in Mark 2:9, we learn that it is easier to heal the body than the soul. Nevertheless, it was harder to heal the body of the paralytic on this occasion because a claim to heal demanded instant proof for verification. When Jesus healed the paralyzed man, the crowd gasped in amazement.

Levi (Mark 2:14; Luke 5:27) and Matthew (Matt. 9:9) are the same individual. The future apostle was a tax collector, likely an agent of Herod Antipas (Luke 23:6–7). This made him an outcast from Jewish society much as the leper (Mark 1:40) had been. The meal was probably a reception given by Levi to introduce his business acquaintances to his new master. Probably the chief reason the Pharisees objected to fellowship with these outcasts was their fear of being defiled (see John 18:28). Jesus defended his contact with them by indicating they had a greater need. Those who defended their own righteousness, like the Pharisees, lacked the sense of need that makes people open to the possibility of healing (see John 5:40).

By the first century, mandatory fasting had become an important display of piety for the Jews. It was natural for the Pharisees to raise the issue of fasting because Jesus and his disciples seemed to be lax in observing this tradition. Jesus answered that just as fasting at a wedding feast was out of place for members of the wedding party, so mandatory fasting while he was present on earth was inappropriate. Further, making fasting mandatory was an effort to take the outmoded traditions of Judaism and impose them on the fresh spiritual life in Christianity. Such a requirement was like pouring new wine into old wineskins, causing the old, brittle skins to burst from the expanding pressure of the new wine.

Healing the Lame Man in Jerusalem (John 5:1–47) #49

John does not name the feast mentioned (5:1), but its identity is a factor in determining the length of Jesus' ministry (see discussion of the "Length of Jesus' Ministry" in chap. 5). Archaeologists have uncovered what may have been the Pool of Bethesda (also named Bethzatha or Bethsaida) with five colonnades or porticos. The best manuscripts omit the statement in verses 3b and 4 about an angel stirring the water.

Rabbinic tradition permitted the treatment of sickness on the Sabbath only if the life of the person was endangered. Jesus violated this prohibition both by healing the invalid and by urging him to pick up his bed. Jesus defended the healing by comparing his work to that of the Father, who was at work sustaining creation, even on the Sabbath (5:17). The Jews regarded Jesus' suggestion that God was his own Father as blasphemous.

Jesus confronted his accusers by claiming that their response to his word determined whether or not they had eternal life. Further, he would execute judgment on the last day (5:27–29). As proof for his claims he cited the testimony of John the Baptist (5:33), his miraculous works (5:36), and the witness of the Father (5:37). He accused them of failing to receive even the words of Moses, whose memory they claimed to cherish. Had they received Moses' words, they would have believed in Jesus as the one to whom Moses pointed.

More Sabbath Controversies
(Matt. 12:1–14; Mark 2:23–3:6; Luke 6:1–11) #50–51

The Old Testament (see Deut. 23:25) permitted hungry people to take grain from fields belonging to others in order to satisfy their needs. The Pharisees did not accuse the disciples of stealing but of violating the Sabbath by working. They reaped the grain by removing it from the stalks, and they threshed it by rubbing the grain in their hands to separate the kernels from the chaff. Jesus responded to the objections of the Pharisees by giving three illustrations, each of which developed more fully than the previous one the theological implications of Sabbath activity.

1. He indicated that there was biblical precedent for the law of human need to assume greater importance than the law of ceremony. He reminded them of the time David ate the sacred shewbread (see 1 Sam. 21:1–6).

2. He pointed out (Mark 2:27) that the Pharisees erred in their understanding of the Sabbath. They forgot that the Sabbath was not a means of testing human obedience to meticulous Sabbath observance but a merciful provision by God for human rest and worship.

3. Jesus claimed that he was Lord of the Sabbath and that he could interpret its regulations as he saw fit. He made it clear

that his Sabbath activities were not mere accidents but were the result of who he was.

The clash in the wheat fields led to a clash in the synagogue. On the Sabbath Jesus met a man whose hand was physically useless. He viewed the meeting as an occasion for ministry, but the Pharisees saw it as an opportunity to accuse Jesus. Logically the Pharisees could not answer Jesus' question in Mark 3:4 without abandoning their theological position. They would have been able only to answer, "It is lawful to do nothing on the Sabbath." Jesus' anger at the Pharisees was mixed with grief for their uncompromising views. Their opposition to Jesus led them to make an alliance with their political enemies, the Herodians, who supported the tyrant Herod Antipas. The Pharisees had previously viewed the house of Herod with contempt.

A Withdrawal to Select the Twelve
(Matt. 12:15–21; Mark 3:7–19; Luke 6:12–16) #52–53

Rejected by the religious leaders of Judaism, Jesus moved away from them to focus on the common people who came from Palestine and regions of the north and south to hear him. After a night of prayer, Jesus appointed twelve of his disciples, corresponding to Israel's twelve tribes, to serve as apostles (Luke 6:13). Their primary purpose was to be with Jesus and to receive formal and informal teaching from him. Their secondary purpose was to be missionaries for him. Bartholomew is probably the Nathanael of John 1:45–51. Thaddeus (Mark 3:18) is likely identical with Judas, the son of James in Luke 6:16.

The Sermon on the Mount
(Matt. 5:1–7:29; Luke 6:17–49) #54

The Sermon on the Mount is a collection of Jesus' sayings that touch on the theme of discipleship. Much of its content is found in three chapters of Matthew. Luke contains roughly half of Matthew's material in parallels located in various parts of the Gospel but particularly in chapter 6. Matthew places the location of the message on a mountain (5:1), but Luke places it on a level place (Luke 6:17), which might easily be a level spot on a mountainside. Many scholars feel that the content of the message is uniquely from

Jesus but that Matthew gave the sermon its present structure. However, note that the ending of the message (Matt. 7:28) conveys the impression that the material was delivered on a single occasion.

Determining the source of the sermon is a complicated process. Has Matthew described the actual historical setting for the discourses in the sermon? Sometimes the material in the Matthean and Lucan writings appears in different contexts. For example, Matthew records the Lord's Prayer as part of a warning against vain repetitions (Matt. 6:7–15) while Luke records the prayer as a response to a disciple's request, "Lord, teach us to pray" (Luke 11:). It is certainly possible that Jesus presented identical teachings in different contexts, but this emphasis must not be used to rule out the unique phrasing given by Matthew.

Some feel the sermon is a compilation by Matthew. They emphasize that Matthew was quite creative in producing the sermon and suggest that he has not demonstrated strict historical accuracy. Others believe that Matthew structured and expanded the sermon around an existing message which Luke knew and presented. In this view, the teachings derive from Jesus, but the structure comes from Matthew. Still others accept the authenticity of the contexts but point out that neither the Matthean nor the Lucan sermon is a verbatim account of Jesus' teachings. They emphasize that the specific idiom may be that of Matthew, but the message carries the voice and authority of Jesus. My own position is very close to the third option.

Two features of the sermon are important for its interpretation.

1. In the sermon Jesus appears in contrast to Moses. Just as Moses went to Mt. Sinai to receive a new law, one greater than Moses delivers new insights into God's law by emphasizing the eternal principles already contained in the writings of Moses. Particularly in Matthew 5:21–22, 27–28, 33–34, 38–39, 43–44 Jesus contrasted his teaching with an erroneous understanding of the original Mosaic writing. By this approach, Jesus claimed to be greater than Moses.

2. The content of the sermon is an ethic for committed disciples of Jesus. It is not a spiritual law for all human beings. It is not a set of rules by which one may earn salvation. The sermon describes the character, duties, and attitude of the Christian

disciple, with a commitment to Jesus at the very center of the call to obedience (Matt. 7:21–23).

Location and Audience (Matt. 5:1–2; Luke 6:17–19). The location of the sermon is on the steep hills west of the Sea of Galilee. Luke's reference to a "level place" probably described a plain on the hillside on which crowds could gather. Matthew focused the sermon on the disciples (5:1), but it is apparent that a crowd of people also gathered around to hear the message (Matt. 7:28–29).

The Beatitudes (Matt. 5:3–20; Luke 6:20–26), Subsections 1 and 2. The Beatitudes in Matthew consist of nine sayings praising the attitudes of a true disciple of Jesus. The second half of each verse or phrase outlines the rewards of discipleship. The predominant use of the future tense in Matthew suggests that the rewards are yet to come, but the use of the present tense in verses three and ten warns us against limiting the fulfillment exclusively to the future. Luke's statements differ from Matthew by being written in the second person instead of the third person. Also, Luke has only four beatitudes balanced by four "woes" which express regret over failure in discipleship. Although Luke's statements are outwardly similar to Matthew's, some of the differences result from Jesus' practice of using similar forms of beatitudes on different occasions and with different emphases. Luke might have been giving a general summary of what Jesus said on several different occasions.

The "meek" to whom Jesus promised the inheritance of the earth are not those who are timid or mousy but those who rely on God instead of human scheming to get their inheritance. The fact that the meek will inherit the earth suggests that ultimately God will vindicate those who trust him for their reward instead of those who by self-seeking try to obtain rewards in their own way.

In Matthew 5:13–16 Jesus outlined the distinctiveness of the life of his disciples and insisted that their character was to have a penetrating, preserving, transforming effect on society. In Matthew 5:17–20 Jesus affirmed the authority of the principles of the Old Testament. Jesus' statement in 5:17 indicates that he brings the Law and the Prophets of the Old Testament to their desired end. His teaching does not abolish the Old Testament, as some of his opponents charged. Rather, his teaching transcends the Old Testament and brings it to its intended completion. Jesus illustrated in

5:21–48 how to apply the Old Testament to the new situations his coming has introduced by making new applications of the Old Testament. His illustrations oppose a legalistic application of the Old Testament, but they retain an emphasis on the principles set forth in the Old Testament. In verse 18 Jesus spoke of the jot, a reference to the smallest Hebrew letter the *yod*, and the *tittle*, the short extension of a stroke on a Hebrew letter resembling the crossing of a "t" in the English alphabet.

The Antitheses (Matt. 5:21–48; Luke 6:27–30, 32–36), Subsection 3. This section consists of six teaching units (vv. 21–26; 27–30; 31–32; 33–37; 38–42; 43–48) in which Jesus' interpretation of Old Testament law is contrasted with erroneous application by those who misused the teachings from Sinai. Several features of this section are significant.

1. The material consists of a series of examples of the application of the principles that Jesus stated earlier in verses 17–20.

2. Jesus' applications are more demanding and inward than popular applications and relate to a person's attitudes rather than to literal conformity to the rules.

3. Jesus is not abrogating the Old Testament law but reinterpreting its application for disciples. Jesus issues his appeal to all disciples, not to a higher level of superior disciples.

The prohibition against insulting a "brother" calls for mutual love among believers and stresses the urgency of reconciliation as a sign of genuine Christianity (vv. 21–26). The warning against adultery and sexual immorality includes hyperbole, acceptable exaggeration, which points out that avoiding temptation will involve drastic sacrifices and self-denial such as cutting off the right hand (vv. 27–32). Jesus was not prohibiting the use of oaths, but he was indicating that the verbal integrity of an individual should be such that an oath is not necessary to convince hearers of truthfulness (vv. 33–37). The original purpose of "an eye for an eye and a tooth for a tooth" was to limit revenge by suggesting that punishment must not exceed the crime. Jesus was not necessarily calling for pacifism, but he was banning an attitude of vindictiveness and appealing for generosity (vv. 38–42). In Matthew 5:40 Jesus called for a disciple to surrender voluntarily his cloak (the outer garment) whenever his coat (the inner garment) was taken by law. He urged this despite the law's permission to keep the cloak on humanitarian grounds (see Exod. 22:25–27). The Old Testament did not command hatred of an enemy, but such an application could have been inferred from particular passages (Ps. 139:19–24). Jesus called for his followers to practice an utterly accepting love.

True Righteousness in Giving, Praying, and Fasting (Matt. 6:1–18), Subsection 4. Jesus warned that the recognition hypocrites receive from their generosity is the admiration of others but their generosity is not rewarded by God. The Lord's Prayer is not a legalistic model for slavish imitation, but it highlights principles relevant for the practice of prayer by each believer. It affirms a family awareness of God ("our Father") along with a concern for God to receive honor in today's world ("Hallowed be thy name"). It expresses an eschatological longing for the time when all human beings will acknowledge God as Lord ("Thy kingdom come"). It contains a petition for the necessities of physical life ("Give us today our daily bread") and for forgiveness. Forgiving others is not a means of earning divine forgiveness but an expression of the genuineness of personal repentance. The prayer, "bring us not into temptation," is a request for the stamina to endure temptation (James 1:2–4) and a warning against the swaggering attitude of Peter (Mark 14:29–31).

Scholars debate the relationship between the prayer in Matthew 6:9–13 and the one in Luke 11:2–4. All the content of the Lucan prayer appears in Matthew. Matthew's additional phrases appear to be more rhythmical, reflecting a possible usage Matthew found among Jewish Christians. It is also important to note that Matthew and Luke record the prayer's usage in two different historical settings. It is reasonable to suggest that Jesus used this prayer on multiple occasions and that Matthew and Luke simply record different instances of its use by Jesus.

Jesus stressed the value of fasting as a sign of repentance before God rather than as an effort to impress others with personal piety. He assumed that his disciples would continue to practice voluntary fasting based on spiritual interest and hunger.

Single-Minded Service to God (Matt. 6:19–34), Subsection 5. Jesus warned against covetousness and anxiety by appealing for loyalty to

God and trust in his compassionate care. Jesus almost personified the eye as a moral arbiter through which either good or evil could enter the body. He called for believers to live a life of devotion to God rather than being swamped by materialism. He also warned that worry was irrational (6:26), unproductive (6:27), and even pagan (6:31–32). He promised that God would supply physical needs for the follower who makes obedient discipleship his chief concern.

Avoiding Critical Attitudes and Spurious Discipleship (Matt. 7:1–8:1; Luke 6:31, 37–49), Subsections 6–8. Jesus prohibited a fault-finding, critical attitude, blind to personal failings. He did not exclude the need for value judgments toward other professing believers (see Matt. 7:6). The "mote" is a speck, and the "beam" is a log or rafter. Jesus urged believers to apply to themselves the insights they used so meticulously on others.

In 7:7–11 Jesus provided an argument from the lesser to the greater (known as a *fortiori*). He argued that if evil earthly parents give good things to their children, how much more will our heavenly Father give good things to those who persistently pray to him.

Jesus warned that true discipleship was a minority movement (Matt. 7:13–14) and urged his followers not to be led astray by false prophets, and to bring forth works that prove genuine discipleship (Matt. 7:15–20). He warned that his words would be used as the touchstone for future judgment of all human beings (Matt. 7:24; Luke 6:47), an indication that Jesus was more than a mere moral teacher.

Healing the Centurion's Servant
(Matt. 8:5–13; Luke 7:1–10) #55

The centurion represents a man whose race would have made him an outsider to God's purposes. Luke's account mentions that the centurion sent two delegations of Jews and friends to seek help from Jesus, but Matthew omitted this detail. The behavior of the centurion proved his moral earnestness (Luke 7:4–5), but he felt a sense of unworthiness in Jesus' presence. His military background provided an analogy for him to explain Jesus' power (Matt. 8:9). Jesus commended the presence of his practical, all-trusting faith. He used the incident to show that membership in God's kingdom was not exclusively a Jewish privilege but was open to believing Gentiles. Jesus demonstrated his power by healing the servant at a distance in response to the centurion's faith.

Raising the Widow's Son (Luke 7:11–17) #56

The presence of crowds shows the popularity of Jesus at this point in his ministry. The loss of an only child made the plight of the mother especially poignant. Jesus' action demonstrated his power and compassion. No one asked Jesus to help, but his sympathy for the mother's grief moved him to action (7:13). The healing inspired awe in the observers, but their response fell short of believing in him as the Messiah.

Jesus and John the Baptist (Matt. 11:2–19; Luke 7:18–35) #57

John's questions about Jesus were prompted by the difference between Jesus' actions and John's expectations (cf. Matt. 3:11–12 and 11:4–6). He also had his own questions about some of Jesus' practices (such as failing to fast in Matt. 9:14–15). Jesus acknowledged John as the promised forerunner of Malachi 3:1. He called him "great" in his own place within God's purpose, but John represented the last of the old order. God's purpose was leading to a new order, and John stood outside this new order. Even the least in this new order was greater in the divine purpose than the great man who proclaimed the new order but remained outside. The imprisonment and martyrdom of John the Baptist showed that violent men sometimes vigorously oppose the entrance of God's kingdom. Jesus rebuked the stubborn Jews for failing to respond either to the stern preacher John or to him the loving servant.

Warning and an Invitation (Matt. 11:20–30) #58

Jesus rebuked the cities that saw his mighty works but did not respond with faith in his message. Even without a verbal message, the residents of these cities should have realized that God was at work in Jesus.

God chose to reveal his message not to proud religious leaders but to the lowly and humble. Jesus invited burdened people to find rest in him. This rest comes not by shirking responsibility but by becoming a servant of Jesus, whose gentleness and meekness provide the rest.

True Worship of Jesus (Luke 7:36–8:3) #59–60

The other three Gospels tell the story of the sinful woman anointing Jesus (Matt. 26:6–13; Mark 14:3–9; John 12:1–8), but that story takes place in the last week of Jesus' life. This incident occurs much earlier in Luke and involves details absent from the other Gospels—such as wetting Jesus' feet with her tears.

The woman was present at the occasion because it was not uncommon for uninvited guests to enter a home and watch a dinner party in progress. The prostitute would have been an unwelcome onlooker, but she could easily have perfumed his feet because Jesus would likely have reclined horizontally on a cushion with his head toward the table. His feet would be stretched out behind him with the sandals removed. In his response to the woman, Jesus claimed to forgive her sins. This claim once again irritated his critics.

The women who followed Jesus in Luke 8:1–3 accompanied him on another tour through Galilee. Their financial support showed the proper spirit of response and worship to him. The Gospels never picture a woman taking malicious action against Jesus. His only enemies were stubborn men.

The Unpardonable Sin
(Matt. 12:22–37; Mark 3:19–30) #61

Matthew's account shows us that the charge against Jesus came in response to his miracle of healing and exorcising a blind, speechless man possessed with a devil. His accusers assumed that the exorcism and healing were empowered by Satan. Jesus first showed that their charge was illogical. If he cast out Satan by Satan, then Satan's kingdom was divided and could not long endure such internal strife. He next showed what his healing truly demonstrated (Mark 3:27). He was the strong man who bound Satan. Finally, he warned the Jewish religious leaders who had accused him of being in league with Satan. If they were so blind as to observe a good work and attribute it to evil power, then they had lost the ability to discern good from bad. If they were unable to discern good from bad, they could not identify their sin and would be unable to confess it. The sin would be unpardonable not because it extended beyond God's grace, but because their own stubbornness prevented them from seeing the evil in their deeds and attitudes.

The Sign of Jonah (Matt. 12:38–45) #62

Because Jesus had already performed many miracles, this request for an additional sign grew out of a closed mind rather than a search for truth. Jesus compared the coming passion of his death, burial, and resurrection to Jonah's three-day stay in the belly of the sea creature. Since Jesus was buried on Friday afternoon and arose on Sunday morning, he spent only about thirty-six hours in the tomb, not seventy-two. In computing time Jews counted any portion of a day on which an activity occurred as a single day. Jesus remained in the tomb for portions of Friday and Sunday and all of Saturday. According to Jewish reckoning this would be three days. Matthew elsewhere speaks of Jesus' arising "on the third day" (16:21) and "after three days" (27:63). To Matthew these two terms must have had the same meaning.

Spiritual Kinship
(Matt. 12:46–50; Mark 3:31–35; Luke 8:19–21) #63

Jesus' family could not approach him because of the crowds surrounding him. When he received the report that his mother and brothers wanted to see him, he responded that his genuine relatives were those who did God's will. Fellowship with God is not based on physical relationship but on spiritual obedience.

The Kingdom of God in the New Testament: An Excursus

All three synoptic Gospels emphasize that the theme of the preaching and teaching of Jesus was the kingdom of God. The phrase "kingdom of God" occurs frequently in Mark and Luke but only four times in Matthew. Matthew used kingdom of heaven, but the two terms are interchangeable (Matt. 19:23–24; cf. with Mark 10:23). Matthew's usage may reflect a tendency to avoid the divine name out of deference to the Jews who considered such usage a desecration.

The primary meaning of the term *kingdom* relates to reign or rule. The kingdom of God is the reign or rule of God over all. This idea is common in the Old Testament (Ps. 145:11, 13). Occasionally the term is also used in the New Testament as a reference to the realm over which a king ruled.

The New Testament suggests that the kingdom (the reign or rule of God) was already present in the person and works of Jesus (Matt. 12:28). However, this kingdom also has an eschatological component, for it is an event to be experienced completely only in the future (see Mark 9:47; 10:23–25).

When Jesus spoke of the coming of the kingdom of God (Matt. 4:17), he was referring to the fact that God was visiting the earth to establish a new order. This present age is a time of sinfulness, evil, and rebellion against God. In the age to come God will perfectly establish his rule and remove all sin and evil. This process of the defeat of evil is already underway through the person and work of Christ (Luke 17:20), but the complete victory will be achieved only in the age to come (Rev. 12:10). When Jesus spoke of the "mystery of the kingdom" (Mark 4:11), he was referring to the fact that the kingdom of God had already appeared on earth before its full manifestation at the return of Christ. Believers can already enjoy the present blessings of this future kingdom (Eph. 1:14).

Jesus initially addressed the Jews in his preaching and offered them the reign of God on the basis of repentance and faith in Jesus (Mark 1:15). The rejection of this offer by most of the Jews resulted in God's transfer of his kingdom to the church (Matt. 21:42–43). The church and the kingdom are not identical. The kingdom refers to the rule of God, and the church represents those people who have received the kingdom in Jesus and witness to its blessings. Israel has not been permanently removed from the experience of divine blessings, but after the completion of the divine purpose among the Gentiles, Jewish people will again be brought back into the divine plan (see this figure in Paul's discussion of the "natural" and "grafted" branches in Rom. 11:19–24).[2]

---

2. For further discussion of the kingdom, its nature, and its relationship to Jesus, see G. R. Beasley-Murray, *Jesus and the Kingdom of God* (Grand Rapids: William B. Eerdmans Publishing Co., 1986); G. E. Ladd, *Crucial Questions About the Kingdom of God* (Grand Rapids: William B. Eerdmans Publishing Co., 1952); *The Gospel of the Kingdom* (Grand Rapids: William B. Eerdmans Publishing Co., 1961); and *The Presence of the Future* (Grand Rapids: William B. Eerdmans Publishing Co., 1974).

The Parables of the Kingdom

The New Testament uses the term *parable* to refer to metaphors (Mark 7:14–17) and analogies (Mark 3:23–27) as well as stories (Mark 4:1–9). The popular understanding is that a parable is a story from daily life used to illustrate a spiritual truth, but the actual usage of the term in the New Testament is more complicated.

Early interpreters used allegory as a method of understanding the parables. At the beginning of the twentieth century Adolph Julicher insisted that a parable could contain only a single teaching point and that other details were simply background information. Contemporary interpreters realize that parables often contain details with hidden symbolism and allow for openness to an allegorical understanding of some features (notice that Jesus used some allegory in interpreting the parable of the sower in Mark 4:3–9, 14–20).

A key issue in discussing parables is understanding their purpose. Jesus discussed this in Mark 4:11–12, but the interpretation of this passage is much disputed. Doubtless, Jesus used parables in order to present his teaching vividly and memorably, but Mark suggested that Jesus also sought to conceal truth as well as to reveal it. The passage does not suggest that Jesus deliberately tried to be vague, but it indicates that Jesus' use of parables confronted people with radical demands about himself. Some who heard those demands refused to comply and were driven further from the kingdom. The responsibility for this opposition belongs to the hearers whose volitional choices kept them from listening to Jesus' demands. Jesus deliberately used parables to clarify the exclusive nature of the call to follow him. Much of Jesus' teaching about the kingdom appeared in parabolic form.[3]

The Parable of the Sower (Matt. 13:1–23; Mark 4:1–25; Luke 8:4–18), #64, Introduction and Subsection 1a. Although huge crowds

---

3. For a valuable introduction to the entire issue of the understanding and interpretation of parables, see R. H. Stein, *An Introduction to the Parables of Jesus* (Philadelphia: Westminster Press, 1981). For a more recent thorough discussion, see Craig L. Blomberg, *Interpreting the Parables* (Downers Grove, Ill.: InterVarsity Press, 1990). For extensive information about the background of parables, see J. Jeremias, *The Parables of Jesus* (New York: Scribner's, 1963). C. F. D. Moule discusses the use of parables in other New Testament writings in "The Use of Parables and Sayings as Illustrative Material in Early Christian Catechesis," in *Essays in New Testament Interpretation* (Cambridge: Cambridge University Press, 1982), 50–53.

gathered to hear Jesus teach (Mark 4:1), he knew that spiritual interest had not driven all of them to listen to him. Jesus wanted to challenge his listeners to apply his message to their lives (4:9), but he also wanted to explain to his disciples why listeners such as the scribes and the Pharisees resisted his message. This parable gives the answer. It is not the message of Jesus that guarantees a response, but rather, the spiritual heart of the listener dictates the nature of the response to the message.

The seed represents the gospel message proclaimed by Jesus. The soil represents the various types of hearers in the world. It is not merely a reference to a member of the church. Palestinian farmers sowed seed without regard to the type of soil on which it fell. Then they plowed the seed under the soil. The hard soil would not allow the seed to penetrate and represented a response in which Satan snatched away the seed before it could bear fruit. The thin, rocky soil let the seed sprout quickly only to cause it to die because it could not penetrate the rock. This soil represented a superficial response that could not endure persecution or hardship. The soil with thorns and weeds sprouted plants that choked the good seed. This described a person whose worldly interests crowded out the word of God. The good soil represented a person who received the gospel message and responded with joyful results. The first three types of soil do not represent believing responses to the message because the recipient did not endure (see Mark 13:13 which describes "endurance" as an identifying badge of the Christian).

Parable of the Growing Seed (Mark 4:26–29), #64, Subsection 1b. This parable explains how God's kingdom will come into the world. Just as the seed grows and develops without help from the farmer, so God's kingdom will not come by human effort or accomplishment. In Jesus' day rabbis tried to bring about the kingdom by obedience to the law. Revolutionaries attempted insurrection to overthrow the established order and install the kingdom. Jesus insisted that only God himself would inaugurate the kingdom.

The Mustard Seed and the Leaven (Matt. 13:31–35; Mark 4:30–34), #64, Subsections 1d–e. Jesus' disciples seem to have expected the establishment of the messianic kingdom in their lifetime as implied in the selfish request of James and John (see Mark 10:35–40). The small beginnings and snail-like progress of the kingdom were beyond their patience or understanding. Jesus emphasized that the kingdom would begin almost imperceptibly but would grow into an all-encompassing movement. The growth of the mustard seed into a tree large enough to hold nesting birds illustrated this principle.

Jesus illustrated the same feature in the parable of the leaven. Three measures of meal were enough to prepare bread for one hundred people. A small amount of yeast placed in the meal would eventually penetrate the entire amount of dough. Similarly the kingdom, though infinitesimally small in its beginning, would ultimately dominate the entire earth.[4]

The Hidden Treasure and the Pearl of Great Price (Matt. 13:44–46), #64, Subsection 2b–c. Both the hidden treasure and the pearl represent the indescribable worth of the kingdom. In the parable of the treasure Jesus focused on the joy that the finder had upon discovering the treasure and his willingness to sacrifice everything to obtain it. Jesus commended the joyful abandonment of everything for the sake of the kingdom. The merchant found a pearl so valuable that it made all other currencies worthless by comparison. Jesus commended the prudent sacrifice of this merchant as the type of response we must make to participate in God's kingdom.

The Wheat and the Tares and the Net (Matt. 13:24–30, 36–43, 47–50), #64, Subsection 1c, 2a, 2d. The parable of the wheat and the tares refers to the entire world rather than to the church alone (Matt. 13:38). Jesus was not speaking about the character of the church but about the coexistence of God's kingdom with Satan's kingdom in the world. The good seed and the tares are now inextricably mixed, but their different origins and destinations will become apparent in the final judgment.

The parable of the net makes the same point. The seine nets trapped both clean and unclean creatures in their sweep. The

---

4. Interpreters differ over their understanding of the birds (Matt. 13:32; Mark 4:32) and the leaven (Matt. 13:33). As indicated in the discussion, the reference to the birds may indicate the size of the mustard plant, but sometimes the term has a derogatory connotation, as in the baker's dream in Gen. 40:19. In this passage, however, the birds are not birds of prey, but are more like the birds of Nebuchadnezzar's dream in Dan. 4:12, 14 and serve as indicators of the size of the tree.

The leaven or yeast is sometimes used as a symbol for evil (see Mark 8:15), but it can have more than one meaning in Scripture. Here its use shows pervasiveness, a feature the kingdom of God will ultimately accomplish.

unclean fish lacked scales or fins. Jesus indicated that just as the fishermen separated the clean from the unclean, so will God's angels separate the "evil from the righteous" in the final judgment.

The Parable of the Householder (Matt. 13:51–53), #64, Subsection 2e. Jesus concluded the parables in Matthew with a challenge to his disciples to serve as scribes of the kingdom of heaven and bring out old and new treasures in order to instruct other followers of Christ. Perhaps the terms "old" and "new" refer to the fact that Jesus' teaching is grounded in the eternal truths of God "the old" now brought to light in a new, revolutionary way.

The Stilling of the Storm
(Matt. 8:18, 23–27; Mark 4:35–41; Luke 8:22–25) #65

This event demonstrates the sovereignty of our Lord over nature (cf. Mark 6:41–44; 8:6–9 for the same emphasis). Mark's account possesses many eye-witness details such as the reference to the "other boats" (v. 36), Jesus' sleeping in the stern on a pillow (v. 38), and the words of Jesus as he calmed the sea (v. 39). Jesus demonstrated his humanity by his weariness and his deity by bringing a great calm with the spoken word. Jesus' supernatural power produced fear in the disciples, for they seemed to relate better to the humanity of Jesus than to his divinity (see this same reaction in Mark 9:2–6 at the transfiguration).

The Gadarene Demoniac
(Matt. 8:28–34; Mark 5:1–20; Luke 8:26–39) #66

Matthew mentions two demoniacs, but Mark and Luke focus on only one of these pitiful creatures. The biblical texts have different readings for the location of the incident. Gerasa was a Roman city at least thirty miles from the sea, but Gadara was a smaller town six miles away. Matthew probably refers to Gadara while Mark refers to Gerasa. One locates the incident by the nearest large city, while the other locates it near a closer small town. Both convey accurate information.

None of the human treatment offered to this man brought any healing (Mark 5:3–5). The demons instantly understood Jesus' nature and recognized the gulf between them and him (Mark 5:7). A Roman legion normally contained six thousand men, but the number (Mark 5:9) need not suggest that six thousand demons possessed the man. This statistic does suggest that Satan completely controlled the man. Sending the demons into the herd of swine was an outward sign that convinced the bystanders of the reality of the exorcism. The herdsmen scattered in fright from Jesus' supernatural power, but residents from nearby later saw the man clothed and sensible. Terrified by Jesus' power and perhaps by the financial loss, they begged him to leave. To their everlasting detriment he honored their requests.

Jesus denied the request of the former demoniac to accompany him. He assigned him a ministry of witness, and the man proclaimed the Lord's mighty power throughout the area. Since the surrounding area was Gentile, the witness of the man would not lead to messianic excitement and new difficulties for Jesus. His presence assured a continued witness in an area of desperate need, where curious people were probably asking questions about Jesus.

Miracles of Healing and Raising to Life
(Matt. 9:18–26; Mark 5:21–43; Luke 8:40–56) #67

The woman with the constant flow of blood was an outcast from society, separated from social contacts even with family and forbidden from worship in the temple (see Lev. 15:19–33). Spending her money on physicians brought no relief but only an aggravation of her problems. Her knowledge of Jesus' works and her sense of need (Mark 5:27) drew her to Christ. Her remarkable faith was revealed in her firm belief that if she could only touch Jesus' robe she would be healed.

Jesus' response (Mark 5:30) suggests that the flow of healing power to the woman cost him spiritual energy. His disciples rebuked him (note their arrogance here as in Mark 6:37!) for asking, "Who touched me?" However, the woman responded by confessing before the entire crowd with great humility both her need and experience of healing. Jesus commended her faith and thus differentiated her response from mere superstition. His acknowledgment of her healing before the crowd would have brought her acceptance after twelve years of rejection.

Jairus had also come to Jesus with faith that if Jesus laid his hands on his daughter she would be healed. Mark and Luke gave longer accounts and indicated that the daughter died while Jesus journeyed to her house. Matthew omitted the details in the other Gospels, abbreviated the account, and indicated that she was already dead when Jairus approached Jesus.

The brief stop to heal the woman with the issue of blood must have been agonizing for Jairus, but Jesus knew that delay would not hinder his ability to carry out God's will in Jairus's home. Jesus described the dead girl as "asleep," for he knew that he would awaken her. His description caused a faithless ridicule from the crowd in the home, and Jesus excluded them from viewing the miracle. Jesus' touch brought the girl to life. Jesus requested that she eat to add further proof of the reality that her life was restored.

Healing the Blind and the Speechless
(Matt. 9:27–34) #68

Matthew alone contains these two miracles. The contrast between them shows that Jesus' miracles caused either wonder or contempt, depending on the viewpoint of the observer.

Jesus apparently did not respond immediately to the request of the two blind men, but their persistence led to their healing. Jesus tried to prevent misguided enthusiasm by ordering them to secrecy, but it would be hard for formerly blind men to keep quiet!

In the second miracle demon possession had made the possessed person mute. The response of the multitudes to Jesus' exorcism showed that the official religious leaders of the nation had no authority such as Jesus had. Criticism by the Pharisees indicates the mounting opposition to Jesus' work.

Rejection at Nazareth
(Matt. 13:54–58; Mark 6:1–6; Luke 4:16–30) #39, 69

Luke 4:16–30 chronologically belongs with the above sections in Matthew and Luke. Luke likely arranged the incident in topical order.

In the synagogue in Nazareth Jesus followed Jewish custom by standing to read Scripture and by sitting to explain it. Two features of his message angered the people: his insistence that he was the

Servant of the Lord who spoke in Isaiah 61:1–2; his suggestion that God would pass over a rebellious Israel and give his blessings to the Gentiles (Luke 4:25–27). The residents remembered him as a hometown boy and were unable to see supernatural power in him.

Jesus quoted a Semitic proverb to indicate that the only place where he could not be acclaimed was in his hometown. He could help only those humbled enough by their pain and sickness to receive the healing he offered.

Sending Out the Twelve
(Matt. 9:35–11:1; Mark 6:6–13; Luke 9:1–6) #70

Jesus' request for prayer for laborers presents a binding challenge for today's disciples. The laborers represent disciples sent to rescue people from the coming judgment. Jesus sent his own disciples as an immediate practical solution to the need for laborers.

The account in Matthew does not narrate the selection of the disciples but rather, their commission for service. Matthew 10:5–15 relates more to the immediate mission of the disciples, and the remainder of the chapter describes the ultimate mission of Christians in the world. Jesus' instructions to them emphasized the priority of a mission to Israel. They were to travel in haste without encumbering possessions and were to depend on God for their provisions.[5] They could expect both acceptance and rejection.

The instructions in Matthew 10:16–42 leap ahead to the mission of Christians and contain encouragement for facing and overcoming persecution. Jesus reminded believers that they could expect the same treatment he received (Matt. 10:24–25).

The Irrational Fear of Herod Antipas
(Matt. 14:1–12; Mark 6:14–29; Luke 9:7–9) #71

When Herod Antipas heard of Jesus' miracles, he feared that John, whom he had beheaded, had risen from the dead to perform

---

5. Matthew and Mark contain differences in specifying the equipment allowed for the traveling disciples. Matt. 10:10 prohibits a staff, and Mark 6:8 permits one. Since the staff was normally essential for the journey, perhaps Matthew is banning the securing of an extra staff beyond the one they already own. The same insight might explain the permission of sandals in Mark 6:9 and their banning in Matt. 10:10. Matthew may have banned procuring an extra pair so that the disciples could travel easily in haste.

them. Even Herod had enough theological understanding to recognize that the miracles Jesus was performing were the logical, even necessary, deduction from a resurrection.

John's condemnation of Herod's immoral behavior brought imprisonment from the monarch who could not tolerate such open opposition in his domain. Herodias waited her time to perpetrate the death of the Baptist. The opportunity came when Herod made a rash promise to his stepdaughter Salome[6] at his birthday celebration. When Salome's request involved the murder of John, Herod granted her wish to prevent losing face with his courtiers.

Feeding the Five Thousand (Matt. 14:13–23; Mark 6:30–46; Luke 9:10–17; John 6:1–15) #72–73

The feeding of the five thousand was a turning point in Jesus' ministry. After this time his popularity with the masses declined, and he devoted more of his time to instructing the disciples. The impressive and crucially important nature of this miracle provides an explanation for its appearance in all four Gospels.

Several features of the feeding led the Jewish audience to recognize messianic overtones in the event. The incident occurred at the time of the Passover, the period when Jews expected the Messiah to appear (John 6:4). The Jews also expected the Messiah to repeat Moses' Old Testament manna miracle by feeding them at a great future banquet (see evidence for this expectation from the discussion in John 6:30–35). After the miracle the Jews attempted to make Jesus into a Messiah according to their military-political pattern. Jesus rejected their advances and withdrew to a mountain to pray. Rejecting the aspirations of the crowd led ultimately to the decline in his popularity (John 6:66).

Jesus' actions in this miracle are similar to his actions at the last supper (cf. Mark 6:41 and Mark 14:22–25). However, the chief purpose of the Gospel writers is not to compare the feeding with the observance of the Supper but to describe a miracle.

---

6. Her name does not appear in Scripture, but Josephus named her as the daughter of Herodias by her first husband in *Antiquities* 18.5.4.

Walking on the Water
(Matt. 14:24–36; Mark 6:47–56; John 6:16–21) #74–75

This incident occurred during the "fourth watch of the night," the period from approximately 3:00–6:00 A.M. The groggy, super-stitious disciples could easily have felt that Jesus' shadowy outline was a ghost. Peter's response to Jesus (Matt. 14:28–31) represents an example of true faith which did not survive through a crisis of temptation. The response of the disciples to Jesus (Matt. 14:33) prepares the way for Peter's fuller confession in Matthew 16:16.

The Bread of Life (John 6:22–71) #76

When the crowds sought Jesus on the day after the feeding of the five thousand, Jesus accused them of showing interest only because he had filled their stomachs (John 6:26). They failed to recognize that the miracle portrayed Jesus as the true bread of life, a fact that Jesus explained to them (John 6:35). His explanation caused discontent among his listeners (John 6:41). Jesus' appeal for the listeners to "eat his flesh" and "drink his blood" (John 6:53–54) demanded that they receive by faith the benefits of his sacrificial death. The response of the multitudes revealed a rejection of Jesus' personal mission (John 6:60–66). However, the disciples, with Peter as their spokesman, saw a believing response to Jesus as their only hope for eternal life.

The Tradition of the Elders
(Matt. 15:1–20; Mark 7:1–23; John 7:1) #77

The Pharisees were on a fact-finding mission to investigate the activities of Jesus. They accused Jesus' disciples of violating rab-binic tradition by eating bread with hands not washed in the proper rabbinic tradition. This was not an accusation of inadequate hygiene!

Jesus responsed by accusing the Pharisees of hypocrisy and of fol-lowing human tradition rather than the divine commandment. To illustrate his charge, he denounced their practice of *corban*. The law commanded that children honor their parents, but Jewish leaders had devised a scheme to avoid the obligation of supporting needy parents by dedicating money or property to God for a future offer-ing. It then became impossible for them to use income so designated to support their parents. In the meantime the child could use the proceeds from the money or property for personal benefit. This practice of corban legitimized selfish behavior and was based only on human tradition.

Jesus warned his disciples that the primary source of evil was internal, from within the evil of the human heart. Ceremonial defilement was of little concern to God. Mark added in 7:19b that Jesus' comment abolished the distinction between clean and unclean foods.

The Faith of the Syro-Phoenician Woman
(Matt. 15:21–28; Mark 7:24–30) #78

Jesus' previous activity had been in Galilee, but he now withdrew into the area of Tyre and Sidon. Information on Jesus' miraculous activity had reached this area, and the desperate mother came with a request for Jesus. Jesus' comment in Mark 7:27 probably represented a popular proverb and not his opinion. He used the comment to lead the woman to recognize that her only hope for help lay in casting herself, Gentile though she was, on God's great mercy. The woman gladly accepted her position as an outsider and claimed healing for her daughter. Jesus' reply highlighted the depth of her faith (Matt. 15:28).

Healing a Deaf Man and Feeding the Four Thousand
(Matt. 15:29–38; Mark 7:31–8:9) #79

The miracle in Mark 7:31–37 took place in the Decapolis, a predominantly Gentile area. In this miracle Jesus opened the ears of the deaf man. He showed the man what he was doing by "putting his fingers into his ears," spitting, and touching his tongue; and glancing upward toward heaven in prayer. In these actions Jesus described to the man his need and the source of his healing in a sign language he could understand. The crowd marveled at Jesus' miracle, but still failed to understand his true nature.

The feeding of the four thousand contains too many differences from the previous feeding to be a variant account of the same incident. This miracle was a response by Jesus to the hunger of a crowd that had followed him for three days. The disciples apparently failed to learn from the first miracle that limited resources did not hinder Jesus' ability to perform miracles. The baskets containing the leftovers from this miracle were flexible bags, the same type used to lower Paul over the wall in Acts 9:25. The baskets used to hold the leftovers in the earlier feeding miracle were stiff wicker baskets. Also, the number of leftover baskets differed from that of the first miracle of feeding. Furthermore, the two incidents occurred on two different shores of the Sea of Galilee (seen most clearly in Mark 8:10). The disciples' response in Matthew 15:33 would seem unusual if they had seen an earlier miracle. We can account for their spiritual obtuseness by realizing that they were slow to recognize religious truth from Jesus (see their response in Matt. 16:5–12).

Some scholars contend that this miracle (also in Mark 8:1–9) is a duplicate account of the feeding of the five thousand in Matthew 14:13–21, a literary feature known as a doublet. They believe that there was only one miracle of feeding, not two. Since this incident occurred in Gentile territory, some suggest that Mark included it to affirm that Gentiles as well as Jews will share in the Messianic banquet. Against this alteration of history for the purpose of making a theological point is Jesus' reference to two such miraculous incidents (see Matt. 16:9–11 and Mark 8:17–19).

Messianic Signs (Matt. 15:39–16:4; Mark 8:10–12) #80

The Pharisees and the Sadducees formed an unholy alliance to take joint action against Jesus. Jesus credited them with the intelligence to discern the signs of changing weather but castigated their failure to recognize the signs of the Messiah already at work in his ministry. The works which they questioned and rejected were a sufficient sign of the divine nature of his ministry (see Matt. 11:4–6).

The Leaven of the Pharisees and the Sadducees (Matt. 16:5–12; Mark 8:13–26) #81

Jesus rebuked the lack of spiritual perception among the disciples, but the very preservation of this story suggests that the disciples applied the lesson to themselves. The leaven of the Pharisees was hypocrisy (see Mark 7:6). The leaven of Herod (leaven of the "Sadducees" in Matt. 16:6) is likely a reference to worldly self-seeking. The mention of the two feedings in Mark 8:19–20 is added evidence for their historicity.

The healing of the blind man in Mark 8:22–26 is the only example of a gradual healing performed by Jesus. Jesus' healing actions in this miracle constituted an acted parable with the purpose of drawing the attention of the man to what Jesus would perform.

Peter's Confession of Jesus' Messiahship (Matt. 16:13–20; Mark 8:27–30; Luke 9:18–21) #82

This section represents the clearest messianic declaration by Jesus up to this point in his ministry, although much of his previous teaching clearly moved in this direction. Peter's answer to Jesus' question shows that the disciples' grasp of Jesus' messianic role had progressed far beyond the nationalistic understanding of the general public, and that Peter understood something about Jesus' special relationship with God.

Jesus' statement in Matthew 16:18 played on the meaning of Peter's name, "rock" or "stone." The metaphor was more a description of Peter's function than his character. Peter was a foundation stone for the early church; he was not being installed as the first "pope." He was representative of the entire apostolic group (see the same metaphor applied to all the apostles in Eph. 2:20). Some interpret the truth of Peter's confession as the rock or Jesus himself as the rock, as distinguished from Peter. "The gates of Hades" refers to the power of death. Jesus affirmed that the process of death would not exterminate the church.

The keys of the kingdom do not represent authority to regulate admission into the church. Nor are they a reference to the binding and loosing of Satan (despite the fact that "binding" is sometimes used in reference to Satan; see Mark 3:27). Binding and loosing represent the right of the church on earth to determine and apply decisions previously made in heaven. Peter exercised this authority when he pioneered the extension of the gospel to Gentile converts (see Acts 10:1–11:18). Ultimately, the authority to bind and loose belongs to the entire church in extending forgiveness to those whom God has pardoned (see Matt. 18:18).

Jesus had to silence the public proclamation of these messianic insights by the disciples because of their inadequate grasp of his messianic role. Peter's response illustrates this deficient view (Matt. 16:22–23).

Predicting the Passion and Bearing the Cross (Matt. 16:21–26; Mark 8:31–37; Luke 9:22–25) #83

After Jesus' first prediction of his passion, Peter revealed his misunderstanding of Jesus' role by giving him a public rebuke. Jesus' stern response to Peter shows that Satan was attempting to use Peter's logical but spiritually erroneous words to divert Jesus from the cross.

Christians have written so idealistically about the cross that Jesus' appeal to "take up the cross" has lost much of its harsh demand. A man condemned to crucifixion carried the horizontal piece of the cross to the site of execution through crowds of mocking, cursing people. For Christians, the cross represents a risk or danger to which we expose ourselves because of our commitment to Christ. Taking up the cross is a decision we must make, and God will provide us many opportunities in our lives to make that choice.

The Transfiguration (Matt. 16:27–17:8; Mark 8:38–9:8; Luke 9:26–36) #84–85

The story of the Transfiguration follows immediately after Jesus' promise that some of those "standing by" would not die before the "kingdom of God had come with power." Since some of the disciples witnessed the Transfiguration, it seems best to suggest that Jesus saw this event as a fulfillment of his promise.

The references to "six days" (Matt. 17:1; Mark 9:2) and "eight days" (Luke 9:28) indicate about a week of time. The Transfiguration was an open display for the disciples of the glory Jesus had before the Incarnation. The event strengthened the flickering faith of the disciples, whose awareness of Jewish opposition was striking terror in their hearts.

John the Baptist and Elijah (Matt. 17:9–13; Mark 9:9–13; Luke 9:36) #86

The question about the appearance of Elijah in the vision of the Transfiguration showed that the disciples were taking seriously the messiahship of Jesus, but also shows that they were interpreting the

Old Testament prediction of Elijah's appearance prior to the Messiah (Mal. 4:5) in a rigidly literal way. They felt that Elijah must somehow come in a bodily form. Jesus' answer to them pointed out that Elijah had already appeared in the ministry and work of John the Baptist.

Faith and Deliverance
(Matt. 17:14–23; Mark 9:14–32; Luke 9:37–45) #87–88

Jesus' words to the crowd (Mark 9:16) were an effort to draw their attention from the failure of the disciples to the power he could offer. The boy's condition resembled epilepsy, but Jesus' response indicated that the power of evil had somehow gripped him. In bringing deliverance, Jesus challenged both the father and the disciples to greater faith and ardent prayer (Mark 9:19, 29). The father's confession of the emptiness of his faith made contact with the riches of Christ's grace (Mark 9:24–25). Jesus' second prediction of his passion reminded the disciples that he was a suffering Messiah rather than a conquering Messiah.

Payment of the Temple Tax (Matt. 17:24–27) #89

Most adult Jewish males paid an annual half-shekel tax for the upkeep of the Jerusalem temple, whether they resided in Jerusalem or not. Paying this tax was a matter of patriotic pride for most of the Jews.

The inquiry to Peter was an effort to determine whether Jesus followed the conventional Jewish practice or an independent path. Jesus argued that since the tax was God's tax, he was technically exempt from it as God's son. However, he put aside his right of exemption in order not to offend the authorities and damage the mission for which he was sent. Jesus sent Peter to obtain the shekel through a miraculous provision and pay it to the proper authorities. Jesus' response illustrates the principle of foregoing rights and privileges in order to allow a ministry to have a wider sphere of influence (cf. 1 Cor. 9:19–23).

Discipleship and Forgiveness
(Matt. 18:1–35; Mark 9:33–50; Luke 9:46–50) #90–92

Jesus presented instructions about discipleship and humility in order to spotlight the self-seeking strife erupting among the disciples (Mark 9:33–34). The child Jesus called to come to him (Matt. 18:2) symbolized a disciple. Jesus' reference to the child did not commend any particular childish trait such as innocence or trustfulness. Rather, he said that a true disciple must appropriate the lowly status of a child instead of adopting a pattern of self-seeking. To "humble oneself" does not demand a phony modesty but the acceptance of an inferior position (just as Jesus did, according to Phil. 2:8). Jesus warned his listeners that they must exert every effort to overcome any sin or habit which could cause another believer to stumble (Matt. 18:7–8). Mark vividly warned that by tripping a struggling believer one thereby showed that he was lost and could expect eternal punishment (Mark 9:43–50).

The fact that the commands of Matthew 18:15 are singular suggest that they relate more to rescuing a sinning believer than to bringing discipline in the church. Discipline, however, in the final analysis might be necessary. Jesus suggested the following steps in the rescue of an erring believer:

1. a private conference;

2. a conference with several witnesses;

3. consideration of the issue before the entire church.

Peter's request in Matthew 18:21 may be paraphrased, "How many times must I forgive my brother when he sins against me? Won't seven times be enough?" Jesus' answer called for unlimited forgiveness.

The parable of the unmerciful servant illustrated this appeal for unlimited forgiveness. The debt of the servant was beyond human imagination. The talent was the largest unit of currency. Ten thousand was the highest Greek number. We might paraphrase the amount as ten billion dollars. To dream that he could repay it was an illusion (Matt. 18:26). The forgiveness of the king illustrates the greatness of God's mercy in offering forgiveness. The paltry debt owed to the servant by his fellow servant amounted to seventeen or eighteen dollars. The stone-hearted response of the lender was to throw his fellow servant into prison. When the king was informed of this financial brutality, he reversed his decision and threw the lender into prison until he could pay all—an utter impossibility.

The point is that we are to forgive others because God has forgiven us. Those who fail to forgive others reveal their own failure to understand and receive divine forgiveness. We forgive others not because they deserve it but because God has graciously forgiven us (Eph. 4:32).

An Appeal for Discipleship
(Matt. 8:19–22; Luke 9:57–62) #93

Luke's story has the most complete account of Jesus' contact with three prospective disciples who lacked whole-heartedness.

- The first candidate had not counted the cost, and Jesus challenged him with the demands of discipleship.

- The second lacked a sense of urgency, and Jesus indicated that following him took precedence even over urgent family responsibilities.

- The third wanted to procrastinate, and Jesus warned that the kingdom had no place for the would-be follower who looked backward when called to move forward.

To Jerusalem for the Feast of Tabernacles
(Luke 9:51–56; John 7:2–10) #94–95

Jesus' brothers showed their unbelief by their failure to grasp the nature of his mission. They reasoned that he could recruit added followers by a spectacular miraculous display at the well-attended Feast of Tabernacles. Jesus knew that he would show his true glory in the humiliation of the Crucifixion. He refused to regulate his activities by their worldly suggestions, and when he did go to Jerusalem, his travel was private and secret.

For Further Discussion

1. Were Jesus' activities on the Sabbath a violation of divine law?

2. Explain why Jesus performed miracles.

3. What was Jesus' purpose in speaking about cutting off a right hand which leads to sin?

4. In what sense must our righteousness exceed the righteousness of the scribes and the Pharisees?

5. Can an individual commit the unpardonable sin today?

6. Present and discuss evidence that the Twelve grew in their spiritual understanding of Jesus' person and work.

Bibliography

Carson, D. A. *The Gospel According to John*. Grand Rapids: William B. Eerdmans Publishing Co., 1991.

Cole, R. Alan. *Mark*. TNTC. Rev. ed. Grand Rapids: William B. Eerdmans Publishing Co., 1989.

Ellis, E. Earle. *Luke*. NCB. Rev. ed. Grand Rapids: William B. Eerdmans Publishing Co., 1981.

France, R. T. *Matthew*. TNTC. Grand Rapids: William B. Eerdmans Publishing Co., 1985.

Geldenhuys, Norval. *Commentary on the Gospel of Luke*. NICNT. Grand Rapids: William B. Eerdmans Publishing Co., 1951.

Hill, David. *Matthew*. NCB. Grand Rapids: William B. Eerdmans Publishing Co., 1981.

Morris, Leon. *Luke*. TNTC. Rev. ed. Grand Rapids: William B. Eerdmans Publishing Co., 1988.

Tasker, R. V. G. *John*. TNTC. Grand Rapids: William B. Eerdmans Publishing Co., 1960.

10 The Later Judean and the Perean Ministry

Guiding Questions

1. List the events that took place in the later Judean ministry of Jesus according to John's Gospel.

2. List and describe the message of the parables of Jesus which appear in Luke's Gospel during this section of his ministry.

3. What evidence do you see in Luke's Gospel to indicate that the content is listed topically more than chronologically?

4. Explain how the rich young ruler demonstrated his unwillingness to repent.

This section of Jesus' ministry is narrated largely by John and Luke. John primarily described Jesus' ministry in Jerusalem, and Luke focused on Jesus' ministry in Judea and en route to Jerusalem. Matthew and Mark also present information about the concluding section of Jesus' travels to Jerusalem. Luke's narrative is a travel document in which Jesus is moving from Judea to Jerusalem (Luke 9:51–56), but the material is loosely connected and is not intended to be a complete chronological account of all of Jesus' travels.[1]

---

1. For a discussion of the relationship between Luke 9:51–18:14 and John 7:2–11:54, see note #10 in Robertson's *Harmony*, 276–79.

Jesus' Discourse at the Feast of Tabernacles (John 7:11–52) #96

Jesus' absence from the Feast of Tabernacles led people to speculate about him. Some, probably impressed by his miracles of compassion, viewed him as a "good man," but others accused him of deception. If the authorities could prove that his deceptions were blasphemy, they could execute him.

Jewish religious leaders accused Jesus of lacking instruction from an acknowledged rabbinic authority; Jesus claimed that the Father was his teacher. He insisted that those who did the Father's will would know the truthfulness of his teaching (John 7:14–18).

Jewish opposition to Jesus developed because he healed the invalid man at the pool of Bethesda on the Sabbath (John 5:1–9). In his defense Jesus explained his Sabbath actions. Jews were accustomed to practicing circumcision on a male child on the eighth day after birth even if that day was the Sabbath. They elevated the law of circumcision over the Sabbath law. Jesus pointed out that if circumcision affecting only part of the body was acceptable on the Sabbath, how much more desirable was a healing that affected the entire body (John 7:19–24).

Some residents of Jerusalem rejected Jesus as the Messiah because they knew of his early childhood in Nazareth, and they believed that the origin of the real Messiah would be a mystery. Their view about Jesus was truer than they knew, for they were unaware that Jesus had been born in Bethlehem. Jesus responded to them by asserting that the Father had sent him (John 7:25–31). When Jesus promised that he was going away, some Jews speculated that he would settle among Diaspora Jews and teach Gentiles (John 7:32–36).

During the Feast of Tabernacles priests carried a golden pitcher filled with water from the Pool of Siloam to the temple for a water-pouring ceremony. It symbolized God's bestowal of physical and spiritual provision for his people. This ceremony continued for seven days, but it was suspended on the climactic day of the feast.[2]

---

2. The Mishnaic passages that discuss this rite appear in C. K. Barrett, *The New Testament Background: Selected Documents*, rev. ed. (London: SPCK, 1987), 199–201.

On that day Jesus presented himself as the true source of life for the people—a reference to the Holy Spirit (John 7:37–39).

Jesus' claims in 7:37–39 created a division among the people. Some identified him as the Messiah, but others denied his messiahship because they felt that he was from Galilee and not from Bethlehem (according to Mic. 5:2). Only their ignorance kept them from learning the truth of Jesus' birth in Bethlehem. Notice also that this passage reflects divergent views among the Jews about the Messiah's birth. Some felt that his origin would be unknown (John 7:27), and others looked for his birth in Bethlehem (John 7:40–44). The authorities as well as the people were divided over who Jesus was.

An Adulteress Brought to Jesus (John 7:53–8:11) #97

Scholars generally agree that John did not include this event in his Gospel. The most accurate manuscripts of the Greek New Testament, which were undiscovered when the King James Version was published in 1611, omit this section. Other later manuscripts place the material either after Luke 21:38, after John 7:36, 44, or at the end of John's Gospel. In its current location the passage might be an illustration of Jesus' words in 8:15, "I judge no one."

Although the story is not in some of the best manuscripts, it may describe an actual event. The actions of Jesus are in character with what we know of him.

The woman brought to Jesus had committed the same sin as the Samaritan woman in John 4. The leaders who brought the woman to Jesus wanted to embarrass him either before the Romans or the people. One might have asked them why they had not already punished the woman themselves according to the guidelines in Deuteronomy 22:23–24.

If Jesus supported the death penalty, the Roman authorities could accuse him of rebellion against their laws that reserved capital punishment as a right only for them. If Jesus rejected the death penalty, the leaders could accuse him of ignoring the Mosaic law. Jesus' answer shifted the attention from a debate about imposing the death penalty to an appeal for mercy. He warned that those who claim to speak for God can be blinded by their own sin. Jesus' reprimand to the woman "not to sin again" prevented his display of mercy from appearing to be an easy acceptance of sexual immorality.

The Light of the World (John 8:12–20) #98

During the seven-day Feast of Tabernacles the Jews burned four large oil lamps in the temple area continuously. The lamps symbolized the pillar of fire that guarded the Jews in their wilderness wanderings (Exod. 13:21-22). This custom provided a background for Jesus' claim to be the light of the world.

The Jews who heard Jesus' claim challenged his authority to make such a sweeping pronouncement. To satisfy the Jewish law demanding two witnesses, Jesus presented himself and the Father as witnesses of a truthful testimony. When the Jews demanded that he produce his Father, Jesus responded that their blindness kept them from understanding and knowing the Father. John highlighted the divine control of the entire sequence of events by explaining that Jesus was not arrested at this time because "his hour had not yet come."

Jesus Claims Preexistence (John 8:21–59) #99

Jesus challenged the Jews to abide by his word permanently and consistently (vv. 31–32). The listeners confidently claimed that their descent from Abraham guaranteed their spiritual deliverance, but Jesus warned that true freedom came only through obedience to him (v. 36).

When Jesus claimed that those who obeyed his word could never die, the Jews dismissed his claim as absurd. "Abraham and the prophets are dead," they retorted. "Are you claiming to be greater than they?" Jesus answered that even Abraham had a vision of the messianic age. He knew Abraham's mind on this subject because of his preexistence. This claim led the Jews to attempt to stone him on the spot, but Jesus slipped away from their murderous intentions.

A Blind Man Finds Jesus as the Light of the World (John 9:1–41) #100

This miracle shows that faith in Jesus can lead a person from darkness to light. Jesus came into the world to reveal himself in word and deed as the light of the world. Some who see the work of Jesus respond in faith, but others reject the revelation offered in him. This incident is an acted parable of belief and disbelief (see 9:39–41).

Jesus' disciples asked the cause of the man's blindness, and Jesus answered that his blindness was due neither to his own sins nor to the sins of his parents. The miracle that healed the blind man is a revelation of God's power to open the eyes of the spiritually blind. The blind man progressively responded to Jesus' words and grew to understand the person of Jesus (see vv. 7, 11, 17, 25, 30–33, 36–38). In contrast, the Pharisees progressively grew in their rage and blindness (see vv. 16, 34, 40–41). Jesus healing the blind man violated regulations against healing on the Sabbath; kneading the clay (v. 11) also involved work.

Some feel that excommunicating the blind man (v. 34) represents a practice which was not used until after the fall of Jerusalem in A.D. 70. They believe that the Jews at that time formulated guidelines for banning Christian Jews from their synagogues. Evidence exists, however, that a ban against permitting heretics to worship in the synagogues had long been in force.[3]

Jesus' answer to the Jews in verses 40 and 41 pictured them as willfully blind to the revelation he had given them. Because they thought they saw, they continued to be guilty, unaware of their lostness and blindness.

The Good Shepherd (John 10:1–21) #101

Jesus used the figure of the good shepherd to provide an added commentary on the blind man (a sheep), the Pharisees (thieves and robbers), and himself (the good shepherd). Shepherds sometimes left their sheep overnight in a walled pen in the care of a porter ("keeper"). The next morning the shepherds came to the pen and

---

3. The ban formulated against Christians, also known as the "Benediction against Heretics," had various translations, but the following is a representative statement: "For the renegades let there be no hope, and may the arrogant kingdom soon be rooted out in our days, and the Nazarenes (i.e. the Christians) and the *minim* ('heretics') perish as in a moment and be rooted out from the book of life and with the righteous may they not be inscribed." The statement appears as the Twelfth Benediction in a Jewish document known as the Eighteen Benedictions. Carson has a lengthy discussion of the issue in *The Gospel According to John* (Grand Rapids: William B. Eerdmans Publishing Co., 1991), 369–72. The ban has also been discussed earlier under "Purpose" in the section dealing with the "Gospel of John" in chapter 7. It may be helpful to compare the translation by Carson with that given in chapter 7.

called their sheep as the keeper opened the gate. The sheep would respond because they recognized the voice of the shepherd. Thieves and robbers would climb over the wall into the pen to cause panic among the sheep, but the shepherd would gently lead his sheep to food, water, and protection.

Jesus' words disclosed three features about his actions for the sheep.

1. He was the door ("gate"), a reference to the fact that some shepherds slept at night in the gateway of their sheep pens and literally became the gate over which marauders would have to enter to reach the sheep.

2. He was the Good Shepherd, a shepherd with genuine attachment to the sheep instead of the merely materialistic concern of the hired hand.

3. Jesus willingly surrendered his life in the Crucifixion in order to take it up again in the Resurrection (v. 17).

The Sending of the Seventy (Luke 10:1–24) #102

Luke records Jesus' instructions to the seventy more fully than he recorded the earlier sending of the Twelve (see Luke 9:1–6). The location of the mission is uncertain, for the sequence of the preceding verses (Luke 9:51–62) suggests that Jesus sent them into the Transjordanean region of Perea, but Robertson suggests a Judean destination for their ministry. The number seventy (some manuscripts read seventy-two) may be a symbol of the nations of the world based on Genesis 10 (seventy names appear in the Hebrew text and seventy-two in the LXX). Since haste and mobility were important, Jesus limited equipment for the disciples and urged rapid, deliberate movement. Jesus' statement that he saw "Satan fall from the sky like lightning" (v. 18) implies that the mission of the seventy was a preview of the ultimate downfall of Satan. The hymn of praise in verses 21–24 resembles the Johannine style and reminds us that this style is not foreign to the Synoptics.

The Good Samaritan (Luke 10:25–37) #103

This parable is unique to Luke and does not appear to be linked chronologically to the preceding or following incidents. The lawyer's question was not an inquiry for information but an effort to see the kind of answer Jesus would give. He might have hoped Jesus would give a poor answer so he could embarrass him. His question, "What must I do?" implies ignorance of divine grace. When Jesus asked him the teaching of the law on the issue of eternal life, the lawyer quoted Deuteronomy 6:5 and Leviticus 19:18. Jesus' commendation of his answer does not suggest a new method of salvation by works but affirms that the person who genuinely trusts God will show the attitude reflected in verse 27.

The lawyer refused to let the issue rest and inquired, "Who is my neighbor?" The parable of the good Samaritan was the answer to his question and not a discourse on how to be saved.

The seventeen-mile road from Jerusalem to Jericho drops more than three thousand feet. It is wild country with many places for robbers to hide. Violent men assaulted the Jewish traveler. Both the priest and the Levite refused to help their injured countryman because they would incur expensive and inconvenient ceremonial defilement by contact with someone who might be dead (see Lev. 21:1–4). Jesus shocked the audience by suddenly introducing a hated Samaritan who showed compassion by dressing his wounds, letting the injured man ride the donkey through dangerous territory while he walked, and paying money to an innkeeper for an extended convalescence for the injured man. He even promised his credit for additional funds if they were needed.

Jesus used the parable to show the lawyer that he had asked the wrong question. The question should not be "Who is my neighbor?" but "To whom can I be a neighbor?" Jesus commended the Samaritan as someone who showed what it meant to love a neighbor as oneself. The prejudice of the surprised lawyer surfaced when he refused to identify the true neighbor as a "Samaritan." He called him "the one who treated him with compassion."

Mary's Good Choice (Luke 10:38–42) #104

Luke alone contains this incident. It does not appear in a chronological or geographical sequence, for Bethany was near Jerusalem, and later in Luke's Gospel Jesus was still far from the city (see 17:11). The story emphasizes that quiet dependence on Jesus is more important than bustling service.

Mary took full advantage of her opportunities to listen to Jesus' teaching. Martha, agonizing over the details of a hostess, was distracted. In her frustration she blurted out to Jesus, "Tell Mary to help me with my tasks." Jesus' tender reply contrasted Martha's fretful preoccupation with Mary's attentive listening. He did not define the "one necessary thing," but the context suggests that what is necessary is learning from him or depending on him.

Persistence in Prayer (Luke 11:1–13) #105

Luke's inclusion of these stories reflects his interest in prayer. The prayer in 11:1–4 resembles the Lord's Prayer of Matthew 6:9–13, but it is an abbreviated form. Perhaps Jesus taught the Lord's Prayer on more than a single occasion.

The first parable (vv. 5–8) underscores the importance of persistence in prayer. The shameless request by a host for bread to feed a late-arriving guest continued until the neighbor surrendered his three loaves. Jesus insisted that tepid prayer will never prevail with God but that perseverance with a God-honored request will bring a positive response. The context makes clear that we do not pressure a reluctant God into responding to our requests; rather, he examines our motives to determine the presence of genuine desire.

The second parable (vv. 9–13) suggests that God always hears true prayer and answers it in the way he deems best. Just as fathers do not give evil gifts to their children, so the heavenly Father does not give harmful things to believers but rewards them with the highest good.

Another Accusation of Being in League with the Devil (Luke 11:14–36) #106

On more than one occasion Jesus' opponents accused him of being linked with the devil (see #61 and #68, or Matt. 9:27–34; 12:22–37). The earlier incidents were clearly in Galilee, and this incident likely occurred in Judea or Perea. Here Jesus omitted the stern warning of blasphemy against the Holy Spirit and the unpardonable sin (see Mark 3:20–30). Jesus' general reply to his accusers resembles his response in the earlier passages. His concluding warning in 11:24–26 shows that a person who expelled the spirit of evil must replace it with a more powerful source of strength. The kingdom of God can bring a full and complete victory over evil.

In 11:33–36 Jesus figuratively pictures the eye as the entrance of either good or evil into the life of a person. A single eye was a "sound" eye that kept its gaze single-mindedly fixed on the good. An evil eye focused its attention on darkness which corrupts life. Jesus called his listeners to dwell with unimpaired devotion on following God's will so that their entire being might be filled with the light of divine presence.

A Clash with the Pharisees (Luke 11:37–54) #107

After Jesus had spoken, he accepted an invitation from a Pharisee to have lunch with him. When Jesus failed to follow rabbinic tradition for hand washing before eating, his host was astonished. Jesus sensed his displeasure and warned the Pharisees of the danger of emphasizing the external over the internal. He reminded them that the way to maintain inner purity was to preserve a right inward state when giving alms. If we give our hearts, we will not merely make an outward gesture. Jesus also denounced other practices by both Pharisees and lawyers which emphasized the outward over the inward and permitted hypocrisy to remain unchanged.

The Urgency of Deciding for Christ (Luke 12:1–59) #108

Jesus continued his warning against the hypocrisy of the Pharisees and urged his listeners to prepare for judgment by cultivating an attitude of commitment to him. When a hearer in the crowd urged Jesus to settle a dispute over inheritance, the Lord responded by using the parable of the rich fool to warn that possessions do not guarantee life. In language resembling a passage in Matthew (6:19–34) he exhorted his hearers not to worry about obtaining possesions (Luke 12:22–34). He then reinforced his teaching about the proper use of wealth with a reminder that the coming of the Son of Man will expose the emptiness of earthly goals and possessions (12:35–40).

Answering a question from Peter, Jesus stressed the responsibility of all of his servants and emphasized that great privilege brought great responsibility (12:47–48). He knew that his message would precipitate division, even within families (12:49–53). He encouraged his hearers to make peace with God rather than risk losing everything in God's final judgment.

The Urgency of Repentance (Luke 13:1–9) #109

Jesus' listeners assumed that human suffering was a punishment for sin. In response, Jesus referred to several disasters in Jerusalem to make the point that sin alone had not caused the disasters. He reminded all of those present that they faced judgment if they failed to repent.

Jesus told the parable of the barren fig tree to emphasize further the urgency of repentance. The Old Testament used the fig tree as a symbol of Israel (see Hos. 9:10). Using agricultural language of cultivating a vineyard, Jesus delivered a stern appeal for the Jews to repent. When the fig tree failed to bear fruit over a three-year period, it was likely that it would never bear fruit. Giving the barren tree another year was an act of agricultural mercy. Jesus stressed that through his ministry God was providing another opportunity for spiritually barren Israel to repent.

A Display of Mercy and the Spread of God's Kingdom (Luke 13:10–21) #110

The debate about proper use of the Sabbath caused continuing controversy between Jesus and his opponents. Jesus took the initiative by healing on the Sabbath (see Mark 2:23–3:6 for other Sabbath controversies) a woman who for eighteen years had been incapable of walking erectly. The action annoyed the synagogue leader who said to the crowd, "People should get their healings over within six days." Jesus denounced his hypocrisy by showing that Jewish legalists violated the Sabbath in feeding their animals. Jesus reasoned, "If animals can be cared for in such ways, is it no more important to care for people?" The joyful response of the people reflected their enthusiastic support of Jesus.

Jesus used the parables of the mustard seed and the leaven to show that the ultimate expansive development of the kingdom of God will be an utter contrast to its present incipient form. (See Matthew 13:31–32, 44–46 [#64] for a discussion of these parables).

Jesus Claims Deity (John 10:22–42) #111–112

The Feast of Dedication (Hanukkah) took place in December and celebrated the rededication of the temple by Judas Maccabeus after its desecration under Antiochus Epiphanes. Jesus offered two responses to an inquiry concerning whether he was the Messiah. First, he indicated that his works witnessed that he came from God. Second, he blamed the failure of the people to believe on their unwillingness to listen to his message. When he claimed, "I and the Father are one," the Jews correctly saw this as a claim to divinity and wrongly tried to stone him. As the Jews apparently stood poised to hurl the stones, Jesus reasoned with them again. He pointed out, "Jewish rulers claim to be 'gods' in a representative sense (Ps. 82:6), and you should not take offense at the claim of the Messiah to be the Son of God." When they rejected his additional argument, he escaped from them because his hour had not come.

Who Will Be Saved? (Luke 13:22–35) #113

In this travel section Luke continued to present events from the teaching ministry of Jesus. When a questioner asked him, "Are the saved only a few?" Jesus directed the questioner away from curiosity about others to concern about his own needs. The listener doubtless felt that his Jewish background provided an entrance into God's kingdom, but Jesus warned him that many Gentiles would be saved. The Jews, who presumed themselves to be "first," would be "last."

In response to a threat concerning the fox Herod Antipas, Jesus refused to be intimidated by the actions of a mere worldling. No human intervention could prevent his divine appointment in Jerusalem. The concluding word in verse 35 may be either a threat of final judgment or a word of hope that Jerusalem will recognize Jesus' lordship in a future conversion.

A Warning to the Excluded Guests (Luke 14:1–24) #114

Luke highlighted the distorted values of the Pharisees, who showed no concern for the sick man (vv. 1–6), maneuvered for status (vv. 7–11), and lacked compassion for the poor and needy (vv. 12–14). He called his hearers to display humility (v. 11) and mercy (v. 13).

The reference to feasts in Jesus' exhortation led a listener to reflect on the messianic banquet, the great feast that Jews expected to inaugurate the kingdom of God (see Matt. 22:1–10 for a similar story). His outburst in verse 15 made the banquet sound like a rally reserved for legalistic Pharisees. Jesus' warning indicated the "religious" Pharisees rejected his invitation to the banquet inaugurating the kingdom. Such "rejects" as publicans, sinners, and even Gentiles would take their places at the feast.

A Call to Discipleship (Luke 14:25–35) #115

The first (vv. 25–27) and final parts (vv. 34–35) have parallels in Matthew (5:13; 10:37–38). The middle section (vv. 28–33) is found only in Luke. The appeal to "hate" one's closest relations probably represents Hebraic hyperbole which suggests that we should completely subordinate everything to our commitment to Jesus. No prudent person would undertake construction or battle without counting the cost, and no thoughtful disciple should assume the position of a disciple lightly. The half-hearted disciple will be tossed out like worthless salt. Jesus' purpose was not to repel sincere seekers but to awaken the superficial follower to the consequences of such half–heartedness.

An Appeal to Sinners (Luke 15:1–32) #116

These three parables show the joy of God in welcoming all penitents into his kingdom. Jesus spoke the parables at this time in order to defend his fellowship with publicans and sinners. Jews scorned the publicans for their graft and their collaboration with the hated Romans. Pharisees regarded as "sinners" any who did not keep the rabbinic ceremonial regulations. The message in Jesus' words is that God loves the confused, squalid, pretentious, mixed-up world. Jesus' mission demonstrates that love. His association with sinners is neither an approval of their actions nor mere humanitarianism. He proclaims his message to sinners and rejoices in welcoming the responsive into God's family.

1. The parable of the lost sheep (cf. Matt. 18:12–14) illustrates two features of Jesus' ministry. First, like the shepherd, Jesus considers no sacrifice or trouble too great in order to rescue lost sheep. Second, Jesus has the same joy as the shepherd in

recovering the lost sheep. Jesus was calling his critics to share his joy rather than to castigate his actions.

2. The parable of the lost coin illustrates the thoroughness of God's search for lost sinners. Jesus was calling his dour listeners to rejoice with him at the happy outcome of the salvation of sinners. The writings of many non-Christian religions emphasize how human beings yearn and search for God. Christianity emphasizes that God through Christ seeks to save lost, stumbling human beings.

3. In the parable of the prodigal son the younger son was to receive one-third of the estate. Normally the father would have maintained the usage of the estate until death. The action of the younger son in turning his inheritance into cash may have represented rash, dishonest action. In a distant country he wasted his inheritance. For a Jew to feed swine was an unspeakable degradation. The son could not obtain enough of the swine's food to satisfy his hunger, another sign of his abject poverty.

A gnawing sense of misery and need led the prodigal to resolve to return to his father with a confession of sin against God and the father. As a sign of his humility he was now willing to assume the lowest place and to follow his father's commands. Without any hope for restoration he threw himself on his father's mercy.

The prodigal underestimated his father's love. Throwing aside all sense of dignity and decorum, the father dashed to embrace his son as soon as he saw him in the distance. Before the prodigal could finish his intended confession and plea, the father had extended forgiveness. The robe, the ring, and the shoes are visible signs of his restoration. The fatted calf, saved for a festive occasion, was killed to be enjoyed at this festive and joyful time. All the household except one joined in the celebration.

The second edge of this parable now appears. The elder brother, who represents the haughty scribes and Pharisees, criticized the festivity for his returned brother. The brother viewed himself as deserving honor and recognition and resented his father's partiality for his younger sibling. Note the contrast between the brother's "this thy son" and the father's "this thy brother." The father's address to the son is compassionate and reassuring. The family's riches had constantly been available to the elder son. The hearty welcome extended to the younger son was not a reward but a spontaneous outburst of joy at the return of one who had wandered away.

The behavior of the older brother showed that he was the one to blame for his failure to enjoy the family's riches. Further, he allowed the relationship with his father to degenerate into a slavish bondage and self-righteousness that lacked a balancing sense of freedom. Jesus thus showed that the root of the Pharisees' error was an insistence on slavish obedience to the law as a basis for earning God's favor. They lacked a concept of responding to a God of love and grace who provided the means of communion with him.

The Unjust Steward, the Rich Man, and Lazarus (Luke 16:1–17:10) #117

The unjust steward was a household business manager for a large landowner. Two features of his actions are noteworthy as examples. First (vv. 1–2), he provided a negative example by squandering his master's goods and losing his job. The dismal example of the steward reminds us that we should make wise use of the talents and opportunities which God gives us. We should labor for the eternal rather than the temporal.

Second, the behavior of the steward (vv. 3–7) received commendation from Jesus because it demonstrated intelligent self-interest. He tried to curry the favor of his master's debtors by reducing their debts and hoping for favorable treatment from them after his dismissal. Even the master commended his prudent foresight. Jesus' command in verse 9 to use "unrighteous mammon" to make "friends for yourselves" urged his listeners to use their worldly goods given them by the Father to bring blessings to others. Doing this would be a sign that they deserved the true riches of eternal life.

Jesus was not appealing for an imitation of the dishonest actions of the unjust steward, but he was commending his prudent action. Jesus called for prudence and unselfishness, not for dishonesty.

In the parable of the rich man and Lazarus Jesus was teaching truths about the kingdom of God, not providing information about life after death. Jesus intended that the rich man serve as a symbol for both the Pharisees and the Sadducees, who loved money. The rich man is sometimes called "Dives," from the Latin name for "rich." The rich man's treatment of Lazarus showed his self-centered, greedy nature. The phrase "Abraham's bosom" describes a heavenly banquet scene with Lazarus as a guest reclining on a cushion in front of Abraham. It presents a picture of supreme blessedness. The term *hell* (Grk. *hades*) represents the place where the unbelieving dead go at death to await final judgment.

The dialogue of Abraham with the rich man underscores two truths. First, God will not admit Jews into heaven merely because they are descendants from Abraham. Second, those who will not believe and repent upon hearing God's Word will not even respond to a miracle like a resurrection.

The Raising of Lazarus (John 11:1–44) #118

The Lazarus in this story is not the Lazarus of the preceding parable. Jesus' disciples objected to the journey to Judea, fearing that the Jews would put him to death. Jesus' answer (vv. 9–10) reflected his faith that God determined the events of his life. So long as he walked in God's will, nothing could hasten the divinely determined time of his death.

Jesus' assurance to Martha (vv. 25–26) sought to deepen her faith in the one who alone could bring resurrection on the last day. His words assured her that he had the power to effect a resurrection and that those who believed in him would never experience death. In human beings, physical life usually ebbs away. The spiritual life Jesus gives never ends.

The Jews felt that Lazarus was irreversibly dead. They believed the human spirit hovered over the body of the deceased for three days, but decomposition began when it departed on the fourth day. Human feelings and divine power stood side by side when Jesus wept for (11:35) and raised Lazarus. His weeping and display of emotion (11:38) stemmed from his anger over the deadly effects of sin. He was outraged at the effects of sin and death on those whom he loved. His reversal of those effects produced faith in some who saw it (11:45). Lazarus was raised with the same physical body which he carried to the grave. He eventually died again, and with other believers awaits the final resurrection at Christ's return.

The Decision to Kill Jesus (John 11:45–54) #119

The Jewish leaders never questioned the reality of the raising of Lazarus. Their problem was ambition and materialism, not disbelief in the miraculous. The Sanhedrin feared that the miracle would stir up messianic excitement, and they feared that this would bring harsh Roman rule upon the nation. They saw their own positions and power at stake. The high priest Caiaphas suggested the death penalty for Jesus so that the death of one man might save the nation from destruction. John noted that his words contained a deeper truth than he realized (vv. 51–52). Unconsciously Caiaphas stated that God would use Jesus to die for the Jewish nation and for all the scattered children of God.

The Presence of the Kingdom (Luke 17:11–37) #120

Jesus warned the speculative Pharisees that the arrival of the coming kingdom of God could not be predicted by easily observable signs. He mentioned two reasons for this. First, unknown to the Pharisees, the kingdom was already present in its incipient form in the person of Jesus. It was already a saving and correcting force in the lives of the Jewish people. Second, it would come so suddenly and unexpectedly that no one could predict its final arrival with any degree of accuracy (vv. 22–37). Jesus intended that people not speculate about the time of the end and that they pay closer attention to his commandments.

Appeals to Prayer (Luke 18:1–14) #121

In the parable of the unjust judge Jesus appealed for believers to persevere without losing heart when making their requests. They must render the obedience that represents God's will. The widow represented a helpless individual whose only asset was her persistence. The judge represented one who had no reverence for God and lacked sympathy for human beings. The persistence of the widow finally triumphed over the tenacious indifference of the judge. The point is not that God will finally answer our prayer or reward our behavior merely to stop us from bothering him. Jesus taught that if a helpless widow could finally obtain justice from a godless, hard-hearted judge, how much more can the children of God expect answers in prayer and ultimate vindication from God. The parable has application to prayer life and also to the final vindication of believers at the time of Christ's return.

In the parable of the Pharisee and the publican, the Pharisee was so busy priding himself on his performance that he failed to realize he lacked the essential requirement of a right attitude. His attitude resembled that of the unconverted Paul, who described himself as "blameless" concerning legal righteousness (Phil. 3:6). The performance of the Pharisee greatly exceeded the normal requirement of fasting once a year and giving tithes only on certain types of income. He tithed all of his possessions. The despised publicans robbed the Jews, made alliances with the despised Romans, and were uniformly detested. Jesus' words must have shocked his audience, which would be partisan to the Pharisees. God relates to those people who have lost their pride and humbled themselves in repentance.

Marriage and Divorce
(Matt. 19:1–12; Mark 10:1–12) #122

Jesus was approaching Jerusalem through the region known as Perea. Jewish rabbis agreed that Deuteronomy 24:1–4 permitted divorce with the right to remarry, though they disagreed on the grounds for divorce. The rabbinic school of Shammai restricted the "indecency" ("uncleanness") of Deuteronomy 24:1 to sexual immorality. The school of Hillel, whose views governed contemporary practices, accepted any action displeasing to the husband as a basis for divorce.[4] The Pharisees wanted to spring a trap on Jesus by luring him into this debate.

Jesus answered his inquisitors by discussing the nature of marriage. Marriage involves a lifelong commitment of a man to a woman (Matt. 19:4–6). Any practice of divorce represents a reversal

---

4. The school of Hillel even allowed burning the husband's dinner or his finding someone more attractive as grounds for divorce. See Mishnah tractate *Gittin* 9:10, edited by Herbert Danby (London: Oxford University Press, 1933).

of the will of God. The Pharisees viewed Moses' statements in Deuteronomy (24:1–4) as a commandment, and they felt that Jesus repudiated what Moses commanded. Jesus pointed out that Moses had not commanded divorce, although his words allowed it. Divorce, however, was a concession to human frailty, not an expression of the will of God.

In Matthew 19:9 Jesus suggested that adultery (see Matt. 5:32) was a basis for dissolving a marriage. The logic behind the permission is that a divorce only recognizes the dissolution that adultery has already brought. Many interpreters infer that in such instances the spouse who has not committed adultery is permitted to remarry. Some point out that the absence of a similar "exception clause" in Mark can be explained because Mark assumed that his readers would have allowed for divorce and remarriage under these circumstances. The "adultery" Matthew described may include either premarital unchastity, incest, or postmarital immorality. Most interpreters who favor an exception to the prohibition of divorce feel that postmarital immorality is the most likely meaning.

The response of the disciples in Matthew 19:10–12 indicated that they felt a commitment so demanding was better avoided. Jesus' answer to them implied that only those who were able to accept the commitment of marriage should undertake it. Some might avoid marriage for physical or spiritual reasons.

Applying Jesus' words in a fallen world is difficult. Christians today must take Jesus' words about the permanence of marriage seriously, but they must not interpret them so to make divorce the unpardonable sin.

Commending the Lowly
(Matt. 19:13–15; Mark 10:13–16; Luke 18:15–17) #123

Jesus had already used little children as an example of the humble attitude that should grace his disciples (Matt. 18:2–3). His indignant protest at the attempts of his disciples to exclude children places value on children themselves. Beyond that, however, Jesus was commending those whose acceptance of a childlike status makes them great on Jesus' scale of values. Only those who come to

Jesus with the humility of little children will enter the kingdom of God.

The Rich Young Ruler and the Laborers in the Vineyard (Matt. 19:16–20:16; Mark 10:17–31; Luke 18:18–30) #124

All three Synoptics contain the story of the rich young ruler, with each of the three making individual contributions to the description of the questioner. The rich young man seemed to feel that he lacked some single heroic act in his quest to obtain eternal life. By telling the young man that only God was "good," Jesus tried to lead him to see that he was divine if he truly was good. Jesus quoted the commandments in Mark 10:19 to lead him to see that he needed to observe faithfully all the commandments. His probing directive in verse 21 to give his possessions to the poor touched the young man at a point of resistance to God's commands for his life. His sorrowful departure showed his unwillingness to repent of his materialistic concerns.

Three lessons from this event touch our lives.

1. One can be interested in eternal life without possessing it (v. 17).

2. Many who claim to have obeyed God have done so only in a superficial sense (v. 20).

3. The young man lacked eternal life because he rejected Jesus' call for repentance (v. 22).

Jesus' words shocked his disciples, for they equated riches with the enjoyment of divine favor. Jesus' statement (v. 25) about the difficulty of a camel passing through a needle's eye is a folk proverb, showing that it is difficult for the wealthy to enter God's kingdom. Despite that difficulty God can perform the impossible and bring the wealthy into his presence (v. 27).

The parable of the laborers in the vineyard closes this passage only in Matthew. The parable serves as a fitting answer to Peter's inquiry in Matthew 19:27 by reminding him that eternal life is a gift, not a payment for service. The penny or denarius represented the normal wage for a day's work. The employer hired employees whose work could not possibly merit the wage he paid, but those who heard the parable should realize that he was a great-hearted employer who had sympathy for the poor and needy. Jesus was teaching the crowd that God was like this. His generosity went far beyond human ideas of fairness. In God's kingdom no persons receive less than they deserve. By God's grace all actually receive more. Most of us can identify with the complaint in verse 12, but we should be filled with joy at divine grace shown to the needy.

An Appeal for Servanthood
(Matt. 20:17–28; Mark 10:32–45; Luke 18:31–34) #125

Jesus' passion prediction in this section is the most detailed observed thus far in the Gospels. Apparently the disciples still failed to understand the information, particularly in reference to the coming Resurrection.

Something about Jesus' manner may have told the disciples that events in his life were coming to a decisive climax. James and John took advantage of this awareness to request favored positions in the kingdom. Although their attitude was wrong, their request showed a confidence in Jesus' ability to establish a kingdom. Jesus promised his disciples suffering and martyrdom (v. 39). The petty selfishness of the group of disciples led Jesus to emphasize that greatness in his kingdom comes by serving, not by ruling.

Blind Bartimaeus
(Matt. 20:29–34; Mark 10:46–52; Luke 18:35–43) #126

Only Mark mentioned Bartimaeus by name. This probably indicates that Bartimaeus had become a recognized disciple among Christians by the time Mark was written. It may also explain why only Mark chose to mention him, while Matthew mentioned that two blind men were sitting by the roadside. Geldenhuys suggests that the difference between Luke's description of Jesus drawing near to Jericho (Luke 18:35) and Matthew and Mark's description of his departure from the city may be attributed to Bartimaeus's actions.[5] He maintains that Bartimaeus heard of Jesus' arrival on

---

5. Norval Geldenhuys, *Commentary on the Gospel of Luke*, NICNT (Grand Rapids: William B. Eerdmans Publishing Co., 1951), 467–68, n. 1.

the outskirts of Jericho, followed him through the city while Jesus spoke with Zacchaeus (Luke 19:1–10), and waited for Jesus as he passed out of the city. Bartimaeus showed great faith by responding to what he heard (Mark 10:47), persisting in his request for help, and standing to his feet when Jesus summoned him.

Zacchaeus and the Parable of the Pounds (Luke 19:1–28) #127

Zacchaeus showed the same determination to contact Jesus as Bartimaeus. He did not come to see Jesus out of mere curiosity or with any skepticism but with an openness to the message of Jesus. His promise to repay fourfold (v. 8) is a confession that he extorted money from his clients (2 Sam. 12:6). His spontaneous act of repentance revealed the magnificent work of grace in his heart and proved that he was now a true son of Abraham (v. 9).

The parable of the pounds echoed two themes: the meaning of discipleship (13, 15–26) and the rejection of the king (12, 14, 27). The disciples shared the Jewish view that Jesus' kingdom would be earthly and centered at Jerusalem. Jesus' arrival near Jerusalem heightened their excitement that the kingdom might appear immediately. The statements of verses 12, 14, and 27 suggest that the rejection of Jesus by the Jews led to an interval during which he would be absent from earth. During this time disciples are to be faithfully serving him (v. 13). When he returns, he will initiate judgment and reward. The true disciple will be a productive servant (vv. 17, 19), and the fearful, timid disciple will experience judgment and rejection (vv. 22–24). Jesus emphasizes that following him involves committing our lives to his service.

For Further Discussion

1. Should the incident of "The Woman Taken in Adultery" (John 7:53–8:11) be included as part of Scripture?

2. Explain how we should apply Jesus' teaching on showing love to our neighbors as taught in the parable of the good Samaritan (Luke 10:25–37).

3. Relate Jesus' attitude toward Scripture shown in his words, "The Scripture cannot be broken" (John 10:35) to your own attitude toward Scripture.

4. What practices toward non-Christians do Jesus' words in the three parables of Luke 15 encourage you to develop?

5. Apply Jesus' teachings on prayer in Luke 18:1–14 to your own prayer life.

6. Explain how the parable of the laborers in the vineyard (Matt. 20:1–16) illustrates God's gracious attitude toward sinners. What attitudes does this parable challenge you to show toward careless, indifferent people?

Bibliography

Barrett, C. K. *The New Testament Background: Selected Documents.* Rev. ed. London: SPCK, 1987.

Carson, D. A. *The Gospel According to John.* Grand Rapids: William B. Eerdmans Publishing Co., 1991.

Geldenhuys, Norval. *Commentary on the Gospel of Luke.* NICNT. Grand Rapids: William B. Eerdmans Publishing Co., 1951

Robertson, A. T. *A Harmony of the Gospels.* New York: Harper & Row Publishers Inc., 1950.

Also see bibliography in chapter 9.

11 The Final Week of Jesus' Life—Crucifixion and Resurrection

Guiding Questions

1. What did the triumphal entry of Christ mean to him? To the crowd who observed it?

2. Describe the actions of Jesus Christ on the days before his crucifixion.

3. Evaluate and compare the evidence for the time of the Passover in the Synoptics and in John's Gospel.

4. Describe the Jewish and Roman phases of the trial of Jesus.

5. List the actions of the Jewish leaders in conducting Jesus' trial that were contrary to their own laws and practices.

6. Explain the historical evidence for the resurrection of Jesus.

Jesus' final week of life on earth began with the triumphal entry on Sunday and included a week filled with teaching, preaching, and confrontation with his enemies. The events include vigorous discussions, penetrating questions, insightful responses by Jesus, the self-sacrifice of the Crucifixion, and the momentous victory of the Resurrection. The week ended with Jesus initiating a post-Resurrection period of instruction and encouragement for his disciples.

Jesus' Arrival at Bethany (Matt. 26:6–13; Mark 14:3–9; John 11:55–12:11) #128a, 141

Jesus' arrival at Bethany near Jerusalem (John 12:1) likely occurred on a Saturday with the meal of John 12:2 taking place on the evening of that day. A. T. Robertson postponed Mary's anointing of Jesus until Tuesday of Passion Week in an apparent agreement with Matthew and Mark. The chronological notes of John, however, require that we place the event on the Saturday before Palm Sunday (John 12:1, 12). Matthew and Mark delay the report of the incident (Matt. 26:6–13; Mark 14:3–9 [#141]) in order to show the relationship between this incident and Judas's determination to betray Jesus. Mary's anointing here has similarities with the anointing by the sinful woman mentioned in Luke 7:36–50 (#59). The lesson that Jesus draws from the anointing in Luke differs from that of the anointing in the other three Gospels. Because of the differing views of the chronology of the events, we will group together those sections that Robertson labels #128a, 141.

Simon the leper may have been the father of Lazarus, Mary, and Martha. If he were still a leper, he would not have been present at this event. Perhaps he had relinquished responsibility for household management to his children. Matthew and Mark mentioned the anointing of Jesus' head, perhaps to suggest his anointing as king. John mentioned the anointing of his feet to show Mary's humility. The value of the perfume (three hundred denarii) represented a year's wages for a working man. Judas expressed the opinion of some of the disciples that the perfume could have been sold and the proceeds given to the poor. John tells us (12:6) that Judas pretended altruism to mask his greed. Jesus' reply to Judas indicated that Mary had begun to anoint his body in anticipation of the coming burial. Mary likely did not understand the necessity of Jesus' death, but she offered humble devotion to Jesus, and her actions signalled more than she knew. Jesus' sharp rebuke prompted Judas to approach the authorities a few days later (Matt. 26:14–16; Mark 14:10–11) with an offer to betray Jesus.

The Triumphant Entry into Jerusalem (Matt. 21:1–11, 14–17; Mark 11:1–11; Luke 19:29–44; John 12:12–19) #128b

The significance of this event for the New Testament writers is obvious since all four Gospels record it. For Jesus the entry was a claim of messiahship, but riding the donkey showed that he did not come as the warrior-king expected by the Jewish people. Matthew mentioned two animals, the donkey and her colt, which had never been ridden (a fulfillment of Zech. 9:9). Bringing along the colt's mother would provide reassurance for the colt in the face of a boisterous crowd. The garments hastily thrown on the colt served as an improvised saddle, and the "carpet" of garments and branches signaled the crowd's messianic expectations. The raising of Lazarus had doubtless heightened messianic expectations. The shouting of "Son of David" by the crowd also reflected messianic hopes, and "Hosanna" was a cry to the Davidic king to save them now. This crowd of Passover pilgrims viewed the salvation they wanted as primarily political—freedom from oppression.

Not all the onlookers shared enthusiasm for Jesus' arrival. The Pharisees asked Jesus to silence the crowd (Matt. 21:15–16; Luke 19:39–40). Jesus' reply that "the stones would cry out" if the crowd were silenced may have been a proverbial saying. It might also have referred to the tumbled stones of the Jerusalem temple from A.D. 70 onward as evidence of his messiahship. After entering the temple briefly, he returned to Bethany for the night.

Cursing the Fig Tree and Cleansing the Temple (Matt. 21:12, 13, 18–19; Mark 11:12–18; Luke 19:45–48) #129

Mark provided the chronological order of these events, showing that both took place on a Monday. The cursing of the fig tree[1] and the cleansing of the temple are signs of divine judgment on the empty religious practices of Israel. Jesus came to the tree hoping to find the small early ripe figs which ripen with the leaves before the main fig crop. Cursing the fig tree was an acted parable by Jesus, not a petty loss of temper.

---

1. See Mic. 7:1 for the fruitless fig tree used as a symbol of Israel's spiritual failure. The parable of the barren fig tree in Luke 13:1–9 used the same symbolism.

The Pharisees were shocked at the outcry of children in the temple (Matt. 21:15), but they were apathetic about the uproar of the merchants and the money-changers. For Jesus it was supreme blasephemy that a place intended for the worship of God should become a house of business. The crowds' support of Jesus prevented the Jewish leaders from taking immediate action against Jesus, but they became more earnest in seeking to get rid of his annoying preaching. For a discussion of the relationship of this cleansing to that in John's Gospel, see section #31 on John 2:13–22.

The Greeks Approach Jesus (John 12:20–50) #130

John 12:19 concludes with a statement by the Pharisees that "the world had gone after him." This statement received a partial fulfillment in the desire shown by some Greek proselytes in John 12:20 to see Jesus. John did not indicate that Jesus actually met with the Greeks, but the report from Philip and Andrew that they wanted to meet him led Jesus to announce that the hour for his glorification had come. Jesus' mention of his coming death by crucifixion (John 12:32) led some of the Jews to conclude that he could not be the Messiah. Basing their views on such statements as Psalm 89:4, they had concluded that the Messiah would live forever. Since Jesus was going to die, they rejected him as the Messiah. Jesus appealed for them to recognize the light among them while it still shined (John 12:35–36).

The Withering of the Fig Tree
(Matt. 21:19–22; Mark 11:19–25; Luke 21:37–38) #131

Mark's reference to the "morning" (Mark 11:20) suggests that the time is Tuesday morning after the initial cursing of the tree on Monday. Matthew linked the cursing of the tree and the discovery of the withered tree together to produce a more dramatic story, but the time indicators in Mark's Gospel point us to the correct chronological order. Jesus used the incident to teach the importance of faith in prayer, perhaps hoping to stimulate the disciples to develop faith for the coming crisis of Jesus' arrest, trial, and death.

The Debate over Jesus' Authority (Matt. 21:23–22:14; Mark 11:27–12:12; Luke 20:1–19) #132

In the temple courtyards, Jesus' opponents tried to outwit him in a theological debate. After Jesus refused to answer their question about the source of his authority, he told three parables:

1. Parable of the two sons (Matt. 21:28–32);

2. Parable of the wicked husbandmen (all three Synoptics);

3. Parable of the marriage feast of the king's son (Matt. 22:1–14).

All three parables were directed against the Jewish leaders and echoed the spiritual failure of official Israel.

The Jewish leaders asked Jesus about his authority for the recent cleansing of the temple. Jesus implied that his authority had the same source as that of John the Baptist and then startled his opponents by asking them about the source of John's authority. They hesitated to answer that his authority was divine because Jesus could then expose their failure to accept John. They were reluctant to cause opposition from the people by saying that John had authority from men. Their answer pretended ignorance. Jesus refused to answer their question, and by this he showed that their problem was not ignorance but intentional opposition to God's will. Jesus also implied that his authority came from the same source as the authority of John.

In the parable of the two sons, the son who refused and later changed his mind represents the irreligious Jews, such as publicans and sinners, who were flocking to Jesus. The son who said, "I go, sir," and did not go represents the Jewish religious leaders who failed to recognize God's saving actions in the ministry of Jesus. Jesus commended the irreligious Jews who were repenting but gave a firm rebuke to the self-righteous Jewish leaders.

In the parable of the laborers in the vineyard, the owner represents God, and the vineyard represents the Jewish nation (Isa. 5:1–7). The husbandmen who rented the vineyard are the Jewish leaders, and the servants beaten and killed refer to the Old Testament prophets. The son who was murdered represents Jesus. The destruction of the husbandmen points to the utter overthrow of the Jewish religious leaders in Jerusalem in A.D. 70. Giving the vineyard to others suggests the transfer of God's kingdom to "God's own people," who would be redeemed Jews and Gentiles (1 Pet. 2:9). Just as the owner expected fruit from the husbandmen, God expected fruit from the nation of Israel. Their fruitlessness led to judgment.

In the parable of the marriage feast, the invited guests who twice refused the invitation to the wedding feast are the Jews who rejected Jesus. The king's destruction of their city represents judgment against the Jews in the events of A.D. 70. Those who were finally brought to the feast are Jewish sinners and Gentile outcasts. The appearance at the feast of the man without a wedding garment illustrates the importance of proper clothing at a marriage feast. The garment represents the change of life that Jesus demands from all his followers. The lesson from the rejection of the improperly clothed guest is that salvation is a gift, but it is not without standards and is not to be taken lightly.

Payment of Taxes to Caesar
(Matt. 22:15–22; Mark 12:13–17; Luke 20:20–26) #133

The Herodians were a loosely knit group of unscrupulous Jews who supported the Herodian family. Here they are linked again (see also Mark 3:6) with their unlikely collaborators, the Pharisees, to outwit and embarrass Jesus.

The tax was the annual poll tax, which the Romans had begun to levy in A.D. 6. The imposition of this tax led to a Jewish rebellion under Judas the Galilean (see Acts 5:37). Romans required the payment of the tax with a special coin imprinted with the head of the emperor. Use of this image-stamped coin angered the Jews. Normal business activities used a copper coin without the image of the emperor.

After fawning flattery to Jesus, the questioners asked him a double-edged question. Jesus knew that affirming the lawfulness of paying tribute to the Romans would alienate him from the Jews. Denying the lawfulness of the tax would bring Roman wrath upon him. His answer sliced through the horns of this dilemma. When the Jews produced a coin in response to Jesus' request, they undercut their objection to the tax. Their use of the coin suggests a tacit acceptance of the emperor's authority. Jesus' logic was that the coin belonged to Caesar, and they should return to him his due. Theologically Jesus was teaching that Christians must accept the state as ordained by God (Rom. 13:1–7; 1 Pet. 2:13–17) and render respect and obedience to the governments.

Affirming the Resurrection
(Matt. 22:23–33; Mark 12:18–27; Luke 20:27–40) #134

Jesus had successfully overcome Pharisaic and scribal questions. Now he encountered the trickery of the Sadducees, who denied the Resurrection. The Sadducees opposed all supernaturalism. They used an illustration intended to demonstrate the absurdity of the Resurrection. The Sadducees rejected the Prophets and the Writings as divine: they received only the Law. Their hypothetical illustration concerned levirate marriage (see Deut. 25:5–10). Telling the story of a woman who was married successively to seven siblings after each previous sibling spouse had died, the Sadducees asked Jesus, "Whose wife will she be in the resurrection?" They intended to make the idea of resurrection a laughing stock.

Jesus presented two objections to the Sadducean questions. They failed to understand the Scriptures and the power of God. He explained his response by illustrating the last example first. They failed to understand the power of God because they assumed that life after death would continue with the same physical needs as in this life. However, the power of God will create a completely new style of life in which the relationship between husband and wife for procreative purposes has no place. Jesus showed that they failed to understand the Scriptures by his reference to Exodus 3:6. When God spoke these words to Moses, the patriarchs Abraham, Isaac, and Jacob had long been physically dead, but God identified himself as their God. He could be their God only if they were still alive. The fact that Jehovah was their God suggested that they had a permanent caring relationship with the God who made that relationship. Jesus' answer silenced his inquisitors, and at least some of the scribes commended his insight (Luke 20:39–40).

The Greatest Commandments
(Matt. 22:34–40; Mark 12:28–34) #135

The scribe who interrogated Jesus had been sent by the Phari-sees. In response to his question about the greatest commandment, Jesus answered with a reference to Deuteronomy (6:4–5) and Lev-iticus (19:18). Jesus summarized that the heart of true religion lay in a positive, loving attitude to God and others. The scribe affirmed Jesus' evaluation of the law as scriptural, and Jesus affirmed his response as an indication that the scribe was not far from the kingdom of God. As we might expect, Jesus' answers sub-dued all questioners.

The Deity of the Messiah
(Matt. 22:41–46; Mark 12:35–37; Luke 20:41–44) #136

Jesus took the offensive in the theological debate by questioning the audience about their designation of Messiah as Son of David. He referred to Psalm 110:1, the most frequently quoted Old Testa-ment text in the New Testament, to show that the use of the title was inadequate and perhaps misleading as a guide to the Messiah's identity. Jesus pointed out that the Messiah was not a mere earthly replica of David but rather was David's Lord. He emphasized that the Messiah was divine as well as human.

Denunciation of the Scribes and Pharisees
(Matt. 23:1–39; Mark 12:38–40; Luke 20:45–47) #137

Matthew provides the most detailed account of Jesus' searing rebuke to the scribes and Pharisees. Jesus attacked the hypocrisy of the scribes and Pharisees. In Matthew 23:2–12 he warned the crowds and his disciples about the evils of the scribes and Phari-sees. Jesus urged his hearers to obey the teachings of the Mosaic law but to avoid the hypocritical example of the scribes and Phari-sees (Matt. 23:2–3). He warned of Pharisaic pretense and status-seeking and suggested that the religious use of the term "father" should not award mere human beings the status due only to God (Matt. 23:9–10).

In Matthew 23:13–36 Jesus denounced the scribes and Pharisees with a series of seven woes. In the first woe Jesus warned that the activities of the Pharisees and scribes prevented seekers from finding the true way of salvation (Matt. 23:13). In the fifth and sixth woes he warned against their failure to distinguish between external propriety and internal purity (Matt. 23:25–26). The seventh woe (Matt. 23:29–34) denounced the hostility of the scribes and Pharisees to God's true messengers and warned them of coming judgment. In Matthew 23:37–39 Jesus lamented the stubbornness of Jerusalem's religious leadership and held out hope only if the leaders acknowledged God's Messiah in an attitude of repentance.

The Widow's Mite (Mark 12:41–44; Luke 21:1–4) #138

Following the series of denunciations against nominal religion, Jesus now presented an example of genuine religion. The treasury was a section in the Court of Women which contained thirteen trumpet-shaped collection boxes. The large offerings of the wealthy must have landed in the boxes with a loud thud. By contrast, the offering of the poor widow must have been inaudible when it landed in the offering box. The mite was a Jewish coin of very small value. The offering of the widow represented true sacrifice, and because of this Jesus said that the widow "cast in more than all of them."

The Olivet Discourse
(Matt. 24–25; Mark 13:1–37; Luke 21:5–36) #139

Occasion of the Prophecy (Matt. 24:1–3; Mark 13:1–4; Luke 21:5–7). The proud reference of the disciples of Jesus to the beauty of the temple led to his comment about the coming destruction of the temple. The disciples then asked what the sign of the temple's destruction and of the end of the world would be. Jesus' answer is found in a section known by many New Testament students as "The Little Apocalypse" or "The Olivet Discourse," from the location of the message on the Mount of Olives. Jesus' answer did not cater to mere curiosity but attempted to meet practical and ethical aims. His reply distinguished the eschatological event of his return from the destruction of the temple.

The Signs of the End (Matt. 24:4–14; Mark 13:5–13; Luke 21:8–19). Jesus taught that signs prior to the end included false teachers, a worsening world political situation, international crises, world-wide calamities, persecutions, and the preaching of the gospel.[2] He promised spiritual help for his disciples, and he added that their perseverance in obedience would be a sign of their final salvation. Believers can take courage from the reminder elsewhere in Scripture that they will endure because God holds them firmly (1 Pet. 1:3–5).

The Abomination of Desolation (Matt. 24:15–22; Mark 13:14–20; Luke 21:20–24). The term *abomination of desolation* is a literal rendering of a phrase in Daniel 11:31 and 12:11, also echoed in Daniel 9:27. The phrase was an Old Testament idiom for anything that insulted the worship of the true God. Daniel referred to the pagan statue erected in the Jerusalem temple in 167 B.C. by the Syrian king Antiochus Epiphanes. The Synoptic writers were probably referring to the Roman standards (seen as idolatrous by the Jews) in the temple in A.D. 70. Luke 21:20 makes a more obvious reference to this event with its description of the armies surrounding Jerusalem.

The use of this abomination identifies a feature in prophetic writings known as double reference. In this passage general symbols of judgment refer to God's judgment on Israel from a Syrian king and a Roman army, and these temporal judgments picture the divine judgment at the final day. God's ongoing judgments against human sin and rebellion serve as pictures of his final defeat of evil. In the final days the abomination of desolation will become incarnate in an evil ruler known in Christian history as the Antichrist— described in 2 Thessalonians 2:4 and Revelation 13:11–17.

After the reference to the abomination of desolation, warnings appear in all three Synoptics urging believers to flee quickly from the horrors of siege and destruction.[3] These words refer both to temporal

---

2. A comparison of this section with Rev. 6:1–8 shows a broad, general agreement between the progress of trouble here and that in Revelation. The passage in Revelation appears to show wars, famine, death, and perhaps the preaching of the gospel as precursors of the end. The events mentioned in the Synoptics and Revelation are best taken as a general picture of the events which believers can expect as they live in this age. Believers can anticipate trouble and persecution, but they can count on divine assistance as they encounter it.

3. The church historian Eusebius probably referred to the phrase, "let them that are in Judea flee unto the mountains" (Matt. 24:16; Mark 13:14; Luke 21:21), when he said, "But the people of the church in Jerusalem had been commanded by a revelation, vouchsafed to approved men there before the war, to leave the city and to dwell in a certain town of Perea called Pella" (Eusebius, *Church History* 3.5.3). The "revelation" may have been a reference to Jesus' words or a command from a Christian prophet who saw the application from the Synoptics. Believers had fled the city before its destruction by the Romans.

judgments and to the final judgment against evil. The statement that the Lord "will shorten" the days of persecution reminds us that even the horrors of warfare and judgment remain under divine control.

The Return of Christ (Matt. 24:23–31; Mark 13:21–27; Luke 21:25–28). Matthew and Mark suggest that false Christs and false prophets will appear. They will perform signs and wonders that will be convincing enough to deceive the gullible. The statements again contain a double reference as they speak of both the pseudo-messianic rebellions preceding and following A.D. 70 and also of similar misleading teachers and wonder-workers who will appear in the final times. These words remind us that even false prophets can perform signs and wonders (see Exod. 7:11), and believers must be wary of accepting signs and wonders as infallible proof that the performer of the deed represents God.

In Mark 13:24–27 astronomical disturbances appear as symbols of political upheavals and also of God's final judgment. The prophetic use of double reference again appears. The upheavals symbolized in these verses may refer to the overthrow of Roman rulers, clashes between nations, and ultimately to the second coming of Christ (Mark 13:26). Jesus' disciples probably understood that Christ referred to himself, but they may have failed to grasp how the second coming might occur. We join them in their failure to understand totally all that God will do in these eschatological events.

Parables of Readiness (Matt. 24:32–25:30; Mark 13:28–37; Luke 21:29–36). Although the fig tree frequently appears in Scripture as a reference to Israel (Mark 11:12–14), its use as a symbol here does not picture Israel. Instead, this story seems to be an agricultural parable suggesting that growth of the fig tree heralds the advent of summer. Jesus warns that the events described in Mark 13:24–25 indicate his coming is near.

In Mark 13:30 the reference to "these things" is best limited to the judgments of A.D. 70. With this interpretation, Jesus was stating that the generation of his earthly ministry would see the destruction of Jerusalem and the temple. Jesus was not promising his return in the lifetime of his hearers. Christians of the first century probably anticipated and longed for Christ's return in their lifetime (2 Pet. 3:12)—as do Christians in this century.

Matthew used the generation in Noah's lifetime as an example of those unprepared for Jesus' return (Matt. 24:37–39). Just as the people of Noah's generation went about their daily activities without any spiritual preparation, many living at the time of Christ's return will be spiritually unprepared. True followers of Jesus demonstrate their preparedness for his return by righteous living.

Jesus' discussions of the timing of his return in Mark 13:32–37 lead to two practical applications. First, we must not allow our interest in Jesus' return to degenerate into an unhealthy date-setting. Second, the very uncertainty of the date should stimulate our moral commitment to Christ.

The parable of the ten virgins (Matt. 25:1–13) presents the challenge of constant readiness for Christ's return. It also teaches that after the return of Christ, symbolized in the parable by the coming of the bridegroom, no time will be left to prepare.

The parable of the talents (Matt. 25:14–30) resembles the parable of the pounds in Luke (19:12–27). Although the details of the parables differ, they make the identical point that readiness for Jesus' return consists of responsible activity, not passive inactivity. Just as the period of the owner's absence gave his servants an opportunity to use their resources, the period of Christ's absence provides his servants the opportunity to serve him in active obedience. In the story the "talent" does not symbolize a natural endowment but a privilege and opportunity in the kingdom of heaven. The opportunities available to disciples differ, but all disciples must earnestly take advantage of their privileges during Christ's absence. In the New Testament the talent represents a sum of money worth thousands of dollars.

A Picture of Future Judgment (Matt. 25:31–46). The "brothers" of Jesus are his spiritual relationships (Mark 3:33–35) and not merely his ethnic relationships, the Jews. This passage does not suggest that the works of kindness mentioned in verses 35 and 36 are the basis of salvation. This interpretation would pit Paul's emphasis on salvation by grace through faith in Christ (Eph. 2:8–9) against Jesus' emphasis on good works. Jesus seems to be saying that works of kindness and mercy to needy believers are evidence of genuine commitment to Christ. His words do not call for mere human philanthropy but for a personal response to Jesus himself

(Matt. 7:21–23). Although other New Testament books use different words, the idea that works of mercy constitute evidence of faith is also echoed in James (2:14–26) and 1 John (3:16–18). The words in Matthew are relevant to conservative evangelicals who often understand the gospel of salvation by grace through faith but fail to emphasize works of mercy which most assuredly will follow saving faith.

The Plot to Kill Jesus
(Matt. 26:1–5; Mark 14:1–2; Luke 22:1–2) #140

The date of two days before the Passover is a reference to a time on Tuesday afternoon or evening. The prime movers of this Passover plot were the priestly Sadducees who later were joined by the Pharisees and the scribes. The priestly leaders feared that an arrest during the feast might provoke a public revolt, so they looked for an opportunity to make an arrest in secret.

Jesus' Actions in Bethany
(Matt. 26:6–13; Mark 14:3–9; John 12:2–8) #141

This incident belongs chronologically with the incident of #128a from John 11:55–12:1, 9–11. See that section for a discussion of the chronological relationship and the significance of these events.

The Agreement to Betray Jesus
(Matt. 26:14–16; Mark 14:10–11; Luke 22:3–6) #142

The plot to kill Jesus became easier when one of his disciples offered to make him available to the priests. Judas' willingness to betray Jesus simplified the task of the Sadducean priests.

What motive led Judas to become the betrayer? The Gospels do not provide an answer, but the picture of Judas is uniformly bad. John 12:6 describes him as a thief, and his willingness to become a tool of Satan highlights his moral complicity (Luke 22:3). Judas might have been disappointed by the failure of Jesus to be a political messiah, so he decided to salvage some personal gain from this disappointing relationship.

Preparation for the Passover
(Matt. 26:17–19; Mark 14:12–16; Luke 22:7–13) #143

Jesus' instructions to the disciples combine supernatural insight and practical preparation. A man carrying the water pitcher would be easy to spot, for normally a woman carried the pitcher. Knowing that this sign would appear at just the right time demanded supernatural knowledge. The readiness of the upper room suggests that Jesus may already have made preparations with the householder. Christian tradition suggests that the last supper took place in the home of John Mark, but no biblical statement supports this tradition. The divine provision did not release the disciples from making practical preparation such as preparing the lamb, the bitter herbs, and the wine for the meal.

The Time of the Passover. The synoptic Gospels make it clear that Jesus and his disciples ate the Passover meal on Thursday of Passion Week (Mark 14:12, 17; Matt. 26:17, 20; Luke 22:7, 14). Several passages in John's Gospel are sometimes interpreted as suggesting that other Jews ate the Passover meal on Friday evening following Jesus' death and burial.

John 18:28 states that the Jews did not enter into Herod's palace, "that they might not be defiled, but might eat the Passover." At first glance it appears that John stated that the Jewish leaders would eat the Passover on the night after Jesus and his disciples. The term "Passover," however, can refer to the week-long festival (Num. 28:16–17) consisting of the Passover celebration and the seven-day Feast of Unleavened Bread (see the usage in Luke 22:1 for evidence of this practice). John's purpose in 18:28 might indicate that the Jews, even though they had eaten the Passover lamb the previous evening, did not want to become ritually impure and unable to observe the remaining portion of the festival.

Some argue that the phrase, "the day of preparation for the Passover," in John 19:14 suggests that the Passover was the following day. It is again possible, however, to view the term "Passover" as a reference to the entire Passover week. In this event the preparation for the Passover becomes the day of preparation for the week-long festival. The day for this preparation is Friday of Passover week. If this interpretation is correct, then John 19:14 is understood to read that Pilate was concluding the trial of Jesus on Friday of Passover week and not on the preceding day. The explanations given for both of these Johannine verses avoid conflict between the Synoptics and John.

Part of the difficulty in interpreting the verses is because the Jewish day ends at sundown. The Jewish time for the slaying of the lamb was the afternoon of 14th Nisan. The feast of Passover and Unleavened Bread began in the evening, which was 15th Nisan. Some early Christians took the position that Jesus did not eat the Passover but was crucified at the time the lamb was slain, which was 14th Nisan. He literally became our Passover. Paul's reference in 1 Corinthians 5:7 to Christ as "our Passover" is viewed as support for this interpretation, but we must realize that Paul was not attempting to settle the issue of the time of the Passover celebration but only to present a picture of the significance of Jesus' death.

Other interpreters have attempted to reconcile John and the Synoptics by suggesting that Jesus and his disciples followed a different calendar in their Passover observance than the calendar of the Jerusalem establishment. According to this view the Synoptics show Jesus eating a Passover meal with his disciples earlier in the week than the official Passover. Jesus therefore came to be crucified at the actual time of the slaughter of the Passover lambs according to the suggested schedule John followed. Thus, both John and the Synoptics are correct.[4] Adopting this understanding involves making specific historical decisions with little hard evidence. It is best to follow the solution already outlined above.

Jesus Washes the Disciples' Feet (Matt. 26:20; Mark 14:17; Luke 22:14–16, 24–30; John 13:1–20) #144–45

Only Luke tells at this point the story of the competition among the disciples for choice positions in the coming kingdom. Jesus reminded his disciples that faithful service in a lowly place demonstrates true greatness. He promised his disciples that they would enjoy a position of prominence in the eschatological messianic banquet with him.

---

4. For additional information on this issue, see the extended note in Robertson's *Harmony of the Gospels* (New York: Harper & Row Publishers Inc., 1950), 279–84. See also the discussion in D. A. Carson, *The Gospel According to John*, 455–58, 589–90, 603–5.

The incident in John's Gospel shows the close attention Jesus gave to his disciples as the end drew near. Jewish custom suggested that a rabbi's pupils should perform chores for him, but they were exempted from the menial task of washing feet. Jesus did for his disciples what the disciples of a rabbi were not expected to do and what his disciples were unwilling to do. Jesus told Peter that his washing symbolized cleansing from sin (John 13:10). He announced to all the disciples that the act symbolized the lowly service Christians should demonstrate toward one another (John 13:14–15).

Identifying the Betrayer (Matt. 26:21–25; Mark 14:18–21; Luke 22:21–23; John 13:21–30) #146

Jesus startled his disciples with the announcement that one of them would betray him. When John asked the identity of the betrayer, Jesus answered that it would be the one who would receive a special morsel of bread from the common dish. Custom called for a host to offer a sop, the morsel of bread, to a specially honored guest. In offering the sop Jesus was overcoming intended evil with good. In receiving the sop Judas showed his stubborn resistance to Jesus' love. From that moment he became Satan's tool (John 13:27). The disciples probably thought Judas's departure was due to instructions to make a purchase from the purse he carried.

The Disciples Claim Loyalty to Jesus (Matt. 26:31–35; Mark 14:27–31; Luke 22:31–38; John 13:31–38) #147

All four Gospels narrate that Jesus predicted Peter's coming threefold denial. Luke alone refers to Satan's role in Peter's downfall. Even though Peter would experience great trials, Jesus indicated that he had prayed for Peter's faith to hold firm. His hopeful words expressed confidence that Peter would retrace his steps and become a source of strength to fellow Christians.

Peter's answer showed that he comprehended neither the serious events fast approaching nor the reality of his own weakness. Jesus' words about taking purses, bags, and swords symbolized the coming dangers. The disciples indicated their readiness to fight for Jesus when they brought out two swords. Jesus' response, "It is enough," was a way of suggesting, "That's enough of this type of talk." Jesus' disciples were so hopelessly out of touch with him at this point that meaningful communication was impossible.

The Lord's Supper
(Matt. 26:26–29; Mark 14:22–25; Luke 22:17–20) #148

Luke's account of the Last Supper takes place prior to the identification and departure of the betrayer Judas. Matthew and Mark place the Last Supper after the identification of Judas. Luke may not have intended to follow chronological sequence at this point. Paul's account of this incident (1 Cor. 11:23–26) resembles Luke's in that it locates the second cup of wine after the supper itself.

Jesus instituted the Lord's Supper at the celebration of the Passover liturgy with his disciples. The liturgy included a blessing; drinking several cups of wine; reciting the Exodus story; eating lamb, unleavened bread, and bitter herbs; and finally, singing psalms.[5] The Passover commemorated Israel's release from Egyptian slavery in the offering of a Passover lamb, signifying freedom for the people of God. The Lord's Supper commemorated the redemption of God's new people, the church, by the sacrifice of Christ's life on the cross.

The phrase, "This is my body," suggests that the bread represented the body of Jesus. The Aramaic language Jesus would have spoken contains no word for "is," and this suggests that Jesus was not identifying the bread with his body. Jesus was certifying that his death had saving significance for believers.

The wine drunk by the disciples represented the shed blood of Jesus. This shedding of blood inaugurated a covenant between God and his people (see Jer. 31:31–34; Heb. 8:7–13). Jesus' blood completely removes sins; the blood of animals could only temporarily cover them. The word for "many" is equivalent in English to "all."

The Lord's Supper represents a backward look at the work of Christ on the cross. It also contains a forward look. Believers will not celebrate the Lord's Supper in heaven, for there the marriage feast of the lamb fulfills it (Rev. 19:9). Each time believers celebrate

---

5. For additional evidence of the Jewish practice, see the references in C. K. Barrett, *The New Testament Background*, rev. ed. (London: SPCK, 1987), 197–98.

the Supper they remind themselves of the significance of Jesus' death and renew their hope of his return.

The Farewell Discourses (John 14:1–17:26) #149–51

In answer to Peter's request to know where he was going, Jesus did not tell the disciples his exact destination. He assured them that his departure was for their advantage, and he promised to return (John 14:1–3). The "mansions" are dwelling places in heaven, not lavishly decorated homes. Jesus was teaching that heaven included room for all believers. Jesus presented himself as the way to the Father and promised his disciples new privileges in prayer. Prayers offered on the authority of Jesus from an obedient heart will receive a divine response. Jesus also promised that his departure would lead to the coming of the Spirit of truth. He identified this Spirit as the "helper" ("comforter"—KJV) who would encourage, strengthen, and aid believers. The command of 14:31, "Arise, let us go from here," suggests that at this time Jesus and his disciples left the upper room to go to the Mount of Olives.[6]

In John 15 Jesus transformed the Old Testament symbol for Israel, the vine, into an allegory of fruitfulness, discipleship, and prayer. Christ himself was the vine, and believers were the branches. Those who remained in him, obeyed him, and followed his commandments produced fruit. Such individuals would have unlimited possibilities in prayer because all their prayers would conform to the divine will. Jesus also warned his disciples of coming persecution and promised them that the Spirit would enable them to witness to him despite hardship and persecution.

In John 16 Jesus added that the work of the Holy Spirit involved convicting the world at large of sin, righteousness, and judgment. The Spirit will expose that the root of unbelief is a desire to live independently of Jesus. The Spirit also teaches believers that Jesus' return to the Father signaled that he successfully completed the Father's will. He will remind all human beings that the defeat of Satan through the Cross and Resurrection is a preview of coming world judgment.

---

6. This is a plausible solution, but it is by no means the only possibility. See D. A. Carson, *The Gospel According to John* (Grand Rapids: William B. Eerdmans Publishing Co.), 477–79 for additional insight.

In John 17 Jesus prayed for himself, the Twelve, and coming generations of believers. For himself Jesus prayed that he might once again enjoy the Father's glory. He could make this daring request because he had completed the Father's will on earth. For the Twelve he prayed that the Father would keep them from the evil one and sanctify them in the truth. For future generations he asked that they enjoy a supernatural unity. The demonstration of this unity will lead the world to understand the spiritual mission of Jesus.

The Struggle in Gethsemane (Matt. 26:30, 36–46; Mark 14:26, 32–42; Luke 22:39–46: John 18:1) #152

It was normal to conclude the Passover liturgy with the singing of Psalms 115–118, known as the Hallel. Although the Mount of Olives was on the route to Bethany, Jesus did not plan to return to Bethany for the evening. He and his disciples intended to spend the night on the slopes of the mount as he had done before (see Luke 21:37).

In the garden of Gethsemane Jesus surrounded himself with two rings of supporters. Eight disciples, excluding Judas, were on the outside. Inside and closest to him were Peter, James, and John. To these three he revealed something of his inner struggle and the Passion that lay ahead. His suffering here and on the cross was real and costly. In this suffering Jesus' true humanity was revealed.

Prostration in prayer showed intense anguish. Standing was the usual position for prayer (see Mark 11:25). Jesus' anguish involved more than a normal fear of pain and death. He foresaw his separation from God which his suffering would bring (see Mark 15:34), and he recoiled from the coming loneliness. Despite the utter anguish, pain, and suffering, he followed the divine plan because doing the will of God was more important than personal comfort.

Luke 22:44 pictures the intense emotions of the moment by observing that Jesus' sweat flowed as profusely as blood from an open wound. Luke did not indicate that Jesus actually sweat blood, but he drew a comparison. Some manuscripts omit the comparison between sweat and blood.

The Arrest of Jesus (Matt. 26:47–56; Mark 14:43–52; Luke 22:47–53; John 18:2–12) #153

Judas appeared leading a mob determined to arrest Jesus. The mob included Roman soldiers, temple police, and representatives of the Jewish leaders. Some in the crowd had already been awed by Jesus' words on an earlier occasion (John 7:45–46). The shock of hearing Jesus give a bold, authoritative self-identification on a sloping hillside in the middle of the night caused some of them to fall backward.

Judas stepped forward to identify Jesus to the authorities with a kiss. The kiss was normally used to show reverence for a rabbi, but Judas's kiss displayed rank hypocrisy. Although Jesus asked that his disciples be permitted to leave without a scene (John 18:8–9), Peter stepped forward with a sword and cut off the ear of a temple servant named Malchus. Jesus healed the wounded servant (Luke 22:51)[7] and ordered Peter to sheath his sword. Peter's actions amounted to a denial of the purpose Jesus had devoted himself to, and Jesus again pledged to do the Father's will. Peter's impetuous behavior made it advisable for the disciples to flee.

Mark did not identify the young man (14:51–52) who left his clothing behind as he fled, but the anonymity may indicate that it was Mark himself. If this were Mark, he may have followed Jesus and the disciples from his home where the Last Supper was held. In Acts 12:12 the home of Mark's mother became a place where Christians met for prayer.

The Trial of Jesus (John 18:12–14, 19–23) #154

Interrogations of Jesus before different groups in connection with his trial appear in the Gospels, but the evidence varies, and different interpreters view the order differently. The following discussion represents one interpretation of the evidence.

Jesus' trial had two parts, a Jewish phase and a Roman phase. The Jewish phase began with a brief appearance before the former high priest Annas and continued with appearances before Caiaphas,

---

7. It is interesting that the medical doctor Luke is the only Gospel writer to record the healing of the servant Malchus. This appears to be an indication of his medical interest.

the current high priest, and the entire Sanhedrin. The Roman phase involved an initial appearance before Pontius Pilate, who was the Roman governor, a second appearance before Herod Antipas of Galilee, and another appearance before Pontius Pilate, who then decreed Jesus' punishment. Although these distinct appearances before different groups are present in the Gospels, some examine the evidence and see a different order of events.

Annas was the most powerful figure in the Jewish priestly leadership. He held the office of the high priesthood from A.D. 6 to 15, was followed in the office by five of his sons, and was the father-in-law of Caiaphas, the high priest at the time of Jesus' arrest. Annas began the interrogation of Jesus; Jesus answered little except to remind all that he had been perfectly open in his teaching. His response in verse 23 was a demand for fair treatment, not an expression of insolence.

Appearance Before Caiaphas and the Sanhedrin (Matt. 26:57, 59–68; Mark 14:53, 55–65; Luke 22:54, 63–65; John 18:24), #155.[8] Annas sent Jesus to Caiaphas for the continuation of the trial. Sadducean members of the Sanhedrin had already been at work to locate witnesses to bring capital accusations against Jesus. Many witnesses brought wild, unsubstantiated charges against Jesus. The charge that Jesus would destroy the temple represented a perversion of the statement in John 2:19. Jesus had described his body as a temple and predicted the resurrection after his crucifixion.

The high priest Caiaphas attempted to force Jesus to convict himself by asking, "Are you the Messiah?" His affirmative answer caused the high priest to tear his garments as a sign that Jesus had spoken blasphemy. Perhaps Caiaphas willfully refused to listen when Jesus claimed that his messiahship was not the political type

---

8. The Sanhedrin violated many rules in their conduct of Jesus' trial. They were obligated to serve as an impartial jury for hearing accusations, but some of them had participated in Jesus' arrest and had sought false witnesses against him (Mark 14:55–56). Jewish laws suggested that verdicts in capital trials must be reached during the daytime, but Jesus' trial began at night, lasted most of the night, and reached a verdict in the dawn hours (Mark 15:1), hardly an evidence of justice! Capital cases also required that a verdict of conviction be reached on a day after the trial, and no trial could be held on a Sabbath or festival eve. For a presentation of Jewish rules for conducting judicial procedure, see Mishnah tractate *Sanhedrin* 4.1 in Danby, *The Mishnah*. Some scholars question whether the rules suggested in the Mishnah were operative in New Testament times.

which the religious leaders expected (Matt. 26:64). Jesus' blasphemy did not consist merely in the affirmation that he was Messiah, for after all his claim might have been true. To the minds of the Sadducean leaders the statement was blasphemy because the one who said it was helpless, lacking followers, and rejected by the religious leaders. How could *he* be the Messiah? The religious leaders could either accept Jesus' claim or reject it. They had no difficulty choosing an option. It also did not matter to them that Jesus was convicted on the basis of his own testimony, a patently illegal procedure.

After Jesus' admission, the Sanhedrin agreed that he deserved death. They erupted into unrestrained abuse of Jesus and would issue a formal decree of death after the morning dawned (Mark 15:1).

Peter's Denial of Jesus (Matt. 26:58, 69–75; Mark 14:54, 66–72; Luke 22:54–62; John 18:15–18, 25–27), #156. Peter's rash self-confidence (Mark 14:29) and his association with Jesus' enemies (Mark 14:54) assured his downfall. The first servant girl who accused him may have seen Peter previously and thus knew him as a disciple of Jesus. The bystanders recognized the rough accent of a Galilean. Peter's display of bravado in Matthew 26:74 was an effort to convince the crowd that he was not Jesus' disciple. Cocks crowed at certain times of the night, and the second cock-crowing came at around 1:30 A.M. Since cock-crowing was important for keeping time in the days of Jesus, it could be described as the cock-crowing. Although Peter's fall is lamentable, his repentance and subseqent service to Christ as recorded in the accounts in Acts provides hope for all Christians.

Jesus' Formal Condemnation (Matt. 27:1; Mark 15:1; Luke 22:66–71), #157. Issuing a formal decree of death after dawn preserved a semblance of legality for Jewish trial procedure; at least the formal condemnation took place in the daytime.

The Jews lacked the authority to impose the death penalty, for the Romans reserved this right for their officials. Moreover, a Roman governor would not normally issue the death penalty for a charge of blasphemy. If Roman security were threatened, however, the Roman government would often be quick to execute. Jewish leaders thought Jesus deserved death for alleged blasphemy, but they accused him before Pilate of being a rebel against Rome (Luke 23:2).

The Suicide of Judas (Matt. 27:3–10; Acts 1:18–19), #158. Judas's "repentance" was mere regret and remorse, not godly sorrow. In an effort to reconcile the accounts of Acts and Matthew, some interpreters suggest that Judas's rope broke as he attempted to hang himself.[9] He then plunged to his death. The moral absurdity of the behavior of the priests following Judas's death is deplorable. They were concerned about putting blood money into the temple treasury, but they had no reluctance about seeking the death of an innocent man.

Jesus Before Pilate (Matt. 27:2, 11–14; Mark 15:1–5; Luke 23:1–5; John 18:28–38), #159. The Synoptics contain a brief account that reveals the cynicism of Pilate and records the multiple accusations against Jesus. John records the preoccupation of the Jews with ritual purity and their recognition that only Pilate had the legal authority to put Jesus to death (John 18:31). The Jewish charge against Jesus carefully omitted any reference to blasphemy and accused him of fomenting political discord in Palestine (Luke 23:2). In an interview with Pilate, Jesus clearly indicated that his kingdom was spiritual, not political. Pilate surmised that a "visionary" such as this was not a threat to Roman imperial might.

Jesus Before Herod Antipas (Luke 23:6–12), #160. Pilate sought a way to avoid the responsibility of deciding Jesus' fate. When he learned of Jesus' Galilean background, he tried to shift the responsibility to Herod Antipas, the ruler of Galilee. Herod was in Jerusalem seeking to win favor with his subjects by attending the Passover. He had a curious interest to see Jesus, but his persistent prodding with questions produced no response from Jesus. In mockery Herod dressed Jesus in royal attire and returned him to Pilate.

The Return to Pilate and the Condemnation (Matt. 27:15–30; Mark 15:6–19; Luke 23:13–25; John 18:39–19:16), #161–62. As the trial of Jesus progressed, Pilate faced the choice of preserving his office or giving justice to Jesus. He finally chose to preserve his

---

9. For additional discussion on relating the statements of Matthew and Acts see I. Howard Marshall, *Acts*, TNTC (Grand Rapids: William B. Eerdmans Publishing Co., 1980), 64–65.

office. Many of Pilate's actions urged the Jewish mob to accept a lesser punishment for Jesus than crucifixion. When he offered to release an offender, either Barabbas or Jesus, Pilate was astounded that the crowd clamored for the release of the rebel leader Barabbas. When he subjected Jesus to scourging, he tried to stir up sympathy for Jesus in the fickle crowd, but the mob shouted out more vigorously, "Crucify him!" When he washed his hands of the entire affair (Matt. 27:24–25), he seemed to feel that the ritual washing would set him free from blame in the matter. When he heard the crowd relate Jesus' claim to be the Son of God, he superstitiously asked him, "Where do you come from?" He finally surrendered his conscience to the Jewish threat of blackmail (John 19:12).

The events preceding Jesus' crucifixion raise several questions of historical and theological significance. Why did this mob call for Jesus' crucifixion when several days earlier Jesus had been acclaimed as the Messiah? It is likely that this was a different mob. Those who greeted Jesus at his entry to Jerusalem were Passover pilgrims. Those who clamored for his crucifixion were collaborators with the Jewish priestly leaders.

Who was responsible for the death of Jesus? Was it the fault of the Jews or the Romans? Both are culpable. Pilate, as the Roman representative, had the power to stop the proceedings. He did nothing. The Jews instigated the entire affair by falsely accusing Jesus and bringing him to Pilate. They accepted the implications of their actions (Matt. 27:25). However, nothing in the actions of the Jews should lead Christians to view them as "Christ-haters."

Jesus was probably scourged with a whip whose leather thongs contained pieces of bone or metal. Some whippings were so brutal the victims died. This whipping was probably less severe, intended to appease the Jews and to teach Jesus a lesson. It is impossible to describe accurately the crown of thorns. Some suggest that date palm branches, twisted together and fashioned into an imitation royal crown, could have caused Jesus intense pain and aided the mockery of the soldiers. The mockery of the soldiers resembles the mockery of the Sanhedrin members after they had condemned the Lord (Luke 22:63–65).

The Cross of Jesus (Matt. 27:31–34; Mark 15:20–23; Luke 23:26–33; John 19:16–17) #163

The Romans reserved the horrors of crucifixion for criminals and slaves. This method of capital punishment was the first-century counterpart to firing squads and electric chairs. The Gospels provide little information on the details of Jesus' crucifixion. Nails were usually driven through the victim's wrists and ankles. The weight of the body rested on a peg that extended between the legs. Death came slowly, and suffocation or cardiac arrest was often the cause.

Jesus probably carried only the crosspiece to the place of execution. The upright beam likely remained in its place. Weakened by scourging, Jesus required help to make the trip to the execution site. Simon, the father of Alexander and Rufus, who apparently had become Christians, helped to carry the load.

The trip to the execution site progressed with loud outcries of grief, particularly from the female followers of Jesus. Jesus' words to the women ended with a statement which suggested, "If the innocent Jesus has suffered such a terrible fate, what will happen to those who are guilty?"(Luke 23:31). Jewish tradition suggests that Jerusalem women provided a narcotic drink to relieve pain among the victims; Jesus refused the offer of the drink.

The place of crucifixion had the Hebrew name "Golgotha," meaning "place of a skull." "Calvary" is the Latin equivalent. In Jerusalem the Church of the Holy Sepulchre has at least a claim to be the crucifixion location, for it was outside the walls of Jerusalem in Jesus' lifetime (see Heb. 13:11–13, which describes a location outside the city walls).

The Early Hours of the Crucifixion (Matt. 27:35–44; Mark 15:24–32; Luke 23:33–43; John 19:18–27) #164.

The Gospel writers believed that Psalm 22:18 was fulfilled when lots were cast to determine the ownership of Jesus' garments. Pilate's trilingual inscription that Jesus was the king of the Jews contained deeper truth than its author realized. The parade of mockers before the cross was described in language from Psalm 22:7. The most positive word recorded by the Gospel writers was the plea for mercy from Jesus' fellow victim, the thief (Luke 23:42).

To designate the "third hour" as the time when Jesus was nailed to the cross (Mark 15:25) does not correspond easily to the "sixth hour" for the conclusion of his trial (John 19:14). Despite many attempts at harmonization, it is probably best to regard both times as approximate. In a day when no one owned a watch, observers made different estimates of the advance of the sun. We should not expect Gospel writers without watches to give time precisely. Their writings reflect the standards of chronological accuracy of their day.

Three of Jesus' seven final sayings appear in this section:

1. In Luke 23:34 Jesus requested forgiveness for his enemies.

2. In Luke 23:43 he offered paradise to the repentant thief on the cross. The term *Paradise* comes from a Persian word meaning garden and is used to refer to the place where believers experience rest and joy immediately after death.

3. In John 19:27 Jesus committed the care of Mary to the beloved disciple, John. Mary had probably identified with her son in such a way that she could not expect assistance from her family members who did not yet believe in him (see John 7:5). John met that need.

The Closing Hours of Jesus' Crucifixion (Matt. 27:45–50; Mark 15:33–37; Luke 23:44–46; John 19:28–30) #165

Darkness fell over Jerusalem from noon until 3 P.M. No Gospel writer specified a cause for the darkness. Four additional final sayings of Jesus appear in this section:

4. Jesus' cry "My God, my God, why have you forsaken me?" suggested that he was aware of his present alienation from God as he died in order to ransom many (Matt. 27:46).

5. Jesus expressed physical agony due to the torture of crucifixion when he uttered, "I thirst" (John 19:28).

6. The exclamation "It is finished" (John 19:30) was a cry of victory. Jesus used a single Greek term that sometimes appeared on receipts to suggest "Paid in Full." By uttering the word Jesus expressed awareness that he had paid the debt of sin.

7. Jesus' final words, "Father, into thy hands I commend my spirit" (Luke 23:46), expressed confidence in the triumphant outcome of the Crucifixion. Jesus expressed the hope of restored fellowship with the Father after death.

The Death of Jesus (Matt. 27:51–56; Mark 15:38–41; Luke 23:45, 47–49) #166

God may have used the earthquake to tear the veil of the temple. Opening the veil represented the open access to God made possible by the death of Jesus. This idea is developed in Hebrews (10:19–20). Matthew recorded the raising and appearance of some Old Testament saints in relation to Jesus' death and resurrection (Matt. 27:51–53). This unique occurrence showed that through Jesus the hope of a better future became a reality. The witness of the centurion was more a response to divine power than a theological understanding of the person and work of Jesus Christ (Matt. 27:54).

The Burial of Jesus (Matt. 27:57–60; Mark 15:42–46; Luke 23:50–54; John 19:31–42) #167

Because the Jews were concerned about violating ritual laws that prohibited the display of the body of a condemned criminal overnight (Deut. 21:22–23), they asked Pilate to hasten the death of the victims. Breaking the legs of crucifixion victims hastened death because the crucified could no longer use the legs to push upward to open the chest cavity. The lack of oxygen led to quick death. The soldiers, who knew death when they saw it, found Jesus already dead when they came to break his legs. One jabbed his spear into Jesus' side, and a mixture of blood and water flowed out. Experts differ on how the blood and water appeared because they disagree on what was pierced. John's record, however, does show the reality of Jesus' humanity. Because Jesus was a real man, blood flowed from his side.

Joseph of Arimathea's request to bury Jesus contains three noteworthy elements:

1. It required great courage.

2. It identified him with the Lord.

3. It was unusual, for Romans normally threw aside without burial the bodies of the victims of crucifixion.

Furthermore, the weight and cost of the spices that Joseph used to anoint Jesus (John 19:39) reflected the extravagance of his devotion, and the use of the clean linen shroud showed much care and reverence. Also, Nicodemus's partnership with Joseph is evidence that he indeed might have been "born again."

The Watch by the Tomb
(Matt. 27:61–66; Mark 15:47; Luke 23:55–56) #168

Matthew probably mentioned this story to offset a rumor that the disciples had stolen Jesus' body. This story demonstrated the difficulty and indeed the impossibility of such action.

The Sadducees and Pharisees requested maximum security, a detachment of Roman soldiers. The stone was sealed, the guard was set, and anyone trying to steal the body would have encountered the armed might of the Roman empire. We cannot imagine that grave robbers were active at this location!

The Emptying of the Tomb
(Matt. 28:1–4; Mark 16:1) #169–70

The Bible never gives a full description of the event of the Resurrection. It emphasizes that the tomb was empty and that the disciples met the risen Lord. The event took place near dawn on Sunday after Jesus' burial on Friday. The outward manifestations of the Resurrection included an earthquake, the appearance of an angel, and moving the stone sealing the tomb. The reality of the event is shown by the paralyzing fright of the normally hardened, tough guards.

The Response of the Women (Matt. 28:5–8;
Mark 16:2–8; Luke 24:1–8; John 20:1) #171

It is impossible to unravel fully the differences of the details in the four Gospels as they report the Resurrection. The variety of details points to the opinions of several eyewitnesses and shows us that the Gospel writers made no effort to present a unified report. This fact provides a firmer basis for believing the truthfulness of the report.

Perhaps John's report of the visit by Mary Magdalene (20:1) describes a visit she made alone before sunrise. She may have returned later with the other women as the sun was rising (Matt. 28:1). Matthew and Mark mention only a single angel at the tomb, but Luke mentions that two were present. The women came to the tomb questioning who would remove the stone to allow them access to the tomb (Mark 16:3). God had already handled the object of their concern and they reacted with fear, joy, confusion, and disbelief.

Disappointment Among the Disciples
(Luke 24:9–12; John 20:2–10) #172

The women's words about the empty tomb spurred Peter and John to dash away to investigate the incident for themelves. The more youthful John won the race, but he remained outside the tomb gazing intently inside. The more impetuous Peter rushed into the tomb. What did they see?

The burial cloth which had covered Jesus' head was rolled up and left in a corner as if the original user no longer needed it. Some have suggested that the cloth covering Jesus' body retained the shape of his body. We can more safely contrast the appearance here with that at Lazarus's resurrection. Lazarus came from the tomb with his grave clothes clinging to his body, but Jesus apparently passed through all the grave coverings and left them behind. John believed in the Resurrection on the basis of the empty tomb, but both disciples left the tomb disappointed (John 20:10).

Mary Sees Jesus
(Matt. 28:9–10; Mark 16:9–11; John 20:11–18) #173–74

The major focus of these verses is Jesus' appearance to Mary. As Mary stood in grief near the tomb, Jesus spoke to her. She recognized him only when he uttered her name. Apparently Mary responded by falling to her knees and clinging to Jesus' feet in a magnificent effort to keep him with her. Jesus' words to her (John 20:17) probably suggest, "Stop clinging to me. I am not yet in the ascended state and am not about to disappear permanently."[10] Mary needed to learn that her relationship to Jesus did not depend on his physical presence.

---

10. For additional information on interpreting this difficult verse, see the discussion in Carson, *The Gospel According to John*, 641–45.

Bribing the Guards (Matt. 28:11–15) #175

The story suggested by the chief priests was an insult to the guards and potentially dangerous to their health and well-being! The priests were so desperate to conceal the absence of Jesus' body that they failed to consider the improbability that the guards would sleep through a grave robbery and, at the same time, know what occurred during their slumber. The priests might have trusted more in their ability to bribe the governor if that proved necessary.

The Emmaus Disciples
(Mark 16:12–13; Luke 24:13–35; 1 Cor. 15:5a) #176–77

The Emmaus disciples glumly reported to Jesus, whom they did not recognize, the frustration of their messianic hopes in the events surrounding his Passion in Jerusalem. The post-Resurrection appearance of Jesus must have been different from his pre-Passion appearance since they were unable to recognize him. Something in Jesus' manner of blessing and distributing the bread (Luke 24:30–31) led them to recognize that the stranger who had so warmed their hearts was the Lord himself.

Jesus Appears to the Eleven (Mark 16:14;
Luke 24:36–43; John 20:19–31; 1 Cor. 15:5b) #178–79

The disciples still feared persecution from the authorities and so they met behind locked doors. Miraculously, Jesus appeared among them despite the locked doors. This miracle resembles the act of Jesus' passing through the grave clothes at his resurrection. Jesus gave the disciples physical evidence to sustain their faith. A week later he appeared to the ten disciples plus Thomas, who had been absent at the first appearance, to give the same evidence to him. It is unfair to label Thomas as "doubting," for all that he demanded was the same evidence that the other disciples had already received.

Jesus' command for his disciples to receive the Holy Spirit is an acted parable pointing to the future outpouring of the Spirit on the disciples at Pentecost. The disciples failed to demonstrate evidence of the dynamic presence of the Spirit until then. The locked doors that protected their meeting (John 20:26) indicate that the disciples did not yet have the boldness we later find in Acts. The power of forgiving and retaining sins refers to the authority of all Christians to declare the terms under which sins can be forgiven. These terms include repentance and faith in Jesus Christ.

More Post-Resurrection Appearances (John 21) #180

Jesus had early in his ministry shown supernatural knowledge about the location of a school of fish (Luke 5:1–11). Since the disciples did not recognize the Lord, his advice to the disciples on this occasion would have been received as the advice of one fisherman to another. John's response revealed that he recognized Jesus (John 21:7), and Peter showed action. By preparing the food for the disciples, Jesus showed that he was continuing to serve them even as he had done earlier in washing their feet (John 13:4–17); and by eating food, Jesus reassured the disciples of the reality of his resurrection.

Jesus asked Peter if he loved him more than the other disciples loved him. Jesus' threefold repetition of the question to Peter, "Peter, do you love me?" was an effort to reassure Peter about his acceptance back into the body of the disciples. Just as Peter had denied the Lord three times, Jesus three times accepted him back with the commission, "Feed my sheep."

Jesus' question about Peter's love also affirmed that a genuine love for Jesus is an indispensable qualification for Christian service. Peter was expected to show his love in his care for the flock. Jesus' command to Peter did not empower him with any primacy over other believers. Nothing in the context suggests that Jesus intended to give Peter any rights for governing the church or for exercising authority.

Jesus predicted to Peter that he would die in old age after a period of confinement during which he would be carried about by others. Some feel that the description in John 21:18 refers to crucifixion as Peter's mode of death. If it does not refer to crucifixion, it at least suggests that Peter will be a martyr. Jesus' comment to Peter led the inquisitive disciple to ask about John, "What will happen to him?" Jesus responded with the wise reminder, "If I desire him to live until I return, what is that to you? You must focus on following me."

Jesus' Final Actions (Matt. 28:16–20; Mark 16:15–20; Luke 24:44–53; 1 Cor. 15:6–7; Acts 1:3–12) #181–84

The conclusion from Mark 16:9 onward likely did not come from Mark's hands. See "The Ending of Mark" in chapter 7 for a discussion of the evidence for rejecting this as a part of Mark's original writing.

Jesus challenged his disciples with the Great Commission in the Book of Matthew (28:16–20). Jesus had received universal authority from his obedience to the Father's plan. His universal lordship demands a univeral mission. So, he commanded his followers to make other disciples. As a part of discipleship they were commanded to baptize as an act of repentance and commitment to God's people. They were also directed to teach the commandments of Jesus, an emphasis on the strong ethical content of his words.

After a postresurrection ministry lasting forty days, Jesus ascended to heaven to be seated at the supreme place of authority in heaven (Eph. 1:20–23). His departing act was to raise his hands as a sign of blessing to the disciples.

Excursus on the Resurrection of Jesus

Thoughtful people rightly ask three important questions about the Resurrection:

1. What is the resurrection of Christ?

2. What is the evidence that this resurrection occurred?

3. Why is the Resurrection important?

In this section we will provide answers to these three questions.

We can understand the nature of Christ's resurrection by comparing it to the raising of Lazarus (John 11:38–44) and the son of the widow at Nain (Luke 7:11–17). These two men were physically dead; Jesus brought them back to life. They did not live forever in the body in which they returned from death. They eventually died physically, and they are physically dead today. The resurrection of Jesus Christ was different. He died physically, but he returned to life. He did not return with the same physical body, but rather, he received a new, glorified body and became the firstfruits of all who have died (1 Cor. 15:20). He lives today in heaven and will continue to live for eternity. The resurrection of Jesus Christ is the historical event by which he came back from physical death to a new quality of life with a new, glorified body, never again to die.

What is the evidence for this resurrection of Jesus Christ?[11] First, the New Testament teaches that Jesus Christ was dead physically. His death occurred after at least three predictions prior to the event (Matt. 16:21; 17:23; 20:17–19). A centurion observed his death and exclaimed, "Truly this man was the Son of God" (Mark 15:39). Other soldiers at the crucifixion observed that he was dead when they attempted to break his legs (John 19:32–37). These professional soldiers possessed the ability to observe and diagnose the presence of death. Joseph of Arimathea received the body of Jesus for burial. If Jesus had been alive, Joseph would have noticed signs of life. Joseph wrapped the body of Jesus in pungent spices which surely would have awakened Jesus if he had only fainted and had not actually died (John 19:39). We can say with confidence that Jesus Christ was dead.

Second, Jesus Christ was buried. Joseph of Arimathea buried him in a new cave cut from rock (Matt. 27:57–61). Guards were placed at the tomb under the orders of Pontius Pilate the governor. A seal was placed on the tomb. A heavy stone was rolled in front of the opening. Women followers of Jesus (Matt. 27:61) observed the location of his burial. Jesus was buried in a tomb, and his followers observed the location.

Third, the tomb was empty. The New Testament explains that an earthquake occurred, an angel descended, and the angel rolled away the stone (Matt. 28:1–2). This incident left the guard detail in a state of paralyzed terror (Matt. 28:4). The angel announced the resurrection to the women who had come to the tomb to complete the process of burial (Matt. 28:5–7). Peter and John raced to the tomb to find it empty (John 20:2–10). The orderliness of the appearance of the burial clothing suggested that no one had stolen Jesus' body. Instead, the empty tomb and the appearance of the

---

11. Michael Green's book *Man Alive* (Chicago: InterVarsity Press, 1967) provided assistance and stimulation in formulating the answer to this question. His practical defense of the Resurrection carries many examples of how a knowledge of the Resurrection served as a tool of evangelism and provided assistance in experiencing divine power in daily living.

grave clothing within convinced the beloved disciple that Jesus had arisen (John 20:8). The effort by the enemies of Jesus to bribe the guards at the tomb to lie about the disappearance of Jesus' body provides evidence for the Resurrection (Matt. 28:11–15). These enemies knew surely that some miracle had led to the disappearance of the body. The soldiers guarding the tomb could not possibly describe an incident which allegedly occurred while they slept!

Fourth, the post-Resurrection appearances of Jesus reveal the reality of the Resurrection. These appearances occurred to many different groups of people, in many places, and at various times. They endured for forty days, suddenly came to an end when Jesus ascended into heaven, and have never occurred since that time. After the Resurrection Jesus appeared to such individuals as Mary Magdalene (John 20:10–18), Peter (Luke 24:34), Thomas (John 20:26–28), and James, the Lord's brother (1 Cor. 15:7). He appeared to such small groups as the Emmaus disciples (Luke 24:13–35), the women as they left the location of the tomb (Matt. 28:8–10), and the seven disciples as they were fishing (John 21:1–14). He also appeared to larger groups such as the entire body of the disciples (John 20:19–23) and a group of over five hundred believers (1 Cor. 15:6). Moreover, these appearances occurred in different places at different times of the day. The variety of these appearances rules out any possibility that these sightings were mere hallucinations.

Finally, we see evidence for the Resurrection in the changes in the disciples. One day they were cowering in terror from the Roman authorities, and after Pentecost God changed them into a group that no degree of persecution could muzzle. The single event that contributed to their change was the resurrection of Christ. Only an event such as the Resurrection could lead the Christian Jews to move their day of worship from the Sabbath to Sunday, the day when the Lord rose from the dead. Only a historical event such as the Resurrection could lead Christians to adopt baptism, an event proclaiming Jesus' resurrection, as the symbol of entrance into the Christian life. All of these features, taken together, provide cumulative certainty of the reality of the Resurrection.

Given that the Resurrection occurred, why is it important?

- The Resurrection provides evidence of the deity of Christ (Rom. 1:4).

- The Resurrection is the event by which Jesus was exalted into heaven (Acts 2:33).

- The Resurrection provides a basis for the justification of believers (Rom. 4:25).

- The fact of Jesus' resurrection provides confidence for the coming resurrection of all believers (1 Thess. 4:14; Rom. 8:11).

- Because of the Resurrection, all believers have an incentive to endure and persist in Christian living (1 Cor. 15:58).

- The fact of Jesus' resurrection is the event which has prompted human beings to believe in Jesus as Lord. The Resurrection has led individuals to experience hope for the future and encouragement and help in this life. The Resurrection has placed Christianity in the unique position of having a historical basis for the supernatural faith which it declares.

For Further Discussion

1. Does the Olivet Discourse (Matthew 24–25; Mark 13; Luke 21:5–38) provide a detailed map or a general summary of God's plans for the end times? Give evidence for your answer.

2. Why did Jesus select Judas to be one of his disciples?

3. Explain how the message of Jesus in the farewell discourses (John 14–17) instructed and encouraged the disciples.

4. Evaluate the character of Pontius Pilate in light of his conduct at the trial of Jesus.

5. Evaluate the importance of the Resurrection for Christian faith and practice.

Bibliography

See the works listed previously in chapters 8–10 and review the footnotes in this chapter. In addition, consult the following works.

Barrett, C. K. *The New Testament Background: Selected Documents.* Rev. ed. London: Society for Promoting Christian Knowledge, 1987.

Beasley-Murray, G. R. *Christ Is Alive!* London: Lutterworth Press, 1947.

Blinzler, Josef. *The Trial of Jesus.* Westminster: Newman, 1959.

Brandon, S. G. F. *The Trial of Jesus of Nazareth.* New York: Stern & Day, 1968.

Carson, D. A. *The Gospel According to John.* Grand Rapids: William B. Eerdmans Publishing Co.,1991.

Craig, William L. *The Historical Argument for the Resurrection of Jesus During the Deist Controversy.* Lewiston, N.Y.: Edwin Mellen Press, 1985.

Green, Michael. *Man Alive!* Chicago: InterVarsity Press, 1967. Popular presentation by an Anglican evangelical of biblical argument for the resurrection of Jesus.

Kunneth, Walter. *The Theology of the Resurrection.* St. Louis: Concordia Press, 1965.

Ladd, G. E. *I Believe in the Resurrection of Jesus.* Grand Rapids: William B. Eerdmans Publishing Co., 1975.

Marshall, Howard I. *Acts.* TNTC. Grand Rapids: William B. Eerdmans Publishing Co., 1980.

Miethe, Terry L., ed. *Did Jesus Arise from the Dead? The Resurrection Debate.* San Francisco: Harper & Row Publishers Inc., 1987. Summary of a debate between Gary R. Habermas and Antony G. N. Flew at Liberty University in 1985.

Milligan, William. *The Resurrection of Our Lord.* London: MacMillan Co., 1899.

Morris, Leon. *The Cross in the New Testament.* Grand Rapids: William B. Eerdmans Publishing Co., 1965.

——————. *The Cross of Jesus.* Grand Rapids: William B. Eerdmans Publishing Co., 1988.

Orr, James. *The Resurrection of Jesus.* London: Hodder and Stoughton, 1909. Reprint, Joplin, Mo.: College Press, 1972.

Robertson, A. T. *A Harmony of the Gospels.* New York: Harper & Row Publishers Inc., 1950.

Stalker, James. *The Trial and Death of Jesus.* London: Hodder and Stoughton, 1894.

12 Introduction to the Acts and the Role of Peter in Early Christianity (Acts 1–12)

Guiding Questions

1. List evidence for the Lucan authorship of Acts.

2. Evaluate the evidence for determining the date of the writing of Acts.

3. What indicators of historical reliability do you find in Acts?

4. Explain the significance of Pentecost for the Christian church.

5. List the actions and contributions of Peter that are narrated in Acts 1–12.

Authorship

The case for Lucan authorship of Acts was discussed in the study of the authorship of Luke's Gospel in chapter 7. We can summarize that discussion in three statements.[1]

1. The author of the Gospel of Luke and the author of Acts are one and the same.

---

1. For expansion and explanation of these statements, see the discussion of authorship of Luke's Gospel, chapter 7.

2. The author of Acts was a companion of Paul during the journey to Rome for his appearance before Caesar.

3. Luke is Paul's companion who is most likely to have written Acts.

Acceptance of Lucan authorship of Acts was generally followed without serious question in the early church. Early Christian leaders such as Irenaeus,[2] Clement of Alexandria,[3] and Eusebius[4] provide evidence for the Lucan authorship of Acts. The Muratorian Canon (A.D. 190) listed Luke as the author of Acts. This combination of internal and external evidence for the Lucan authorship of Acts remained relatively unchallenged until critical approaches to the New Testament appeared at the end of the eighteenth century. Since that time critics have increasingly questioned Lucan authorship.

Challenges to the Lucan Authorship of Acts

Some have questioned Lucan authorship by challenging the idea that the author of the "we" sections of Acts was a companion of Paul.[5] In these sections the author used the first person plural "we" to describe his actions. (The passages appear in Acts 16:10–17; 20:5–21:18; and 27:1–28:16.) One critic of Lucan authorship suggested that the author of Acts used a source written in the first person plural by another individual in the "we" sections. This suggestion becomes less convincing when we remember that Luke frequently put his own stamp on his sources. Because of this tendency we would not expect Luke to be reluctant to dispense with the first person plural if he used other sources. Another opponent of Lucan authorship feels that the use of the first person plural is a stylistic device that makes a rhetorical point rather than a historical point. However, this suggestion fails to explain why the author decided to use a stylistic device in the places he did.

---

2. Evidence in Irenaeus appears in *Against Heresies* 3.14.1–4.

3. The evidence in Clement appears in *Stromata* 5.12, where Clement designates the author of Acts 17:22–23 as "Luke."

4. Eusebius designates Luke as the author of Acts in his *Church History* 3.4.

5. For the significance of these sections, see the discussion of the authorship of Luke, chapter 7.

Other challengers to Lucan authorship focus on theological differences between the Paul of Acts and the Paul of the Epistles. They reason that a man such as Luke who knew Paul intimately could not have written Acts with a picture of Paul that differs from the Paul of the Epistles. In Acts 17 Paul used Stoic ideas about God and the world to make a case for natural theology. In Romans 1 Paul used natural revelation to support his belief that pagan people are responsible for their sins. Which is the proper view of Paul? Did he suggest that natural theology could lead to God, or did he support that having God's revelation in nature only produced guilt and contributed to lostness?

The differences can be explained by pointing out that Paul in Acts may have been building a thought bridge to the sophisticated pagans in Athens in preparation for preaching the gospel. On the other hand, Paul may have wanted to warn his Roman readers that the revelation of God in nature does not bring a saving understanding of Jesus. Only God's revelation given at the cross as portrayed in Paul's letter to the Romans explains how Jesus brings people to God. This explanation for the differences between Paul in Acts 17 and Romans 1 seems reasonable. Paul used more than one method to present the gospel.

Despite some modern objections to Luke as the author of Acts, the ancient view of the early church still carries weight. External evidence and internal evidence in Acts suggest that Luke authored the book.[6]

Luke the Man

What information do we have about Luke? Luke was probably a Gentile.[7] His name is Greek, and Paul's reference to Luke in Colossians 4:10–14 seems to link him with Gentiles rather than Jews. Luke's exceptionally refined use of Greek also suggests that he was Greek. Paul's reference to Luke in Colossians 4:14 indicates that he was a physician. No other certain information about Luke's background exists, but the Anti–Marcionite prologue to Luke's Gospel, dating from the second century A.D., states that he was a

---

6. For a more comprehensive discussion of the problem of Lucan authorship of Acts, see Carson, Moo, and Morris, *An Introduction to the New Testament*, 185–90.

7. For a contrary opinion, see Earle Ellis, *The Gospel of Luke*, NCB (Grand Rapids: Eerdmans, 1981), 52–53, who says, "The balance of probabilities favours the view that Luke was a Hellenistic Jew."

native of Antioch, Syria, never married, and died in Boeotia at the age of eighty-four.[8]

Date of Writing Acts

The date for writing Acts is linked with the date for writing Luke. Both books have the same author, and Luke's Gospel is the first volume of a two-volume work. In the earlier discussion of Luke's Gospel, a date in the early sixties was suggested as the likely time of writing.[9] The most significant factor contributing to this date is the abrupt ending of Acts. The most cogent explanation of why Luke ended Acts with Paul still imprisoned is that Paul's imprisonment was still unresolved. The fact that Paul had spent two years (Acts 28:30) in a Roman prison at the conclusion of Acts provides help in dating Acts in the early sixties.

A suggested date for writing Acts used by many contemporary scholars is A.D. 80, or even later. Scholars select this time because of their difficulty in dating Luke prior to A.D. 70. The later date for writing Luke is popular because of the commonly held view that Luke's Gospel reflects the circumstances of the Roman destruction of Jerusalem in A.D. 70. The reference in Luke 21:20 to the "surrounding of Jerusalem by armies" leads many scholars to date Luke after this event occurred. It is difficult for them to accept such a prophecy prior to the event. However, we should be able to accept that Jesus had such prophetic gifts and that the statement in Luke 21:20 is a genuine prophecy of the future. If we accept this passage of Scripture as prophecy, we should have little difficulty in accepting an earlier date for the writing of Luke and Acts.

At the conclusion of Acts Paul was still awaiting trial. Nero had not yet turned against the Christians as he did in A.D. 64. Luke wrote Acts at some time in the early sixties.

Literary Questions About Acts

The term *genre* is used to describe a literary style of a writing. Acts belongs to the history genre. Luke wrote history with a pur-

---

8. For the full quotation of this prologue, see Ellis, *The Gospel of Luke*, 41.
9. For more complete discussion of the issue of dating Luke-Acts, see the discussion of the date of Luke in chapter 7.

pose. He was not interested in outlining each facet of the development of the early church. Rather, he focused on how the gospel spread from Jerusalem to Rome. He also paid close attention to the work and ministry of Paul. Although Luke had a theological purpose for writing, we must understand that Acts contains reliable, trustworthy historical information.

The Quality of Greek

The Greek of Acts reflects cultured usage. At times, however, Luke used a Greek style heavily influenced by contact with Semitic culture. In the many speeches of Acts, Luke did not present verbatim reports of what was spoken. He presented an accurate summary of the messages he heard. One source of evidence for the accuracy of Luke's report is that Peter's sermons in Acts use expressions that also appear in 1 Peter.[10] Luke did not compose speeches. Rather, he accurately summarized the words which his speakers used.

The Sources of Luke

The first four verses of Luke's Gospel indicate that Luke used sources to write his Gospel. We might infer from this statement that sources also lay behind the book of Acts, but Luke used them with such skill that we cannot easily detect their presence. At times Luke used his own memory of events as his basis for writing. He also gained information from Paul, from Christians in various locations such as Jerusalem, Syria, Antioch, and Rome, and from such companions of Paul as Timothy and Silas. Many unnamed Christians probably shared information with Luke. Some documents, such as the Jerusalem Decree (Acts 15:23–29), were also available for Luke to use. The fact that Luke used sources does not mean that Acts is only a research project. We should recognize divine guidance in each part of the process of writing. Luke was a willing recipient and user of this guidance.

---

10. For example, in Acts 4:11 Peter referred to Ps. 118:22, a reference describing Jesus Christ in terms of "stone." Peter refers to the same Psalm in 1 Pet. 2:7. This practice, of which other examples appear in Acts, shows that Luke has carefully and accurately summarized what Peter said.

Historical Accuracy of Acts

Luke's purpose for writing Acts was to show the progress of the gospel through the ministry of the risen Christ. We will explore evidence for this purpose in a later section. We also need to recognize as we read Acts that the book describes certain events that occurred in history. Acts provides information about the coming of the Holy Spirit at Pentecost, the conversion of Paul, and the growth and spread of early Christianity throughout the Roman world. Futhermore, the impact of the ministry of Peter, James, and Paul on the early church is clearly shown in historical events.

What is our basis for trusting the information given in Acts? Are the accounts of events in Acts reliable? Was Luke an accurate historian?

Answering these questions involves investigating Luke's knowledge of the Roman government and the personalities involved in it. We must look at the reports of miracles and speeches in Acts. Did Luke accurately report what Paul and the early church said and did? Many past and current biblical scholars have discussed the problem of the historical reliability of Acts.

W. M. Ramsay was a leading defender in an earlier generation in studying the historical reliability of Acts. Ramsay wrote at a time when the study of Roman history was making great strides, and unusual insights into the character of events in the Roman Empire were forthcoming. He noted that it was not uncommon for scholars in his generation to assume that the Romans first persecuted Christians during the time of Emperor Trajan in A.D. 112. Trajan's letter to the younger Pliny indicated the existence of this persecution.[11] This evidence led to the assumption that any references to persecution belonged to a period later than A.D. 112. Ramsay noted that research into Roman history proved that persecuting Christians was a standing policy of Rome. Therefore, references to persecution do not necessarily indicate late dates. Rather, such references are indications that Roman policy was being carried out even during the apostolic period.

---

11. W. M. Ramsay, *Pauline and Other Studies in Early Christian History* (New York: A. C. Armstrong, 1906; reprint, Grand Rapids: Baker Book House, 1970), 195.

Scholars also examined the nautical terms used to describe Paul's voyage to Rome (Acts 27). Many had questioned the reliability of the account of Paul's journey to Rome, but intensive investigation showed that Luke's account reflects unusual accuracy in reporting nautical practices and insightful awareness of weather conditions in the Mediterranean area. Those who have studied and examined the navigational practices in Acts 27 conclude that the author had an intimate acquaintance with sailing on the Mediterranean during the fall and winter of the year.[12]

The classical scholar A. N. Sherwin-White examined Luke's knowledge of Roman provincial government, the legal treatment of Roman citizens, and the trials of Paul before various government representatives. After a massive study, he commented that "any attempt to reject its [Acts's] basic historicity even in matters of detail must now appear absurd."[13]

The most ambitious study concerning the historical reliability of Acts is the work by the late Colin Hemer.[14] Hemer discussed the evidence of historical details, names and titles, the question of theological differences between Luke and Paul, and the issue of the presence of historical errors in the narratives describing Paul's ministry. Based on his research, he decided in favor of the historical reliability of Acts.

Below are four sources of evidence that have led scholars to affirm the reliability and trustworthiness of the events recorded in Acts.

1. Luke is fully aware of the correct terms to use in designating Roman officials and provinces. In Acts 18:12 Luke accurately designated Gallio as a "proconsul," the ruler of a senatorial province. In Acts 23:26 (and in other places in Acts) Luke correctly used the term "governor," the title for the ruler of an imperial province. Pontius Pilate served in this capacity in the Gospels. Sometimes the classifications of the provinces

---

12. For additional information on this issue, see the monograph by James Smith, *The Voyage and Shipwreck of Paul*, 4th ed. (London: Longman, Brown, Green & Longmans, 1880; reprint, Grand Rapids: Baker Book House, 1978).

13. A. N. Sherwin-White, *Roman Society and Roman Law in the New Testament* (London: Oxford University Press, 1963; reprint, Grand Rapids: Baker, Twin Books, 1978), 189.

14. Colin J. Hemer, *The Book of Acts in the Setting of Hellenistic History*, WUNT 49 (Tubingen: Mohr, 1989).

changed, demanding accurate research to keep abreast of the situation. Luke seems to have taken great care to remain informed and accurate in his reporting of historical events.

2. Some believe Luke is wrong in his report in Acts 5:36 that the Jewish rabbi Gamaliel could describe the activities of the rebel leader Theudas. Josephus also mentions a Theudas, but Josephus places his actions in the period from A.D. 44 to 46—ten years after the setting of Acts 5. Acts 5:37 mentions the activities of another rebel leader, Judas of Galilee, who can be dated about A.D. 6, 7. Probably the Theudas mentioned by Gamaliel was unknown to contemporary writers like Josephus but he may well have been dated near the time of Judas of Galilee. Josephus mentioned another Theudas was active forty years after the first Theudas. Rather than calling Luke's reference to Theudas an error, we should recognize that he and Josephus are referring to two different men.

3. Some who question the historicity of Acts point out that the speeches in Acts are not historically reliable. They note that the speeches are uniform in character, and they suggest that Luke composed speeches without a keen interest in historical accuracy. Competent ancient historians such as Thucydides usually narrated the essential elements in historical events. We have every reason to believe that Luke followed a similar pattern using firsthand accounts from Paul and others. He had a foundation of information and did not need to resort to the creation of events that never occurred. Moreover, the uniformity of style that we see in Luke suggests only that he paraphrased the speeches in his own words. Luke was not giving verbatim reports of the speeches, but he included accurate summaries. Luke's intention to give his readers a certainty about what they had been taught (Luke 1:4) suggests that he wanted to be accurate in reporting the speeches and events of Acts.[15]

---

15. For a more complete discussion on the comparison of Luke's concern for historical accuracy to that of Thucydides, see the discussion in Carson, Moo, and Morris, *An Introduction to the New Testament*, 206–10. See also F. F. Bruce's defense of the historical trustworthiness of Acts in "Paul's Apologetic and the Purpose of Acts," in *A Mind for What Matters* (Grand Rapids: William B. Eerdmans Publishing Co., 1990), 166–78, and his discussion of the speeches of Acts in "The Significance of the Speeches for Interpreting Acts," *SwJT* 33, no. 1 (1990): 20–28.

4. Many scholars have questioned the accuracy of the reports of the miracles in Acts. Hemer suggested that the miracles performed and reported in Acts often serve as a testimony to the fact of Jesus' messiahship and also demonstrate the love and power of God over every rival claim.[16] He cites Peter's reference to Jesus' resurrection as an example of the first type of miracle (Acts 2:24–36). As examples of the second type, he refers to the healing of the lame man at the beautiful gate (Acts 3:1–10), the temporary blinding of Elymas (Acts 13:11–12), and the raising of Eutychus at Troas (Acts 20:8–12). Hemer warns against rejecting Luke's historical accuracy just because he reported a miracle as an event and insists that for those who accept the reality of an incarnation, the presence of miracles is a corollary of that viewpoint.[17]

An investigation of Luke's knowledge of Roman government practices, navigational practices, and local history shows him to be remarkably well informed about these issues. At the same time, a willingness to accept his narration of miracles develops as a by-product of a Christian worldview.

Characteristics of Acts

Acts is clearly a missionary document, whose main purpose (Acts 1:8) dominates the structure of the book. We read about the preaching of the gospel, the formation of the church, and the spread of the church in Jerusalem, Judea, Samaria, and throughout the world.

Luke abbreviated the story of the spread of the gospel. Mentioning every detail of the expansion of Christianity in all directions was not part of his purpose. In some sections his report is quite condensed. A mere sentence may trace movements that lasted weeks (Acts 19:1). In other instances events are elaborated in much greater detail (Paul's voyage and shipwreck in Acts 27). The presence or absence of Luke at the events is an important factor in determining the extent of the detail that is presented.

---

16 Hemer, *Book of Acts*, 430–31.
17 Ibid., 442.

Rome and Antioch, two centers of mission, dominate Acts. Most of the biographical material is about Peter and Paul, the two leading apostles. Speeches are common in Acts. Some of the messages are evangelistic with an emphasis on the resurrection of Christ. Others deal with deliberations about church order and internal disagreements (see Acts 15). Still others are either personal defenses (Acts 7:2–60) or exhortations to congregations (Acts 20:18–35).

The role of the Holy Spirit is prominent in Acts. The Holy Spirit provides miraculous power (13:9–11), wisdom (15:28), and guidance (16:6–10). The Holy Spirit also guided the important administrative decisions that the church carried out (13:2).

The Purposes of Acts

Luke's statement in the first two verses of Acts contrasts the purpose of the Third Gospel with the purpose of Acts. The Gospel was an account of what Jesus began to do and to teach up to the Ascension. Acts is an account of the continuation of Jesus' work through the Holy Spirit at work in the early church. Luke traced the gospel from its beginning in Jerusalem into the very center of power in the empire, Rome. He traced the development of the gospel on an axis from Jerusalem to Rome. Luke's account is selective, not comprehensive. He omitted discussions of the progress of the gospel in Egypt and Arabia, but he did include many summaries of the success of the gospel (see Acts 6:7; 9:31; 12:24; 16:5; 19:20; 28:30–31), to the credit of the Holy Spirit. Gundry clearly described the purpose of Acts: "The overall purpose of Luke-Acts, then, is the presentation of the beginnings of Christianity in Jesus' life and the extension of Christianity in early church history so as to convince readers by the irresistible advance of the gospel that God through His Spirit really is working in human history for the redemption of all people."[18]

Luke may also have had several subsidiary purposes.

1. The significance given to Paul in the second half of Acts suggests that Luke wanted to highlight Paul's contributions to the spread of Christianity.

---

18. Robert H. Gundry, *A Survey of the New Testament*, 212.

2. Luke demonstrated the innocence of Christians as they faced various false accusations.

- In Ephesus, Paul enjoyed friendly relationships with local leaders, and the town clerk found him guiltless of any illegal actions (19:35–41).

- In Philippi, city officials apologized for imprisoning Paul wrongly (16:35–40).

- In Corinth, Gallio indicated that he found Paul guiltless of any criminal actions (18:12–17).

- The Roman governor Festus and the Jewish king Agrippa agreed on Paul's innocence of the charges brought against him by the Jews (26:30–32).

3. Luke sought to silence some of the groundless accusations made by caustic critics of Christianity (see 1 Pet. 2:15) and to commend the faith to such "noble" people as Theophilus (Luke 1:3).[19]

The Text of Acts

Two textual forms of Acts have been preserved. Comparing these two forms presents interesting contrasts. The uncial manuscripts *Sinaiticus* and *Vaticanus* provide the foundation for all modern Greek texts of Acts and the English translations that come from them. A second text form is in the uncial manuscript *Bezae* (known by the text symbol D) and is about ten percent longer than the commonly received text. This second text form is known as Western because of its supposed geographic origin. Additions and changes to the standard text vary from single words to entire sentences.

Readings in the Western Text. In Acts 19:9 the *Bezae* manuscript adds the detail that Paul used the lecture hall of Tyrannus in Ephesus from 11 A.M. to 4 P.M. The addition is likely an accurate statement because this time was normally the warm part of the day when Tyrannus himself would not have used the hall. In Acts 15:29 this text adds to the apostolic decree the words, "and not to do to

---

19. For a survey of recent study and current questions in Acts see Carson, Moo, and Morris, *An Introduction to the New Testament,* 202–6.

others what they do not want to be done to themselves." This addition indicates an interest in ethical behavior, a common feature of the *Bezae* manuscript.

Although some of the information in the Western additions may be accurate, in all likelihood the material did not come from Luke himself. Generally, the additions tend to remove grammatical difficulties, clarify ambiguities, add references to Christ, and insert historical details. Such features normally indicate that the text is secondary and was not written by Luke.[20]

The Content of Acts

The Ascension of Jesus (1:1–11)

Luke's opening words in Acts provided a brief summary of his Gospel before he proceeded with his story of the church. The Gospel describes what Jesus began to do and teach. Acts relates what he continued to do and teach through the apostles and other witnesses. In verses one through five Luke emphasized the commandments that Jesus gave to the disciples (v. 2), the genuineness of the Resurrection appearances (v. 3), and the promised coming of the Spirit (v. 5). Luke's use of the term "baptism of the Spirit" describes the pouring out of the Spirit by God on his people at Pentecost. Paul's use of the term later in 1 Corinthians 12:13 refers to an experience at conversion by which all believers are transformed by the presence of God and united into the body of Christ.

In verses six and seven Jesus warned his disciples not to indulge their curiosity about God's future plans for Israel but to use their energy to spread the gospel. He promised that the Holy Spirit would provide power for carrying the gospel throughout the earth. The Ascension was a visible event in which Jesus received exaltation to God's right hand (Acts 2:33–35). The upward movement of Jesus showed the transcendence of God, and the cloud represented God's heavenly glory (cf. Luke 9:34). The reality of the Ascension pointed to the hope of Jesus' return, and during the interim of Jesus' absence his disciples are to be involved in spreading the gospel.

---

20. For additional information on Codex *Bezae* and the Western text, see Bruce M. Metzger, *The Text of the New Testament* (Oxford: Oxford University Press, 1964), 49–51, 132–33.

The Choice of Matthias (1:12–26)

Peter insisted that the election of a replacement for Judas was necessary since Judas had defected (v. 20). Apostasy rather than death was the occasion for selecting a new apostle.[21] The responsibility of declaring the resurrection of Jesus demanded the full representation of the apostles.

The New Testament does not indicate any role later played by either Justus or Matthias in the history of the early church. After prayer and deliberation, the apostles left the choice to the Lord, by casting lots. While casting lots appears to have had an honorable history in Judaism (Prov. 16:33), the church never used it again after this incident. Some have suggested the church should have waited for God to demonstrate that Paul was his choice to be the twelfth man, but Paul did not meet the requirements listed by Peter in verses 21 and 22. Before Pentecost casting lots might have been a proper procedure, but believers are now led by the Spirit of God (Rom. 8:14).

The Day of Pentecost (2:1–47)

The Feast of Pentecost celebrated the wheat harvest among the Jews and also became for them the traditional day on which Moses received the law at Sinai. Those present at Pentecost heard a noise that resembled rushing, violent wind; and saw a sight that resembled tongues of fire resting on the individuals. The filling of the Holy Spirit appears to be a state in which a person is controlled by the Holy Spirit for service. Subsequent usage in the New Testament (Eph. 5:18) implies that those already filled with the Spirit can receive a fresh filling to carry out a specific task. Verses 6, 8, and 11 suggest that the disciples spoke in human languages, and those who had come together for the Feast of Pentecost heard the words in their own vernacular. The crowds were puzzled by the speaking of the Spirit-filled Christians, but some mockers made the accusation, "They are drunk."

The Sermon of Peter. Peter was the spokesman for the disciples; he indicated that the events of Pentecost were a fulfilment of Joel's

---

21. No successor was selected to take the place of James after his martyrdom (Acts 12:2).

prophecy (Joel 2:28–32) that God would pour out his Spirit on all kinds of people who would then prophesy and see visions. Peter referred to miracles that authenticated Jesus' person (Acts 2:22), his death according to God's plan (2:23), and his resurrection (2:24–33). The outpouring of the Spirit showed the exaltation of Jesus and pointed to his messiahship and lordship.

Response to the Sermon. When Peter's listeners asked, "What shall we do?" Peter urged them to repent and submit to baptism as a sign of the faith which they had in Christ. Peter counseled baptism as a sign of the forgiveness of sin and not as a means to obtain it.[22] Comparing this passage with other New Testament passages (see Eph. 2:8–9) affirms that repentant faith in Christ is the means of salvation, and baptism is one way to demonstrate this faith.

A Healing and an Imprisonment (Acts 3:1–4:31)

After healing the lame man (3:1–10), Peter proclaimed that the strength of the risen Christ had provided the power for the healing (3:12–26). The preaching of the Resurrection disturbed the Sadducees, who denied the doctrine of resurrection. Thus, the Jewish religious leaders jailed the apostles and brought them out the next morning to warn them to cease preaching in the name of Jesus (4:16–18). Peter and John insisted that they would continue to preach what they had seen and heard, and after their release by the Jews they returned to a small group of friends and supporters to pray for additional boldness (4:23–31).

Generosity and Hypocrisy in the Early Church (Acts 4:32–5:42)

The Christians at this time demonstrated their love for God, their unity, and their love for one another by generous sharing. Christians continued to own their goods until they felt that it was necessary to sell them for the benefit of the body. Sharing goods was voluntary, perhaps occasioned either by a sudden influx of pov-

---

22. The interpretation turns on the proper meaning of the Greek preposition *eis*, translated as "for." The usage in Acts 2:38 can be compared to the usage in Matt. 3:11, where baptism in water is a sign of repentance and not the basis or cause of repentance. For further information on the grammatical aspects of this issue, see H. E. Dana and J. R. Mantey, *A Manual Grammar of the Greek New Testament* (New York: Macmillan Co., 1942), 104.

erty-stricken converts or a widespread economic downturn. The generosity of Barnabas received special commendation (4:36–37).

Ananias and Sapphira tried to gain credit for greater generosity than they had shown by giving only part of the proceeds of a sale and claiming to have donated the full amount. Peter here appears as a man of supernatural insight who becomes the agent to announce God's displeasure to sinners. The shock of Peter's strong rebuke led to the deaths of both Ananias and Sapphira.

The Appointment of the Seven (6:1–7)

The church grew rapidly and was increasingly unable to meet all the physical needs of its members. Both Hebraists (Jews who spoke primarily a Semitic language) and Hellenists (Jews who spoke primarily Greek) were among those who responded to the message of the gospel. When the Hellenists complained that their widows were being neglected in the daily distribution of food, the church acted quickly to avoid division. Seven men were selected, principally if not totally, from the Greek-speaking element of the church. These men were responsible for distributing food, and thus the apostles were freed to devote their full attention to prayer and preaching. The result (6:7) was the continued spread of the gospel, even among Jews normally unresponsive to the message.

These seven men are sometimes called "deacons," even though the text does not use that name for them. It may be more accurate to say that these seven were responsible for functions from which the later office of deacon developed (1 Tim. 3:8–13).

Stephen's Sermon and Martyrdom (6:8–8:4)

Stephen was one of the original seven who refused to limit his ministry exclusively to caring for the needy. His vigorous preaching caused him to be charged with teaching that Jesus would destroy the temple and change the customs dating back to Moses (6:14). In his defense Stephen asserted that the Jews had rejected and disobeyed those whom God raised up to deliver his people (7:25, 39–43). He also warned that the Jews fell into idolatry and assumed that God inhabited their temple (7:44–50). He accused his audience of having the stubborn attitudes of their predecessors (7:51–53).

The audience responded with predictable violence and stoned Stephen.[23] Since the Jews lacked the power to carry out capital executions (John 18:31), it is probable that the stoning of Stephen was a spontaneous mob action outside the law. The martyrdom of Stephen led to persecution against the Jerusalem church, and all except the apostles fled the city (8:1).

The Widespread Ministry of Philip (8:5–40)

The preaching of Philip in Samaria resulted in many converts to Christianity as manifested in the obvious miraculous signs and moral changes in the Samaritans (8:7–8).

Simon the sorcerer (8:9–11) professed a genuine belief in Christianity, but he seems to have been more impressed by the power of the miraculous than by a genuine belief in Christ (8:13). His greed and materialistic interest suggest that he came to Christianity only to be able to retain his profitable financial control over the people (8:18–24).

The delay in bestowing the Spirit on the Samaritans did not establish a pattern followed consistently in the church. Normally the Spirit came to the believer at conversion (Rom. 8:9; Eph. 1:13–14). Two reasons explain the delay on this occasion.

1. A delay in giving the Spirit to the Samaritans gave the Jews, who saw the physical evidence of the Spirit's coming, confidence that even outcast Samaritans could be converted.

2. The bestowal of the Spirit to the Samaritans by the hands of Jewish Christians provided a foundation for unity between believers who might have viewed one another with suspicion.

Philip also shared the gospel with a Gentile government official from Ethopia (8:26–40). The official was the treasurer of his country. As a eunuch he would have been banned from entering the temple (see Deut. 23:1), but Isaiah 56:3–5 offered the promise of a better future hope for eunuchs. Even if he could not have become a complete proselyte, he was seeking and serving God to the best of his ability.

---

23. For information on the Jewish practice of stoning see the Jewish document *Sanhedrin* 6.1–4, printed in C. K. Barrett, *The New Testament Background: Selected Documents*, rev. ed (London: SPCK, 1987), 215–17.

God twice gave directions to Philip as he journeyed in order to lead him to contact this official. First (8:26), God directed him to travel the road extending from Jerusalem to Gaza. Second (8:29), he urged Philip to approach the chariot the eunuch was riding in. As Philip approached the chariot, he heard the eunuch reading aloud from Isaiah 53:7–8. When Philip inquired if he understood what he was reading, the official invited Philip to sit beside him, perhaps with the hope of gaining an interpretation of the passage. After the eunuch's opening question (8:34), Philip declared the story of Jesus to the attentive official. We do not have the text of Philip's teaching, but he probably reflected the content of Peter's sermon in Acts 2. The eunuch must have given Philip some indication of his faith in Jesus, for when the convoy approached a body of water, he requested baptism. Although the content of 8:37 provides sound theology, the words lack solid textual support. They were likely written by a later hand.

In 8:38 Philip baptized the new believer. The description of Philip and the eunuch both going down into the water suggests immersion as the mode Philip used for baptism. When they had come up from the water, the Holy Spirit snatched Philip away from the eunuch. This need not suggest that Philip "dematerialized" and "rematerialized" in a new location. It may simply mean that Philip was led to move to another place of ministry at Azotus.

This story has incredible value in revealing the leadership of the Spirit in the missionary expansion of the early church. It also provides evidence of the power of the prophetic Scriptures in witnessing to the work of Jesus. The church father Irenaeus stated that the converted eunuch became a missionary to his own people, but we do not have records of an Ethiopian church prior to the fourth century.[24]

The Conversion and Early Preaching of Paul (Acts 9:1–31)

The importance of Paul's conversion is underscored by the fact that the event is narrated three times in Acts (9:1–31; 22:3–16; 26:4–18). Because Jewish communities had some rights to main-

---

24. Irenaeus, *Against Heresies* 3.12.8.

taining law and order among themselves, Paul requested a letter from the high priest to authorize his persecution of Christians. The Christian claim that Christ was the way to God probably led to Christianity being named "the Way" in Acts 9:2.

As Paul approached Damascus, he was suddenly surrounded by an intensely bright light. He heard a voice speaking to him, but those traveling with him could hear only a sound without understanding the separate syllables (cf. Acts 9:7 and 22:9). The sight, sound, and subsequent blinding of Paul left his companions speechless, and they led him by the hand into Damascus, where he fasted for three days. God instructed a devout Jewish Christian named Ananias to go to Paul with a message of encouragement and to heal his blindness.

Immediately after his conversion Paul began to preach in Damascus. According to Galatians (1:16–17), he also journeyed to Arabia for a period of time.[25] Paul may have received additional revelation and insight into Christian principles during the Arabian visit. He eventually returned to Damascus, where Jewish opposition made it advisable for him to leave the city for Jerusalem. In Jerusalem, Barnabas served as a character reference for Paul when he testified before the apostles, who were still unconvinced about Paul's conversion, that Paul had become a genuine believer. Opposition to Paul's preaching in Jerusalem led the disciples to send him away to his native Tarsus, where he dropped out of the story of Christian mission until Acts 11:25. Paul was likely active in Tarsus during this period, but the New Testament does not indicate what he did there.

The Miracles, Vision, and Preaching of Peter (Acts 9:32–11:18)

Luke likely recorded the miraculous activity of Peter at this place to prove that God had performed mighty works through Peter in the period leading up to his ministry among the Gentiles. Luke

---

25. Paul's visit to Arabia probably occurred during the interval between Acts 9:22 and 23. The "many days" of verse 23 would allow for a period of time away from Damascus, after which Paul could have returned to the city. Paul did not journey to Jerusalem until three years (Gal. 1:18) after his conversion. We do not know how much of this three-year period took place in Arabia.

wanted his readers to know that Peter had not fallen into spiritual compromise as he shared the gospel with the Gentiles. Peter showed that he had outgrown Jewish legalism by residing with Simon the tanner (9:43) in Joppa. Tanners were ceremonially unclean because of their contact with dead animals; most scrupulous Jews avoided them. Such scruples did not seem to hinder Peter.

Peter Preaches to the House of Cornelius. Peter had a vision that convinced him that contact with Gentiles was acceptable to God. During a time of prayer near lunch (Acts 10:9–13), Peter fell into a trance and saw a vision of a sheet being lowered from heaven by its four corners. The sheet contained ceremonially impure animals. In the vision God commanded Peter to kill and eat them. The vision convinced Peter that God had nullified the Mosaic dietary restrictions. The Gentile failure to observe these restrictions had been a chief reason for the reluctance of Jews to fellowship with Gentiles. Abolishing these restrictions opened the way for fellowship of Jewish Christians with Gentiles. Peter grasped this truth and followed divine leadership to preach in the home of Cornelius, a Roman centurion.

Peter's sermon to the Gentiles is an excellent example of C. H. Dodd's definition of the *kerygma*.[26] In this sermon Peter stressed God's acceptance of people from every nation. Before the conclusion of Peter's message God poured out the Holy Spirit on the largely Gentile audience. The presence of the Spirit was demonstrated by the physical evidence of glossalalia, which prompted Peter to declare that the Gentiles were to be baptized in the name of the Lord.

Peter Defends His Preaching. Several days later the Jewish Christians in Jerusalem accused Peter of unlawful fellowship with the Gentiles. In defense of his actions Peter recounted God's revelation in Cornelius's home. He wisely had taken with him six other Jewish Christian believers (Acts 11:12), and their combined testimonies of God's work convinced most of the audience that God had granted salvation to the Gentiles. The church would have other clashes in the future over the relationship of Christianity to the law (see Acts

---

26. See the discussion of Dodd and his emphasis on the *kerygma* in chapter 6 under the "Evaluation of Form Criticism."

15:1–2), but this incident provided a first step toward bringing the gospel to the Gentiles and abandoning strict Jewish legalism.

The Gospel in Antioch (11:19–30; 12:25)

A breakthrough in the declaration of the gospel to the Gentiles took place in Syrian Antioch. Jewish Christians, driven from Jerusalem by persecution linked with the death of Stephen, began sharing the gospel in Antioch with Gentiles. When the Jerusalem church learned of conversions among the Gentiles, Barnabas was sent to investigate. Barnabas discovered a growing, challenging Christian community, and he enlisted Paul to assist him in teaching and instructing the Gentile Christians (Acts 11:25–26). The attachment of the believers to Christ led unbelieving Antiochenes to dub them "Christ's people," or simply "Christians." The reality of Christianity among the Gentiles was demonstrated by their generosity for the famine victims among believers in Judea. Paul and Barnabas carried the offering to Judea and then returned to Antioch, bringing John Mark back with them (Acts 12:25). This famine visit to Jerusalem probably took place sometime between A.D. 45 and 48.

Persecution by Herod Agrippa I (Acts 12:1–23)

The Herod who martyred James, the brother of John, was Herod Agrippa I, grandson of Herod the Great. He curried favor with the Jews by his martyrdom of James and his imprisonment of Peter. The fervent prayer of the church led to Peter's miraculous release from prison. After his release Peter went into hiding (Acts 12:17). The Jewish historian Josephus parallels Luke's account of Herod's death with information that both confirms and supplements the Acts narrative.[27]

This event shows two characteristics of God's action. First, God responded to the prayers of the church, even when his followers could not believe he was at work. Second, those who oppose God's work face his judgment.

---

27. Josephus, *Antiquities* 19.8.2.

For Further Discussion

1. Evaluate the truthfulness of the statement, "Christians are obligated to follow the practices observed by the church in the book of Acts."

2. Is baptism a symbol of the new birth or a means of experiencing regeneration? Give evidence for your conclusion.

3. Which of the practices of the Jerusalem church in Acts 2:42–47 should be considered indicators of a healthy church today? Give reasons for your answer.

4. Are the differences in the accounts of Paul's conversion in 9:1–19; 22:3–16; 26:8–19 only normal variations involved in retelling an important event, or are they clear indicators of a fabrication? Give evidence for your conclusion.

5. Explain the importance of the conversion of Cornelius for the Gentile mission of the church.

Bibliography

Barrett, C. K. *The New Testament Background: Selected Documents*. Rev. ed. London: SPCK, 1987. Useful collection of documents illustrating the history, culture, and religious practices of the apostolic period.

Bruce, F. F. *A Mind for What Matters*. Grand Rapids: William B. Eerdmans Publishing Co., 1990.

———. *The Book of Acts*. NICNT. Rev. ed. Grand Rapids: William B. Eerdmans Publishing Co., 1988.

———. "The Significance of the Speeches for Interpreting Acts." *SwJT* 33, no. 1 (1990): 20–28.

Carson, D. A., Douglas J. Moo, and Leon Morris. *An Introduction to the New Testament*. Grand Rapids: Zondervan Books, 1992.

Dana, H. E., and J. R. Mantey. *A Manual Grammar of the Greek New Testament*. New York: Macmillan Co., 1942.

Ellis, Earle. *The Gospel of Luke*. NCB. Grand Rapids: William B. Eerdmans Publishing Co., 1981.

Gundry, Robert H. *A Survey of the New Testament*. Rev. ed. Grand Rapids: Zondervan Books, 1981.

Harrison, Everett F. *Acts: The Expanding Church*. Chicago: Moody Press, 1975.

Hemer, Colin J. *The Book of Acts in the Setting of Hellenistic History.* WUNT 49. Tubingen: Mohr, 1989.

Marshall, I. Howard. *Acts.* TNTC. Grand Rapids: William B. Eerdmans Publishing Co., 1980.

Metzger, Bruce. *The Text of the New Testament.* Oxford: Oxford University Press, 1964.

Munck, Johannes. *The Acts of the Apostles.* AB. Garden City, N.Y. : Doubleday, 1967.

Rackham, R. B. *The Acts of the Apostles.* WC. London: Methuen and Co. Ltd., 1901. Reprint, Grand Rapids: Baker, Limited Editions Library, 1953.

Ramsay, W. M. *Pauline and Other Studies in Early Christian History.* New York: A. C. Armstrong, 1906. Reprint, Grand Rapids: Baker Book House, 1970.

Reicke, Bo. *The New Testament Era.* Philadelphia: Fortress Press, 1968.

Sherwin-White, A. N. *Roman Society and Roman Law in the New Testament.* Oxford: Oxford University Press, 1963. Reprint, Grand Rapids: Baker, Twin Brooks Series, 1978. A defense of the reliability of the historical records in Acts.

Smith, James. *The Voyage and Shipment of Paul.* 4th ed. London: Longman, Baker Book House, 1978.

Stott, John R. W. *The Spirit, the Church, and the World: The Message of Acts.* Downers Grove, Ill.: InterVarsity Press, 1990. Exposition of the biblical text with a special effort to apply it to contemporary life.

Tenney, Merrill C. *New Testament Times.* Grand Rapids: William B. Eerdmans Publishing Co., 1965. Information on Jewish and Graeco-Roman times in the New Testament era.

Theron, Daniel J. *Evidence of Tradition.* Grand Rapids: Baker Book House, 1958. Information from Jewish, Roman, and early Christian sources illustrating the Jewish and Graeco-Roman background of the New Testament.

Williams, David J. *Acts.* NIBC. Peabody, Mass.: Hendrickson, 1985.

13 The Role of Paul in the Spread of Christianity (Acts 13–28)

Guiding Questions

1. List the major events and their locations during each of Paul's missionary journeys.

2. Explain why Paul changed the focus of his preaching from the Jews to the Gentiles.

3. Explain how Paul attempted to relate to the culture of his audience in his speech on Mars Hill in Athens.

4. What evidence did Luke present (Acts 13–28) to show that Christianity did not pose a threat to the Roman government?

5. List the appearances that Paul made in his own defense during his arrest in Jerusalem and in Caesarea. What was his message on each occasion?

6. What did Paul do during his imprisonment in Rome?

The second half of Acts focuses on two features which are in contrast with the opening twelve chapters.

1. Luke presents the missionary ministry of Paul in its broad sweep, showing his work in Cyprus, Galatia, Ephesus, Macedonia, and Achaia on three separate missionary trips. The

ministry of Paul and not Peter receives the chief attention in this section.

2. He gives special attention to the rippling effects of the gospel in the large cities of the Gentile world and finally in Rome itself.

Luke's purpose in the latter half of Acts was to show Paul's ministry of preaching and planting churches, culminating finally in his imprisonment and two-year ministry in Rome, the center of the empire.

Paul's Missionary Journeys
Harmonized with the Pauline Epistles

For additional information on the chronology of Paul's life, see "A Chronology of Paul's Life" in chapter 14.

Date	Epistle	Event
A.D. 29	Acts	Death and resurrection of Christ.
A.D. 32		Conversion of Paul, followed by three-year period of preaching in Damascus and Arabia. Escaped a Jewish death plot in Damascus by being lowered over wall in city.
		Barnabas introduced Paul to Jerusalem church.
		Paul returned to Tarsus.
		Barnabas brought Paul to Syrian Antioch. Both took famine relief to Jerusalem.

Date	Epistle	Event
A.D. 47	Acts	**I. FIRST MISSIONARY JOURNEY** Syrian Antioch Cyprus—Blinding of Elymas and conversion of proconsul Sergius Paulus.
		Perga—Departure of John Mark. Pisidian Antioch—Paul turned to Gentiles after preaching in synagogue.
		Iconium—Driven from city after preaching in synagogue. Lystra—After Paul healed a cripple, crowd tried to worship Barnabas and Paul as Zeus and Hermes. Paul was stoned.
		Derbe Lystra Iconium Pisidian Antioch Perga Attalia Syrian Antioch
A.D. 49	Galatians (under S. Galatian theory)	Jerusalem Council (Acts 15)
A.D. 50–52		**II. SECOND MISSIONARY JOURNEY** Antioch in Syria Derbe Lystra—Paul took Timothy (Acts 16:1).

Date	Epistle	Event
A.D. 50–52	Galatians (under S. Galatian theory)	Iconium Pisidian Antioch Troas—Paul received Macedonian vision. Philippi—Conversion of Lydia and exorcism of demon-possessed girl.
		Jailing of Paul and Silas. Earthquake at midnight. Conversion of jailer.
		Thessalonica—Paul driven from city by mob attack on Jason's house.
		Berea—Jews listened to Paul's message and searched Old Testament to verify it.
		Athens—Paul preached sermon on Hill of Ares (Mars' Hill).
	1 and 2 Thess.	Corinth—Paul involved in tent-making with Priscilla and Aquila.
		Conversion of Crispus, the synagogue ruler.
		Paul remained one and a half years in Corinth after the Roman governor Gallio refused to condemn his preaching.
		Cenchrea—Paul took a Nazarite vow by shaving his head.
		Ephesus—Left Priscilla and Aquila behind here.
		Caesarea Jerusalem Syrian Antioch

Date	Epistle	Event
A.D. 53–57	1 and 2 Thess.	III. THIRD MISSIONARY JOURNEY Syrian Antioch Galatia and Phrygia (Derbe, Lystra, Iconium, Pisidian Antioch)
	1 Cor.	Ephesus—Preaching in school of Tyrannus. Converts renounced the occult by burning magical books. Demetrius led riot of silversmiths on behalf of goddess Artemis (Diana).
		Paul ministered for three years (20:31).
	2 Cor.	Macedonia (Philippi, Thessalonica)
	Romans	Greece (Athens and Corinth)—Jews plotted to kill Paul on voyage to Palestine.
		Macedonia Troas—Healing of Eutychus after a fall from window during Paul's sermon.
		Miletus—Farewell to Ephesian elders.
		Tyre—Paul warned to avoid Jerusalem.
		Caesarea—Agabus warned Paul of suffering in Jerusalem.
		Jerusalem—Jews rioted in temple against Paul. He was rescued and arrested by Roman soldiers. Defended himself before Sanhedrin. Sent to Felix in Caesarea.

Date	Epistle	Event
A.D. 53–57	Romans	Caesarea—Paul defended himself before Felix, Festus, and Agrippa. He appealed for trial in Rome.
		IV. JOURNEY TO ROME Crete—Paul advised not to sail onto Mediterranean. Storm hit ship in which Paul was traveling.
		Malta—Paul's ship wrecked. Paul and companions remained here during winter.
A.D. 61	Philemon Colossians Ephesians Philippians	Rome—Paul is housed in a rented home. Preached to Jews and Gentiles. Waited two years for trial before Nero.
A.D. 63	1 Timothy Titus	Release from prison. Ministry in east.
A.D. 67	2 Timothy	Reimprisonment.
		Martyrdom.

Paul's First Missionary Journey

Paul's first penetration into the Gentile world began in Antioch in Syria and took him to the island of Cyprus and the mainland cities of Perga, Antioch in Pisidia, Iconium, Lystra, and Derbe. After reaching Derbe, Paul reversed his travels, returning through the cities which he had just visited, and finally disembarking from the port of Attalia for the return trip to Antioch in Syria. Although we call Paul's trips "missionary journeys," we would be mistaken to view them as hasty dashes from one city to the next. Paul's missionary policy involved entering a city, establishing a foundation among the residents who responded to his preaching, and moving to another city only under pressure from local authorities or other evident signs of divine leadership. Barnabas accompanied Paul throughout this first journey, and John Mark served as a coworker for a portion of the trip.

Antioch in Syria (Acts 13:1–3)

Leaders in the church at Antioch came from a multiethnic background, but all seemed to possess a remarkable sensitivity to divine leadership. The church set aside special periods to concentrate on receiving divine leadership for ministry. As the believers sought divine guidance, they learned that God was calling two of their outstanding leaders for a special task. The departure of Paul and Barnabas was accompanied by another period of prayer and fasting. The laying on of hands was neither a formal ordination nor a commission to apostolic office but an act of blessing in which the church expressed its unity in supporting the ministry of Paul and Barnabas.

Ministry in Cyprus (Acts 13:4–13)

Paul practiced two principles of missions in Cyprus that he used in all subsequent missions.

1. He traveled primarily to the great population or political centers as he preached the gospel. On the island of Cyprus he first went to the eastern city of Salamis and then to the seat of government at Paphos.

2. He began his ministry in the synagogues of the cities he travelled to. There he found Jews and some proselytes who accepted the Old Testament Scriptures and had at least some foundation for understanding what he meant when he called Jesus the "Messiah."

In the government center of Paphos Paul was opposed by a Jewish magician named Bar-Jesus (Hebrew for "son of Joshua") or Elymas, a term which designated him as a magician. Elymas opposed Paul's preaching when he saw it as a threat to his livelihood. Paul met his opposition with strong action and brought judicial blindness on him. The Roman proconsul Sergius Paulus was so overwhelmed by this display of power that he responded in faith to the gospel.

Paul left Cyprus for Perga on the mainland of Asia Minor. Luke noted that John Mark, who began the journey as Paul's helper, left from Perga and returned to his home in Jerusalem (13:13). Luke did not explain why Mark departed.

Luke's report of the ministry in Cyprus highlighted two significant features.

1. Paul assumed the leading role in ministry. We see this shift in the order in which the names of the missionaries are presented. In 13:7 the order is "Barnabas and Saul"; in 13:13 the order is "Paul and his companions."

2. Luke designated "Saul" as "Paul" for the first time in 13:9. Hereafter this name is used to describe his work among the Gentiles. "Saul" was a Jewish name and would have been more acceptable in that environment.

Paul elsewhere tells us that he was born a Roman citizen in Tarsus in southeastern Asia Minor (Acts 22:3, 28; 23:6; Phil. 3:4–6). We do not know how Paul's father obtained Roman citizenship, but being a Roman citizen gave Paul protection and many privileges in his ministry (see Acts 16:36–40). His father was a Pharisee, and he reared Paul by the standards of strict Judaism. Paul had studied in Jerusalem under the celebrated rabbi Gamaliel. We do not know if Paul saw Jesus before the Crucifixon, nor do we know if Paul was married. Bachelorhood was rare among Jewish men, and we might surmise that he had been married, but perhaps lost his wife through death.[1]

Paul in Pisidian Antioch (Acts 13:14–52)

Antioch was a leading city in this interior area of Asia Minor, but it was not technically in Pisidia. Since many cities bearing the name Antioch existed in the New Testament era, this city carried the name "Antioch towards Pisidia" or Pisidian Antioch in order to distinguish it from similarly named cities. Paul's message presented the ministry of Jesus as a fulfillment of prophecy. He ended with an appeal for his hearers to avoid the error of the Jerusalem

---

1. See 1 Cor. 7:7–8, which implies Paul was single. Later in 1 Cor. 7:32–35 Paul suggested that the single state provided the unmarried person additional freedom in serving the Lord.

Jews who had rejected Jesus. Jews and Gentile proselytes responded to Paul's message and asked him to return on the next Sabbath. When Paul and Barnabas returned the next Sabbath, envious, unbelieving Jews opposed his preaching. Paul was led to turn his ministry specifically to the Gentiles. Opposition against Paul forced him to leave the city before he had completed the development of the church. He later returned to consolidate the results of his first visit (Acts 14:21–24). The pattern in Antioch— preaching in the synagogue, success among the Gentiles, Jewish hostility, withdrawal from the synagogue, additional ministry among the Gentiles, persecution, departure—became the pattern he followed in most of his visits. Wherever Paul preached, either a revival or a rebellion followed.

Ministry in Iconium, Lystra, Derbe, and Return to Antioch (Acts 14:1–28)

After Paul experienced initial success in preaching at Iconium, a reaction from unbelieving Jews drove him from the synagogue and eventually from the city. Not intimidated by the opposition, Paul continued to preach the gospel in the neighboring cities of Lystra and Derbe, both located in the area of Lycaonia.

In Lystra Paul preached primarily to a pagan audience, healed a lame man, and was overwhelmed by the public response that identified him and Barnabas as Greek gods come to earth. The superstitious crowds called Paul Hermes, the messenger of the gods, and Barnabas Zeus, the principal Greek god. Horrified by their idolatrous response, Paul instructed the crowd about the true nature of God and succeeded in restraining them from their intended sacrifices to the missionaries. The fickle crowds, filled with propaganda from venomous Jews who arrived in Lystra from Antioch and Iconium, turned against Paul and apparently joined in stoning him. Paul, left for dead by the vengeful mob, revived, returned to Lystra, and departed to preach in Derbe, over fifty miles from Lystra.

After completing the preaching circuit, Paul and Barnabas retraced their steps, strengthened the groups of believers, and appointed local leadership in the churches. The churches were organized according to the pattern of the synagogues, but the leaders were selected more by prayer and fasting than by congregational vote (v. 23). After returning through the cities they had previously visited, Paul and Barnabas sailed to Antioch, proclaiming how God had opened a door of opportunity for work with the Gentiles.

The Jerusalem Council (Acts 15:1–35)

Apparently the Antioch church did not impose separate conditions on Gentiles who converted to Christianity. This freedom of spirit did not please some Jewish Christians from Judea who visited Antioch and insisted on obedience to the Mosaic law as a condition for Gentile salvation. Those who expressed this attitude probably had been Pharisees in their pre-conversion days. The resulting dissension led the Antioch church to send Paul and Barnabas to Jerusalem to discuss and clarify the issue. In Jerusalem Paul and Barnabas related how the Gentiles responded to the gospel, and they argued for exempting Gentiles from an enforced obedience to the Mosaic code. They were opposed by converted Pharisees (15:5) who insisted on obedience to the Mosaic laws as a condition for conversion. Peter threw his powerful influence behind the policy of accepting in the church those Gentiles whose hearts were cleansed by faith.

The Decision of James. The church looked expectantly to James, the Lord's brother, to bring wisdom and insight into the disagreement. He drew on Amos (9:11–12) to support his position and insisted that Gentiles could become believers without following Jewish laws and practices. He asked the Gentiles to show respect for Jewish scruples by avoiding food used in idolatrous practices, rejecting food that came from strangled animals, refusing to consume blood, abstaining from sexual immorality and marriage to near relatives (See Lev. 18:6–18). The members of the church accepted James's suggestions, inscribed their decision in a letter to Antioch, and sent the letter with Judas and Silas, who would be able to explain and interpret the letter. The members in Antioch rejoiced when they received the letter.

Results of the Conference. Three important decisions emerged from the Jerusalem Council.

1. The church decided that obedience to the Mosaic law was not a condition for salvation to be imposed on Gentiles.

2. The church urged that Gentile Christians avoid certain practices for the sake of harmonious Jewish-Gentile relationships.

3. The church preserved a unity that gave credibility to its witness of the gospel.[2]

Second Missionary Journey

The Beginning of the Journey (15:36–41)

After a period of ministry in Antioch, Paul invited Barnabas to join him on a return visit to those cities contacted during the earlier journey. The two men agreed on the need for the trip but disagreed on the role of Mark, who had left them on the first journey (13:13). Barnabas, a cousin of Mark (Col. 4:10), saw potential in the young man despite his earlier failure. Paul, unwilling to be deserted again by Mark, refused to consider taking him on this journey. The two men could not resolve their disagreement, and the division produced two missions. Barnabas took Mark and departed for Cyprus, never again to be a companion with Paul on a journey.[3] Mark's future performance justified Barnabas's risk in taking him (Col. 4:10; 2 Tim. 4:11). Mark did not need to serve on another missionary team headed by Paul. He needed to spend more time in the company of an encourager such as Barnabas. His subsequent rehabilitation offers an illustration of God's ability to bring good out of human errors and mistakes (Rom. 8:28).

Paul took Silas with him as they traveled through Syria and Cilicia encouraging the churches. Their journey became Paul's second missionary trip.

The Ministry in Philippi (Acts 16:1–40)

When Paul visited Lystra, he added Timothy to his team. Timothy was the son of a Jewish mother and a Gentile father. To facili-

---

2. John Nolland uses the Jerusalem Conference as a case study of relating the Bible to our traditions in changing circumstances. His article suggests how a church can collectively seek God's will. See his "Acts 15: Discerning the Will of God in Changing Circumstances," *Crux* 27 (March 1991): 30–34.

3. The later mention of the name of Barnabas in 1 Cor. 9:6 and Col. 4:10 suggests that his departure from Paul was not a departure from Christian service and obedience to the Lord.

tate his acceptance in ministry among the Jews, Paul (probably through the resources of a synagogue) had Timothy circumcised. Whenever doctrinal issues were not at stake, Paul was willing to be flexible to encourage the spread of the gospel (1 Cor. 9:19–22). However, if any practice endangered the truth of the gospel, Paul was adamant in his refusal to yield (Gal. 1:6–9).

The Macedonian Vision. After Paul arrived at Troas, he received a vision of a Macedonian man urging him, "Come to Macedonia and help us." Paul recognized the vision as a call from God and made his way to Macedonia. He eventually arrived in Philippi, a colony in Macedonia where Roman war veterans could retire to live under Roman law with freedom from taxes.

In Jail in Philippi. Philippi had such a small Jewish population that the city lacked the ten Jewish men necessary to build a synagogue (16:13). Among the women who had gathered for prayer, Lydia was the one responsive to the gospel. Her offer of hospitality to Paul and his missionary team demonstrated the reality of her conversion (v. 15). After Paul exorcised a divining spirit from a slave girl, her owners accused him of practicing customs illegal for Romans to observe. The indignant crowd, with the support of the magistrates, had Paul and Silas beaten and jailed. Despite the misery of their imprisonment, Paul and Silas were praising God at midnight when an earthquake shook the jail, causing the doors to be thrown open and the chains to be unfastened. The jailer, fearing that all of his prisoners had escaped, prepared to take his life, for Roman custom held him accountable for his prisoners on penalty of death. Paul's cry to him (v. 28) saved his life and led the jailer to ask dramatically, "How may I be saved?" The response of the jailer and his household to the gospel led to their baptism. The jailer demonstrated the genuineness of his conversion by his hospitality and compassion for the prisoners. Paul refused to leave his imprisonment until the magistrates apologized for imprisoning him, a Roman citizen, without a proper trial and investigation of his citizenship. The fact that a "we" section of Acts ends after this narrative (extending from 16:10–17) and begins again when Paul passes through Philippi in 20:5–6 suggests that Luke remained in Philippi, perhaps to minister among the Christians there.

Ministry in Thessalonica and Berea (Acts 17:1–15)

In Thessalonica, the capital city of Macedonia, Paul successfully ministered both to Jews in the synagogue and to the Gentiles. Jealousy of Paul's success caused unbelieving Jews to take Paul's friends before the city authorities and accuse them of treason. The authorities required Jason and the others to post bond before releasing them. Christians in Thessalonica responded by sending Paul and Silas to the city of Berea, forty-five miles away.

In Berea the Jews listened to Paul's preaching with open-mindedness. The Bereans did not respond uncritically, but they examined the Scripture to check on the arguments that Paul developed from them. Large numbers of Jews and Gentiles responded to the gospel. No opposition among Berean Jews seems to have developed, but Thessalonian Jews came to the city, stirred up crowds, and made it wiser for Paul to leave for another location.

The Ministry in Athens (Acts 17:16–34)

Paul was concerned when he saw the city of Athens filled with idols. He shared Christian truth in the synagogue and in the market place with some of the Epicurean and Stoic philosophers. Those who heard Paul preach might have thought he was preaching about two separate deities named "Jesus" and "resurrection," or they may have used these two terms as a scornful dismissal of the concept of resurrection. Paul's listeners took him to the *Areopagus* to investigate his teaching. The term "Areopagus" may refer either to a court that examined Paul's teaching or to an informal meeting of Athenians on the Areopagus (the Greek term for "hill of Ares," named for the Greek god of war).

In his explanation Paul acknowledged the truth of some Greek philosophical ideas, particularly from the Stoics, and suggested that the thinkers did not go far enough. Paul asserted:

1. God was lord of the world and did not need a temple (vv. 24–25);

2. God created human beings, and they need him (vv. 26–27);

3. The divine nature cannot be captured in an idol (vv. 28–29).

Paul concluded that God raised Christ from the dead in order to call all people to repent. The Athenians responded to Paul's message in typical fashion: some believed, some sneered, others reflected.

Ministry in Corinth (Acts 18:1–22)

Corinth was the capital city of the Roman province of Achaia. The ancient city of classical times was destroyed by the Romans in 146 B.C., but Julius Caesar began to build a new city in 46 B.C. In New Testament times Corinth was a commercial center with a reputation for immorality.

Paul had two encouraging experiences after his arrival in Corinth.

1. He met Priscilla and Aquila, a tentmaking couple who became immensely useful to him in future ministries. The emperor Claudius had expelled them from Rome in A.D. 49 or 50 because of rioting in the Jewish section of Rome in connection with a man named "Chrestus."[4]

2. Timothy and Silas rejoined him from Macedonia. The resulting evangelistic thrust led to strife with the Jews, but a ruler of the synagogue converted to Christianity. The Jews, doubtless spurred by jealousy, brought Paul before Gallio, the new proconsul of the senatorial province, to accuse him of illegal behavior.[5] The nature of their accusation is unclear. The Romans provided Judaism a measure of legal protection by

---

4. The Roman historian Suetonius described the action of Claudius in *The Lives of the Caesars* 5.25.4. He said, "Since the Jews constantly made disturbances at the instigation of Chrestus, he expelled them from Rome." Suetonius appears to feel that Chrestus himself started the rioting. The name "Chrestus" could easily be confused with the Greek name for Christ, "Christus." It is possible that Suetonius confused preaching about Christ for rioting led by Chrestus and that he was really describing rioting by unbelieving Jews over the preaching of the gospel about Christ. Barrett has a translation and discussion of the section from Suetonius in *The New Testament Background: Selected Documents*, rev. ed., 13–14. For a contrary opinion, see Bruce W. Winter, ed., *The Book of Acts in Its First-Century Setting*, vol. 2, *Graeco-Roman Setting*, ed. by David W. J. Gill and Conrad Gempf (Grand Rapids: William B. Eerdmans Publishing Co., 1994), 469–71.

5. A Latin inscription found at Delphi in Greece indicated that Gallio's term as proconsul was from approximately A.D. 51 to 53. Paul visited Corinth sometime during his proconsulship, probably during A.D. 51. This find provided an important foundation for determining New Testament chronology. For translation and discussion of the inscription see C. K. Barrett, *The New Testament Background: Selected Documents*, rev. ed., 51–52.

classifying it as a lawful religion. Up to this point Christians had received the same protection from the Romans, who viewed Christianity as a segment of Judaism.

The Jews may have requested Gallio to ban Christianity as an illegal religion, or they may have insisted that Paul led people to worship contrary to general Roman law. Gallio classified their dispute as an internal Jewish issue and refused to give any attention to the matter. Gallio's decision set a precedent that was followed by Roman provincial governors for several decades, a measure of tolerance for Christianity.

The Third Missionary Journey

Paul began his third missionary journey from Antioch. He traveled through Galatia and Phrygia, provinces he had visited on his previous missionary journeys. In 18:24–28 Luke mentioned the arrival in Ephesus of the eloquent Jew Apollos. Apollos had a thorough knowledge of Scripture and spoke with fervor; however, he knew only the baptism of John. After Priscilla and Aquila instructed him on this issue, Apollos traveled to the province of Achaia and the city of Corinth, where he provided significant help to those who had believed and also refuted unbelieving Jews. Paul's third journey concluded with his arrival in Jerusalem in Acts 21:17.

Ministry in Ephesus (Acts 19:1–20:1)

In Ephesus Paul met some disciples of John who had not received the Holy Spirit and understood only the baptism of John. These disciples comprehended John's emphasis on repentance, but they failed to see the role of Christ as the object of their faith. After they understood that Jesus Christ was the coming one in whom they were to place their faith, they received Christian baptism. The appearance of the gifts of tongues and prophecy revealed the reality of the Spirit's coming. In Acts, whenever special groups were received into the church, the Holy Spirit came on them in an unusual manner, signifying God's acceptance of each group. We see this unusual coming of the Spirit on the occasion of the conversion of four other groups:

1. the first Jewish believers (chap. 2);

2. the Samaritans (chap. 8);

3. the Gentiles (chap. 10);

4. the partially-taught disciples in Ephesus (chap. 19).

We should guard against expecting the manner by which God bestowed the Holy Spirit upon the groups of people as recorded in Acts to be normal or usual today.

Spread of the Gospel in Ephesus. After Paul had preached for three months in the synagogue in Ephesus, resistance to his message forced him to withdraw. He moved into a lecture hall used by a teacher whose name or nickname meant "tyrant." For two years the gospel spread throughout Asia from this location. Healings and exorcisms accompanied Paul's preaching. The seven sons of a self-styled Jewish high priest named Sceva attempted to cast out demons by using the name of Jesus. In a bizarre incident an evil spirit confessed that he knew both Jesus and Paul but did not know the sons of Sceva. Under demonic influence the possessed man became violent and attacked Sceva's sons. The incident produced fear and respect for Jesus among the superstitious people, and many abandoned pagan and occult practices by publicly burning magical handbooks and collections of curses and imprecations. The word of God continued to spread throughout the region.

The Riot of the Silversmiths. The incident in 19:23–41 demonstrated the rapid spread of the Christian message. Demetrius, a silversmith who made statues of the goddess Artemis, protested that Paul's preaching led people to deny the existence of man-made idols. This fact had severe economic consequences for his craft and the tourist traffic in Ephesus. Artemis was the name used for a local fertility goddess who had become linked with the Greek goddess Artemis, the patron of hunting. The temple in Ephesus, one of the seven wonders of the ancient world, held an image of Artemis, probably a meteorite which to the superstitious Ephesians resembled a many-breasted female. The incident showed the utter lack of a concerted plan of action by the supporters of Artemis and also the impact of Christian preaching on the public. The officials of the city declared their opposition to action against the missionaries unless the proper procedures were followed. The story indicates that Christians were not seen as a threat to the state and that they should be treated with tolerance in a religiously pluralistic society. After the trouble ceased, Paul left Ephesus for Macedonia.

Into Greece and Back to Jerusalem (20:2–21:16)

After nearly three years of ministry in Ephesus (Acts 20:31), Paul journeyed into Macedonia and Achaia. Under his direction the churches of Macedonia and Achaia collected money to be used to relieve poverty among the Jews in Jerusalem (2 Cor. 8:1–9:15). While in Corinth, Paul learned of a plot against him by the Jews, and he decided to return to Jerusalem through Macedonia. After a memorable incident of bringing Eutychus back to life in Troas, he arrived in Miletus, where the elders of the Ephesian church came to visit him.

Farewell to the Ephesian Church from Miletus. In his farewell address to the Ephesian church leaders, Paul reviewed his work as a missionary (20:18–27) and prepared the leaders for the time when he would no longer be with them (20:28–35). He pointed to his own example of faithful service as a pattern for them to imitate (20:35).

Paul continued the journey to Jerusalem after leaving Miletus. As he travelled, Paul was welcomed enthusiastically by the Christian communities he visited (21:7–8). However, he also heard predictions about trouble he would meet in Jerusalem as well as warnings not to go to the city (21:4, 10–12). Paul's friends were accurate in predicting the trouble that awaited him in Jerusalem. However, they were wrong in assuming that the expected trouble should alter his plans. Paul continued on his journey to Jerusalem, convinced that he was following the will of God.

Resumption of the "We" Sections. The resumption of a "we" section in Acts 20:5 indicates that Luke again began to travel with Paul in Philippi and accompanied him to Jerusalem. After Paul's arrival in Jerusalem (21:17–18) and subsequent arrest, the "we" sections disappear until Paul boards a ship at Caesarea bound for Rome (27:1).

Arrest and Imprisonment in Jerusalem (Acts 21:17–23:35)

Paul received a warm welcome from the Christians in Jerusalem when he arrived, and the leaders of the church rejoiced when they learned of his successful ministry among the Gentiles. Paul's arrival represented the completion of his third missionary journey. Church leaders were aware that many Jewish Christians harbored suspicions against Paul for his alleged laxity toward the law. They suggested a plan to overcome these suspicions by asking Paul to pay the expenses of four young men who had taken a Nazarite vow (Num. 6:1–21). Paul's action would not involve him in compromise and would certify that he lived according to the law. Further, it would illustrate his principle of "becoming all things to all men" (1 Cor. 9:19–22). After agreeing to the request, Paul went to the temple to begin his own period of cleansing from ritual defilement. Jews from outside Jerusalem (perhaps from Ephesus) saw him in the temple and assumed that he had defiled the temple by bringing in a Gentile. Gentiles were prohibited from entering the inner courts of the temple under penalty of death. Accusations were made against Paul, and a mob formed. In the uproar they seized Paul and dragged him from the temple. Roman soldiers garrisoned at the Fortress of Antonia near the temple kept watch for such disturbances, and they acted quickly to quench the riot and to rescue Paul. The Roman tribune, sensing that Paul was the focus of the trouble, arrested him and carried him through the violent mob to be questioned in the relative quiet of the barracks.

Paul's Defense in Jerusalem

In 21:37–22:29 Paul defended himself before the crowd and also before the Roman officials. The Roman tribune granted Paul permission to speak to the people as he requested. Paul's speech emphasized that he was raised as a devout Jew and had shown zeal for Judaism by his persecution of Christians. In the second sharing of his conversion story in Acts, Paul related that he had been on the way to Damascus when Jesus met him in an experience of blinding light and led him to realize that he had been persecuting the Lord. Further, Paul learned that God had a task for him to fulfill. The witness of Ananias, a devout Jew in Damascus, confirmed this call. God gave further confirmation to Paul in a temple vision in Jerusalem in which he learned that God intended for him to go to the Gentiles. Mentioning Gentiles aroused the restless crowd to riot, and the Roman tribune determined to scourge Paul in order to learn the truth about what happened. When he learned that Paul was a Roman citizen,[6] the tribune abandoned his plans to scourge him and decided to involve the Jewish authorities to help settle the issue.

Paul's appearance before the Jewish Sanhedrin (22:30–23:10) provoked another outburst from the Jews. Paul was given an opportunity to speak. He divided the assembly, which included Pharisees and Sadducees, when he spoke concerning the hope of the resurrection. When dissension spread among the Jews, the Roman tribune again rescued Paul and returned him to the barracks.

Assurance in the Face of Danger

In 23:11–35 Paul learned two facts that both sustained and unsettled him. He was sustained when he received divine assurance that his faithful witness in Jerusalem would also lead him to a similar opportunity for witness in Rome (23:11). He was unsettled when he learned of a plot against him by the Jews (23:12–16). When Paul shared information about this plot with the Roman tribune, the commander moved Paul under heavy Roman guard from Jerusalem to the Roman capital of Caesarea. There Paul would defend himself before the Roman procurator Felix, who summoned Jewish leaders to his court to listen to their charges against Paul.

Paul's Appearance Before Felix (Acts 24:1–27)

The governor Felix was a former slave whose term of service in Judea was characterized by an unwise use of violence to put down

---

6. We do not know how Paul proved his citizenship to Claudius Lysias. Some citizens had identity cards, and others could point to local birth records. The wearing of a toga was also the mark of Roman citizenship. Paul indicated that he received Roman citizenship at birth, for he inherited it from his father. By contrast, Claudius Lysias paid a price or a bribe to obtain his citizenship. For information on the issue of citizenship, see A. N. Sherwin-White, *Roman Society and Roman Law in the New Testament* (Oxford: Clarendon Press, 1963; reprint, Grand Rapids: Baker, Twin Brooks Series, 1978), 144–71.

rebellion and by alienation from the Jews. He married Drusilla, the daughter of Herod Agrippa I (12:1–4, 21–23), as his third wife. Their marriage had a sordid history because Felix had used a Cypriot magician to persuade Drusilla to leave her husband to become his wife. Paul reasoned before Felix about righteousness (24:25) and touched the governor at a vulnerable point.

The Jews appeared before Felix with a hired attorney, Tertullus, who described Paul as a troublemaker who profaned the temple. Paul conducted his own defense by denying the charges against him and affirming that he worshipped God according to what was written in the Law and the Prophets. Felix refused to act on flimsy evidence and indicated his preference to wait for a full report from the tribune Claudius Lysias. Without any evidence against Paul, he retained him in custody. On one occasion when Paul was summoned to present his views before Felix, Paul touched the governor's conscience when he discussed faith in Christ, righteousness, and judgment. Felix's conscience quickly became calloused again, and he retained Paul as a prisoner, hoping for a bribe. Even when he left as governor, as a favor to the Jews he did not release Paul.

Paul Before Festus (Acts 25:1–12)

Festus appears to have been a good ruler who served too brief a period in Judea to make permanent contributions to Roman relationships with the Jews. He served from the late fifties until his death in A.D. 62.

The Jews had not forgotten Paul during the two-year delay in his trial. On Festus's first visit to Jerusalem they discussed Paul's case with him. He properly held an initial examination in Caesarea. There Festus tried to curry favor with the Jews by offering to conduct a trial in Jerusalem, but Paul balked at this dangerous concession to Jewish demands. As a Roman citizen Paul could appeal for a trial to be conducted before Caesar, where a determination of the violation of any Roman law would be made. Although Paul was willing to die for his faith (21:13), he did not want to become a needless sacrifice. After conferring with his colleagues, Festus granted Paul's appeal.

Paul Before Festus and Herod Agrippa II
(Acts 25:13–26:32)

While Festus was making arrangements to send Paul to Rome for trial, Herod Agrippa II made a state visit to Festus. Herod was the son of Herod Agrippa I (12:1–4) and ruled over small territories in the northeast part of Palestine. Herod had a younger sister, Bernice, whose husband had died. After his death, she went to live with her brother, and many scandalous rumors about their relationship circulated.

Defense Before Herod Agrippa II

Festus related his perplexity about handling Paul's case, and Agrippa asked for the opportunity to hear Paul present his defense. The opportunity came the next day, and Paul used the occasion to present again the testimony of his conversion (the third narrative of this story in Acts). Paul described for Agrippa his early life as a devoted Jew and his initial persecution of the church. He related the details of the Damascus road experience and emphasized that God had called him as apostle to the Gentiles. With rising enthusiasm Paul declared that his message was nothing other than what Moses and the prophets had declared, the suffering and resurrection of the Messiah.

An Appeal for Agrippa's Conversion

During Paul's testimony Festus interrupted him to say that Paul was out of his mind, a charge Paul denied. In order to confirm that his words were truthful and sober, Paul turned to Agrippa with the query, "Agrippa, do you believe the prophets?" A ruler of Agrippa's status could scarcely affirm or deny Paul's question, and he parried Paul's verbal thrust with the comment, "In short you want to persuade me to become a Christian."[7] After Paul expressed the hope that all his listeners might become Christians as he was, the interview was concluded. Agrippa (a Jewish expert) and Festus (a Roman expert) later agreed on Paul's innocence.

---

7. This translation assumes that Agrippa was too embarrassed by Paul's appeal to profess belief in the Christian message. He turned aside Paul's question by suggesting that he was not about to be maneuvered into conversion. The translation of v. 28 in the KJV ("Almost thou persuadest me to be a Christian") is too optimistic of Agrippa's conversion. Agrippa was not "almost" persuaded. He was quite far from the kingdom. For additional information, see F. F. Bruce, *The Book of Acts*, NICNT, rev. ed (Grand Rapids: William B. Eerdmans Publishing Co., 1988), 471.

The Voyage to Rome (Acts 27:1–28:16)

Note the appearance again of the "we" sections of Acts. Luke, the author of Acts, joined Paul for this trip to Rome and remained with him until Paul was delivered to the custody of soldiers in Rome (28:16).

The journey to Rome involved typical navigational practices and patterns of the first century.[8] Due to dangerous weather conditions, no sailing occurred on the Mediterranean during the period from mid-November to early March. Paul's voyage was near the beginning of this dangerous period, and the trip to Rome was interrupted by the advent of a sudden storm known as the "Euroaquilo," a term for the northeast wind. The gale blew the boat for two weeks before the ship struck a reef at the island of Malta and broke apart.

Paul's Prominent Role

Four times during the voyage Paul's intervention showed his growing leadership on the boat and finally his utter domination of events due to his spiritual foundation.

1. He predicted danger ahead if the ship left its port at Crete (v. 10).

2. After the ship was caught in the violent storm, he predicted that no one would die, but that the ship would run aground (vv. 21–26).

3. He pointed out that the sailors must remain with the boat to preserve the lives of the passengers (v. 31).

4. He encouraged all the passengers to eat in preparation for the strenuous task of getting ashore (vv. 33–35).

In the confusion that erupted after the boat struck the reef, the soldiers wanted to kill the prisoners to prevent their escape, but the centurion, who was responsible for Paul's safe transport, intervened

---

8. For additional information on this issue, see the monograph by James Smith, *The Voyage and Shipwreck of Paul*, 4th ed. (London: Longman, Brown, Green & Longmans, 1880; reprint, Grand Rapids: Baker Book House, 1978).

to save the lives of all the prisoners. All the passengers reached the shore by floating, swimming, and wading.

On the Island of Malta

The passengers and crew remained on the island of Malta for three months, where Paul continued to minister by healing and helping (28:8–9). When conditions for sailing improved, Paul sailed to the Italian mainland and journeyed overland under guard to Rome. He made a brief stop to visit the Christians at Puteoli, and other believers, learning of Paul's arrival, met him as the party neared Rome. In Rome Paul received permission to live in a private dwelling under military guard rather than in a prison.

Paul in Rome (28:17–31)

Luke's concluding section of Acts has no information on the progress of Paul's appeal to Caesar or his relationship with Roman Christians. The fact that Christians met Paul upon his arrival (28:15) indicates that Christianity existed in Rome prior to Paul's arrival. Luke focused on Paul's relationship with the non-Christian Jews in Rome.

Meeting with the Jews

Soon after his arrival in Rome, Paul summoned the Jewish leaders to explain to them the events that led him to Rome and to declare the Christian message. The Jews indicated that no one from Judea had communicated with them about Paul. They were interested in knowing more about Christianity because of its controversial nature. At a later date Jews returned to Paul's residence to listen to his message again. Their response was the same as before. Some were persuaded; others refused to listen. The stubbornness of the Jews led Paul to focus on the more responsive Gentiles.

Imprisoned for Two Years

For two years Paul remained in his own private dwelling (vv. 30–31). Here God supplied him with basic needs.

- He provided Paul with a source of income to rent the private dwelling.

- He fortified Paul spiritually with boldness and openness to proclaim the gospel. We cannot conceive of Paul moping around in self-pity during his confinement.

- God marvelously provided an audience to listen to his preaching. The armed might of Rome did not prevent the crowds from swarming to his home.

Paul was transported to Rome at government expense; there he found a group of Gentiles receptive to the gospel.

After Two Years, What?

What happened at the conclusion of two years? Luke does not tell us. The Jews may have failed to prosecute their case. The Roman government may have tried Paul and acquitted him, or they may have dropped their case. It hardly seems likely that Paul was tried and executed at this time. The likely possibility is that he was released, enjoyed an additional time of ministry, wrote the Pastorals, and finally was arrested, tried, convicted, and executed.

Outline of Acts

I. Witness in Jewish Culture (1:1–12:25)

  A. Birth of the church (1:1–2:41)

    1. Ministry of the risen Christ to the disciples (1:1–11)
    2. Choice of Matthias to replace Judas (1:12–26)
    3. Advent of the Holy Spirit at Pentecost (2:1–13)
    4. The sermon of Peter (2:14–41)

  B. Initial spread of the gospel in Jerusalem (2:42–6:7)

    1. Vitality of the early church in Jerusalem (2:42–47)
    2. Peter's healing of the crippled man (3:1–10)
    3. Peter's second sermon (3:11–26)
    4. Peter's defense of the healing (4:1–22)
    5. The church at prayer (4:23–31)
    6. The unity of the Jerusalem church (4:32–37)
    7. Hypocrisy of Ananias and Sapphira (5:1–11)
    8. Public ministries of the apostles (5:12–16)
    9. Apostolic appearance before the Sanhedrin (5:17–42)
    10. The appointment of the seven (6:1–7)

C. Three leaders: Stephen, Philip, and Paul (6:8–9:31)
    1. Accusations against Stephen (6:8–15)
    2. Stephen's defense to the Sanhedrin (7:1–53)
    3. The stoning of Stephen (7:54–60)
    4. The exodus of the church (8:1–4)
    5. Philip's ministries throughout Palestine (8:5–40)
    6. The conversion and preaching of Paul (9:1–31)

D. Initial spread of the gospel among Gentiles (9:32–12:24)
    1. Peter's miracles in Judea (9:32–43)
    2. Peter's preaching of the gospel to Gentiles (10:1–48)
    3. Peter's defense of his preaching to Gentiles (11:1–18)
    4. Spread of the gospel among the Gentiles in Antioch (11:19–30)
    5. Peter's miraculous escape from prison (12:1–19)
    6. Death of Herod Agrippa (12:20–23)
    7. Spread of the gospel (12:24)

II. Witness in Gentile Culture (12:25–28:31)

A. First missionary journey (12:25–15:35)
    1. The initiation of the journey (12:25–13:3)
    2. The ministry at Cyprus (13:4–12)
    3. Paul's sermon in Pisidian Antioch (13:13–43)
    4. Gentile response to the gospel (13:44–52)
    5. Ministry at Iconium (14:1–7)
    6. Stoning at Lystra (14:8–20)
    7. Strengthening the new churches (14:21–28)
    8. Jerusalem Council (15:1–29)
    9. Return to Antioch (15:30–35)

B. Second missionary journey (15:36–18:22)
    1. Initiation of the journey (15:36–41)
    2. Involvement of Timothy (16:1–5)
    3. Entrance into Macedonia (16:6–10)
    4. Ministry at Philippi (16:11–40)
    5. Ministry at Thessalonica (17:1–9)
    6. Ministry at Berea (17:10–15)
    7. Ministry at Athens (17:16–34)
    8. Ministry at Corinth (18:1–17)
    9. Travels to Antioch (18:18–22)

C. Third missionary journey (18:23–21:17)
  1. Ministry of Apollos (18:23–28)
  2. Paul's ministry with the disciples of John the Baptist (19:1–7)
  3. Ministry at Ephesus (19:8–41)
  4. Journey through Macedonia to Troas (20:1–6)
  5. Ministry from Troas to Miletus (20:7–16)
  6. Ministry with the Ephesian elders at Miletus (20:17–38)
  7. Trip from Miletus to Jerusalem (21:1–17)

D. Events in Jerusalem (21:18–23:35)
  1. Paul's participation in purification rites in the temple (21:18–26)
  2. Riot by the Jews (21:27–36)
  3. Arrest and address of Paul (21:37–22:29)
  4. Paul's appearance before the Sanhedrin (22:30–23:10)
  5. Paul's movement to Caesarea (23:11–35)

E. Events in Caesarea (24:1–26:32)
  1. Paul's defense before Felix (24:1–27)
  2. Paul's defense before Festus and the appeal to Caesar (25:1–12)
  3 Paul's defense before Agrippa (25:13–26:32)

F. Journey and ministry to Rome (27:1–28:32)
  1. Journey to Rome (27:1–28:16)
  2. Ministry to Rome (28:17–31)

For Further Discussion

1. Using the evidence of the Gallio Inscription (see footnote 4 in this chapter), determine the time of Paul's appearance before Gallio in Corinth. Use that date to prepare a chronology of Paul's life.

2. Summarize your own conclusions about how Luke might have become aware of such privileged information as appears in Acts 23:25–30; 25:14–22; 26:30–32.

3. Explain the evidence for the authenticity of the story of Paul's voyage and shipwreck in Acts 27.

4. Evaluate the options used to explain what might have happened to Paul after the conclusion of the two years of imprisonment in Rome (Acts 28:30).

Bibliography

Barrett, C. K. *The New Testament Background: Selected Documents*. Rev. ed. London: SPCK, 1987.

Bruce, F. F. *The Book of Acts*. NICNT. Rev. ed. Grand Rapids: William B. Eerdmans Publishing Co., 1988.

Nolland, John. "Acts 15: Discerning the Will of God in Changing Circumstances." *Crux* 27 (March 1991): 30–34.

Sherwin-White, A. N. *Roman Society and Roman Law in the New Testament*. Oxford: Clarendon Press, 1963. Reprint. Grand Rapids: Baker, Twin Brooks Series, 1978.

Smith, James. *The Voyage and Shipwreck of Paul*. 4th ed. London: Longman, Brown, Green and Longmans, 1880. Reprint, Grand Rapids: Baker Book House, 1978.

Also, see the bibliography in chapter 12.

14 An Overview of Paul's Life

Guiding Questions

1. Discuss the materials and methods used to produce letters in the New Testament era.

2. Summarize chronologically the chief events in the life of Paul.

3. List some of the data that can be used to establish a chronology of Paul's life.

4. Summarize Paul's theology of the person and work of Christ.

Individuals influence life through their actions, character, and writings. Jesus Christ permanently influenced history more through his actions and character. He left no writings, but his disciples faithfully recorded his words. His sinless life and redemptive death permanently altered the course of world history.

Paul is an example of someone who influenced history through actions, character, and writings. He was the most significant missionary in the history of the Christian church. He brought to the missionary task an intense, driving personality with a commitment to and faith in the Lord Jesus Christ. His writings provide a portrait of a warm-hearted pastor, insightful theologian, and passionate evangelist.

The Literary Contributions of Paul

Paul as a Letter Writer

Paul, using the style of a letter, authored thirteen of the twenty-seven books of the New Testament. Paul's letters, like other letters both in and outside the New Testament, contain an address and greeting, a body, and a conclusion. The address and greeting were normally quite brief and usually followed the formula, "A to B, greetings." The address contained not only the name of Paul the sender but also the name of the recipients. The formula for the address and greeting appears in the letter sent by the apostolic council to the early churches in Acts 15:23 and also in James 1:1. Some New Testament letters lack the address and greeting in their beginning (Hebrews, 1 John), but most New Testament letters expand the address and greeting considerably. The addresses and greetings in Romans 1:1–7 and in 1 Corinthians 1:1–3 reflect this expanded beginning.

The bodies of Paul's letters varied according to his purpose in writing. Most of Paul's letters are considerably longer than their contemporary secular models. The Roman writer Cicero authored 776 letters which vary in length from 22 to 2,530 words. Paul's letters varied in length from 335 words in Philemon to 7,114 in Romans. The average length of his letters was around 1,300 words.[1] Ancient letters closed with greetings, and many New Testament letters have this feature. Many New Testament letters also contain a doxology or a benediction. The final chapter of Romans is largely a greeting with a doxology at the conclusion.

Although Paul's letters are similar to typical secular letters of the time, the apostle added some features that reflect his own creativity. Sometimes the opening section of Paul's letters reflects the purpose of the letter (Gal. 1:1–5; Titus 1:1–4). The reference to the writer and to the addressees contains specifically Christian greetings and other elements not found in secular letters (see 1 Tim. 1:1–2). Paul also frequently included an expression of thanksgiving concerning the addressees (see 1 Cor. 1:4–9).

---

1. Carson, Moo, and Morris, *An Introduction to the New Testament*, 232.

During Paul's time the expense of writing material and the low level of literacy led to the use of trained scribes for writing letters. The trained scribe was called an *amanuensis*. Tertius identified himelf as the amanuensis who wrote Romans (16:22). After an amanuensis completed the writing of the letter, the author often added a final greeting in his own hand (see Gal. 6:11 and 2 Thess. 3:17).

How much freedom did an amanuensis have in writing? This much-debated question is difficult to answer. A reasonable answer is that the amanuensis had the freedom to make his own contributions based on his skill and the nature of the relationship which he had with the author. We can assume that Paul certainly checked the wording of each of his letters to verify that it accurately represented his thought. Those who wrote for Paul were close personal friends rather than professional scribes. Paul might have given a close associate some freedom in choosing words. This freedom might account for some of the differences in the Greek used in the Pastorals and the Greek in Paul's other letters.[2]

Words were transcribed on papyrus, which measured about 9 1/2" x 11". Depending on the size of the letters, each sheet could hold 150–250 words. Since all of Paul's letters are longer than a page, it was necessary to join the pages at the edges to form a scroll. The writing instrument was probably a reed pen. The amanuensis used a crude form of ink with a carbon base made from soot, gum, and water.[3] Paul usually asked a trusted friend to take the completed letter to its destination (see Eph. 6:21; Col. 4:7 for the name "Tychicus" as the carrier of Ephesians and Colossians). The lack of a public postal service made it necessary for Paul to use this delivery system.

Several generations ago the German New Testament scholar Adolf Deissmann suggested a distinction between "epistles" and "letters." He viewed "epistles" as carefully composed public pieces

---

2. For a brief study of the theory of ancient letter writing, see Abraham J. Malherbe, *Ancient Epistolary Theorists* (Atlanta: Scholars Press, 1988). For a comparison of New Testament and secular letters, see David Aune, *The New Testament in Its Literary Environment* (Philadelphia: Westminster Press, 1987), 116–225.

3. For information on the process of preparation and the materials used in making ancient books, see Bruce M. Metzger, *Manuscripts of the Greek Bible* (New York: Oxford University Press, 1981), 14–19.

of literature. He saw "letters" as private communications, written for specific purposes to specific groups.[4] Most scholars today do not follow the rigid distinctions Deissmann suggested, but they do recognize that some letters are more literary and some more personal. Romans would be among the most literary of Paul's writings. The letter to Philemon reveals its personal and circumstantial nature.

The Sources of Paul's Thought

Paul affirmed that his gospel came to him as a revelation from Jesus Christ (Gal. 1:12). Any analysis of Paul's thought that ignores this statement cannot do justice to his theology. Paul made it clear that the specific revelatory event to which he referred was his encounter with Christ on the Damascus Road and in Arabia (Gal. 1:16–17).[5] He also indicated his dependence on other Christians for insights in his teaching. He clearly expressed his debt to other believers in 1 Corinthians 15:1–3.

Any apparent contradiction between the revelatory nature of the gospel and its dependence on tradition can be clarified by distinguishing between the form and content of Paul's gospel. The content of Paul's gospel, received by direct revelation, affirms that Jesus was the Son of God and that he died to redeem sinners from the curse of the law (Gal. 3:13). The form of Paul's gospel reflects knowledge of the historical background of the gospel events and it involves the use of certain phrases and statements to communicate the truth.

Scholars have suggested that some of the forms Paul used to express his message might have included hymns (Phil. 2:6–11; Col. 1:15–17; and 2 Tim. 2:11–13) and statements of faith (1 Cor. 15:1–7 and Rom. 10:9–10) from the early church. Although it is reasonable to suggest that Paul used early hymns and statements of faith, it is difficult to identify these passages with certainty.[6]

---

4. Adolf Deissmann, "Prolegomena to the Biblical Letters and Epistles," *Bible Studies* (Edinburgh: T & T Clark, 1901), 1–59.

5. A contemporary defense of the divine origin of Paul's gospel appears in Seyoon Kim, *The Origin of Paul's Gospel*, 2 ed. (Tubingen: J. C. B. Mohr, 1984).

6. An excellent discussion of Paul's possible sources appears in Ralph P. Martin, *New Testament Foundations* (Grand Rapids: Eerdmans, 1978), 2:248–75.

It is not likely that Paul had contact with the earthly Jesus. It would be wrong, however, to use Paul's statement in 2 Corinthians 5:16 to suggest that he received no information from the earthly teaching of Jesus. Paul used that passage to state that he no longer viewed Christ from a "fleshly" point of view. Though he probably did not meet Jesus personally, he was clearly influenced by Jesus' teaching. The ethical teaching of Romans 12 has sections similar to the Sermon on the Mount. The eschatological teaching in 1 Thessalonians 4–5 and 2 Thessalonians 2 resembles Jesus' teaching in the Olivet Discourse of Mark 13.

As Paul interprets, quotes, and alludes to the Old Testament in his writings, he views it in the light of the new revelation of God in Christ. The Greek world in which Paul was raised contributed philosophical understandings (note the statement in Acts 17:28) and linguistic distinctives to his writings. Paul's own Jewish background also influenced his viewpoint and outlook. Neither Greek nor Hebrew thought, however, could provide the complete basis for Paul's teaching. He clothed some of his statements in words taken from his Greek and Hebrew background, but his conversion to Christ caused him to view all of his background in the light of his new faith.[7]

The Arrangement of Paul's Writings

The New Testament generally arranges Paul's letters according to length, not chronology. As the longest letter, Romans is first. The shortest letter, Philemon, is last.

Paul's first nine letters are addressed to seven churches (Romans, 1 and 2 Corinthians, Galatians, Ephesians, Philippians, Colossians, 1 and 2 Thessalonians). The last four letters are addressed to three individuals (1 and 2 Timothy, Titus, and Philemon).

The Collection of Paul's Letters

Paul wrote his letters over a period of at least fifteen years to people separated from each other by hundreds of miles. How were

---

7. W. D. Davies has suggested that Paul's contact with rabbinic Judaism and Pharisaism influenced his theology. See *Paul and Rabbinic Judaism*, 4th ed. (Philadelphia: Fortress Press, 1980). For a classic statement of a contrary view, see J. G. Machen, *The Origin of Paul's Religion* (New York: Macmillan Co., 1928). Machen investigates possible influence from both Paul's Jewish and Greek background but affirms the supernatural origin of Paul's message.

these letters gathered together into a single group? When did the collection come together? Who was responsible for it? Scholars differ widely in their answers to these questions, but two basic theories have been proposed to answer these questions.

1. Some suggest that Paul's letters were suddenly gathered together after a period of neglect following their initial writing. Many feel that the publication of the canon of the early heretic Marcion (c. A.D. 144) stimulated the collection of the Pauline letters. Marcion omitted the Pastorals, and his Pauline corpus contained ten letters. The Muratorian Canon, dated at the end of the second century, is seen by some as an "orthodox" response to the more heretical canon of Marcion. E. J. Goodspeed advocated that the publication of Acts (dated by him around A.D. 90) led the runaway slave Onesimus to collect Paul's writings and to produce Ephesians as a cover letter for the entire corpus.[8] Goodspeed's views are subject to questions and disagreement at several points. Many disagree with his A.D. 90 date for Acts. Others point to New Testament evidence of widespread circulation and usage of Paul's writings. Thus, a period of neglect following these writings is doubtful. A reference to the reading of Paul's letters in Colossians 4:16 and to the writing of letters falsely attributed to Paul (2 Thess. 2:2) suggest that Paul's writings had widespread early circulation.

2. A second theory for the collection of Paul's letters supports a gradual development of the Pauline canon.[9] If, as seems likely, Paul's letters began to circulate widely soon after they were written, it is reasonable to anticipate a gradual collection of his writings. Who initiated the collection and what precipitated it remain speculative. Guthrie suggests that Timothy may have collected the Pauline writings after the apostle's death.[10] Although Guthrie's suggestion supports a sudden

---

8. E. J. Goodspeed, *An Introduction to the New Testament* (Chicago: University of Chicago Press, 1937), 210–21. For additional discussion of this issue, see under "Readers of Ephesians" in chap. 17

9. Carson, Moo, and Morris, *An Introduction to the New Testament*, 235.

10. Donald Guthrie, *New Testament Introduction*, 2nd ed. (London: Tyndale House Publishers, 1963), 998–1000.

rather than a gradual collection, it is possible that Timothy made public a collection of Paul's writings which previously had been accepted as authored by the apostle. The collection of Paul's writings likely was not a complex editorial process but a simple experience of gradually bringing together and copying letters accepted as Pauline.

The Practice of Pseudonymous Authorship

Pseudonymous authorship occurs whenever a writer deliberately uses a name other than his own on a literary document.[11] Many current New Testament scholars advocate pseudonymous authorship for such writings as Colossians, Ephesians, the Pastorals, James, and 1 and 2 Peter. Those who advocate pseudonymity suggest that the writers used the practice to gain acceptance for their own views by attributing them to respected authors of the past. Some also suggest that the disciple of a noted leader might use pseudonymity to honor the leader after his death by writing a document styled in the patterns of the deceased leader. Others suggest that writers used pseudonymity to conceal unpopular opinions that might endanger the author.

In our discussion of pseudonymity, we must acknowledge the practice of anonymity. The Gospels, Acts, Hebrews, and the Johannine Epistles are anonymous because these writings use no personal name for the author within the book. The question of pseudonymous authorship arises only when an author deliberately uses the name of a person other than himself as the stated author of a particular writing.

Advocates of pseudonymity justify this practice in the New Testament by pointing to the widespread use of this method in extrabiblical writings. Others bring ethical, psychological, historical, and theological objections against the acceptance of this practice in the New Testament.

Our investigation of this practice will begin with Jewish writings and extend through the New Testament period. We also will discuss

---

11. For a more complete discussion of this issue, see my article, "Pseudonymity and the New Testament," in *New Testament Criticism and Interpretation,* eds. David Alan Black and David S. Dockery (Grand Rapids: Zondervan Books, 1991), 535–59.

contemporary views of this issue and then frame a conclusion to our discussion.

Pseudonymity in Jewish Writings. Jews used pseudonymity more frequently in apocalypses than in epistles. Names such as Enoch, Baruch, and Ezra were attached to apocalyptic writings, perhaps to encourage acceptance for the documents. Only two examples of epistolary pseudepigraphy appear among Jews in the pre-Christian era. The *Epistle of Jeremy* used the name of the prophet to denounce idolatry and add to the content of the canonical book. The *Letter of Aristeas* contained a defense of the Jews written for a Gentile environment. The author wrote to his brother Philocrates about the Jewish translation of the Hebrew Old Testament (Septuagint, abbr. LXX) into Greek. Readers of the letter would link the writer with the translation of the LXX during the time of Ptolemy II Philadelphus of Egypt (285–247 B.C.). Scholars generally give the writing a later date, usually between 250 B.C. and A.D. 100.[12]

Internal Evidence for Pseudonymity in the New Testament. The scant evidence for the practice of pseudonymity in the New Testament questions the idea that writers and readers of the New Testament accepted this practice.

In 2 Thessalonians 2:2 Paul warned against the acceptance of the content of a letter "supposed to have come from us." In 3:17 he stated that a greeting in his own handwriting was a sign of the letter's authenticity. His chief reasons for warning against the acceptance of the pseudonymous letter concerned the letter's heretical content. If Paul attacked the use of pseudonymity to prevent the spread of heresy, he likely would not sanction its use to help spread the gospel.

In 1 Timothy 4:1–2 Paul warned against accepting the teachings of "hypocritical liars" and "deceiving spirits." These pointed words also seem to apply to banning the acceptance of literary forgeries which spread false teachings.

Many New Testament writings contain an appeal for truth that would be difficult to harmonize with the work of a pseudonymous writer.

---

12. James H. Charlesworth, ed., *The Old Testament Pseudepigraphy* (Garden City: N.Y.: Doubleday, 1985), 2:8.

- In Ephesians 4:25 Paul urged his readers to "put off false-hood and speak truthfully."

- In Ephesians 4:15 he instructed his readers to "speak the truth."

- In Colossians 3:9 he warned, "Do not lie to each other."

Such warnings as these make it quite unlikely that a New Testament writer would use a deceptive literary method.

Pseudonymity and the Ante-Nicene Writers. Were Christian writers of the post-apostolic era concerned that the name of the correct author appear on their writings? Apparently they regarded the claim to authorship as important, and they used several tests to demonstrate that their writings bore the name of the correct author.

Eusebius is not regarded as an Ante-Nicene father, but he related events that came from that period. In his discussion of the authorship of the Shepherd of Hermas, he noted that the acceptability of the book was linked with the certainty of authorship. Some identified Hermas with the disciple of the same name in Romans 16:14, while others debated this identification. Eusebius indicated that uncertainty about the authorship caused the book to be omitted "among the acknowledged books."[13] Known pseudonymous authorship of this document would certainly have led to its exclusion from the list of accepted writings.

Eusebius also told the story of Serapion and the Gospel of Peter. In the late second century, Serapion, bishop of Antioch, wrote to the church at Rhosse in Cilicia about their use of the apocryphal Gospel of Peter. Serapion had initially allowed the church to use the book, but later he realized that the writing contained heresy. He banned its usage with this comment: "We brethren, receive both Peter and the other apostles as Christ; but we reject intelligently the writings falsely ascribed to them, knowing that such were not handed down to us."[14]

Tertullian insisted that the apostles should serve as the source of the orthodox teachings of Christianity. He wrote: "It remains, then,

---

13. Eusebius, *Church History* 3.3.6.
14. Ibid., 6.12.3.

that we demonstrate whether this doctrine of ours, of which we have now given the rule, has its origin in the tradition of the apostles, and whether all other *doctrines* do not *ipso facto* proceed from falsehood."[15] He scrutinized the authorship of a book before accepting it as authentic.

Tertullian also examined the content of a writing before admitting its usefulness among Christians. He discussed the apocryphal writing, The Acts of Paul, and indicated his rejection of the book—because of its authorship *and* content. The author of the work, a presbyter in Asia who presented himself as a friend of Paul, elaborated some of the accounts he had received about Paul. Upon realizing the falsehood of the authorship and much of the content of his book, the church removed the presbyter from office. Tertullian indicated that the document went wrongly "under Paul's name."[16] He also questioned the book because it included the record of a woman teaching and baptizing. Since the authenticity of both the authorship and content of this document was questionable, Tertullian did not accept it as Scripture.

In his discussion of the corporeality of God, Origen referred to *The Doctrine of Peter.* He rejected the use of this document because he believed that the book "was not composed by either Peter or by any person inspired by the Spirit of God."[17]

The *Constitution of the Holy Apostles* was sometimes accepted as the work of Clement, bishop of Rome. Scholars viewed the book as a third-century document with later additions. The writing contains laws or instructions on various moral issues and directives for church leaders. Some sections offer encouragement for those facing martyrdom. One section includes a warning against pseudonymous writings:

"For you are not to attend to the names of the apostles, but to the things, and their settled opinions. For we know that Simon and Cleobius, and their followers, have compiled poisonous books under the name of Christ and of his disciples, and do carry them about in order to deceive you who love Christ, and us his servants."[18]

---

15. Tertullian, *On Prescription Against Heretics,* 21.
16. Tertullian, *On Baptism,* 17.
17. Origen, *De Principiis* Preface 8.
18. *Constitutions of the Holy Apostles,* 6.16.

These words reveal the attitude of an unknown early Christian writer who did not accept as genuine a writing known to have come from a pseudonymous author. This view appears to represent the position of Christian orthodoxy.

Evidence from the early fathers indicates that two factors were important in assessing the church documents: orthodoxy of content and genuineness of authorship. Thus, a book with heretical teaching or pseudonymous authorship was rejected. These two criteria were used together when evaluating a document. F. F. Bruce surveyed the criteria of canonicity and suggested that "it is doubtful if any book would have found a place in the canon if it had been known to be pseudonymous. . . . Anyone who was known to have composed a work explicitly in the name of an apostle would have met with . . . disapproval."[19]

Pseudonymity and Modern Scholarship. Although such Christian leaders as Luther and Calvin commented on the possibility of pseudonymous writings in the New Testament, serious discussion of this issue became more common in the 1800s. The following statement of F. C. Baur indicates that he advocated pseudonymous authorship for the Pastorals: "What gives these Epistles their claim to the name of the apostle is simply the circumstances that they profess to be Pauline, and make the apostle speak as their author."[20] Baur maintained that the reality of pseudonymity in the Pastorals should prepare students to anticipate it in other New Testament writings. He actually rejected the apostolic authorship of most of Paul's letters.

Martin Dibelius, an influential German scholar who lived in the early twentieth century, felt that pseudonymity was clearly present in the New Testament. Regarding the authorship of 2 Peter, he wrote: "Obviously in this case we have the beginning of pseudonymity in the literary sense."[21] His investigation of the Pastorals led him to conclude that a "Paulinist makes use here of conceptions

---

19. F. F. Bruce, *The Canon of Scripture* (Downers Grove, Ill.: InterVarsity Press, 1988), 261.
20. F. C. Baur, *Paul: The Apostle of Jesus Christ*, trans. A. Menzies (London: Williams and Norgate, 1875), 2:109.
21. Martin Dibelius, *A Fresh Approach to the New Testament and Early Christian Literature* (New York: Charles Scribner's Sons, 1936), 207.

which are foreign to the Pauline letters which have come down to us."[22]

Questions concerning apostolic authorship of New Testament books were not limited to European scholars. James Moffatt, born in Great Britain but a longtime New Testament teacher in America, explained the presence of pseudonymous writings by referring to Jewish and Greek antecedents. He took the position that Christian writers who practiced pseudonymity adopted a practice widely accepted in the ancient world, and the primary motive leading to pseudonymity was modesty. This modesty prevented a follower of a noted master from presenting his own ideas about the master's teachings under his own name.[23] He emphasized that classical historians did not feel guilty when composing writings that were true to "the general spirit of the situation"[24] and reflected the creative imagination of the author for their details. Moffatt insisted that this practice in the writing of ancient literature led to the production of speeches in the New Testament that were more or less free compositions reflecting the writer's judgment in each particular situation. In summary, Moffatt contended that Christian writers may have adopted the literary practice of pseudonymity, a practice similar to that of non-Christian writers.

A voice in opposition to pseudonymous authorship in the New Testament comes from the British scholar R. D. Shaw. He included a section, "Pseudonymity and Interpolation," in a discussion of the Pastorals and rejected the concept of pseudonymous writings based on the ethical inconsistency of the act. Shaw felt that a writer who made a determined effort to mislead his readers concerning his identity violated a basic moral principle and that "the claim to a place in the canon must go with it."[25]

More recently, Kurt Aland advocated that pseudonymous writing is the natural development of the idea that the Holy Spirit is the author of Scripture. Aland felt that if the Holy Spirit is the author of a writing, the identity of the human author makes little

---

22. Ibid., 232.
23. James Moffatt, *Introduction to the Literature of the New Testament* (New York: Charles Scribner's Sons, 1911), 41.
24. Ibid., 42.
25. R. D. Shaw, *The Pauline Epistles: Introductory and Expository Outlines* (Edinburgh: T & T Clark Ltd., 1903), 482.

difference. In this view it naturally follows that a human writer would designate a pseudonymous author without creating conflict. If we take Aland's viewpoint to its logical conclusion, then pseudonymity becomes the normal practice, and the presence of the name of the true author is exceptional.[26] For Aland, it is improper to charge a writer who uses pseudonymity with dishonesty or unethical actions.

David Meade has made the most aggressive recent attempt in English to advocate the practice of pseudonymity in the New Testament. He feels that the literary attribution to an author "must be regarded more as a claim to authoritative tradition . . . and less a claim to actual authorship."[27] Meade sees no moral culpability in the practice, for he feels that the actual author viewed his beliefs as faithful to and continuous with the teachings of the indicated author. He does not use apostolic authorship as a basis for identifying canonical authority. He locates authority in the religious community that interprets tradition and is nurtured by it.

Michael Green offers ethical and historical objections to admitting the presence of pseudonymous writings in the New Testament. He speaks in a conciliatory manner to those who might disagree with him:

> If . . . it could be conclusively proved that 2 Peter is that otherwise unexampled thing, a perfectly orthodox epistolary pseudepigraph, I, for one, believe that we should have to accept the fact that God did employ the literary genre of pseudepigraphy for the communicating of His revelation.[28]

Donald Guthrie is the most prolific recent writer who opposes the acceptance of the presence of pseudonymous material in the New Testament. He investigates the attitude of the early church concerning the acceptance of pseudonymous writings and concludes that "where the pseudonymous device was recognized it was

---

26. Kurt Aland, "The Problem of Anonymity and Pseudonymity in Christian Literature of the First Two Centuries," in *The Authority and Integrity of the New Testament* (London: SPCK, 1965), 8.

27. David G. Meade, *Pseudonymity and Canon* (Grand Rapids: William B. Eerdmans Publishing Co., 1986), 43.

28. Michael Green, *The Second Epistle of Peter and the Epistle of Jude*, TNTC, ed. R. V. G. Tasker (Grand Rapids: William B. Eerdmans Publishing Co., 1968), 33.

not merely not tolerated but emphatically condemned."[29] He also objects to the practice of pseudonymity on the ethical basis that the "deception" involved in writing such literature "is difficult to reconcile with the high spiritual quality of the New Testament writings concerned."[30] For both historical and ethical reasons, Guthrie rejects the idea that pseudonymous writings are included in the New Testament.

Those who find pseudonymous writings in the New Testament defend their viewpoints by suggesting that the practice was common in the ancient world. They also suggest that the church accepted the Holy Spirit as the true author of Scripture and would not find it offensive to use the name of someone other than the actual author as the writer.

Those who oppose the idea that pseudonymous writings appear in the New Testament suggest that the practice is ethically objectionable to the Christian church. They also point out that historically the church refused to allow pseudonymous writings in the canon whenever they were detected.

Conclusion. Some New Testament writings are anonymous, but they are not pseudonymous. The absence of the name of an author in the four Gospels and Hebrews indicates that these writings are anonymous. Pseudonymity occurs when we encounter the deliberate use of a name other than the genuine author. Is there evidence that the church permitted this practice?

Available evidence indicates that the church historically opposed the acceptance of pseudonymous writing into the New Testament. Those who suggest that the practice was so common in the New Testament period that it would be seen as harmless must explain why early Christian writers seemed to reject those documents bearing spurious names as authors. The church's opposition to the acceptance of pseudonymous writings makes it difficult to argue that we should accept such writings as the Pastorals, 2 Peter, and perhaps others as examples of pseudonymous New Testament literature.

---

29. Donald Guthrie, *New Testament Introduction*, 2d ed. (London: Tyndale House Publishers, 1963), 290.
30. Ibid., 291.

Students who endorse pseudonymity must not ignore the ethical dilemma that its acceptance involves. It is difficult to accept the existence of a church that urged it members to practice truth and at the same time condoned the obvious deceit involved in pseudonymous writings. A church that could urge its members to "put off falsehood" (Eph. 4:25) would not seem to be able to accept pseudonymous writings as genuine candidates for canonical material.

The Personality of Paul

Paul's personality was as varied and sparkling as a multifaceted diamond.[31] In matters of doctrinal importance he could be as unbending as hardened steel. In debatable issues he was as pliable as rubber. His relationships with his churches alternated between supportive love and strong but compassionate rebuke.

Paul's love for his converts shines brilliantly in each of his letters. He compared his gentleness to that of a mother caring for her children (1 Thess. 2:7) and his firmness to that of a father (1 Thess. 2:11). He wrote to the Philippians a thank-you note from prison (Phil. 4:10–20). He showed compassion and love for even the worldly Corinthian believers (2 Cor. 7:8–12).

Paul's will could be unyielding under pressure. He was not easily discouraged, nor did trials fill him with self-pity. The Christlike character that graced his life was not merely the product of steadfast willpower. It sprang from the work of the Holy Spirit within him (1 Cor. 15:10; Gal. 5:22–24).

Paul also had unusual physical stamina. In Lystra of Asia Minor he was stoned, dragged out of the city, and left for dead by his attackers. However, the next day he left for Derbe with Barnabas (Acts 14:19–20). In 2 Corinthians 11:23–29 he listed an unbelievable sampling of hardships he had personally suffered. His ability to withstand this variety of rigorous experiences testifies to his resilience and durability.

Paul also possessed unusual emotional stamina. He had learned how to be content in the extremes of both poverty and plenty (Phil. 4:12–13). He could function tactfully in various delicate situations,

---

31. Taken from Thomas D. Lea and Tom Hudson, *Step by Step Through the New Testament* (Nashville: Baptist Sunday School Board, 1992), 138–39.

as when he was discussing the subject of giving with the Corinthian Christians (2 Corinthians 8–9). His flexibility did not indicate weakness, but he attempted to understand the viewpoint and needs of other believers. In his personal relationships Paul maintained his principles without showing deceit (2 Cor. 4:2).

Paul aimed his fiercest outbursts at those who tried to mislead his converts. He fired a vehement rebuke at Jewish legalists who tried to trick Christians into following all aspects of the law as a means of salvation (Gal. 1:9). He spoke forcefully and firmly to any who willfully tried to turn young Christians from their commitment to Christ (Gal. 5:12; Phil. 3:2–3).

The Life of Paul

Paul does not leave us without information about his background. Information about his birthplace, home, education, and pre-Christian experiences appears in speeches in Acts 22:1–21 and 26:2–23. Paul also described his religious background in a brief statement in Philippians 3:4–8.

Birth and Early Life

Paul was born in Tarsus, a prosperous city and educational center in the province of Cilicia. From his family he inherited Roman citizenship (Acts 22:28). Perhaps his father or grandfather had performed some special service for the Romans. Paul used his Roman citizenship to escape confinement (Acts 16:37–39), avoid punishment (Acts 22:23–29), and claim the right to plead his case in the emperor's court in Rome (Acts 25:10–12). Somewhere in his life Paul learned the trade of tentmaking (Acts 18:3), but whether he learned it in his hometown or in Jerusalem is uncertain. Paul used his skill at this trade to avoid burdening the churches with supporting him financially (1 Thess. 2:9).

Rabbinic Training

Paul received rabbinic training in Jerusalem, but at what age he began this training is uncertain. The phrase, "this city," in Acts 22:3 may refer either to Tarsus or Jerusalem. Paul could have been exposed to Hellenistic ideas either in Tarsus or in Jerusalem. Jerusalem, despite its intense Jewish fervor, was not free from Hellenistic influence. Paul, however, insisted that he was a "Hebrew of Hebrews" (Phil. 3:5), a phrase which suggests that culturally and linguistically he and his parents were Jewish in their religious and social expression. He probably learned Aramaic and traditional Jewish customs in his home.

Paul's rabbinic training in Jerusalem came from the rabbi Gamaliel (Acts 22:3), who was a Pharisee of the school of Hillel. Hillel and his followers showed openness and generosity, traits demonstrated in Gamaliel's irenic advice in Acts 5:34–39. Paul became a Pharisee of the most rigorous persuasion (Phil. 3:5), and his persecution of Christians led him to deviate from the openness of his teacher (Acts 26:9–11). His fierce persecution of Christians was an effort to destroy the church (1 Cor. 15:9).

Conversion

Paul's conversion occurred near the city of Damascus in Syria. The account of this conversion is repeated three times in Acts (9:1–9; 22:4–16; 26:9–17). The accounts include several details about Paul's conversion.

- Paul was an active persecutor of Christians who had not expected to convert to Christianity (Acts 9:5).

- Christ initiated the change in Paul by a revelation made to him.

- Soon after receiving the revelation from Christ, Paul was baptized in Damascus, probably by a devout Jew named Ananias (Acts 22:16).

- Paul received an immediate call to take the gospel to the Gentiles (Gal. 1:15–16).

Missionary Activity

Paul began to preach that Jesus was "Son of God" (Acts 9:20) and went into Arabia for a period not exceeding three years (Gal. 1:17–18). He later went to Jerusalem, where he remained for fifteen days (Acts 9:22–26; Gal. 1:18). From Jerusalem he went to Tarsus, where he remained for an uncertain length of time (Acts 9:30). At the request of Barnabas, Paul joined him in the developing work among the largely Gentile church in Antioch of Syria

(Acts 11:22–26). While they were in Antioch, Paul and Barnabas took gifts from the church at Antioch to relieve poverty among Jerusalem believers (Acts 11:28–30).

During their time in Antioch Paul and Barnabas were called by the Holy Spirit to undertake the first missionary journey. Taking John Mark with them, they left Antioch and visited Salamis and Paphos on the island of Cyprus. Paul and Barnabas visited Antioch, Iconium, Lystra, and Derbe on the mainland of Asia Minor. In each city Paul and Barnabas first entered the synagogue to preach the gospel. When they were rejected by the Jews, they turned to the Gentiles. Frequently a rebellion by the Jews drove the pair from a city after large numbers of Gentiles were converted. Paul and Barnabas established largely Gentile churches on Cyprus and the mainland of Asia Minor. Paul was greatly disappointed that John Mark left them at Perga (Acts 13:13) during this significant missionary experience.

After completing this journey Paul and Barnabas went to Jerusalem at the request of the Antioch church to help settle the question of the relationship of Gentiles to the observance of the Mosaic law (Acts 15). The arguments of Peter and James and the reports of Paul and Barnabas led to the decision that observance of the law was not a requirement for salvation. The council required a minimal sensitivity by Gentiles to Jewish religious scruples (Acts 15:19–21, 28–29). The decision promoted unity between the Judean churches and the largely Gentile churches of Syria and Asia Minor.

Paul and Barnabas were unable to agree on including John Mark in a second missionary journey (Acts 15:36–41). Paul took Silas with him on his second journey, and Barnabas left with John Mark on a separate trip. On the second journey Paul visited the churches of Asia Minor in Antioch, Lystra, Iconium, and Derbe. He also entered new territory by crossing the Aegean Sea into Macedonia and Greece. Paul visited Philippi, Thessalonica, Berea, Athens, and Corinth. He remained in Corinth for eighteen months (Acts 18:11) before leaving there to return ultimately to Antioch (Acts 18:22).

On a third missionary trip Paul passed through the same territory in Asia Minor that he had previously visited, and spent three years in Ephesus (Acts 20:31). He later visited Macedonia and

Greece before returning to Jerusalem with offerings for the relief of the poor (Rom. 15:26–27). His arrest and imprisonment ended his travels for several years.

Arrest and Imprisonment

The Jerusalem Jews insisted on Paul's arrest under the suspicion that he had profaned the temple by allowing a Gentile into its interior (Acts 21:27–32). The Romans imprisoned Paul, and he was forced to defend his innocence before the Jerusalem Sanhedrin (Acts 23:1–10); the Roman governor Felix (Acts 24:10–21); and his successor Festus (Acts 25:8–12). When Paul sensed that he might not receive justice from Festus, he insisted on his right as a Roman citizen to have his case heard in Rome (Acts 25:12). Festus asked the Jewish king Agrippa II to evaluate Paul's defense (Acts 26:2–29); he then sent Paul to Rome for the continuation of the trial.

The trip to Rome was a harrowing experience. A violent northeast wind (Acts 27:14) blew the ship across the Mediterranean for two weeks (Acts 27:27). The ship was demolished when it struck the shore of the island of Malta. After remaining there for the winter (Acts 28:11), Paul and his friends journeyed on to Rome, where he was delivered to judicial and military representatives (Acts 28:16). Paul's imprisonment in Rome lasted two years (Acts 28:30–31). Early church tradition suggests that Paul was released after this period, but the New Testament is silent about this issue.[32] The tradition of a release allows for the possibility of a later Pauline ministry in Greece and Asia Minor during which time Paul wrote the Pastorals.

---

32. In the *First Epistle of Clement* 5, Clement wrote of Paul's activities: "Paul also obtained the reward of patient endurance, after being seven times thrown into captivity, compelled to flee, and stoned. After preaching both in the east and west, he gained the illustrious reputation due to his faith, having taught righteousness to the whole world, and come to the extreme limit of the west, and suffered martyrdom under the prefects." Some suggest that the "limit" to which he went included Spain (Rom. 15:28).

The church historian Eusebius also suggests a time of release for Paul after an initial imprisonment and martyrdom after a second imprisonment in *Church History* 2.22.

A Chronology of Paul's Life

The absence of clear chronological statements in Acts and the Pauline writings makes it difficult to establish accurately the dates for events in Paul's life. Paul used chronological statements such as "three years" (Gal. 1:18) and "fourteen years" (Gal. 2:1), but these time indicators are rare. In Acts, Luke uses general chronological indicators such as "after some days" (Acts 15:36) and sometimes more precise statements such as "a year and six months" (Acts 18:11). These indicators are only randomly mentioned and do not provide a basis for constructing an accurate chronology of Paul's life and ministry. However, historical sources outside the New Testament provide us with enough data to attempt a chronology of Paul's life.

Chronological Date

The Gallio Inscription (see chapter 13, n. 4) provides an important foundation for establishing Pauline chronology. This inscription gives information suggesting that Paul appeared before Gallio in Corinth (Acts 18:12–17) either in the summer of A.D. 51 or A.D. 52.

The Claudius edict (Acts 18:2) is reported by the Roman historian Suetonius,[33] but he gives no date for the edict. Scholars frequently date the edict banning Jews from Rome in A.D. 49–50.

The date for Paul's martyrdom is certainly during the reign of Nero. Evidence from 1 Clement 5–6 suggests that Peter and Paul suffered under Nero at the same time other multitudes were tortured. Scholars generally date this event in A.D. 64. Guthrie prefers an earlier date for Paul's martyrdom.[34] Eusebius, however, places Paul's martyrdom in Rome after a second imprisonment.[35] Following a later date allows more time for Paul to engage in other activities after his release from a Roman imprisonment—perhaps a ministry in Ephesus and Greece and writing the Pastorals.

Paul was in a Caesarean prison for two years (Acts 24:27) and was sent to Rome shortly after Festus replaced the Roman governor Felix. Using evidence from Josephus and Tacitus, many schol-

---

33. Suetonius, *The Lives of the Caesars* 5.25.
34. Guthrie, *New Testament Introduction*, 1,004.
35. Eusebius, *Church History* 2.22. See also the additional discussion in Eusebius about Paul's death in 2.25. The evidence in that section for a martyrdom in A.D. 68 is less compelling.

ars suggest that Festus arrived in Caesarea in A.D. 59 or 60, although some accept a date of A.D. 58.

A Suggested Chronology

The Gallio Inscription and the Second Journey. The most important evidence for establishing the chronology of Paul's life is the Gallio Inscription, which allows us to give a probable estimate of his appearance before Gallio during his second missionary journey (Acts 18:12–17). Paul's appearance before Gallio in Corinth likely occurred during the summer of A.D. 51, the probable year in which Gallio assumed the proconsulship of Achaia. If Paul remained in Corinth eighteen months (Acts 18:11), the likely dates for his second missionary journey are A.D. 50–52.

The Apostolic Council and the First Journey. The Apostolic Council probably occurred in A.D. 49, shortly before the beginning of the second missionary journey. Paul's first missionary journey preceded the council and probably took place in A.D. 47–48.

Paul's Conversion and Early Ministry. Information in Galatians 1:13–2:10 allows us to arrive at probable dates for earlier activities in Paul's ministry. In Galatians 2:1 Paul mentioned a visit to Jerusalem made fourteen years after his conversion.[36] Scholars differ over whether this visit is the same as Paul's visit to Jerusalem mentioned in Acts 11:28–30, known as the famine relief visit, or the visit of Paul and Barnabas in Acts 15:4 for the Jerusalem Council. Since the description of the visit in Galatians 2:1–10 seems more like the setting for the Jerusalem Council, I assume that the visit mentioned in Galatians 2:1 is the Apostolic Council visit in A.D. 49. Paul's conversion can then be dated at A.D. 35, although it could possibly have occurred as early as A.D. 32 if we subtract the three years of Galatians 1:18. Information in Josephus allows us to date the famine relief visit of Acts 11:28–30 in A.D. 45 or 46.[37]

---

36. It is debatable whether the fourteen years are to be marked from his conversion or from Paul's first visit to Jerusalem mentioned in Galatians 1:18. If the fourteen-year interval dates from the first visit to Jerusalem, then the visit mentioned in Galatians 2:1 occurred seventeen years after Paul's conversion. Since the conversion of Paul is the significant event which the apostle is considering in this section, it is likely that the fourteen years are dated from Paul's conversion and not from his first visit to Jerusalem.

37. Josephus, *Antiquities* 20.2.5.

The Third Missionary Journey. We can identify probable dates for later periods of Paul's ministry by examining material in Acts and in Paul's writings. Paul began his third missionary journey in Acts 18:23, and during this period he remained at Ephesus for approximately three years (see Acts 19:8, 10; 20:31). After leaving Ephesus Paul journeyed into Macedonia and Achaia. The only time notation for this section is a three-month period he spent in Achaia (Acts 20:3). The third journey probably took place between A.D. 53 and 57.

Arrest, Imprisonment, and Later Ministry. Paul returned to Palestine probably in the spring of A.D. 57. We know that this return took place sometime in the spring, for Paul wanted to reach Jerusalem in time for Pentecost (Acts 20:16). Paul's two-year imprisonment in Caesarea (Acts 24:27) lasted from A.D. 57 until 59, and Paul spent A.D. 60 in his travels to Rome (Acts 27:1–28:16). His two-year detention in Rome took place from A.D. 61 to 63 (Acts 28:30–31). It is probably best to view Paul's imprisonment in Rome as a detention, for he enjoyed great liberties during this time which were not evident in his previous imprisonment in Caesarea. Following this detention, we have no biblical evidence to determine further dating, but Christian tradition allows for the possibility of a release from prison with an extended ministry in the east. Paul could have written the pastoral Epistles during A.D. 64 through 67 and suffered martyrdom in either 67 or 68.

Given the available information, we now suggest the following chronology for Paul's life:

Conversion of Paul	35 (32)[a]
Famine Visit to Jerusalem	45 or 46
First Missionary Journey	47–48
Apostolic Council	49
Second Missionary Journey	50–52
Third Missionary Journey	53–57
Imprisonment in Caesarea	57–59

Conversion of Paul	35 (32)[a]
Voyage to Rome	60
Captivity in Rome	61–63
Release from Captivity and Ministry in East	64–67
Martyrdom	67 or 68

a. The date of A.D. 32 for Paul's conversion becomes a possibility if the figure of fourteen years in Galatians 2:1 is dated from the visit to Jerusalem made three years following Paul's conversion (see Gal. 1:18). For more complete information on all the chronological issues raised in this section, see Guthrie, *New Testament Introduction* (1990 ed.), 1,001–1,010.

For additional information on the chronology of Paul's life, see "Paul's Missionary Journeys Harmonized with the Pauline Epistles" in chapter 14.

A New Proposal for Pauline Chronology

John Knox suggested a new approach to Pauline chronology by relying primarily on the evidence of the Pauline Epistles. Knox does not entirely ignore or reject evidence from Acts, but he is highly suspicious of its accuracy and prefers statements from Paul's letters wherever he detects a conflict between Acts and Paul. Knox suggests this chronology for the life of Paul.[38]

Conversion and Call to Apostleship	34
first Jerusalem Visit (Gal. 1:18)	37

---

38. John Knox, *Chapters in a Life of Paul*, rev. ed. (Macon, Ga.: Mercer University Press, 1987), 68. F. F. Bruce insists that "we can continue to take the chronology of Acts seriously" in "Chronological Questions in the Acts of the Apostles," in *A Mind for What Matters* (Grand Rapids: Eerdmans, 1990), 149.

Arrival in Macedonia	40
Arrival in Corinth	43
Arrival in Ephesus	46
Second Jerusalem Visit (Jerusalem Council after seventeen years)	51
Final Visit to Corinth (Completion of Collection)	54
Final Visit to Jerusalem and Arrest (Acts 21:17, 30–33)	54 or 55

In the revision of his earlier work Knox altered his original proposal. He now suggests that the second visit to Jerusalem, the visit for the Jerusalem Council, occurred seventeen years after the first visit. He also feels that the interval between the second and third Jerusalem visits must be at least three years and possibly as many as four.

At least two differences between Knox's chronology and my chronology are obvious. First, Knox places the apostolic council of Acts 15 after the second missionary journey. Knox insists that the data of the Pauline letters support this move. Second, Knox differs in the number of visits Paul made to Jerusalem.

Knox accepts a three-Jerusalem-journey framework. The Pauline letters mention three visits, and these visits can be paralleled with visits mentioned in Acts: three years after Paul's conversion (Gal. 1:18; Acts 9:26–31); the apostolic council (Gal. 2:1; Acts 15:3–5); and delivering the collection money from Corinth at the conclusion of the third missionary journey (Rom. 15:25–28; Acts 21:17–19). Acts mentions two additional visits. These include the famine relief visit in Acts 11:28–30 and the visit between the second and third missionary journeys in 18:22.

Although Paul's writings supply the primary material for a study of his life, information in his writings must be supplemented by the material in Acts. Luke was Paul's companion, and we have already seen reasons why we may regard his accounts as accurate.[39] It appears to be wholly unwarranted to reduce the accounts in Acts to a level of historical suspicion.

Knox's proposal places the second missionary journey prior to the Jerusalem Council. This placement disregards Luke's account of the incident in Acts 15. Knox suggested that Luke may have placed the council prior to the second missionary journey in order to dispose of the question of Gentile relationship to the law before the mission to the Gentiles. If this explains the placement of the council in the chronology of Acts, why didn't Luke place it prior to the first missionary journey which also included a mission to the Gentiles?

The Theology of Paul

Paul's belief system is Christocentric.[40] We can accurately summarize Paul's thought by using "in Christ," a frequent phrase in Paul's writings. The foundation for Paul's theology was not ethics, anthropology, soteriology, ecclesiology, or eschatology. Underlying all of these important themes was Paul's view that salvation was "in Christ" and that the church is the body of Christ, only existing because believers are first "in Christ."

Paul's thought can be described as historical, functional, and dynamic.[41] His thought was historical because it was grounded in the historical events of the incarnation, life, death, and resurrection of Jesus (Gal. 4:4). Paul's theology is functional primarily because he emphasized the functional aspects of Christ's work and assumed the ontological categories. Normally Paul entered into a descripton of Christ's being or essence only when he met a heretical challenge to his preaching. His description of Christ's person in Colossians 1:15–19 and 2:9–10 was chiefly a response to a depreciation of Christ's person. Paul's theology also led to a dynamic, redemptive encounter with Christ. He did not emphasize theology for its own

---

39. See the discussion of the "Historical Accuracy of Acts" in chapter 12.

40. Among useful studies of Pauline theology are Donald Guthrie, *New Testament Theology* (Downers Grove, Ill.: InterVarsity Press, 1981), which treats theology by topics divided according to sections of the New Testament, and Leon Morris, *New Testament Theology* (Grand Rapids: Zondervan Books, 1986), 19–90.

41. R. N. Longenecker, "Pauline Theology," in *Zondervan Pictorial Encyclopedia of the Bible* (Grand Rapids: Zondervan Books, 1975). This following summary of Paul's theology reflects an indebtedness to many of Longenecker's ideas.

sake but to stress the urgency of a vital, living encounter with Christ (see Col. 3:1–5).

Human Sin

Paul's discussion of human sinfulness emphasized two features.

1. Paul emphasized a relationship between human depravity and the sin of Adam (Rom. 5:12–21). Through Adam's act of disobedience, sin and death affected all human beings.

2. Paul emphasized personal responsibility for choosing to express that depravity.

In Romans 1:18–3:8 he insisted that the Gentiles rejected God and made their own choices absolute. He pointed out that the Jews, who made the law absolute, were also alienated from God. The result was that both Jews and Gentiles were hopelessly separated from God. Because of the sin of Adam and by personal choice, human beings received and demonstrated a separation from God which provided an occasion for God to demonstrate his grace in the person and work of Jesus Christ.

The Law

Paul viewed the law in itself as holy, righteous, and good (Rom. 7:12). It reflected the standard of righteousness of a holy God and was inscribed in the human conscience (Rom. 1:19–20). Giving the law in the Mosaic code clarified, amplified, and applied God's will to the new situation of the nation of Israel.

Without rejecting this aspect of the law, Paul found another use for the Mosaic covenant. God had earlier promised Abraham that all the nations of the world would be blessed in him (Gen. 12:3). Giving the law 430 years after this covenant did not nullify the promise to Abraham (Gal. 3:17). God added this covenant because of human transgressions and not to negotiate anew the promise he had earlier given (Gal. 3:18–19). The coming of the Messiah terminated the function of the Mosaic covenant (Gal. 3:19). The covenant itself prepared individuals to exercise faith in Jesus Christ (Gal. 3:24) and clarified the exceeding sinfulness of sin (Rom. 7:13). Stated more positively, the law kept people under protection until Christ came (Gal. 3:23–25). Some Jews in Paul's day tended to view their possession of and obedience to the law as a badge of merit with God (Rom. 2:17–25). Paul pointed out that the law only revealed human sinfulness and prepared an individual to be open to faith in Christ.

E. P. Sanders, in an important work, rejected the idea that the Jews believed that keeping the law would merit salvation.[42] He stressed the Jewish idea that God chose the Jews and gave them the law. He insists that Jewish obedience to the law was motivated more by their desire to continue enjoying the benefits of the covenant than by a desire to enter under the covenant. Sanders's work warns us to guard against having too negative a view of the law, but he fails to provide a satisfactory explanation for the practice of legalism that permeated the Jewish system.

The Person and Work of Christ

Paul's discussion of the person of Christ was primarily functional. The personhood of Christ was intimately related to what Jesus did. This becomes apparent in Romans 10:9–10, when the affirmation that Christ is Lord is linked with the resurrection of Christ. Paul viewed Jesus as divine and as the proper object for the faith of believers (Rom. 10:11).

The chief emphasis in Paul's message is that the work of Jesus Christ constitutes the focal point of God's plan of redemption. Christ came under the law to take the curse of the law on himself (Gal. 3:13). He became sin for us so that we might become the righteousness of God in him (2 Cor. 5:21). Not only does Christ obliterate the curse of the law; he also fulfills the legal demands of the law. The result of his life and work is that believers in God's sight are holy, blameless, and irreproachable (Col. 1:22). The effect of responding to God's gracious work in Christ is that believers receive the righteousness of Christ and experience peace with God (Rom. 5:1).

The Church

Paul's concept of being "in Christ" also has corporate significance. This concept includes participation in a community in which the members are closely linked with Jesus Christ and vitally

---

42. E. P. Sanders, *Paul and Palestinian Judaism* (Philadelphia: Fortress Press, 1977).

related to one another. Paul used the expression "the body of Christ" to describe the church (Eph. 1:23; Col. 1:18, 24). Continuing the analogy, Paul described Christ as the "head" of the church (Eph. 1:22–23) and a source of strength for individual believers (Eph. 4:15–16). The fact that all believers are "in Christ" established a vital relationship between Christ and individual believers and between all the members of the body. Being in Christ is to affirm Christ as the one Lord over the church (Eph. 4:5).

The close link between all believers is an encouragement for Christians not to wound one another by personal sin (1 Cor. 8:12) and to show concern for the needs of fellow believers (1 Cor. 12:25–26). This unity is also demonstrated by a recognition and acceptance of the abilities and gifts of other believers (Rom. 12:5–8; 1 Cor. 12:12–31). Recognizing the gifts of other believers leads to the development of mutual dependence.

Pauline Ethics

Paul calls all believers to express their new life in Christ. Their position in Christ enables them to live this new life (Gal. 5:22–23). The love of Christ motivates them to express this life (2 Cor. 5:14). The law of Christ points the way for demonstrating this life (Rom. 8:3–4). Christians face the challenge of expressing the life of heaven even though they live on planet earth (Eph. 2:6). We live on earth today conscious of the depravity that lies within our nature and challenged by the prospects of victories and conquests "in Christ."

The one who is "in Christ" has a new lifestyle. Believers avoid old vices (Gal. 5:19–21; Eph. 4:17–21) and exhibit qualities worthy of Christ's followers (Gal. 5:22–23; Col. 3:12–14). Believers demonstrate a new life in the Christian household (Eph. 5:21–6:9) and reflect concern for the impact of their behavior on other believers (1 Cor. 8:9–12). They reflect a humility with one another for which Christ himself is the chief example (Phil. 2:1–11).

Pauline Eschatology

Throughout Paul's ministry his expectation of the return of Christ, the *parousia*, was the driving force of Paul's future hopes (1 Thess. 4:13–18). This return brings the resurrection of the believer's body (1 Cor. 15:12–58) and a permanent union for the believer with Christ (1 Thess. 4:17). It also brings judgment, but the issue of judgment for the believer has already been decided (Rom. 8:1). For the believer this judgment brings purging (1 Cor. 3:13–15) and some form of reward (2 Cor. 5:10). For the unbeliever the parousia brings wrath and condemnation (1 Thess. 1:10; 2 Thess. 2:10–12). At the return of Christ all authority and power will be subjected first to the Lord and then will be delivered to the Father (1 Cor. 15:24, 27).

Some have suggested that Paul's eschatological views changed during his ministry. They suggest that his views developed from an emphasis on a future parousia to a more existential grasp of the return that stressed fulfillment for the present and the experience of immortality at death. However, Paul's writings, from his earliest to his latest, include both of these elements, making one hesitant to accept major changes in his views. In his earlier letters he described the parousia with imagery similar to Jewish apocalyptic thought (2 Thess. 2:1–12), but he also emphasized that Christ presently lives in the believer (Gal. 2:20). In his letters to Rome and Corinth, written after several years of ministry, Paul emphasized the full completion of events at Christ's return (1 Cor. 15:12–58), and he also stressed his hope of immortality at death (2 Cor. 5:1–10). This variety in emphasis likely reflects the changing circumstances to which he wrote and is not an indication of massive shifts in his eschatology.

The work of Christ can be described as "finished" (John 19:30), but in another sense it is still being applied to the life of believers. Christians alive today experience power, joy, and spiritual renewal in Christ, and they will also know fellowship with Christ after death (1 Thess. 5:10). The complete experience of a relationship with Christ and the completion of the divine purpose await the return of Christ. For this event Paul and all believers can join in the early prayer: "Our Lord, come!" (1 Cor. 16:22).

For Further Discussion

1. Be able to defend your answer to the question, "Were any of the New Testament writings authored pseudonymously?"

2. What evidence do you see in the conversion accounts of Paul that supernatural influence caused the transformation?

3. Discuss the evidence concerning Paul's release from the confinement of his first Roman imprisonment and his subsequent ministry in the church.

4. Using only the letters of Paul, construct a chronology of his life.

5. Relate the influence of the concept of being "in Christ" to the theology of Paul.

Bibliography

Aland, Kurt. "The Problem of Anonymity and Pseudonymity in Christian Literature of the First Two Centuries." In *The Authority and Integrity of the New Testament*. London: SPCK, 1965.

Aune, David. *The New Testament in Its Literary Environment*. Philadelphia: Fortress Press, 1987. A comparison of letter writing in the New Testament and in secular literature.

Barrett, C. K. *Essays on Paul*. Philadelphia: Westminster Press, 1982. Pauline studies, primarily dealing with people and places in Paul's life, by a noted British scholar.

Baur, F. C. *Paul: The Apostle of Jesus Christ*. Translated by A. Menzies. London: Williams and Norgate, 1875.

Beker, J. C. *Paul the Apostle*. Philadelphia: Fortress Press, 1980. A study of Paul's theology by a Princeton theologian who suggests that the triumph of God and the imminent redemption of the created order are themes of Paul's thought.

Bruce, F. F. *A Mind for What Matters*. Grand Rapids: William B. Eerdmans Publishing Co., 1990.

———. *The Canon of Scripture*. Downer's Grove, Ill.: InterVarsity Press, 1988.

———. *Paul and Jesus*. Grand Rapids: Baker Book House, 1974. Study of the teachings of Jesus and Paul with a greater emphasis on their unity than their diversity.

———. *Paul: Apostle of the Heart Set Free*. Grand Rapids: William B. Eerdmans Publishing Co., 1977. Historical study of the life of Paul presenting Paul as a preacher of spiritual freedom compelled by Jesus' love.

Carson, D. A., Douglas Moo, and Leon Morris. *An Introduction to the New Testament*. Grand Rapids: Zondervan Books, 1992.

Charlesworth, James H., ed. *The Old Testament Pseudepigraphy*. Garden City, N.Y.: Doubleday, 1985.

Davies, W. D. *Paul and Rabbinic Judaism.* 4th ed. Philadelphia: Fortress Press, 1980. Forceful presentation of Jewish influence on Pauline thought.

Deissmann, Adolf. "Prolegomena to the Biblical Letters and Epistles." In *Bible Studies.* Edinburgh: T & T Clark Ltd., 1901. A classical discussion of the distinction between letters and epistles. Although Deissmann's discussion is useful, scholars today generally no longer accept his definitions of the terms.

Dibelius, Martin. *A Fresh Approach to the New Testment and Early Christian Literature.* New York: Charles Scribner's Sons, 1936.

Goodspeed, E. J. *An Introduction to the New Testament.* Chicago: University of Chicago Press, 1937.

Green, Michael. *The Second Epistle of Peter and the Epistle of Jude.* TNTC. Edited by R. V. G. Tasker. Grand Rapids: William B. Eerdmans Publishing Co., 1968.

Guthrie, Donald. *New Testament Introduction.* 2d. ed. London: Tyndale House Publishers, 1963.

———. *New Testament Theology.* Downers Grove, Ill.: InterVarsity Press, 1981. Presentation of New Testament theology by topics with contribution of each New Testament author treated under the topic.

Hagner, Donald A., and Murray J. Harris. *Pauline Studies: Essays Presented to Professor F. F. Bruce on His 70th Birthday.* Grand Rapids: William B. Eerdmans Publishing Co., 1980. A variety of theological and exegetical studies on Paul.

Kim, Seyoon. *The Origin of Paul's Gospel.* 2d ed. Tubingen: J. C. B. Mohr, 1984. Contemporary discussion of the argument for the divine origin of Paul's gospel.

Knox, John. *Chapters in a Life of Paul.* Rev. ed. Macon, Ga.: Mercer University Press, 1987. Defends chronology of Paul's life using the letters of Paul as source of information.

Kummel, W. G. *The Theology of the New Testament.* Translated by John E. Steely. Nashville: Abingdon Press, 1973. A study of the theology of Jesus, Paul, and John by a leading German theologian.

Lea, Thomas D. "The Early Christian View of Pseudepigraphic Writings." *JETS* 27 (March 1984):65–75. A study of the early church's opinion of pseudepigraphy, suggesting that it rejected pseudonymous writings as authentic.

———. "Pseudonymity and the New Testament." In *New Testament Criticism and Interpretation.* Edited by David Alan Black and David S. Dockery. Grand Rapids: Zondervan Books, 1991.

———, and Tom Hudson. *Step by Step Through the New Testament.* Nashville: Baptist Sunday School Board, 1992.

Longenecker, Richard. *The Ministry and Message of Paul.* Grand Rapids: Zondervan, 1971. Brief summary of the ministry and message of Paul for the beginning theological student, working pastor, and alert Christian layman. Most of the content was originally published in the *Zondervan Pictorial Bible Encyclopedia.*

————. "Pauline Theology." In *Zondervan Pictorial Encyclopedia of the Bible.* Grand Rapids: Zondervan Books, 1975.

Ludemann, Gerd. *Paul: Apostle to the Gentiles.* Philadelphia: Fortress, 1984. A study of Pauline chronology which pieces together an outline of his life using the evidence of the Pauline letters.

Machen, J. G. *The Origin of Paul's Religion.* New York: Macmillan Co., 1928. Classic defense of the divine origin of Paul's gospel.

Malherbe, Abraham J. *Ancient Epistolary Theorists.* Atlanta: Scholars Press, 1988. A discussion of the content of letters in ancient times.

Martin, Ralph P. "Paul and His Predecessors." *New Testament Foundations,* 2:248–75. Grand Rapids: William B. Eerdmans Publishing Co., 1978. Discussion of the sources of Pauline thought.

Meade, David G. *Pseudonymity and Canon.* Grand Rapids: William B. Eerdmans Publishing Co., 1987. Defends view that the use of the author's name in connection with a book of the Bible asserts authoritative tradition and not literary authorship.

Metzger, Bruce M. *Manuscripts of the Greek Bible.* New York: Oxford University Press, 1981. A discussion of the process and tools of letter writing in ancient times.

Moffatt, James. *Introduction to the Literature of the New Testament.* New York: Charles Scribner's Sons, 1911.

Morris, Leon. *New Testament Theology.* Grand Rapids: Zondervan Books, 1986. Discussion of New Testament theology by surveying the views of the New Testament authors.

Ridderbos, H. N. *Paul, an Outline of His Theology.* Translated by John R. DeWitt. Grand Rapids: William B. Eerdmans Publishing Co., 1975. Theology of Paul by a major Dutch theologian, who surveys the chief themes in Paul's thought viewed from their position in the history of redemption.

Sanders, E. P. *Paul and Palestinian Judaism.* Philadelphia: Fortress Press, 1977. Defends view which he names as "covenantal nomism." Suggests that Jews did not seek to keep the law in order to earn merit from God but in order to continue to enjoy the benefits of the covenant God had initiated with them.

Shaw, R. D. *The Pauline Epistles.* Edinburgh: T & T Clark, 1903.

Stowers, Stanley K. *Letter Writing in Graeco-Roman Antiquity*. Philadelphia: Westminster Press, 1986. A study focusing chiefly on the way in which letters were used in antiquity.

15 Paul's First Writings (A Survey of Galatians and 1 and 2 Thessalonians)

Guiding Questions

1. Explain the meaning of the German term *Hauptbriefe*.

2. What occasion led Paul to write Galatians?

3. What three major arguments did Paul present in defending his gospel to the Galatians?

4. List Paul's purposes for writing 1 and 2 Thessalonians.

5. What incidents occurred when Paul first visited Thessalonica (Acts 17:1–9)?

6. Explain how to determine the dates for writing 1 and 2 Thessalonians.

The letters of Paul to the Galatians and Thessalonians date from the early years of Paul's work as a missionary. All three letters are characterized by expressions of intense feelings (Gal. 1:8–9), demonstrations of pastoral concern (1 Thess. 2:19–20), and warnings of serious consequences (2 Thess. 3:6–15). The circumstances that produced the writings are usually clearly evident, and the proof of Pauline authorship is indisputable.

The Letter to the Galatians

In Galatians Paul describes the origin of his gospel and the freedom of God's saving grace. The concerns of Galatians are theological and practical. In the letter Paul models an ideal pastor, an articulate teacher of Christian truth, and a stalwart defender of Christian freedom.

Authorship

Galatians is one of four Pauline writings to which the German term *Hauptbriefe* is applied.[1] The term describes the letters to the Romans, 1 and 2 Corinthians, and Galatians as so obviously Pauline that Paul's authorship has never been seriously challenged. Galatians was accepted as Pauline from very early on, and references to this letter appear in the writings of Barnabas, Polycarp, Justin Martyr, and 1 Clement. In some early lists of Paul's epistles (such as that of Marcion), Galatians appears first, thus supporting its internal claim for Pauline authorship (1:1). New Testament scholars do not question Paul's authorship of Galatians.

Occasion

Paul and Barnabas had undertaken their first missionary journey in cities of Asia Minor such as Antioch, Iconium, Lystra, and Derbe. In these cities the Jews reacted strongly against Paul's preaching (Acts 13:50; 14:2, 19). After Paul and Barnabas left this region, apparently some Jewish Christians entered the area and taught the believers that those who desired to receive Christian salvation must also submit to Jewish law. This interpretation meant that Gentile Christians had to follow the same rituals as Jewish converts. They would be forced to practice circumcision and obey Mosaic laws and customs. A corresponding situation also developed in Antioch of Syria (Acts 15:1), but Paul did not write Galatians to deal with the issue there. Jewish Christians from outside the Gala-

---

1. F. C. Baur, the radical German critic, used this term in the German original of *Paul: His Life and Works*, 2d ed. rev., trans. by Eduard Zeller (London: Williams & Norgate, 1876), 1:245–49. As used by Baur, the term designated Galatians, Romans, and 1 and 2 Corinthians as Paul's "great epistles" which he accepted as indisputably Pauline. Baur found reasons for questioning the authenticity of the remainder of Paul's writings.

tian communities probably spread the false teaching. These false teachers are called Judaizers, and their teaching is known as "legalism." Local Jews seemed more interested in opposing the preaching of Christ rather than subverting what Paul taught.

Paul was deeply concerned that his Galatian converts were losing their grip on the gospel of grace which he had taught them (1:6–7). His opponents apparently attacked the legitimacy of his apostleship in order to undermine his authority to proclaim the gospel (1:13–2:10). Consequently, Paul had to defend both his understanding of the gospel and his apostleship. The doctrinal section of Galatians teaches that believers are accepted by God through faith in Christ and not by legalistic works (2:16). Paul explained that God had not given the law as a means of justification but to prepare for the coming of Christ (Gal. 3:23–24). He also insisted that the Holy Spirit allowed believers to keep the law (Gal. 5:5).

The large influx of Gentiles into the church made the theological issues Paul addressed in Galatians enormously important. Many of the first Jewish believers continued to practice their Jewish lifestyle, attend the synagogue and temple, follow Jewish dietary laws, and remain aloof from the Gentile Christians. The Judaizers against whom Paul wrote in Galatians wanted to require Gentile Christians to follow Jewish practices. Was this the correct route to become a believer? What about those Gentiles who refused to follow Jewish rites? Were they true believers? Should they be regarded as "second-class" Christians?

Had the views of the Judaizers won the day, the gospel of salvation as a free gift from God received by faith would have been seriously undermined. The church might well have divided into Jewish and Gentile communities, which would have resulted in disunity and heresy among Christians. Providentially God raised up this farsighted apostle who argued for salvation by grace through faith, the unity of all believers in Christ, and dependence on the Holy Spirit to develop Christian character and discipleship.

Destination

Paul addressed this letter to the churches in Galatia (1:2), but the precise location of Galatia is disputed. In the fourth century B.C. a number of people of Celtic origin left their homeland in Gaul

(France) and moved southward and eastward. Eventually they migrated to north central Asia Minor where several tribes settled in and around the centers of Ancyra (modern Ankara), Pessinus, and Tavium. The Gauls gave their name to the area they inhabited and it eventually became known as *Galatia*. The Romans used men from these tribes to help them fight in local wars and allowed them to expand their territory southward. Under their ruler Amyntas, the Gauls extended their influence into Pisidia, Lycaonia, and other southern provinces.

When Amyntas died in 25 B.C., the Romans took the territory the Gauls had previously controlled and formed the province of Galatia. In the north, this Roman province was much larger than the original area the Galatians had initially migrated to. Toward the end of the third century B.C. the Romans separated the southern area and reduced the province to the northern sector. At the time Paul wrote, the term Galatia could have referred to North Galatia, the territory originally occupied by the migrant Gauls. This area corresponds to the original ethnic usage of the term. It could have also referred to the Roman province of Galatia which included the cities of Antioch, Iconium, Lystra, and Derbe, all of which Paul evangelized on his first missionary journey. This area corresponds to the Roman provincial use of the term. To which of these places did Paul write?

Through much of the nineteenth century scholars contended that Paul wrote to the area of North Galatia, but the arguments of W. M. Ramsay helped to establish the acceptance of the South Galatian destination for the letter to the Galatians.[2] Settling this question of destination is really a matter of answering the question, "What did Paul mean when he used the term Galatia?" Several features favor a South Galatian destination.

- When Luke reported Paul's visit to South Galatia in Acts 13–14, he did not mention a visit to cities in the north. It is much more likely that Paul wrote his letter to a place he visited.

---

2. W. M. Ramsay, *The Church in the Roman Empire* (Grand Rapids: Baker Book House, 1954), 97–111.

- We know the Galatian churches contributed to the collection of funds for the poor of the Jerusalem church (1 Cor. 16:1). The list of those who accompanied Paul to Jerusalem to deliver the offering contains the names of two men from South Galatia (Timothy and Gaius in Acts 20:4) but no representative from North Galatia. Including South Galatian representatives favors this location, but the point is not conclusive because not all of the giving churches sent representatives with Paul.

- South Galatia was more vulnerable to the false teaching of the Judaizers than was North Galatia. Cities in South Galatia were situated on a busy trade route, while cities in the north were relatively isolated.

- The mention of Barnabas in Galatians 2:1, 9, 13 points to a South Galatian destination because Barnabas accompanied Paul to this region but not beyond it. Although the presence of his name is not conclusive evidence,[3] the suggestion in Galatians 2:13 that "even Barnabas" was led astray strongly implies that the readers had personal contact with him.

Those who follow a South Galatian destination for the letter understand the references to "the region of Phrygia and Galatia" (Acts 16:6) and "the region of Galatia and Phrygia" (Acts 18:23) as the old territory of Phrygia now located in Roman Galatia. This would be the area Paul would pass after he left the cities of Lystra and Iconium (Acts 16:2). Followers of this interpretation contend that Acts does not include an account of a visit by Paul to North Galatia.

Those who favor a North Galatian destination present several elements to support their views.

- Luke's record of Paul's visits to this region (Acts 13–14) suggested severe persecution, but Paul did not mention persecution in his letter to the Galatians. This omission favors a North Galatian destination.

---

3. Paul referred to Barnabas in 1 Cor. 9:6 even though we have no record of Barnabas's visit to Corinth. The mere mention of the name Barnabas is not conclusive, but it is a factor to tilt one's decision toward a southern destination.

- Paul mentioned a sickness he suffered when he visited Galatia (see Galatians 4:13), but Acts does not mentions this illness. Again, the omission points to a letter addressed to a location other than South Galatia.

- Paul's use of "O foolish Galatians" in 3:1 to refer to his readers is thought to be inapplicable to residents in Lystra and Derbe, cities of Lycaonia (Acts 14:6), and to residents in Antioch of Pisidia (Acts 13:14). However, the provinces known as Lycaonia and Pisidia were older designations of the area. During the time of Paul's writing, the term "Galatia" could be used to refer to inhabitants of the cities of Paul's first journey to Asia Minor mentioned in Acts 13–14.

Those who follow a North Galatian destination for Galatians insist that "the region of Phrygia and Galatia" (Acts 16:6) and "the region of Galatia and Phrygia" (Acts 18:23) refer to the provinces of Phrygia and Galatia. They reason that Paul went to the province of Galatia in the north after having first visited Phrygia in the south. The question of the intended destination of Galatians cannot be settled with finality, but in my judgment the arguments for a South Galatian destination are more compelling than those for a North Galatian destination.[4]

Date

The determination of the date for Galatians depends on its destination. If we accept a North Galatian destination, then we cannot date Galatians until during or after Paul's second missionary journey, A.D. 50–52. Sometime during the second journey, on his way from Pisidian Antioch to Troas (Acts 16:6–10), Paul may have visited North Galatia, and he could then have written Galatians at any time after his visit. Because of the similarity in content between Romans and Galatians some interpreters tend to place the two writings in the same general period, the mid-to-late fifties.

If we accept a South Galatian destination the letter can be dated as early as A.D. 49–50. By this time Paul would have completed his first missionary journey, which included a visit to South Galatia.

---

4. For a more complete discussion of these issues, see Donald Guthrie, *New Testament Introduction* (1990 ed.), 465–72.

Accepting a South Galatian destination, however, opens other possibilities for dating the letter.

In Galatians Paul mentioned two visits to Jerusalem, the visit of Galatians 1:18 and 2:1. The visit of Galatians 1:18 is most likely the same visit of Paul mentioned in Acts 9:26–30, but Luke also indicated visits by Paul to Jerusalem in Acts 11:28–30 and 15:4–21. With which of these visits should we link the visit of Galatians 2:1?

On the one hand, if the visit of Galatians 2:1 refers to the visit of Acts 15:4–21, then it is strange that Paul did not use the decree from the Jerusalem Council to support his position in the letter. It is also unlikely that Peter would have behaved with the same degree of compromise described in Galatians 2:11–14 if the Jerusalem Council had already taken place. These elements favor identifying the visit of Galatians 2:1 with the visit of Acts 11:28–30.

On the other hand, the subject discussed in Galatians 2:1–10 is similar to the subject discussed in Acts 15:4–21; and the conclusion reached in Galatians 2:9–10 seems similar to the conclusion in Acts 15:22–29. These features favor the identification of the visit of Galatians 2:1 with the visit of Acts 15:4–21.

If we date the writing of Galatians prior to the completion of the Jerusalem Council, then we can suggest that the visit of Galatians 2:1–10 is identical with that of Acts 15:4–21. Perhaps the meetings described in Galatians 2:2, 9–10 were preliminary private meetings held during the conference and prior to the announcement of the decison of the council. Paul may have felt that the issue confronting the Galatians was so important that he had to write his letter before the conclusion of the Jerusalem Council. If we follow this understanding of the incidents in Galatians and Acts, it becomes possible to date Galatians in A.D. 49–50, but the date cannot be maintained with certainty.[5] The following chart suggests the order of events leading to the writing of Galatians based on one's view of its destination.

---

5. For a more complete discussion of these issues, see Guthrie, *New Testament Introduction* (1990 ed.), 472–81.

North Galatian Theory	South Galatian Theory
1. Paul's first missionary journey	1. Paul's first missionary journey
2. Jerusalem Council	2. Writing of Galatians[a]
3. Paul's second missionary journey	3. Jerusalem Council
4. Writing of Galatians	4. Paul's second missionary journey

a. This order is favored by the present writer. The arguments presented suggest that Paul wrote Galatians during the Jerusalem Council. Those who link the journey of Gal. 2:1 with that of Acts 11:28–30 would generally follow the same order as listed here, but they would date the writing before the beginning of the council. Some who accept a South Galatian destination, however, place it at the end of the second journey or at some time before or during the third journey. Their dating of the epistle approximates the date held by those who follow the North Galatian destination.

The Message of Galatians

Greeting and Occasion (1:1–10)

Paul's greeting to the Galatians is more abrupt than in most of his epistles. He omitted his usual commendation to the readers and presented a lengthy statement defending the divine origin of his apostleship. His statements emphasized that he was presenting more than the opinions of a mere man (1:1–5).

Paul was astonished that the Galatians so quickly responded to a counterfeit gospel, which he designated as "really no gospel at all." In proclaiming a divine curse on those who were declaring a false message, Paul was not merely disturbed over a challenge to his personal prestige; he was concerned for the truth of the gospel. He reinforced his trenchant denunciation of the false teachers by insisting that his commitment to Christ banned any thought of his seeking popular approval (1:6–10).

The Experiential Argument (1:11–2:21)

Paul used an autobiographical argument to defend the divine origin of his message. He insisted that his gospel did not develop from his background, for before his conversion he persecuted the church and had been concerned only in making great strides of advancement in Judaism (1:13–14). Furthermore, he had not learned his gospel from the apostles, for he saw none of them until three years after his conversion (1:18). When he finally visited Jerusalem, the trip was only a "get-acquainted" meeting with Peter and James which lasted fifteen days (1:19).

Paul again visited Jerusalem after fourteen years (either from his conversion or from the visit of 1:18). During this visit, the Jerusalem leaders (James, Peter, and John) demonstrated their acceptance of Paul's gospel by refusing to insist that the Gentile Titus be circumcised (2:3–5).[6] They also recognized the legitimacy of Paul's ministry by accepting his gospel and apostleship (2:9). Paul's mention of this acceptance helped to certify the divine origin of his message.

Additional confirmation of the divine origin of Paul's message appeared in Peter's acceptance of Paul's rebuke for inconsistent behavior. When Peter came to Antioch, he initially ate with Gentiles, but under pressure from Judaizers he withdrew from table fellowship with them. Peter's behavior was tantamount to a public announcement that Gentiles were second-class citizens and suggested that they lacked the fulness of the gospel. The implication of Paul's argument is that Peter understood his rebuke (2:11–16).

Paul concluded his experiential argument in 2:17–21 and laid the foundation for a new theological position. He insisted that those Jews who again introduced law-keeping as essential to salvation were erecting the structure of human achievement. This structure had crashed into ruins for Paul in his Damascus road experience (v. 18).

---

6. The grammatical statements of vv. 3–5 are difficult to unravel, and the verses contain some textual variation. It is difficult to know with certainty whether or not Titus was circumcised, but the logic of Paul's statement compels the conclusion that Titus did not undergo circumcision.

For Paul the experience of conversion so transformed him that he found Christ's work to be the sole sufficient source for his salvation and sanctification (v. 20). To return to law-keeping after such a life-transforming discovery would be a declaration that Christ had died for no purpose (v. 21). Paul was now prepared to argue his point with greater theological precision.

The Theological Argument (3:1–5:1)

Paul's argument in this section fulfilled three purposes.

1. He wanted to show the Galatians that their contemplated return to law-keeping as a method of relating to God was a contradiction of their experience (3:1–5).

2. He wanted to convince his readers that their experience had been identical with that of their forefather Abraham (3:6–9).

3. He wanted to explain the purpose and intent of the law (3:19–25).

How had the Galatians begun their Christian life? Paul insisted (and the Galatians would remember) that they had received the Spirit by believing the message of Christ crucified. The Galatians were mistakenly acting as if they received the Spirit as a reward for their obedience to the law. They had experienced the Spirit as God's free gift, and their present behavior contradicted their past experience (3:1–5).

What about Abraham? What had been the experience of the fabled patriarch? Abraham received a right standing with God by humble dependence on the divine promise. Those who put their faith in Jesus Christ would receive the same blessing of God inherited by the faithful Abraham because of his faith (3:6–9). The justification given to Abraham was a right relationship with God. Demonstrating the faith expressed by Abraham led to the imputation of the righteousness of Christ to the Galatian believers. This justification would produce sanctification, a change in individual moral behavior.

Paul's Judaizing readers would confront him with the question, "What about the law? Where does it fit into God's scheme?" Paul answered their question with three statements.

1. The law could not bring a blessing but a curse, for it demanded perfect obedience (3:10).

2. The statement of the Old Testament was that faith, not the law, brought right standing with God (3:11).

3. Christ's death had delivered believers from the curse of their own disobedience (3:13).

Those who disagreed with Paul suggested that the appearance of the law annulled the earlier agreement with Abraham. "Not so," retorted Paul. He insisted that God would never contradict himself by annulling an earlier promise with the appearance of the law 430 years later (3:15–17).

The use of the law was only temporary, but it was real. Negatively, God gave the law to show that all wrongdoing was an offense against God (3:19, 22). The law clearly revealed the moral bankruptcy of all human beings. Stated more positively, the law was a companion to usher us into the presence of Christ (3:23–24).

A response in faith abolished all ethnic, social, and sexual distinctions and made believers members of God's family (3:26–29). As children of God believers received the complete rights and privileges of family members (4:6–7). Believers now had privileges and responsibilities like adult family members. Why, asked Paul, should the Galatians now enter again the spiritual slavery from which they had escaped (4:8–11)?

Paul briefly interrupted his theological argument with a personal appeal based on his relationship with the Galatians. At one time they had welcomed him as "an angel of God" (4:14). Paul himself was as concerned for the Galatians as a father for his own children (4:19). By contrast, the false teachers were only interested in creating a rift between Paul and the Galatians in order to turn the Galatians into fanatical Judaizers (4:17). The contrast in motives should make Paul's genuine love much more appealing.

Paul concluded his theological argument with an appeal based on the Old Testament story of Hagar and Sarah (4:21–31). Hagar, the slave woman, symbolized Mt. Sinai, the system of obedience to the Mosaic law. Her son Ishmael represented those enslaved to legalism. Sarah corresponded to the freedom of Christianity. Her son Isaac represented the spiritual children of Abraham, who were freed from the law by faith in Christ. The Galatians were the children born in freedom, but they acted as if they were the descendants of the slave-wife.[7] Paul urged them to take their stand in freedom and to avoid the harness of slavery (5:1).

The Practical Argument (5:2–6:10)

In this final section Paul warned against the cavalier attitude that freedom from the law created in some who lived in disobedience. He reminded the Galatians that they must respond to the urgings of the Holy Spirit and not be captured by the cravings of the flesh. He also entreated them to show concern for one another and to demonstrate persistence in their commitment to Christ.

Expressing himself vigorously, Paul warned that those who practiced circumcision to receive spiritual help would get no help from Christ. Their action demonstrated that they were no longer trusting Christ; they were trusting themselves. By this action they broke the bond of faith in God's grace, and they could not develop any other relationship with Christ (5:3–4).[8] For Paul, the Holy Spirit, not legalistic behavior, was the source of Christian character (5:5–6).

In 5:7–12 Paul made another personal reference to the Galatians. He encouraged them by commending their early progress in Christian growth. He also warned the Galatians that the leaven of legalism could spread infectiously through their entire band (5:9), but he was confident that the Galatians would overcome their

---

7. Paul's use of the term "figuratively" (4:24) does not diminish his interest in the literal truth of the Old Testament story. He technically does not use the story as an allegory, but he accepts the historicity of the Old Testament events. Behind these events he finds the example of a great spiritual truth. What Paul offers is an illustration of God's dealings with human beings. For further discussion, see R. Alan Cole, *Galatians*, TNTC, rev. ed. (Grand Rapids: William B. Eerdmans Publishing Co., 1989), 179–81.

8. Paul's literal statement in 5:4 is that they have "fallen away from grace." The expression of "falling from grace" is familiar to many Protestants as a description of living an immoral lifestyle which supposedly severs one's personal relationship to Christ. Notice that immoral living is not Paul's concern at this point. He is concerned about the object of trust of the readers, and he is stating that they must trust Christ completely or not at all. Those who trust legal activity such as circumcision as a means of relating to God have indeed committed apostasy.

It is true that individuals may so place their trust in their own personal performance that they do not have salvation. We might question whether those who do this were ever God's children in a saving sense.

inclination for legalism as they rested more completely in Jesus Christ (5:10).

Although most of the trouble in the Galatian church came from the legalists, others in the church may have tried to press Christian freedom beyond its limits. Paul now referred to this group (5:13–18). First, he described the right use of freedom—serving one another in love (5:13). Second, he pointed out that the source of this freedom comes not by rendering obedience to a set of rules but by living continually in a Spirit-controlled existence (5:16).

Paul then proceeded to discuss the vast benefits bestowed upon the believer by the presence of the Spirit. Human nature left to itself produces an astonishing variety of vices (5:19–21). In complete contrast, human beings enabled by the Holy Spirit produce a bountiful harvest of qualities that fulfill God's laws (5:22–24). Paul emphasized that it was imperative for Christians to keep step with the Spirit (5:25).

Paul knew that his readers would listen to his words, and he wanted to help them deal with some of the ringleaders of the legalistic heresy once they repented of their actions. How should the church deal with those legalists who saw the error of their actions? Paul urged his readers to "restore" those who fell into sin and to help bear their burdens (6:1–2). Those who took pride in their legalistic teaching should permit the scrutiny of God to evaluate their actions (6:4). The apparent contrast of Paul's statements in 6:2 and 6:5 is only on the surface. In 6:2 Paul insisted that some burdens are so heavy that they require help. In 6:5 he pointed out that Christians must answer for their own behavior at the final judgment.

The Galatian Christians also needed instruction about Christian giving and a reminder of the benefits of consistent obedience. Christians who receive instruction from their pastor-teacher must make a financial contribution for his support (6:6). Christians who have been led astray into legalism must know that they will reap from God what they sow in their behavior (6:7–8). Paul also included a word for the faint-hearted. Those tempted to grow weary in their practice of obedience and generosity received the promise of reaping if they endured in obedience (6:9).

Conclusion (6:11–18)

With the main part of the letter concluded, Paul took the pen of his scribe to flesh out the ending in his own handwriting (6:11). The "large letters" emphasized the authenticity of his writing. He charged the Judaizers with spreading their teaching only to avoid persecution and to gain converts about whom they could boast (6:12–13). Paul's object of boasting was the cross, and he pointed to his suffering in obedience as a mark of the purity of his motive (6:14–17).

Outline of Galatians

I. Introduction: Greetings to the Galatians and a Stern Warning to Those Who Were Perverting the Gospel by Preaching Legalism (1:1–10)

II. Experiential Argument (1:11–2:21)
- A. Direct revelation of the gospel from Jesus to Paul (1:11–12)
- B. Impossibility of Paul learning the gospel from his Jewish background (1:13–14)
- C. Impossibility of Paul obtaining the gospel from apostolic sources (1:15–24)
- D. Acceptance of Paul's gospel by Jerusalem Christian leaders (2:1–10)
- E. Ability of Paul to rebuke Peter successfully when Peter compromised (2:11–16)
- F. Experience of spiritual life through Christ, not legalism (2:17–21)

III. Theological Argument (3:1–5:1)
- A. Completeness of faith (3:1–5)
- B. Example of Abraham's faith (3:6–9)
- C. Inability to experience justification by obeying the law (3:10–14)
- D. Priority of the promise to Abraham over the covenant of the law (3:15–18)
- E. Purpose of the law (3:19–29)
- F. Availability of sonship through faith alone (4:1–7)
- G. Emptiness of legalism (4:8–11)
- H. Paul's personal appeal to the Galatians (4:12–20)

I. Illustration of Hagar and Sarah as an example of freedom (4:21–5:1)

IV. Practical Argument (5:2–6:10)
   A. Contrasting effects of legalism and faith (5:2–6)
   B. Personal appeal (5:7–12)
   C. Genuine freedom (5:13–18)
   D. Works of the flesh (5:19–21)
   E. Fruit of the Spirit (5:22–26)
   F. Proper treatment of offenders (6:1–5)
   G. Appeals for generosity, obedience, and persistence (6:6–10)

V. Conclusion: Contrast Between the Pride of the Judaizers and the Humility of Paul (6:11–18)

For Further Discussion

1. Explain the difference between the North Galatian and the South Galatian theory of the destination of Galatians.

2. Defend your view of the date of writing Galatians.

3. Why is the content of Galatians important in Christian history?

4. Compare Paul's account of his visit to Jerusalem (Gal. 2:1–10) with Luke's account of Paul's visit for the Jerusalem Council (Acts 15:1–29). Point out similarities, differences, and suggest means of harmonization.

5. What forms of legalism do you observe in contemporary Christianity? Explain some principles from Galatians which would successfully combat this legalism.

The Letters to the Thessalonians

The City and the Church

The city of Thessalonica was founded in 315 B.C. by Cassander, a general of Alexander the Great. He named the city for his wife Thessalonica, the daughter of Philip of Macedon and the sister of Alexander. The city was located on a protected bay in the northwest corner of the Aegean Sea. Its favorable location led to its development as a seaport and contributed to its growth in population, wealth, and importance. During Roman times the Ignatian Way *(Via Egnatia)* passed through Thessalonica and linked the city with Philippi to the east and with Dyrrhachium on the Adriatic Sea to the west. After 146 B.C. it served as capital of the Roman province of Macedonia. In Paul's day the city may have had a population of two hundred thousand people. In modern Greece the city of Salonika, built on the same location and reflecting the ancient name, is the second largest city in the country.

Paul's initial ministry in Thessalonica is narrated in Acts 17:1–9. The apostle located a synagogue in the city, and for three successive Sabbaths he preached there. His assertion that Jesus was the Messiah led some Jews, Greeks, and particularly some of the women, to faith. His success provoked hostility among unbelieving Jews, who started a riot, hauled some believers before the city authorities, and charged them with disloyalty to Caesar. Paul's host, Jason, had been among those brought before the city judiciary, and Jason made a pledge to these leaders. The nature of the pledge is unclear. Perhaps he promised to send Paul and his friends away, or he may have guaranteed that the preaching of Paul would cause no further trouble. He could not have promised Paul's permanent absence from the city because Paul attempted to return on another occasion (1 Thess. 2:18) and probably visited there again (Acts 20:1–2).

The length of Paul's stay in Thessalonica is much debated. Luke mentions a three-week ministry in the city (Acts 17:2), but his description does not limit Paul's stay to only three weeks. Several facts suggest that Paul remained in Thessalonica for more than three weeks—perhaps several months.

- The large number of Gentile converts in the city suggests a longer stay (1 Thess. 1:9).

- Paul's manual labor in the city suggests a stay of more than three weeks (2 Thess. 3:8).

- Paul's acknowledgment that he had received aid from the Philippians more than once while in Thessalonica points toward a longer stay (Phil. 4:16).

- The sheer variety of Paul's teaching during his stay in Thessalonica suggests a longer stay.

Apparently Paul's instruction about the return of Christ left room for unanswered questions. Some scholars suggest that Paul's teachings on eschatology would require longer than three weeks (1 Thess. 4:13–18).

Authorship

Both 1 and 2 Thessalonians claim Pauline authorship. The vocabulary, style, and theology are Pauline. If Paul were not the author of these writings, determining a reason for so many Pauline elements would be difficult. Why would someone write letters such as these to imply that they came from Paul? The claim of the letters and the obvious evidence of Pauline authorship should be accepted as true.

The more radical school of German higher criticism led by F. C. Baur challenged Pauline authorship of 1 Thessalonians primarily for its lack of doctrinal emphasis. This objection is overstated, since the doctrine of Christ's return is quite prominent in 1 Thessalonians 4:13–18. However, it is true that Paul wrote more about pastoral concerns than doctrinal concerns in the letter.

Some have questioned the Pauline authorship of 2 Thessalonians because of variations with 1 Thessalonians in the doctrine of Christ's return. They point out that 1 Thessalonians anticipates an imminent return of Christ, while 2 Thessalonians suggests that the return follows a time of apostasy and the appearance of the man of lawlessness. Paul, however, was not attempting to formulate a systematic approach to eschatology but only to respond to the needs of the church. A misunderstanding about those who would participate in Christ's return prompted Paul's statements in 1 Thessalonians. The belief by some that the day of Christ had already begun prompted Paul's teachings in 2 Thessalonians. Dealing with problems in the church necessitated different emphases and language.

No decisive objections to Pauline authorship have swayed the convictions of centuries of Christian opinion. My judgment is that we should accept Pauline authorship as claimed in both letters.

Occasion

After Paul left Thessalonica, he had a brief ministry in Berea and Athens (Acts 17:10–34). In Athens Silas and Timothy rejoined Paul, but he apparently sent them back to Macedonia for further ministry (Acts 17:15–16; 1 Thess. 3:2). They later met him in Corinth (Acts 18:5), and Timothy brought a favorable report on the growth of the converts in faith and love (1 Thess. 3:6). Timothy also may have brought with him a letter requesting instruction from Paul on several subjects, but we have no way to prove this suggestion. After receiving information about the church, Paul wrote 1 Thessalonians to accomplish several purposes.

- He wanted to encourage believers as they faced intense persecution (1 Thess. 2:14; 3:1–4).

- He responded to criticism against his motives in Christian service by explaining how he had conducted his ministry in Thessalonica (1 Thess. 2:1–12).

- The presence of low moral standards in Thessalonica led Paul to explain Christian standards for sexual morality (1 Thess. 4:1–8).

- The death of some members in the congregation led to questions about how they would participate in the coming return of Christ and Paul answered their questions (1 Thess. 4:13–18).

- The church needed instruction about the healthy use of spiritual gifts (1 Thess. 5:19–22).

No information in Acts or 2 Thessalonians fully explains how the renewal of fresh contacts between Paul and the Thessalonians led to the writing of the second letter. In 2 Thessalonians Paul indicated his knowledge that some believers in Thessalonica were suggesting that the day of the Lord had already occurred, apparently from a letter wrongly attributed to him (2 Thess. 2:2). Paul had also heard of unhealthy idleness among the Thessalonians (2 Thess. 3:11–13). When he learned this information, Paul was probably still in Corinth on his second missionary trip. He wrote 2 Thessalonians not too long after writing the first letter. The development of eschatological fanaticism and disruptive laziness prompted his writing.

Date

Paul's stay in Corinth can be dated with the help of the Delphi Inscription, which provides information about the service of the proconsul Gallio.[9] Gallio probably assumed office in the summer of A.D. 51 and served through the summer of A.D. 52. Paul was brought before Gallio shortly after the governor's arrival in Corinth, and this was near the end of Paul's eighteen-month stay in the city (Acts 18:9–18). Paul's Corinthian ministry likely began in A.D. 50, and Paul wrote 1 Thessalonians either in this year or the following year.

Some have suggested that 2 Thessalonians was written before 1 Thessalonians. Neither letter claims to come before or after the other, and it is possible that the suggestion is correct. Some indications in 2 Thessalonians seem to suggest an awareness of an earlier letter (2 Thess. 2:15; 3:17). It would be natural to take these as references to 1 Thessalonians. In the absence of adequate reasons to support a reversal of the order of writing these two letters, it is better to retain the traditional order.

Assuming the priority of 1 Thessalonians, we can place the writing of 2 Thessalonians at a time just a few months later than the first letter. Silas and Timothy are still with Paul (2 Thess. 1:1). A date of 51 or 52 is likely, and the earlier is more probable.

The Message of First Thessalonians

Thanksgiving for the Conversion of the Thessalonians (1:1–10)

After a brief greeting and an expression of gratitude for the faith, love, and hope of the Thessalonians, Paul described their exemplary response to the gospel (1:1–10). Despite severe suffering, the response of the Thessalonians provided a model for all believers in Macedonia and Achaia. Like the sound of a trumpet the evangelistic emphasis of the Thessalonians penetrated the entire Grecian peninsula. They had left the worship of idols and turned to the worship of the living God. With patience and confidence they anticipated Christ's return.

---

9. For information on this inscription, see chapter 13, n. 5.

Explanation of Paul's Motives and Actions (2:1–12)

Apparently Paul had his detractors in Thessalonica, and he had to defend his motives, actions, and general behavior (2:1–12). Paul insisted that his motives were pure. His preaching was free from error, motivated by pure reasons, and was untainted by trickery or deceit (2:3). His actions resembled those of a mother gently caring for her children, and the Thessalonians could remember his faithful toil to provide his own support (2:7–9). His general behavior resembled a father who offered encouragement and comfort to his struggling children (2:10–12).

Paul's Relationship to the Thessalonians (2:13–3:13)

Paul pictured his relationship with the Thessalonians with gratitude, joy, and prayer (2:13–3:13). He expressed gratitude because the Thessalonians, after responding to the gospel as God's message, endured savage persecution from other Gentiles (2:13–15). Paul longed to see the Thessalonians again with the joyful anticipation of parents eager to look upon their firstborn (2:17–20). Greatly distressed at the intensity of the persecution they faced, Paul sent Timothy to strengthen them. Timothy's return with a report of their steadfastness produced renewed gratitude to God and fervent prayer for an opportunity to see them (3:6–10). Paul prayed also for the multiplication of their love for each other so that they might face trials with renewed strength (3:11–13).

Exhortation to Sexual Purity (4:1–8)

Regardless of the spiritual fervor in Thessalonica, problems existed in the fellowship. The prevailing sexual laxity that Paul witnessed throughout the Roman Empire caused him to remind his readers that sexual purity was the will of God (4:3). Anyone who violated God's standards at this point faced certain punishment from him. Paul made it clear that God had not called believers to trifle with impurity but to live a holy life (4:6–8).

Exhortation to Mutual Love and Hard Work (4:9–12)

In addition to maintaining moral purity, the Thessalonians needed to deepen their love for one another (4:9–10). Paul also urged them to win the respect of outsiders and secure their own living by hard, steady work at their occupations (4:11–12). The fact that laziness was a serious shortcoming by the time 2 Thessalonians was written suggests that already the seeds of sluggishness were sprouting in Thessalonica (see 2 Thess. 3:11–13).

Questions About the Parousia[10] (4:13–5:11)

The most potentially damaging problem that Paul addressed in 1 Thessalonians involved a serious misunderstanding of the impact of the Lord's return. Some believers had died since Paul visited the city. What would happen to them when Christ returned? Would they miss out on the benefits of the return? Perhaps they feared that death before Christ's return represented punishment for sin or indicated a loss of salvation. To overcome the fears of his readers, Paul assured them that at the return of Christ the dead would rise first and go to meet the Lord. The dead would be joined in the Lord's presence by living believers, and both would remain with the Lord forever (4:13–18). Paul's new revelation to his readers concerned the order of the resurrection. Deceased believers would be raised prior to the transformation of living believers.[11]

Readiness for the Lord's Return (5:1–11)

Believers in Thessalonica were asking, "When will the Lord return?" Paul indicated that they did not need additional instruc-

10. The term *parousia* is the most generally used New Testament word for the return of Christ. The expression is a transliteration of the Greek word which literally means "coming" or "presence." Other terms used in the New Testament to describe the return of Christ are translated as "appearing" (the Greek term used in Titus 2:13 is transliterated *epiphaneia*) and as "revelation" (the Greek term used in 2 Thess. 1:7 is transliterated *apokalypsis*).

11. The section in vv. 13–18 is closely examined for its teaching about the order of events at the return of Christ. Those who hold to a dispensational view of eschatology use the term "rapture" (derived from the Latin word translated "caught up" in v. 17) to describe a secret return of Christ to remove living believers prior to the persecution and suffering of the tribulation period. They feel that raptured believers will escape the grueling hardship of the difficulties described in Rev. 13:5–17. To them the events of vv. 13–18 are a pretribulation return of Christ.

Others of different eschatological persuasion view this as the glorious second advent of Christ occurring *after* the events of the tribulation (Matt. 24:4–31). They view the events of vv. 13–18 as after the tribulation. Still others identify the tribulation as a time of persecution in this age and do not regard it as a special time of difficulty at the end of the age. They would generally be postmillennial in their eschatology.

For additional discussion of this issue, see Robert G. Clouse, ed., *The Meaning of the Millennium: Four Views* (Downers Grove, Ill.: InterVarsity Press, 1977).

tion about the timing of the return. For most human beings that event would occur unexpectedly (5:1–3). Believers should prepare for the Lord's return by disciplined, godly living supported by attitudes of faith, love, and hope. Paul's instructions discouraged rationalistic speculation about the timing of the parousia and insisted that watching for Jesus' return involved consistent living in obedience to the Lord's commands (5:4–11).

Final Exhortations (5:12–22)

Toward the end of his letter Paul offered several instructions for his Christian friends.

- He urged the church at large to show respect for its leaders (5:12–13).

- He urged the leaders to demonstrate understanding and acceptance to all members, especially those who persisted in trying behavior (5:14–15).

- He directed all of his readers to acknowledge God's sovereignty and providence by expressing thanks in all circumstances (5:16–18).

- He urged his readers to accept the gifts of the Spirit with an openness characterized by a discerning evaluation of the gift (5:19–22).

Conclusion (5:23–28)

Paul concludes his letter with a prayer for the consecration of his readers and a reminder of God's faithfulness in directing their sanctification (5:23–24). He requested prayer for himself and urged his friends to greet one another with warmth and love (5:25–28).

Outline of First Thessalonians

I. Greeting (1:1)

II. Gratitude for the Conversion of the Thessalonians (1:2–10)
   A. Moral transformation of the Thessalonians (1:2–5)
   B. Endurance of suffering by the Thessalonians (1:6)
   C. Spiritual model provided by the Thessalonians (1:7–10)

III. Explanation of Paul's Motives and Actions (2:1–12)

  A. Motives of Paul (2:1–6)
  B. Actions of Paul (2:7–9)
  C. Encouragement provided by Paul (2:10–12)
 IV. Relationship of Paul to the Thessalonians (2:13–3:13)
  A. Gratitude for their endurance of persecution (2:13–16)
  B. Intense longing to see them again (2:17–20)
  C. Concern for their stability in facing trial (3:1–5)
  D. Encouragement in faith during hardship (3:6–10)
  E. Prayer for spiritual growth (3:11–13)
 V. Confronting Problems Among the Thessalonians (4:1–5:22)
  A. Need to maintain sexual purity (4:1–8)
  B. Demonstration of brotherly love (4:9–10)
  C. Maintenance of diligent habits (4:11–12)
  D. Concern for believers who died before the parousia (4:13–18)
  E. Moral preparedness for the Lord's return (5:1–11)
  F. Demonstrating respect, joy, and discernment (5:12–22)
 VI. Conclusion (5:23–28)

The Message of Second Thessalonians

Paul's Concern for the Persecuted Thessalonians (1:1–12)

Following a brief introduction (1:1–2), Paul explained his prayer concerns for his readers. He expressed thanksgiving for their growth in faith and love for each other in spite of their intense sufferings (1:3–5). Paul explained the certainty of divine judgment on their persecutors and the equal certainty that God would provide ultimate relief for the persecuted (1:6–10). He assured his readers that he prayed constantly that their way of living would ensure God's final commendation of their actions and life purpose (1:11–12).

The Return of Christ (2:1–12)

Paul used the term "day of the Lord" to describe the complex of events that will occur at Jesus' return. He assured the Thessalonians that these events had not yet begun even though someone had used devious methods to suggest that the events were already unfolding (2:1–2). Paul insisted that a moral rebellion against God and the appearance of the man of lawlessness[12] would occur before the day of the Lord came (2:3–4). This man of lawlessness will demand worship as God, display satanically-inspired, counterfeit miracles, and inspire all types of evil in his followers (2:5, 9–10). Those who follow him will face condemnation because they loved wickedness and accepted lies rather than divine truth (2:11–12). Jesus will render this lawless one utterly powerless at his return, but for the present the spirit of the man of lawlessness was already at work (2:7, 9). The display of power by the man of lawlessness will increase after the restrainer is removed (2:7).[13]

Paul's statements here make a direct contribution to the question of whether or not the return of Christ can occur at any moment. Can the return of Christ take place immediately, or must certain events occur before we can expect the Lord's appearance? Paul's answer here suggests that a falling away from God and the appearance of the man of sin will precede the return of Christ.

Gratitude and Prayer for the Thessalonians (2:13–17)

Paul expressed gratitude for God's work among the Thessalonians and anticipated a glorious spiritual future for them. He urged them to stand firm in their obedience to the teaching he had given them, and he prayed for God to encourage them to fulfill that purpose.

---

12. The identification of this man of lawlessness is a much-disputed question. In the history of interpretation, many individuals of outstanding evil actions have been linked with this man of lawlessness. Paul was not concerned with evil persons who appear periodically in world history but with the person who would appear in the final times. Paul did not use the name Antichrist, but he was obviously thinking of the same person whom John pictured in Rev. 13:5–10, often called the Antichrist. Paul distinguished him from Satan (2:9), but he viewed him as Satan's tool. Paul appears to refer to a historical personality, but it is difficult to prove this dogmatically from Paul's description. For a fascinating study of the use of the term "Antichrist" in the Bible and in church history, see F. F. Bruce, "Antichrist in the Early Church," in *A Mind for What Matters* (Grand Rapids: Eerdmans, 1990), 181–97.

13. Identifying the restrainer presents a vexing problem. The most accurate answer is that we do not know. Among possible suggestions for the restrainer are the Roman Empire or any human government personified in the form of its ruler or leader, the restraining influence of the Holy Spirit, or the missionary preaching of Paul. For additional discussion of the issue, see David J. Williams, *1 and 2 Thessalonians*, NIBC (Peabody, Mass.: Hendrickson Publishers, Inc., 1992), 126–28.

Final Concerns for the Church (3:1–15)

As he concluded this letter, Paul was concerned about three needs in the Thessalonian church. After requesting prayer for his own ministry and protection (a true demonstration of spiritual humility!), Paul expressed confidence that his readers would persevere in their obedience (3:1–5). Endurance in commitment to Christ in the presence of coming hardships would be a constant need. A second concern involved inappropriate conduct by some of the believers. Paul urged the Thessalonians to avoid a habit of idleness, settle into productive labor, and earn their own living (3:6–13). His third concern involved the outwardly disobedient. He urged that the church administer firm but sensitive discipline to those who rebelled against his teaching (3:14–15).

Conclusion (3:16–18)

Paul reminded his readers that only divine strength would allow them to accomplish the goals he had set before them. He took the pen to add a personal greeting and provide a sign of authenticity for his letter.

Outline of Second Thessalonians

I. Greeting (1:1–2)

II. Concern for Persecuted Thessalonians (1:3–12)
   A. Thanksgiving for growth in faith and love (1:3–5)
   B. Certainty of divine judgment on the persecutors of the Thessalonians (1:6–10)
   C. Prayer for the fulfillment of God's purpose in their lives (1:11–12)

III. The Return of Christ (2:1–12)
   A. Denial that the day of the Lord has occurred (2:1–2)
   B. Explanation of precedents to the day of the Lord (2:3–12)
      1. Rebellion against God (2:3a)
      2. Manifestation of the man of lawlessness (2:3b–10a)
      3. Deception among followers of the man of lawlessness (2:10b–12)

IV. Gratitude and Prayer for the Thessalonians (2:13–17)
   A. Gratitude for God's work in their lives (2:13–15)

    B. Prayer for God's continued encouragement and strength in their lives (2:16–17)

V. Final Concerns for the Church (3:1–15)

    A. Obedience and perseverance of the Thessalonians (3:1–5)

    B. Disciplined labor by the idle (3:6–13)

    C. Sensitive discipline to the disobedient (3:14–15)

VI. Conclusion (3:16–18)

For Further Discussion

1. Contrast the pretribulational and posttribulational interpretations of 1 Thessalonians 4:13–18.

2. Contrast the view of Antichrist in 2 Thessalonians with that in 1 John and the Book of Revelation.

3. Is the return of Christ imminent? Defend your views by a comparison of the teachings in 1 Thessalonians 4:13–18; 2 Thessalonians 2:1–12; and Matthew 24–25.

4. How much depth does the instruction in the Thessalonian writings suggest for Paul's teaching ministry in Thessalonica? Compare your observations on Paul's instruction with the level of instruction in your own church.

Bibliography (Galatians)

Baur, F. C. *Paul: His Life and Works*. 2d ed. rev. Translated by Edward Zeller. London: Williams & Norgate, 1876.

Bruce, F. F. *The Epistle of Paul to the Galatians*. NIGTC. Exeter: Paternoster Press, 1982.

Cole, R. Alan. *Galatians*. TNTC. Rev. ed. Grand Rapids: William B. Eerdmans Publishing Co., 1989. Solid but not exhaustive exegesis of Galatians.

Fung, Ronald Y. K. *The Epistle to the Galatians*, NICNT. Grand Rapids: William B. Eerdmans Publishing Co., 1988.

Guthrie, Donald. *Galatians*. TCB. London: Thomas Nelson & Sons Ltd., 1969.

Longenecker, Richard. *Galatians*. WBC. Dallas: Word Inc., 1990. Thorough treatment of form, setting, exegesis, and application of Galatians.

Ramsay, W. M. *The Church in the Roman Empire*. Grand Rapids: Baker Book House, 1954.

Thielman, Frank. *From Plight to Solution: A Jewish Framework for Understanding Paul's View of the Law in Galatians and Romans.* NovTSup 61 (Leiden: Brill, 1989). An analysis of Paul's understanding of the law, insisting that Paul derived his understanding from the Old Testament and the Judaism of his day.

Bibliography (1 and 2 Thessolonians)

Best, Ernest. *A Commentary on the First and Second Epistles to the Thessalonians.* HNTC. New York: Harper & Row Publishers Inc., 1972.

Bruce, F. F. *A Mind for What Matters.* Grand Rapids: William B. Eerdmans Publishing Co., 1990.

————. *1 and 2 Thessalonians.* WBC. Waco, Tex.: Word, 1982.

Clouse, Robert G., ed. *The Meaning of the Millennium: Four Views.* Downers Grove, Ill.: InterVarsity Press, 1977.

Jewett, Robert. *The Thessalonian Correspondence.* Philadelphia: Fortress Press, 1986.

Morris, Leon. *1 and 2 Thessalonians.* TNTC. Rev. ed. Grand Rapids: William B. Eerdmans Publishing Co., 1984. Brief but helpful exegesis of 1 and 2 Thessalonians.

————.*The First and Second Epistles to the Thessalonians.* NICNT. Rev. ed. Grand Rapids: William B. Eerdmans Publishing Co., 1991.

Stott, John R. W. *The Gospel and the End of Time.* BST. Downers Grove, Ill.: InterVarsity Press, 1991. An exposition of the Thessalonian writings which focuses on applications to contemporary life.

Wanamaker, Charles. *The Epistles to the Thessalonians.* NIGTC. Grand Rapids: William B. Eerdmans Publishing Co., 1990. Thorough commentary on Greek text of the Thessalonian writings.

Williams, David J. *1 and 2 Thessalonians.* NIBC. Peabody, Mass.: Hendrickson Publishers Inc., 1992.

16 Paul's Chief Writings (A Survey of Romans and 1 and 2 Corinthians)

Guiding Questions

1. Explain some of Paul's purposes in writing Romans.

2. Identify the approximate time and place for the writing of Romans. Be able to defend your answer.

3. Be able to present a general outline of Romans.

4. Explain the factors that contributed to the growth and influence of first-century Corinth.

5. Explain the two events that led Paul to write 1 Corinthians.

6. List the problems Paul addressed in 1 Corinthians.

7. Discuss the major critical problem in 2 Corinthians.

8. Explain the visits Paul made to Corinth. Explain the letters Paul wrote to Corinth.

9. List some of the charges against which Paul defended himself in 2 Corinthians.

Romans contains the doctrinal marrow of Paul's writings. In this letter Paul set forth a system of theology that begins with the sinfulness of man and concludes with the glory of God. Corinth was the most troubled church with which Paul worked. Both letters to the Corinthians are filled with Paul's responses to specific questions raised by the church and to specific needs caused by the behavior of individuals in the church. Information in 2 Corinthians indicates that Paul faced determined opposition from a segment in the church there.

The Epistle to the Romans

Importance of the City

Rome had grown from a small village on the River Tiber founded in 753 B.C. to a powerful metropolis of over a million people. The military successes of Roman leaders brought fabulous wealth to the city. This wealth is revealed by the presence of numerous impressive buildings. People from many ethnic backgrounds practicing many religions walked the streets of Rome. Reaching this great metropolis for Christ was an important goal for Paul. Paul indicated his desire to visit Rome to preach the gospel (Acts 19:21; Rom. 15:23–25), but when he wrote Romans he had not yet visited the city. He was convinced that his missionary activity would lead him to Rome, and he wrote with the coming visit in mind.

Founding the Church at Rome

Although some early church fathers state that Peter and Paul founded the Roman church, it is likely that neither apostle had a role in its establishment.[1] Paul's failure to include a greeting to Peter in Romans suggests that Peter was not in Rome at the time. Nothing in this epistle suggests that Peter had anything to do with establishing the church. If Peter had founded the church, it seems dishonest for Paul to claim that his policy was not to build on the foundation of another (Rom. 15:20).

Paul's statements in 1:13 and 15:23 suggest that he had not been involved in establishing the church and imply that the church had existed for some time when he wrote. The expulsion of the Jews

---

1. Irenaeus states in *Against Heresies* 3.1.1. that Peter and Paul were responsible for "laying the foundations of the Church" at Rome. He probably was not referring to the actual founding of the church, but was suggesting that both Peter and Paul enjoyed ministries in Rome which more firmly established a work begun earlier.

from Rome under the emperor Claudius in A.D. 49–50 may indicate that a Christian church had already been established by that time.[2] Paul clearly had not visited Rome by this date.

If neither Peter nor Paul established the church, how did Christianity reach the city? Although we cannot prove this point beyond dispute, Jews and proselytes from Rome might have carried the gospel back to the city after their conversion in Jerusalem on the Day of Pentecost (Acts 2:10).

Authorship

Like all of Paul's writings, Romans opens with a claim of Pauline authorship. No critics have presented satisfactory reasons for rejecting this claim. In 16:22 Tertius identified himself as the scribe or amanuensis for the letter. The content and Pauline traits of the letter make it unlikely that Tertius selected his own wording in writing. Tertius served more as a secretary recording the words of Paul than as a creative editor expressing Pauline ideas. The letter's obvious Pauline traits make it one of the *Hauptbriefe*,[3] and support for an author other than Paul has little acceptance among New Testament scholars.

Date and Provenance

Just as the authorship of Romans is relatively uncontested, the circumstances for writing the book are also generally quite clear. Paul's description of his activities in Romans 15:23–29 suggests that he had completed the collection of funds for the Jerusalem believers. His plan was to take this money to Jerusalem. These facts suggest that Paul wrote Romans after 2 Corinthians, for the collection of funds was still anticipated when 2 Corinthians was

---

2. The decree of expulsion was discussed in chap. 14 (see the section entitled "A Chronology of Paul's Life"). Suetonius stated that the reason for the expulsion order was unrest being caused by someone named Chrestus. It is widely assumed that the name Chrestus is a corrupted spelling for Christus (Christ) and that the reference in Suetonius related to controversy over Jesus as the Messiah. If this is so, the presence of the agitation would signal that Christians were already in Rome. For a contrary opinion, see Bruce W. Winter, ed., *The Book of Acts in Its First-Century Setting*, vol. 2, *Graeco-Roman Setting*, ed. by David W. J. Gill and Conrad Gempf (Grand Rapids: William B. Eerdmans Publishing Co., 1994), 469–71.

3. For an explanation of this term, see the discussion in chapter 15 under "The Letter to the Galatians, Authorship" and also n. 1 of the same chapter.

written (see 2 Cor. 8–9). Paul most likely wrote the letter during the three months he spent in Greece on his third missionary journey (Acts 20:3). Although the date might vary by a year or two, it seems likely that Romans was written in A.D. 57.[4]

Several features in Romans suggest that Paul wrote the letter from Corinth. His commendation of Phoebe of Cenchrea implies a Corinthian origin for the letter (Rom. 16:1–2). Cenchrea was the Aegean seaport of Corinth. The Gaius who sent greetings in 16:23 may be the same person mentioned in 1 Corinthians 1:14. The Gaius mentioned in the Corinthian letter was certainly a resident of Corinth. The Erastus mentioned as the director of public works in 16:23 may be the Erastus mentioned on an inscription found at Corinth. The Corinthian inscription concerned an Erastus who served as an *aedile* in Corinth and laid a section of pavement at his own expense. Some suggest that the term *aedile* was the Latin name for commissioner of public works, but the identification is uncertain.[5] We have adequate information for accepting the Corinthian origin of Romans even if we do not identify the Erastus mentioned in Romans with the man memorialized in the Corinthian inscription.

The Composition of the Roman Church

Did Paul write chiefly to Jews or to Gentiles in Romans? Evidence from the book indicates that Paul indeed was writing to some Jews. His argument in 9–11 presupposes the importance of the Jewish people in the divine plan, and in many passages he appears to argue against Jewish objections (2:17–3:8; 6:1–7:6). Also, his use of the example of Abraham (chap. 4) and his frequent references to the Old Testament would have more appeal to a predominantly Jewish congregation.

On the other hand, many passages in Romans suggest that the congregation was predominantly Gentile. Specifically, his references in 1:5–6, 1:13, and 15:15–16 single out Gentiles in the congregation and leave the impression that they comprised a major

---

4. For assistance in locating this date within the general scheme of Paul's writings, see "Paul's Missionary Journeys Harmonized with the Pauline Epistles" in chapter 13 and "A Chronology of Paul's Life" in chapter 14.

5. For a discussion of this issue, see David Gill, "Erastus the Aedile," *TynBul* 40 (1989): 293–301.

segment of the church. In 11:28–31 the unbelief of the Jews brought God's mercy to the Gentiles, and Paul's statement in 11:13 indicates that he was focusing on this element in his ministry.

Although a substantial number of Jews were living in Rome, it seems more likely that the congregation consisted of a Gentile majority with a strong Jewish minority.[6]

Purpose

Some New Testament writings contain a clear statement of purpose (John 20:30–31), but the purpose of many books of the New Testament must be deduced from their contents. Both of these approaches are useful in determining the purpose of Romans.

Paul stated his longtime desire to visit Rome (1:13), but circumstances had prevented the fulfillment of this desire (15:22). He shared with the Romans his intention to come to them as he traveled through Rome to Spain. One intent of his letter was to seek the full cooperation of the Romans for his projected mission to Spain. He was hoping for financial support (Rom. 15:24, 28).

Paul had also experienced a rough and tumble struggle in Galatia and perhaps in Corinth with opponents who emasculated his gospel. Perhaps he wanted to set before the Romans his mature theological thought in order to build up stability in the congregation. In addition, Paul wanted to unify the Roman believers who appear to have been divided over some social issues of the day (Rom. 14:1–15:13).

Paul, therefore, wrote Romans with a threefold purpose.

1. He was seeking support for his projected visit to Spain (15:24, 28).

2. He wanted to explain his theology to the Romans and apply it to practical issues in daily life.

---

6. One uncertain point is the effect of the Claudius edict (see n. 2 in this chapter) on the number of Jewish Christians in Rome. Claudius's edict would affect both believing and unbelieving Jews alike, but it apparently did not remain in force for long. Approximately a decade after the edict, Aquila and Priscilla (Rom. 16:3; Acts 18:2–4) are back in Rome. During the time of its enforcement it would have substantially reduced the number of Jewish Christians in the Roman church, and Jewish Christians returning to Rome would not immediately assume places of congregational leadership.

3. He wanted to urge the Romans to a greater unity than they presently had (14:1–15:13).

Textual Problems

Romans and Colossians are the only letters Paul wrote to Christian communities he had not yet visited.[7] Romans lacks the personal expressions of interaction with individuals and circumstances we find, for example, in a letter like Philippians. Many scholars question the reason for Romans 16 in the letter, for it is composed almost entirely of a series of greetings to Roman friends whom Paul apparently had known elsewhere. Some insist that Romans 16 may have been omitted from Paul's original letter, but no textual evidence supports this claim. It seems more appropriate to view the extensive greetings in Romans 16 as an effort by Paul to establish friendship and credibility with Christians in a city he had not visited.

Other textual problems also appear in Romans. Some evidence indicates that a fourteen-chapter form of Romans existed without chapters 15 and 16. Those who support the original fourteen-chapter form suggest that Paul first wrote chapters 1 through 14 as a general doctrinal treatise but later added chapters 15 and 16 when he sent the letter to Rome. One explanation for the origin of the briefer edition of Romans is that the heretic Marcion excised the final two chapters of the letter because of his bias against the Old Testament. Quotations from the Old Testament in 15:3 and 15:9–12 might have led Marcion to take this action.

The benediction of 16:20 is not always in the same place in different manuscripts. Some manuscripts place it at 16:24, and others place it at the end of the chapter. The doxology of 16:25–27 also appears in multiple locations. Most manuscripts have it at the end of Romans, but some place it after 14:23, and others in both locations. One manuscript has it at the end of chapter 15.

Although dogmatism about these textual issues is not wise, it can be concluded with some certainty that Paul's original text of Romans ended with a benediction in 16:20 and a doxology in 16:25-27. The benediction of 16:24 probably did not appear in the

---

7. Paul had not visited the hometown of Philemon. He addressed this letter more to Philemon personally than to the Colossian church.

original text. We are on solid ground in insisting that Paul's original letter included all sixteen chapters.

Recent Study of Romans

Recent study of Romans has been greatly affected by a viewpoint introduced by E. P. Sanders in his 1977 monograph *Paul and Palestinian Judaism*.[8] Sanders contends that the Jews of Paul's time did not view works as a means of salvation but as a means of maintaining status in their covenant relationship with God. Sanders names his view "covenantal nomism," and he insists that first–century Jews felt that their election by God as His covenant people was the source of their salvation. He maintains that interpreters of Romans must consider that Paul wrote against a background of covenantal nomism rather than against legalism.

Critics of Sanders point out that his view still allows a role for works so that they are somehow required for salvation.[9] Also, even if first–century Jews were nomistic in their viewpoints, we would expect that some were more legalistic than nomistic.[10] It also seems rather tenuous to permit a proposed construction of first-century Judaism to force our exegesis into a singular mold. It is wisest to base our understanding of Scripture on the text that lies before us rather than to subject it to certain interpretations based on a proposed construction. The work of Sanders, nevertheless, has made a positive contribution toward correcting caricatures of first–century Jewish theology.

The Message of Romans

Students of Romans have suggested many dominant themes as the chief emphases of the book. The reformers focused on

---

8. E. P. Sanders, *Paul and Palestinian Judaism* (Philadelphia: Fortress Press, 1977).

9. See R. H. Gundry, "Grace, Works, and Staying Saved in Paul," *Biblica* 66 (1985): 1–38. Gundry admits that "Sanders has certainly put us in his debt" (p. 1), but he insists that Paul's understanding of good works makes them "evidential of having received grace through faith, not instrumental in keeping grace through works" (p. 11).

10. Richard Longenecker in *Paul, Apostle of Liberty* (New York: Harper & Row Publishers, Inc., 1964), 65–85, insists that Judaism contained both an "acting legalism" and a "reacting nomism" (p. 78). He suggests that "to both classes, the Law was of great importance; but it was important for different reasons" (p. 78). Despite the fact that Longenecker published his work before the appearance of Sanders's studies, his viewpoint makes a contribution to resolving the issues raised by Sanders.

justification by faith as the theme. Others identified Paul's chief emphasis as the experience of union with Christ discussed in chapters 6–8. Still others discovered the chief theme in the history of salvation narrated in chapters 9–11. Perhaps it is wisest to conclude that Romans does not contain a single theme but discusses several topics. Justification by faith, union with Christ, and the history of salvation certainly appear in the text of Romans, and we can also emphasize that a clear explanation of the gospel and an appeal for unity (14:1–15:13) are also discussed.

Introduction (1:1–17)

Paul's salutation (1:1–7) follows the general formula of all of his letters: A to B, greeting. In Romans, each section of the introduction is expanded, including the sender's name, the recipient's name, and the greeting. Although the same form of the salutation is found in secular letters of his time, Paul included a specific Christian emphasis in each section.

The introduction (1:8–15) contains three features of interest.

1. Paul commended the Romans for their renowned faith and assured them of his constant prayers for them.

2. Paul expressed his long-standing desire to visit Rome so that both he and the Romans might be encouraged by their mutual faith.

3. Paul emphasized his eagerness to preach the gospel in Rome.

In 1:16–17 Paul introduced the righteousness of God as one of the themes he would develop in the letter. In this context the righteousness that Paul described was not so much a moral quality as it was a legal standing. Righteousness referred to a right standing before God, and Paul indicated that this righteousness was based on the principle of faith described in Habakkuk 2:4.

The Sinfulness of All Human Beings (1:18–3:20)

Human beings need to know how to get right with God. Paul explained that God had revealed his wrath against sinners because they were living in moral disobedience and rebellion. He presented evidence that men and women are all transgressors in God's sight and seriously in need of his mercy and pardon.

Paul began by offering evidence for the sinfulness of the Gentiles (1:18–32). He charged the Gentiles with holding wrong ideas about God and underscored that their ideas developed from a willful rejection of the truth they had known. The deliberate ignorance of the Gentiles led them to abysmal immorality, and God allowed them to follow their choice (v. 28). We should not compare the wrath of God (1:18) to sinful, human passions. God's wrath is a response to human wickedness and disobedience. Although wrath is God's strange work (Isa. 28:21), it is necessary to understand it in relation to his mercy.

After proclaiming the sinfulness of all Gentiles, Paul emphasized that the Jews were just as guilty before God (2:1–3:8). Paul observed that many Jews tolerated in themselves the same vices and sins they quickly condemned in others (2:17–24). He explained that true Jews were not just physical descendants of Abraham or those who practiced circumcision outwardly. Rather, true Jews were those who had a right spiritual relationship with God (2:28–29).

Paul anticipated that some Jews would respond to his teaching in 2:17–29 by asking inwardly, "What is the advantage of being a Jew if we too are guilty?" Paul answered that the Jews had many advantages, particularly their possession of the Scriptures (3:2). More of these Jewish advantages are described in Romans 9–11, but for now he is content to point out that Jews, like Gentiles, are sinners.

Paul concluded his argument by forcefully asserting the sinfulness of Jews and Gentiles (3:9–20). He quoted a collection of verses largely from the Psalms to prove that human beings are sinful, merchants of violence, and dispensers of inhumanity. Paul insisted that the law brought to light the sinfulness of all human beings, but it could do nothing to bring healing to those sick with sin. Paul warned those who trusted their presumed obedience to the law that God has erected a sign reading "Dead End" at the end of the path of legal obedience. Paul is now prepared to present the hope that the mercy of God makes available to sinners.

The Path of Righteousness (3:21–5:21)

Paul developed the theme of God's initiative to provide humanity with righteousness using four major points (3:21–31).

1. This righteousness was apart from the law (v. 21).

2. This righteousness was founded on faith in Jesus Christ (v. 22).

3. This righteousness applied to all human beings (v. 23).

4. This righteousness was made possible by the redemptive, atoning death of Jesus Christ (vv. 24–26).

Since salvation comes by God's grace through faith, no one can boast before God (v. 27). No one has secured salvation by personal obedience to the law. Salvation is a gift of God by faith in Jesus Christ.

In this section Paul uses the word "justification" to describe the act of God that granted righteousness (3:24). Justification is a divine act by which God declares as righteous anyone who places trust in Jesus Christ. This justification leads to a new standing before God, and it provides an incentive for holy living.

Paul illustrated the principle of justification by faith as it operated in the lives of Abraham and David (4:1–25). Basing his argument on the experience described in Genesis 15:1–6, Paul insisted that Abraham's faith in the divine promise provided justification with God (4:3). He also pointed out that David's experience in Psalm 32:1–2 reflected an experience of pardon available only to those who cast themselves in faith on God's mercy (4:7–8).

Paul next presented a list of blessings that God makes available to those who experience justification (5:1–11). Among these are peace (v. 1), joy (v. 2), hope (vv. 4–5), and love (v. 5). Paul concluded his argument to this point in Romans with a contrast between the work of Adam and the work of Christ (5:12–21). To Paul, Adam was a historical figure who represented humanity. Paul believed that all of humanity first existed in Adam. Adam stood at the head of sinful humanity. Christ, by contrast, stood at the head of redeemed humanity. Paul pointed out that the old relationship of sin and death in Adam had been broken and was replaced by grace and life in Christ. The presence of the law caused sin to increase (v. 20), but the experience of grace through Christ removed the accumulated reign of sin (v. 21).

The Path of Holy Living (6:1–8:39)

Should someone object to Paul's explanation of the way of salvation by grace through faith, the objection might take this form: "If sinners receive grace, can't they experience grace all the more by continuing to sin?" Paul answered this rhetorical question (6:1) with a pointed "God forbid!" He then clarified that salvation as exemplified in baptism so changes individuals that they receive a new nature which delights in serving God (6:3–14). Furthermore, even though Christians are under grace, they are not free to sin (6:15–23). In conversion Christians pass from an experience of slavery to sin to the service of God (vv. 16–18). They also come to recognize that the practice of sin leads to death, but the experience of God's grace in Christ leads to eternal life (v. 23).

In chapter 7 Paul continues his argument for holy living with an analogy from marriage. Just as death terminates the marriage bond between husband and wife, so the death of the believer with Christ gives the believer freedom to enter into union with Christ. This union produces a freedom to serve in the new way of the Spirit (7:1–6). Paul argues that the presence of the law stimulated in him and in all human beings an awareness of and desire for sin (vv. 7–13). Paul pictures himself and all believers as those who long to live on a higher plane, but who are constantly dragged to the abyss of disobedience by the power of sin (vv. 14–25).

But, thanks be to God, there is a way to victory. Christians, controlled by the Spirit of God, can experience life and strength in the struggle against sin (8:1–4). Furthermore, the indwelling presence of the Spirit provides the hope that the body of the believer will one day experience resurrection even as Christ did (v. 11). The present experience of the Spirit and the hope for the future resurrection become twin foundations to help believers bear patiently the trials of the present (vv. 18–30). The recognition of present victory and future hope because of God's gracious actions in Jesus inspired Paul to burst into a paean of praise and worship to God (8:31–39).

The Problem of Israel's Unbelief (9:1–11:36)

Paul now centered his discussion on a poignantly personal point. Why had the Jews, his own people, rejected the gospel? After all, they were the chosen people. The incidents leading to the development of the gospel had all originated in their midst. How had they reached such a degraded state of unbelief? Paul must have wrestled often with this problem on a personal level. He also must have had Jewish believers who asked him for answers.

Paul's answer to this problem began with an expression of deep concern for the Jews (9:1–5). He expressed unceasing anguish at the contrast between the Jewish heritage and their present state of unbelief. The law, the covenants, the temple, the patriarchs, and the Lord Himself had come from among them. Paul's love and concern had such depth that he wished condemnation for himself if it meant salvation for Israel (9:3).

Paul explained that Israel's unbelief was part of the plan of God (9:6–29). He indicated that divine election was the reason some responded to the light of the gospel and some did not. He warned that no human being should question the justice of God concerning this divine election, because it is not appropriate for humans to question God on this matter. God showed his mercy and compassion by electing some to salvation.

Paul insisted that Israel was responsible for her rejection of the gospel (9:30–10:21). Paul thus introduced that mystifying connection between divine sovereignty and human responsibility. The Jews were rejected because they stubbornly persisted in seeking justification with God by keeping the law (9:32). Paul believed that human beings were responsible for responding to the gospel. That need motivated Paul to involve himself in world-wide proclamation (10:14–21).

Paul concluded by emphasizing that God had not completely forsaken Israel (11:1–16). The presence of a remnant of the saved, including Paul himself, was evidence for believing that God still had great future purposes for Israel. Further, if Israel's rejection of the gospel produced such blessings for the Gentiles, how much more glorious their own response to the gospel would be (11:17–32). Reflecting on the wisdom of the divine plan led Paul to burst into a doxology of praise for God (11:33–36).

Practical Christian Living (12:1–15:13)

The major doctrinal section of Romans has now come to completion. Paul appealed to his readers to remember the mercy of

God and present themselves to God as living, obedient sacrifices (12:1–2). In this section Paul explored the practical applications of the doctrines he taught in the previous section. He also used ethical admonitions similar to the ethical demands of Jesus in the Gospels.

Paul recognized the spiritual diversity in the church, and he urged his readers to use wisely the spiritual gifts God had bestowed on them (12:3–8). He appealed for his readers to show love both within and outside the Christian body (12:9–21). Concerning secular government, Paul asked his readers to practice obedience and respect and to pay their taxes (13:1–7). You will notice the similarity between this section and the words of Jesus in Matthew 22:15–22. Paul urged his readers to owe nothing to anyone except love (13:8–10) and to live in a state of moral watchfulness for Christ's return (13:11–14).

Christians in Rome had different opinions about such issues as what foods to eat and how to observe the significance of various holy days (14:1–15:13). Paul urged Christians with different convictions, first of all, to show respect for one another (14:10). He also encouraged them not to hinder the growth of other believers by offending the religious scruples of different minded brothers or sisters. They were to undertake particularly those actions which served to build up one another (14:19–21). They had the example of Christ to encourage them to seek the good of fellow believers (15:1–13).

Conclusion (15:14–16:27)

In this closing section Paul shared some of his personal plans with the Roman believers. He intended to make a missionary trip to Spain and would pass through Rome as he traveled westward (15:23–29). He welcomed their assistance in completing the projected journey to Spain (15:24). He commended Phoebe for her service in the church at Cenchrea and probably committed this letter to her for delivery (16:1–2). After singling out Phoebe for praise he sent personal greetings to a large number of his friends and acquaintances in Rome (16:3–16). He warned against false teachers (16:17–20), added greetings from fellow Christians with him in Corinth (16:21–24), and concluded with a doxology praising the plan of salvation and the wisdom of God (16:25–27).

Outline of Romans

I. Introduction (1:1–17)
   A. Greeting (1:1–7)
   B. Paul's desire to visit Rome (1:8–15)
   C. Theme of God's righteousness (1:16–17)

II. The Sinfulness of All Human Beings (1:18–3:20)
   A. Sinfulness of the pagan world (1:18–32)
   B. Sinfulness of the Jews (2:1–3:8)
   C. Proof of universal sinfulness (3:9–20)

III. The Path of Righteousness (3:21–5:21)
   A. God's provision in the work of Christ (3:21–31)
   B. Faith of Abraham and David (4:1–25)
   C. Blessings of justification (5:1–11)
   D. Contrast between Adam and Christ (5:12–21)

IV. The Path of Holy Living (6:1–8:39)
   A. Victory over sin (6:1–23)
      1. A question about sin (6:1–2)
      2. Baptism—the illustration of union with Christ (6:3–14)
      3. Slavery—the illustration of devotion to Christ (6:15–23)
   B. Victory over the law (7:1–25)
      1. Illustration of release from marriage (7:1–6)
      2. Inner struggle with sin (7:7–25)
   C. Victory over death (8:1–39)
      1. New life in the Spirit (8:1–17)
      2. Anticipation of coming glory (8:18–30)
      3. Confidence of victory (8:31–39)

V. The Problem of Israel's Unbelief (9:1–11:36)
   A. Paul's concern for Israel (9:1–5)
   B. Sovereignty of God in election (9:6–29)
   C. Responsibility of human beings (9:30–10:21)
      1. Stubbornness of Israel (9:30–33)
      2. Contrast between legal and faith righteousness (10:1–13)

    3. Proclaiming the gospel world-wide (10:14–21)

  D. God's plan for Israel (11:1–32)

    1. Election of the remnant (11:1–10)

    2. Coming restoration and salvation of Israel (11:11–32)

  E. Praise for divine wisdom (11:33–36)

VI. Practical Christian Living (12:1–15:14)

  A. Appeal for consecration (12:1–2)

  B. Use of spiritual gifts (12:3–8)

  C. Love within and outside the Christian community (12:9–21)

  D. Responsibility to secular government (13:1–7)

  E. Imperative of love (13:8–10)

  F. Moral readiness for Christ (13:11–14)

  G. Love and Christian liberty (14:1–15:13)

    1. Practice of Christian liberty (14:1–12)

    2. Demonstration of Christian charity (14:13–23)

    3. Example of Christ (15:1–13)

VII. Conclusion (15:14–16:27)

  A. Paul's plans for future visits (15:14–33)

  B. Commendation of Phoebe (16:1–2)

  C. Greetings to Christian friends (16:3–16)

  D. Warning against false teachers (16:17–20)

  E. Greetings from Christian friends (16:21–24)

  F. Doxology (16:25–27)

For Further Discussion

1. Does Paul pursue a single theme in writing Romans? Be able to defend your answer.

2. Explain what Paul means in Romans 1:17 by the term "righteousness of God."

3. Explain the theological meaning of the terms *justification*, *redemption*, and *propitiation*.

4. Can Christians experience justification without also experiencing sanctification?

5. Was the return of the Jews to Israel in 1948 the conversion of the Jews to which Paul referred in Romans 11:26? Defend your answer.

The Corinthian Letters

The City of Corinth

The city of Corinth was located on a narrow strip of land that connected the Peloponnesian Peninsula with northern Greece. It had two seaports, Cenchrea on the Aegean side in the east and Lechaeum at the edge of the Gulf of Corinth on the west. The city's location made it a crossroads for travel and commerce and contributed to its prosperity. Ship captains, eager to avoid the stormy dangers of sailing around the Peloponnesian Straits in the south, would dock at one port of Corinth. Their cargo was unloaded, hauled overland, and then loaded in another vessel on the opposite side. They avoided the risk of losing ships and lives in the dangerous voyage along the southern route.

Corinth was also known for hosting athletic events known as the Isthmian Games. These events took place every two years and provided great financial rewards for the victors. Huge crowds thronged to the city for the festivities.

Rome destroyed Corinth in 146 B.C., but a century later it was rebuilt on the same location. The city developed rapidly as a Roman colony, and its population in the New Testament period was estimated to be as much as one-half million. In the New Testament period Corinth was also the capital of the Roman province of Achaia.

In ancient times the city of Corinth had a temple dedicated to the worship of the goddess Aphrodite. It was located on the Acrocorinth, a massive outcropping of rock jutting upward about eighteen hundred feet above Corinth. Ancient writers indicated that one thousand sacred prostitutes offered their bodies in the temple in the service of the goddess Aphrodite. Such immorality attracted to the city many people interested only in licentious living, but evidence suggests that this temple was in ruins during the New Testament era when Paul visited. Immorality was still prominent in the city, however.

Corinth obtained a well deserved reputation for fast, profligate living. Realizing the costliness and moral turpitude involved in visiting Corinth, the Roman geographer Strabo quoted an ancient proverb about the city: "Not for every man is the voyage to Corinth."[11] Moralists used the name of the city to coin the Greek verb *korinthiazesthai*, which meant "to practice fornication."[12]

Building a Christian church in this loose, licentious city would not be an easy task. Immorality, contentiousness, heresy, and brutality were all prevalent in this prosperous, pagan community.

Authorship

The opening verses of both Corinthian letters identify Paul as the author. Few have contested this claim to Pauline authorship. Some scholars have insisted that various parts of 2 Corinthians may not all have been written on the same occasion, but they generally accept Pauline authorship even for the sections in question. One exception to this is 2 Corinthians 6:14–7:1, which some scholars view as an insertion added by a Pauline disciple. We will discuss this issue later in the chapter under the heading "Integrity."

Founding the Church at Corinth

Paul went to Corinth from Athens on his second missionary journey (Acts 18:1). There he met Aquila and Priscilla, who were tentmakers like Paul. They were among those Jews expelled from Rome by the Emperor Claudius (Acts 18:2).[13] This couple became strongly involved with Paul in the ministry among the Gentiles (Acts 18:18–19; Rom. 16:3–4). Each day they made tents together, and each Sabbath Paul presented the gospel in the synagogue. Silas and Timothy assisted with the preaching when they arrived from Macedonia (Acts 18:5; 2 Cor. 1:19).

Jewish opposition drove Paul from his synagogue ministry, but he found another location for evangelizing nearby (Acts 18:7–8).

---

11. Strabo, *Geography* 8.6.20.

12. Jerome Murphy-O'Connor, *St. Paul's Corinth* (Wilmington, Del.: Michael Glazier Books, 1983), 56. Murphy-O'Conner collected and printed all references to the city of Corinth in secular writings. His work provides a helpful resource for almost any question one could ask about ancient references to Corinth.

13. For information on the Claudius edict banning Jews from Rome, see "Chronological Date" in the section "A Chronology of Paul's Life," chapter 14.

The resistance to his ministry must have been extremely intense, and Paul received considerable encouragement from a divine vision (Acts 18:9–11). Paul remained in Corinth for eighteen months, but near the end of this period his Jewish opponents brought him before Gallio, the Roman proconsul of Achaia.[14]

Gallio characterized the Jewish opposition to Paul as an internal matter to be settled by the Jews. He cleared Paul of any wrong-doing before Roman law. This decision of Gallio gave Paul free-dom to continue his ministry for some time (Acts 18:18).

The Corinthian church did not have many members who were locally prominent, wealthy, or otherwise influential (1 Cor. 1:26). Sosthenes (Acts 18:17; 1 Cor. 1:1) and Erastus (Rom. 16:23) were the likely exceptions.[15] Most Corinthian believers came from degrading backgrounds (1 Cor. 6:9–11), but they experienced the transforming power of the gospel.

Paul's Relationship with the Corinthian Church

Notes and suggestions from the Corinthian letters allow us to piece together the story of Paul's relationship with the church. Since Paul did not provide us with a detailed explanation of the relationship, my suggested outline must be regarded as tentative. New Testament scholars have generally accepted this outline—with some variations.

After Paul's eighteen month ministry in Corinth, he returned to Antioch (Acts 18:23) and then began his third missionary jour-ney. During this journey he remained in Ephesus for approxi-mately three years (Acts 20:31). This period probably parallels the time of Apollos's ministry in the city of Corinth (Acts 18:24–28). When problems arose in the church, some Corinthian friends contacted Paul as founder of the church. Chloe's servants (1 Cor. 1:11) brought him word about disagreements in the fellowship. Others in the church sent Paul a letter requesting information about several issues of behavior and doctrine (1 Cor. 7:1, 25; 8:1; 12:1; 15:1; 16:1, 12). It is possible but not certain that the three

14. Paul's appearance before Gallio provided an occasion for establishing a chro-nology of Paul's life and ministry. An inscription mentioning the name of Gallio al-lows us to date the time of his service in A.D. 51/52. For information on the Gallio Inscription and its relationship to a chronology of Paul's life, see chapter 13, n. 4.
15. For information on the identity of Erastus, see n. 5 in this chapter.

men mentioned in 1 Corinthians 16:17 carried this letter to Paul. The report from Chloe's servants and the letter from friends prompted Paul to write 1 Corinthians. In 1 Corinthians Paul promised a forthcoming visit (1 Cor. 4:19), which he hoped to make after visiting Macedonia (1 Cor. 16:5).

In 1 Corinthians 5:9 Paul referred to an earlier letter to Corinth in which he had warned the church against association with immoral people. His earlier letter had caused some misunderstanding, and Paul now clarified his earlier statements (1 Cor. 5:10–11). The letter mentioned in 1 Corinthians 5:9 is no longer extant.

Paul sent Timothy to Corinth to deal with the misunderstandings of the Corinthian Christians concerning the Christian life (1 Cor. 4:8–17). Paul even requested the Corinthians to assist Timothy in accomplishing the aim of the visit (1 Cor. 16:10). Although we learn nothing more from either Corinthian epistle about Timothy's visit, few productive results seem to have come from his efforts.

Paul finally decided to go to Corinth to deal with some of the developing problems in the city. His own visit was both unpleasant and unsuccessful. New Testament scholars often call this visit the "painful" visit, and they believe that it is described in 2 Corinthians 2:1. Since the words of 2:1 cannot refer to the founding of the church, they must apply to a visit preceding his final visit reported in Acts 20:2. Additional evidence for this visit is the fact that Paul's final visit to Corinth is described as his third visit (2 Cor. 12:14; 13:1–2).

Back in Ephesus Paul wrote a strongly worded letter to the Corinthians urging them to change their attitudes toward him and toward God. Paul also urged the Corinthian church to enforce discipline against an unmanageable individual who led opposition against Paul (2 Cor. 2:5–11). Titus carried the letter to Corinth and must have planned to return to Ephesus through Macedonia. Paul, anxious to know the results of his letter, left Ephesus. He waited in Troas and then in Macedonia for Titus (2 Cor. 2:12–13). In Macedonia, Titus met Paul and shared with him the good news that the Corinthians had repented of their rebellious attitudes against Paul (2 Cor. 7:4–16). This exuberant report from Titus prompted Paul to write 2 Corinthians while still in Macedonia. He sent the letter with Titus back to Corinth with the understanding that Paul himself would follow soon (2 Cor. 13:1–4; Acts 20:2).

A Chronology of Paul's Relationship with the Corinthian Church

1. Paul evangelized Corinth during his second journey (Acts 18:1–11).

2. Paul wrote a letter to Corinth, now lost, in which he urged Christians to avoid association with professing believers who were immoral (1 Cor. 5:9–11).

3. Paul wrote 1 Corinthians from Ephesus during his third missionary journey to advise the Corinthians on handling problems in the church.

4. Paul made a "painful" visit to Corinth from Ephesus to correct problems in the church. His visit failed to achieve its aim (2 Cor. 2:1).

5. Paul sent another letter, also lost, calling the Corinthians to repentance and urging discipline for an opponent in the church (2 Cor. 2:4–11). Titus carried the letter to Corinth. Scholars have named this letter the "severe" letter.

6. Paul left Ephesus, for Troas and then to Macedonia, to await word on the success of Titus's visit (2 Cor. 2:12–13).

7. Titus met Paul in Macedonia with the report of the Corinthian church's warm acceptance of Paul's letter and eagerness to see him (2 Cor. 7:5–16).

8. Paul wrote 2 Corinthians from Macedonia and sent it to Corinth by Titus.

9. Paul went to Corinth for his third visit (2 Cor. 12:14; 13:1; Acts 20:2).

The Nature of Paul's Opponents in 1 and 2 Corinthians

Paul acknowledged that he faced opposition in both 1 and 2 Corinthians, but his opponents in the two letters came from different backgrounds. In 1 Corinthians Paul's opponents were within the church. They were divided against one another and also against Paul. The fact that members were taking each other to court (6:1–8) suggested that support for each side of the issue existed in the church. Also, some engaged in sexual license (6:12–20), but others advocated celibacy (7:1). They seem to have regarded their sexual activities as morally indifferent because they had already experienced a spiritual resurrection in their present existence.[16] The most likely source of this particular false teaching is the pagan background of the Corinthians.

In 2 Corinthians Paul's opponents appear to have infiltrated the church from the outside (2 Cor. 11:4). They had a background in Judaism (2 Cor. 11:22), but they were also influenced by the Hellenistic world. In these opponents Paul confronted a Hellenistic Jewish movement that opposed him but was not as concerned with circumcision and the Mosaic law as the Galatians had been. The views of these new opponents on power, prestige, and position reflected values adopted from the Hellenistic world. Particularly, they seem to have emphasized Hellenistic views of speaking and communicating, for they suggested that Paul's clear emphasis on the gospel was unimpressive and insignificant (2 Cor. 10:10; 11:6).[17]

First Corinthians

Authenticity

Affirmation of the existence of this letter appeared early. Around A.D. 95 Clement of Rome wrote the Corinthians concerning the existence of a rebellious spirit in the church. He referred to Paul's letter with the words: "Take up the epistle of the blessed Apostle Paul. What did he write to you at the time when the Gospel first began to be preached?"[18] Clement went on to rebuke the church for allowing the persistence of a contentious spirit to which Paul

---

16. The identical position appears in the description of the false teaching in 2 Tim. 2:17–18. There Paul suggested that the offenders asserted the resurrection was past, apparently affirming that they had already received the spiritual experience the resurrection would bring.

17. For additional information on the nature of Paul's opponents in Corinth, see Carson, Moo, and Morris, *An Introduction to the New Testament*, 279–82.

18. Clement, *The First Epistle of Clement* 47.

had first referred. Both the early church and the modern church have accepted 1 Corinthians as genuinely Pauline.

Date and Provenance

We suggested in the outline that 1 Corinthians is actually Paul's second letter to Corinth. He wrote it from Ephesus during his third missionary journey. Paul was nearing the end of his stay in the city, for he was making plans to leave (1 Cor. 16:5–8). Some have suggested that Timothy carried the letter (1 Cor. 16:10), but this is uncertain. The date would be A.D. 55 or 56.

Occasion

Two features contributed to the writing of 1 Corinthians. First, Paul received from the servants of Chloe a report about disagreements in the church (1 Cor. 1:11). Second, he received a letter from the church requesting information about certain issues of practical and doctrinal significance (1 Cor. 7:1, 25; 8:1; 12:1; 15:1; 16:1). Perhaps the three men mentioned in 1 Corinthians 16:17 brought the letter from the church to Paul.

The Message of First Corinthians

Introduction (1:1–9)

Paul's opening address to the Corinthians followed the traditional pattern of: A to B, greetings. Paul gave a Christian twist to each segment of the salutation, and followed his salutation with his normal expression of thanksgiving for the church (1:4–9). Notice that Paul expressed gratitude for God's work among the Corinthians rather than for the performance or actions of the Corinthians themselves.[19] Paul's less than abundant expression of satisfaction with their activities should alert us that all was not well in Corinth.

---

19. A comparison of the object of thanksgiving in 1 Cor. 1:4–9 with that in 1 Thess. 1:4–10 should make this point clear. Paul was lavish in expressing gratitude for the actions and performance of the Thessalonians. This element is absent in the opening section of 1 Corinthians.

Factions in the Church (1:10–4:21)

Paul began his letter by stating the fact of the division (1:10–17). The factions developed from loyalty to personalities rather than to Jesus himself (v. 12). Paul even depreciated the loyalty of those who professed allegiance to him (v. 13). Those who followed Apollos might have been attracted by his eloquence (Acts 18:24–28). Peter probably appealed to those who were more legalistic in their attitudes. The "Christ" party probably represented a group of believers who viewed themselves as more spiritual than others.

Paul highlighted three factors that contributed to the factions in the church:

1. misunderstanding the nature of the gospel (1:18–3:4);

2. misunderstanding the nature of the ministry (3:5–4:5);

3. human pride (4:6–13).

The Nature of the Gospel (1:18–3:4)

In explaining the nature of the gospel, Paul pointed out the need to understand its content (1:18–31), and he insisted that the central theme of the gospel was the cross of Christ. This message was a contradiction to the Jews, who could not conceive of a crucified Messiah. The message was folly to the Gentiles, who refused to regard as divine someone too weak to prevent so horrible a death as crucifixion (vv. 22–24). The recipients of the gospel in Corinth illustrated the nature of the gospel. The world regarded those who had become believers as lacking influence, position, and power (v. 26).

The nature of the gospel demanded a divine demonstration of power (2:1–5). Paul offered a simple, unpretentious presentation of the truth when he ministered in Corinth. The mighty results of his preaching demonstrated that God's power lay behind the message.

Paul also argued that the nature of the gospel demonstrated divine wisdom (2:6–3:4). The gospel contained God's true wisdom (v. 7). The wisdom of the gospel was revealed by the Holy Spirit (v. 10), and produced believers of maturity. The performance of the Corinthians, however, indicated that they had not yet reached the proper level of maturity (3:1–4).

The Nature of the Ministry (3:5–4:5)

The Corinthians apparently understood the nature of the ministry as a competition. They viewed Paul and Apollos as competitors seeking to gain followers for themselves. To overcome this concept of the ministry, Paul pictured himself and Apollos as "servants" (3:5) and "fellow-workers with" God (3:9). As a master builder Paul laid a foundation, and the Corinthians must build on this foundation with great care (3:10). Rather than boasting of the traits possessed by mere human beings, the Corinthians should realize that all of God's resources belong to them (3:22–23). Only God can deliver an accurate evaluation of the contributions of human beings (4:1–5).

Pride (4:6–13)

Human pride was the final element contributing to disunity in the Corinthian church. Paul reminded the Corinthians that they had received all of their endowments from God. It was sheer stupidity to boast of what they had. God had given it all to them as a gift of grace. To boast about their gifts from God would be like heirs who boasted that they had worked to earn the fortune they inherited.

Paul's Personal Appeal (4:14–21)

After Paul's careful reasoning about problems in the church, he made a personal appeal for unity. Many of the Corinthians were converted through his ministry. They could properly call him their spiritual "father" (4:15). As a father appealing to his children, Paul urged them to imitate him as he followed Christ (4:16).

Moral Problems in the Church (5:1–6:20)

Paul focused on three moral problems in the congregation: incest (5:1–13); lawsuits among believers (6:1–11); and sexual immorality (6:12–20).

Incest (5:1–13). Paul dealt with this issue by writing more about the church's toleration of the practice than about the offender who was involved. The problem concerned a man who persisted in sexual relationships with his father's wife, probably his stepmother. The Corinthian church was tolerant—even the pagans did not accept such behavior. Paul advised the church to expel the sinning member and to cast him into that arena where Satan held sway and to cease all contact with the erring member. Paul may have felt that ceasing all contact with the member would cause him to recall the blessedness of fellowship with God's people. The growing hatred of his fleshly lusts and habits might lead him to forsake his immoral habits and return to fellowship with God's people.

Lawsuits Among Believers (6:1–11). Paul was shocked that Christians were taking one another to court, perhaps in an effort to settle financial claims. He did not deny the jurisdiction of the courts over believers, but he expressed grief that Christians could not settle their disputes within the fellowship.[20] Paul suggested two alternatives instead of court: arbitration (v. 5) and taking a loss on the claim (vv. 7–8). He warned his readers that those who persisted in immoral activities would not inherit the kingdom of God (vv. 9–11).

Sexual Immorality (6:12–20). Paul joyfully maintained that the Christian life was an experience of freedom and liberty. Everything was permissible for him. To distinguish this statement from sexual license, Paul added two qualifiers. First, he would do nothing that was not beneficial to his Christian life. Second, he would not allow any habit to dominate him. In the case of sexual immorality, Paul warned that this sin destroyed individual personality (v. 18). Christians are to view their bodies as a residence for the Spirit of God (v. 19).

Marriage (7:1–40)

Paul now treated the question of marriage—a topic about which the Corinthians had written to him for advice. Many in ancient times admired celibacy as a higher calling, and Paul admitted that celibacy was a good, acceptable option. Marriage, however, was the more normal expectation even though celibacy had some distinct advantages (7:32–35).

Paul urged the unmarried and the widows to remain single if they had the gift of continence (7:8–9). He urged Christians to

---

20. Bruce Winter suggests that Paul was concerned that Christians were endorsing a corrupt legal system in Corinth by taking cases to court for resolution. These Christians were guilty of granting a false status to a system that spawned injustice. See his "Civil Litigation in Secular Corinth and the Church," *NTS* 37 (1991):559–72.

remain married without contemplating separation or divorce (7:10–11). Paul did not mention the exception discussed by Jesus in Matthew 5:32 and 19:9 because he was answering questions, not preparing a systematic statement.

He urged Christians who were married to unbelievers to remain married. If the unbeliever left, the Christian was released from the bond of marriage and apparently free to remarry (7:12–16).

Paul urged Christians to live contentedly in the state in which God had placed them (7:17–24). To those who were single, Paul counseled the preference of the single state over marriage (7:25–28). Those who married might face troubles that would limit their Christian usefulness. Marriage, however, was always an acceptable option (7:36–38). Widows were free to remarry, but only to believers (7:39–40).

Meat Offered to Idols (8:1–11:1)

Christians in the first century faced the challenge of relating to their friends and neighbors who practiced idolatry. Pagan shrines, which received sacrifices for their gods, supplied meat for public consumption. This meat had been used in the worship of a pagan god, and some Christians would offend their consciences if they ate it. Sometimes Christians would be invited to eat private meals in homes where meat used in idol worship was served. How should a Christian respond to this? What should Christians do when they were asked to attend services in an idol temple? Paul dealt with all of these issues.

Paul suggested three limitations to personal freedom concerning the consumption of meat offered to idols.

1. He indicated that one Christian should never eat meat if the eating offended a weaker Christian (8:13).

2. He suggested that a believer should limit the right to eat meat if that freedom hindered the spread of the gospel (9:19–23).

3. He warned that a Christian should never indulge the freedom to eat meat if that action threatened the personal spiritual life of the individual (9:24–27).[21]

---

21. Bruce Winter provides directions for contemporary application of these passages to Christians facing the rise of pluralism in their social worlds. See his "Theological and Ethical Responses to Religious Pluralism—1 Corinthians 8–10," *TynBul* 41 (1990): 209–26.

Concerning the attendance of services in temples of idol worship, Paul advised Christians to flee idolatry. He felt that some demonic reality lurked behind the idolatrous offerings in a temple. He did not want Christians to trifle with this reality (10:14–22).

Paul's general advice was that it was acceptable to eat meat offered to idols because ultimately everything belongs to God (10:25–26). If another believer raised a question about consuming this meat, the sensitive believer was to abstain from eating it (10:28). Whatever they ate or drank, believers must do so for the glory of God without injuring even one of God's children (10:31–11:1).

Disorders in Public Worship (11:2–14:40)

The Corinthians revealed their disunity and self-seeking by creating three separate problems in worship.

1. Corinthian women refused to cover their heads in worship in defiance of the custom of the times (11:2–16).

2. The church members engaged in unacceptable revelry and contentiousness in their observance of the Lord's Supper (11:17–34).

3. The church placed an excessively high priority on the more public and flashy spiritual gifts (12:1–14:40).

Covering the Head in Worship (11:2–16). Paul directed Christian women in Corinth to cover their heads in worship and Christian men to worship with uncovered heads (vv. 6–7). His intent seems to have been to follow accepted customs in Corinth so long as these practices did not interfere with obedience to the divine commandments.

What was the nature of the covering? Some suggest that the covering was long hair for the women. Others indicate that the covering was a veil. This veil covered the head but not the face and was customarily used by Greek women in ancient times. It is likely that Paul was urging the Corinthian women to use some type of veil.[22]

---

22. Leon Morris, *1 Corinthians*, TNTC, rev. ed. (Grand Rapids: Eerdmans, 1985), 150–51.

What was the purpose of veiling the women? Some suggest that the veil showed the submission of a woman to her husband. Others maintain that it demonstrated her new authority as a Christian woman (see v. 10). Although Paul clearly wanted women to respect their husbands, showing submission does not seem to be the primary purpose for wanting the women in Corinth to be veiled. Paul wanted women to wear the veil as a sign of their new authority to pray and worship in public.[23]

Paul's chief interest in insisting on the veil for women and the uncovered head for men was to urge Corinthians to follow accepted customs in the city. He saw no need for Christians to overturn accepted customs that did not interfere with serving Christ. Our application of this principle in the twentieth century does not mean that we insist that women wear veils. Rather, it means that women should be dressed in modest, respectable clothing for the public worship of God.

Disunity at the Lord's Supper (11:17–34). The Corinthians celebrated the Lord's Supper as part of a fellowship meal, and each participant contributed some food for the meal. The wealthy brought much, while the poor brought little or nothing. The purpose was to share a communal meal. The wealthy, however, were privately eating to excess, while the poor could only gaze at the gluttony with empty stomachs. Corinthian Christians did not share fellowship during the celebration of the supper as they were called to do. Their practices only established factions and created disruptions.

Paul warned the Corinthians about their practice of factionalism and gluttony in their observance of the Lord's Supper. He counseled them to participate worthily in the supper by being morally fit (vv. 27–28). The observance of the supper also helped believers to focus on the death of Christ in the past and the return of Christ in the future (vv. 23–26). Paul advised those who could not avoid factionalism and gluttony as they participated in the supper to stay away from its public observance (vv. 33–34).

The Exercise of Spiritual Gifts (12:1–14:40). Apparently the Corinthians never learned to do anything in moderation. Once they were aware that they had spiritual gifts, they prized the more spectacular

---

23. For additional explanation of this viewpoint, see Morna D. Hooker, "Authority on Her Head: An Examination of 1 Cor. 11:10," *NTS* 10 (1963–64): 410–16.

gifts (such as tongues) above all the others. Christian worship and service could easily degenerate into an experience of frenzy and flamboyance with little moral substance. Paul's instructions were designed to correct the abuses the Corinthians allowed.

- He emphasized the diversity of spiritual gifts (12:1–11). Each believer possessed spiritual gifts to be used for the common good, not to promote rivalry and mindless ecstasy (v. 7).

- He stressed the interdependence of all believers (12:12–31). Paul recognized that the human body had many varied parts, and each part made a vital contribution to the function of the body. Within the body of Christ each gifted person made contributions, and God blended all of the diverse elements into a single, harmonious whole.

- Paul taught the priority of love within the Christian fellowship (13:1–13). Love in the body of Christ displaced envy and self-seeking (vv. 4–5). Paul stressed that the practice of love produced a lasting result. In the presence of God, Christians would have no need for the revelation that tongues provided.

- Paul stressed the superiority of prophecy (14:1–40). The practice of tongues allowed a believer to speak to God, but the gift of prophecy permitted a believer to encourage and strengthen fellow believers (vv. 2–3). Believers should seek prophecy because it promoted understanding and intelligent response (vv. 18–19). Women who desired instruction on doctrinal issues were urged to talk with their husbands at home rather than disturb worship by outrageous inquiries (vv. 34–36).

Two features of Paul's teaching provide helpful direction for contemporary Christians. First, Paul stressed that believers should seek the gifts that build up and edify other Christians rather than seek showy, ecstatic gifts. Second, he urged all believers to love one another.

The Resurrection (15:1–58)

Some Christians in Corinth denied that the dead would rise (v. 12).[24] Such denial resulted in rejecting Christ's resurrection and robbed Christianity of its future hope. Those who died with no hope for a future resurrection were to be pitied (v. 19). Paul corrected the misunderstanding of this matter in Corinth by making the following points.

- Paul insisted on the reality of Christ's resurrection (15:1–11). Christ's resurrection was verified by post-Resurrection appearances of the Lord before many different groups (vv. 4–7). Also, belief in the Resurrection was a foundation of Christian faith (v. 11).[25]

- Paul pointed to the consequences of denying the experience of resurrection (15:12–19). If human beings cannot be raised from the dead, Christ has not been raised. If Christ has not been raised, our preaching is in vain, and Christians are still in their sins (vv. 14, 17). Those who denied the Resurrection chopped away at the heart of Christianity.

- Paul taught the results of Christ's resurrection (15:20–28). The resurrection of Christ implied the resurrection of believers (v. 22). The resurrection of Christ was the first step in the establishment of God's kingdom and the destruction of death (vv. 23–26).

- Paul emphasized the resurrection of believers (15:29–58). The hope of a future resurrection gave believers the courage to endure danger and hardship for the sake of Christ (vv. 31–34). He insisted that believers would experience resurrection with an imperishable body suited for life in the world beyond (vv. 35–49). Since Christ's resurrection

---

24. For a discussion of the difference between resurrection and reincarnation, see H. W. House, "Resurrection, Reincarnation, and Humanness," *BSac* 148, no. 590 (1991): 131–50.

25. For an excellent summary of the historical evidence for and the importance of the resurrection of Christ, see George E. Ladd, *I Believe in the Resurrection of Jesus* (Grand Rapids: Eerdmans, 1975).

provided victory over death, Christians have an incentive for unceasing labor to the glory of God (v. 58).

Conclusion (16:1–24)

After Paul concluded his response to the needs of the Corinthian church, he focused on a few additional matters of practical significance.

- He provided instructions for receiving the offering for impoverished believers in Jerusalem (16:1–4; cf. Rom. 15:25–27).

- He outlined his plans for a coming visit to Corinth (16:5–9).

- He instructed them about receiving Timothy and explained Apollos's inability to visit them at that time (16:10–12).

- He commended Stephanas and his fellow workers (16:15–18).

- He sent final greetings to the church (16:19–24).

Outline of 1 Corinthians

I. Introduction: Greeting to and Thanksgiving for the Church at Corinth (1:1–9)

II. Factions in the Church (1:10–4:21)
- A. The fact of the division (1:10–17)
- B. Reasons for the factions (1:18–4:13)
    1. Misunderstanding the nature of the gospel (1:18–3:4)
        a. Content of the gospel (1:18–31)
        b. Demonstration of divine power (2:1–5)
        c. Demonstration of divine wisdom (2:6–3:4)
    2. Misunderstanding the nature of the ministry (3:5–4:5)
    3. Human pride (4:6–13)
- C. Paul's personal appeal to the church (4:14–21)

III. Moral Problems in the Church (5:1–6:20)
- A. Incest (5:1–13)
- B. Lawsuits among believers (6:1–11)
- C. Moral problems among believers (6:12–20)

IV. Marriage (7:1–40)
- A. Desirability of marriage (7:1–7)

B. Advice to the single (7:8–9)

C. Advice to the married (7:10–16)

D. Advice to all believers (7:17–24)

E. Additional insight for the single (7:25–38)

F. Advice to the widows (7:39–40)

V. Limiting Personal Liberty (8:1–11:1)

A. Concern for fellow believers (8:1–13)

B. Concern for spreading the gospel (9:1–23)

C. Concern for individual temptation (9:24–10:13)

D. Participating in idol feasts (10:14–22)

E. Summary of arguments (10:23–11:1)

VI. Disorders in Public Worship (11:2–14:40)

A. Covering the head in worship (11:2–16)

B. Observing the Lord's Supper (11:17–34)

C. Abuse of spiritual gifts (12:1–14:40)

   1. Diversity of spiritual gifts in the church (12:1–11)

   2. Interdependence of Christians in the church (12:12–31)

   3. Priority of love (13:1–13)

   4. Superiority of prophecy (14:1–40)

VII. The Resurrection (15:1–58)

A. Resurrection of Christ (15:1–28)

   1. Reality of Christ's resurrection (15:1–11)

   2. Denial of the possibility of resurrection (15:12–19)

   3. Results of Christ's resurrection (15:20–28)

B. Resurrection of believers (15:29–58)

   1. Affirming the reality of the resurrection (15:29–34)

   2. Nature of the resurrection body for believers (15:35–49)

   3. Victory of Christ over death (15:50–58)

VIII. Conclusion (16:1–24)

A. Collection of the gift for believers in Jerusalem (16:1–4)

B. Paul's future journeys (16:5–9)

C. Instructions concerning Christian leaders (16:10–18)

D. Final greetings (16:19–24)

Second Corinthians

Authenticity

Authors in the early church referred to 2 Corinthians less often than they did 1 Corinthians. Although Clement of Rome provided the earliest evidence for the existence of 1 Corinthians, he did not mention 2 Corinthians. Irenaeus, writing in the late second century, quoted 2 Corinthians and attributed it to Paul.[26] An internal comparison of 1 and 2 Corinthians also suggests that Paul authored both epistles. The Pauline authorship of 2 Corinthians is accepted by both the early and the present church.

Date and Provenance

The content of 2 Corinthians suggests that Paul wrote it soon after writing 1 Corinthians. Following his meeting with Titus (2 Cor. 7:4–16), and while still in Macedonia (2 Cor. 7:5), Paul wrote to the church at Corinth. We would date the letter in A.D. 56 or 57.

Occasion

Paul wrote 2 Corinthians after receiving the enthusiastic report from Titus that his Corinthian friends had repented of their former hostility toward him (2 Cor. 7:8–11). In a very personal way, his letter expressed joy at the favorable response of the majority of the church (2 Corinthians 1–7). Paul then emphasized his desire to complete the collection of money he was gathering for the Christians in Jerusalem (2 Corinthians 8–9). He also defended himself against determined detractors who represented a substantial threat (2 Corinthians 10–13).

Integrity of the Text

Many contemporary New Testament scholars question the integrity of the text of 2 Corinthians. They question whether the letter was originally written as a single unit. Some contend that various sections of the letter were written separately and then patched together to produce a single document.

Some have suggested that 2 Corinthians 6:14–7:1 was the lost letter originally mentioned in 1 Corinthians 5:9. In 1 Corinthians

---

26. Irenaeus, *Against Heresies* 4.28.3.

5:9 Paul indicated he had written to warn the Corinthians against associating with professing believers who were living immorally. However, the passage from 2 Corinthians 6:14–7:1 is clearly written to deal with separation from those who are unbelievers. This fact makes it unlikely that 2 Corinthians 6:14–7:1 was originally the letter mentioned in 1 Corinthians 5:9 and supports the view that it was an integral part of 2 Corinthians.

More frequently, scholars have insisted that 2 Corinthians 10–13 was written at a different time than 2 Corinthians 1–9. Some argue further that 2 Corinthians 10–13 is the "severe" letter mentioned in 2 Corinthians 2:4. They point to the change in tone expressed by Paul as evidence of their belief. For example, in 2 Corinthians 7:16 Paul expressed unreserved confidence in the Corinthians. In 2 Corinthians 10–13 (particularly evident in 12:19–21) Paul expressed great concern for the Corinthians. How could the apostle express both opinions in the same letter? They also see evidence of a "severe" response by Paul in 2 Corinthians 10:12–18; 11:7–15, and 12:11–13.

No manuscript evidence exists to prove that 2 Corinthians circulated in a form different from our present canonical writing. The differences between chapters 1–9 and 10–13 are real, however. How can we explain them?

Some explain the differences by suggesting that in the first section Paul addressed primarily the repentant majority of the church. Then he addressed the reactionary minority in the second section.[27]

Another explanation of the differences between the two sections is the suggestion of a delay in writing chapters 10–13. During the delay, it is supposed, Paul received additional information about Corinth which indicated that the church had once again fallen into divisiveness and opposition to Paul. Paul's abrupt change of tone at 10:1 might suggest the point at which he began to respond to this new information. Paul nowhere indicated that he had received new information for writing chapters 10–13, but he may have failed to mention the new information because of the personal nature of the attacks against him (2 Cor. 10:7–11; 11:1–6).[28]

---

27. See Robert H. Gundry, *A Survey of the New Testament*, rev. ed. (Grand Rapids: Zondervan Books, 1981), 272.

28. Carson, Moo, and Morris, *An Introduction to the New Testament*, 271–72.

It seems best to me to accept the integrity of 2 Corinthians but to remain open to the possibility that a delay in writing the final chapters allowed for the arrival of new information that led to Paul's change of tone.

The Message of Second Corinthians

Preface (1:1–11)

Paul's preface contained a brief greeting that followed his general form for the salutation of a letter (1:1–2). He also expressed thanksgiving to God for the encouragement and protection he had received (1:3–11).

Confrontation with Paul's Former Opponents (1:12–7:16)

Paul defended himself against his former detractors in Corinth. He answered some of the attacks directed against him. He explained some of his motivations in ministry. He opened up his heart in an outpouring of spiritual compassion for this stubborn church which caused him such grief. God had given Paul a glorious ministry among the Corinthians, and he wanted them to know his aims, goals, and motivations for service.

Paul defended himself to some whose behavior changed because of the strong words he wrote in his "severe" letter (2:4). His tone is earnest, but he also expressed hope for the future because of their changed actions and attitudes.

Paul's Failure to Visit Corinth (1:12–2:4)

Paul's opponents in Corinth had attacked his character. Paul answered with a general defense of his integrity (1:12–14). He insisted that all of his relationships with the Corinthians were motivated by divine holiness and sincerity.

Apparently Paul had changed his plans for visiting Corinth. In 1 Corinthians 16:5–9 he outlined plans to visit Corinth after first passing through Macedonia. In 2 Corinthians 1:15–16 he shared his revised plans. He first intended to go to Corinth, proceed to Macedonia, and then return to Corinth. Paul had not followed this plan. Indeed, he went to Corinth on the "painful" visit (2 Cor. 2:1) and then returned to Ephesus. Perhaps someone had suggested that a leader who was so fickle lacked the necessary qualifications for the Christian ministry.

Paul insisted that he had not acted with light-hearted purposes in making his visits (1:17). He explained that he had not visited them because he had wanted to avoid an unpleasant encounter by making too quick a return to Corinth (1:23). He genuinely loved the Corinthians and wanted them to know the depth of that love (2:4).

Restoring Paul's Opponent (2:5–11)

Paul did have an opponent in Corinth, and his "severe" letter had instructed the church to discipline him. The church had disciplined him (2:6), and the offender had been overwhelmed with sorrow (2:7). Paul now urged the church to affirm love for this opponent. Otherwise, Satan might scheme to take advantage of the situation (2:8, 11).

Triumph in Ministry (2:12–17)

Paul recounted his anxiety while awaiting the reply to his "severe" letter to Corinth. He journeyed to Troas and ultimately to Macedonia to learn the results of Titus's visit (2:12–13). In Macedonia Paul learned the good news of the repentance of the Corinthians toward him (7:5–16). Remembrance of that victory caused Paul to rejoice in the triumph through which God always leads his servants. Paul had shared the gospel with the Corinthians, not like a hawker peddling wares, but with the sincerity of a God-sent spokesman (2:17).

The Transformed Lives of the Corinthians (3:1–3)

Some had apparently attacked the legitimacy of Paul's apostleship toward the Corinthian church. Paul insisted that he needed no special recommendation for his work with the Corinthians. The planting of the church and the transformation of their lives were Paul's recommendations for ministry and apostleship.

The Superiority of the New Covenant (3:4–18)

Paul continued to defend his ministry before some of his detractors. He insisted that his competence in ministry came from God (3:6). Paul proclaimed that the ministry of the new covenant was superior to that of Moses because the new covenant featured the ministry of the Spirit (3:8), produced righteousness (3:9), and provided permanence (3:10–11). Anyone who attacked Paul's ministry must reckon with its superior nature.

The Motivation for Ministry (4:1–18)

Paul explained that God had given him a superior motivation for ministry. Despite the drain on his physical strength, God was providing him spiritual renewal each day (4:16). The afflictions Paul faced were light in contrast with the "heavy" glory God was storing up for him (4:17). God also gave him an ability to view events from an eternal rather than a temporal viewpoint (4:18).

The Heavenly Hope of Christians (5:1–10)

Paul's ministry radiated with the hope of receiving the resurrection body at Christ's return (5:1–4). His present possession of the Holy Spirit was a deposit assuring him of future victory (5:5). Paul's knowledge that he ultimately would be "at home with the Lord" filled him with a desire to please God through his present actions (5:9–10).

The Ministry of Reconciliation (5:11–7:4)

God had given Paul a ministry of reconciliation to proclaim the gospel to all people. Christ's love compelled him to carry out that ministry (5:14). In spite of the difficulties he faced, Paul viewed himself as an ambassador urging people to be reconciled to God (5:20–21). This clear perception of his ministry motivated Paul to endure unbelievable hardships (6:3–10). It led him to purify himself from any contaminating alliance and practice (6:14–7:1). Paul used all of these elements to assure the Corinthians of his delight in sharing the gospel with them (7:2–4).

Joy over Titus's Report (7:5–16)

Paul had waited anxiously for Titus to bring information about the response of the Corinthians to his strongly worded letter. Would they reject the letter and their apostle? Would God use Paul's words to change the Corinthians? Paul rejoiced when Titus told him that God had used his strong words to bring about repentance in the

Corinthians. He affirmed his unchanged devotion for the Corinthians and expressed confidence in them (7:12, 16).

Collection for the Jerusalem Christians (8:1–9:15)

Paul, for some time, had urged the Corinthians to complete the collection of funds for impoverished Jewish Christians in Jerusalem (Rom. 15:25–27). Now Paul pressed home to his Corinthian friends the urgency of completing that task.

As incentives for completing the collection of funds, he commended the unselfish example of the Macedonians to the Corinthians (8:1–7) and referred to Jesus' example of self-giving (8:8–9). His intent in urging the Corinthians to take part in the offering was to allow their "plenty" to offset the "poverty" of the Jewish Christians in Jerusalem (8:14). He made wise, honest plans for receiving and transporting the collection to Jerusalem so that no one could accuse him of dishonesty (8:16–24).

Paul explained some features about the proper manner of giving to the needy Jerusalem Christians (9:1–5). He wanted a generous offering rather than a grudging donation (9:5). God's generosity to them should be an incentive for their own generous giving (9:8). Their giving would be a thanksgiving to God (9:11); meet the needs of God's people (9:12); and unify Jewish and Gentile believers (9:13–14).

Paul's Words to a Rebellious Element in the Church (10:1–12:21)

Paul's tone changed radically as we move from chapters 8–9 to chapters 10–13. Paul's words became defensive and displayed a lack of confidence in the genuine response of the group he was addressing. His change of tone came because he was speaking to a still rebellious group in the church. The group either had ignored his appeals in the "severe" letter, or they had begun to express additional rebellion which came to Paul's attention after he wrote the first nine chapters.

Paul's Defense Against Charges of Timidity and Inconsistency (10:1–11)

Paul referred to the charges made against him by opponents in the Corinthian church. Some accused him of showing timidity in face-to-face contacts, but acting with excessive boldness in the safety of a letter. Paul insisted that his attitude and behavior would be the same whether he was present with them or absent from them. Consistency of behavior was his practice.

An Explanation of Paul's Missionary Practices (10:12–18)

Paul's opponents in Corinth apparently boasted of their ministerial accomplishments in the city. They wished to claim credit for the work Paul had started. Paul insisted that he would not boast of the work of another but would boast only of what the Lord had done through him (10:15–17). Paul refused to commend himself for his work (10:18).

Warning Against Gullibility (11:1–6)

Cunning, deceitful teachers were going to the Corinthians and enticing Paul's friends away from their pure commitment to Christ. Their methods included attacking Paul's speaking abilities and claiming for themselves a greater knowledge of God's plans and workings than Paul had (v. 6). Paul was concerned that the Corinthian believers might accept the claims of these false apostles uncritically (v. 4).

A Defense of Financial Independence (11:7–15)

Paul had not accepted financial support from the Corinthians and insisted that he had never been a financial burden to them (v. 9). His opponents interpreted his financial independence as evidence of Paul's lack of love for the Corinthians. Paul insisted that he would never change his practice because his refusal to accept funds from the Corinthians prevented his enemies from boasting that they worked on the same basis as Paul (v. 12).

Paul's Apostolic Credentials (11:16–12:13)

This section contains Paul's celebrated "fool's speech." Paul encountered opponents who boasted of their apostolic credentials and questioned those of Paul. In such circumstances Paul had no option but to resort to the foolish practice of boasting of his own credentials as an apostle in ministry.

- Paul focused on his Jewish background and his suffering (11:16–33). Paul was a true descendant of Abraham, but he boasted that he had worked with greater zeal and had suffered more painfully than his opponents (11:22–23).

- Paul cited his visions and revelations (12:1–10). Apparently his opponents boasted of intimate visions and revelations from the Lord as evidence for their authority. Paul answered that he had also experienced visions from the Lord, particularly a vision that provided him with encouragement to deal with his "thorn in the flesh." Nevertheless, Paul preferred to delight in his weaknesses and hardships rather than in his visionary experiences.

- Paul concluded his "fool's speech" by referring to the miraculous signs and miracles that characterized his ministry (12:11–13). His opponents whom Paul named "super-apostles" claimed to perform miracles and wonders in their ministries. Paul indicated that these same signs had marked his ministry. He was in no sense inferior to these enemies who were attacking him.

The Purpose of Paul's Speech (12:14–21)

Paul assured his friends in Corinth that he had no interest in their money or material possessions. He gladly poured out his own possessions and personality for their benefit (v. 15). Neither did he use other people such as Titus to exploit the Corinthians.

Paul had written and spoken strongly to them in order to strengthen them and build them up. He knew that jealousy, factions, and disorder characterized the Corinthians in the past. He had spoken like a "fool" so they might humble themselves and repent of their previous sins (vv. 19–21).

Paul's Coming Visit (13:1–10)

Paul insisted that on his third visit he would not spare any offenders from his rebuke (v. 2). He assured them that he would speak with the power of Christ. He challenged his readers to examine themselves to make certain that they were following the faith (v. 5).

Conclusion (13:11–14)

Paul's final exhortation urged the Corinthians to practice Christian unity. He closed with a trinitarian benediction (v. 14).

Outline of Second Corinthians

I. Preface (1:1–11)

    A. Salutation (1:1–2)

    B. Thanksgiving for God's comfort and deliverance (1:3–11)

II. Confrontation with Paul's Former Opponents (1:12–7:16)

    A. Paul's failure to visit Corinth (1:12–2:4)

    B. Restoration of Paul's opponent (2:5–11)

    C. An experience of triumph in ministry (2:12–17)

    D. Transformed lives of the Corinthians (3:1–3)

    E. Superiority of the new covenant (3:4–18)

    F. Superior motivation for ministry (4:1–18)

    G. Heavenly hope of Christians (5:1–10)

    H. Ministry of reconciliation (5:11–7:4)

    I. Joy over Titus's report (7:5–16)

III. Collection for the Jerusalem Christians (8:1–9:15)

    A. Incentives for giving (8:1–9)

    B. Purpose of giving (8:10–15)

    C. Process of collection (8:16–9:5)

    D. God's reward for generosity (9:6–15)

IV. Confrontation with Paul's Present Opponents in Corinth (10:1–12:21)

    A. Defense against charges of timidity and inconsistency (10:1–11)

    B. Explanation of Paul's missionary practices (10:12–18)

    C. Warning against gullibility (11:1–6)

    D. Defense of financial independence (11:7–15)

    E. Paul's apostolic credentials (11:16–12:13)

    F. Purpose of Paul's speech (12:14–21)

V. Paul's Coming Visit (13:1–10)

IV. Conclusion (13:11–14)

For Further Discussion

1. How can churches practice discipline in a meaningful way today?

2. Discuss the question, "Was Paul prejudiced against marriage?"

3. To what modern issues of behavior do Paul's words about eating meat offered to idols (1 Cor. 8:1–11:1) relate today?

4. Are the gifts of prophecy and glossolalia still available for the church today?

5. Did Paul believe in a bodily resurrection for believers? Give evidence for your conclusion.

6. Compare and contrast Paul's teaching about Christian giving (2 Corinthians 8–9) with the Old Testament practice of tithing.

7. How does Paul's discussion of his "thorn in the flesh" (2 Cor. 12:1–10) help us to understand God's purposes in permitting personal suffering?

Bibliography (Romans)

Bruce, F. F. *Romans*. TNTC. Rev. ed. Grand Rapids: William B. Eerdmans Publishing Co., 1985. Useful, brief commentary by a noted English scholar.

_____. "The Romans Debate—Continued." In *A Mind for What Matters*. Grand Rapids: William B. Eerdmans Publishing Co., 1990. Bruce suggests that a chief purpose for Paul writing Romans was to involve the Romans as partners in ministry.

Cranfield, C. E. B. *Romans: A Shorter Commentary*. Edinburgh: T & T Clark Ltd., 1985. Useful, brief commentary on Romans by a noted English scholar.

Dunn, James D. G. *Romans*. WBC. 2 vols. Dallas: Word Inc., 1988. Massive, technical commentary on Romans.

Gill, David. "Erastus the Aedile." *TynBul* 40 (1989): 293–301.

Johnson, Alan F. *Romans: The Freedom Letter*. EBC. Rev. ed. 2 vols. Chicago: Moody Press, 1985.

Longenecker, Richard. *Paul, Apostle of Liberty*. New York: Harper & Row Publishers Inc., 1964.

Moo, Douglas. *Romans 1–8*. WEC. Chicago: Moody Press, 1991.

Morris, Leon. *The Epistle to the Romans*. Grand Rapids: William B. Eerdmans Publishing Co., 1988.

Bibliography (1 and 2 Corinthians)

Barnett, Paul. *The Message of 2 Corinthians*. BST. Downers Grove, Ill.: InterVarsity Press, 1988. Suggestions for the exposition of 2 Corinthians.

Betz, Hans Dieter. *2 Corinthians 8 and 9*. Hermenia. Philadelphia: Fortress Press, 1985.

Bruce, F. F. *1 and 2 Corinthians*. NCB. Grand Rapids: William B. Eerdmans Publishing Co., 1980.

Carson, Donald A. *From Triumphalism to Maturity*. Grand Rapids: Baker Book House, 1984. Exegetical studies of 2 Corinthians 10–13.

Carson, D. A., Douglas J. Moo, and Leon Morris. *An Introduction to the New Testament*. Grand Rapids: Zondervan Books, 1992.

_____. *Showing the Spirit*. Grand Rapids: Baker Book House, 1987. Exegetical studies of 1 Corinthians 12–14.

Coleman, Lyman, and Richard Peace. *Study Guide for the Book of 1 Corinthians in Mastering the Basics*. Littleton, Colo.: Serendipity, 1986.

_____. *Pastor/Teacher Commentary: 1 Corinthians in Mastering the Basics*. Littleton, Colo.: Serendipity, 1986.

Conzelmann, Hans. *A Commentary on the First Epistle to the Corinthians*. Hermenia. Philadelphia: Fortress Press, 1975.

Gundry, Robert H. *A Survey of the New Testament*. Grand Rapids: Zondervan Books, 1981.

Hooker, Morna D. "Authority on Her Head: An Examination of 1 Cor. 11:10." *NTS* 10 (1963–64): 410–16.

House, H. W. "Resurrection, Reincarnation, and Humanness." *BSac* 148, no. 590 (1991):131–50.

Hughes, Philip E. *Paul's Second Epistle to the Corinthians*. NICNT. Grand Rapids: Eerdmans, 1961.

Kruse, Colin. *2 Corinthians*. TCNT. Grand Rapids: William B. Eerdmans Publishing Co., 1987. Excellent brief exegetical survey of 2 Corinthians.

_____. "The Relationship Between the Opposition to Paul Reflected in 2 Corinthians 1–7 and 10–13." *EvQ* 61 (July 1989):195–202.

Ladd, George E. *I Believe in the Resurrection of Jesus*. Grand Rapids: William B. Eerdmans Publishing Co., 1975. Defense of the historicity of Jesus' resurrection.

Martin, Ralph P. *2 Corinthians.* WBC. Waco, Tex.: Word Inc., 1986. Thorough exegetical study of 2 Corinthians.

Morris, Leon. *1 Corinthians.* TNTC. Rev. ed. Grand Rapids: William B. Eerdmans Publishing Co., 1985. Excellent brief exegetical material on 1 Corinthians.

Murphy-O'Connor, Jerome. *St. Paul's Corinth.* Wilmington, Del.: Michael Glazier Books, 1983. Collection of evidence from secular writers concerning history and significance of Corinth. Excellent resource material.

Prior, David. *The Message of 1 Corinthians.* BST. Downers Grove, Ill.: InterVarsity Press, 1985. Suggestions for the exposition of 1 Corinthians.

Winter, Bruce. "Civil Litigation in Secular Corinth and the Church." *NTS* 37(1991): 559–72.

Winter, Bruce. "Theological and Ethical Responses to Religious Pluralism—1 Corinthians 8–10." *TynBul* 41(1990):209–26.

17 Paul's Captivity Epistles (Ephesians, Philippians, Colossians, and Philemon)

Guiding Questions

1. Explain the evidence for the provenance of the captivity Epistles.

2. What evidence suggests that Ephesians, Colossians, and Philemon were written at approximately the same time?

3. List the similarities in the content of Ephesians and Colossians.

4. List the characteristics of the heretical teaching that Paul opposed in Colossians.

5. Explain Paul's relationship with Philemon and Onesimus.

6. List some of Paul's purposes in writing Philippians.

Paul refers to himself as a prisoner or "in bonds" in four of his letters (Philem. 1, 9; Col. 4:18; Eph. 3:1; 4:1; 6:20; Phil. 1:7, 13, 14). Sometimes these writings are called "prison epistles," but Paul was not in prison as much as he was in detention. The term *captivity* more accurately expresses Paul's condition as he wrote these letters. Paul was probably awaiting trial and had the freedom to welcome visitors during this time.

Three of the letters are closely linked to the same place and time in Paul's life. Statements in Colossians 4:7 and Ephesians 6:21 suggest that Tychicus carried both of these letters to their destination. Similarities in the content of these letters (cf. Eph. 5:22–6:9; Col. 3:18–4:1) imply that Paul wrote them at about the same time. In Colossians 4:9 Paul mentioned Onesimus as a companion of Tychicus. The fact that Onesimus was probably the courier for Philemon (Philem. 8–10) suggests that this letter comes from the same circumstances that produced Ephesians and Colossians. The Archippus mentioned in Philemon 2 also received a message from Paul in Colossians 4:17. This fact further ties the two letters together. Although the time and place of writing for these three letters are the same, the identification of their place of writing is much disputed. We will evaluate the possible places from which the captivity Epistles could have been written.

Time and Place

Acts mentions two locations of lengthy imprisonment for Paul (Acts 24:27; 28:30–31), Caesarea and Rome. Some sources of early church tradition and some scriptural references have led a few expositors to suggest that Paul was imprisoned in Ephesus (1 Cor. 15:32; 2 Cor. 1:8–11; 11:23—note his reference here to "more frequent imprisonments"). We will examine the evidence for the possibility that Paul could have written from each of these locations.

Caesarea

The slave Onesimus fled from his master Philemon, who lived in Colossae (note that Archippus mentioned in Philem. 2 lived in Colossae according to Col. 4:17). Onesimus could have escaped to Caesarea or to Ephesus more easily than he could have to Rome. Several features suggest, however, that Paul did not write the captivity Epistles from Caesarea.

In Caesarea Paul had access only to his friends (Acts 24:23). In the captivity letters Paul appears to have enjoyed wide opportunities to preach the gospel to crowds who came to hear him (Eph. 6:19–20; Phil. 1:12–13; Col. 4:3–4). These passages seem to resemble more closely the liberty Paul had at Rome (Acts 28:30–31).

In Philemon 22 Paul requested Philemon to prepare a guest room for him. Paul evidently expected to be released in the near future. At no time during his Caesarean imprisonment did Paul suggest any hope of release. After he made his appeal to Caesar (Acts 25:10–11), release would have been out of the question.

It is questionable if a former slave such as Onesimus would have access to Paul under the rather strict conditions of his imprisonment in Caesarea. In Rome Paul's detention was more informal (Acts 28:30–31). Visitation by a former slave would be a more likely possibility in that location.

Although Paul theoretically could have written the captivity Epistles from Caesarea, nothing in his letters supports this hypothesis. In my judgment we should reject Caesarea as an option for the provenance of the captivity Epistles.

Ephesus

Paul endured more imprisonments than mentioned in Acts (see 2 Cor. 11:23). His references to fighting with wild beasts in Ephesus (1 Cor. 15:32) and a crisis experience in Asia (2 Cor. 1:8–11) have led some to suggest that he was imprisoned in Ephesus. Fighting with wild beasts, however, might be a figurative expression for a difficult experience rather than evidence for a gladiatorial battle. As a Roman citizen Paul should not have had to face wild beasts. Thus, the reference to "wild beasts" is not definite proof of an Ephesian imprisonment for Paul.

Paul had serious difficulties at Ephesus and was probably greatly discouraged there. The experience in Acts 19 and his description of the crisis experience in 2 Corinthians 1:8–11[1] suggest this discouragement. Nothing in the biblical text, however, clearly indicates an Ephesian imprisonment for Paul.[2] Even if we could prove an Ephesian imprisonment, this fact would not necessarily suggest that he wrote the captivity Epistles from that location. The fact that Paul suffered imprisonment at Philippi does not prove that he wrote any letters from that city. His brief imprisonment in Philippi did not allow enough time

---

1. Asia in 2 Cor. 1:8 probably refers to Ephesus. Ephesus was the most prominent city of the Roman province of Asia.
2. For a discussion of the evidence of an Ephesian ministry for Paul, see George S. Duncan, *St. Paul's Ephesian Ministry* (New York: Charles Scribner's Sons, 1930).

to write from that location (Acts 16:22–40). If Paul were imprisoned in Ephesus, he probably experienced only a brief time of detention.

Little evidence exists to support an Ephesian origin for Ephesians, Colossians, or Philemon. A stronger case, however, can be made in support of an Ephesian origin for Philippians.

The content of Philippians presupposes several journeys over a great deal of time.

- News of Paul's imprisonment had to reach Philippi.

- Epaphroditus needed time to travel to Paul with a gift from the church (Phil. 2:25–30).

- The church had to learn of Epaphroditus's illness.

- Paul had to learn that the church was concerned about Epaphroditus's illness.

The communication of these facts and the delivery of the gift to Paul required four one-way trips between Paul's imprisonment location and Philippi. It would be much easier to account for these journeys if Paul were in Ephesus rather than Rome, since travel between Ephesus and Philippi required little more than a week, and the trip between Ephesus and Rome required at least a month. We should point out, however, that the trips between Philippi and Paul's imprisonment location could still have occurred even if Paul were in Rome. An imprisonment of two years (Acts 28:30–31) allows plenty of time for communication between Paul and the Philippians. Such multiple journeys would be easier to make, though, if Paul wrote from Ephesus.

In addition, Paul's mention of the "Praetorium" (Phil. 1:13) and Caesar's household (Phil. 4:22) could refer to Ephesus and not specifically to Rome. The reference to the "praetorium" might be understood as a reference to the Praetorian Guard, since we know that this guard had a contingent at Ephesus.[3] Some have found evi-

---

3. The term *praetorium* may refer to the palace of the Roman emperor or the provincial governor (in John 18:28 the praetorium is Pilate's palace in Jerusalem), or it may refer to the body of persons known as the Praetorian Guard. In Phil. 1:13 the NIV prefers the translation "the palace guard," but it also includes an alternate reading: "the palace." The Praetorian Guard was a special detachment of troops assigned to the emperor or to a Roman provincial governor. Inscriptions noting the presence of the Praetorian Guard have been found in Ephesus. See A. H. McNeile and C. S. Williams, *An Introduction to the Study of the New Testament*, 2d ed. rev. (Oxford: Clarendon Press, 1953), 182.

dence that household slaves of Augustus lived in Ephesus.[4] Further, Paul's expressed interest in visiting Philippi would be easier to accomplish from Ephesus than from Rome (Phil. 2:24).

There is little tangible evidence for the Ephesian origin of any of Paul's letters, however. Although some features of Philippians are easier to explain if we assume an Ephesian origin, there is no clear evidence to support this viewpoint. If Paul had written from Ephesus, he would have written at the time he received a collection from the Corinthians for believers in Jerusalem. He mentioned this offering in every other letter written during this period, but he did not mention it in Philippians. The omission of any discussion of this offering further weakens the idea that Philippians was written from Ephesus.

The hypothesis of an Ephesian origin for Philippians and the other captivity Epistles is purely speculative. Of course, one might argue that the same statement is true of the suggested Roman origin, but the balance of evidence tilts more to Rome than to any other place.

Rome

Rome is the traditional location for the provenance of the captivity Epistles. Though evidence for a Roman origin exists, it by no means solves all the questions of origin. Acts 28:30–31 describes Paul's two-year imprisonment in Rome, a sufficient length of time for Paul to have authored all four epistles. Also, the names of Paul's traveling companions on the trip to Rome appear in the captivity Epistles. Luke's presence in Rome is attested by the "we" sections in Acts 28. Also, Luke is named in Philemon 24 and Colossians 4:14 as being with Paul when he wrote these epistles. Aristarchus, who accompanied Paul to Rome (Acts 27:2), is mentioned in Philemon 24 and Colossians 4:10.

One feature that detracts from the theory of a Roman origin is Paul's announced purpose to visit Philemon in Colossae (Philem. 22). If Paul wrote from Rome, it seems contradictory to his announced plans (Rom. 15:28) to visit Spain. Perhaps the circum-

---

4. Apparently some of Augustus's personal slaves may have settled in Ephesus after they received freedom. See A. H. McNeile and C. S. Williams, *An Introduction to the Study of the New Testament*, 182.

stances surrounding Paul's imprisonment led him to change his mind. It is also possible that the needs of the Colossian church became more important than making a trip to Spain. Paul had changed his mind about his earlier plans to visit Corinth (1 Cor. 16:5–7; 2 Cor. 1:15–17), and he could have responded to the changing situation in Colossae by altering his plans in order to go there.

Even though a Roman origin for the captivity Epistles cannot be fully proven, this location has more supporting evidence than any other place. Positive evidence for an origin in any other city is lacking as well.

Date of the Captivity Epistles

The captivity Epistles were written in the early 60s.[5] We have already presented evidence for considering Ephesians, Colossians, and Philemon as a group of letters written at approximately the same time. Philippians was probably written at a later time than the other three, because Paul's attitude toward his release was more optimistic in Philippians. In Philemon 22, Paul expressed a hope for release, but in Philippians 1:25 he was confident that it would occur. If we assume that Philippians was written after Philemon, it is easy to account for Paul's optimism. If we assume that Philemon, Ephesians, and Colossians followed Philippians, it would be difficult to account for the omission of any reference to the outcome of Paul's trial.

We may date Ephesians, Colossians, and Philemon near the middle of Paul's captivity in Rome. Philippians was probably written near or at the end of the two-year period.

The Epistle to the Ephesians

Authorship

The Ephesian letter claims Pauline authorship. The existence of the letter was known from the early days of Christianity, and its Pauline authorship was not seriously questioned at that time. Many of the themes in Ephesians such as grace, the reconciling work of

---

5. For additional discussion of the date of Paul's captivity in Rome see chapter 14 under "A Chronology of Paul's Life."

Christ, and the spiritual struggle with the flesh also appear in other letters of Paul.

Some modern scholars have questioned Pauline authorship for several reasons.

- Some point to the vocabulary used in Ephesians. Words are included that are rare in Paul's other writings (e.g., *politeia* used in Eph. 2:12 and translated "citizenship").

- The sentences in the Greek of Ephesians are long and somewhat cumbersome, and they lack the passionate quality so evident in a letter such as Galatians.

- Ephesians does not reflect an ardent expectation of the return of Christ, an element obviously present in many of Paul's other writings (e.g., Rom. 13:11–12; 1 Thess. 4:13–18).

Despite the difficulties, the questions about Pauline authorship are not sufficient to overcome the claim of the letter or the opinion of the early church. H. J. Cadbury put it well when he wrote, "Which is more likely—that an imitator of Paul in the first century composed a writing ninety or ninety–five per cent in accordance with Paul's style or that Paul himself wrote a letter diverging five or ten per cent from his usual style?"[6] I believe the content of Ephesians is easier to understand if Paul is accepted as the author of the letter.[7]

Date, Provenance, and Carrier

Ephesians was written from Rome during the early 60s while Paul was imprisoned there. References in Ephesians 6:21–22 suggest that Tychicus carried the letter to its destination.

---

6. H. J. Cadbury, "The Dilemma of Ephesians," *NTS* 5 (1958–59): 101.

7. Luke Johnson opts for the authorship of Ephesians by Paul or one of his followers. His argument for authorship by Paul or one of his followers could support Paul as sole author as well. He says, "There is nothing in it that cannot be accounted for by the special circumstances and purpose of the letter. If, in fact, Ephesians is a circular letter written to Gentile communities under the authorization of the captive Paul, then the lack of personal references, the distinctive stylistic traits, the use of tradition, and the perspective on the church are not only all intelligible but virtually necessary." See Luke Johnson, *The Writings of the New Testament* (Philadelphia: Fortress Press, 1986), 371–72.

Readers of Ephesians

The phrase "in Ephesus" (Eph. 1:1) is absent from some of the most significant manuscripts of this letter. Generally, the tone of the letter is impersonal. Some of Paul's statements seem to imply that the writer may not have known the readers (e.g., 1:15; 3:2; 4:21—in each instance the reference to "heard" suggests a lack of contact with the readers by the writer). The picture of Paul's relationship with the Ephesians in Acts 20:36–38 is warm and affectionate. How can we explain the contrast between the impersonal content of the letter and the obvious compassion in Acts?

Some have suggested that Ephesians was originally a circular letter, sent perhaps to churches throughout Asia. The church at Ephesus kept a copy of this letter without an address. As time passed, readers outside of Ephesus might have assumed that Ephesus had initially received the letter. A few scholars have suggested that the letter "from Laodicea" (Col. 4:16) may actually be the Ephesian letter coming to Colossae from Laodicea. If Ephesians were originally written as a circular letter, however, it is strange that it would contain very personal references to Paul's contact with Ephesus (see Eph. 3:13). Such personal touches would not be expected in a general circular letter.

E. J. Goodspeed suggested that an admirer of Paul penned Ephesians near the end of the first century. He believed the author possessed a collection of Paul's letters and wrote Ephesians to serve as an introduction to Paul's thinking. Goodspeed argued that the appearance of Acts caused a renewed interest in Paul's role in early church history and led to the collection of his writings. He felt that Onesimus, the converted slave mentioned in Philemon, was the admirer who wrote Ephesians. If his hypothesis were true, we would expect Ephesians to be first in the collection of Paul's letters.[8] No manuscript evidence has ever placed Ephesians first.

The hypothesis of a circular letter, though not without problems, provides the most logical explanation for the omission of "in Ephesus" from the greetings of the letter. The importance of Ephesus in the province of Asia would make it the logical city to be

---

8. See E. J. Goodspeed, *The Key to Ephesians* (Chicago: University of Chicago Press, 1956).

mentioned as the recipient in any copy of the letter which left a blank for the destination.

Relationship to Colossians

The letters of Ephesians and Colossian resemble each other more closely than any other pair of Paul's writings. Both letters refer to Christ as the head of the church (Eph. 1:23; Col. 1:18). Both contain discussions of the domestic responsibilities of believers (Eph. 5:22–6:9; Col. 3:18–4:1). Both begin with a chiefly doctrinal section and conclude with a chiefly practical section. These similarities suggest that the two letters were written at nearly the same time.

By way of contrast, Colossians contains a rebuttal of false teaching that minimizes the person of Christ. Ephesians emphasizes the unity of all believers and offers praise for the blessings shared in Christ.

Purpose of Ephesians

Determining the precise purpose for which Paul wrote Ephesians is difficult. Most of Paul's letters were written to meet specific needs in the churches, but it is hard to discover the specific occasion for which Ephesians was written. The letter has a solemn, serious tone as it outlines the important practices and doctrines for believers to keep in mind. Paul did not aim his statements in Ephesians against any specific false teaching. Ephesians is a general statement of Christian truth concerning the church, Christian unity, and the Christian walk. The understanding of this truth is as necessary for the church today as it was in Paul's day.

The Content of Ephesians

The content of Ephesians falls naturally into two divisions.

1. Chapters 1–3 discuss the spiritual privileges of the church.

2. Chapters 4–6 present the responsibilities of believers for the Christian walk.

After his usual introduction in 1:1–2 Paul outlined the spiritual blessings available to believers in Christ (1:3–14):

- the election of the Ephesians by the Father;

- redemption through the Son;
- the seal of the Holy Spirit.

After listing the divine resources available for believers, Paul prayed that his readers might grow in their knowledge of God (1:15–23). He specifically wanted them to understand the hope of their calling, the riches of God's inheritance in believers, and the greatness of the divine power available to believers.

The mention of the divine power of God revealed in Christ's resurrection led Paul to discuss the illustration of that power in the transformation of believers from spiritual death to heavenly life (2:1–10). In their pre-Christian state, the Ephesians were dead in sin, enslaved to evil, and the objects of divine wrath (2:1–3). In Christ, they received divine mercy which made possible a life of good works (2:4–10). These good works were not an option for believers; they were necessary.

The experience of conversion applied to Gentiles as well as Jews (2:11–22). Prior to conversion, Gentiles lived without hope—as did the Jews. In Christ they have been reconciled to God and are at peace with God (2:13–18). Because of the experience of reconciliation, Gentiles and Jews became citizens of God's kingdom. They were also members of God's family, and God was building them into a holy temple for his habitation (2:19–22).

Gentiles were also heirs of God along with the Jews (3:1–13). Through Christ, they share in all the promises God has made available (3:6). Paul's mission was to declare that gospel to the Gentiles. He saw this work as a special stewardship entrusted to him in spite of the suffering to which it led (3:2, 13). Paul believed his involvement in God's plan was an unspeakable privilege (3:8).

Paul prayed that the Ephesians would experience strength through the Holy Spirit and grasp the depth of God's love for them (3:14–21). He assured them that God was able to carry out his work more abundantly than they could ever imagine (3:20–21).

The proclamation of these spiritual blessings now led Paul to show his readers how they should apply them to their lives. A practical section filled with exhortations, words of encouragement, and specific details of application now follows (beginning at 4:1).

Paul described the new life that God's blessings would produce within the church (4:1–16). Christians were to work hard to maintain unity in the fellowship (4:1–6). All members of the church had received spiritual gifts for use in the fellowship (4:7). Leaders of the church were to prepare all people for works of service so that the entire body might experience growth and unity (4:11–12).

- Paul outlined the new behavior expected of all believers with one another (4:17–32). Christians were to put off their old pre-conversion lifestyle (4:20–24), and to practice truth, honesty, wholesome talk, kindness, and forgiveness with one another (4:25–32).

- Paul demanded a new life of believers before unbelievers (5:1–21). Believers were to walk in love, sexual purity, the light of holy behavior, and wisdom. The Holy Spirit provided the spiritual dynamic for energizing these demands (5:18–21).

- Paul taught that this new life revolutionizes the Christian home (5:22–6:9). Husbands and wives were to practice mutual submission to one another. Paul appealed to husbands to love their wives sacrificially and transcendently (5:25–32). Children were to obey their parents, and parents were to provide consistent discipline and instruction for the children (6:1–4). Christian servants were to obey their owners from the heart, and the owners were to treat their slaves with the confidence that the Lord would reward their mercy and compassion (6:5–9).

Christians were engaged in an unending struggle against Satan's deceit and treachery (6:10–20). Paul urged his readers to put on all of God's armor and to live in a state of prayerful readiness.

In conclusion (6:21–24) Paul pointed out the role of Tychicus as the carrier of the letter. He also offered peace, love, and grace to all his readers.

Outline of Ephesians

I. Salutation (1:1–2)

II. The Privileges of the Christian (1:3–3:21)

    A. Spiritual blessings in Christ (1:3–14)

    B. Prayer concerning divine resources (1:15–23)

    C. New life in Christ (2:1–10)
    D. Life as reconciled persons (2:11–22)
    E. Life as God's heirs (3:1–13)
    F. Experience of God's love and power (3:14–21)
III. The Responsibilities of the Christian (4:1–6:20)
    A. Unity and spiritual growth in the church (4:1–16)
    B. New walk with other believers (4:17–32)
    C. New walk before unbelievers (5:1–21)
    D. New standard for the home (5:22–6:9)
    E. New strength for spiritual warfare (6:10–20)
IV. Concluding Greetings (6:21–24)

The Epistle to the Philippians

Background

Philip II of Macedon seized the valuable mining territory around this city sometime after 400 B.C. and named the city for himself. After 200 B.C. the city passed under Roman control. In 42 B.C. Philippi was the site of a battle between the forces of Octavian (later Augustus Caesar) and Antony, who defeated the armies of Brutus and Cassius. In 31 B.C. Octavian defeated the forces of Antony at Actium. He settled some of his defeated opponents in Philippi and made the city into a Roman colony.

Paul first visited the city on his second missionary journey (Acts 16:12). On the Sabbath he attended a prayer meeting on the banks of the river, where Lydia and others responded to his message (Acts 16:13–15). Those who attended the prayer meeting were probably Jews or proselytes to Judaism who had come to this location because the city had no synagogue. Jewish tradition suggested that if ten Jewish men lived in a city, a synagogue would be built there. The absence of the synagogue points to the small number of Jews in the area.

Paul's additional experiences in Philippi revealed the Roman and pagan character of the city. After Paul freed a slave girl from demonic possession, her owners charged Paul and his friends with teaching unlawful customs (Acts 16:21). Paul and Silas were thrown into prison, but an earthquake set the stage for their freedom. The jailer was converted as a result of these remarkable events.

On the day following the earthquake the city magistrates sent word to the jailer to release Paul (Acts 16:35–36). Paul protested that he had been unlawfully jailed as a Roman citizen and insisted that the magistrates personally come and escort him from the area. After receiving what amounted to an apology from the magistrates, Paul left (Acts 16:38–40).

Authorship

Philippians claims Pauline authorship and reflects the apostle's personality. Early acceptance of Pauline authorship by such leaders as Clement of Rome and Ignatius provides additional support for this position. The testimony of the letter concerning authorship should be received as it stands.

Date and Provenance

Reasons have previously been discussed for accepting Rome as the place from which Paul wrote Philippians. The epistle was probably written near or at the end of Paul's two-year imprisonment in the city. A date near the mid 60s is likely.

Occasion and Purpose

The Philippian church sent Epaphroditus to Paul with a gift (2:25–30). After recovering from a serious illness, Epaphroditus was ready to return to Philippi. Paul sent a note of gratitude for the gift by this trustworthy friend (4:10–18).

Paul also wanted to ease the anxieties and concerns the church felt for him in his imprisonment. Paul outlined his circumstances (1:12–14) and suggested that God had overruled the imprisonment for spiritual progress (1:15–18).

The members of the Philippian church had shown a tendency toward disunity and contentiousness. Paul rebuked them for having this spirit (2:1–11), and he encouraged them to practice humility in their relationships with one another.

The church faced a challenge from Judaizers who diluted or added to the requirements for salvation (3:1–6). In addition to rebuking the Judaizers, Paul used severe language to rebuke a group of perfectionists in the city (3:12–16). Another group reflected tendencies toward sensuality and materialistic greed (3:18–19), and Paul addressed a strong warning to them. Each of these groups required strong resistance, and Paul intended to help the church deal with them.

Paul's letter also prepared for a forthcoming visit to the church by both Timothy and himself (2:19–24). His expression of hope to see his Christian friends soon (2:24) indicated that Paul's long imprisonment in Rome was nearing its end.

Issues in Interpreting Philippians

The Hymn in 2:6–11. Modern scholars call the words of 2:6–11 a hymn, suggesting that it may have come from the worship of the early church. The purpose and content of the hymn have produced mixed evaluations. Though most agree that Paul used the hymn to urge humility upon his readers, interpreters disagree over the number of verses in the hymn, the original source of the words, and the theological meaning of its content.

The hymn appears to divide the life of Christ into a period of preexistence, a time on earth, and exaltation to heaven. Paul taught that Christ did not regard his equality with God as a position to be used for his own advantage.[9] He urged Christians to imitate in their relationships with one another the humility Christ showed in his incarnation and crucifixion.[10]

The Identity of Paul's Opponents. Paul's descriptions of his opponents in Philippians might refer to a variety of movements. First, his reference in 1:15–18 seems to describe church members who were creating trouble for him. Later, however, he refers to these opponents as opposing the church (1:28–29). His discussion in 3:1–6 appears to be a reference to Judaizers. The opponents in 3:12 are advocates of their own perfection. In 3:18–20 he pictures libertines and materialists. Who are these opponents? Do all of these descrip-

---

9. This interpretation is offered by Roy W. Hoover, "The Harpagmos Enigma: A Philological Solution," *HTR* 64 (1971): 118.

10. Ralph P. Martin disagrees with this statement. He feels that the words of Paul are an appeal for the Philippians to become the type of persons who, by the death and exaltation of Jesus, have a place in the church. He insists that the motive in Paul's ethics is not imitation of Christ but death and resurrection. See Martin, *Carmen Christi*, rev. ed. (Grand Rapids: Eerdmans, 1983), 288, 291.

Although it is true that Paul does use death and resurrection as a motive for ethics (Rom. 6:1–14), he also appealed to imitation (1 Cor. 11:1). It is not inappropriate to see his use of imitation here.

tions refer to a single group? Was Paul attacking his enemies on more than one front?

The latter question suggests a multifaceted solution.

- Paul was dealing with more than one type of problem group in the church.

- Paul seems to have opposed some individuals in the church who made life miserable for him.

- Paul was opposing Judaizers who may have been ethnic Jews, whose practices were similar to some practices that appear later in Gnosticism.

- Paul warned against those who pretended to practice perfectionism and libertinism.

The Unity of Philippians. Some interpreters find evidence in the text of Philippians of several documents linked together after being written separately. They suggest that the phrase "finally" in 3:1 and 4:8 normally signals a conclusion, but in Philippians it signals the move to another topic of discussion. Those who favor a composite letter also point to the shift in mood from encouragement to warning (between 3:1 and 3:2). Some see evidences of three separate fragments in the letter. These fragments include:

1. expression of gratitude for the gift of money (4:10–20);

2. warning against church divisions (1:1–3:1; 4:4–7; 4:21–23);

3. attack against false teachers (3:2–4:3; 4:8–9).

Luke Johnson rejects this effort to divide Philippians into separate fragments. He denies that textual evidence compels this fragmentation and insists that earlier parts of the letter prepare for later developments. For example, the warning against disunity (1:15–17, 28; 2:21–22) prepares for the attack against false teachers (3:2–4:3). Johnson says, "There is no reason, therefore, to treat Philippians as a composite of three letters."[11] It is reasonable to see Philippians as a single letter written for multiple purposes.

---

11. Johnson, *The Writings of the New Testament,* 339.

The Content of Philippians

Salutation

Paul opens the letter with his traditional style of salutation (1:1–2). He identifies himself and Timothy as "servants of Christ Jesus." He mentions both the Philippian believers and their congregational leaders. His reference to the leaders as "overseers and deacons" is unusual in a salutation. His greeting of "grace" and "peace" is a normal wish for believers.

Gratitude and Prayer for the Philippians (1:3–11)

Paul was grateful for his close fellowship with the Philippians in the work of the gospel (1:3–5). Their sharing of this labor with him was a sure sign that God's work was continuing in them. Paul was confident that God would continue this good work until Christ's return.

Paul developed a rich, deep affection for the Philippians through his contact with them (1:7–8). This affection led Paul to pray for the growth of their love, the maturity of their insights, and the extension of their righteousness (1:9–11).

Paul's Personal Experiences (1:12–26)

The Philippians were concerned about Paul's welfare during his confinement. Paul assured them that his detention had accelerated the spread of the gospel (1:12–14). He recognized that some people preached the gospel with false motives, and others preached with true commitment. Paul rejoiced that, whether with false or true motives, Christ was preached (1:18). A person with Paul's flexibility in God's purposes would hardly succumb to self-pity, resentment, and bitterness.

Paul was in a dilemma as he wondered whether or not his present imprisonment would end in his death (1:19–26). His own preference would be to die and be with Christ (1:23), but the reality was that the Philippians needed him. He expressed confidence that God would preserve him to help develop their joy and maturity (1:25).

Appeals to the Philippians (1:27–2:18)

The Philippians faced intimidating opposition. Paul urged them to show steadfastness and stamina as they endured suffering (1:27–30).

Paul appealed for the believers in Philippi to show greater unity. He warned them against selfish ambition and pompous conceit (2:1–5). As an object lesson to demonstrate humility, Paul pointed to the example of Christ (2:6–11), who had shown humility in his incarnation and crucifixion. God honored him as the exalted Lord.

Paul urged the Philippians to give attention to the spiritual health of the church with reverence and respect (2:12–13). God would provide the desire and power to develop this attitude. Paul was so concerned for the continuing spiritual health of the Philippian church that he was willing to offer his own life as a means to nourish the faith and purity of the church (2:15–18).

The Visit of Two Friends (2:19–30)

Paul hoped to be released soon from prison and to visit the Philippians (2:24). Before his visit, Paul planned to send Timothy, who shared with Paul a passionate concern for the welfare of the Philippian Christians (2:19–23).

Another messenger was also ready to depart. Epaphroditus, who had carried a gift to Paul, had recovered from his serious sickness (2:25–27). Paul planned to send this courageous Christian to Philippi with a message from him (2:28). He expected the compassionate Philippians to receive Epaphroditus with joy and honor.

Warning Against False Teachers (3:1–21)

False teachers were confusing the Philippians. Paul warned against the legalism of the Judaizers, who stressed circumcision and fleshly ordinances (3:1–3). If personal merit could have earned righteousness with God, Paul had an impeccable background (3:4–6). He had learned that God provided true righteousness only to those who trusted Christ without any hope of self merit.

Paul realized that the only goal worth pursuing was the personal knowledge of Jesus Christ. He was eager to share in the power of Christ's resurrection. He knew that the path to such power involved identifying with Jesus in death to self (3:7–11).

For Paul the road to maturity involved pressing on toward that goal to which Christ had called him (3:12–16). He did not look back at his achievements, but he pressed forward toward Christ's future call. Spiritually mature people will imitate Paul's attitude. God will show such mature people any deficiencies or shortcomings in their lives.

Paul warned the Philippians against other troublemakers lurking around Philippi (3:17–21). Some indulged gluttony and sexual vice with their minds set on earthly goals. True believers must set their minds on heaven and live as responsible members of a heavenly community (3:20–21).

Appeals for Unity, Prayer, and High-Mindedness (4:1–9)

Paul mentioned two members of the church who needed to put aside their disagreements (4:2–3). He urged a third member to help lead them to concord and harmony.

Confidence in Christ's return should lead the Philippians to pray with courage about every issue bothering them (4:6–7). Those who practice such prayer will find that God's peace guards them like a sentry.

Paul knew that the object of a person's thoughts colors individual character. He urged the Philippians to have noble, pure, and praiseworthy ideas as food for their thoughts (4:8–9).

Gratitude for a Gift (4:10–20)

On more than one occasion the Philippians sent financial support to Paul (4:16). This support lapsed for a while, but the Philippians had renewed their support (4:10). Paul rejoiced in their generosity, not merely because he had received a gift, but also because God would notice their generosity and credit it to their account (4:17).

Conclusion (4:21–23)

Paul concluded with personal greetings to all the Philippian believers. He also sent greetings to the Philippians from some converted slaves or servants who had been members of Caesar's imperial family. He ended with a grace benediction.

Outline of Philippians

I. Salutation (1:1–2)

II. Expression of Gratitude and Prayer for the Philippians (1:3–11)

    A. Thanksgiving for partnership with the Philippians (1:3–6)

    B. Paul's genuine affection for the Philippians (1:7–8)

    C. Paul's prayer for their growth in love, discernment, and righteousness (1:9–11)

III. Paul's Personal Experiences (1:12–26)

    A. Outcome of Paul's imprisonment (1:12–14)

    B. Rejoicing at the progress of the gospel (1:15–18)

    C. Readiness for future ministry (1:19–26)

IV. Appeals to the Philippians (1:27–2:18)

    A. Urging them to steadfast behavior (1:27–30)

    B. Appeal for unity (2:1–5)

    C. Imitation of Christ's humility (2:6–11)

    D. Development of a healthy congregation (2:12–18)

V. Future Visits of Timothy, Paul, and Epaphroditus (2:19–30)

VI. Warning Against False Teachers (3:1–21)

    A. Warning against Judaizers (3:1–3)

    B. Rejection of legalism (3:4–6)

    C. Importance of gaining Christ (3:7–11)

    D. Pressing toward the spiritual goal (3:12–16)

    E. Warning against immorality (3:17–21)

VII. Appeals for Unity, Prayer, and High-Mindedness (4:1–9)

    A. Encouragement for unity (4:1–3)

    B. Urging to prayer (4:4–7)

    C. Need for lofty thinking (4:8–9)

VIII. Gratitude for a Gift (4:10–20)

IX. Conclusion (4:21–23)

The Epistle to the Colossians

The Growth of City and Church

Colossae was located in the southwest corner of Asia Minor in the Roman province of Asia, one hundred miles east of Ephesus. The cities of Hierapolis and Laodicea were nearby. Colossae, Heirapolis, and Laodicea were situated in the Lycus River valley. An important road reaching eastward from Ephesus passed through the region.

Colossae had been a prominent city during the Greek period, but by Paul's time much of its importance had faded. Earthquakes in the area had been detrimental to all cities in the region, but the neighboring cities had grown more in Roman times than Colossae had. Colossae was the least important city to which Paul addressed a letter.

Paul may have passed through the city during his travels, but nothing in the letter indicates that Paul founded the church in Colossae. Epaphras (1:7) apparently founded the church. When Paul wrote Colossians, Epaphras was with him, but he continued to have great concern for the Colossian believers. Paul learned of the faith of his audience through a report (1:4); they had not met him personally (2:1).

Colossae was probably evangelized during the time of Paul's long stay in Ephesus (Acts 19:10). Epaphras may have been converted during this time and might have returned to his native city to preach the gospel.

Gentiles made up the majority of the church's membership (1:27; 2:13). Jews must have been either in the church or in the area, for some of the church's problems appear to be related to Jewish misundertandings of the gospel (2:16–17, 20–21). At the time Paul wrote, Archippus appears to have been in charge of the church (4:17).

Authorship

Until the nineteenth century no scholars raised serious questions about Pauline authorship of Colossians. In recent decades, some scholars have asserted that the author was an associate of Paul rather than the apostle himself.[12] Several features contribute to this assertion.

- The language and style of Colossians are described as un-Pauline. Colossians has many *hapax legomena*,[13] but all of Paul's writings contain some of these. Some of the stylistic

---

12. Johnson, for example, credits "the letter to an associate of Paul during his lifetime." See Johnson, *The Writings of the New Testament*, 359.
13. This transliteration of a Greek phrase means "spoken only once." It refers to a word appearing only once in the New Testament.

features of the Greek usage differ from other Pauline writings, but scholars evaluate these phenomena differently.

- Some refer to the variations in the theology of Colossians. They observe the absence of discussion of such common Pauline terms as justification, salvation, and righteousness. They also note the presence of such ideas as the cosmic aspects of Christ's person (1:16–19). This observation is subjective, for an author is not required to discuss each of his characteristic themes in a particular writing. Also, Paul's discussion of the cosmic aspects of the person of Christ in Colossians is similar to his discussion of this subject in other, universally accepted letters (see 1 Cor. 8:6).

- Colossians and Ephesians are quite similar, and scholars argue that one person would not write two letters with so much similarity. The similarities in content can be explained by pointing out that Paul repeated these ideas on two occasions in the same time frame. Similarity of content between Ephesians and Colossians is not necessarily a basis for opposing Pauline authorship of Colossians

The arguments against Pauline authorship are indecisive. The letter claims Pauline authorship (1:1) and concludes with a distinguishing statement by Paul (4:18). We should accept the claim as it stands.

Provenance and Date

Reasons have already been discussed for accepting Rome as Paul's location for writing the letter. A date in the early 60s is likely. The statements in 4:7–8 suggest that Tychicus carried the letter to its destination.

The False Teaching in Colossae

Paul does not present a systematic response to the false teaching permeating Colossae at the time. We can identify some of the false teaching by noting the responses Paul gave to the heretics.

- Paul emphasized the supremacy of Christ (1:15–19), and this emphasis suggests that the false teachers undercut the high

Christology Paul advocated. They may even have spoken warmly and appreciatively of Christ, but to them he could have been only a created being. For Paul, all the divine fullness dwelt in Christ.

- Paul warned against being deceived by human philosophy (2:8)—empty human speculations without divine revelation. This error may have been an early development of Gnosticism, which became fully developed in the second century.

- Some effort was made to impose Jewish practices on the Colossian believers. Paul mentioned circumcision (2:11), dietary regulations and religious festivals (2:16), and human tradition (2:8).

- Asceticism was a characteristic of the heresy (2:21–23). This asceticism imposed restrictions on the body and demanded abstinence from certain objects or practices.

- The false teaching involved the worship of angels (2:18). Perhaps this feature described the worship of angels as intermediaries between the highest God and the physical universe. This development of an angelic hierarchy was a characteristic of later Gnosticism.

The content of the heresy was eclectic. It contained a mixture of Jewish legalism, Greek speculation, and the mysticism of the Orient. Some of the elements seen in Colossae emerge fully developed in later Gnosticism or in the Oriental mystery religions. However, we must avoid identification of this heresy as Gnosticism, for the Jewish features of the false teaching do not resemble Gnosticism. The location of Colossae near an important trade route between East and West may have allowed the city to become a collecting point for ideas from several different cultures.

The Importance of Colossians

Christians of every generation encounter the philosophies of their era. Colossae was touched by a syncretistic contemporary philosophy. As we examine Paul's efforts to meet the errors of his time, we can learn how to grapple with wrong thinking in our time. When thinking falls out of step with God's ideas, we must allow him to help us to correct error.

Paul also emphasized some realities with a transcultural appeal. Relationships between husbands and wives, parents and children, and employers and employees must reflect the impact of our Christian commitment. Paul reminded his readers in Colossae of these important relationships.

The Content of Colossians

Salutation (1:1–2). Colossians and Ephesians share a similar general outline. Both letters have a section of theology or doctrine and a section of application and ethical behavior.

Paul began his letter to the Colossians with a salutation similar to those in his other letters (1:1–2). He identified himself as an apostle and bestowed divine authority on his teachings.

Thanksgiving (1:3–8). A thanksgiving such as we find in 1:3–8 is a normal part of Paul's letters. Paul omitted the thanksgiving in the Galatian letter and went straight into verbal battle with the Judaizers there. Here Paul expressed gratitude for the faith and love among the Colossians. These fruits were a product of the gospel they believed.

Prayer for the Colossians (1:9–12). In 1:9–12 Paul prays for the Colossians. This prayer developed into a meditation on the person of Christ in the following section (vv. 13–23). Paul prayed that the Colossians might be filled with the knowledge of the divine will and lead a life pleasing to God in every way.

The Supremacy of Christ (1:13–23). Paul proclaimed the supremacy of Christ in 1:13–23. He emphasized Christ as the redeemer (1:13–14) and as supreme over all creation (1:15–16).[14] He described him as the sustainer of the universe and head of the church (1:17–18). Since the fullness of God resided in him, Christ was the source of reconciliation with the Father (1:19–20).[15] Those

---

14. The interpretation of 1:15 ("firstborn of every creature" [KJV]) is of vital significance in establishing the deity of Christ. Cultic groups refer to this verse as proof that Christ was created by the Father and thus lacked eternal existence. At issue is the question of whether the passage refers to priority in time or in status. The translation "supreme over all creation" shows a preference for understanding the passage as a reference to Christ's priority in status. For additional information on the text, see Larry R. Helyer, "Arius Revisited: The Firstborn over All Creation (Col. 1:15)," *JETS* 31 (March 1988): 59–67.

15. Norman T. Wright analyzes the poetic structure of this passage and concludes Paul wrote to warn against a heresy which stemmed from Judaism rather than Gnosticism. See his "Poetry and Theology in Colossians 1.15–20," *NTS* 36 (1990): 444–68.

who responded to these truths about Christ were reconciled to God (1:21–23).

The Ministry of Paul (1:24–2:7). The Colossians did not know Paul personally, and Paul now explained his place in relation to them. He insisted that his ministry of preaching and endurance of suffering were intended to assist the Colossians (1:24–25). His own special call was to proclaim Christ, and his goal was to present each believer mature in Christ (1:28–29).

His concern for the Colossians and other neighboring believers was that they might develop a unity of love and a complete understanding of Christ. He insisted that all of God's purposes centered in Jesus, and he did not want any spurious arguments to divert their attention from Jesus (2:1–5).

The Colossians had responded to the proclamation of Christ as Lord. They were to continue their devotion to that truth and to be rooted and built up in Christ as the source of their strength (2:6–7).

The Antidote to False Teaching (2:8–23). Much of what Paul taught in this section is anticipated by his teaching in 1:13–20. Paul first emphasized the all-sufficiency of Christ (2:8–15). He stressed that all of the divine fullness dwells in Christ so that we do not need to worship any supernatural being except Christ (2:9).[16] He emphasized that no other supernatural beings should receive any form of homage or worship because Christ had conquered them (2:15).

In 2:16–23 he warned against submission to a legalism resembling Judaism. If the Colossians submitted to Jewish regulations concerning foods, festivals, and asceticism, they would permit the opinions of human beings, rather than Christ, to dominate their behavior. As believers they had been released from the power of any supernatural being other than Jesus (2:20–23). It made no sense to put themselves again under the rules and authority of a power from which they had escaped.

---

16. One of the key issues in interpreting Colossians is the identity of the "basic principles of this world" ("rudiments" [KJV]) mentioned in 2:8. The term "basic principles" comes from the Greek word *stoicheia*, which sometimes referred to the letters of the alphabet. In this context, however, Paul used the term to refer to local gods or deities who presided over different areas and races of the world. Paul did not believe that these deities existed, but pagans did, and some pagan thought may have influenced the Colossians. For discussion of this issue, see N. T. Wright, *Colossians and Philemon*, TNTC (Grand Rapids: Eerdmans, 1986), 100–102.

Union with Christ in New Life (3:1–4). Christians have entered the new spiritual age in Christ. They must now allow that life to produce its results in them. Christians must keep their minds in accord with God's holy purposes for them.

Identity with Christ by Death to Old Ways (3:5–11). The new life to which Paul appealed in 3:1–4 must be seen in the present behavior of Christians. Paul calls on Christians to abandon their pre-conversion style of living. His imperative, "Put to death," (3:5) calls for vigorous action and cooperation by Christians. The habits Paul insisted on putting to death include sexual sins (3:5) and sins of anger (3:8).

Embracing the New Life (3:12–17). Believers must not only cut themselves loose from old habits of lust, hate, and rage; they must also adopt positive traits such as compassion, kindness, and humility. The crowning virtue is love, and the presence of this love produces peace throughout the Christian community (3:14–15).

New Life at Home (3:18–4:1). Paul called on believers to follow the same household practices he outlined in Ephesians 5:18–6:9. Here in a briefer summary, he appealed to wives to follow their husbands with respect and for husbands to love their wives. Children were to obey their parents, and parents were not to use such harsh discipline that children become bitter. Slaves should offer a heartfelt obedience to their masters, and masters should treat their slaves with justice.

General Instructions for Believers (4:2–6). Paul's words focused on prayer, wisdom, and speech. He requested prayer for the Colossians and for himself. He urged wise, thoughtful action toward unbelievers. He reminded them to let their words be zestful and salty but filled with the grace of God.

Conclusion (4:7–18). In his conclusion Paul spoke of the coming of Tychicus and Onesimus to Colossae (4:7–9). Since he was bringing the letter from Paul, Tychicus would be able to give the Colossians a report on Paul's circumstances.

Paul included a list of greetings from various friends who surrounded him during his confinement (4:10–17). Paul's imprisonment location appears to be a beehive of Christian activity.

He concluded with his own signature as a sign of genuineness and offered a benediction to his readers (4:18).

Outline of Colossians

I. Salutation (1:1–2)

II. Person and Work of Christ (1:3–23)
- A. Gratitude for the faith of the Colossians (1:3–8)
- B. Prayer for the growth of the Colossians (1:9–12)
- C. Supremacy of Christ (1:13–23)
  1. Work of Christ (1:13–14)
  2. Person of Christ (1:15–20)
  3. Effect of Christ among the Colossians (1:21–23)

III. Ministry of Paul (1:24–2:7)
- A. Explanation of Paul's function (1:24–29)
- B. Reassurance of Paul's concern (2:1–5)
- C. Encouragement to continue in Christ (2:6–7)

IV. Antidote to False Teaching (2:8–23)
- A. Sufficiency of Christ (2:8–15)
- B. Warning against legalism and mysticism (2:16–19)
- C. Encouragement to escape asceticism (2:20–23)

V. New Conduct of the Believer (3:1–4:6)
- A. Union with Christ in new life (3:1–4)
- B. Identity with Christ by death to old ways (3:5–11)
- C. Embracing the new life (3:12–17)
- D. New life at home (3:18–4:1)
  1. Between wives and husbands (3:18–19)
  2. Between children and parents (3:20–21)
  3. Between servants and masters (3:22–4:1)
- E. General instructions for believers (4:2–6)

VI. Conclusion (4:7–18)
- A. Coming of Tychicus and Onesimus (4:7–9)
- B. Christian greetings (4:10–17)
- C. Expression of genuineness and benediction (4:18)

The Epistle to Philemon

Authorship

No scholars have ever seriously questioned the Pauline authorship of Philemon. The tone throughout the letter sounds like Paul.

Philemon is the most nearly private letter in all of Paul's known writings. Paul intended his letter primarily for Philemon, although the church meeting in Philemon's house was also to read it. The letter grows naturally out of the circumstances it describes. We should accept its claim to be Pauline.

Recipients

Mentioning Archippus both in Colossians 4:17 and here in verse 2 suggests that the recipients lived in Colossae. Philemon was the principal recipient. He apparently was a slave-owner from whom Onesimus had fled. Probably Philemon had been converted during Paul's three-year ministry in Ephesus (Acts 20:31).

We cannot positively identify Apphia and Archippus. Some have supposed that Apphia is the wife of Philemon, and Archippus is their son. Paul also addressed the letter to the house church meeting at Philemon's home.

Occasion

The content of Philemon suggests that Onesimus fled from Philemon, probably robbing him as he fled (v. 18). Although this fact cannot be proven, it is a reasonable inference from the context of the letter. Philemon possibly sent him on a mission from which he failed to return. In any case, he was a runaway slave.

Somehow Onesimus came into contact with Paul and was converted (v. 10).[17] Paul was now returning Onesimus to Philemon, but he included a request for the gracious treatment of Onesimus (v. 17). Philemon would have been permitted to punish Onesimus, but Paul urged him to receive the slave "as a dear brother" (vv. 15–16).

Onesimus was useful to Paul in evangelism (v. 13), and Paul clearly wanted to keep Onesimus with him. He did not request Philemon to release Onesimus, although he left the impression that this was his wish.

How did Philemon respond to the letter? The preservation of the text suggests that Philemon followed Paul's wishes and released Onesimus. If he had not, Philemon or Paul probably would have

---

17. Luke Johnson suggests the presence of Epaphras with Paul (Col. 1:7; 4:12–13) may have drawn Philemon to Rome. See Luke Johnson, *The Writings of the New Testament*, 353–54.

destroyed the letter, and we would know nothing about the incident.

Recent Study of Philemon

In a small but important volume, John Knox suggested a novel approach to the interpretation of the letter to Philemon.[18] Knox suggested that Philemon was a leader of the churches in the Lycus Valley in which Colossae, Laodicea, and Hierapolis were situated. He feels that Philemon lived in Laodicea rather than Colossae. He also suggested that Archippus was the actual owner of Onesimus and was therefore the chief recipient of the letter. He feels that Paul sent the letter to Philemon so that this influential leader might use his authority to persuade Archippus to release Onesimus. The "ministry" Archippus was to exercise (Col. 4:17) was releasing Onesimus to become Paul's helper. Knox identified the letter to Philemon with the letter "from Laodicea" mentioned in Colossians 4:16. This letter first went to Philemon in Laodicea and then was forwarded to Archippus in Colossae.

Knox's understanding of the text is not the most natural interpretation. Philemon appears to be the primary recipient since his name appears first in the letter. Perhaps Paul included Apphia, Archippus, and the house church in the letter to surround Philemon with additional moral pressure to release Onesimus. Most scholars have not followed Knox's approach.

The Value of Philemon

Two features of this letter make it of great value in New Testament study. First, the letter provides an example of a Christian approach to the social problem of slavery. Attacking the institution forthrightly would have been futile. Paul, both in Philemon and in Colossians 4:1, urged masters to treat their slaves with compassion. Paul sounded no call for slaves to rise in armed rebellion, but he melted the resistance of both groups with a lavish outpouring of Christian love. He urged Philemon to receive Onesimus as a "dear brother." When a slave owner could refer to his slave as a brother in Christ, emancipation should not be far away. Christianity thus

---

18. John Knox, *Philemon Among the Letters of Paul* (Chicago: University of Chicago Press, 1935).

established conditions that made it impossible for slavery to endure.[19]

This letter also presents an intimate, personal account of Paul. He writes not so much as a theologian or apostle to the Gentiles. Rather, he writes as a Christian man applying the gospel he has preached. His words show his integrity (v. 19) and genuine compassion for both Philemon (v. 7) and Onesimus (v. 16).

The Content of Philemon

Paul began with a greeting addressed to Philemon, Apphia, Archippus, and the church meeting in Philemon's house (vv. 1–3). He then expressed thanksgiving for the faith and love of Philemon (vv. 4–7).

On the foundation of love Paul appealed for Philemon to give merciful treatment to Onesimus, who had been converted under Paul's influence while Paul was in prison (vv. 8–10). The name Onesimus means "profitable." Paul coined a pun on the name by suggesting that Onesimus was formerly useless but had now become useful (v. 11).

Paul discovered Onesimus to be a useful servant in ministry, but he refused to retain Onesimus with him illegally. He returned Onesimus to Philemon as a beloved brother (vv. 12–16).

Paul requested that Philemon receive his former runaway as he would have received Paul. Paul promised repayment of any debt that Onesimus owed to Philemon. Without making a specific request for the release of Onesimus, Paul was nevertheless confident that Philemon would do more than he had asked (vv. 17–21).

Paul included a request that Philemon prepare him a guest room (v. 22). He thus expressed confidence of his release from prison. He concluded with greetings and an expression of grace (vv. 23–25).

Outline of Philemon

I. Introduction (vv. 1–3)

II. Gratitude for Philemon (vv. 4–7)

---

19. For an interesting analysis of the dilemma facing Christians in their ownership of slaves, see John M. G. Barclay, "Paul, Philemon, and Christian Slave-Ownership," *NTS* 37 (1991): 161–86.

III. Odyssey of Onesimus (vv. 8–21)

    A. Conversion of Onesimus (vv. 8–11)

    B. Return of Onesimus (vv. 12–16)

    C. Request for Onesimus (vv. 17–21)

IV. Paul's Personal Request (v. 22)

 V. Greetings and Benediction (vv. 23–25)

For Further Discussion

1. Compare New Age thinking with the heresy Paul faced in Colossae.

2. Should Paul have opposed slavery more forcefully in his time? How would his letter to Philemon affect the existence of slavery? How should churches challenge social evils today? How should individuals challenge social evil?

3. Compare Paul's description of the function of spiritual gifts in the church (Eph. 4:7–16) with the expression of these gifts in your church.

4. After studying Philippians 2:1–11, explain the "Kenotic" theory of Christ's incarnation.

Bibliography

Barclay, M. G. "Paul, Philemon, and Christian Slave-Ownership." *NTS* 37 (1991):161–86.

Barth, Marcus. *Ephesians*. AB. 2 vols. Garden City, N.Y.: Doubleday, 1974.

Bruce, F. F. *The Epistles to the Colossians, to Philemon, and to the Ephesians.* NICNT. Grand Rapids: William B. Eerdmans Publishing Co., 1984.

_____. *Philippians*. NIBC. Peabody, Mass.: Hendrickson Publishers Inc., 1983.

Cadbury, H. J. "The Dilemma of Ephesians." *NTS* 5 (1958–59): 101.

Duncan, George S. *St. Paul's Ephesian Ministry*. New York: Scribner's Sons, 1930.

Foulkes, Francis. *The Letter of Paul to the Ephesians*, TNTC. Rev. ed. Grand Rapids: William B. Eerdmans Publishing Co., 1989. Brief, exegetical commentary on Ephesians.

Goodspeed, E. J. *The Key to Ephesians*. Chicago: University of Chicago Press, 1956.

Harris, Murray J. *Colossians & Philemon*, EGGNT. Grand Rapids: William B. Eerdmans Publishing Co., 1991.

Helyer, Larry R. "Arius Revisited: The Firstborn over All Creation (Col. 1:15)." *JETS* 31(March 1980): 59–67.

Hoover, Roy W. "The Harpagmos Enigma: A Philological Solution." *HTR* 64 (1971): 118.

Johnson, Luke. *The Writings of the New Testament*. Philadelphia: Fortress Press, 1986.

Knox, John. *Philemon Among the Letters of Paul*. Chicago: University of Chicago Press, 1935.

Lincoln, Andrew T. *Ephesians*. WBC. Dallas, Tex.: Word Inc., 1990. Thorough exegetical commentary on Ephesians.

Lohse, Eduard. *Colossians and Philemon*. *Hermenia*. Philadelphia: Fortress Press, 1971.

Martin, Ralph P. *Carmen Christi*. Rev. ed. Grand Rapids: William B. Eerdmans Publishing Co., 1983.

_____. *The Epistle of Paul to the Philippians*. TNTC. Rev. ed. Grand Rapids: William B. Eerdmans Publishing Co., 1987. Brief exegetical commentary on the epistle.

_____. *Philippians*. NCB. Grand Rapids: William B. Eerdmans Publishing Co., 1980.

McNeile, A. H., and C. S. Williams. *An Introduction to the Study of the New Testament*. 2d ed. rev. Oxford: Clarendon Press, 1953.

Mitton, C. Leslie. *The Epistle to the Ephesians*. NCB. Greenwood, S.C.: Attic, 1976.

Motyer, Alec. *The Message of Philippians*. BST. Downers Grove, Ill.: Inter-Varsity, 1984. Expositional commentary on Philippians.

Moule, H. C. G. *Studies in Ephesians*. Grand Rapids: Kregel Publications, 1977. Expositional studies by a noted English scholar and church leader.

_____. *Studies in Philippians*. Grand Rapids: Kregel Publications, 1977. Studies emphasizing the art of expounding and applying the text from a noted English scholar.

O'Brien, Peter T. *The Epistle to the Philippians*. NIGTC. Grand Rapids: William B. Eerdmans Publishing Co., 1991. Thorough exegetical commentary on Philippians.

Schweizer, Eduard. *The Letter to the Colossians*. Minneapolis: Augsburg Press, 1982.

Silva, Moises. *Philippians*. WEC. Chicago: Moody Press, 1988.

Stott, John R. W. *The Message of Ephesians*. BST. Downers Grove, Ill.: InterVarsity Press, 1979. Expositional commentary on Ephesians.

Wright, Norman. "Poetry and Theology in Colossians 1:15–20." *NTS* 36 (1990): 444–68.

Wright, N. T. "Colossians and Philemon." TNTC. Grand Rapids: William B. Eerdmans Publishing Co., 1986.

_____. *The Epistles of Paul to the Colossians and Philemon.* TNTC. Grand Rapids: Eerdmans, 1986. Brief exegetical commentary on the epistles.

18 The Pastoral Epistles

Guiding Questions

1. Why do we call 1 and 2 Timothy and Titus the "pastoral Epistles"?

2. Discuss the evidence investigated to determine the authorship of the Pastorals. Give your own evaluation of the evidence.

3. What evidence is available to support a second Roman imprisonment for Paul?

4. What problems did Timothy face in Ephesus? How did Paul instruct him to deal with the problems?

5. What problems did Titus face on Crete? How did Paul instruct him to deal with the problems?

The three letters of 1 and 2 Timothy and Titus form the only group of writings in the New Testament directed to individuals with pastoral responsibilities. Since the early 1700s scholars have called them the "pastoral Epistles." Some of the content in these letters deals with subjects other than pastoral duties. However, the term so aptly describes the major emphasis of the letters that it has become a widely accepted descriptive title.

The pastoral Epistles have a long history of acceptance as genuine Pauline literature. Clement of Alexandria (ca. 155–ca. 220) referred to 1 Timothy 6:20–21 as written by "the apostle," a clear reference to Paul.[1] The church historian Eusebius included the pastoral Epistles among Paul's genuine writings.[2] Other early church leaders accepting Pauline authorship of the Pastorals included Irenaeus and Origen. The list of New Testament books in the Muratorian Canon, a document dated about 180–200, referred to the Pastorals as Pauline.

The canon of Scripture assembled by Marcion omitted the Pastorals. This omission has led some scholars to assume that the Pastorals had not been written by the time of Marcion (ca. 140). However, Marcion's omission of these letters might well be due to his own theological bias. He also omitted Matthew, Mark, and John from his canon and mutilated Luke's Gospel. It is possible that Marcion had read the Pastorals but chose to exclude them from his canon because he disagreed with their content.

One issue debated by New Testament scholars beginning in the nineteenth century is the authorship of the Pastorals. In the nineteenth century those who rejected Pauline authorship cited the style, vocabulary, theology, and level of church organization in the Pastorals as arguments against Pauline authorship.

Some contemporary New Testament scholars accept Pauline authorship of the Pastorals; others reject it. Among those who accept Pauline authorship are Donald Guthrie, J. N. D. Kelly, and C. Spicq. Among those who reject Pauline authorship are P. N. Harrison, C. F. D. Moule,[3] M. Dibelius, H. Conzelmann, and A. T. Hanson. It is important for us now to explore the question of authorship.

Authorship of the Pastorals

Many contemporary interpreters maintain that the name "Paul" in the Pastorals is a pseudonym. Most who advocate

---

1. Clement of Alexandria, *Stromata* 2.11.
2. Eusebius, *Church History* 3.3.
3. Moule suggests, "Luke wrote all three Pastoral epistles. But he wrote them during Paul's lifetime, at Paul's behest, and, in part . . . at Paul's dictation." See his "The Problem of the Pastoral Epistles: A Reappraisal," *Essays in New Testament Interpretation* (Cambridge: Cambridge University Press, 1982), 117.

pseudonymity feel that an admirer of Paul wrote the letters at some time after Paul's death.[4] Some suggest that the writer used Paul's name to secure acceptance of his ideas. Others suggest that the writer may have intended a tribute to Paul by writing with a Pauline style to some of the churches the apostle had founded and developed.

Some who view the Pastorals as pseudonymous also maintain that they do contain genuine fragments written by Paul. These scholars regard those fragments that contain personal information about Paul or his recipients as genuinely coming from the apostle (e.g. 1 Tim. 1:13–15; 2 Tim. 1:16–18; 3:10–11; Titus 3:13–15).[5] They contend that the Pastorals are comprised of pieces that are stitched together by a disciple of Paul.

Those who question or oppose Pauline authorship usually present five arguments to support their views:

1. differences in vocabulary and style between the Pastorals and other Pauline materials;

2. the nature of the heresy refuted in the Pastorals;

3. the ecclesiastical structure present in the letters;

4. conflicting circumstances between the Pastorals and other New Testament books;

5. theology.

Different Vocabulary and Style

The pastoral Epistles contain many *hapax legomena*. Such words as "slave traders" (1 Tim. 1:10; *andrapodistai*) and "integrity" (Titus 2:7; *aphthoria*) are *hapax legomena*. Some words rare in Paul's ten other writings are key terms in the Pastorals. The word "godliness" is one such word (1 Tim. 6:11; *eusebeia*). Further, some of Paul's most important words are absent from the Pastorals, or they appear

---

4. For a brief discussion of the practice of pseudonymity in the New Testament, see the presentation in chapter 14 on "The Practice of Pseudonymous Authorship." For additional information on the subject, see Carson, Moo, and Morris, *An Introduction to the New Testament*, 367–71.

5. A leading advocate of this theory was P. N. Harrison, whose views passed through several changes over several decades. See his book, *The Problem of the Pastoral Epistles* (London: Oxford University Press, 1921).

with a different meaning. The term "son" as a reference to Christ does not appear in the Pastorals. The term "righteousness" *(dikaio-syne)* is defined in the Pastorals as a virtue to be sought (1 Tim. 6:11), but in Paul's other writings it is a gift of right-standing with God (Rom. 3:21–26).

P. N. Harrison has collected impressive statistics related to the linguistic peculiarities of the Pastorals. He suggested that the language of the Pastorals was the speech of the second century A.D. Harrison contends that many words used in the Pastorals, though found in the first century, were more common in the second century.[6]

In rebuttal to Harrison, J. N. D. Kelly pointed out that most of the *hapax legomena* in the Pastorals were used by other Greek writers prior to A.D. 50. He also observed that the proportion of *hapax legomena* in second-century writings is nearly the same in the Pastorals and those Pauline epistles whose authorship is not questioned, such as 1 Corinthians.[7] The noted scholar Bruce Metzger suggested that the Pastorals are too brief to be a source of accurate information about the writing habits of the author.[8]

Any change in Paul's style in the Pastorals can be attributed to three causes.

1. Paul's subject matter, age, and life experiences might have led him to express a mood different from that expressed in his other writings. We would not expect a minister to use the same words on Father's Day and Easter or a younger pastor to use the same vocabulary as a mature minister.

2. The needs of Paul's readers could have led him to omit terms and ideas he used in other writings. Paul faced new challenges as he wrote the Pastorals, and he used a vocabulary appropriate to those challenges.

3. Paul may have used an amanuensis or secretary in writing the Pastorals. That amanuensis could have chosen some of the

---

6. Ibid., 67–86.

7. J. N. D. Kelly, *A Commentary on the Pastoral Epistles* (London: Adam & Charles Black, 1963; Grand Rapids: Baker, Thornapple Commentaries, 1981), 24.

8. Bruce Metzger, "A Reconsideration of Certain Arguments Against the Pauline Authorship of the Pastoral Epistles," *ET* 70 (1958): 93–94.

words unique in the Pastorals.[9] In Romans 16:22 Paul mentioned Tertius as the scribe for that epistle. Paul was imprisoned and awaiting death while writing 2 Timothy (2 Tim. 4:6–8), and likely required help to complete the task.

These considerations suggest that it is precarious and unnecessary to reject Pauline authorship based on contrasts in style and vocabulary between the Pastorals and other Pauline writings. Alternate explanations of the differences can be presented.

The Problem of Heresy

In the second century, Christianity became involved in a fierce struggle with a heretical movement known as Gnosticism. This false teaching denied the resurrection of Christ, vacillated between moral license and rigid asceticism, and insisted that sinful human beings could not enjoy fellowship and full contact with the transcendent God. Those who question Pauline authorship find evidence of some of these beliefs in the Pastorals, and conclude that the Pastorals were a product of the second century and thus not authored by Paul.

Those who link the heresy with second-century Gnosticism cite the denial of the future resurrection in 2 Timothy 2:17–18 as support for their position. Others note the presence in 1 Timothy 6:20 of the term "opposing ideas" (*antitheseis*). This term is identical to the title of a work by the second-century heretic Marcion, and the similarity leads them to date the Pastorals in the second century. Although most scholars agree that Marcion was not a true Gnostic, they contend that his negative attitude toward the body and the physical world is similar to that of the Gnostics.

The heresy Paul described in the Pastorals was characterized by an interest in Jewish law (1 Tim. 1:6–7) and showed the influence of "those of the circumcision group" (Titus 1:10). Marcion and his followers adamantly resisted having any element of Judaism in their

---

9. Richard N. Longenecker has an important discussion on the role of the amanuensis in "Ancient Amanuenses and the Pauline Epistles," in *New Dimensions in New Testament Study*, ed. R. N. Longenecker and M. C. Tenney (Grand Rapids: Zondervan Books, 1974), 281–97. Longenecker says, "Just how closely the apostle supervised his various amanuenses in each particular instance is, of course, impossible to say. . . . Paul's own practice probably varied with the specific circumstances of the case and with the particular companion whom he employed at the time" (294).

teachings. This fact makes it unlikely that the false teaching challenged in the Pastorals had any link to the heresies originating with Marcion.

Marcion omitted the Pastorals from his New Testament canon. Some who question Pauline authorship see this omission as evidence of the non-Pauline origin of the Pastorals. However, Marcion could well have omitted the Pastorals because he disagreed with some of their theological content. For example, Paul's affirmation that "the law is good" (1 Tim. 1:8) contradicted Marcion's adamant rejection of the Old Testament. Furthermore, Paul's reference to knowledge (*gnosis*) as "what is falsely called 'knowledge'" would be an irritant to Marcion, who viewed his own system as a new form of gnosis. We can find adequate reasons for Marcion's omission of the Pastorals from his canon without suggesting they were non-Pauline in origin.

Kelly's examination of the heresy in the Pastorals led him to conclude that "in general there is nothing in the sparse, vague hints we are given to indicate that the doctrine attacked had the elaboration or coherence of the great Gnostic systems."[10]

The Pastoral heresy clearly contained a strain of heterodox Judaism. False teachers may not have held ideas similar to those Paul found in Galatia, but they were ascetics who disparaged marriage and some types of food (1 Tim. 4:1–5). Paul found another heresy similar to the Pastoral heresy in Colossae (see Col. 2:16, 21–23). Paul was not opposing a second-century form of Gnosticism. Rather, he was wrestling against an erroneous form of Judaism that contained features similar to later Gnosticism.

The Church Organization

Ignatius served as bishop of Antioch during part of the first half of the second century A.D. He was martyred in Rome around 115. While journeying under armed guard to Rome, he wrote his letter to the Ephesians in which he stated: "We ought to receive every one whom the Master of the house sends to be over His household, as we would do Him that sent him. It is manifest, therefore, that we should look upon the bishop even as we would look upon the Lord Himself."[11] Some have seen a similarity between the position of

---

10. Kelly, *Pastoral Epistles*, 11–12.
11. Ignatius, *Letter to the Ephesians* 6.

the bishops in the Pastorals and the position of church leaders described by Ignatius. This perceived similarity leads them to date the Pastorals beyond the time of Paul and into the second century A.D.

Further, those who date the Pastorals in the second century maintain that an excessive interest in church organization appears in the Pastorals. They cannot accept that the same person wrote 1 Corinthians, which has little interest in church organization, and the Pastorals, which show great interest in the subject.

However, Paul was always interested in proper organization for the churches. He and Barnabas appointed elders in the Galatian churches during their return visit to the area on the first missionary journey (Acts 14:23). In the Philippian church Paul recognized the presence of both bishops (overseers) and deacons (Phil. 1:1). In 1 Thessalonians, Paul described church leaders as those "who are over you in the Lord" (1 Thess. 5:12). Paul consistently showed an interest in and an awareness of church organization. In my judgment, it is quite tenuous to conclude that the discussions of roles for bishops and deacons in the Pastorals indicate a second-century date of writing.

Nothing in Paul's discussion about bishops and deacons (1 Tim. 3:1–13; Titus 1:5–9) suggests that they had the relatively autocratic power described by Ignatius. Paul certainly viewed these bishops and deacons as having authority, but their authority was not excessive. Paul gave these leaders authority that they might serve as his representatives in correcting errors and abuses in the churches (1 Tim. 5:17–20). Since the Pastorals are the final writings of Paul, it should not surprise us that Paul would discuss requirements for the office of bishop and deacon. Paul was only showing his usual pastoral concern for his people.

Conflicting Circumstances

In 1 Timothy and Titus we see evidence that Paul had traveled extensively in the eastern half of the Roman Empire. In 1 Timothy 1:3 Paul left Timothy in Ephesus to deal with false teachers. In Titus 1:5 Paul left Titus in Crete and eventually traveled to Nicopolis (Titus 3:12), where he intended to remain during the winter. In 1 Timothy 3:14 Paul expressed the hope that he might return to Ephesus. When we open 2 Timothy, Paul was again in prison, probably in Rome, and he expected that death was a clear possibility (2 Tim. 1:16–17; 4:6–8, 16–18). He also asked Timothy to bring him his cloak and books from Troas and described Trophimus's illness at Miletus as if it had occurred only recently (2 Tim. 4:13, 20).

I believe that it is impossible to correlate these journeys with Paul's journeys in Acts. While it is possible that Paul visited Crete on his journey to Rome (Acts 27:7–12), we find no indication in Acts that Paul began missionary work there. Acts presents no evidence that Paul ever visited Nicopolis. In Acts 20:4–6 Timothy accompanied Paul during his journey to Ephesus, and he could not have received a letter from Paul in Ephesus during the same time period. The difficulty of harmonizing these journeys with Acts has led some to conclude that a pseudonymous writer added these incidents to Paul's life.

The traditional response to these observations is that Paul was released from his imprisonment of Acts 28, returned to the east for a period of ministry, was later arrested and imprisoned, and was finally returned to Rome. Those who question this solution point out that Paul had intended to travel westward to Spain from Rome but indicated no plans for a trip eastward (Rom. 15:23–29).

Paul probably changed his mind about making the journey to Spain. In Philemon 22 he expressed an interest in returning to Asia Minor. Paul also expected a release from his first imprisonment and an additional period of service (Phil. 1:18–19, 24–26; 2:24). Acts does not record all of Paul's activities. Therefore, we should not be surprised that many significant events in Paul's life are not fully described in Acts (see 2 Cor. 11:22–33 for examples).

Some early Christian leaders presented evidence of more than a single imprisonment in Rome. For example, Eusebius wrote: "Paul spent two whole years at Rome as a prisoner at large, and preached the word of God without restraint. Thus, after he had made his defense it is said that the apostle was sent again upon the ministry of preaching, and that upon coming to the same city a second time he suffered martyrdom."[12]

We can conclude from the examination of available evidence that the Pastorals should not be faulted for not being in agreement with the account of events in Acts. It is certainly possible that Paul min-

---

12. Eusebius, *Church History* 2.22.

istered in the eastern half of the Roman Empire after release from a first imprisonment in Rome. During this period Paul might have stayed for a time in Ephesus, worked in Crete, and finally visited Nicopolis. At some point he was arrested again and returned to Rome, from which he wrote 2 Timothy. The Pastorals do not necessarily conflict with Acts, but rather they deal with a period of Paul's life after the writing of Acts.

Theology

Some who question the Pauline authorship of the Pastorals emphasize that the theological content of the Pastorals varies too much from the genuine Pauline writings to be viewed as Pauline. Two important issues surface from these discussions.

1. Scholars observe that many common Pauline phrases and ideas from Paul's other epistles are not mentioned in the Pastorals.

2. The writer, whoever he may have been, is viewed as using a hackneyed, trite style of writing to communicate Christian doctrine.

On the first issue scholars note, for example, the different context in the discussion about union with Christ. In Paul's other writings the term "in Christ" refers to persons in their relationship to the Lord (see Eph. 1:3). In the Pastorals the term refers to qualities more than to persons. For example, in 2 Timothy 1:1 and 3:12 Paul wrote of "life in Christ Jesus." However, the experience of having "life in Christ Jesus" need not be distinguished from the personal experience of being "in Christ." A person who has life in Christ is in Christ.

Further, although the Pastorals do not have frequent references to the Cross or the death of Christ, the concept is not completely absent. The statement about the "ransom" of Christ (1 Tim. 2:6) refers to his death as does the metaphor of redemption in Titus 2:14.

Concerning the second issue of using hackneyed or trite phrases, some scholars mention the use of words such as "the faith," "the deposit," or "sound teaching." They maintain that terms like *faith* (1 Tim. 3:13) and *deposit* (2 Tim. 1:14) sound like a reference to an official body of doctrine. In many of Paul's other writings the term *faith* refers to personal commitment to Christ (see Rom. 3:22, 26). However, in Philippians 1:27 and Colossians 2:7 Paul used the term *faith* in reference to Christian doctrine. Therefore, using these terms in the Pastorals is not unique.

The Pastorals do contain a change in Paul's theological emphases. Paul's advancing age, the needs of the readers, and the subject matter being discussed might have contributed to these changes. It is not necessary to insist that variations in theological emphases are so great that they demand an author other than Paul. Some of Paul's emphases in the Pastorals, while significantly different from his emphases in his other writings, may be explained by the needs of the audience or other circumstances. Also, some phrases in the Pastorals have parallels with statements found in Paul's earlier writings.

Conclusion of Arguments Concerning Authorship

The arguments against Pauline authorship of the Pastorals are not compelling. Internal claims from the letters suggest Paul as the author. External evidence from church history presents a uniform tradition naming Paul as author. The fact that the Pastorals had many witnesses to their existence indicates that they must have had a wide circulation and that their date of origin reaches back to the earlier years of the church. The best evidence suggests that Paul wrote the Pastorals in the closing years of his ministry.[13]

Chronology for the Pastorals

Assuming Pauline authorship of the Pastorals, we must place the letters in the shadowy period between Paul's release from his first Roman imprisonment and his execution. Presenting an exact chronology of Paul's life is an impossibility. Scholars reach different conclusions for the date of his arrival in Rome. Assuming Paul arrived in Rome for his first imprisonment in A.D. 61, we can conclude that his release from prison occurred around A.D. 63 (Acts 28:30). However, the only certainty is that Paul's death occurred during the reign of Nero (54–68), likely between 64 and 67.

---

13. A useful discussion supporting Pauline authorship of the Pastorals appears in E. E. Ellis, "The Pastorals and Paul," *ExpTim* 104 (November 1992): 45–47.

The exact nature of Paul's movements during this period is unknown. Paul probably wrote 1 Timothy from Macedonia (1 Tim. 1:3). In 2 Timothy he is a captive, perhaps for the second time. The apostle apparently is in Rome expecting death (2 Tim. 4:6–8, 13–18). The Epistle to Titus indicates Paul had an extensive missionary tour of Crete (see 1:5). When Paul wrote Titus, he planned to remain at Nicopolis during the winter (3:12).

We do not know if Paul ever visited Spain (Rom. 15:24). He may have returned to Asia Minor after his release from an initial imprisonment. Since 1 Timothy and Titus cover similar subjects (cf. 1 Tim. 3:1–13; Titus 1:5–9), Paul likely wrote them close together. Paul must have written 2 Timothy as his final letter, while he was in prison staring death in the face (2 Tim. 4:6–8). Below is a suggested chronology for Paul's writing of the Pastorals (with possibilities for wide variations).

- A.D. 61–63. Paul's first imprisonment. Writing of the prison Epistles, including Ephesians, Philippians, Colossians, and Philemon.

- A.D. 63–65/66. Paul freed for additional missionary work. Writing of 1 Timothy and Titus.

- A.D. 65/66. Paul arrested again. Writing of 2 Timothy, a second Roman imprisonment, and martyrdom following this arrest.

Occasion and Purpose

General Occasion and Purpose for the Pastorals

During the period following his release from the first Roman imprisonment, Paul returned to the East for further ministry. On the island of Crete he experienced a successful ministry, then departed, leaving Titus to complete the task of organizing and instructing the infant churches.

Paul traveled with Timothy to Ephesus and learned that the church there was facing great spiritual difficulty. After a period of ministry, Paul departed from Ephesus, leaving Timothy in charge. Paul proceeded to Macedonia, where he wrote 1 Timothy. This letter presented additional instructions for Timothy as Paul's representative in Ephesus, and also emphasized the meaning and significance of some of Paul's initial oral statements about Timothy. As he wrote 1 Timothy, Paul probably also reflected on the needs of Titus in Crete. He likely penned Titus at about the same time as 1 Timothy, with the intention of clarifying and adding to earlier oral instructions to Titus.

Paul's mood in 2 Timothy differs from that in the other two Pastorals. His personal struggles and imprisonment are reflected in his writing (see section on the occasion and purpose of 2 Timothy).

1 Timothy

The Occasion and Purpose of 1 Timothy

Paul indicated two purposes for writing 1 Timothy.

1. He wrote to urge Timothy to provide firm personal resistance to the false teaching spreading its influence in Ephesus (1:3–4). To help Timothy follow this command, Paul included information on the identity of the false teachers and the nature of their teaching. Paul identified certain influential leaders of the church who had fallen under the influence of the false teaching (1:18–20). His insistence on maintaining high standards for church leaders suggested that erring church leaders were among those who were helping to spread the heresy. The false teachers urged dietary restrictions and asceticism (4:3), and seemed to be influenced by Jewish thought in their interest in the law (1:7–8). The teachers also displayed a type of mysticism in their emphasis on superior knowledge (6:20–21).

2. Paul wrote to encourage the Ephesian Christians to live as members of "God's household" or family (3:15). He was eager for them to present a committed lifestyle for others to imitate in order to provide a contrast with the corrupt, self-seeking actions of the false teachers. Paul warned against apostasy and asceticism (4:1–4). He urged church members to consistently demonstrate Christian behavior (4:11–16). He encouraged churches to take proper care of true widows (5:3–8), and he warned against greed and materialism (6:6–10).

It is incorrect to interpret 1 Timothy or either of the other two Pastorals as a church organization manual. Paul was not writing a text on church administration; rather, he was preparing Timothy to deal wisely with false teachers who were threatening the vitality and accomplishments of the Ephesian church.

Provenance

Paul most likely wrote this letter from Macedonia. Nothing in the letter explicitly identifies this area, but Paul indicated that he left Timothy in Ephesus as he went into Macedonia (1:3). Paul and Timothy had been in Ephesus together, and Paul apparently left Timothy behind and traveled to Macedonia. From this location he wrote to reinforce the instructions given to Timothy prior to his departure.

Destination

Paul apparently wrote 1 Timothy to his younger associate in Ephesus (1:3). Although Paul sent grace greetings to the entire church (in 6:21 the "you" is plural), he obviously addressed these words primarily to Timothy. His personal words to Timothy in 1:18–19 and in 4:12–16 suggest that Paul focused chiefly on meeting Timothy's needs. Timothy may well have shared with the entire church the advice and insights from Paul, but their chief impact fell on Timothy himself.

Contributions of 1 Timothy

Two features of this letter make important contributions to contemporary Christian living.

1. Paul provided an example of one Christian offering help to another as a mentor in his personal words to Timothy. He addressed Timothy as his "true son" in the faith (1:2), and gave him specific instructions for carrying out ministerial tasks (4:11–16). Much of the advice he gave to Timothy was eminently practical (5:1–2).

2. Paul had more to say about Christian ministry in this letter than in any other letter he wrote. He focused chiefly on the character of those who minister to others. If he mentions ordination at all (1:18; 4:14), he does not clearly explain its

method or purpose. Paul presumed that church leaders would be individuals with unimpeachable character (3:1–13), a highly visible lifestyle of commitment, and a disciplined home life. Furthermore, he insisted that leaders be experienced believers with a good reputation even among unbelievers.

2 Timothy

The Occasion and Purpose of 2 Timothy

Paul's mood in 2 Timothy was deeply influenced by his personal circumstances. He apparently had been arrested again, had undergone a preliminary hearing (4:16–18), and expected to die soon (4:6–8). Some Christian friends had cared for him at great sacrifice (1:16–18), while others had abused and ignored him (4:14–16). Paul found himself alone; many of his close friends had left on specific ministries (4:10–12). The false teaching in the Ephesian church had continued to spread. The church leader Hymenaeus, excommunicated in 1 Timothy 1:20, continued to exert his evil influence on the church, and he had reinforcements (2:17–18).

Paul dealt with the heresy, but was not preoccupied with it. He chose to focus his attention on Timothy. Paul reminded Timothy of their lengthy friendship (3:10–11) and insisted that he be loyal to Paul's teaching and practice (1:13–14; 2:1–13). He urged Timothy to focus his efforts on developing faithful followers of Christ (2:1–2). Paul appealed for Timothy to come to his side (4:9). He courageously faced the future and prepared Timothy to continue the work of ministry even after Paul's death.

Provenance

Paul mentioned that his friend Onesiphorus had searched for him and located him in Rome (1:16–17), and that he had recently made a "defense" (4:16), a suggestion that he was confined in a prison in connection with a trial. He anticipated his death in the near future (4:6–8).

Paul's mention of leaving a cloak in Troas (4:13) and departing from Trophimus who was sick in Miletus (4:20) suggests that Paul was in Asia Minor not long before writing 2 Timothy.

All of these factors imply that Paul had been arrested again somewhere in the East and transported to imprisonment in Rome. He wrote 2 Timothy from this city.

Destination

Paul clearly wrote this letter as a personal exhortation and encouragement to Timothy (1:2). We cannot tell from the letter where Timothy was living at this time. Timothy was possibly still in Ephesus, where he was in 1 Timothy 1:3. However, the most honest answer is that we do not know where he was when he received 2 Timothy.

Contributions of 2 Timothy

The value of 2 Timothy consists largely in its important, helpful challenges for Christian living.

1. We observe Paul courageously facing death and giving contemporary believers an example to imitate (4:6–8). Even in this circumstance Paul encouraged suffering for the gospel (1:8). His words add a dimension of reality to the issue of suffering for Christians who live in the West with little to fear from governmental persecution. Martyrdom is still a reality for Christians in some areas, and Paul's words are an encouraging example for those who might face this possibility.

2. Paul's images of discipleship show that its cost to the believer could be significantly high (2:3–7). He compared Christian commitment to the dedication of a soldier, an athlete, and a hardworking farmer, and prepared Timothy for the cost of commitment (2:20–21). Paul's words should remind us that, although salvation is free, the believer's response to salvation demands commitment and endurance.

Titus

The Occasion and Purpose of Titus

In Titus 1:5 Paul stated his purpose for writing. He had left Titus behind to appoint elders in a church that was younger and less organized than the church at Ephesus. False teaching swirled through the area, but its threat was not as menacing as that mentioned in 1

Timothy. This judgment is based on the fact that Titus lacks the urgent appeals of 1 Timothy, such as "fight the good fight" (1 Tim. 6:12) and "guard what has been entrusted to your care" (1 Tim. 6:20). Paul described the false teachers and their teaching in 1:10–16 and 3:9–11. He outlined for Titus the importance of appointing and training new leaders for the Cretan church (1:5–9). He also encouraged Titus to rebuke his erring opponents (1:13).

Provenance

Paul had just left Crete (1:5) and was going toward Nicopolis, where he intended to spend the winter (3:12). Nothing in the letter tells us exactly where Paul was when he wrote, but he was traveling somewhere between Crete and Nicopolis.

Destination

The statement in 1:5 suggests that Paul wrote specifically to Titus, who was left behind for ministry on the island of Crete. The method and timing of Titus's arrival with Paul on Crete is unclear, but his location on this small island is firmly established.

Contributions of Titus

Paul's instructions in Titus demonstrate the transforming power of the gospel on Christians. In 2:1–10 Paul outlined the new life-style that should characterize the life of a Christian, whether young or old, male or female, slave or freeman. Paul's portraits show that the gospel transformed people of reckless, lawless behavior into individuals who put aside self-destructive habits and developed a concern for one another.

Paul's discussion also emphasized the relation between salvation and good works (2:11–14; 3:3–8). In this discussion, Paul taught that God's grace produces upright behavior, not careless living. Furthermore, God's kindness and the regeneration of the Holy Spirit develop new behavior in people previously enslaved to their passions.

The Content of 1 Timothy

Salutation (1:1–2)

Paul's salutation follows his usual pattern. He identified himself as the author and Timothy as the recipient. Calling Timothy his "true son" need not suggest that Timothy was converted through Paul's ministry. Apparently Timothy was already a believer when he met Paul (Acts 16:1–3). Paul could legitimately view him as his spiritual child or "son" in the ministry.

The threefold greeting of "grace, mercy, and peace" highlighted the desperate needs of Timothy to complete the tasks Paul had given him.

The Explanation of Timothy's Task (1:3–20)

Paul gave a threefold task to his young Christian friend.

1. Paul directed Timothy to prevent the spread of false teaching (1:3–11). Paul wanted Timothy to warn the leaders of the heretical group in Ephesus to stop spreading their speculative ideas which promoted controversy.

2. Paul explained to Timothy the necessity of preaching the gospel vigorously in Ephesus (1:12–17). He thanked God for his own salvation and explained that the salvation of a sinner like himself would encourage other despairing sinners to turn to God in faith and receive eternal life.

3. Paul urged Timothy to call the Ephesians to renewed obedience so they might recapture the excitement of their earlier commitment (1:18–20). Paul reminded Timothy of the spiritual failure of two Ephesian leaders who had trifled with the false teaching he denounced.

In the first chapter, Paul outlined the task Timothy faced. He then explained to him how to accomplish the task. Paul's emphases were intended to aid Timothy in opposing the false teaching and in calling his Ephesian friends to renewed commitment.

Prayer for All People (2:1–7)

Paul urged Timothy to lead the Ephesians to pray for all people, particularly those in positions of leadership. These prayers would help believers to live in godliness and commitment and would also help unbelievers come to know the God who delights in the salvation of the lost.

Holy Living by Men and Women (2:8–15)

Both men and women in Ephesus had been self-seeking, gullible, and disobedient in their behavior. Paul urged the men to pray from a pure heart and to renounce their inclination for contempt and controversy (v. 8). He directed the women to produce good works (v. 10), show more interest in learning than in leading (vv. 11–12),[14] and focus on their roles as Christian mothers (v. 15).

Church Leadership (3:1–13)

Strong-willed leaders in the Ephesian church had caused problems for Paul. Consequently, he took steps to guarantee that new leaders would have a firm commitment to Christ and work to develop godliness and unity within the congregation by presenting qualifications for the offices in the church. These offices included bishops or overseers (3:1–7), deacons (3:8–10, 12–13), and women helpers (3:11), and the qualifications for these offices focused on the development of the proper character for leadership. Among the traits mentioned are: observable obedient behavior (vv. 2–3); exemplary home leadership (vv. 4–5); spiritual maturity (v. 6), and respect from unbelievers (v. 7). Paul's discussion tells us little about the responsibilities and duties of the leaders.

Correct Application of Christian Truth (3:14–16)

Paul explained that one purpose for writing was to encourage the Ephesians to live in a manner appropriate to those in God's household (v. 15). Paul was not merely outlining how Christians should behave in church—as if he were about to deliver a lecture on church manners. He saw Christians as members of God's family, and he urged them to conduct themselves in a manner consistent with this transforming relationship.

---

14. The meaning of 1 Tim. 2:11–12 is a much debated issue in New Testament interpretation. Paul did not intend to ban teaching by all women for all time. In Corinth women prophesied (1 Cor. 11:5), and Priscilla must have participated in teaching Apollos (Acts 18:24–26). The teaching which Paul commended for women is more informal and less "official" (2 Tim. 1:5; Titus 2:3–4).

For contrasting opinions on this issue, see D. J. Moo, "1 Timothy 2:11–15: Meaning and Significance," *TJ* n.s. 1 (1980): 62–83, and P. B. Payne, "Libertarian Women in Ephesus: A Response to Douglas J. Moo's Article: 1 Timothy 2:11–15: Meaning and Significance," *TJ* n.s. 2 (1981): 169–97.

Paul also presented a hymnic expression of Christian truth to prepare Timothy for dealing with false teaching (v. 16). In the hymn Paul emphasized the earthly ministry of Christ, including his incarnation, resurrection, and triumphant ascension. He also mentioned Christ's ongoing ministry, including the proclamation and response to the gospel and the glory Christ received in heaven after his ascension.

Understanding False Practice (4:1–5)

In 4:1–3 Paul warned against an asceticism that prohibited marriage and he expressed concern over insistence on abstinence from eating certain foods. Paul was not dealing with nutrition; he was arguing against a theologically-based abstinence. Against asceticism and abstinence, Paul declared that all of God's creation was good (v. 4). He also insisted that the gratitude expressed in thanksgiving sanctified everything God had made (v. 5).

Timothy's Performance of His Task (4:6–16)

Paul now explained Timothy's role in combating errors among the Ephesian false teachers. First, he explained how Timothy would face and overcome falsehood (4:6–10). Paul urged Timothy to make a positive presentation of the truth and to develop his own habits of personal integrity.

Second, he specified certain Christian actions for Timothy to undertake (4:11–16). Timothy was to be the example of a godly young man. He was to proclaim God's message, use his spiritual gifts, and practice consistent spiritual growth.

Responsibilities Toward Special Groups in the Church (5:1–16)

Paul gave instructions to Timothy for meeting the needs of three special groups within the church. First, Paul urged Timothy to treat men and women, young and old, as family members (5:1–2). Second, he outlined how the church should meet the needs of genuine widows in the church. Paul insisted that genuine widows deserved financial help and honor from the church (5:3–8).[15] Third, Paul focused on the special needs facing younger widows (5:9–16). He suggested that younger widows not receive financial help from the church but that they plan to remarry and assume domestic responsibility.

Proper Handling of Leaders (5:17–25)

Paul was aware of a severe leadership crisis in the Ephesian church. In 5:17–20 he described how the church is to honor and protect deserving elders. He provided practical assistance for dealing with leaders who strayed from their commitment to Christ. In 5:21–25 Paul issued warnings and directives Timothy could use in dealing with the problems of the Ephesian church. Some of Paul's exhortations consisted of common-sense advice for Timothy. Other insights prepared Timothy to respond wisely to the tricky practices of the straying elders.

A Warning to Slaves and Sinners (6:1–10)

Paul addressed two groups with special needs in the Ephesian church. He spoke to the slaves (6:1–2), calling them to honorable Christian behavior and providing guidelines for appropriate actions under a Christian and a non-Christian owner.

In 6:3–10 Paul focused on the behavior of false teachers. He warned Timothy of the contentious, greedy habits of false teachers (6:3–5), and exposed the evils of materialism (6:6–10). Paul affirmed that godliness, not wealth, brought great gain. He showed that the desire for wealth created a spiritual trap that would ensnare the careless and carry them to utter ruin. Paul did not condemn wealth, but he warned that those who desired it would bring great sadness on themselves.

Instructions to Timothy and the Wealthy (6:11–21)

To prepare Timothy to meet the rigors of dealing with proud, greedy controversialists, Paul outlined a program for developing godliness (6:11–16). He urged Timothy to complete the ministry assigned to him in Ephesus, and reminded him to respond to this challenge in the sight of God (6:13).

---

15. Bruce Winter provides useful first-century historical information to increase our understanding of the church's task in providing for needy widows. See his "*Providentia* for the Widows of 1 Timothy 5:3–16," *TynBul* 39 (1988): 83–99.

In 6:17–19 Paul wrote to those who had already accumulated wealth. What should they do? Paul did not condemn wealth, but he described the hazards wealth might encourage. He urged the wealthy to be "rich in good deeds" (v. 18).

In 6:20–21 Paul's concluding word of caution was directed specifically to Timothy. He urged Timothy to faithfully carry out his task of opposing false teachers, and to ignore their silly jargon.

Outline of 1 Timothy

I. Salutation (1:1–2)

II. Explanation of Timothy's Task (1:3–20)

    A. To prevent the spread of false teaching (1:3–11)

        1. Content of the warning (1:3–4)

        2. Goal of the warning (1:5–7)

        3. Reason for the warning (1:8–11)

    B. To preach the gospel (1:12–17)

        1. Thanksgiving to God (1:12–14)

        2. Statement of the gospel (1:15)

        3. Purpose of divine mercy (1:16)

        4. Doxology (1:17)

    C. To prevent a decline in commitment (1:18–20)

III. Emphases that Will Accomplish the Task (2:1–6:21)

    A. Prayer for all people (2:1–7)

        1. Objects and content of prayer (2:1–2)

        2. Goal of prayer (2:3–4)

        3. Goodness of the goal of prayer (2:5–7)

    B. Holy living (2:8–15)

        1. Appeal to men (2:8)

        2. Appeal to women (2:9–15)

    C. Church leadership by committed servants (3:1–13)

        1. Qualifications of overseers (3:1–7)

        2. Qualifications of deacons (3:8–10, 12–13)

        3. Women helpers (3:11)

    D. Correct application of Christian truth (3:14–16)

        1. Plans for a visit (3:14)

2. Purpose for writing (3:15)
3. Hymn for believers (3:16)

E. Understanding false practice (4:1–5)
1. Warning against apostasy (4:1–3)
2. Argument against asceticism (4:4)
3. Argument for blessing food (4:5)

F. Timothy's performance of his task (4:6–16)
1. Facing falsehood (4:6–10)
2. Demonstrating Christian behavior (4:11–16)

G. Responsibilities toward church groups (5:1–16)
1. Proper treatment for all ages (5:1–2)
2. Care of true widows (5:3–8)
3. Warning to younger widows (5:9–16)

H. Proper handling of leaders (5:17–25)
1. Recognition and discipline of leaders (5:17–20)
2. Special directions to Timothy (5:21–25)

I. Warning to slaves and sinners (6:1–10)
1. Responsibility of Christian slaves (6:1–2a)
2. Indictment of the false teachers (6:2b–5)
3. Greed of the false teachers (6:6–10)

J. Instructions to Timothy and the wealthy (6:11–21)
1. Program for godliness (6:11–16)
2. Promise for the prosperous (6:17–19)
3. Final caution (6:20–21)

The Content of 2 Timothy

Salutation (1:1–2)

The salutation in 2 Timothy followed the standard form for greetings in letters. Its content is brief and similar to the greeting in 1 Timothy. The threefold wish for "grace, mercy, and peace" also appears in 1 Timothy but not in any of Paul's other letters.

The Gratitude of Paul (1:3–5)

Paul began this letter, filled with personal exhortations to Timothy, by expressing gratitude for Timothy's faithfulness in ministry.

In most of Paul's letters, he moved from salutation to thanksgiving. But here Paul expressed gratitude for his own spiritual attachment to Timothy, the attachment Timothy had to him, and the indisputable faith of Timothy.

Paul moved from gratitude to an appeal for Timothy to show stamina in Christian work. He called for Timothy to show courage, stamina, and continuing commitment to proper doctrine.

Qualities Needed in Ministry (1:6–18)

Paul urged Timothy to show loyalty despite the hardships he faced. He called upon Timothy to show courage (vv. 6–7) by overcoming the natural hesitancy which seemed to characterize him. He also prepared Timothy for the possibility of suffering (vv. 8–12), by pointing out his own suffering as an incentive to promote steadfastness in Timothy. Paul encouraged Timothy to follow his pattern of teaching (vv. 13–14) and to note the positive example of faithfulness shown by Onesiphorus (vv. 15–18). This positive incentive was an important factor in Paul's efforts to encourage Timothy.

Images of Effective Ministry (2:1–7)

Paul used illustrations from daily life to describe the qualities needed for effective Christian service. He urged Timothy to select reliable leaders who would receive the truths which he had learned from Paul (2:1–2). He encouraged Timothy to endure hardship like a soldier with the single-minded goal of pleasing his commanding officer (2:3–4). He directed Timothy to demonstrate the stamina and discipline of an athlete (2:5). Paul used the analogy of a hardworking farmer to show that the one who worked hard has the first claim on the fruits of the work. This final illustration strengthened the expectation of recognition from God for a job faithfully done.

Truths that Promote Effective Ministry (2:8–13)

Paul presented three truths to encourage ministerial excellence.

1. He reminded Timothy that Jesus Christ was God's resurrected Messiah (v. 8).

2. He reminded Timothy that all the hardship he endured assisted God's people in obtaining their salvation. Timothy was to copy Paul in maintaining such an unrelenting purpose.

3. He reminded Timothy of the certainty of reward from God for faithful living.

In 1:6–2:13 Paul appealed for Timothy to display stamina in Christian service. The focus will now shift to the need for doctrinal soundness as the stubborn false teachers Timothy encountered in his ministry are described.

Confrontation of False Teaching and Living (2:14–26)

Timothy's clash with error is much less obvious in 2 Timothy than in 1 Timothy. Nevertheless, Paul knew that error still lurked in the background among those with whom Timothy worked. Thus, he urged Timothy to take the lead in opposing falsehood by warning of the dangers from heresy and exposing its errors (2:14–19). He then advised Timothy to avoid the evil influence of false teachers by refusing to learn their teaching (2:20–21). Finally, he directed Timothy to respond to error by avoiding contentious debates and by trying to teach the truth to those false teachers willing to listen (2:22–26).

The Stubborn Character of the False Teachers (3:1–9)

Paul wanted Timothy to understand the stubbornness and deceitfulness of the heretics he opposed. He pictured these false teachers as self-centered, loveless, conceited, and pretentious. He warned Timothy to avoid the actions and attitudes of false teachers (3:1–5). He also described the methods they used to spread their views. These false teachers were men who worked primarily among gullible women. Their opposition to God sprang from their depraved natures (3:6–9).

Sources of Strength for Endurance (3:10–17)

How could Timothy hold up under the relentless onslaught of such powerful purveyors of false teaching? Paul proposed that Timothy would be encouraged by observing his example in facing numerous persecutions, hardships, and difficulties. Timothy should count on persecution as the expected experience for believers (3:10–13). Paul also directed Timothy to experience the nurture Scripture could give him (3:14–17). Timothy's ongoing response to the promises and directives of Scripture could make him a godly man prepared for any ministry to which God might call him.

Charge for Consistent Behavior (4:1–5)

In this section Paul continued his emphasis on doctrinal soundness which began in 2:14. He directed Timothy to continue declaring the gospel message with patience and care. Paul knew the time would come when some of Timothy's hearers would pay more attention to novelty and error than they would the truth. In these difficult situations Timothy was to remain alert and carry out his responsibilities.

Reward for Self-Sacrifice (4:6–8)

In the closing section of 2 Timothy, Paul revealed his expectation of approaching death and explained the sacrifice of his life and energies for Christian service. He expected divine recognition for the service he had rendered.

Personal Appeals from Paul to Timothy (4:9–18)

Paul requested Timothy to visit him (v. 9), to bring Mark with him (v. 11), and to bring Paul's cloak and books (v. 13). He warned Timothy of the strong opposition Alexander the metalworker had shown in the past (vv. 14–15). He reminded Timothy of the magnificent strength God provides to his people in their trouble and hardship (vv. 16–18).

Conclusion (4:19–22)

Paul concluded with a personal greeting to his faithful friends Priscilla and Aquila (v. 19). He shared information with Timothy about mutual friends and sent greetings to Timothy from other Christians. Paul included a closing benediction in verse 22.

Outline of 2 Timothy

   I. Salutation (1:1–2)

  II. Gratitude of Paul (1:3–5)

 III. Appeals for Stamina in Ministry (1:6–2:13)

     A. Qualities needed in ministry (1:6–18)

       1. Call for courage (1:6–7)

       2. Readiness to suffer (1:8–12)

3. Imitation of Paul's example (1:13–14)
4. Incentive for faithfulness (1:15–18)

B. Images of effectiveness in ministry (2:1–7)

1. Teacher (2:1–2)
2. Soldier (2:3–4)
3. Athlete (2:5)
4. Farmer (2:6)
5. Application (2:7)

C. Truths that promote effectiveness in ministry (2:8–13)

1. Correct understanding of Christ (2:8)
2. Goal of Paul's suffering (2:9–10)
3. Certainty of reward (2:11–13)

IV. Appeals for Doctrinal Soundness (2:14–4:8)

A. Confronting false teaching and living (2:14–26)

1. Resist the false teachers (2:14–19)
2. Appeal for separation (2:20–21)
3. Respond to error (2:22–26)

B. The stubborn character of the false teachers (3:1–9)

1. What they are (3:1–5)
2. What they do (3:6–9)

C. Sources of strength for endurance (3:10–17)

1. Example of Paul (3:10–13)
2. Enrichment of Scripture (3:14–17)

D. Charge for consistent behavior (4:1–5)

1. Basis of the charge (4:1)
2. Timothy's charge for ministry (4:2)
3. Reason for the charge (4:3–4)
4. Timothy's personal charge (4:5)

E. Reward for self–sacrifice (4:6–8)

1. Sacrifice of life (4:6)
2. Service of ministry (4:7)
3. Reward for obedience (4:8)

V. Personal Appeals from Paul to Timothy (4:9–18)

A. Requests and warnings (4:9–15)
B. Reminder of God's delivering power (4:16–18)

VI. Conclusion (4:19–22)
  A. Greetings to friends (4:19)
  B. Information about mutual friends (4:20)
  C. Final request and greetings to Timothy (4:21)
  D. Benediction (4:22)

Content of Titus

Salutation (1:1–4)

The salutation followed the general form of Paul's other letters. In addition, Paul included a lengthy section describing the scope and nature of God's redemptive plan, a feature not always present in the salutations in his other letters. Paul greeted Titus with phrases similar to those he used for Timothy in 1 Timothy 1:2.

Directions for Appointing Church Leaders (1:5–16)

Paul had left Titus on Crete to work through some of the difficulties in the Christian church there. He identified the qualifications of elders or overseers of the church (1:5–9). The Cretan church needed upright, mature leaders because of the deceitful, stubborn opponents they faced among the false teachers (1:10–16). Driven by a desire for gain, these false teachers were spreading their errors widely. The false teaching spread by these teachers consisted of Jewish myths (v. 14).

Instructions for Teaching Groups Within the Church (2:1–10)

Paul focused on five groups in the Cretan church who needed instructions.

1. He urged Titus to teach the older men to persevere in upright living.

2. Titus was to instruct the older women to be worthy examples for the younger women.

3. The younger women were to be encouraged to love their husbands and children and to accomplish needed domestic responsibilities.

4. Titus was to teach the younger men to show self-control in every area.

5. Titus was to urge slaves to be obedient to their owners and to work honestly in order to make the Christian life-style attractive to all.

A Theological Foundation for Christian Living (2:11–15)

Paul named three factors that inspired committed Christian living.

1. The grace of God (v. 11). A knowledge of divine grace does not promote carelessness but disciplined, self-controlled living.

2. The blessed hope for Christ's return (vv. 12–13). The knowledge of Christ's return provided an incentive for alert commitment to Christ.

3. The position of Christians as God's special people (v. 14). Recognition of this special relationship should motivate believers to be eager to obey God.

Christian Standards of Behavior (3:1–11)

Paul began this section with an insistence on Christian submission to governmental authorities and an emphasis on considerate conduct toward all people (3:1–2).

Paul described two incentives to encourage believers to express their new relationship to Christ.

1. He suggested that the kindness and love of God in rescuing Christians from an aimless existence should produce full commitment (3:3–4).

2. He focused on the renewal authored by the Holy Spirit in regeneration as a source of strength for holy living (3:5–7).

He warned the Cretans to avoid empty discussions about insignificant issues. He encouraged them to confront false teachers who troubled their churches but to avoid them if they persisted in their wrong practices (3:9–11).

Conclusion (3:12–15)

Paul informed Titus that he was sending Artemas or Tychicus to him and that he wanted Titus to spend the winter with him in Nicopolis (v. 12). He encouraged Titus to show Christian hospitality to traveling Christians who were presently on the island of Crete (vv. 13–14). He closed with personal greetings to his disciple and an expression of grace (v. 15).

Outline of Titus

I. Salutation (1:1–4)
  A. Author (1:1–3)
  B. Recipient (1:4a)
  C. Greeting (1:4b)

II. Directions for Appointing Church Leaders (1:5–16)
  A. Qualifications for church leaders on Crete (1:5–9)
  B. False teachers on Crete (1:10–16)
    1. Nature of the false teachers (1:10, 12, 14–16)
    2. Method of spreading false teaching (1:11)
    3. Method of resisting false teaching (1:13)

III. Instructions for Teaching Groups in the Church (2:1–10)
  A. Older men (2:1–2)
  B. Older women (2:3)
  C. Younger women (2:4–5)
  D. Younger men (2:6–8)
  E. Slaves (2:9–10)

IV. Theological Foundations for Christian Living (2:11–15)
  A. Understanding the grace of God (2:11–12)
  B. Expecting the return of Christ (2:13)
  C. Living as God's special people (2:14–15)

V. Christian Standards of Behavior (3:1–11)
  A. Toward rulers and other believers (3:1–2)
  B. Motivation of divine mercy (3:3–4)
  C. Strength supplied in the new birth (3:5–8)
  D. Avoiding divisive issues and people (3:9–11)

VI. Conclusion (3:12–15)

A. Instructions for Titus (3:12–14)
B. Greetings to Titus (3:15)

For Further Discussion

1. Explain the difference between Paul's directions for dealing with false teachers in 2 Timothy 2:24–26 and Titus 3:10.

2. Analyze the role of women in the church today on the basis of Paul's discussion in 1 Timothy 2:11–15.

3. To what extent are churches today obligated to reproduce the church organization described in 1 Timothy 3:1–13?

4. Some have accused Paul of being stubborn and inflexible in his desire to maintain orthodoxy in the Pastorals. How would you respond to this charge?

Bibliography

Barrett, C. K. *The Pastoral Epistles*. NCLB. Oxford: Clarendon Press, 1963.

Carson, D. A., Douglas J. Moo, and Leon Morris. *An Introduction to the New Testament*. Grand Rapids: Zondervan Books, 1992.

Coleman, Lyman, and Richard Peace. *Pastor/Teacher Commentary for 1 & 2 Timothy*. Littleton, Colo.: Serendipity, 1988. Guidance for leading group Bible study of the Pastorals.

_____. *Study Guide for the Book of 1 & 2 Timothy*. Littleton, Colo.: Serendipity, 1988.

Dibelius, Martin, and Hans Conzelmann. *The Pastoral Epistles*. Hermenia. Philadelphia: Fortress Press, 1972.

Ellis, E. E. "The Pastorals and Paul." *ExpTim* 104 (November 1992): 45–47.

Fee, Gordon D. *1 and 2 Timothy, Titus*. NIBC. Peabody, Mass.: Hendrickson, 1988. Excellent exegetical commentary on the Pastorals.

Guthrie, Donald. *The Pastoral Epistles*. TNTC. 2d ed. Grand Rapids: William B. Eerdmans Publishing Co., 1990. Brief exegetical commentary on the Pastorals.

Harrison, P. N. *The Problem of the Pastoral Epistles*. London: Oxford University Press, 1921.

Kelly, J. N. D. *A Commentary on the Pastoral Epistles*. London: Adam and Charles Black, 1963. Reprint, Grand Rapids: Baker, Thornapple Commentaries, 1981.

Knight, George W. *The Pastoral Epistles*. NIGTC. Grand Rapids: William B. Eerdmans Publishing Co., 1992. Thorough exegetical commentary on the Greek text of the Pastorals.

Lea, Thomas D., and Hayne P. Griffin. *1, 2 Timothy, Titus*. NAC. Nashville, Tenn.: Broadman & Holman Publishers, 1992.

Longenecker, R. N., and M. C. Tenney, eds. *New Dimensions in New Testament Study*. Grand Rapids: Zondervan Books, 1974.

Metzger, Bruce. "A Reconsideration of Certain Arguments Against the Pauline Authorship of the Pastoral Epistles." *ExpTim* 70 (1958):93–94.

Moo, D. J. "1 Timothy 2:11–15: Meaning and Significance." *TJ* n.s. 1(1980):62–83.

Moule, C. F. D. *Essays in New Testament Interpretation*. Cambridge: Cambridge University Press, 1982.

Oden, Thomas C. *First and Second Timothy and Titus*. Int. Louisville, Ky.: John Knox Press, 1989.

Payne, P. B. "Libertarian Women in Ephesus: A Response to Douglas J. Moo's Article: 1 Timothy 2:11–15: Meaning and Significance." *TJ* n.s. 2(1981):169–97.

Spicq, C. *Les Epitres Pastorales*. 4th ed. rev. Paris: Gabalda, 1969. Thorough exegesis and discussion of critical problems of the Pastorals by a French Catholic who supports Pauline authorship.

Stott, John R. W. *The Message of 2 Timothy*. BST. Downers Grove, Ill.: InterVarsity Press, 1973. Guidelines for exposition of 2 Timothy.

Ward, Ronald. *Commentary on 1 & 2 Timothy & Titus*. Waco, Tex.: Word Inc., 1974.

Winter, Bruce. "*Providentia* for the Widows of 1 Timothy 5:3–16." *TynBul* 39 (1988): 83–99.

19 The Epistle to the Hebrews

Guiding Questions

1. Present evidence for and against the chief candidates for the authorship of Hebrews.

2. Show how the writer of Hebrews explains the theme, "the superiority of Jesus."

3. Explain the purpose for writing Hebrews.

4. Explain why the author of Hebrews refers to Melchizedek (Heb. 7:1–3).

The New Testament writings from Hebrews through Jude are not addressed to specific locations (except for 2 and 3 John). The Epistle to the Hebrews has no specific address or salutation, but takes its name from the traditional addressees. The letters including James, 1 and 2 Peter, 1, 2, and 3 John, and Jude are called the general or catholic Epistles. This is because they are not addressed to a specific location. These letters are named after the author who is identified in the writing as in James, 1 and 2 Peter, and Jude, or is traditionally associated with the letter such as in 1, 2, 3 John.

Authorship

Hebrews is an anonymous epistle because the author is not named. The readers of the book obviously knew who the writer was, but the name has not been preserved for us.[1]

The early church was uncertain about the author of this anonymous letter. Eastern Christendom usually regarded Paul as the author, while western Christendom doubted Pauline authorship, and initially excluded Hebrews from the canon because of this uncertainty. Later leaders in the West such as Jerome and Augustine accepted Pauline authorship. Their influence eventually led the West to accept Hebrews into the canon.

Several doctrinal similarities between Hebrews and the Pauline Epistles can be identified. Among these similarities favoring Pauline authorship, are:

1. the work of Christ in creation (Heb. 1:2; Col. 1:16);

2. the humiliation of Christ in the Incarnation and Crucifixion (Heb. 2:14–17; Phil. 2:5–8);

3. the place of the new covenant (Heb. 8:6; 2 Cor. 3:4–11);

4. the work of the Holy Spirit in distributing gifts (Heb. 2:4; 1 Cor. 12:11);

5. the negative example of Israel's conduct during the wilderness wanderings (Heb. 3:7–11; 4:6–11; 1 Cor. 10:1–11).

In addition to doctrinal similarities, the conclusion of the letter contains several elements suggesting Pauline authorship. The reference to a clear conscience and request for personal prayer (13:18) are similar to statements of Paul in Romans 15:30 and Acts 23:1. The reference to God as the God of peace (Heb. 13:20) is similar to the statement in 1 Thessalonians 5:23. The reference to Timothy in 13:23 sounds more like a statement from Paul than from any

---

1. The use of the first person plural (2:1–4; 4:14–16) suggests that both the writer and the readers shared certain experiences in common. The statements in 6:9–11; 10:25, 32–34 suggest that the writer knew intimate details about the spiritual lives of the readers. The statement in 13:23 suggests that the readers knew the identity of the writer who was planning to visit them. The request for prayer in 13:19 also suggests that the readers knew the writer.

other writer. Some of the suggested similarities carry more weight for supporting Pauline authorship than others.

Differences between Paul and Hebrews are also apparent. For example, the conduct of Israel is characterized as "unbelief" (Heb. 3:19) in Hebrews, but Paul places more emphasis on the idolatry and licentiousness of the people (1 Cor. 10:7–8). These differences in emphasis weaken arguments used to support Pauline authorship.

Other considerations that make Pauline authorship unlikely include:

1. The anonymity of Hebrews. None of Paul's other writings is anonymous.

2. The appeal for authority to those who were eyewitnesses of Jesus' ministry (Heb. 2:3). As an apostle Paul insisted that he had not obtained his gospel from others (Gal. 1:1, 11–12).

3. The classical style of Greek in Hebrews. Paul normally used a simpler form of Greek than is found in Hebrews.

4. The emphasis in Hebrews on Jesus as our great high priest (4:14–16) is absent from Paul's writings.

5. Old Testament quotations in Hebrews are regularly taken from the LXX, but Paul does not always follow this practice.

Even when the Western church accepted Hebrews into the canon of Scripture, it continued to express doubts about Pauline authorship. The Council of Hippo (A.D. 393) and the Third Council of Carthage (A.D. 397) listed thirteen epistles authored by Paul and added: "Of the same to the Hebrews, one." In this way they put Hebrews in a different category even as they affirmed the possibility of Pauline authorship. After the Sixth Council of Carthage (A.D. 419), it became routine to accept fourteen letters as Pauline without separating Hebrews for special recognition.

During the Reformation, Calvin argued that Clement of Rome or Luke wrote Hebrews. Luther proposed Apollos. Virtually no New Testament scholar today supports Pauline authorship.

Some have suggested Barnabas as the author of Hebrews. His Levitical background (Acts 4:36) would explain the presence of interest in priestly functions found in Hebrews. The relationship between Barnabas and Paul could explain similarities in theology.

The African Christian father Tertullian championed Barnabas as a candidate for authorship. Weakening the argument for authorship by Barnabas, however, is the fact that Barnabas probably heard and saw Jesus. The author of Hebrews suggested that he depended on others for his testimony about Jesus (2:3). It also is difficult to explain how the name of a leader as well known as Barnabas could have been lost if he were the author of Hebrews. The lack of early references to Barnabas is a major hindrance in accepting him as the writer.

Luke is a candidate for authorship because of the similarities in the polished Greek of Hebrews and Luke-Acts. But, since Luke is a Gentile, it is less likely that he would write with the Jewish outlook of Hebrews.

Luther's suggestion of Apollos, who was acquainted with Paul (1 Cor. 16:12), would explain similarities to Pauline thought in Hebrews. His reputation for eloquence (Acts 18:24–28) would explain how he could have written in the polished literary style of Hebrews. As a native of Alexandria he may also have used the LXX in Old Testament quotations. The LXX was produced in Alexandria. Weakening the argument for authorship by Apollos is the lack of early tradition favoring him.[2]

Adolf Harnack, eminent German scholar of the nineteenth century, suggested Priscilla as the author of Hebrews because of her close ties with Paul. He argued that she wrote the letter anonymously because authorship by a woman would have been unacceptable to the early church. There is little external evidence to support this thesis. The reference by the writer to himself (11:32), using the masculine participle of the word "tell," makes authorship by Priscilla unlikely.

It is best to admit that we do not know the identity of the author of Hebrews. The third-century Christian leader Origen was correct when he stated, "Who wrote the epistle, in truth, God

---

2. Qualified contemporary support for Apollos comes from Luke Johnson, who says, "The suggestion (that Apollos wrote Hebrews) . . . has just enough piquancy not to be dismissed entirely." Johnson suggests that authorship of Hebrews by Apollos could explain connections between Hebrews and 1 Corinthians. See Johnson, *The Writings of the New Testament*, 416. Johnson's theory is similar to views advocated earlier by Hugh Montefiore, *A Commentary on the Epistle to the Hebrews*, HNTC (New York: Harper and Row Publishers Inc., 1964).

knows."[3] Our failure to decide on this issue, however, does not diminish the value of the book or its authority. Regardless of the identity of the author, God still speaks forcefully through the message of Hebrews.

Destination

The heading of Hebrews in Greek reads "To the Hebrews." Considerable evidence supports the idea that Hebrews was written to Jewish Christians. The frequent appeals to the Old Testament, the presumption that the readers knew Jewish ritual (see Hebrews 9), the warning against returning to Judaism (see Heb. 6:1–2), and the early tradition for the title point to the Jews as the intended recipients.

Some, however, maintain that Hebrews was originally addressed to Gentiles. The polished Greek and the extensive use of the LXX are used to support this viewpoint. However, these features do not communicate any insight about the readers; they only indicate the background of the author. Hebrews does not refer to the temple (as distinguished from the tabernacle in the wilderness). This fact plus the references to the LXX make it likely that the readers did not live in Palestine. Jews in Palestine would have an interest in events surrounding the temple and would also show more interest in Hebrew or Aramaic than the Greek of the LXX.

Where did the readers live? The suggestion in 2:3 that the readers had not seen or heard Jesus during his earthly ministry make it less likely that they were Palestinians. Also, the statement in 6:10 suggests that the recipients of the epistle had assisted poverty-stricken Christians, but Palestinian Christians were poor and normally received aid from others (Acts 11:27–30; Rom. 15:26; 2 Corinthians 8–9). The statement in 13:24, "Those from Italy send you their greetings," implies that those away from their native Italy are sending greetings back to their home, likely in Rome.[4] The fact that the evidence for the knowledge of

---

3. Eusebius, *Church History* 6.25.14.

4. In fairness, it should be observed that Heb. 13:24 can also be interpreted to suggest that Christians then residing in Italy were sending greetings to other believers outside the country.

Hebrews first appeared in Rome also supports the likelihood of a Roman destination.[5]

Although we cannot select Rome as the destination with great certainty, among the options it is an intelligent guess.[6] Fortunately, the interpretation and value of Hebrews is not dependent on determining the specific destination of the letter.

Purpose

The question of the purpose of Hebrews is closely linked to the identity of the recipients. All agree that the book is written for Christians who are being urged to continue their profession (Heb. 3:6, 14).

The extensive references to the Old Testament could be used in relation to Gentile believers who had made a careful study of the Scriptures. Some scholars suggest that the warning against turning "away from the living God" (3:12) could be directed to former pagans who were now in danger of committing apostasy. However, most scholars have not felt that these warnings were addressed to Gentiles. The fact that the writer mentions the generation of Israelites under Moses' leadership in this passage (3:12) seems to relate the warning to first-century Jews. The "elementary teachings" of 6:1 presuppose a background in Judaism. The insistence that the new covenant has superseded the old (Hebrews 8) makes more sense if applied to Jewish recipients.

Some who favor a Jewish audience have attempted to identify a specific group of Jews to whom the author might have written. Some have contended that the readers consisted of a group of converted Jewish priests (Acts 6:7) or former members of the Qumran community. However, none of these specific identifications seems viable among New Testament scholars.

The author wrote about the readers as if he knew them well. He described their generosity (6:10), their persecution (10:32–34;

---

5. Clement of Rome, toward the close of the first century A.D., referred to Hebrews in his *First Epistle of Clement*. Some of his most moving references use the language of Hebrews to describe the blessings available through Christ. See *First Epistle of Clement* 36.

6. A convincing defense of the Roman destination for Hebrews appears in William Manson, *The Epistle to the Hebrews: An Historical and Theological Reconsideration* (London: Hodder & Stoughton, 1951), 159–97.

12:4), their immaturity (5:11–6:12), and his hope of visiting them (13:19, 23). He rebuked them for not meeting together enough (10:25). It is possible that the author wrote to a group of Jewish Christians who had broken off from a body of Christians in their locality and no longer met with them. They could have broken away and contemplated returning to Judaism to avoid persecution and harassment. The author wrote to warn them against apostasy (10:26–31) and to bring them back into orthodox Christianity.

Date

Determining an exact date for the writing of Hebrews is an impossibility, but certain indicators suggest that the book was written prior to A.D. 70. The reference to Timothy in 13:23, if this is Paul's younger companion, requires a date in Timothy's lifetime. The reference in 10:1–2 to the sacrifices in the Jewish temple seems to imply clearly that sacrifices were still being offered. Although the writer does not specifically refer to the temple, he probably would not have made these comments if the temple had been destroyed.

The author used the present tense in 7:8; 9:6–7, 9, 13; and 13:10 to describe the rituals of the sacrifices. Some understand this verb tense as evidence that the temple was still standing. Although the temple might still have been standing, this argument has shortcomings. First, other authors writing after the temple's destruction used the present tense to describe temple ritual. Here the use of the present tense does not primarily suggest time but serves as a vivid description of temple activity. Second, the author of Hebrews is obviously discussing the tabernacle rather than the temple, and his use of the present tense has little relationship to the debate about whether or not the temple had been destroyed at the time he was writing.

Whatever date we accept, we must place the letter prior to A.D. 95, the approximate date for *First Clement*. The use of Hebrews by Clement indicates that the author must have written it prior to this time.

Any date between A.D. 60 and 95 is possible. Most of the evidence, however, points to a time of writing prior to A.D. 70.

Literary Form

Letters in the New Testament period began with specific salutations and concluded with benedictions and farewells. They were written to meet needs in the life of the church. Hebrews has some, but not all, of these characteristics.

The letter begins without a salutation and omits the naming of the author and addressees. The book concludes with a benediction, some personal observations, and a farewell (13:20–25).

The oratorical style and remarks such as "I do not have time to tell" (11:32) suggest a sermon or a general address. The statement in 13:22, "I have written to you briefly," suggests a letter written in the style of a sermon. Also, the specific nature of the warnings and moral appeals in the book (2:1–4; 5:11–6:10; 10:32–34) suggest that the author wrote for circumstances clearly known to him. It is best to view this document as a letter, but the author may have used portions of sermons or addresses to complete the writing.[7]

Special Characteristics

The Greek used in Hebrews has high literary qualities and reflects an elegant vocabulary. It also makes frequent allusions to and quotations from the Old Testament. Some passages such as Psalm 110:1, 4 appear repeatedly (1:13; 6:20; 7:17, 21; 10:12–13). The quotations do not serve as mere confirmations of the author's opinions; they provide the foundation for the presentation itself.

The Christology of Hebrews is incredibly rich and varied. Over twenty titles or names are used for Christ. Both the humanity and the deity of Christ are emphasized in Hebrews.

A group of five warnings appear in the argument of Hebrews. These warnings are found in 2:1–4; 3:7–4:13; 5:11–6:20; 10:26–39; and 12:15–29. The writer is anxious that his listeners pay special attention to the voice of the living God. Most of the warnings deal

---

7. Adolf Deissmann distinguished between the letter and the epistle. He viewed the letter as a more informal communication written for a specific purpose and the epistle as a more formal expression for general literary circulation. Although Hebrews has some characteristics Deissmann sees present in epistles, it is best to view it as a letter. For further information about Deissmann's views, see the discussion in "Paul as a Letter Writer" in chapter 14.

with the danger of neglecting the salvation in Christ or missing out on it because of unbelief, apostasy, or compromise.

Content

The author focused on the superiority of Christ throughout Hebrews. He showed that Christ was superior to the Old Testament prophets, to angels, to Moses and Joshua, and to the Old Testament priesthood. His aim was to warn his readers that those who abandoned Christianity to return to Judaism were forsaking a religion that offered superior benefits and promises, and they were trading Christianity for a religion that lacked hope, failed to lead to a deep knowledge of God, and could not provide the power for holy living.

The Superiority of Christ to the Prophets (1:1–3)

The revelation of God given through Christ is both superior and final. The majestic descriptions of Jesus given by the writer in these verses implied that in both quality and quantity God had no more revelation to give other than what he had given in Jesus. God could say nothing better than he said in Jesus.

The writer asserted that Christ was superior to the Old Testament prophets because he was the Son of God, the Heir of the universe, the Creator, the Radiance of divine glory, the Sustainer of the universe, the Redeemer from sin, and the Exalted One. Christ is God's final and most complete message to human beings.

The Superiority of Christ to Angels (1:4–2:18)

Jewish readers would have had a high regard for angels. The writer demonstrated that Christ was superior to angelic messengers by making several points.

- The writer contrasted Jesus with angels (1:5–14). He described Jesus as the Son and as the Creator who himself received worship from the angels. Angels were God's servants, created beings, and spirits who ministered to believers (v. 14).

- The author presented the first exhortation to remain faithful to Christ (2:1–4). His argument moved from the lesser to the greater. If the giving of the law in the Old Testament (v. 2) led its violators to be punished, how much greater will be the punishment for those who neglect the great salvation in Christ.

- The writer admitted that in the Incarnation Jesus had briefly become "lower than the angels" (2:9). The Incarnation resulted in two benefits for believers. First, the death and resurrection of Jesus made it possible for all believers to overcome the fear of death (2:14–15). Second, because the incarnate Christ suffered and overcame temptation, he is able to help believers when they are tempted (2:18).

The Superiority of Christ to Moses and Joshua (3:1–4:13)

The author of Hebrews contrasted Moses and Joshua with Christ and clearly proved the superiority of Christ to both of these men and their ministries. He also mentioned the unbelief shown by the Jewish generations in the time of Moses and Joshua and warned his readers not to follow their evil example.

In comparing Jesus to Moses, the writer pointed out that Moses was a servant of God *in* God's house, that is, among the people of God. In contrast, however, Jesus was God's son serving *over* that house. The superiority of Jesus' position is obvious (3:5–6).

Joshua led the Jews of his generation to rest in Canaan. Jesus, however, brought the people of God into a resting place that provided eternal spiritual benefits (4:1–10). The superiority of the destination provided by Jesus is again obvious.

The writer was aware that a crisis faced his readers just as the Jews in the lifetime of Moses and Joshua confronted crises. He warned that unbelief could prevent them from entering a relationship of promise just as it had in an earlier generation. The problem earlier was unbelief (3:18; 4:11), and he wanted his readers to avoid the spiritual defeat caused by unbelief.

The Superiority of Christ's Work (4:14–10:18)

The writer of Hebrews focused on three features of Christ's work that revealed his superiority.

1. He pointed to the superior priesthood of Christ (4:14–7:28).

2. He explained the superior covenant Christ founded in relationship to human beings (8:1–13).

3. He described the superior sacrifice Christ offered for our redemption (9:1–10:18).

The Superior Priesthood of Christ (4:14–7:28). The unknown author described Jesus as a great high priest who had entered the very presence of God (4:14). Jesus offers an unrestricted supply of grace to anyone who will acknowledge a need for it and claim it (4:15–16).

The writer began by outlining two similarities between Christ as high priest and the priests after Aaron. Both showed the ability to understand sympathetically the needs of human beings before God (5:1–3; 7–10). Both were called by God to carry out their work (5:4–6).

In 5:11–6:20 he issued his most serious warning against committing apostasy and turning away from Christ. He described his readers as immature and urged them to move beyond spiritual infancy into maturity (5:11–12; 6:1–2). He warned that if they finally renounced Christ, they would forfeit all hope of eternal salvation (6:3–6). He reminded his readers that they had borne fruit which demonstrated salvation, but he wanted them to avoid becoming lazy and careless in their Christian profession (6:7–12).[8]

The author pointed out two features that proved the superiority of the priesthood of Jesus over that of the Aaronic priests. First, Christ became a high priest by a divine oath which established him in a new priestly order, the order of Melchizedek (7:11–22).[9]

---

8. For additional discussion of this problem passage see the section below entitled "The Exegesis of Hebrews 6:4–12."

9. Melchizedek is a little-known Old Testament figure whose story appears in Gen. 14:18–20 with a later reference in Ps. 110:4. He is a historical personality, whose life illustrates or typifies several truths about Christ. First, the name of Melchizedek, meaning "King of Righteousness," typifies Christ. Second, the absence in the Old Testament of an account of his birth and death typifies the eternal nature of Christ (Heb. 7:3). Third, Melchizedek's receiving a tithe of battle spoils from Abraham and blessing him in return typifies the greatness of Christ over Aaron. The fact that the priestly Levites descended ultimately from Abraham showed that the priesthood of Melchizedek was superior to that of the Aaronic priests (Heb. 7:9–10). Since Melchizedek is a type of Christ, Christ himself becomes superior to the Aaronic priesthood.

Second, Christ's own personal superiority to the Aaronic priests made him more significant than they were (7:23–28). Christ was an eternal priest, but the priests of Aaron died and required successors to follow them. Christ was also sinless, but the priests of Aaron were sinners.

The Superior Covenant of Christ (8:1–13). The covenant of Christ was superior in three areas.

1. The new covenant offered an internalization of the law. God wrote the law in the hearts and minds of his people (8:10).

2. Christ's covenant provided a new, direct knowledge of God (8:11).

3. The new covenant promised complete forgiveness of sin (8:12).

The Superior Sacrifice of Christ (9:1–10:18). The author of Hebrews shared several effects of Christ's sacrifice to demonstrate its superiority. The death of Christ was more effective than the sacrifices offered by the Aaronic priests because Christ's sacrifice cleansed the conscience, brought forgiveness, and dealt with heavenly realities, not mere earthly symbols (9:11–28). Christ's sacrifice was also superior because he offered himself voluntarily in a never-to-be-repeated death (10:1–14). The fact that Aaronic priests regularly repeated animal sacrifices showed that these sacrifices could not remove sin.

Exhortations to Obedient Living (10:19–13:25)

The superiority of Christ resulted in an appeal to endure because of the excellencies of Jesus (10:19–39). The faith of earlier believers was a living example to be imitated (11:1–40). The example of Christ provided stamina to lead believers to endure hardship and opposition (12:1–17). The majestic nature of the new covenant introduced by Christ could produce such reverence and awe that believers would serve Christ faithfully (12:18–29). The writer concluded with a collection of exhortations to his readers that affected their social life, home life, religious life, and their relationship to church leaders (13:1–25).

In 10:19–39 the writer urged his readers to draw near to God and to experience fellowship with one another without neglecting corporate fellowship (10:19–25). Those who openly repudiate their Christian profession will fall into the hands of the living God (10:26–31). He noted that their own past experiences had taught them the need for endurance in their profession of commitment (10:32–39).

In 11:1–3 the author described the nature of faith as a conviction of certainty about what we do not see. This kind of faith motivated the godly men and women of the past to move toward the promises even though they did not inherit them (11:4–40).

As incentives for enduring hardships, the author mentioned the example of Jesus (12:1–3) and the benevolent discipline of God (12:4–11). He described the dramatic circumstances under which the Old Covenant began, but he presented Jesus as the mediator of a new and better covenant (12:18–29). He noted that the character of God resembled a consuming fire in order to promote holiness and fear in the readers.

In his closing exhortations, the writer urged his readers to show mutual love in their social life and purity in their married lives (13:1–6). In their religious life, they were to serve the unchanging Christ (13:7–9). In their worship of God, they were to offer praise and unselfish service to others (13:10–16). In his concluding words, the writer called for obedience to congregational leaders, requested prayer for himself, commended Timothy to their hospitality, and offered a benediction (13:17–25).

The Exegesis of Hebrews 6:4–12

This difficult passage is a battleground for exegetes. On the surface it appears to suggest that believers can commit apostasy or turn against the Christ whom they have professed. Is this a possibility? Does the writer of Hebrews say that a saved person can become lost? Let us explore these questions.

First, note the word "impossible." The writer of Hebrews used the adjective impossible at least three other times in Hebrews (6:18; 10:4; 11:6). In each passage he described an issue in an absolute sense. The statement suggests that a compromise in ideas is impossible. The fulfillment of this impossibility depends on several other events mentioned in vv. 4–6.

The terms "enlightened," "tasted" (used twice, in v. 4 and in v. 5), and "shared" suggest someone who has professed Christ. The term "taste" describes a full profession of salvation. To share in the Holy Spirit describes one who has professed to be a believer. All of these terms refer to someone who claims to be a believer.

The term "fall away" refers to committing apostasy. Individuals who fall away cannot be brought back to Christ because they are openly disgracing Christ by their actions and are trying to recrucify the Son of God, an act which is impossible (see Heb. 10:12).

In 6:7–8 the writer illustrated the statements of 6:4–6 by contrasting fruitful and unfruitful soil. Unproductive soil can expect judgment. Unproductive professing believers can also expect judgment.

In 6:9–12 the writer assured the readers that he was confident they would persevere in their faith. Their previous compassion and love for others demonstrated the reality of their faith. The author indicated that he did not want his readers to become lazy or listless but to endure in their commitment.

Can believers actually lose their salvation? Professing believers can appear to lose their salvation. If they abandon the faith they profess, the consequences are severe (10:26–31). However, the moment professing believers abandon Christianity, they reveal that their faith was not real. The distinctive evidence of true Christianity is endurance (3:14).[10]

A true believer will not abandon Christianity. True believers will endure in their commitment to Christ because God will preserve them by his power (1 Pet. 1:5).

The author of Hebrews was not dealing primarily with the question of the endurance of believers in their faith. He was dealing with the life-style of his readers. He wanted them to know that the consequences of abandoning Christianity were quite serious. If they turned from Christ, they would not find salvation anywhere

---

10. For additional discussion of the exegesis of this passage, see Donald A. Hagner, *Hebrews*, NIBC (Peabody, Mass.: Hendrickson Publishers Inc., 1990): 90–96. Hagner refers to the statement of 1 John 2:19 to illustrate that those who abandon Christianity show that they never were believers. John pointed out that those who left the fellowship had never been among the believers (p. 92).

else. He did not feel, however, that they would prove to be apostates.

An Outline of Hebrews

I. The Superiority of Christ's Person (1:1–4:13)

   A. The superiority of Christ to the prophets (1:1–3)

   B. The superiority of Christ to angels (1:4–2:18)

       1. The superiority of Christ's nature (1:4–14)

       2. A warning against neglecting Christ (2:1–4)

       3. The value of Christ's incarnation (2:5–18)

   C. The superiority of Christ to Moses and Joshua (3:1–4:13)

       1. The superiority of Jesus to Moses (3:1–6)

       2. The failure of God's people under Moses (3:7–19)

       3. The superiority of Jesus to Joshua (4:1–8)

       4. The urgency of seeking God's rest (4:9–13)

II. The Superiority of Christ's Work (4:14–10:18)

   A. The superior priesthood demonstrated in Christ (4:14–7:28)

       1. The value of Christ's high priesthood (4:14–16)

       2. The comparison of Christ and Aaron (5:1–10)

       3. The warning against falling away (5:11–6:20)

       4. The Melchizedek order of Christ's priesthood (7:1–28)

   B. The superior covenant introduced by Christ (8:1–13)

   C. The superior sacrifice offered by Christ (9:1–10:18)

       1. A sacrifice that cleanses conscience (9:1–14)

       2. A sacrifice that removes sin (9:15–22)

       3. A sacrifice that affects heavenly realities (9:23–28)

       4. A voluntary sacrifice (10:1–10)

       5. An unrepeatable sacrifice (10:11–18)

III. The Superiority of Christ's Power (10:19–13:25)

   A. An appeal for endurance (10:19–39)

       1. By approaching God through Christ (10:19–25)

       2. By fearing the living God (10:26–31)

       3. By considering past experiences (10:32–39)

   B. The experience of faith (11:1–40)

       1. The nature of faith (11:1–3)

2. Examples of the faithful (11:4–40)
C. The experience of discipline (12:1–13)
   1. The example of Christ (12:1–3)
   2. The purpose of God (12:4–13)
D. Warning against rejecting God (12:14–29)
E. Final exhortations and conclusion (13:1–25)
   1. Exhortations for social life (13:1–3)
   2. Exhortations for home life (13:4–6)
   3. Exhortations for religious life (13:7–9)
   4. Sacrifices that please God (13:10–16)
   5. Obedience to leaders (13:17)
   6. Benediction and conclusion (13:18–25)

For Further Discussion

1. Defend your views on the authorship of Hebrews.

2. Defend your views on the interpretation of Hebrews 6:4–12.

3. How can Christians be assured of their own salvation?

4. Is it necessary to determine the author of Hebrews in order to use it authoritatively? Give reasons for your answer.

Bibliography

Attridge, Harold W. *The Epistle to the Hebrews. Hermenia.* Philadelphia: Fortress Press, 1989.

Brown, Raymond. *The Message of Hebrews.* BST. Downers Grove, Ill.: InterVarsity Press, 1982. Guidelines for the exposition and application of Hebrews.

Bruce, F. F. *Hebrews.* NICNT. Grand Rapids: William B. Eerdmans Publishing Co., 1965.

Guthrie, Donald. *Hebrews.* TNTC. Grand Rapids: William B. Eerdmans Publishing Co., 1993. Brief, exegetical commentary on Hebrews.

Hagner, Donald A. *Hebrews.* NIBC. Peabody, Mass.: Hendrickson Publishers Inc., 1990.

Hughes, Philip Edgcumbe. *A Commentary on the Epistle to the Hebrews.* Grand Rapids: William B. Eerdmans Publishing Co., 1977. Commentary focusing on the theological significance of Hebrews.

Johnson, Luke. *The Writings of the New Testament.* Philadelphia: Fortress Press, 1986.

Lane, William L. *Hebrews*. WBC. 2 vols. Dallas: Word Inc., 1991. Thorough exegetical commentary on Hebrews.

Manson, William. *The Epistle to the Hebrews: An Historical and Theological Reconsideration*. London: Hodder & Stoughton, 1951.

Montefiore, Hugh. *A Commentary on the Epistle to the Hebrews*. HNTC. New York: Harper and Row Publishers Inc., 1964.

20 The Epistle of James

Guiding Questions

1. Which James is the author of this epistle?

2. Describe the purpose for writing the Epistle of James.

3. Contrast Paul's doctrine of faith and work with James 2:14–26.

4. List the issues James discusses in his epistle and the advice he gives concerning each issue.

The Epistle of James emphasizes the practical side of Christianity and includes only overt references to theological issues. James, however, assumes a theological foundation even though he does not explain it at length. His aim is to show that anyone who makes a commitment to Jesus Christ must present moral evidence of that commitment.

Authorship

Two elements emerge from the author's identification of himself in 1:1. First, he must be a prominent, well-known leader named James, since he limited the introduction of himself to his first name and gave no other qualifying features. Second, he reflected Christian humility by identifying himself as "a servant of God and of the Lord Jesus Christ."

Four men named James appear in the New Testament:

1. James, the son of Zebedee and brother of John, who is one of the Twelve Apostles (Mark 1:19; 5:37; 9:2; 10:35; Acts 12:2);

2. James, the son of Alphaeus, also one of the Twelve (Mark 3:18—He may be identical with "James the younger" in Mark 15:40).

3. James, the father of Judas (Luke 6:16; Acts 1:13);[1]

4. James, the Lord's brother (Gal. 1:19; Acts 12:17; 15:13; 21:18).

Of these four, James, the father of Judas, is too shadowy a figure to be considered seriously as the author of the epistle. To a smaller degree this objection is also true of James, the son of Alphaeus, a somewhat insignificant figure among the Twelve. James, the son of Zebedee, held a prominent role among the apostles, but he was martyred quite early—about A.D. 44 (Acts 12:2). The early date of his death removes him from consideration.

The most likely candidate is the Lord's half brother. Several features of the book are consistent with a presumed authorship by this James.

- The epistle contains several references that plainly reflect influence from the teaching of Jesus, especially the Sermon on the Mount (cf. James 4:11 and Matt. 7:1–2; James 1:22 and Matt. 7:24–27). In these and other instances, James did not quote Jesus' words, but he clothed his language with words suggesting that he remembered the oral teachings he had previously heard. We would expect such similarities to appear in a book authored by the Lord's brother.

- The general Jewish atmosphere of the epistle and its frequent references to the Old Testament point to the likeli-

---

1. The expression "Judas son of James" in Luke 6:16 reads more literally "Judas of James." It is an example of a Greek construction known as a genitive of relationship. The construction states a relationship, but it leaves the nature of that relationship to be determined from the context. Most translators feel that the expression should read "Judas son of James," but it could possibly read "Judas brother of James."

hood that it was written by someone from a Jewish background. The author has several direct quotations from the Old Testament (2:8; 4:6), as well as many indirect references to the Old Testament (5:11, 17). The term "Lord of Sabaoth" (5:4) is a phrase that was familiar to the Jews. The reference to God's unity reflects a major Jewish creed (2:19). Such evidence points to a Jewish writer, and we can presume that the Lord's brother is the most viable candidate.

- The early church generally supported the identification of this James as the author. Origen was the earliest Christian writer to refer to this letter as the work of James, the Lord's brother. Eusebius classified the letter among the disputed books, but he referred to it as if it were genuine.[2] We can assume from his evidence that not all the Christians he knew considered it to be genuine. We also can understand that some Christian leaders would find it easy to ignore a letter written by a Jew primarily for Jewish Christians and appearing to contradict Paul's doctrine of justification by faith. (For additional information on this issue, see the discussion of canonicity in this chapter.)

- We find parallels between this epistle and the speech of James in Acts 15. The same Greek word is translated "greeting" in Acts 15:23 and James 1:1. Believers are called "brethren" in James 2:5 and Acts 15:13. The parallels extend even to the use of isolated words.[3] These verbal similarities are not indisputable evidence of authorship by the Lord's brother, but they do support his authorship.

Some scholars today have suggested that the name "James" is a pseudonym.[4] They believe that some early unknown Christian wrote in the name of James. Advocates of this view feel that the unknown author was pointing to James the brother of the Lord,

---

2. Eusebius, *Church History* 2.23.25; 3.25.3.

3. For a more detailed listing of linguistic similarities, see Donald Guthrie, *New Testament Introduction*, 2d ed., vol. 3, *Hebrews to Revelation* (London: Tyndale House Publishers, 1964), 66–67.

4. For a general discussion of this subject, see "The Practice of Pseudonymous Authorship," in chap. 14.

but they claim that the Lord's brother did not write this letter. They point to at least three facts to support their claims.

1. They suggest that the Lord's brother would not have written this epistle without referring to his relationship to Jesus. However, the identification of James as the Lord's brother is always made by someone other than James himself (see Matt. 13:55; Mark 6:3; Gal. 1:19). This fact indicates that the relationship to Jesus was not an important issue for James himself. Also, the author's identification of himself as a "servant . . . of the Lord Jesus Christ" shows his genuine humility.

2. Some support pseudonymity because the discussion of faith and works (James 2:14–26) appears to represent a misunderstanding of Paul's view of the relationship between faith and works. They argue that the Lord's brother would not have been so ignorant of Paul's meaning. However, if James authored the epistle quite early, even before he met Paul, it would be understandable if he did not have a full grasp of Paul's teaching. In later contact with Paul, James could have learned that Paul's view of justification by faith did not lead to moral laxity.[5]

3. Support for pseudonymous authorship comes from the high quality of Greek used in the epistle. Proponents of pseudonymity suggest that a simple Galilean such as James could not have written the literary-style Greek. However, Palestinian Jews, especially those of Galilee, lived in bilingual areas and needed to know Greek as well as Hebrew. James could have developed this skill for Greek in his own Galilean background.[6]

We have examined several features used in support of the pseudonymous authorship of James. We have offered alternate explana-

---

5. James seems to be writing in 2:14–26 in opposition to a view that emphasized salvation by faith but minimized the importance of works. James emphasized that saving faith will always produce works. Paul agreed that the experience of God's grace must not lead to sin (Rom. 6:1–2).

6. Concerning the possibility of James's learning Greek well enough to author the epistle, J. N. Sevenster says, "Even though absolute certainty cannot be attained on this point, in view of all the data made available in the past decades the possibility can no longer be precluded that a Palestinian Jewish Christian of the first century A.D. wrote an epistle in good Greek." See J. N. Sevenster, *Do You Know Greek?* NovTSup 19 (Leiden: E. J. Brill, 1968), 191.

tions for each feature instead of relying on the hypothesis of pseudonymity. We also have suggested reasons for accepting the Lord's brother as author. There is no need to resort to the hypothesis of pseudonymous authorship when cogent reasons for accepting the Lord's brother as the author are evident.

James was a younger half brother of Jesus. The fact that his name appears first in the list of Jesus' half brothers (Matt. 13:55; Mark 6:3) suggests that he is the oldest of the half brothers.

What was his relationship to the mother of Jesus? He likely was a child of Joseph and Mary. It is possible that he was an older stepbrother of Jesus by a conjectural marriage of Joseph prior to his marriage to Mary. However, we have no evidence of an earlier marriage. The primary support for this view is the dubious claim by Roman Catholics that Mary remained a perpetual virgin. However, the most natural interpretation of the terms "brother" and "sister" in Mark 6:3 suggests that these are the children of Mary and Joseph.

James was not a believer in the Lord Jesus during the public ministry of Jesus (John 7:2–10). He saw the risen Christ (1 Cor. 15:7) and became his follower. He met with those awaiting the Holy Spirit on the day of Pentecost (Acts 1:14). He carefully observed the demands of Jewish law (Gal. 2:12; Acts 21:17–26). At the Jerusalem Council he placed his support behind Paul's position that observance of the law was not a condition for the salvation of Gentiles (Acts 15:12–21). The church historian Eusebius recorded the story of his martyrdom (ca. A.D. 62) and included the tradition that James spent so much time on his knees that they became as hard as those of a camel.[7] Although this statement is likely an accurate picture of James as a man of piety, we probably should not take his testimony literally.

Provenance

Assuming that the Lord's half brother authored the epistle, it is likely that he wrote from Jerusalem. This view is more of an inference than a statement from Scripture. James became the leader of the Jerusalem church (Acts 15:12–21; Gal. 2:9). Social conditions assumed in the letter suggest an origin of Jerusalem or Palestine. The letter pictures greedy merchants eagerly searching for profits

---

7. Eusebius, *Church History* 2:23.4–18.

(4:13–17) and describes landlords giving unjust treatment to the poor (2:5–7; 5:1–6). These conditions would be typical of Palestine in the decade of the fifties.

Destination

The epistle lacks an address to a specific church. Several features, however, suggest that James wrote to a generally Jewish audience. James used the Greek word for synagogue (the term "meeting" [synagogue] in 2:2 refers to a church) to describe where Christians met. He also used the Old Testament and references to other Jewish customs frequently (see 4:6; 5:11, 17).

James addressed his epistle to "the twelve tribes scattered among the nations" (1:1). This general designation does not specify a location for the recipients, but it suggests a Jewish-Christian audience outside of Palestine. Perhaps James wrote to some of the Jewish believers who scattered from Jerusalem after early persecutions there (Acts 11:19).

Date

Josephus dated the martyrdom of James on the basis of events in A.D. 62.[8] We must date the writing of James prior to this time. Several features point to an early date. First, James described economic conditions in Palestine which ceased to exist after the outbreak of the war against Rome (A.D. 66). Among the features he stressed were the chasm between the rich and the poor and the unjust treatment of laborers by landowners (2:5–7; 5:1–6). Second, mentioning only the term "elders" as a description of church leaders (5:14) suggests a simple church organization. This fact supports an early date. Third, the use of the term "synagogue" (2:2) to describe the meeting place for Christians suggests a time prior to the use of the term "church." Though none of this information identifies a specific date for the writing of James, it does dictate an undetermined early date for the epistle.

Canonicity

The Epistle of James experienced some difficulty being accepted into the canon of Scripture. Eusebius put it among the disputed

8. Josephus, *Antiquities* 20.9.1.

books of the New Testament, but he accepted it. In the West it was generally ignored until Jerome and Augustine endorsed it as canonical. The book received its harshest treatment from Martin Luther. Luther emphasized Paul's doctrine of justification by faith so strongly that he had difficulty accepting James (cf. Rom. 3:27–30; James 2:20–26). Luther regarded James as an "epistle of straw," but he did quote it approvingly on several occasions.[9]

Despite Luther's criticism, James deserves to be included in our canon. It presents a needed appeal for believers to demonstrate their faith through a life-style that reflects their faith commitment. It provides a needed corrective for those who emphasize correctness of doctrine without an equal emphasis on purity of life.

Literary Style

The content of James moves quickly from one subject to another. James discussed trials, hearing and doing God's word, the practice of showing favoritism, faith and works, the tongue, and many other topics. This rambling style of dealing with moral issues resembles Proverbs in the Old Testament and makes James difficult to outline.

James began with an introduction which resembled a letter, but he omitted the conclusion normally accompanying letters at that time. The epistle also lacks personal references, prayer requests, and travel plans. James might have intended his epistle for several Christian groups scattered over a large area, which may explain why his letter is written in a more impersonal style.

James frequently used rebuke and exhortation to encourage specific behavior in his readers (2:1–4; 3:9–12; 4:1–6). This approach has caused some to designate the epistle a *parenesis*, that is, an unstructured collection of moral admonitions. Whether or not we use this term, we can still see James writing a series of messages to share pastoral advice to scattered groups of Christians who were retreating from their initial commitment to Christ.

The Content of James

Finding a single theme that ties together the warnings and commands of James is difficult. At times James shows the atti-

---

9. For additional discussion of Luther's views on James, see Carson, Moo, and Morris, *An Introduction to the New Testament*, 417–18.

tude of a compassionate pastor as he shepherds his flock through trials (1:1–18). At other times he speaks with the fire of an Old Testament prophet as he warns, denounces, and calls for changed behavior (1:19–27; 4:1–12). I feel it is best to view James as a loose collection of messages or homilies that deal with various subjects.

How to Face Trials (1:1–18)

After a brief and somewhat impersonal introduction (1:1), James moved into a discussion of the trials of Christian life. We must distinguish between his discussion of trials in 1:2–4 and 1:13–18. In the former passage he focused on external afflictions, persecutions, or various hardships in life. James's advice as we face these trials is that we must let them accomplish the divine purpose in our lives (1:4). His discussion of the experience of temptation and trial in the latter passage dealt with enticements to sin. James warned against blaming the enticements on God (1:13). He clearly pointed out that encouragement to sin comes from a personal response to evil (1:14). Believers must resist being led astray by their own desires.

In 1:5–8 James discussed the relationship between wisdom and prayer. Christians need wisdom to face their trials. James urged his readers to ask God for that wisdom in faith. The believing prayer warrior will experience a generous bequest of wisdom from God, but the unstable doubter can expect nothing.

James focused on a specific example of a type of trial in 1:9–11. Humble, poor individuals should rejoice in the spiritual wealth available to obedient believers (Matt. 5:3, 5). They should not regard their poverty as an insurmountable trial. Wealthy individuals, on the other hand, must realize the temporary nature of their wealth (1:11).

Responding to God's Word (1:19–27)

This section contains two divisions. The first division focuses on controlling speech and anger (1:19–20). James urged his readers to be quick to listen but slow to speak. Further, they were to be slow to indulge the kind of anger that does not produce God's righteousness.

The second division focuses on "doing" God's word (1:21–27). "Word" refers to the proclaimed message from Scripture. James warned his readers to avoid merely hearing the message. With vivid imagery he compared the hearers who did not perform to those who saw their face in a mirror but quickly forgot what they had seen. He called the message of Scripture the "perfect law that gives freedom" (1:25) and urged his readers to continue to obey it.

James concluded this section with two examples of the kind of deeds that are pleasing to God. First, caring for the poor and needy imitated God's own concern for these people. Second, avoiding the polluted value system of the world showed the importance of preserving a pure heart.

Avoiding Partiality (2:1–13)

In verses 1–4 James prohibited the demonstration of partiality toward the rich and against the poor. The remainder of the paragraph presented two reasons for this prohibition. First, such partiality stood in contrast to God's treatment of the poor as "rich in faith" (2:5–7). Second, the "royal law" (Lev. 19:18) condemned such partiality (James 2:8–13) by demanding that believers love the poor as well as the rich.

Producing Good Works (2:14–26)

Three times in this section James made the point that genuine faith produced works (vv. 17, 20, 26). A faith that did not produce works was dead.[10]

James began the section with an illustration showing that faith without action was lifeless. Good wishes expressed to a hungry, poorly clothed man or woman did not provide him or her with needed food and clothing (vv. 14–17).

Using a style of argument known as *diatribe*, James introduced an imaginary objector who expressed a viewpoint in opposition to that of James (vv. 18–19). James insisted on the impossibility of showing

---

10. Many evangelicals turn to this passage for insight in answering the question, "Must Christ be Lord to be Savior?" For a presentation suggesting that James demanded a works-producing faith as the basis for salvation, see John F. MacArthur, Jr., "Faith According to the Apostle James," *JETS* 33 (March 1990): 13–34. Note also the responses to MacArthur's position by Earl D. Radmacher and Robert L. Saucy, ibid., 35–47.

faith without deeds. He used two biblical examples to support his point. Abraham's willingness to offer Isaac (vv. 21–23) and Rahab's hosting the Jewish spies (v. 25—see Joshua 2) showed the reality of their faith. James insisted that faith without deeds was dead.

Throughout this section James was probably combating false teachers who were familiar with Paul's doctrine of justification by faith (Rom. 3:27–30), and interpreted Paul to support a faith that did not produce works. James vigorously attacked this error. James's definitions of faith and justification were different from Paul's. James attacked faith that emphasized only intellectual belief (James 2:19), whereas Paul emphasized faith as personal commitment to Christ (Rom. 3:28). James clarified the means by which justification is demonstrated to others, that is, the performance of good deeds (James 2:24). Paul spoke of what justified a person before God, faith in Christ alone.

James and Paul were friends who were fighting two different theological errors. James fought against a type of antinomianism. Paul opposed legalism.

Controlling the Tongue (3:1–12)

James introduced the subject of the tongue in 1:19 and 1:26. Here he expanded on his earlier statements.

First, he described the difficulty of controlling the tongue (vv. 1–2). He warned those who aspired to a teaching office that they placed themselves in a greater danger of judgment, because their office required them to use the most difficult part of the body to control, the tongue.

Second, he used vivid images from nature to show the potential for evil from the tongue (vv. 3–6). A small spark can cause a conflagration in a great forest; the tongue can set ablaze the course of life on earth.

Third, he showed that human beings can tame animals but they cannot tame the tongue (vv. 7–8).

Fourth, James taught that humans use the tongue inconsistently (vv. 9–12). Human beings use the tongue to praise God, but they also use the tongue to curse those created in God's likeness. Blessing and cursing come from the same tongue. James said, "This should not be."

False and True Wisdom (3:13–18)

In this section James emphasized some values that most Jews of his time would readily identify with. He contrasted earthly wisdom with heavenly wisdom.

Earthly wisdom, whose source was satanic, was characterized by jealousy and arrogance (3:14–15), and resulted in every kind of evil practice (3:16). In the opening verses of the next section James will show an additional sample of the harvests of earthly wisdom (4:1–3).

Heavenly wisdom loved peace and showed consideration for others (3:17). It showed mercy in personal relationships and listened to the reason of others. Its fruit included a rich harvest of righteousness (3:18).

Renouncing Worldliness (4:1–12)

Apparently James was writing to several congregations permeated with worldly habits. He now described how these habits were expressed and urged his readers to repent.

First, he warned that the evil desires of the readers led to disagreements and quarrels (4:1–3). They needed to learn to ask God for what they needed with the proper motive.

Second, James prescribed repentance for his contentious readers (4:4–10). He denounced their spiritual adultery and urged them to submit to God (4:4, 7). The series of staccato commands in verses 7–10 shows the passion with which James wrote.

Dissension among the church members had produced slanderous, critical speech (vv. 11–12). James responded to this by forbidding slander. He warned that the believers to whom he was writing were attempting to usurp God's role by acting as judges, a role that they were not qualified to fulfill.

Renouncing Arrogance (4:13–5:6)

James denounced two forms of arrogance in these verses. First, he denounced arrogance that stemmed from presumptuous planning (4:13–17). He warned his readers against an arrogant, self-sufficient attitude which failed to consider the uncertainties of life and reminded them that they lived under God's will rather than their own prideful planning.

Second, he warned against the arrogance that came from the misuse of wealth (5:1–6). James condemned rich landowners for their selfishly hoarding wealth (5:2–3), their dishonest treatment of workers (5:4), and their self-indulgence (5:5).

The warnings of 4:13–17 may apply both to Christians and non-Christians. Both groups can be guilty of presumptuous planning. The warnings of 5:1–6 most likely apply to non-Christians. James did not hold out any hope of deliverance for those he warned in 5:1–6, and this sounds like a warning to unbelievers.

Demonstrating Endurance (5:7–20)

In 5:1–6 James had warned the rich landowners who oppressed the poor. Now he shifted his emphasis to speak a word of encouragement to the poor (5:7–11).

The poor are tempted to be impatient when the rich do not receive judgment for their evil ways. James urged his readers to seize hope from the anticipation of the Lord's return. They should be patient and avoid grumbling against one another (5:8–9). The patient endurance of the Old Testament prophets and Job should encourage perseverance.

James warned against invoking God's name to guarantee the truthfulness of individual statements (cf. Matt. 5:34–37). He insisted that the truthfulness and trustworthiness of our words should be so obvious that we would not need an oath to support them.

All believers face the alternating circumstances of trouble, happiness, and sometimes sickness. How should followers of Christ meet each of these situations? James advised those in trouble to pray. Those blessed with happiness should praise God (5:13). Those afflicted with sickness should call the leaders of the church to seek mutual prayer for physical healing (5:14–16). The oil used in anointing and praying was a symbol that set apart the individual for special care and attention from God. Any expression of prayer for the sick must always include the tacit acknowledgment of dependence on God's will (see 1 John 5:14–15).[11] James included the

---

11. Douglas J. Moo, *James*, TNTC (Grand Rapids: William B. Eerdmans Publishing Co., 1985), 176–87, contains helpful insights concerning the many issues involved in these verses, such as the role of the anointing oil and the link between faith and healing.

example of Elijah's bold prayers as a motivation for his readers (5:17–18).

James's final words were a call for action (5:19–20). He wrote to his readers about the tongue, worldliness, arrogance, and greed. Now he urged each believer to help restore any who had wandered from the truth. He encouraged them actively to seek the conversion of those who left the truth and assured them that God would approve and bless their efforts.

Outline of James

I. Greeting (1:1)

II. The Testing of the Believer (1:2–18)
   A. The attitude in testing (1:2–4)
   B. The use of prayer in testing (1:5–8)
   C. The correct estimate of testing (1:9–11)
   D. The result of testing (1:12)
   E. The source of testing (1:13–18)

III. The Evidences of Faith (1:19–5:20)
   A. The evidence of inner obedience (1:19–2:13)
      1. Hearing and doing God's word (1:19–27)
      2. Avoiding partiality (2:1–13)
   B. The Evidence of Outer Obedience (2:14–5:20)
      1. Practicing good works (2:14–26)
      2. Controlling the tongue (3:1–12)
      3. Following true wisdom (3:13–18)
      4. Avoiding worldliness (4:1–10)
      5. Avoiding judgement of others (4:11–12)
      6. Avoiding arrogance (4:13–17)
      7. Resisting injustice (5:1–6)
      8. Practicing endurance (5:7–11)
      9. Demonstrating honesty (5:12)
      10. Engaging in believing prayer (5:13–18)
      11. Reclaiming erring christians (5:19–20)

For Further Discussion

1. Does the Epistle of James have an outline, or is it a disconnected series of exhortations?

2. Give your opinion concerning the date for writing James.

3. What is the relationship between faith and healing?

4. Discuss the statement, "The Greek of James is too elegant to have come from a Palestinian fisherman." Give reasons either for or against the statement.

Bibliography

Adamson, James. *The Epistle of James*. NICNT. Grand Rapids: William B. Eerdmans Publishing Co., 1976.

_____. *James: The Man & His Message*. Grand Rapids: William B. Eerdmans Publishing Co., 1989. Excellent discussion of critical issues and content of the Epistle of James. Information in this book helps prepare one to read a commentary.

Carson, D. A., Douglas J. Moo, and Leon Morris. *An Introduction to the New Testament*. Grand Rapids: Zondervan Books, 1992.

Davids, Peter H. *The Epistle of James*. NIGTC. Grand Rapids: William B. Eerdmans Publishing Co., 1982. Thorough, exegetical commentary on James.

_____. *James*. NIBC. Peabody, Mass.: Hendrickson Publishers Inc., 1983.

Dibelius, Martin, and Heinrich Greeven. *James*. *Hermenia*. Philadelphia: Fortress Press, 1976.

Guthrie, Donald. *New Testament Introduction*. 2d. ed. Vol. 3, *Hebrews to Revelation*. London: Tyndale House Publishers, 1964.

Johnson, Luke Timothy. "The Mirror of Remembrance (James 1:22–25)." *CBQ* 50 (October 1988): 632–45. Excellent example of historical and literary study which illuminates Scripture.

Laws, Sophie. *A Commentary on the Epistle of James*. HNTC. San Francisco: Harper & Row Publishers Inc., 1980.

MacArthur, John F., Jr. "Faith according to the Apostle James." *JETS* 33(March 1990):33-34.

Moo, Douglas J. *James*. TNTC. Grand Rapids: William B. Eerdmans Publishing Co., 1985. Excellent, brief exegetical commentary on James.

Motyer, Alec. *The Message of James*. BST. Downers Grove, Ill.: InterVarsity Press, 1985. Expositional help in applying James.

Ross, Alexander. *The Epistles of James and John*. NICNT. Grand Rapids: William B. Eerdmans Publishing Co., 1954.

Sevenster, J. N. "Do You Know Greek?" *Supplement to Novum Testamentum* 19. Leiden: E. J. Brill, 1968.

21 The Epistles of 1 and 2 Peter

Guiding Questions

1. Describe the major purpose for writing 1 and 2 Peter.

2. Summarize the arguments for the Petrine authorship of both epistles.

3. Prepare an outline of the major points of 1 Peter.

4. What evidence does Peter present to support the reality of Christ's return?

Two problems faced by many early Christians were persecution and the pernicious spread of false teaching. The Epistles of 1 and 2 Peter confront these two problems. First Peter provided a message of encouragement for Christians in northern Asia Minor who faced unbelievable opposition and persecution. Second Peter warned and instructed Christians, perhaps in the same area, who were being invaded by aggressive false teachers.

The Epistle of First Peter

Authorship

First Peter begins with an affirmation of Petrine authorship (1:1). Other claims made in the letter support this affirmation. The author identified himself as an elder and a witness of Christ's sufferings (5:1). His description of Christ's crucifixion appears to contain expressions that only an intimate disciple would consider (2:21–24). Such early church leaders as Irenaeus, Tertullian, and Clement of Alexandria referred to sections of 1 Peter as a work by the apostle Peter. External evidence for Petrine authorship is strong.

Several themes in 1 Peter also appear in the speeches attributed to Peter in Acts. In both places Peter affirmed that God is no respecter of persons (Acts 10:34; 1 Pet. 1:17). Christ is identified as the stone rejected by the builders (Acts 4:10–11; 1 Pet. 2:7–8), and the "name" of Christ has a prominent place (Acts 3:6, 16; 4:10, 12; 5:41; 1 Pet. 4:14, 16).

First Peter also contains information we can link to the gospels. We would expect this to be true in a letter written by an "insider" such as Peter. Jesus' conversation with Peter in John 21 is reflected in the author's description of Christian leaders as shepherds under the control of Christ the Chief Shepherd (1 Pet. 5:2–4). The designation of Jesus as the "Chief Shepherd" (5:4) may also show the influence of Jesus' statements in John 10:14. The command to be clothed with humility (5:5) may be related to the scene in the upper room when Jesus wrapped a towel around his waist and washed the disciples' feet (John 13:2–17).

Despite such evidence, many New Testament scholars today either question or reject Petrine authorship. These scholars view the epistle as a pseudonymous document, and they cite four features to support their views.

First, some scholars claim that the Greek of 1 Peter is too refined to have come from the hands of an unlettered Galilean fisherman. The Greek of 1 Peter does reflect a reasonably polished style, influenced by the Greek of the LXX which the author knew well. Many scholars doubt the ability of Peter to master the style of Greek used in this epistle. They also feel that the use of the LXX would not be normal for a Galilean writer. In addition, they note the description of Peter in Acts 4:13 as "uneducated and untrained." Such a picture of Peter casts doubts on his ability to use Greek. How shall we answer these questions about Petrine authorship?

Most scholars date 1 Peter at least thirty years after Jesus' lifetime. Peter could have made remarkable progress in his use of Greek during those years. The description of Peter as "uneducated" need not indicate a lack of mental skills but only that he lacked formal training. Thirty years of study and reflection could have moved him forward with remarkable progress in his ability to use Greek.

Furthermore, Palestinians used Greek in the first century, and Peter's work as a fisherman would put him in contact with Greek-speaking businessmen who purchased his fish.[1] It is not unreasonable that a Palestinian Jew would use the LXX, for this version was the Bible used in Gentile churches. Peter tells us in 5:12 that he used Silvanus as his secretary, but we do not know if Silvanus supplied language help to Peter. Silvanus is commonly identified with the Silas of Acts, whom Paul mentioned in the first verse of both Thessalonian letters. Silvanus may well have functioned as a literary helper for Peter, but we lack sufficient evidence to draw this conclusion with confidence. In any case, we have adequate responses for those who reject Petrine authorship for linguistic reasons, and we have compelling answers for their objections.

Second, some suggest that the author of 1 Peter is too dependent on Paul. Those who advocate this viewpoint insist that Peter and Paul supported different theological systems (see Gal. 2:11–14 for evidence of differences between Peter and Paul). They point to the similarity between the views of submission to the state in 1 Peter 2:13–17 and Romans 13:1–7 as evidence of dependence on Paul's views. Scholars point out that we lack evidence for a close relationship between Peter and Paul. How then is it possible that Peter, who on at least one occasion was in opposition to Paul, could have ideas so closely related to those of Paul?

---

1. For additional discussion of this issue, see the work by J. N. Sevenster, *Do You Know Greek?* NovTSup 19 (Leiden: E. J. Brill, 1968). Note also the comments on this issue from Johnson, *The Writings of the New Testament*, 432–33: "As Galileans, John and Peter were, from every indication, successful small-time entrepreneurs, who would have had some command of at least marketplace Greek in order to do business. . . . Peter could have improved his Greek during the years of his ministry. To deny him this capacity is cultural condescension. Two of the great English stylists of the twentieth century (Conrad and Nabokov) learned and mastered English only as adults."

There are several ways to respond to the doctrinal objections concerning Petrine authorship. Though 1 Peter does agree with Paul on many issues, a discussion of such Pauline ideas as the law, the doctrine of justification, and the flesh is missing. Moreover, Peter presents his own unique contributions when he focuses on the doctrine of Christ's journey to speak to the "spirits in prison" (1 Pet. 3:19). Too much can be made of the similarities between Peter and Paul unless the differences and unique features of each author are highlighted as well.

Rather than being indebted primarily to Paul for the views expressed in 1 Peter 2:13–17, both Paul and Peter might have reflected the teachings of Jesus (see Matt. 22:15–22). Stated another way, we may affirm that many of the similarities between Peter and Paul reflect not Peter's slavish reliance on Paul but rather the common doctrinal tradition of the early church. It is also possible that any similarities between the statements in Peter's writings and those in Paul's could be due to the assistance both of them received from Silas, who served as scribe for both men (cf. 1 Thess. 1:1; 2 Thess. 1:1; 1 Pet. 5:12).

Although I question the use of the doctrinal argument as a basis for rejecting Petrine authorship, I recognize that the writings of Peter and Paul have much in common theologically. Nothing that we currently know makes it impossible for these two men to have had a close relationship. Paul was a compelling source for theological insights, and Peter may well have been more a man of action than a person of theological reflection. The similarities in doctrine between the writings of Peter and Paul could be used as an objection against Petrine authorship only if we uncovered something to make it psychologically inconceivable that Peter might succumb to Paul's influence. Both Peter and Paul made significant contributions to Christianity, and we find no facts to force us to acknowledge that the author of 1 Peter lacked originality on such a scale that the Apostle Peter could not have written the document.

Third, some find it unacceptable that a writer such as 1 Peter would make so few references to the teachings of Jesus. This objection flounders over two issues. First, the so-called absence of references to Jesus' teaching is overstated. Numerous references and allusions in 1 Peter can be traced to the influence of Jesus. The statements in 1 Peter 2:12 are remarkably similar to Jesus' words in Matthew 5:16. Peter's discussion of the blessedness of the godly sufferer in 3:14 resembles Jesus' discussion in Matthew 5:10–12. Furthermore, we would not expect the teachings of Jesus to be prominent in a book written to encourage suffering Christians. It was not Peter's purpose to present a handbook of Jesus' teaching. This objection is too subjective to provide a stable foundation for opposing Petrine authorship.

Fourth, some claim that the letter reflects official Roman persecution which developed only in the second century A.D. If this were the date of the epistle, Peter could not have written it. Those who advocate this position insist that the description of suffering in 1 Peter 4:12–16 resembles that described by Pliny the Younger in his letter to the emperor Trajan in the early second century A.D.[2] In Pliny's time it had become a crime for one to be a Christian. Some view the reference to a "fiery trial" (4:12) as a specific indication of government-sponsored persecution. Was the persecution described in 1 Peter clearly beyond Peter's lifetime?

We lack sufficient information about early persecutions to identify clearly the persecutions in this epistle with those in Pliny's time. During Pliny's term of service, it was a crime for a Roman citizen to bear the name of Christian, but the evidence of 1 Peter does not clearly indicate that the issue had reached this level when Peter wrote. The reference to "being reproached for the name of Christ" (4:14) pictured a situation that existed for believers from the beginning of the church. All Christian suffering had resulted from the loyalty of a believer to Jesus Christ. Nothing in Peter's description clearly indicates a condition that was new or beyond the lifetime of the apostle.

Just as it is impossible to link the suffering of Christians in 1 Peter with the persecution of Christians under Pliny, it is also impossible to link this suffering with that inflicted on Christians by Nero. The deliberate persecution of Christians by Nero was limited largely to Rome and its environs. However, it is possible that Nero's harsh treatment of Christians in Rome may have inspired similar treatment

---

2. For a copy of the correspondence between Trajan and Pliny, see Henry Bettenson, *Documents of the Christian Church* (New York: Oxford University Press, 1947), 5–7.

in the provinces. Peter might have been warning his readers of this realistic possibility.

I believe it is difficult to prove that the persecutions mentioned in 1 Peter resulted from the intentional policy of the Roman government. It is much more likely that the persecution came from unbelieving neighbors of Christians who, because of their anger and resentment, made scapegoats of the Christians. The "defense" Peter called on them to give (3:15) might have been a general Christian testimony rather than a legal defense before the Roman government. The suffering described in 4:15–16 sounds more like jealous accusations by unbelieving neighbors or acquaintances of Christians who were living a life-style of Christian commitment to Christ. The position that these persecutions took place during Peter's lifetime is tenable.

The objections against Petrine authorship are inconclusive and can be answered with alternative explanations. If Peter were not the author, we have no convincing reason to explain the use of his name in 1:1. It is best to accept the testimony of the book concerning Petrine authorship and regard the work as a genuine product of the Apostle Peter.

Readers of First Peter

The readers of 1 Peter are identified in 1:1. They lived in that area of Asia Minor north of the Taurus mountains. Paul had labored in at least two provinces of Asia Minor, Galatia and Asia. It is possible that the one who carried this letter to its destination may have traveled in areas of Asia and Galatia not visited by Paul, and thus it is possible that he may not have had contact with those places in which Paul had exerted such significant influence.

Nothing in 1 Peter suggests that the author had worked among his readers. In fact, the statements in 1:12 seem to dissociate Peter from those who preached there. Even though Peter had not lived or worked among the readers, he was able to write a compassionate letter expressing deep concern for them.

We do not know how the people in this area first heard the gospel. Perhaps some of those converted at Pentecost (Acts 2:9–10) might have returned to their homes with the Christian message.

Even though the chief ministry of Peter took place among Jews, this letter appears to have been written chiefly to Gentiles. In their pre-conversion years, the readers had been involved in idolatry (4:3), a sin more characteristic of Gentiles than Jews. The description of their earlier life as a time of "ignorance" (1:14) and "empty" (1:18) sounds more appropriate for Gentiles than for Jews. In 2:9–10 Peter suggests that they were formerly not a people but were now the people of God. All of these references more likely refer to Gentiles than to Jews.

From the beginning, Peter intended that this letter be circulated among churches in several locations. He did not address it to a single congregation, but he did have certain individuals in mind (1:6–9). However, he addressed the needs of different groups scattered in several different areas.

Date and Provenance

The theme of suffering appears in every chapter of 1 Peter. In four of its five chapters the sufferers are the readers. The likelihood is that the storms of suffering linked with the Neronian persecution of A.D. 64 were beginning to gather when this letter was written. Perhaps ripples from the policies Nero was pursuing emboldened the pagan population in northern Asia Minor to make life miserable for the growing Christian population in their midst. The most probable date for the letter is just before A.D. 64. Those who reject Petrine authorship generally suggest the late first century under Domitian (A.D. 81–96) or the early second century under Trajan (A.D. 98–117).

Peter identified Babylon as the location from which he wrote (5:13). Old Testament Babylon in Mesopotamia was deserted in this period. Another Babylon existed in northern Egypt, but it was an insignificant Roman military outpost with no possibility of being the place of origin for this letter. The most likely suggestion is that the term Babylon was used symbolically to refer to the arrogant idolatry and lust for power that characterized biblical Babylon. The term Babylon was used in this sense in Revelation 17:5. Peter probably used the term as a cryptic designation for Rome. It is uncertain why Peter felt it necessary to use this symbolic term for Rome.

The Role of Silas

The name Silas is the Aramaic equivalent to the Latin name *Silvanus*. The Silas (Silvanus) in Peter's reference is probably the same person who accompanied Paul on his second missionary journey (Acts 15:40). Silas served either as an amanuensis for writing 1 Peter, or he may have delivered the letter to its destination. As an amanuensis he even may have assisted in the choice of words.[3]

Canonization of First Peter

The church historian Eusebius regarded 1 Peter as indisputably authentic.[4] No tradition contrary to this view appeared in the early church. The first reference to 1 Peter may be the statement of 2 Peter 3:1, which refers to that letter as the "second letter" by Peter. Scholars have found possible references to 1 Peter in some of the early fathers. The first explicit reference appears in Irenaeus.[5] Marcion omitted 1 Peter from his canon, but his practice was to confine the epistolary section of his collection of inspired writings to Paul's letters. The omission of 1 Peter under these circumstances is not surprising. The Muratorian Fragment omitted 1 Peter from its list, but some scholars contend that the text of the Muratorian Canon is not complete.[6] In general, the external evidence for the authenticity of 1 Peter is impressive.

Form, Unity, and Purpose

Some recent writers interpret 1 Peter as a sermon or liturgy used on the occasion of a baptism. Those who support this view point out the break in the letter's argument in 4:11. They note that in the earlier section of the letter suffering is seen as potential, but from 4:12 forward it becomes actual. The anticipated suffering in 3:13 is described in a future tense, but in 4:12 the suffering is narrated in a present tense.[7] These writers place the baptism after 1:21 and see a

---

3. For information about the role of the amanuensis in writing Paul's epistles, see Richard N. Longenecker, "Ancient Amanuenses and the Pauline Epistles," in *New Dimensions in New Testament Study*, ed. Richard N. Longenecker and Merrill C. Tenney (Grand Rapids: Zondervan Books, 1974), 281–97.

4. Eusebius, *Church History* 3.3.4.

5. Irenaeus, *Against Heresies* 4.9.2.

6. See the discussion in Carson, Moo, and Morris, *An Introduction to the New Testament*, 425–26.

7. It is important to note that not all of 1:1–4:11 views suffering as a future experience. The suffering mentioned in 1:6–9 was already underway for the readers. It is unacceptable to suggest that all references to suffering in 1:1–4:11 are future, while from 4:12 onwards the references are to a present experience.

reference to the act in the experience of "purification" mentioned as a past event in 1:22. F. L. Cross has made a specific application of this view by insisting that 1 Peter is a liturgy for a baptismal service at Easter.[8]

Those who view the book as a sermon or liturgy for baptism should note that the act of baptism is mentioned only in 3:21. Such a sparse reference would be unusual if the subject of baptism were the heart of the letter. Those who place an emphasis on the past tense in 1:22 should also note that the act of regeneration is described as a past event as early as 1:3. It seems improper to use tense distinctions alone as a basis for insisting that the act of baptism occurs in the interval between 1:21 and 1:22.

The fact that many other epistles mention baptism (e.g., Rom. 6:3–4; 1 Cor. 1:13–17; Col. 2:12) has not led New Testament scholars to suggest a liturgical link for each reference to the act of baptism. In the early church baptism represented the public expression of an abandonment of paganism. It should not be surprising that Christians viewed baptism as an important act. Although some of the teaching of 1 Peter may be connected with baptism, it appears to extend beyond the evidence to insist that the book was intended as a baptismal sermon or liturgy.

The approach of E. G. Selwyn to 1 Peter represents a more complete use of the internal evidence. He views the baptismal aspect of 1 Peter as peripheral, and believes the letter was written primarily as an encouragement for persecuted and suffering Christians.[9] Peter showed his readers that Christ left believers an example for facing suffering (2:21). Persecuted Christians can follow Christ's example and present themselves to God in obedient living (4:19).

The Content of First Peter

Peter wrote to Christians in the northern part of Asia Minor who were experiencing persecution because of their faith. He described the conduct they should demonstrate as they faced hostility and persecution. His letter alternated between sections

---

8. F. L. Cross, *1 Peter: A Paschal Liturgy* (London: Mowbray, Imprint of Cassell PLC, 1954).

9. E. G. Selwyn, *The First Epistle of St. Peter* (New York: St. Martin's Press, 1964).

devoted to teaching doctrinal truths and sections designed to exhort and encourage Christian faithfulness and commitment. The exhortations resemble sermons or preaching sections.

Salutation (1:1–2)

Peter identified himself as an apostle of Jesus Christ without additional emphases or descriptions. He addressed his readers who had been scattered throughout the five provinces of Pontus, Galatia, Cappadocia, Asia, and Bithynia. They were temporarily away from their heavenly home, but one day they hoped to reach it. Peter wished for them an abundant experience of grace and peace.

The Method and Nature of Salvation (1:3–12)

Peter alternated between teaching his readers doctrinal truths and urging them to holy living and faithful witness. In this teaching section he focused on the doctrine of salvation.

The salvation Peter described began with a new birth based on the resurrection of Jesus Christ. It produced a living hope for a future heavenly reward that would never perish, spoil, or fade. Peter taught that the reward was kept for his readers in heaven. They would be guarded by divine power until Christ's return.

At the present time, the readers were experiencing trials, but the outcome of those trials would strengthen and refine their faith in Jesus. Their faith in Jesus led them to a present experience of glorious joy despite the persecutions they faced. The result of their faith would be the full possession of the blessings of salvation at the end time.

This salvation had been predicted by the prophets who outlined the sufferings of Christ and the glories that would follow. The readers learned the good news from preachers empowered by the Holy Spirit. Even as Peter wrote, angels were longing to look into and learn about the glories of Christ's kingdom.

A Demand for Holiness (1:13–2:3)

Peter appealed to his readers to respond to God's great salvation by living a life of holiness because God himself is holy. They were to demonstrate holiness by living in reverent fear (v. 17), loving one another deeply (v. 22), ridding their lives of all hindrances

(2:1), and craving the strength which God's written Word could give them (2:2). As incentives to experience that holiness, Peter pointed to the fear of God as judge (1:17), the high cost of redemption (1:18–19), the power of the Resurrection (1:21), and the goodness of God (2:3).

A Description of the People of God (2:4–10)

In this second teaching section Peter used Old Testament imagery to prove that his readers were God's new people who had received the blessings of Old Testament Israel in greater measure. Peter taught that the new position God had appointed for believers should motivate them to glorify God.

He described believers as "living stones" in God's new temple. As living stones they offer to God sacrifices influenced by the character of the Holy Spirit (v. 5). In verse 6 he used Isaiah 28:16 to describe Jesus as a precious cornerstone. Believers who trusted this chosen cornerstone would never experience disappointment. God has appointed unbelievers to suffer the consequences of their unbelief and rejection of Christ (vv. 7–8). Believers comprise a royal priesthood, a holy nation, and God's own people (Exod. 19:5–6). They are to live a life that demonstrates the work of the God who called them from darkness to light (v. 9).

Christian Witness in the World (2:11–3:12)

Peter introduced his second preaching section with a discussion of the role of God's special people in living a holy, godly life before unbelievers. He began by identifying the principles of holy living in 2:11–12 and continued with an application of specific behavior in different life settings.

The general principles are both positive and negative statements (2:11–12). On the negative side, believers were constantly to keep away from all sinful passions. On the positive, their good lives were to commend the Christian faith and thereby be an influence to lead to the conversion of unbelievers.

Believers are to demonstrate obedient, respectful behavior toward the representatives of government in order to silence the irrational slander of fault-finding unbelievers (2:13–17). Slaves are to show obedience and respect to their owners in imitation of the humility of Christ (2:18–25). Wives are to demonstrate such a winsome obedience to God in marriage that husbands will be won to obey God in all areas of life (3:1–6). Husbands are to live considerately with their wives, recognizing that they are coheirs of God's grace (3:7). All believers are to live in harmonious forgiveness with one another by turning from evil and devoting themselves to the peace of God (3:8–12).

Peter's intent in this section was to urge his readers to demonstrate their Christianity in such areas as respect for government, performance of social duties, and the practice of forgiveness. These changes in life-style could compel unbelievers to see and respond to the power of Christianity.

Appeals and Promises to the Persecuted (3:13–4:19)

In a third teaching section Peter prepared his readers for suffering by suggesting that, in the will of God, it was better to endure misunderstanding for obedient living than to suffer the consequences of disobedient and lawless actions (3:13–17). As an incentive to endure such unjust suffering, Peter presented the example of Christ's victory over the powers of evil (3:18–22).

The words of Peter in 3:18–22 are among the most difficult in the New Testament to interpret. In the will of God, Christ died—the righteous one for the unrighteous (3:18). At some time after his resurrection he proclaimed his victory to fallen angels who were awaiting final judgment (3:19). Through the power of the Cross and Resurrection Christ triumphed over Satan, death, and all His enemies. Peter was attempting to encourage his readers by suggesting that just as Christ triumphed over his enemies, so his readers would ultimately triumph over their persecutors if they endured in obedient living.

Some interpret these words to mean that during the interval between his death and resurrection, Christ went to Hades to preach a gospel of repentance and forgiveness. If this had happened, it would offer the opponents of Jesus another chance to believe. Nothing in the text suggests that Christ went to Hades to preach. Rather, the text suggests that Jesus preached after the Resurrection when he was "alive in the Spirit." Also, the idea that the dead have a second chance to hear the gospel is foreign to Scripture. The next event facing those who died without Christ is judgment, not another opportunity to hear the gospel (Heb. 9:27).[10]

In comparing baptism to the flood, Peter suggested that God did not use baptism to remove the defilement of the flesh (v. 21). Baptism served as the outward expression of an inner attitude of faith and repentance.

In 4:1–6 Peter urged his readers to decide that they were willing to suffer just as Christ himself had suffered. The "dead" who heard the preaching of the gospel (4:6) were not the "spirits in prison" (3:19) but believers who had died physically and were enjoying spiritual life with God in heaven. The nearness of the final judgment should lead believers to pray, love one another, and make vigorous use of their spiritual gifts (4:7–11).

In 4:12–19 Peter presented a threefold perspective to encourage his readers not to be surprised at the prospect of the painful trials that lay ahead.

1. Peter reminded his readers that their suffering could lead them to share in Christ's own experiences, a development that would link them more closely with the Savior (4:13).

2. Peter suggested that bearing insults for the name of Christ could lead to a richer supply of the Holy Spirit in their lives (4:14).

3. Peter reminded his readers of the faithfulness of God as a motivation for obedient, trusting service (4:19).

Assurances for Faithful Servants (5:1–14)

In this final preaching section Peter focused on directives to church leaders, and general exhortations and warnings to all Christians. He closed with a final greeting.

Peter urged church leaders to be faithful shepherds from a willing heart with a desire to serve as an example to the flock (5:1–4). He sin-

---

10. For a thorough discussion of the exegetical and theological issues of 1 Peter 3:18–22, see R. T. France, "Exegesis in Practice: Two Samples," in *New Testament Interpretation*, ed. I. Howard Marshall (Grand Rapids: William B. Eerdmans Publishing Co., 1977), 264–81. See also C. E. B. Cranfield, "The Interpretation of 1 Peter 3.19 and 4.6," in *The Bible & Christian Life* (Edinburgh: T & T Clark, 1985), 176–86.

gled out young men and urged them to submit to the older leadership of the church (5:5). He urged humility and trust on all believers (5:6–7). Christians were to be alert against the deceitful practices of Satan and to resist him firmly (5:8–9). Peter promised that God would bestow eternal glory on those who endured suffering (5:10–11).

Peter's final words acknowledged the help of Silas in completing the letter and included a greeting from all the believers in Rome, but especially from John Mark.

Outline of First Peter

I. Salutation (1:1–2)

II. First Teaching Section: Method and Nature of Salvation (1:3–12)
- A. A salvation kept for those preserved by God's power (1:3–5)
- B. A salvation producing joy in the presence of suffering (1:6–9)
- C. A salvation announced by the prophets (1:10–12)

III. First Preaching Section: A Demand for Holiness (1:13–2:3)
- A. A holiness patterned after the divine character (1:13–16)
- B. A holiness procured at great cost (1:17–21)
- C. A holiness demonstrated in brotherly love (1:22–25)
- D. A holiness demonstrated by moral transformation (2:1–3)

IV. Second Teaching Section: A Description of the People of God (2:4–10)
- A. Offering spiritual sacrifices to God (2:4–5)
- B. Trusting in Christ, the chief cornerstone (2:6–8)
- C. Declaring the praises of a merciful God (2:9–10)

V. Second Preaching Section: Christian Witness in the World (2:11–3:12)
- A. General principles of Christian witness (2:11–12)
- B. Submission to government authorities (2:13–17)
- C. Submission and respect by slaves for masters (2:18–25)
- D. Submission by wives to husbands (3:1–6)
- E. Considerate treatment by husbands to wives (3:7)
- F. Compassion and forgiveness among all Christians (3:8–12)

VI. Third Teaching Section: Appeals and Promises to the Perse-
cuted (3:13–4:19)
  A. Appeal for fearless witness under persecution (3:13–17)
  B. The hope for triumph in the face of persecutors (3:18–22)
  C. Appeal to follow Christ's example of suffering (4:1–6)
  D. Warning of the nearness of the final judgment (4:7–11)
  E. Reminder of the faithfulness of God (4:12–19)

VII. Third Preaching Section: Assurances for Faithful Servants
(5:1–11)
  A. Recognition for faithful service by elders (5:1–4)
  B. Grace given to humble believers (5:5)
  C. God's love for all believers (5:6–7)
  D. Alertness for victory over Satan (5:8–9)
  E. Promise of future glory (5:10–11)

VIII. Final Greetings and Conclusion (5:12–14)

The Epistle of Second Peter

Authorship

The authorship of no book in the New Testament has been more
seriously questioned than 2 Peter. Carson, Moo, and Morris join
with B. F. Westcott and E. M. B. Green in recognizing that no
book in the New Testament is as poorly attested as 2 Peter, but the
support for its inclusion is more widespread than the support for
the best attested of the rejected books. [11]

Some opponents of Petrine authorship of the letter note that the
external attestation of 2 Peter is weak. Origen is the first Christian
leader to attribute the work to Peter.[12] Origen noted that the
authenticity of 2 Peter was disputed, but he did not view the objections as serious enough to cause him to reject the book. Although
earlier writers such as Clement of Rome and Irenaeus contain possible allusions to 2 Peter, it is impossible to prove that they used the
book for their references. Eusebius placed the epistle among the disputed writings.[13] Jerome and Augustine accepted it as genuine. The

11. Carson, Moo, and Morris, *An Introduction to the New Testament*, 434.
12. Eusebius, *Church History* 6.25.8.
13. Ibid., 3.3.1.

lack of references to 2 Peter in the early Christian fathers is offset by its use in the Nag Hammadi texts. Two writings from this collection, the *Gospel of Truth* and the *Apocryphon of John* dated in the second century, include probable quotations or allusions to 2 Peter.[14] The external evidence for the authenticity of 2 Peter shows that the church was hesitant to embrace it as authentic, but we find no evidence that any part of the church ever rejected it as spurious.

What does an examination of the internal evidence regarding Petrine authorship reveal? First, it is important to explore the personal allusions to Peter in the epistle. The author describes himself as Symeon (or Simon) Peter, a servant and apostle of Jesus Christ. His reference to learning about the coming of his own death in 2 Peter 1:14 appears to be a recollection of Jesus' statements to Peter in John 21:18–19. The author claims to have been an eyewitness of the Transfiguration (1:16–18), and he mentions a previous letter he had written (3:1). He refers to Paul as "our beloved brother" (3:15). All of these statements point to the apostle Peter as the author, but those who reject Petrine authorship challenge the veracity of these statements and present other evidence to dispute apostolic authorship.

Many who reject Petrine authorship maintain that the personal allusions are a literary device to present the appearance of authenticity in a document that is actually pseudonymous. Those who take this position point out the prevalence of pseudepigraphic literature in early Christian history. They contend that the author of 2 Peter used the personal allusions to add an appearance of truth to his claim for Petrine authorship. They indicate that if 1:14 is a reference to John 21:18–19, this actually rules out Petrine authorship because of the general tendency to date John's gospel after Peter's death. However, if Peter himself heard the statement from Jesus, there is nothing improbable in his reference to the prediction. Also, we find nothing unseemly in Peter's reference to the Transfiguration, since the reference to his presence at the event appears to verify the truthfulness of the observations he will make. Some pseudepigraphic authors did refer to known events in the lives of assumed authors, but my impression of the reference in 2 Peter is

14. A. M. Helmbold, *The Nag Hammadi Gnostic Texts and the Bible* (Grand Rapids: Baker Book House, 1967), 90–91.

that the apostle mentioned it in order to attest truthfully to what actually happened. None of the personal references in 2 Peter need be taken as proof of a pseudepigraphic writing, for alternate explanations of their purposes are possible.

A second question about authorship based on internal content concerns Peter's reference to Paul and "the other Scriptures" (2 Peter 3:15–16). Some scholars maintain that the allusion to Paul's writings refers to a collection of all of his epistles. Since all of Paul's epistles could not have yet been collected during Peter's lifetime, they reject Petrine authorship. However, Peter's reference to "all his letters" may only refer to those letters he had read or seen. Some scholars also suggest that Christian leaders were not calling the New Testament writings "Scripture" in Peter's lifetime, and the reference to Paul's letters as Scripture raises questions about Petrine authorship. It is possible that the word translated "Scripture" might be better translated "writings." If this were accurate, then Peter was only suggesting that the false teachers showed no respect for any religious writings, including those of Paul. However, the usual translation of the Greek word *graphai* is "Scriptures." If this is the correct translation of the term, then Peter was putting Paul's writings on a level with the authoritative Old Testament. Is this a possibility during the apostolic period?

Paul himself viewed his own writings as inspired (1 Cor. 7:40; 14:37), and he expected his readers to recognize the authority of his statements (2 Thess. 3:14; 1 Cor. 7:17). These statements reveal that Paul knew God was inspiring his writings. If this assumption is true, it should not be surprising that Peter himself would recognize the inspired nature of Paul's letters. It is true that the apostolic fathers did not explicitly designate Paul's writings as inspired on a level with the Old Testament documents. It is possible, however, that Peter recognized the inspiration implicit in Paul's writings and may have preceded the later fathers in this insight. As Donald Guthrie suggested, "Is it not more reasonable to suggest that in the apostolic period Peter may have recognized the value of Paul's Epistles even more fully than the later sub-apostolic Fathers?"[15] It is likely that the apostle Peter would recognize the unique nature of Paul's writings as Scripture.

---

15. Donald Guthrie, *New Testament Introduction*, 2d ed., vol. 3, *Hebrews to Revelation* (London: Tyndale House Publishers, 1964), 157.

A third question about authorship based on internal evidence is the relationship of 2 Peter to Jude. Second Peter and Jude share similar content, and most New Testament scholars contend that Peter copied or at least used Jude. Since many date Jude after the death of the apostle Peter, this eliminates Peter as the author of the epistle. However, it is possible that Jude copied Peter or that both used a common source. In favor of the first possibility is Peter's reference to a future coming of the false teachers (2 Pet. 2:1) and Jude's reference to their appearance as already underway (Jude 4).[16] Some argue for the priority of Jude on the grounds that its language is simple and more direct, but it is hard to prove that Jude's words in verses 12 and 13 are more simple and direct than the related words in 2 Peter 2:17. Some find it difficult to account for the existence of Jude if he used 2 Peter, for Jude, under this hypothesis, would have taken most of his words from Peter and would have added only a few thoughts of his own. Jude, however, implied that he wrote hurriedly, and it may have suited him to use Peter's material.

It might be useful to explore further the possibility that both 2 Peter and Jude used a common source. Matthew and Luke have considerable material in common. Many scholars suggest that they used Mark and a document named *Q* as sources. If a common source is the correct explanation for the similarities between 2 Peter and Jude, we lack evidence for that common source— although it still is a possibility. Michael Green argues for the use of a common source by stating, "If both authors drew independently on some standardized form of catechesis denouncing false teaching of an antinomian type, the similarities and differences between the two presentations will be easy to understand, since neither writes in slavish dependence on his outline."[17]

We lack sufficient evidence to establish the dependence of either 2 Peter or Jude on the other, and we are unable to determine with certainty if both used a common source. Similarities between the

---

16. This argument works both ways. Jude 18 refers to the appearance of the false teachers as a future event, and 2 Pet. 2:12 describes them in the present tense. These facts suggest that the use of tense differences to determine the relationship between Jude and 2 Peter is a precarious venture.

17. Michael Green, *The Second Epistle General of Peter and the General Epistle of Jude*, TNTC (Grand Rapids: William B. Eerdmans Publishing Co., 1968), 54.

two letters clearly exist, but it is impossible to be dogmatic about the source of the similarities. In any case, we should not use the similarities between 2 Peter and Jude as a basis for rejecting Petrine authorship of the epistle.

We now note some distinctive vocabulary usage which appears to support Petrine authorship. Such personal allusions that appear in 1:12–18 claim eyewitness insight into the events of the Transfiguration. The use of the Greek word *exodus* (v. 15)[18] to refer to Peter's death reminds us of the use of the term in Luke 9:31 to refer to Christ's death. The term "godliness" (2 Pet. 1:3, 6, 7; 3:11) also appears in Acts 3:12 in a speech given by Peter. This rare word appears elsewhere only in the Pastorals. This linguistic evidence maintains that the distinctive usages of Peter in Acts can be found in 2 Peter. Additional linguistic similarities between 2 Peter and other Petrine material can also be identified.[19]

Although much contemporary scholarship questions and rejects Petrine authorship, it seems best to me to accept the opinion of the early church that the apostle Peter authored this epistle shortly before his martyrdom.

Provenance, Date, and Destination

The epistle contains no evidence to support a specific place of writing. Assuming that Peter wrote the letter, it is logical to suggest a Roman origin, for church tradition places Peter in Rome in his latter days. Nothing in the letter contradicts the suggestion of a Roman origin for 2 Peter.

The apostle spoke of his death as near (1:14), and this suggests a date just prior to his martyrdom. A commonly accepted date for Peter's martyrdom is A.D. 68.

Second Peter lacks a specific destination such as we see in 1 Peter 1:1. If the letter in 2 Peter 3:1 is 1 Peter, then we may conclude that Peter wrote the second letter for the same group. If the letter written before the second letter is an unknown writing of Peter, we cannot determine what destination he intended.

---

18. The term is translated "departure" in the NIV translation of both 2 Peter and Luke.

19. For a listing of linguistic similarities between 2 Peter and the Petrine speeches of Acts and also between 1 and 2 Peter, see Harrison, *Introduction to the New Testament*, 424–25.

Recent Study of Second Peter

Most recent studies of 2 Peter have assumed that the work is a pseudonym, a writing ascribed to a significant figure from the past. Many who advocate pseudonymity do not regard the book as a willful forgery. Barker, Lane, and Michaels view 2 Peter as a testament, a farewell discourse by one who is about to die. They suggest that it contains genuine material from Peter "put together in testamentary form by one or more of the apostle's followers after his death."[20] They insist that posthumous publication in Peter's name does not suggest any intent to deceive because the tradition in the epistle is genuinely Petrine.

This position, however, is still in conflict with the historical evidence from the early church. Existing evidence suggests that the early church insisted on authorship by an apostle or his associate and rejected as deceitful and unacceptable any writing by someone other than the named author.[21] It is certainly possible to maintain that this unknown disciple of Peter could have written an inspired letter just as Mark, who was not an apostle, could have written an inspired gospel. The assertion, however, remains hypothetical and is unprovable.

Michael Green, who has published a thorough survey of the possibility that 2 Peter is a testament written by a follower of Peter and published posthumously, concludes: "I have yet to see a convincing pseudepigraph from the early days of Christianity, and . . . there are few arguments brought against the authenticity of 2 Peter which do not equally militate against the view that it was the product of a pseudepigrapher."[22]

The Content of Second Peter

Peter warned against false teachers who peddled heretical doctrine and practiced an immoral life-style. He urged his readers to be diligent in cultivating Christian growth, warned against denials

---

20. Glenn W. Barker, William L. Lane, and J. Ramsey Michaels, *The New Testament Speaks* (New York: Harper & Row, 1969), 352. For another discussion advocating the "testament" view of 2 Peter, see Richard J. Bauckham, *Jude, 2 Peter*, WBC (Waco, Tex.: Word, 1983), 158–62.

21. See the discussion of "The Practice of Pseudonymous Authorship" in chapter 14.

22. Green, *Second Epistle General of Peter*, 33–34.

of Christ's return, and exposed the consequences of following the false teachings of the heretics.

Salutation (1:1–2)

The salutation in 2 Peter differs from the one in 1 Peter at two points. Using his full name, Peter identified himself as Simon Peter in 2 Peter. Also, he did not address his letter to a specific geographic location, although it is obvious that he had a specific group in mind.

Becoming a Fruitful Christian (1:3–11)

Peter reminded his readers that God provides everything Christians need for spiritual life and godly living (1:3–4). This generous provision led Peter to encourage his readers to develop the Christian graces of goodness, knowledge, self-control, perseverance, godliness, kindness, and love by climbing the "ladder of faith" (1:5–7). Fruitful Christians have an abundance of these qualities. Barren Christians often forget the background from which God delivered them (1:8–9). Peter urged his readers to prove the reality of their election by God as they lived a life consistent with the holy call of the gospel (1:10–11).

The Testimony of Peter (1:12–21)

Peter knew that he did not have long to live on earth, and he promised he would leave a written witness as a reminder of the truth he taught (1:14–15). Some conclude that Peter referred to 2 Peter as the promised writing, but many others believe this statement was a reference to Mark's Gospel. By promising to leave behind some written record, Peter probably helped precipitate the writing of such New Testament apocryphal works as the Gospel of Peter, Acts of Peter, and Apocalypse of Peter.

Peter insisted that his words about Jesus were not clever myths. Peter himself had been an eyewitness of such an event as the Transfiguration (1:16–18). He also suggested that the Scriptures themselves confirmed the apostolic witness.[23] He believed that

---

23. Ibid., 86–87. Does Peter say that the Scriptures confirm the apostolic witness, or does he say that the apostolic witness confirms the Scripture? Although either option would be theologically sound, Green gives reasons to support the first option.

Scripture was authoritative because it was written by men "carried along by the Holy Spirit" (1:19–21).

A Warning Against False Teaching (2:1–22)

Peter began this warning section with a description of false teachers as purveyors of destructive heresies who denied the sovereign Lord who had bought them. Their greed drove them to invent stories with which they exploited their listeners (2:1–3).

Peter solemnly recounted examples of judgment and deliverance to urge his readers to sober reflection and action. Peter indicated that God had judged the sinning angels (Gen. 6:1–4), the ancient world at the time of the flood (Gen. 7:17–23), and the cities of Sodom and Gomorrah (Gen. 19:23–29). God had delivered Noah (Gen. 7:13–16) and Lot (Gen. 19:29). In the same way, God was capable of rescuing the readers from the pernicious false teaching of the heretics who had invaded their territory (2:4–10a).

Peter next outlined characteristics and practices of these false teachers.

- They were arrogant and insolent (2:10b–11).

- Brute-like in their understanding, they were dominated by lust and greed (2:12–16).

- Despite their promise of freedom, these false teachers only led their listeners to spiritual slavery and depravity (2:17–19).

- Although these false teachers claimed to know Jesus Christ as Lord and Savior, their behavior showed that they had never been converted (2:20–22).

The Certainty of Christ's Return (3:1–10)

Peter reminded his readers not to forget the "wholesome teaching" they had received from the apostles (3:1–2). This teaching included an acceptance of Christ's return, a belief thoroughly rejected by the false teachers. Peter insisted that God had always interrupted history with demonstrations of his power, and he would do it again at Christ's return (3:5–7). The delay in Christ's return should not cause believers to question its reality, for God views time with a different perspective than human beings (3:8). The reason for the delay in Christ's return was that God was patiently providing opportunities for more sinners to respond to the gospel (3:9). The promise of Christ himself (see Matt. 24:43–44) added support for accepting the reality of his return (3:10).

An Encouragement to Godly Living (3:11–18)

Peter insisted that the expectation of the Lord's return ought to inspire Christians to holy living (3:11–14). Furthermore, the teachings of Paul supported Peter's emphasis that the patience of the Lord led to salvation (3:15–16). Peter appealed to his readers not to be surprised at the appearance of false teachers, to be on their guard, and to grow in the grace of Christ (3:17–18).

An Outline of Second Peter

I. Salutation (1:1–2)

II. Becoming a Fruitful Christian (1:3–11)
   A. Provisions for the Christian (1:3–4)
   B. Ladder of faith (1:5–7)
   C. Fruitfulness vs. barrenness (1:8–9)
   D. Result of fruitful Christianity (1:10–11)

III. Warning Against False Teachers (2:1–22)
   A. Activities of the false teachers (2:1–3)
   B. Examples of judgment and deliverance (2:4–10a)
   C. Character of the false teachers (2:10b–22)
      1. Arrogant (2:10b–11)
      2. Lacking understanding (2:12)
      3. Lustful and greedy (2:13–16)
      4. Promising what they cannot deliver (2:17–19)
      5. Demonstrating their unconverted condition (2:20–22)

IV. Certainty of Christ's Return (3:1–10)
   A. Based on the promises of the prophets and apostles (3:1–2)
   B. Denied by the false teachers (3:3–4)
   C. A certainty based on God's action in history (3:5–7)
   D. A certainty based on God's view of time (3:8)
   E. A certainty based on God's character (3:9)
   F. A certainty based on the promise of Christ (3:10)

V. Encouragement to Godly Living (3:11–18)

A.   Moral imperative of Christ's return (3:11–14)
B.   Paul's support for Peter's teaching (3:15–16)
C.   Final warnings and appeals (3:17–18)

For Further Discussion

1. Did Christ visit Hades? Give your views of the interpretation of 1 Peter 3:18–19.

2. List the evidence in 1 Peter for the influence of the teaching of both Jesus and Paul. What decision does this evidence lead you to reach about the authorship of 1 Peter?

3. What is the early evidence for the citation of or allusion to 2 Peter? How does this evidence affect your view of the authorship of 2 Peter?

4. Is 2 Peter a testament? Study the question of pseudonymous authorship of 2 Peter and give your own opinions.

Bibliography

Barker, Glenn W., William L. Lane, and J. Ramsey Michaels. *The New Testament Speaks*. New York: Harper and Row Publishers Inc., 1969.

Bauckham, Richard J. *Jude, 2 Peter*. WBC. Waco, Tex.: Word Inc., 1983. Exhaustive exegetical commentary on Jude and 2 Peter. Most thorough recent work in English.

_____. *Word Biblical Themes: Jude, 2 Peter*. Dallas: Word Inc., 1990.

Best, Ernest. *First Peter*. NCB. London: Oliphants, 1971.

Bettenson, Henry. *Writings of the Christian Church*. New York: Oxford University Press, 1947.

Carson, D. A., Douglas J. Moo, and Leon Morris. *An Introduction to the New Testament*. Grand Rapids: Zondervan Books, 1992.

Clowney, Edmund P. *The Message of 1 Peter*. BST. Downers Grove, Ill.: InterVarsity Press, 1988. Provides help for the exposition of 1 Peter.

Cranfield, C. E. B. "The Interpretation of 1 Peter 3:19 and 4:6." In *The Bible and Christian Life*. Edinburgh: T & T Clark Ltd., 1985.

Cross, F. L. *1 Peter: A Paschal Liturgy*. London: Mowbray Imprint of Cassell PLC, 1954.

Dalton, William J. *Christ's Proclamation to the Spirits: A Study of 1 Peter 3:18–4:6*. 2d ed. Rome: Pontifical Biblical Institute, 1989.

Davids, Peter H. *The First Epistle of Peter.* NIC. Grand Rapids: William B. Eerdmans Publishing Co., 1990. Thorough exegetical commentary of 1 Peter.

France, R. T. "Exegesis in Practice: Two Samples." In *New Testament Interpretation.* Edited by I. Howard Marshall. Grand Rapids: William B. Eerdmans Publishing Co., 1977.

Green, Michael. *The Second Epistle General of Peter and the General Epistle of Jude.* TNTC. 2d ed. Grand Rapids: William B. Eerdmans Publishing Co., 1987. Brief exegetical study of 2 Peter.

Grudem, Wayne. *1 Peter.* TNTC. Grand Rapids: William B. Eerdmans Publishing Co., 1988. Brief exegetical commentary on 1 Peter.

Guthrie, Donald. *New Testament Introduction.* 2d ed. Vol. 3, *Hebrews to Revelation.* London: Tyndale House Publishers, 1964.

Harrison, Everett. *Introduction to the New Testament.* Grand Rapids: William B. Eerdmans Publishing Co., 1964.

Helmbold, A. M. *The Nag Hammadi Gnostic Texts and the Bible.* Grand Rapids: Baker Book House, 1967.

Hillyer, Norman. *1 and 2 Peter, Jude.* NIBC. Peabody, Mass.: Hendrickson Publishers Inc., 1992.

Johnson, Luke. *The Writings of the New Testament.* Philadelphia: Fortress Press, 1986.

Kelly, J. N. D. *Commentary on the Epistles of Peter and of Jude.* BNTC. New York: Harper and Row Publishers Inc., 1969.

Longenecker, Richard N. "Ancient Amanuenses and the Pauline Epistles." In *New Dimensions in New Testament Study.* Edited by R. N. Longenecker and Merrill C. Tenney. Grand Rapids: Zondervan Books, 1974.

Marshall, I. Howard. *1 Peter.* IVPNTC. Downers Grove, Ill.: InterVarsity Press, 1991.

Mounce, Robert H. *Born Anew to a Living Hope.* Grand Rapids: William B. Eerdmans Publishing Co., 1982.

Selwyn, E. G. *The First Epistle of St. Peter.* 2d ed. New York: St. Martin's Press, 1964.

Sevenster, J. N. *Do You Know Greek? Supplement to Novum Testamentum 19.* Leiden: E. J. Brill, 1968.

22 The Johannine Epistles

Guiding Questions

1. Defend your view of the author and date of the Johannine Epistles.

2. List the chief themes of 1 John.

3. To whom does the term "antichrist" (1 John 2:18) refer?

4. Explain the purpose for writing 2 and 3 John.

The New Testament contains five books whose authorship is traditionally linked to the apostle John. We call three of these writings epistles and include them among the documents called the catholic or general Epistles. Although they are called general Epistles, each of these letters refers to a specific situation, and two of them designate addressees. The most important of the Johannine Epistles is 1 John, which lacks the name of a specific addressee but contains evidence of the writer's knowledge of local circumstances (1 John 2:19; 5:13–14, 21).

The Epistle of 1 John

First-century Christians needed considerable guidance in distinguishing truth from falsehood and heresy from orthodoxy. John formulated several tests—including righteous living, the demonstration of love, and proper Christology—as evidence of genuine Christian profession.

Authorship

External evidence for the authorship of 1 John consistently points toward the apostle John. Early use of 1 John, without naming the apostle John as the author, appears in Clement of Rome and in the *Didache*. Irenaeus attributed 1 and 2 John to the apostle,[1] and Origen was the first to include all three epistles.[2]

Internal evidence also supports Johannine authorship although the epistle does not name an author. First John has many similarities to John's Gospel. Both writings use the contrasts of "light and darkness," "life and death," and "love and hate." Both employ a relatively simple Greek syntax. First John begins with a section in which the writer suggests that he had close personal contact with Jesus during his earthly ministry (1:1–4). This statement appears to rule out a disciple of John as the author. The authoritative tone expressed in the epistle also supports apostolic authorship.

Some who oppose apostolic authorship see subtle differences between the Gospel of John and the epistle. They note, for example, that the Gospel uses the Greek term *logos* (translated "word" in John 1:1, 14) as a personal reference to Jesus, but 1 John uses the term as a reference to a message or a word that produces life (1 John 1:1). However, John's Gospel also uses *logos* with the meaning of "message" (John 8:31, translated "teaching" in NIV). Some suggest that *logos* in 1 John 1:1 ("word of life") contains a deeper personal reference than has sometimes been acknowledged.

It is best to accept the traditional position that the apostle John is the author of 1 John.

---

1. Irenaeus, *Against Heresies* 3.16.8. Irenaeus attributed both First and Second John to the apostle John by quoting verses from each epistle and identifying John as the author. He did not refer to the quotes as coming from two different Johannine writings, but identified them as coming from the "Epistle."

2. Eusebius, *Church History* 6.25.10. Eusebius was reporting the opinions of Origen, who designated John as the author of all three epistles but suggested that "not all consider them genuine."

Literary Form

First John lacks characteristic elements of a letter. It does not name an author, designate recipients, or express personal greetings. Some have called it a homily; however, the document does include references to the act of writing (1 John 2:1, 12–14). Furthermore, the expression "my dear children" (2:1) identifies a circle of Christians with whom the writer had a close relationship. Early church tradition suggests that John lived in Ephesus in his latter days.[3] He knew some of the special crises and challenges facing the recipients of this letter (1 John 2:19; 5:13–14, 21).

This epistle was probably a general letter written to Christians John knew in the region near Ephesus. The omission of designated recipients may be due to John's intent that it be sent throughout the general area he had ministered to.

Provenance

First John does not indicate its origin. However, church tradition suggests a period of residence for John in Ephesus. This is a likely origin for the epistle, but the issue cannot be settled with certainty. Determining a specific provenance for 1 John is not essential to affirm either the canonicity or usefulness of the epistle.

Date

We have assumed that the author of the epistle is also the author of the Gospel of John. The issue of the date of 1 John is linked with the date for writing the Gospel. Which came first?

We have already assigned John's Gospel to the final decade and a half of the first century.[4] The relationship of the date for 1 John to that of the Gospel is determined by one's view of the purposes of the respective documents. First John appears to have been written to confirm the faith of believers facing the challenges of proto-Gnostic teaching. This movement was growing during the last part of the first century, but it reached its peak of influence in the second century. Some of the later Gnostics used John's Gospel for their own purposes, even though the teachings of the gospel (such

---

3. Eusebius, *Church History* 3.31.3; 5.24.3. Eusebius, quoting Polycrates of Ephesus in a letter written to Victor of Rome, mentions John's burial at Ephesus.
4. See the discussion of "Gospel of John, Date" in chapter 7.

as Jesus' incarnation in John 1:14) destroyed the speculation of the Gnostics.

The development of proto-Gnosticism in the late first century suggests that 1 John may have been written during this time. The use of John's Gospel by some Gnostics suggests that some time had passed after the writing of the Gospel before 1 John was written. John may have been answering some of these false teachers in his epistle. Although we cannot be certain about the exact dating, it is acceptable to suggest a date for 1 John in the early- to mid-nineties.

Purpose

John states several purposes for writing 1 John.

1. John indicates that he wrote so his readers might have fellowship with him (1:3) and that his own joy and the joy of the Christians he represented might be full (1:4).[5]

2. John wanted to provide a foundation for the assurance of salvation for his readers (1 John 5:13).

3. John warned of false teachers who reflected the spirit of antichrist (1 John 4:1–3).

The growing movement of Gnosticism, which later proved to be so troublesome to Christianity, reflected a variety of beliefs in the different Gnostic groups. One group of Gnostics, known as Docetics, rejected the incarnation of Christ. They assumed that flesh was evil by nature and rejected that Christ, who was totally good, could ever assume a nature with the presence of any evil. An affirmation of Christ's incarnation such as we have in 1 John 4:1–3 could well be directed against the teachings of Docetic Gnosticism. John also affirmed the Incarnation as evidence of its reality by citing three of the human senses (1 John 1:1–2).

Another Gnostic falsehood came from the teachings of Cerinthus who distinguished between an immaterial, divine Christ-spirit and a human Jesus with a physical body. Cerinthus asserted that the

---

5. An alternate reading of 1 John 1:4 is "to make *your* joy complete." The NIV text adopts the reading "to make *our* joy complete" (italics mine). The first person plural is probably a reference to John and the Christians who were linked with him through the local church he represented.

divine Christ-spirit came on the man Jesus at his baptism and left him just prior to his suffering on the cross.[6] The statements in 1 John 5:6 might have been directed against Cerinthian Gnosticism. In this verse John asserted that the same Jesus Christ who began his ministry with the water of baptism ended his ministry with the blood of the Crucifixion.

John was probably directing his epistle against a variety of Gnostic teachings heavily influenced by either Docetism or Cerinthian Gnostic elements. John insisted that Jesus had come in the flesh, and those who were followers of Jesus Christ demonstrated the incarnation by obedience to God's commandments and love for other believers.

The Text

The most important textual variant of 1 John is found in the omission of 1 John 5:7–8a: "in heaven: the Father, the Word, and the Holy Spirit; and these three are one. And there are three that bear witness on earth." Perhaps it is easiest to see the effect of this omission by comparing the text of the NIV with that of the KJV.

Textual critics call this passage the *Comma Johanneum*. It bears explicit witness to the Trinity. This passage is obviously not part of the original text of the epistle and is not found in any Greek manuscript prior to the fourth century. In a single manuscript of the eleventh century and another of the twelfth century, the words have been added in the margin by a later hand. No early Greek fathers quote the omitted words.

Metzger tells the story of the inclusion of these words in the Greek text of Erasmus, which influenced their appearance in the KJV.[7] Catholic leaders had criticized Erasmus's omission of these words from earlier editions of his text. He indicated he had not found any Greek manuscripts with these words, but he promised that he would include them if he found a single Greek manuscript that supported the disputed reading. In due time such a manuscript

---

6. Eusebius told the story of John's flight from a public bath house on one occasion when he learned that Cerinthus was inside. John urged others to flee with him as he said, "Let us flee, lest the bath fall; for Cerinthus, the enemy of the truth, is within." See Eusebius, *Church History* 3.28.6.

7. Bruce M. Metzger, *The Text of the New Testament*, 3d ed. (New York: Oxford University Press, 1992), 101.

appeared, but it might well have been produced just to force Erasmus to add the passage. Erasmus included the disputed text in his third edition of the Greek New Testament published in 1522.

Including this passage is not essential to the preservation of the doctrine of the Trinity. Such passages as Matthew 28:19–20 and 2 Corinthians 13:14 also refer to the Trinity.

The Content of First John

Most commentators agree that John used three tests to identify those who belonged to God.

1. The test of right belief demanded that an individual believe that Jesus Christ had come in the flesh (1 John 4:1–3).

2. The test of right behavior demanded righteous living (1 John 2:29).

3. The test of right attitude demanded the evidence of love (1 John 3:11).

In 1 John, the apostle repeatedly introduced these tests to help his readers come to an assurance about their relationship to God. John insisted that an individual must experience and demonstrate reality in all three of these areas in order to show a genuine Christian profession.

The Foundation of Fellowship (1:1–4)

The historical manifestation of God's Word, Jesus Christ, provided the basis for enjoying fellowship with God. John insisted that Jesus Christ, who lived in Palestine, had existed in the beginning. John proclaimed the message of this Word of life so that his readers might enjoy fellowship with him and with the Father. The act of proclamation completed John's joy.

The Necessity of Obedience (1:5–2:6)

As a first test, John highlighted the moral effect of the Christian message (1:5–2:2). He showed that sin ruptured fellowship with God, but the Father promised forgiveness and purification to those who confess their sin. He applied the moral test of obedience to those who profess Christianity (2:3–6). Those who claim to know

Christ make this claim credible not by words only but by righteous conduct.

The Urgency of Love (2:7–17)

John applied a second test to determine the reality of Christian profession. Those who are genuine Christians will demonstrate true love for other believers. John was insisting that genuine faith was expressed first in obedience to God (2:6) and second in love for other believers (2:9–11).

John admitted that Christians could love the world instead of loving one another (2:15–17). However, real Christianity is expressed by rejecting love for the world and practicing deep Christian love for others.

The Importance of Right Belief (2:18–27)

John applied a third test to discriminate between true and false believers. Even as John wrote, "antichrists" who denied that Jesus was God's eternal Son were at work among the believers. To combat this denial of Christian truth, John urged his readers to continue to believe the message they had initially received and to give attention to the illuminating knowledge of the Holy Spirit (2:24–27).

Another Demand for Right Action (2:28–3:10)

John's first test involved the moral test of obedient living. He now urged his readers to produce the righteousness demanded by obedient living.

First, he reminded them of Christ's future appearance (2:28–3:3). The hope of being like Jesus should lead believers to pursue holiness in their present behavior. Second, he reminded his readers of Christ's previous appearance (3:4–10). In his first appearance Christ had come to remove sins and to destroy the work of the devil. These facts made the practice of sin incongruous in believers and provided an incentive to put aside unholy living.

John's statement in 3:6 did not imply that a single act of sin proves that an individual is not a Christian. He warned, however, that the continued practice of sin demonstrates that an individual is not a believer.

Another Demand for Right Attitude (3:11–24)

John's second test of genuine Christianity involved the social test of the practice of love. John pointed out that the presence of love was evidence of spiritual life (3:14–15). Christ's sacrifice for his people provided an example of selflessness which believers should copy (3:16–18). Christians are to love in deed and in truth. The deed involved is unselfish sharing with those in need.

The practice of love for other believers was an assurance of a relationship with God and an experience of rich communion with him (3:19–24). This communion resulted in confidence in prayer (3:21–22).

Another Demand for Right Belief (4:1–6)

In this section John elaborated on the doctrinal test for genuine Christianity. He underscored the importance of the teaching and the character of the audience. John insisted that Christian teaching must contain a bold proclamation that Jesus is the incarnate Lord (4:1–3). He also instructed his readers that those who followed God would heed the teaching of godliness, while those who followed the world would heed the teaching of falsehood (4:4–6). John's readers could test the genuineness of teachers by evaluating the content of their message and the character of their listeners.

A Concluding Appeal for Love (4:7–12)

In this section John applied the social test of love for the third time in the letter. Each application of John's tests has become more probing. He presented three incentives for displaying love.

1. He insisted that we must love others because this is the nature of God (4:8). One who claims to be born of God must display a nature of love.

2. He urged the practice of love because of the historical demonstration of love in Christ's death (4:10–11).

3. He called for a life-style of love because the practice of love makes the presence of the unseen God a reality (4:12).

Combining a Right Belief and a Right Attitude (4:13–21)

Toward the end of 1 John, the breaks and links in his arguments become harder to detect. In this section John appears to insist that believers give evidence of right belief and right attitude. He asserts that the Spirit of God enables true believers to acknowledge that Jesus is God's Son, Christ come in the flesh (4:15). This is a repetition of the doctrinal test.

He also discussed the subject of perfect love for God. Perfect love for God showed itself in confidence before God (4:17) and a deep love for other believers (4:20–21). This is an application of the social test.

The Relationship Between the Tests (5:1–5)

The letter now affirms that it is important for the believer to demonstrate all three signs of the presence of genuine Christianity. John intended to show that the three tests are closely woven together into an essential unity.

First, John insisted that a belief in Jesus as the Christ will result in a love for the Father and his children (5:1–2a). Second, John taught that as we love the Father, we will obey his commands and overcome the world (5:2b–4a). Third, he reminded his readers that the only way to overcome the world was to believe in Jesus Christ (5:4b–5).

The Full Assurance of Our Relationship to God (5:6–17)

How does a person come to faith in Jesus as the Son of God? John's answer is that faith depends on having the right kind of witnesses.

John insisted that we have an adequate testimony for believing that Jesus is the Son of God (5:6–9) because the Spirit of God leads us to believe the truths stated about Jesus at his baptism ("water" is a symbol for Jesus' baptism) and at his death ("blood" is a symbol for Jesus' death). The believer who responds to the testimony of God receives eternal life (5:10–12). Those who have responded to the testimony about God receive an assurance that they possess eternal life, and they experience confidence concerning answers to prayer (5:13–17).

Three Christian Certainties (5:18–21)

John concludes with three "we know" statements that highlight three assurances possessed by Christians. These statements summarize the truths contained in 1 John.

1. Anyone born of God does not continue to sin (5:18).

2. Everyone is either a child of God or a child of the devil. He allowed for no middle-ground position (5:19).

3. The Son of God had come and had given believers the privilege of understanding and knowing him (5:20).

The sin unto death mentioned in 5:16–17 might refer to blasphemy against the Holy Spirit which is unpardonable. John suggested that such a sin did not deserve intercessory prayer. He was emphasizing that some sins are so heinous that prayer to God would not lead to the repentance of the individual involved.

Outline of First John

I. Preface: The Foundation of Fellowship (1:1–4)

II. First Application of the Tests of Life (1:5–2:27)

    A. The necessity of obedience (1:5–2:6)

    B. The urgency of loving one another (2:7–17)

    C. The importance of right belief (2:18–27)

III. Second Application of the Tests of Life (2:28–4:6)

    A. Another demand for right action (2:28–3:10)

    B. Another demand for right attitude (3:11–24)

    C. Another demand for right belief (4:1–6)

IV. Third Application of the Tests of Life (4:7–5:5)

    A. Concluding appeal for love (4:7–12)

    B. Combining a right belief and a right attitude (4:13–21)

    C. Relationship between the tests (5:1–5)

V. The Full Assurance of Our Relationship to God (5:6–17)

VI. Three Christian Certainties (5:18–21)

The Epistles of 2 and 3 John

Authorship

The external evidence for the authorship of 2 and 3 John is not as strong as it was for 1 John. The brevity of these writings and their more personal character probably contributed to their neglect by the early church. Eusebius classified both of them with the disputed epistles, but he acknowledged that they were accepted by many.[8] We have already suggested that Irenaeus attributed both 1 and 2 John to the apostle and that Origen mentioned all three epistles. No early writer attributed the authorship of 2 and 3 John to anyone other than the apostle John.

The similarities in vocabulary and general theme between these two writings and 1 John suggest a similarity in authorship. Both 1 and 2 John speak of Christ as "having come in the flesh" (1 John 4:2; 2 John 7). Both 1 and 3 John indicate that those who do good show that they are God's children (1 John 3:10; 3 John 11).

Why does the author in both 2 and 3 John speak of himself as the elder? This fact does not necessarily point to authorship by another John who is named the elder. It was not uncommon for an apostle to call himself an elder (1 Pet. 5:1). It would certainly be appropriate for John the Apostle to use the term to describe himself as an old man.

It is best to accept the general evidence that points to the apostle John as author of both 2 and 3 John.[9]

Purpose

John wrote 2 John to warn against showing hospitality to false teachers (v. 10). He also warned against the spread of false teaching by proto-Gnostic groups who appear to be similar to those in 1 John 4:1–3 (see 2 John 7). When John prohibited hospitality, he did not oppose offering food or demonstrating kindness to the hungry or

---

8. Eusebius, *Church History* 3.25.3.

9. Luke Johnson described some of the uncertainties about our knowledge of the three epistles. He wrote, "Although it is likely that these documents had a common authorship, we cannot be utterly certain that they did. . . . Nor can we be totally confident that the letters were written in a particular sequence. . . . It is far more likely that they were all sent at once." See *The Writings of the New Testament*, 501.

needy. Rather, he prohibited offering any kind of assistance, such as lodging, which might help the heretics spread their false views.

In 3 John the apostle confronted a church dispute. He commended Gaius for his hospitality and kindness to itinerant missionaries (vv. 5–6). He denounced the self-seeking actions of Diotrephes, whose concern was for his own control over the church (vv. 9–10). He also commended Demetrius, who probably carried the letter to its destination (v. 12).

Recipients

In 2 John the "chosen lady and her children" are probably a local congregation. Some have viewed them as personal friends of the apostle. However, the "elect lady and her children" are beloved by all of those who know the truth (v. 1). It is unlikely that a single family could be this well-known among Christians, but it is likely that a single congregation might acquire this reputation. We do not know where the church was located, but it was probably near Ephesus.

In 3 John the recipient of the letter is Gaius (v. 1). The city in which Gaius lived is unknown, but the location also may be near Ephesus.

Date

It is best to date these two epistles later than the Gospel of John, but it is difficult to know their relationship to 1 John. The reference to "antichrist" in 2 John 7 appears to require the explanation of 1 John for its clarification (1 John 2:18–23). An undetermined time in the early- to mid-nineties is my suggested date for the letters.

Content of 2 John

The letters of 2 and 3 John are the shortest writings in the New Testament. Each one could have been written on a single papyrus sheet. Many of the themes John mentioned in 1 John also appear in these epistles, but 2 and 3 John are more obviously written to deal with specific situations and needs in the local church.

Introduction (vv. 1–3)

Instead of his name, John used the term "elder," which could refer either to his position or his age. The "chosen lady and her children" represent a local church in which John had exercised his influence. His description of the lady is more appropriate to a Christian congregation than to a person.

The Purpose of the Letter (vv. 4–11)

John commended those in the church who were obeying God's commands and urged them to continue their obedience, especially the practice of love for one another (vv. 4–6). He also warned of a doctrinal heresy that threatened the church from the outside (vv. 7–11). Using language similar to 1 John 4:1–3, he warned his readers about the "antichrists" who did not confess the Incarnation. John warned his readers not to give any assistance that would allow the teachers of false doctrine to make progress in spreading their errors.

Conclusion (vv. 12–13)

John expressed the hope that he would be able to visit his readers and talk with them face to face. He anticipated a renewal of Christian fellowship.

Outline of 2 John

I. Introduction (vv. 1–3)

II. Purpose of the Letter (vv. 4–11)

    A. Concern for the internal life of the congregation (vv. 4–6)

    B. Concern for the external threat to the congregation (vv. 7–11)

III. Conclusion (vv. 12–13)

Content of 3 John

In 3 John the apostle wrote to a prominent member of a local church. He also referred to two others who were members of churches. It is interesting to contrast John's instructions concerning the hospitality to be offered to traveling Christians (3 John 5–8) with his instructions forbidding such hospitality to false teachers (2 John 7–11).

The Commendation to Gaius (vv. 1–8)

After greeting Gaius, John commended him for his faithfulness in harmonizing his profession and practice of Christianity (vv. 2–4). He urged him to continue to show hospitality to traveling missionaries (vv. 5–8).

The Warning Against Diotrephes (vv. 9–10)

John warned against the domineering, self-centered actions of Diotrephes. Diotrephes apparently was a leader whose desire for control and recognition caused him to spread malicious gossip against his opponents and excommunicate them from the church. The problems caused by Diotrephes were personal rather than theological. His prideful actions were based on personal vanity and sin.

Commendation of Demetrius (vv. 11–12)

After urging Gaius to avoid imitating the actions of Diotrephes, John commended Demetrius, whose favor with the church and conduct among the people demonstrated his genuine Christianity. Demetrius may have carried the letter to its destination.

Conclusion (vv. 13–14)

John indicated that he had more to write, but he did not want to do so with pen and ink. He looked forward to future contact with the church in a visit he hoped to make.

Outline of Third John

I. Commendation of Gaius (vv. 1–8)

II. Warning Against Diotrephes (vv. 9–10)

III. Commendation of Demetrius (vv. 11–12)

IV. Conclusion (vv. 13–14)

For Further Discussion

1. Evaluate the evidence for identifying the author of John's Gospel and the epistles of John.

2. Defend your view of the "sin unto death" in 1 John 5:16–17.

3. Present the evidence for determining the content of the teachings against which 1 John was written.

4. Defend your view of the identity of the "elder" in 2 and 3 John.

5. Defend your view of the identity of "the chosen lady and her children" in 2 John.

Bibliography

Brown, Raymond. *The Epistles of John*. AB. Garden City, N.Y.: Doubleday, 1982.

Bruce, F. F. "Antichrist in the Early Church." In *A Mind for What Matters*. Grand Rapids: William B. Eerdmans Publishing Co., 1990.

Bultmann, Rudolph. *The Johannine Epistles*. *Hermenia*. Philadelphia: Fortress Press, 1973.

Jackman, David. *The Message of John's Letters*. BST. Downers Grove, Ill.: InterVarsity Press, 1988. Excellent expositional help for applying the content of John's letters.

Johnson, Luke. *The Writings of the New Testament*. Philadelphia: Fortress Press, 1986.

Law, Robert. *The Tests of Life*. 3d ed. Edinburgh: T & T Clark, 1914. Reprint, Grand Rapids: Baker, Twin Brooks Series, 1968. One of the first modern commentators to insist that John wove together in a "spiral" form the tests of righteousness, love, and belief.

Marshall, I. Howard. *The Epistles of John*. NICNT. Grand Rapids: William B. Eerdmans Publishing Co., 1978. Full exegetical commentary on the Johannine Epistles.

Metzger, Bruce M. *The Text of the New Testament*. 3d ed. New York: Oxford University Press, 1992.

Smalley, Stephen S. *1, 2, 3 John*. WBC. Waco, Tex.: Word Inc., 1984.

Stott, John. *The Letters of John*. TNTC. Rev. ed. Grand Rapids: William B. Eerdmans Publishing Co., 1988. Brief exegetical commentary on John's epistles with a profound analysis of structure.

23 The Epistle of Jude

Guiding Questions

1. Identify the author of the epistle by presenting evidence for his background.

2. Discuss the date for writing the epistle.

3. List two major critical problems in the epistle.

4. What does Jude mean by the expression "contending for the faith"?

The content of Jude resembles 2 Peter in that it is largely a warning against false teachers who were invading the church. Jude warned his readers against the heretics who so convincingly spread their errors. He urged his readers to "build themselves up" in the Christian faith as an effective antidote against the spread of falsehood.

Authorship

Jude identified himself as a "servant of Jesus Christ and a brother of James." The James to whom Jude claimed to be related is probably not the son of Zebedee. James, the son of Zebedee, was martyred at such an early time (see Acts 12:1–2) that a reference to him would not be a likely possibility. The James to whom he referred was probably the leader of the Jerusalem church (Acts 15:13–21; Gal. 2:9). This James was a half brother of Jesus (Mark 6:3). Jude was also a half brother of Jesus, but his description of himself as a "servant" reflected his modesty. Both James (see James 1:1) and Jude preferred to present themselves as servants of Jesus Christ rather than claim kinship with the Lord.

Jude may have mentioned his relationship to James in order to commend himself to the public on the basis of the reputation of his better-known brother. Jude would not have been a well-known figure in the early church. He probably engaged in itinerant preaching (1 Cor. 9:5) and wrote this epistle to those he had ministered to.

Neither the New Testament nor early Christian history provides much information about Jude. He was an unbeliever prior to Jesus' resurrection (John 7:5; Acts 1:14). Paul described him as an itinerant missionary accompanied by his wife on his journeys (1 Cor. 9:5). The fact that Jude had contemplated writing another letter to his readers about a different subject before he penned the epistle (see v. 3) suggests that he knew his readers well.

It has become common for scholars to suggest that the name "Jude" is a pseudonym, but those who advocate this view fail to provide an acceptable explanation for the pseudonymity of this letter. Jude, the brother of Jesus, was not a prominent figure in the early church. Anyone wishing to pen a pseudonymous writing would surely have selected some person more prominent than Jude.

Some reject authorship by Jude by advocating that the epistle appeared too late to have been written by one of Jesus' relatives. Eusebius records the evidence from Hegesippus that Jude's grandsons appeared before Domitian, who was Roman emperor from A.D. 81–96.[1] Some use this fact as evidence that Jude would have died before the epistle could have been written. However, this information does not prove with certainty that Jude was dead. It is at least possible that Jude was alive and in his seventies at the beginning of Domitian's reign. Assuming that we can date the epistle before the 90s, we have a strong possibility that Jude could have written the document.

---

1. Eusebius, *Church History* 3.19–20.

The dating of Jude has an important bearing on the issue of authorship. Three features related to dating the epistle are sometimes used as a basis for questioning authorship by the Lord's half brother.

1. Jude refers to the "faith . . . delivered to the saints" (v. 3). Some understand this reference to refer to a time when correct belief was measured by adherence to a fixed body of doctrine. Such a time would likely have come after Jude's lifetime. However, the reference to "faith" need not indicate the passage of a long period of time. Paul's reference to "doctrine" in Romans 16:17 indicates that in his lifetime the Roman believers already knew of a standard of belief to which they were committed. Nothing in Jude's statement demands a time beyond his lifetime.

2. Another objection to Jude as author based on dating focuses on the reference to the "words . . . spoken . . . by the apostles" in verse 17. Some interpreters view this statement as an indication that the apostolic age had passed. However, Jude's words do not mean that a long period of time had passed since the apostolic era; rather, they indicate that the apostles had predicted that scoffers would arise in the church. It would not require a lengthy period for Christians to recognize what the apostles were saying about scoffers if the apostolic writings had been distributed. Nothing in Jude's statements about apostolic predictions demands a date after his lifetime.

3. A final objection to authorship by Jude based on date comes from investigating the identity of the false teachers who have infiltrated the congregations to which Jude wrote (v. 4). Some scholars have viewed the false teachers as Gnostics, and they date the epistle in the second century. The description of false teachers in Jude 5–16, however, could refer to any teachings in which immorality was a prominent feature. Jude's description is not sufficiently clear to link it with certainty to the Gnostics. It is precarious to make Jude's brief description of false teachers a firm basis for dating the epistle in the second century.

Since the rejection of authorship by Jude rests on rather flimsy foundations, accepting the traditional view of authorship by a half brother of the Lord is a wiser choice. If this identification is rejected, we have no way of knowing the identity of the Jude who wrote this letter.[2]

Recognition by the Early Church

Jude's letter had a rather mixed reception in the early church. Early Christian leaders did not generally reject it, but they expressed some hesitation about it, particularly because of Jude's reference to the apocryphal writings of 1 Enoch and the Assumption of Moses.[3]

Early Christian leaders such as Clement of Rome, Polycarp, and Barnabas appear to refer to the letter, but the allusions are not definite enough to clearly identify the source. The Muratorian Canon mentioned Jude by name, but some feel that the way the reference is made raises doubt about its acceptability. Tertullian and Clement of Alexandria cite Jude, and Tertullian went so far as to accept 1 Enoch as inspired Scripture because of Jude's reference to it.[4] Origen described Jude as "a letter of few lines," but he added it was "filled with the healthful words of heavenly grace."[5] Eusebius placed it with the disputed books,[6] but he also placed other canonical writings such as James, 2 Peter, and 2 and 3 John in this category.

The brevity of the book might explain the limited number of references in early Christian writings. It was not long enough to become an important source of quotations or allusions.

Jude's reference to apocryphal writings created difficulty for its inclusion in the canon. In time, Christian leaders came to see that

---

2. Luke Johnson says, "There is nothing about Jude that would prohibit its being a letter written by a follower of Jesus in Palestine during the first generation of the Christian movement." His words indicate that it is not possible to be dogmatic in the identification of Jude as Jesus' half brother. The letter could well have been written by an unknown Jude in the early years of the church, but identifying Jude as Jesus' half brother seems a wiser option. See Johnson, *The Writings of the New Testament*, 444.

3. See the discussion below on "Use of Pseudepigraphical References."

4. Tertullian, *On the Apparel of Women* 1.3.

5. Origen, *Commentary on Matthew* 10.17.

6. Eusebius, *Church History* 3.25.3.

this was no reason for excluding the book, and its acceptance became widespread.

Date

Jude contains very little internal evidence to assist us in determining a date for its writing. Those who accept authorship by a half brother of Jesus must date it during his lifetime. The letter must also have been written late enough to allow the false teachings to develop. A reasonable date for the writing of the letter is between A.D. 65 and 80.[7]

Some suggest that the statements in verse 17 point to a date after the apostolic period. Nothing in the verse demands a time after the death of all the apostles. Others appeal to the Gnostic teaching of the heretics as indicative of a late date. However, nothing in Jude points to the developed Gnostic teaching of the second century.

Relationship to Second Peter

The relationship between Jude and 2 Peter is a much-disputed issue, and conclusions reached about this relationship influence views of authorship and date. Most of Jude is included in 2 Peter, but word-for-word agreements are less common than a general agreement in thought and vocabulary. If 2 Peter used Jude, and Jude were dated as already suggested, the author of 2 Peter could not be the apostle Peter. If Jude used 2 Peter, we would have no chronological difficulty in identifying Jude as Jesus' half brother.

Nevertheless, it is difficult to determine which writer borrowed from the other or whether both may have utilized a third source. For additional information on this subject see the discussion, "Second Peter, Authorship," in chapter 21.

Use of Pseudepigraphical References

Jude identified Enoch as the source for one of his statements (14–15). His words contain a quotation from 1 Enoch 1:9. In verse 9 Jude apparently referred to an incident from another pseudepigraphical book, the Assumption of Moses. We refer to both writings

---

7. This is the time suggested by Guthrie, who discusses at length the various possibilities for dating and settles for an unspecified date between A.D. 65 and 80. See Guthrie, *New Testament Introduction* (1990 ed.), 908.

as pseudepigraphical because the probability is that neither Enoch nor Moses wrote the books. The fact that Jude referred to such writings caused early Christian writers to view the book of Jude with skepticism.

We should not be surprised that Christian writers referred to noncanonical material. Paul quoted a heathen poet in his sermon at Athens (Acts 17:28). He also referred to a Jewish midrash (an exposition that elaborates the content of Scripture) on the water-supplying rock that followed the Israelites in their wilderness wanderings (1 Cor. 10:4). In both of these instances, Paul used these references to illustrate his points in the text. Jude's use of noncanonical materials need not imply that he viewed them as inspired even though the early Christian leader Tertullian called them inspired because of Jude's reference to them. He may have recognized that his readers knew them well, and found them helpful in making his point. It is questionable whether or not Jude viewed the events in the apocryphal sources as actual historical occurrences. Like Paul, Jude may have used the incidents as apt illustrations for his purpose without suggesting that they took place in the indicated manner.

Content of Jude

A major portion of Jude is devoted to a denunciation of false teachers who have infiltrated a group of Christians. The chief intent of Jude is to rally Christians to contend for the faith against the heretics and to make spiritual preparation to resist the inroads of their deceiving errors.

Introduction (vv. 1–2)

Jude identified himself as a servant of Christ the Messiah and a brother of James. Although Jude had once been an unbeliever (John 7:5), his aim as a Christian was to make his life available to Jesus. He was also willing to serve in a less prominent position than his more widely-known brother.

Jude identified the believers as those who had been loved by God, kept by Christ, and called. He wished his readers an abundant supply of mercy, peace, and love. This threefold wish demonstrates Jude's preference for triads, groupings of threes.

The Purpose of the Letter (vv. 3–4)

Jude had intended to write a primer on the subject of salvation to his friends, but the inroads of false teachers changed his plans for the letter's content. When he learned of the presence of heretics who denied Christ, he wrote to urge his friends into a continuous, vigorous defense of the faith. In verses 5–19, he summarized the imperative for contention. He outlined how to contend for the faith in verses 20–23.

Three Examples of Punishment (vv. 5–7)

Jude warned his opponents by presenting three historical instances of divine judgment which had befallen those who opposed God's will:

1. the judgment of Israel in the wilderness (Num. 32:10–13);

2. the angels who sinned (Isa. 14:12–15);

3. the destruction of Sodom and Gomorrah (Gen. 19:24–29).

He suggested that the same punishment lay ahead for the false teachers.

The Description of the False Teachers (vv. 8–10)

The false teachers practiced lust, rebellion, and irreverence. Their own pride and arrogance lay beneath these traits. Jude referred to Michael's respectful response to the devil and compared it to the high-handed disdain of the heretics for angels. He also compared the heretics to unreasoning animals who destroyed themselves.

A Warning Against Leading Others Astray (vv. 11–13)

Jude had previously attacked the sinful life-style of the heretics; now he charged them with leading others astray. He referred to Cain (Gen. 4:4–5, 8–9), Balaam (Num. 31:16), and Korah (Num. 16:1–35) as examples of Old Testament deceivers who led many astray. With vigorous denunciations Jude pictured the heretics as shepherds who only fed themselves, as barren fruit trees, and as waves who washed up their refuse in the lives of their listeners.

The Ultimate Judgment on the Heretics (vv. 14–16)

The false teachers faced inescapable doom, and Jude underscored this by quoting a picture of judgment from 1 Enoch 1:9. In verses 5–11 Jude denounced the evil deeds of the false teachers; in verse 16 he stated that God would hold the heretics accountable for their selfish, boastful, deceitful words.

A Prophetic Application to the Heretics (vv. 17–19)

Jude applied the words of the apostles to the false teachers just as he had applied the words of Enoch to them in the previous section. Jude probably referred to such general warnings as Acts 20:29–30 and 1 Timothy 4:1–3 in order to show that the apostles foretold the coming of evil men who would belittle those who refused to follow their own paths of lust and evil. He also described the heretics as people who created divisions and were controlled by the natural life.

Contending for the Faith (vv. 20–23)

Contending for the faith does not demand perpetual argument. Jude's definition of contending for the faith included Christian growth. He urged his readers to practice five disciplines as they prepared to resist the heretics:

1. to build themselves up in their knowledge of Christian truth;

2. to pray fervently;

3. to live in the sphere of God's love by obedience to divine commands;

4. to fan the flames of Christian hope;

5. to practice evangelism and pastoral care on those who might be enticed into following false teachings (vv. 22–23).

Doxology (vv. 24–25)

Christians will learn best how to resist false teaching when they are fully aware of the power of God available to them. In the concluding doxology, Jude encouraged his readers to remember divine power. Jude pictured God as one who could both guard them and give them a glorious entrance into his heavenly presence. We can best learn to give glory, majesty, power, and authority to God when we experience the salvation he offers through Jesus Christ.

Outline of Jude

I. Introduction (vv. 1–2)
II. Purpose of the Letter (vv. 3–4)
III. Urgency of Resisting the Heretics (vv. 5–19)
    A. Three examples of judgment (vv. 5–7)
    B. Sinful life-style of the heretics (vv. 8–10)
    C. Deceitful attraction of the heretics (vv. 11–13)
    D. Ultimate judgment upon the heretics (vv. 14–16)
    E. Apostolic warning about the heretics (vv. 17–19)
IV. Contending for the Faith (vv. 20–23)
V. Doxology (vv. 24–25)

For Further Discussion

1. Did Jude copy from 2 Peter? Did 2 Peter use Jude? Present evidence to support your chosen viewpoint.

2. What was Jude's purpose in referring to apocryphal writings? Did he view the writings as inspired? Did he feel that the events to which he referred actually occurred?

3. Develop a plan for the discipleship of young Christians from Jude's discussion in vv. 20–23.

Bibliography

Guthrie, Donald. *New Testament Introduction*, 2d ed. Vol. 3. *Hebrews to Revelation*. London: Tyndale House Publishers, 1964.
Also, consult commentaries listed at the end of chapter 21 that deal with 2 Peter and Jude.

24 The Revelation

Guiding Questions

1. Discuss the similarities between John's Gospel and Revelation.

2. Defend your view of the date for writing Revelation.

3. Explain the major interpretive options for approaching Revelation and evaluate their strengths and weaknesses.

4. Give a general outline of the content of Revelation.

5. Explain the relationship between the judgments involving the seals, the trumpets, and the bowls.

6. Explain the differences between the interpretation of Revelation 20:1–6 by various groups, including premillennialists, postmillennialists, and amillennialists.

Authorship

The Revelation, also known as the Apocalypse, names John as its author (1:2, 4, 9; 22:8). John was a prophet (22:9) and a servant of Jesus Christ (1:1). Although the book does not use the term "apostle" to identify him, the early church generally accepted the apostle John as author. Among those who accepted him were Justin, Irenaeus, Tertullian, and Origen. Marcion rejected the book, but he rejected most of the New Testament, including John's Gospel. The most important early rejection of the apostle John as author came from Dionysius, a bishop of Alexandria in the third century.

Dionysius argued, "Therefore that he was called John, and that this book is the work of one John, I do not deny. And I agree also that it is the work of a holy and inspired man. But I cannot readily admit that he was the apostle, the son of Zebedee, the brother of James, by whom the Gospel of John and the Catholic Epistle were written."[1] Dionysius rejected the apostle for three reasons.

1. The author never called himself an apostle.

2. The ideas, words, and arrangement of the content in Revelation differed from that in the Gospel and the First Epistle.

3. The Greek of Revelation contained barbarous language and solecisms not found in the other Johannine writings.

As further support for his idea that some other John may have authored the book, he mentioned the report that the tombs of two Christian leaders in ancient Ephesus bore the name John. Many modern scholars who question apostolic authorship highlight the same concerns expressed by Dionysius.

Dionysius's rejection of the apostle John as author was based on a theological bias. He vehemently opposed the doctrine of Christ's thousand-year reign on earth, known as chiliasm.[2] Early Christian leaders such as Justin, Irenaeus, and Tertullian interpreted Revelation 20:1–6 as support for an earthly millennium. Sometimes their interpretations emphasized the physical and material aspects of the millennium more than the spiritual. Dionysius viewed their doctrine as too materialistic. He rejected the apostolic authorship of Revelation to discredit the chiliastic teaching based on Revelation 20:1–6.

Revealing the theological bias of Dionysius does not suggest that his arguments about authorship are pointless. It does alert us, however, to look for other strong arguments supporting his position in

---

1. Eusebius, *Church History* 7.25.7. Eusebius records a complete range of Dionysius's opinions about the Revelation in this section (chap. 25) of his history.

2. The English term "chiliasm" is derived from the Greek word *chilios*, meaning one thousand.

order to overcome our suspicion that his bias overly influenced his judgment on the issue of authorship.[3]

While the author of Revelation does not speak of himself as an apostle, his assumption that the readers will accept his teaching on the basis of his name alone naturally points to an apostle. The failure of the author to mention his apostleship might be due to the fact that he knew his readers did not need for him to call attention to his apostleship.

Those who take the position that the apostle wrote the Gospel and the Epistles point out that the theological content of Revelation differs in several significant areas from the other Johannine writings. They note that Revelation shows a God of majesty and judgment, but the Gospel and the Epistles present a God of love. Such differences are too greatly magnified, for the Gospel and Revelation teach that God is both loving and judging (John 3:16, 36; Rev. 3:9; 14:7; 16:7). In the Gospel and Revelation Christ is presented as redeemer and ruler (John 8:31–36; 17:1–2; Rev. 1:5; 19:11–21). It is true that the theological emphases of Revelation differ from those of the Gospel and the Epistles, but these differences can be explained by pointing to the different purposes for writing the various books.

The Greek of the Gospel and the Epistles is clear and forthright, but the Greek of Revelation is sometimes irregular.[4] Many feel that these differences in Greek do not suggest that a different author penned the Revelation but that he may have been influenced by his imprisonment (1:9) or by the excitement of a visionary experience (4:1–2). Some scholars claim that the author wrote in the style of someone who spoke Hebrew.

Recognizing the similarities between Revelation and the other Johannine writings is also important. The Gospel (1:1) and Revelation

---

3. Dionysius's concern about the theological content of Revelation 20:1–6 is particularly evident in his actions against the followers of the Egyptian chiliast Nepos described in Eusebius, *Church History* 7.24.

4. One example of this is the use of a case other than the ablative after the first appearance of the preposition *apo* in 1:4. John, however, understood the proper case usage after the preposition, for in a second appearance of the preposition in the same verse he correctly used the ablative case. Some argue that no irregularity in case usage appears in 1:4 because the divine name which follows the first appearance of *apo* is indeclinable.

(19:13) are the only New Testament books that identify Jesus as the "Word." Both John 1:29 and Revelation 5:6 describe Jesus as the "lamb," even though the texts use different Greek words for lamb. In both the Apocalypse and the Gospel, Jesus identified himself with "I am" sayings (Rev. 1:8, 17; 21:6; 22:13, 16; John 6:35; 8:12; 10:7, 11).

If apostolic authorship of Revelation is rejected, the book was probably written by another well-known John in the early church. Some feel that the "elder John" mentioned by Papias may have written the book, but the evidence for his existence is uncertain at best.[5] Others have suggested that the book was written by an unknown member in the circle of John's followers or a Johannine "school of writing." Following the idea that a school of writers loyal to John wrote Revelation involves more difficult assumptions than accepting Johannine authorship of the Apocalypse. Accepting Johannine authorship is a simpler option than a more complicated "school" theory.[6]

The differences between Revelation and other Johannine writings can be explained without requiring a different author. The testimony of the early church presents a strong witness to apostolic authorship. Some of the unique features of Revelation may have resulted from its purpose and setting. It is best to name John the Apostle as the author of Revelation.

Date

The internal conditions evident in Revelation have led scholars to suggest two different time periods for its writing. Some suggest that after the fire in Rome, Nero's persecution of Christians in A.D. 64 led to the writing of Revelation to encourage believers during this difficult time. Those who support this period usually favor a date around A.D. 68 or 69. Among the reasons presented for this position are the following observations.

- The Hebrew practice of *gematria* is used to transform the number 666 of Revelation 13:18 into a symbol for Nero Caesar. Gematria assigns a numerical value to the letters of a word. If we write the name Nero Caesar in Hebrew and alter

---

5. Eusebius, *Church History* 3.39.4–5.
6. For a previous presentation of the issue of a "school" of Johannine writing, see the discussion of the authorship of John's Gospel in chapter 7.

the spelling slightly, we get a numerical value of 666. This fact proves little except that if you tinker enough with the spelling or the language of a word, you can manipulate its numerical value to almost any desired figure.

- Some have suggested that the crude Greek of the Apocalypse came at a time before John learned the smooth Greek of the Gospel and the Epistles. This suggestion does support an earlier date. However, we can explain the rough style of the Greek of Revelation in other ways (see the previous section). Furthermore, archaeological and literary evidence point to the widespread use of Greek in first-century Palestine.

- Some refer to the language of Revelation 17:9–11 and point to the description of the beast who "once was," "now is not," and yet "is" an eighth king. They relate this language to the myth, contemporary in New Testament times, that Nero did not die but would appear again in the East to assert his power. However, the actual story, known as the *Nero-redivivus* myth (Latin for the "resurrected" Nero), does not resemble the description of the beast in Revelation.[7]

The other suggestion for the date of Revelation is during the reign of the emperor Domitian (A.D. 81–96). Those who advocate this period usually propose a date in the 90s. Evidence to support this viewpoint includes the following observations.

- External evidence supports this view. Irenaeus placed the time of writing "almost in our day, towards the end of Domitian's reign."[8] The church historian Eusebius approvingly quoted Irenaeus's view.[9]

- This date allows for an interval between the founding of the churches in the days of Paul and the declension of these same churches in Revelation 2–3. Ephesus had left its first love. Laodicea was lukewarm.

---

7. For an explanation of the content of this myth, see R. H. Charles, *The Revelation of St. John*, ICC (Edinburgh: T & T Clark, 1920), 1:xcv–xcvii.

8. Irenaeus, *Against Heresies* 5.30.3.

9. Eusebius, *Church History* 3.18.3.

- During his reign, Domitian promoted emperor worship. Although we cannot prove that he persecuted Christians on a wide scale, his attempt to encourage emperor worship warned of persecutions to come. Revelation prepared Christians to offer resistance to this coming threat.

Evidence in the Apocalypse suggests a church girding itself for coming trials and persecution (Rev. 3:10). By this time, the churches had time to fall away from the excitement of their initial commitment.

Early Christian leaders explicitly supported a date during the lifetime of Domitian. The most likely date for writing Revelation was between A.D. 81 and 96, probably in the 90s.[10]

Provenance

John stated that he wrote from the island of Patmos, a rugged, rocky island located in the Aegean Sea, forty miles southwest of Ephesus. Roman authorities used the island as a place of exile for offenders and criminals. John clarified that he was in Patmos because of his faithful witness to the gospel (Rev. 1:9).

Destination

John wrote to seven churches in the Roman province of Asia (Rev. 2–3). He probably knew the churches from his years of ministry in the area. Each of the cities mentioned in this section was a center of communication. A messenger carrying Revelation to the seven cities would arrive in Ephesus, travel north to Smyrna and Pergamum, then travel east to Thyatira, Sardis, Philadelphia, and Laodicea.

Canonicity

The Christian West was generally favorable to the contents of Revelation, but the reception in the East was mixed. In the West,

---

10. Evidence for dating Revelation in the time of Domitian is inconclusive, but accepting this general date seems to be the best option. For a warning against too great a presumption for this date, see the article by D. Warden, "Imperial Persecution and the Dating of 1 Peter and Revelation," *JETS* 34 (June 1991): 203–12. Warden notes the difficulty of dating persecution against Christians in Domitian's reign and concludes that the dates of Revelation and 1 Peter are uncertain.

Papias, Justin, and Irenaeus referred to the book as authoritative. The Muratorian Canon included it in the list of canonical writings. Marcion's rejection of the book is not significant, for he frequently rejected any book which, like Revelation, showed dependence on the Old Testament.

In the East, Origen and Clement of Alexandria recognized the book, but Dionysius of Alexandria (see the discussion on the authorship of Revelation) questioned its apostolic authorship. Dionysius influenced Eusebius to question Revelation, and the church historian classified it as both accepted and spurious. His inconsistent attitude showed that he was personally ready to reject it as spurious, but the influence of such teachers as Origen led him to classify it among the accepted.[11]

This mixed reception for Revelation should not greatly trouble us because most of those who were suspicious of the book had a distaste for its eschatology. Such early leaders as Dionysius contended that the book taught a final state that was too materialistic and focused on an earthly reign of Christ. Their rejection of the book represented an effort to minimize its theological influence. One may accept the book as canonical without adopting the extremes of interpretation which so vexed Dionysius.

The reversal of a negative trend toward Revelation in the East began with the influence of Athanasius, the bishop of Alexandria during the fourth century. He knew that the church at large held the Apocalypse in high regard, and he endorsed it. After his lifetime those church councils that issued opinions about the canon endorsed Revelation.

Purpose

Revelation presented a broad, sweeping portrait of future events (1:3) in order to strengthen the church, promote endurance in the face of trials, and encourage suffering believers. John was not merely trying to satisfy curiosity about the future; he wanted to instill a moral earnestness among his readers. He wrote to urge his readers to obey the word of his prophecy (1:3; 22:11–12).

---

11. Eusebius, *Church History* 3.25.1–4.

Form

Three different genres or styles of literature appear in Revelation. The opening verse suggests that the book is an apocalypse, but the writer also declares that his work is a prophecy (1:3), and he writes in the style of a letter (1:4).

The literary form of apocalypse appeared in the second century B.C. and was used to encourage persecuted followers of God. Many authors of apocalypses claimed to be passing on mysteries revealed by an angel or other heavenly being. Some apocalypses are pseudonymous and use the name of a great figure from Israel's past such as Adam, Moses, or Enoch. The writers typically used considerable symbolism, contrasted this age of sin and rebellion with the world to come, and culminated their narrative with the entrance of God's kingdom into history. Revelation differs from other apocalypses in that it is not pseudonymous, and it grounds its hope in the past event of Jesus' sacrificial death. Most apocalypses support their hope with references to a future entrance of God into history.

Revelation clearly contains elements of prophecy. John was in the line of the prophets with his awareness of inspiration and assumption of authority. He also wrote as a prophet to change the moral actions of his listeners (1:3).

Revelation may have circulated as a letter to seven churches in Asia Minor. The opening address and salutation (1:4–5, 9–11) have the form of a letter, and the content of chapters 2 and 3 clearly functions in an epistolary form.

Harrison's description of the book is: "It is an apocalypse with respect to its contents, a prophecy in its essential spirit and message, and an epistle in its form."[12] His statement, citing the presence of all three genres in Revelation, is an accurate assessment of its form.

Recent Study of Revelation

Recent studies of Revelation have focused on the social setting of the book at some length. Adela Yarbro Collins suggests that the social setting out of which the book arose greatly influenced John's writing. She insists that the purpose of Revelation was to resolve

---

12. E. F. Harrison, *Introduction to the New Testament,* 458.

tensions aroused by a perceived social crisis. She does not view the crisis as external but as resulting from the clash between the expectations of John and his Christian friends as they faced the social realities of the first century.[13]

Colin J. Hemer studied the seven churches of Revelation 2 and 3 and presented helpful background information which aids us in understanding the text. Hemer undertook a rigorous historical study of these churches and included material drawn from classical literature, archaeology, coin collections, and inscriptions in order to clarify the text of Revelation.[14]

Gerhard Maier has a useful survey of the history of interpretation of Revelation in the church. He has provided new information strongly supporting the apostolic origin and canonical status of Revelation.[15]

The Interpretation of Revelation

The difficulty in understanding the many symbols and actions described in Revelation led to the development of four major schools of interpretation. Three of these views differ in their time perspective for the events in Revelation. The fourth view regards the contents of Revelation as largely symbolic and thus as having little connection with actual historical events.

1. Those who follow the preterist view affirm that Revelation related primarily to the period of time in which it was written. Preterist interpreters maintain that John described the coming struggle between the church and the Roman government. They limit the historical references in Revelation to the first century. The strength of this approach is that it makes the message of Revelation relevant to the life situation of the early church. Its limitation is its inability to find a significant message for the church beyond the first century except by glancing at God's actions in the first-century church and assuming

---

13. Adela Yarbro Collins, *Crisis and Catharsis* (Philadelphia: Westminster, 1984).
14. Colin J. Hemer, *The Letters to the Seven Churches of Asia in Their Local Setting*, *JSNT* Supplement Series 11 (Sheffield: *JSOT*, 1986).
15. Gerhard Maier, *Die Johannesoffenbarung und die Kirche*, WUNT 25 (Tubingen: Mohr, 1981).

that he might repeat the same pattern in the contemporary church.

2. The historicist interpreters regard Revelation as a continuous chronicle of church history from apostolic times until Christ's return. Those who interpret Revelation from this viewpoint believe that opening the seals, blasting the trumpets, and pouring out the bowls represent different events in world and church history. The strength of this viewpoint is that it gives readers a strong impression of the sovereignty of God in world events. Its weakness is its subjectivity and the widespread disagreement among its interpreters. Those who support this view display a wide variety of interpretations in their efforts to relate the symbols of Revelation to world events.

3. Followers of the futurist view approach Revelation with the understanding that the bulk of its content refers to the future action of God in history. Futurists accept the fact that Revelation arose out of the pressures of the first century, but they insist that Revelation 4–22 refers to events leading up to Christ's return, the coming of Christ's kingdom, the final judgment, and the eternal state. Several interpretative approaches can be identified among the futurists. Futurists themselves disagree about whether the church will be removed from the earth during a "secret" return of Christ known as the Rapture (dispensationalism) or will be left on the earth to face the judgments of the tribulation (historical premillennialism). The strength of the futurist approach is its emphasis on the progressive activity of God in world history. A major limitation is that it leaves the original hearers of Revelation with a limited message of encouragement. How could the original hearers receive much encouragement from having information about the return of Christ at least two thousand years into the future?

4. The fourth approach to Revelation omits references to history and time as the specific focus of God's activities. This approach is called idealist or spiritual. Those who follow this viewpoint feel that the language of Revelation does not predict future events but paints a picture of the continuous strug-

gle between good and evil in the church and the history of the world. It emphasizes basic principles of God working in history rather than specific events. Those who follow this approach contend that God was strengthening the church with a promise of ultimate victory rather than referring to specific events in time. One advantage of this view is its recognition of the presence of many symbols in Revelation. A weakness is the often skeptical attitude of its followers toward predictive prophecy and their failure to develop a perspective on the action of God in history.

Interpretations of Revelation[a]			
Viewpoint	Chapters 1–3	Chapters 4–19	Chapters 20–22
Preterist	Actual churches	Symbols of first-century conditions	Symbols of heaven and victory
Idealist	Actual churches	Symbols of conflict of good and evil	Triumph of righteousness
Historicist	Actual churches	Symbols of historical events; fall of Rome, papacy, Reformation	Final judgment; eternal state
Futurist	Stages of church history	Future tribulation	Millennial kingdom; final judgment; eternal state

a. This chart and the following are adapted from Merrill Tenney, *New Testament Survey*, 391.

Which of these approaches to Revelation is correct? Each contains an element of truth. The preterist interpreter emphasizes the significance of Revelation for the first hearers of the message. The futurist and the historicist interpreters emphasize the action of God in history. The idealist view emphasizes the great principles by which God has operated in history. It is not possible to maintain one approach to interpretation consistently throughout the entire book. It is wisest to use the approach that the specific text of Revelation demands. For example, it is important to read the message of Revelation 2 and 3 from the perspective of the original readers, and it is also important to catch the hope of Christ's future return mentioned in Revelation 19:11–21.

Millennial Perspectives of Revelation

Many who study the book of Revelation are familiar with the terms premillennialism, postmillennialism, and amillennialism. These terms describe the relationship of the return of Christ to the millennium, the thousand-year reign of Christ mentioned in Revelation 20:1–6.

Premillennialists insist that the return of Christ will take place before the millennium begins. Dispensational premillennialists emphasize that the return of Christ will occur in two stages. The first stage will take place prior to the period of final judgment known as the tribulation. This first stage of Jesus' return is called the Rapture. The second stage of Jesus' return will occur at the end of the tribulation in the events described in Revelation 19:11–21. Historical premillennialists believe that the return of Christ is a single-stage event that will occur at the close of the tribulation but prior to the beginning of the millennium.

Postmillennialists emphasize that the return of Christ will take place at the conclusion of the millennium. They feel that the return will occur at the close of a lengthy period of human progress (the millennium) in which the moral climate of the world is changed by a sweeping conversion of the world to Christianity.

Amillennialists teach that the picture of Christ's thousand-year reign in Revelation 20:1–6 is a symbol of his present spiritual kingship at the right hand of God in heaven. Many amillennialists suggest that the millennium is this present period of world history in which the gospel can spread freely and influence history by bringing people to faith in Christ.

The millennial position an individual brings to the interpretation of Revelation will affect the exegesis of the book. Generally those who prefer a premillennial approach will follow a more literal interpretation. Those who follow an amillennial approach will emphasize the importance of a proper understanding of the various symbols in Revelation.

Millennial Perspectives of Revelation			
Viewpoint	Chapters 1–3	Chapters 4–19	Chapters 20–22
Postmillennial	Actual churches	Usually historicist	Symbol of victory of Christianity over the world
Amillennial	Actual churches	Usually historicist	Return of Christ; final judgment;eternal state
Premillennial	Actual churches or seven stages of history	Usually futurist	Millennial reign; final judgment; eternal state

The Value of Revelation

Revelation highlights a profound sense of the sovereignty of God in history, a high view of the person of Christ, and a clear sense of God's actions in the eschatological events that will consummate world history.

The vision of God on the throne (Rev. 4–5) shows that God alone is worthy of our ultimate worship and praise. The powerful, majestic portrait of God in these chapters can provide encouragement to those who face persecution and other hardships connected with their commitment to Christ.

The designation of Christ as the Son of God (2:18) and the Word of God (19:13) expresses the deity of Christ and his revelatory role in God's plan. Identifying him as the Lamb of God (5:6) focuses on the importance of his sacrifice. His majesty is underscored by naming him King of Kings and Lord of Lords (19:16).

Eschatology is a broad term which includes all the events that will secure God's plans for both the individual and the world. Revelation never provides a detailed list of final events in history, but it

reminds us of events that will profoundly affect our present existence. The promised return of Christ provides a sense of hope and
reverence for contemporary believers. The description of final
judgment (20:11–15) shows the seriousness with which God treats
sin and encourages obedience among believers.

Christians who regularly read and reflect on Revelation will discover challenge, hope, encouragement, warning, and insight. This
rich promised harvest is an incentive for believers to study the book
diligently and obey the words of its prophecy (1:3).

Content of Revelation

Several years ago one of my teachers told the story of reading
through the book of Revelation in a single sitting. When he had
finished his rapid survey, he reflected on what he had read. The
words, "Victory in Jesus," came to his mind. Those words are an
excellent theme statement for the Apocalypse. Revelation
describes the ultimate victory of Jesus over all the cosmic forces
of evil. This encouraging affirmation brings hope and
confidence to all believers who face the antagonism of an unbelieving world.

Introduction (1:1–8)

The introduction to Revelation contains a superscription (vv. 1–3)
that identifies the book as a disclosure from the Father to the Son
through an angel to his servant John. The salutation (vv. 4–5a)
identifies the author and recipients and offers a theologically
impressive greeting from the triune God. John addressed a doxology
to Christ (vv. 5b–6) and identified the events related to the return of
Christ as the theme of the book (v. 7–8).

The Glorified Christ (1:9–20)

Revelation contains four distinct visions. The first vision begins
in this section and extends through 3:22. John had a vision of the
exalted and glorified Christ that came to him on the Lord's Day
(Sunday) while he was a prisoner on the island of Patmos (vv. 9–10).
This vision revealed his priestly majesty (v. 13), his deity (v. 14), his
strength (v. 15), and his care for the churches (v. 16). John
responded to the appearance of the Lord by prostrating himself

before Christ (vv. 17–18). Many of the terms used to describe Christ in this section appear again in the letters to the seven churches in chapters 2–3.

As John trembled in fear before Christ, the Lord affirmed his commission to explain the vision he saw, had seen, and was about to see. He was to send the vision's message to the seven churches of Asia (vv. 19–20).

The seven golden lampstands represent the seven churches under Christ's care. The seven stars symbolize the "angels" of the churches, either guardian angels or some symbol of the supernatural character of the church.

Seven Letters to Seven Churches (2:1–3:22)

Each of the messages to the seven churches includes a description of Christ that is relevant to the needs of the particular church, a commendation and/or rebuke, an exhortation, and a promise. For example, the outline of the message to the church in Ephesus (2:1–7) has five elements.

1. description of Christ (2:1);

2. commendation to church (2:2–3, 6);

3. rebuke to church (2:4);

4. exhortation to church (2:5);

5. promise to church (2:7).

The message to the church at Philadelphia (3:7–13) has no rebuke. The message to the church at Laodicea (3:14–22) has no commendation to the church.

We know little about the identity of the Nicolaitans mentioned in 2:6. Early church fathers speculated that they were founded by Nicolas, a proselyte of Antioch (Acts 6:5). Other than the fact that they were a heretical sect, we have very little information. The ten days of persecution for the church at Smyrna symbolize a brief period of affliction (2:10). Satan's throne, in the message to the church at Pergamum, may refer to the city as a center of emperor worship or to other pagan practices in the city (2:13). The woman Jezebel, who caused such hardship for the Thyatiran Christians (2:20–23), referred to a female member of the church whose authoritative teaching enticed many into moral compromise. The Christians at Sardis had a sagging spirituality. They had a good reputation for spiritual vitality, but they were attempting to live off their previous accomplishments rather than change their compromising practices (3:1–6).

The promise to the church members at Philadelphia that Christ will "keep them from the hour of trial" is interpreted according to the millennial viewpoint of the interpreter (3:10). Dispensational premillennialists understand the promise to involve the removal of the church from the world prior to the judgment known as the tribulation. Historical premillennialists understand the passage to mean that the church, while remaining physically on earth, will be preserved from the wrath of God during the tribulation.

The economic prosperity of Laodicea blinded Christians in that city to their spiritual poverty (3:15–18). Christ urged the members of this smug, lifeless church to experience the realities of spiritual life (3:20).

Some interpreters of Revelation claim that the dominant traits of the seven churches are predictions of the unique character of Christianity during subsequent periods in church history. For example, the church at Ephesus symbolizes the energetic apostolic church. The church at Smyrna represents the persecuted postapostolic church. Sardis represents the Reformation church with a love for doctrinal orthodoxy but a lack of spiritual vigor. Although some facets of this interpretative scheme seem to fit, the approach breaks down particularly in the case of the Reformation church. The church at Sardis received almost no commendation in Revelation, and most interpreters feel that the Reformation church deserves more commendable marks than Sardis received.

The Throne in Heaven (4:1–11)

The vision of Christ among the churches is replaced by a vision of God on a heavenly throne as he carries out his judgments in history. This vision extends to 16:21 and concludes with the destruction of all that opposes God. The vision of chapter 4 answers the question, "Who is in charge of history?" The picture of the Lord God Almighty provides the answer to the query.

For John the experience in 4:1 represents the opening of a new door of revelation before God. It does not imply the physical removal of John from earth to heaven. The twenty-four elders represent a group of angels who carry out the rule of God in the universe. The four living creatures resemble the Old Testament seraphim (Isa. 6:1–3), and they symbolize another order of angels who assist in extending the rule of God throughout the universe. The elders praise the character of God. The living creatures praise the works of God. The portrait of God in this chapter is one of indescribable majesty.

The Scroll and the Lamb (5:1–14)

The scroll in this chapter symbolizes the final events of history which will be brought to completion by the work of Christ. The lamb is clearly a symbol for Christ, and taking the scroll from the hand of God represents the commitment of Christ to bring the prophecies of the end to completion. The hymns in verses 9–14 contain a rising chorus of praise for Christ from all of God's creation. The content of this vision answers the question: "Who will carry out the plan of God in history?" The activity of the Lamb in receiving the scroll provides an answer.

The Seals and Their Aftermath (6:1–8:1)

Chapters 6–16 contain three series of seven plagues or judgments that are related to opening seals, sounding trumpets, and overturning bowls. Interpreters differ in their explanation of the relationship of the plagues. Some interpreters claim that the plagues follow one another consecutively. In this approach the seals are followed by the trumpets, and the trumpets are followed by the bowls. The return of Christ and other final events follow the last judgments. From this perspective the trumpets represent the seventh seal; the bowls represent the seventh trumpet; and the coming of Christ and the other final events represent the seventh bowl. The relationship between the various judgments could be diagrammed in this way:

Seals 1 2 3 4 5 6 7

      Trumpets 1 2 3 4 5 6 7

            Bowls 1 2 3 4 5 6 7

                  Return of Christ

Examination of the seals, trumpets, and bowls shows that the final elements in each series bring nearly identical results. This fact suggests that the seals, trumpets, and bowls overlap somewhat in their fulfillment. The following diagram expresses this viewpoint.[16]

Return of Christ

| Seals | 1 | 2 | 3 | 4 | 5 | 6 | | 7 |

| Trumpets | 1 | 2 | 3 | 4 | 5 | 6 | 7 |

| Bowls | 1 2 3 4 5 6 7 |

The judgments of the seals will be spread throughout world history and will include some of the great affliction known as the tribulation. The trumpet judgments will be scattered over the latter days of the world's history, largely during the tribulation, and the bowl judgments will take place at the end. The conclusion of the bowl judgments leads to the return of Christ and all other final events.

The seal judgments symbolize the following:

- Seal 1 (6:2): militaristic conquest, although some view this seal as a symbol of the victorious spread of the gospel;

- Seal 2 (6:3–4): warfare;

- Seal 3 (6:5–6): scarcity, developing from warfare;

- Seal 4 (6:7–8): death, developing from war;

- Seal 5 (6:9–11): the blessedness of Christian martyrs;

- Seal 6 (6:12–17): cosmic events preceding Christ's return (see Mark 13:24–26; Matt. 24:29–31; Luke 21:25–27);

- Seal 7 (8:1): silence in heaven.

Historical premillennialists usually regard the 144,000 Israelites in chapter 7 as symbolic of the church. They maintain that 7:1–8 shows the spiritual protection given to the church upon entering the tribulation, and that 7:9–17 pictures the triumph of the church before God as it emerges from the tribulation. Dispensational premillennialists regard the 144,000 as Jewish evangelists who

---

16. This chart and the preceding are adapted from Robert Gundry, *A Survey of the New Testament*, 353.

spread the gospel in the world during the tribulation. They interpret the vast multitude mentioned in 7:9–17 as Gentiles who respond to the message of the Jewish evangelists and are converted.

The Trumpet Judgments (8:2–11:19)

The trumpet judgments sound the beginning of God's wrath on a civilization which has rejected him. God's wrath is his judgment on sin and sinners. Believers are exempt from experiencing this wrath (Rom. 5:9), but they might still be subject to the normal afflictions and trials all believers experience because of their commitment to Christ (Acts 14:22). We must beware of pressing an overly literal interpretation on the events in these judgments. These events actually happen in history, but it is difficult to understand exactly how each judgment will occur.

The first four trumpet judgments appear primarily to affect the earth. The final three extend the wrath of God to human beings who have rejected the rule of God in their lives (9:20–21). The trumpet judgments represent the following events:

- Trumpet 1 (8:7): hail, fire (perhaps lightning) burning one third of the earth;

- Trumpet 2 (8:8–9): a blazing mountain thrown into the sea with one third of the sea turning to blood and the destruction of one third of sea life and ships;

- Trumpet 3 (8:10–11): falling of a burning meteorite which poisons one third of the rivers and springs on land;

- Trumpet 4 (8:12): darkening of one third of the heavenly bodies;

- Trumpet 5 (9:1–12): opening the bottomless pit so that demonic torment brings misery on human beings;

- Trumpet 6 (9:13–21): death of one third of human beings in a plague caused by demonic horsemen;

- Trumpet 7 (11:15–19): kingdoms of the world becoming the kingdoms of Christ accompanied by lightning, thunder, earthquake, and hailstorm.

An interlude in chapter 10 allowed John to receive a renewed commission to communicate God's saving plan to humanity. The communion with God which produced the message was an experience of sweet intimacy for John. The message warned the church of the persecution and hardship that lay ahead and produced the sensation of bitterness for John (10:9–11).

New Testament scholars have developed a variety of interpretations for chapter 11. Dispensationalists emphasize the restoration of the Jewish temple in Jerusalem at the end of the age. Historical premillennialists usually see this chapter as a prophecy of the fate of the church at the hands of a rebellious world order. They interpret it to mean that believers will suffer persecution and martyrdom during the tribulation, but God assures his people of ultimate triumph.

Measuring the temple (11:1) symbolizes the protection of believers from the wrath of God. The forty-two months (or 1,260 days) represent that period of the tribulation when the dominion of evil reaches its apex. The two witnesses (11:3) symbolize either the power of the witnessing church or an actual reappearance of Moses and Elijah in a display of prophetic power. The resurrection of the two witnesses (11:11–12) may symbolize the power of the church to persevere through persecution, or it may refer to an actual resurrection that will cause the enemies of God's people to experience great fear and terror. The message of the chapter is that the church of God, though oppressed by persecution, will receive divine power to witness for him and endure hardship.

Interlude (12:1–14:20)

This section shows the heavenly warfare that leads to perpetual conflict between Satan and the people of God (12:7–9). Christians receive the assurance that Satan has been conquered even though he will work through his agents to bring unprecedented persecution on the church (13:9–10). John encouraged his readers by describing visions that assure victory (chap. 14).

The dragon in chap. 12 is a symbol for Satan (12:3–4, 9). The woman symbolizes the people of God, the church. The child born to the woman is the Messiah (12:4–5). The woman's flight to the wilderness symbolizes the church's spiritual protection from demonic wrath (12:6). The heavenly battle (12:7–9) pictures the unrelenting warfare between the forces of Satan and the forces of God. Hurling Satan from heaven shows his defeat. Christians understand that ultimately Satan's defeat occurred at Calvary (Heb. 2:14), and they can overcome Satan only in the strength of the power released in Christ's death and resurrection (12:10–12). The remainder of the chapter outlines the efforts of Satan to destroy the church, efforts continually frustrated by God's power.

Satan continues his efforts to destroy the church through his two representatives who appear in chapter 13. Interpreters have named the "beast from the sea" (13:1) the Antichrist. Some interpreters see him as a symbol of the persecuting power of the Roman Empire. Others view the description as a reference to an evil personality who will use political power to lead oppression against Christians during the evil days of the tribulation. John suggested that the beast would have worldwide authority in leading persecution against believers (13:7).

The second beast (13:11) is the servant of the first, and he uses religious persuasion, miraculous signs (13:13–15), and economic threats (13:16–17) to entice believers away from their loyalty to Christ. The number 666, a symbol for the second beast, denotes the apex of evil. One interpretation of this perplexing number suggests that the number 6 represents evil. A triad of 6s implies the completeness of evil, and the number 666 thus refers to the full development of evil in an effort to force Christians into disobedience.

Chapter 14 contains a series of short visions, all of which provide assurance and encouragement for persecuted believers. If the 144,000 represent the total number of the people of God, then the vision of 14:1–5 shows that believers who endure severe persecution will receive salvation from God. The angels who appear in 14:6–13 call God's people to repentance and warn of the doom that will come to those who follow the beast of chapter 13. A concluding pair of visions (14:14–16) shows the gathering of the righteous for salvation and the condemnation of the wicked (14:17–20). Each of these visions provided spiritual encouragement for a harassed and beleaguered church.

The Bowl Judgments (15:1–16:21)

The bowl judgments present a full demonstration of the wrath of God on an unbelieving world. Whereas the trumpet judgments were often partial (as seen by the frequent use of fractions such as "1/3"), the bowl judgments are universal. The trumpet judgments first affected primarily the earth and then human beings. The bowl judgments affect human beings from the outset. The statement in 16:11 suggests that the judgments are not merely vindictive but are intended to promote repentance among those being judged. The term "bowl" describes a wide-mouthed household container that can be compared to a contemporary soup bowl or mixing bowl. John symbolized "wrath" as a liquid poured onto the earth when an angel overturned the bowl. We must exercise great caution in interpreting John's symbols.

Pouring out the contents of each bowl resulted in the following:

- Bowl 1 (16:2): painful sores on people;

- Bowl 2 (16:3): sea turning to blood and killing all sea life;

- Bowl 3 (16:4–7): rivers and springs turn to blood;

- Bowl 4 (16:8–9): scorching heat of the sun;

- Bowl 5 (16:10–11): darkness on the kingdom of the beast and pain on human beings;

- Bowl 6 (16:12–16): gathering of the armies of the East for the Battle of Armageddon;

- Bowl 7 (16:17–21): lightning, thunder, earthquake, and destruction of pagan power.

The plague of the seventh bowl is a proleptic (anticipatory) picture of God's judgment on Babylon, the seat of the power of the beast. The next two chapters in Revelation present a detailed account of the fall and judgment of Babylon.

The Destruction of Babylon (17:1–18:24)

This section begins the third vision in Revelation. Within this vision, which extends through 21:8, John records the consummation of God's redemptive purpose. This present section shows the results of the fall of Babylon mentioned in 16:19. Babylon symbolized a society organized in opposition to God. In the first century this opposition centered in Rome, but John used the term primarily to describe an eschatological destruction.

These two chapters explain the causes for the downfall of Babylon. Chapter 17 shows the religious reasons for the downfall; chapter 18 emphasizes the contributions of commercialism and materialism to the downfall.

John described Babylon as the source of all efforts to entice human beings away from God (17:5). From the evil society which Babylon fostered came all kinds of abominations that permeated the entire earth. Babylon fostered persecution which produced martyrs (17:6). The civilization Babylon developed was founded on principles that rested ultimately on Satan (17:7). The evil Babylon produced would ultimately lead to its own destruction (17:16). Such internal destruction is the method God will use to destroy the proud, self-centered society of human beings living without dependence on God (17:17).

The fall of Babylon completely destroys the economic prowess of pagan society. John described the lament of political leaders (18:9), merchants (18:11), and seamen (18:17) at the destruction of their means of financial livelihood. All meaningful social life in Babylon will disappear (18:22–23). The greed, love of luxury, pride, and immorality of Babylon will contribute to its downfall.

Events Surrounding the Return of Christ (19:1–21)

This chapter opens with a shout of thanksgiving for the destruction of Babylon (19:1–5). John used the picture of a marriage to illustrate the new intimacy believers would soon begin to enjoy with Christ (19:6–10). Christ is the Lamb. The church is the bride. The guests at the wedding banquet are another symbol for the church (19:9). John did not describe the wedding supper. This event may not occur until 21:3, at a time when believers will enjoy full intimacy with God.

John narrated the glorious return of Christ in 19:11–16. The "armies" accompanying Christ are heavenly angels (19:14). The majesty of the return of Christ will effectively destroy all opposition to him (19:15–16).

The eschatological battle of Armageddon is described in 19:17–21. Rather than describe the battle itself, John pictured its results as a sweeping triumph for the forces of Christ. The battlefield metaphor shows the greatness of Christ's victory (19:18). Christ does not obtain his victory by using conventional military weapons but by a dazzling display of spiritual power. Not only are the armies of the Antichrist destroyed, but the Antichrist himself and the false prophet ("the beast from the earth" in 13:11) will be thrown into the lake of fire.

The Millennium and the Final Judgment (20:1–15)

A variety of Christian interpretations for 20:1–6 exists. Premillennialists view this section as a description of the binding of Satan for a thousand years during which time believers are sharing with Christ in his millennial reign over the earth. Postmillennialists view this passage as a symbolic description of the triumph of Christ in human affairs. Amillennialists view this passage as a symbolic description of the present era between the resurrection of Christ and his return.

The millennial reign will be followed by the final destruction of Satan (20:10) and the final judgment (20:11–15). At the final judgment, the "book of life" represents a record of those who have responded in faith to Christ. Following the final judgment, unbelievers will experience the second death. Their first death was physical; their second death in the lake of fire represents eternal separation from God.

The Consummation (21:1–22:5)

John pictured the entrance of believers into a final state of blessedness in the new heaven and the new earth (21:1–8). This section completes the third vision in Revelation by showing that the final destiny of believers is a redeemed earth. The abolition of grief, pain, and other evil results of sin points to the beginning of the eternal state (21:4). The establishment of the new order means that God will live among his people, and they will enjoy uninterrupted fellowship with him (21:3). In this eternal state, all unbelievers are banned from fellowship with God (21:8).

The fourth vision, which concentrates on the heavenly Jerusalem, provides a detailed description of life in the eternal state (21:9–22:5). John pictures life in terms of the majestic brilliance of precious stones and metals (21:18–21). He was overwhelmed in his description by the glory of the divine presence (21:23). John portrayed the experience of believers as including life, healing, and uninterrupted fellowship with God.

Epilogue (22:6–21)

John's epilogue accomplishes four purposes.

1. John urged his readers to heed the words of his prophecy (22:7). He had made this same emphasis in 1:3 as he began Revelation.

2. John reminded his readers of the certainty of Jesus' return (22:10–13, 20).

3. John affirmed that the message was for all to hear and receive. Anyone who wished could receive the free gift of life (22:17).

4. John stressed the authenticity of the prophecy and warned against willfully tampering with it and changing its intent (22:18–19).

He concluded with a benediction in 22:21.

Outline of Revelation

Theme: The Victory of Christ

I. Introduction (1:1–8)
    A. Superscription (1:1–3)
    B. Salutation (1:4–5a)
    C. Praise to Christ (1:5b–6)
    D. Theme of book (1:7–8)

II. The First Vision (1:9–3:22)
    A. The glorified Christ (1:9–20)
    B. The seven letters (2:1–3:22)
        1. The letter to the church in Ephesus (2:1–7)
        2. The letter to the church in Smyrna (2:8–11)
        3. The letter to the church in Pergamum (2:12–17)
        4. The letter to the church in Thyatira (2:18–29)
        5. The letter to the church in Sardis (3:1–6)
        6. The letter to the church in Philadelphia (3:7–13)
        7. The letter to the church in Laodicea (3:14–22)

III. The Second Vision (4:1–16:21)
    A. The picture of God on his throne (4:1–11)

B. The picture of Christ who takes the sealed scroll (5:1–14)
C. The seals and their aftermath (6:1–8:1)
  1. Opening the first seal (6:1–2)
  2. Opening the second seal (6:3–4)
  3. Opening the third seal (6:5–6)
  4. Opening the fourth seal (6:7–8)
  5. Opening the fifth seal (6:9–11)
  6. Opening the sixth seal (6:12–17)
  7. Sealing the 144,000 (7:1–8)
  8. Multitude coming out of the tribulation (7:9–17)
  9. Opening the seventh seal (8:1)
D. The trumpet judgments (8:2–11:19)
  1. Preparation for the trumpets (8:2–6)
  2. Sounding the first trumpet (8:7)
  3. Sounding the second trumpet (8:8–9)
  4. Sounding the third trumpet (8:10–11)
  5. Sounding the fourth trumpet (8:12–13)
  6. Sounding the fifth trumpet (9:1–12)
  7. Sounding the sixth trumpet (9:13–21)
  8. Reaffirming John's commission (10:1–11)
  9. Measuring the temple and the appearance of the two witnesses (11:1–14)
  10. Sounding the seventh trumpet (11:15–19)
E. Interlude (12:1–14:20)
  1. Vision of spiritual struggle between the dragon and the offspring of the woman (12:1–17)
  2. Vision of the two beasts who lead persecution against the people of God (13:1–18)
  3. Visions of reassurance and victory (14:1–20)
F. The bowl judgments (15:1–16:21)
  1. Preparation for the bowl judgments (15:1–8)
  2. First bowl judgment (16:1–2)
  3. Second bowl judgment (16:3)
  4. Third bowl judgment (16:4–7)
  5. Fourth bowl judgment (16:8–9)
  6. Fifth bowl judgment (16:10–11)
  7. Sixth bowl judgment (16:12–16)

8. Seventh bowl judgment (16:17–21)

IV. The Third Vision (17:1–21:8)

A. Vision of the spiritual bankruptcy of Babylon, society in opposition to God (17:1–18)

B. Judgment of Babylon (18:1–24)

C. Joy over Babylon's destruction (19:1–5)

D. Announcement of the marriage of the Lamb (19:6–10)

E. Return of Christ (19:11–16)

F. Battle of Armageddon (19:17–21)

G. Binding of Satan, the resurrection, and the millennial kingdom (20:1–6)

H. Destruction of Satan (20:7–10)

I. Final judgment (20:11–15)

J. New heaven and new earth (21:1–8)

V. The Fourth Vision (21:9–22:5)

A. Description of the new Jerusalem, the eternal state (21:9–21)

B. Worship in the new Jerusalem (21:22–27)

C. Privileges of believers in the new Jerusalem (22:1–5)

VI. Epilogue (22:6–21)

A. Exhortation to obey the message of the book (22:6–7)

B. Certainty of Christ's return (22:8–13, 20)

C. Invitation to respond (22:14–17)

D. Warning against changing the message of the book (22:18–19)

E. Benediction (22:21)

For Further Discussion

1. Explain how obedience to the prophecy in Revelation can influence human behavior.

2. List some guidelines for interpreting and applying the symbols used in Revelation.

3. Give your response to the statement: "The Revelation contains a roadmap of the future." Articulate your position and defend it.

4. Defend the approach to Revelation 20:1–6 that is most acceptable to you.

5. Is the Battle of Armageddon a future historical event fought with conventional military weapons, or is its description in Revelation 19:17–21 a symbolic picture of Christ's ultimate victory over evil? Defend your position.

Bibliography

Beasley–Murray, G. R. *The Book of Revelation*. NCB. Rev. ed. Grand Rapids: William B. Eerdmans Publishing Co., 1981. A premillennial approach to Revelation.

Beasley–Murray, G. R., Herschel H. Hobbs, and Ray Frank Robbins. *Revelation: Three Viewpoints*. Nashville, Tenn.: Broadman & Holman, Publishers, 1977.

Boring, M. Eugene. *Revelation*. *Int*. Louisville, Ky.: John Knox Press, 1989.

Bruce, F. F. "Antichrist in the Early Church." In *A Mind for What Matters*. Grand Rapids: William B. Eerdmans Publishing Co., 1990.

Caird, G. B. *A Commentary on the Revelation of St. John the Divine*. HNTC. New York: Harper & Row Publishers, Inc., 1966.

Charles, R. H. *The Revelation of St. John*. ICC. 2 vols. Edinburgh: T & T Clark Ltd., 1920.

Chilton, David. *The Days of Vengeance*. Ft. Worth, Tex.: Dominion, 1987. A postmillennial approach to Revelation.

Collins, Adela Yarbro. *Crisis and Catharsis*. Philadelphia: Westminster Press, 1984.

Ford, J. Massyngberde. *Revelation*. AB. Garden City, N.Y.: Doubleday, 1975.

Gundry, Robert. *A Survey of the New Testament*. Rev. ed. Grand Rapids: Zondervan Books, 1981.

Guthrie, Donald. *The Relevance of John's Apocalypse*. Grand Rapids: William B. Eerdmans Publishing Co., 1987.

Harrison, Everett F. *Introduction to the New Testament*. Grand Rapids: William B. Eerdmans Publishing Co., 1964.

Hemer, Colin J. *The Letters to the Seven Churches of Asia in Their Local Setting*. *JSNT* Supplement Series 11. Sheffield, U.K.: *JSOT*, 1986.

Hendriksen, William. *More than Conquerors*. 6th ed. Grand Rapids: Baker Book House, 1952. An amillennial approach to Revelation.

Ladd, George E. *A Commentary on the Revelation of John.* Grand Rapids: William B. Eerdmans Publishing Co., 1972. A historical premillennial approach to Revelation.

Maier, Gerhard. *Die Johannesoffenbarung und die Kirche.* WUNT 25. Tubingen: Mohr, 1981.

Morris, Leon. *The Book of Revelation.* TNTC. Rev. ed. Grand Rapids: William B. Eerdmans Publishing Co., 1987.

McDowell, Edward A. *The Meaning and Message of the Book of Revelation.* Nashville, Tenn.: Broadman & Holman Publishers, 1951.

Mounce, Robert H. *The Book of Revelation.* NICNT. Grand Rapids: William B. Eerdmans Publishing Co., 1987.

Tenney, Merrill C. *Interpreting Revelation.* Grand Rapids: William B. Eerdmans Publishing Co., 1957.

———. *New Testament Survey.* Grand Rapids: William B. Eerdmans Publishing Co., 1961.

Wall, Robert W. *Revelation.* NIBC. Peabody, Mass.: Hendrickson Publishers Inc., 1991.

Walvoord, John F. *The Revelation of Jesus Christ.* Chicago: Moody Press, 1966. A dispensational premillennial approach to Revelation.

Warden, D. "Imperial Persecution and the Dating of 1 Peter and Revelation." *JETS* 34 (June 1991):203–12.

Wilcock, Michael. *The Message of Revelation.* BST. Downers Grove, Ill.: InterVarsity Press, 1975.

Glossary of Terms

Agrapha. Sayings of Jesus not recorded in the Gospels. The term literally means "unwritten sayings," but any of these sayings we find today are written. Acts 20:35 includes an example of *agrapha*.

Amanuensis. Copier of New Testament writings. Writers such as Paul used an amanuensis to copy or write down their words (see Rom. 16:22 for the name of Tertius as an amanuensis).

Amillennialist. Interpreter of Revelation 20:1–6 who believes the passage presents a symbolic picture of Christ's present kingship in heaven and the present age of the church. Amillennialists maintain that the millennium is being realized in the events of this age.

Antichrist. Term used in 1 John 2:18 to describe those who deny Jesus is God's eternal Son. Used in Christian history to describe the ultimate incarnation of evil in the last days. The "beast from the sea" in Revelation 13:1 has usually been designated as the Antichrist by Christian historians although the Scripture does not use the term.

Apocalyptic. Style of writing used largely during the intertestamental period. It employed vivid symbols to show the divine control of history. Daniel is an Old Testament example of this style, and Revelation is a New Testament example.

Apocrypha. Term used to designate certain intertestamental writings as "hidden books." Catholics call them "deuterocanonical," but Protestants generally do not regard them as canonical.

Examples of these books are 1 and 2 Maccabees, Ecclesiasticus, and Tobit.

Autographs. Original texts of the New Testament. We no longer possess autographs of the New Testament.

Canon. Collection of authoritative books for both testaments. The New Testament canon includes those books accepted by the church as having a message from God about Jesus.

Captain of the Temple Guard. Jewish official (see Acts 4:1) who commanded the Jewish police force at the temple.

Century. Unit of the Roman army with one hundred soldiers at full strength. The commander was called a centurion (Acts 10:1).

Chiliasm. Term derived from the Greek word *chilios*, meaning one thousand. Chiliasm is the belief in the literal reign of Christ on earth during the period described in Revelation 20:1–6. Some modern premillennialists hold similar views to those once called chiliasts.

Claudius Edict. Directive issued in A.D. 49–50 by the Roman Emperor Claudius banishing all Jews from Rome. The thrust of this edict is mentioned in Acts 18:2.

Cloak. Outer garment of clothing worn in Palestine usually over another garment known as a tunic (q.v.). Normally the cloak could not be taken from a person by legal proceedings (see Matt. 5:40).

Codex. Style of binding collections of New Testament writings that resembles book bindings of today. Prior to using codex bindings, many New Testament writings had been put on scrolls.

Corban. Term used to describe an offering presented to God. Wealthy Jews sometimes declared personal property or land as corban so they would not have to use the proceeds from it to support others in need (such as aged parents) but could use the funds for themselves. The property was given to God on the death of the owner. The practice became a means of encouraging greed (see Mark 7:9–13).

Cursive. Style of handwriting featuring the connection of letters. It was quicker and less expensive to copy the New Testament in cursive.

Dead Sea Scrolls. Ancient manuscripts found in late 1940s at Qumran near the Dead Sea. The manuscripts contained biblical, sectarian, and apocryphal writings and are believed to have belonged to the Jewish sect known as the Essenes (q.v.).

Diachronic. Adjective describing an approach that investigates the development of a field of study over a period of time. A diachronic study of the Gospels focuses on their historical development. Often used in contrast with synchronic (q.v.).

Diadochi. Derivative from a Greek word meaning successors. Used to describe the generals who inherited the territory of Alexander the Great after his death.

Diaspora. Term used to refer to Jews who lived outside of their homeland in Palestine. Diaspora Jews outnumbered Palestinian Jews.

Didache. Transliteration of Greek word for teaching. Used as a technical term to describe instructions needed for Christian growth and spiritual maturity. Often contrasted with *kerygma* (q.v.). Also the title of an early Christian writing viewed by some sections of the church as canonical.

Dominical. Expression whose literal meaning is "lordly". Used to describe sayings in the Gospels uttered by Jesus. The Lord's Prayer in Luke 11:2–4 is a dominical saying.

Egnatian (Ignatian) Way. Roman road used by Paul in his travel through Macedonia. It linked the Aegean and Adriatic Seas and provided a quick route across Macedonia to Rome.

Epicureans. Philosophical movement in Greece advocating pleasure as the chief good of life. Most Epicureans defined pleasure as the absence of pain, not as sensual immorality (see Acts 17:18).

Eschatology. Division of Christian theology that focuses on the doctrine of the final events of time. Eschatology studies what happens to persons and what happens to the world in the end times. The names "personal" and "cosmic" eschatology are used for the two emphases.

Essenes. Jewish religious sect comprised of members who followed a theology similar to the Pharisees but insisted on separation from the activities of the Jerusalem temple. Many link them with the ascetics living at Qumran who possessed the Dead Sea Scrolls (q.v.).

Ethnarch. Technical term used for a ruler over an ethnic group. Used in reference to Archelaus, son of Herod the Great, who ruled over Judea and other smaller provinces from 4 B.C. to A.D. 6.

Form Criticism. Method of study that focuses on the period of oral transmission of the Gospels. Emphasizes that the Gospels originally circulated in varying forms of literary styles.

Futurist. Method of interpreting Revelation that suggests that most of the events in the book will occur at the end of time and thus in the future for readers today. Many futurists suggest that Revelation 1–3 refers to the first-century church.

Gallio Inscription. Inscription found in Delphi, Greece, dating the term of the Roman governor Gallio in Achaia from A.D. 51 to 53. Paul appeared before this governor in Acts 18:12–17, and his appearance, probably in A.D. 51, provides a firm date for determining the chronology of his ministry.

Gematria. Method for interpreting Scripture used at times by various Jewish and Christian groups. This practice assigns numerical values to letters used in words and suggests that these numerical values have interpretive significance. Gematria has been used to suggest that the number 666 in Revelation 13:18 refers to Nero Caesar.

General Epistles. New Testament writings from James through Jude that usually refer to a general rather than a specific geographical location. Such general Epistles as 2 and 3 John contain an address to a specific but unnamed location.

Genre. Style, form, or content of a literary product. In the New Testament the four chief genres are biography in the Gospels, history in Acts, letters in the Pauline writings, and apocalyptic in Revelation.

Gnosticism. A religious movement that promised salvation to its followers by providing them a special form of personal knowledge. Some Gnostics were ascetics; others were libertines. Gnosticism developed fully in the second half of the second century A.D., but the ideas that led to Gnosticism appeared in the first century. Some scholars use the term "incipient Gnosticism" to describe the evidence of Gnosticism in the New Testament.

Hapax Legomena. Transliteration of Greek phrase meaning "spoken only once." Used to refer to Greek words appearing only once in the New Testament. Sometimes used in the shortened form of "Hapaxes."

Hasidim. Devout Jewish opponents of Hellenism. They became the opponents of the policies of the Hasmonean family in Jewish history.

Hasmonean. Term derived from an early ancestor of the Maccabean family named Hasmon. Used of the largely secular leaders who ruled Palestine during the period from 142 to 37 B.C. They were descendants of the earlier Maccabean family.

Hauptbriefe. German word meaning chief letters. Used by the German critic F. C. Baur to refer to Galatians, Romans, and 1 and 2 Corinthians as genuinely written by Paul.

Hazzan. Jewish synagogue official who cared for the synagogue building and its contents.

Hellenism. Culture and influence of the Greek world.

Herodians. Jewish political group that supported the dynasty of the Herods and the Roman government as a result of this support.

Historicist. Method of interpreting Revelation that suggests that the book contains a forecast in symbols of church history from the time of the apostles until Christ's return.

Idealist. Method of interpreting Revelation that suggests the book does not refer to specific events in history but paints a picture of general principles of God's governance of the world. Sees the struggle in Revelation as a symbol of the continuing struggle in history between good and evil rather than a specific event in time.

Intertestamental Period. Period between the writing of the final books of the Old Testament and the beginning of the New Testament era.

Judaizers. False teachers in Galatia who emphasized that salvation for the Gentiles demanded obedience to the law.

Kerygma. Transliteration of Greek word for "preaching." Used as a technical term for the evangelistic preaching done by the early church. Often contrasted with *didache* (q.v.).

Lectionaries. Collection of New Testament readings used in the liturgy of the early church.

Legion. Unit of the Roman army with six thousand soldiers at full strength.

Levirate Marriage. Jewish custom by which the brother or next of kin of the deceased was bound under certain circumstances to marry the widow. Jesus responded to a question relating to levirate marriage as he defended the reality of a future resurrection in Mark 12:18–27.

Metaphor. Figure of speech comparing two objects without the use of "like" or "as." Jesus' statement that believers are "the light of the world" (Matt. 5:14) is a metaphor.

Millennium. Period of a thousand years of Christ's reign described in Revelation 20:1–6. Christian interpreters differ in their understanding of whether the millennium is a special period of history or is a symbol of Christ's present reign.

Minuscules. Style of writing New Testament manuscripts in small letters.

Mystery Religions. Religious movements popular in the first-century world and originating largely in the East. Participants were promised personal contact with a deity. The name originated because of its secret ceremonies.

Negev. Geographical term referring to the southern part of Palestine. Beersheba was the most prominent city in the Negev.

Ostraca. Broken pieces of pottery. Sometimes these bits of pottery were used as writing material.

Papyrus. Writing material made from a plant available in the Middle East. Papyrus, although inexpensive, proved quite durable in dry climates.

Parable. An extended story using familiar facts from daily life to convey spiritual truth. The story of the good Samaritan in Luke 10:25–37 is an example of a parable. Scholars today have extensive debates about more complex meanings of the term.

Parataxis. Style of writing used especially in John's Gospel. John used parataxsis when he wrote more with coordinate conjunctions (such as "and") than with subordinate conjunctions (such as "because"). This writing style gives John an appearance of simplicity when it is read.

Parchment. Writing material usually made from the skins of sheep and goats. This costly material became more common as the church grew in size and influence.

Parousia. Transliteration of Greek word meaning presence or coming. Used to refer to the return of Christ in 1 Thessalonians 4:15.

Pericope. Individual unit or story in the Gospels. The parable of the good Samaritan (Luke 10:25–37) is an example of a pericope.

Pharisees. Members of a Jewish religious movement insisting on obedience to the oral law and the written law of the Old Testament. Prominent in New Testament times, they became even more influential after the destruction of the Jerusalem temple in A.D. 70.

Postmillennialist. Interpreter of Revelation who believes the return of Christ will occur after the events described in Revelation 20:1–6. Postmillennialists generally expect the preaching of the gospel to improve the quality of life in the world. They anticipate the return of Christ to climax the period of the millennium (q.v.).

Praetorian Guard. Elite personal military troops for the Roman Emperor.

Premillennialist. Interpreter of Revelation 20:1–6 who believes the return of Christ will occur prior to the beginning of the millennium (q.v.). Premillennialists expect the millennium to be a separate period of world history. They differ in their understanding of the role of Israel in the millennium and on the question of the number of stages in Christ's return.

Preterist. Method of interpreting Revelation that suggests the events in the book occurred during the apostolic age and were symbols of the struggle between the church and Rome.

Provenance. Place from which a New Testament writing originated. For example, the probable provenance of Philippians is Rome, where Paul was imprisoned.

Pseudepigrapha. Term used for writings, many of which are ascribed with the name of a false author. None was ever seriously considered as canonical. Examples of these writings include 1 Enoch and the Assumption of Moses, referred to in Jude 9, 14–15.

Publicans. Tax collectors in Palestine who were widely despised by the Jews. They were viewed as dishonest and as collaborators with Rome.

Q (Quelle). German word for source. Used as a symbol for the material in Matthew and Luke absent from Mark. An example of this material is in Matthew 3:7–10 and Luke 3:7–9.

Realized Eschatology. Idea that Christians have already experienced the final blessings God gives to believers by receiving them in this life. A Scripture such as John 5:24 emphasizes that believers already have eternal life, but many interpreters view this blessing as only a foretaste of the final inheritance that believers will receive at the end times.

Redaction Criticism. Method of study of the Gospels that focuses on the activities of the writers of the Gospels. It investigates the purposes of the Gospels and forms conclusions based on the unique omissions and inclusions in each Gospel.

Sadducees. Members of a Jewish religious sect who accepted the Torah as the only authoritative Old Testament Scripture. They denied supernaturalism in their theology and controlled many priestly activities of the temple in New Testament times. They lost their influence after the temple's destruction in A.D. 70.

Scribes. Professional writers who became students and copiers of the Old Testament law.

Septuagint. Greek Old Testament translated in Egypt during the reign of Ptolemy Philadelphus (285–246 B.C.). Often referred to with the letters LXX.

Shema. Basic creed of Judaism from Deuteronomy 6:4–5.

Sheol. Jews believed that the dead went to a place called Sheol after death to await final judgment. Similar in meaning to English expression, "the grave" (see Ps. 16:10).

Sign. Usual word used in John's Gospel to describe a miracle. Signs prompted disciples to put their faith in Jesus. The first sign was changing water into wine at the wedding feast in Cana of Galilee (John 2:11).

Stoicism. Philosophical movement in New Testament times that emphasized the importance of self-control. Stoics also were fatalistic, believing that a sovereign force directed their lives (see Acts 17:18).

Subapostolic Writings. Title used to describe materials written just after the period of the apostles by Christian leaders known as the apostolic fathers. Among their writings were *1 and 2 Clement*, the *Didache*, and the *Shepherd of Hermas*.

Synagogue. Place for Jews to worship, provide education for children, and enjoy social fellowship. Developed during captivity in Babylon after destruction of the temple.

Synchronic. Adjective describing an approach to study that places documents side by side and examines them as they appear. In a synchronic study of the Gospels, one is concerned only with the material written in the Gospels, not with the process of writing them. Often contrasted with diachronic study of the Gospels (q. v.).

Synoptic. Comes from a term meaning to look at together. The synoptic Gospels refer to Matthew, Mark, and Luke. These Gospels present the life of Christ in a generally similar manner.

Talmud. Collections of rabbinic interpretations of Old Testament laws that became authoritative in later Judaism of the fourth and fifth centuries A.D.

Targums. Oral translations of the Old Testament written in Aramaic. They often contain material not found in the canonical Old Testament.

Tetrarch. Designation of the ruler of a subordinate province. Used to describe the sons of Herod the Great, Herod Antipas and Herod Philip. Both of these sons ruled smaller divisions of their father's territory.

Trade Guilds. Organization of professionals working in a similar craft. The guild sought better provisions and working conditions for its members and provided help for needy members (see Acts 19:24–26).

Tribulation. Period of judgment during the final times of history that will bring God's wrath on unbelievers and severe persecution on believers. Some biblical interpreters use Daniel 9:24–27 to support that this period lasts for seven years, while others suggest that it is a period of undetermined length.

Tunic. Loose-fitting garment for men and women that extends from the shoulder to the knee or the ankle (Matt. 5:40). It was worn as an undergarment under the cloak (q.v.).

Uncials. Style of writing using capital letters for producing New Testament manuscripts. The earliest manuscripts of the New Testament appear in uncial script.

Vellum. Material made from calfskin, used when copying New Testament manuscripts. Sometimes vellum is called parchment (q.v.). Used for copying New Testament writings after the church had grown in size and wealth.

Zealots. Revolutionary Jewish sect dedicated to overthrowing Roman authority. They led the war against Rome that ended in the destruction of Jerusalem by the Romans in A.D. 70.

Names Index

A

Agrippa 323
Agrippina 19
Alexander the Great 9
Amanuensis 72
Antiochus Epiphanes
    Antiochus IV 11, 233, 254
See Herod Antipas
Antipater 15
Antony 448
Aphrodite 408
Apollos 415, 416, 504
Apostolic Council 351
Archelaus 21
Aristobulus I 15
Aristobulus II 16
Aristotle 9
Artemis 318
Athanasius 591
Augustus 6, 16

B

Bar Cochba 22
Bartimaeus 242
Baur, F. C. 366
Bernice 323
Bethany 246
Bornkamm, Gunther 117
Brown, Raymond 155
Bultmann, Rudolph 85, 109

C

Caesar, Julius 16
Caligula 18
Calvary 269
Cerinthus 562, 563
Christ 180
Claudius 18
Clement of Rome 413
Cleopatra 10
Collins, Adela Yarbro 592
Constantine 36
Conzelmann, Hans 117, 149
Cross, F. L. 556

Culpepper, R. Alan 155
Cynics 51
Cyrus 8

D

Darius the Persian 5
Decapolis 83, 214
Deissmann, Adolf 333, 508
Delphi 316
Didache 560
Dionysius 90, 586, 587, 591
Dives 237
Dodd, C. H. 123, 159, 299
Domitian 20, 539, 576, 589, 590
Drusilla 322

E

Enoch 579, 582
Epistle of Jeremy 338
Erasmus 563, 564
Essenes 52, 55
Eusebius 339, 349, 470, 476, 540, 547, 591
Ezra 8

F

Felix 321, 322, 349
Festus 322, 323
Fortress of Antonia 320

G

Gallio 316, 351, 383, 410
Gamaliel 347
Gnostic 473
Golgotha 269
Good Samaritan 228
Goodspeed, E. J. 336
Gospel of Thomas 81, 116
Griesbach, J. J. 107, 114

H

Haggai 8
Harnack, Adolf 504
Harrison, P. N. 471, 472
Hasmonean 13
Hebraists 61
Hellenists 61
Hemer, Colin J. 287, 289, 593
Hermes 44
Herod 90, 195, 267
Herod Agrippa I 22, 300, 322, 323
Herod Agrippa II 22, 323
Herod Antipas 21, 195, 233, 267
Herod Philip 22
Herod the Great 20, 90, 300
Herodians 55, 195, 250
Hillel 239, 347
Hobart, W. K. 145
Hume, David 182
Hyrcanus II 15
Hyrcanus, John 15

I

Ignatius 474, 475
Infancy Gospels 81
Inscription 351
Isthmian Games 408

J

James 312
Jason 11
Jerusalem Council 312, 351
Jonathan 14
Josephus 53, 90, 300, 351
Judaizers 367
Judas 13
Jupiter 43

K

Knox, John 464

L

Lazarus 237, 246
Letter of Aristeas 338
Levirate marriage 251
Lewis, C. S. 182
Lysias, Claudius 39, 321

M

Maccabeus, Judas 13, 233
Machen, J. G. 171
Magdalene, Mary 272
Magi 175
Magnificat 149
Malchus 264
Marcion 336, 470, 473, 474
Martha 246
Marxsen, Willi 117
Mary 246
Mattaniah 7
Mattathias 13
Matthias 293
Melchizedek 511
Menelaus 12
Mercury 44
Messiah 180, 309
Messianic Secret, The 141, 165
Metzger, Bruce 472
Muratorian Canon 70, 470, 578

N

Nag Hammadi 50
Nazarite vow 320
Nebuchadnezzar 7
Nehemiah 8
Nero 19, 539, 588, 589
Nicolaitans 599

Nicolas 599

O

Octavian 16, 448
Onesimus 438, 439, 463, 464, 465
Onias III 11
Origen 504, 547, 560
Oxyrhynchus papyri 81

P

Palm Sunday 246
Perea 228
Pharisees 54, 321
Philip 9
Philip II of Macedon 448
Philo 53
Pliny the Younger 537
Polycarp 153
Pompey 16
Pontius Pilate 17, 267, 277
Ptolemy I 10
Ptolemy Philadelphus 10

Q

Quest for the Historical Jesus 84
Quirinius 90, 174

R

Ramsay, W. M. 286
Rich man 237
Robinson, J. A. T. 156

S

Sadducees 54, 251
Sanhedrin 59
Satan 179
Schweitzer, Albert 84
Scribes 55
Selwyn, E. G. 557

Shammai 239
Sherwin-White, A. N. 287
Simon 14
Simon the leper 246
Skeptics 51
Strauss, D. F. 84
Streeter, B. H. 115
Synagogue 59

T

Targums 51
Tertullian 340
Third Council of Carthage,
     The 70
Tiberius 17

Titus 20
Trajan 537, 539
Tychicus 438

V

Vespasian 19

W

Westcott, B. F. 154
Wrede, W. 116, 141

Z

Zealots 55
Zechariah 8
Zedekiah 7
Zeus 43

Subject Index

A

Abomination of desolation 254
Abraham's bosom 237
Agrapha 80
Allegory 205
Amanuensis 333, 472, 540
Amillennialism 596
Amillennialists 596, 608
Antichrist 570, 605, 608
Antichrists 565, 571
Anti-Marcionite 140
Antitheses 198
Apocalypse 585, 592
Apocrypha 51
Apocryphon of John 548
Apophthegm 110
Areopagus 315
Armageddon 607
Asceticism 458, 487
Assumption of Moses 578, 579

B

"Benediction against Heretics"
    161, 227
Benedictus 173
Bezae 291
Book of life 608

C

Canon 66
Captivity Epistles 437
Celibacy 417
Centurion 39
Chiliasm 586
Christ of faith 85
Comma Johanneum 563
Court of Women 253

D

Day of Pentecost 293
Dead Sea Scrolls 52
Deep structures 120
Delphi Inscription 382
Diadochi 10

Diaspora 32
Diaspora Jews 60
Diatribe 527
Didache 113
Dispensational premillennial-
    ists 596, 600, 602
Dispensationalism 594
Dispensationalists 604
Docetic Gnosticism 562
Docetics 562
Dominical 81
Dominical saying 110
Doublet 215

E

1 Enoch 578
Emperor worship 45
Epicureanism 50
Epistles 333, 508
Ethnarch 21

F

Feast of Dedication (Hanuk-
    kah) 233
Feast of Pentecost 293
Festivals 57
First death 608
Form Criticism 109
Futurist 594

G

Gemarah 53
Gematria 588
Genre 74, 284
Gnosticism 48, 458, 473
Gnostics 561, 562, 577
Gospel of Truth 548
Graeco-Roman religion 44

H

Hallel 263
Hanukkah 14, 233
Hapax legomena 456, 471, 472
Hasidim 12
Hasmonean 15
Hauptbriefe 366, 395
Hebraists 295
Hellenism 9
Hellenists 295
Hill of Ares 315
Historical premillennialism 594
Historical premillennialists
    600, 604
Historicist 594
Holy Days 57
Hyperbole 87, 198, 234

I

Idealist 594
Ipsissima verba 119
Ipsissima vox 119

J

Jerusalem Decree (Acts 15
    23–29) 285
Jesus of history 85
Justification 402

K

Kerygma 85, 113, 299
Keys of the kingdom 216
Kingdom of God 203

L

Laws of transmission 111
Legalism 367
Legend 110
Legions 39

Letter 508
Letters 334
Literary Criticism 119
Logos 168, 560

M

Magnificat 172
Marcion 591
Millennial 608
Miracle story 110
Mishnah 53
Mite 253
Muratorian Canon 336, 591
Muratorian Fragment 540
Mystery Religions 46–47

N

Nag Hammadi 68, 548
Nero-redivivus 589
New Testament Apocrypha 68

O

Olivet Discourse, The 253
Oniads 11

P

Papyrus 34
Parable 87, 205
Paradise 270
Parataxis 158
Parenesis 525
Parousia 359, 385
Passover 258
Pax Romana 16
Pentecost 293
Perean ministry 95
Pericope 110
Pharisees 15
Pool of Siloam 224
Postmillennialism 596

Postmillennialists 596, 608
Praetorian guard 18, 40
Praetorium 440
Premillennialism 596
Premillennialists 596, 608
Preterist 593
Prison epistles 437
Proconsul 17
Proleptic 606
Prophecy 592
Propraetor or prefect 17
Proto-Gnostic 561, 569
Proto-Gnosticism 562
Pseudepigrapha 52
Pseudepigraphic literature 548
Pseudepigraphic writing 549
Pseudepigraphical 580
Pseudonym 552, 576
Pseudonymity 471, 522, 576
Pseudonymous 548, 592
Pseudonymous Authorship 337
Pseudonymous document 534
Ptolemaic 10

Q

Q 115, 130
Quelle 115

R

Rabbinic Judaism 335
Realized eschatology 159
Redaction criticism 116, 118, 130

S

Sadducees 15
Sanhedrin 265, 349
Second death 608
Seleucid 10

Septuagint 11
Sermon on the Mount, The 195
Signs 158
Source criticism 114
Stoicheia 460
Stoicism 50
Stoics 315
Structuralism 120
Subapostolic 68
Synoptic Gospels 107

T

Talmud 53

Temple 56
Tetrarch 21
Textual Criticism 72
Tobiads 11
Transfiguration 217, 548
Tribulation 602, 604
Two-Source 115

W

Western text form 291
Word 168